THE Television READER

THE Television READER

Critical Perspectives in Canadian and US Television Studies

Edited by

Tanner Mirrlees
& Joseph Kispal-Kovacs

OXFORD
UNIVERSITY PRESS

OXFORD
UNIVERSITY PRESS

Oxford University Press is a department of the University of Oxford.
It furthers the University's objective of excellence in research, scholarship,
and education by publishing worldwide. Oxford is a registered trade mark of
Oxford University Press in the UK and in certain other countries.

Published in Canada by
Oxford University Press
8 Sampson Mews, Suite 204,
Don Mills, Ontario M3C 0H5 Canada

www.oupcanada.com

Library and Archives Canada Cataloguing in Publication
The television reader : critical perspectives in Canadian and US
television studies / edited by Tanner Mirrlees and Joseph Kispal-Kovacs.

Includes bibliographical references.
ISBN 978-0-19-544687-6

1. Television—Canada. 2. Television—United States. 3. Television
broadcasting—Canada. 4. Television broadcasting—United States.
I. Mirrlees, Tanner, 1977– II. Kispal-Kovacs, Joseph, 1963–

PN1992.3.C3T44 2012 791.450971 C2012-902505-4

This book is printed on permanent (acid-free) paper ∞.

Printed and bound in the United States of America
2 3 4 — 15 14 13

Contents

Preface and Acknowledgements

This reader began as an idea by Oxford University Press to produce a Canadian television studies reader that could be used by instructors in Canadian colleges and universities to survey some of the enormous changes taking place in the production, consumption, and reception of twenty-first-century television (and the critical study of TV itself). The two editors, Tanner Mirrlees and Joseph Kispal-Kovacs, realized that there was not only a shortage of critical Canadian TV studies articles available for re-publishing, but also that it would be difficult to address Canadian TV without extensive reference to American TV as well. They also thought it would be dubious to assemble a distinctively "Canadian" TV studies reader given Canada and English-Canadian television's economic, technological, cultural, political, and geographical proximity to the United States and US television.

The book brings together contemporary scholarship on American and Canadian television. It examines TV in Canada and the United States as part of two nationally constructed but asymmetrically interdependent TV systems. The book's focus on Canadian and American TV systems (as opposed to one or the other) provides a much-needed comparative analysis of the similarities and differences between two national yet increasingly integrated and interdependent TV systems. In a sense, this book tries to look at TV in North America as a whole. The book is thus an attempt to complicate the cultural imperialism hypothesis, particularly as it tends to be applied to the Canadian and American TV relationship. It works against the grain of nationalist orthodoxy, which regularly incites moral panics about the threat of American TV to Canada's cultural well-being. Though Canadian and American TV industries, texts, and audiences are converging, Canada is not a helpless victim. In the twenty-first century, Canadian TV is being exported to the United States and the world.

Joseph Kispal-Kovacs has been teaching film and television studies at York University for more than two decades. Over the years, he has learned much from the many thousands of students he has taught and he is grateful for the many difficult questions posed by them. He is also grateful to his colleague and former PhD dissertation supervisor, Scott Forsyth, for his generous help and encouragement over the years. Finally, he thanks his immediate family, Joanne and Alex, for their love and support.

Tanner Mirrlees teaches communication and media studies at the University of Ontario Institute of Technology (UOIT) in the Communication Program. He is grateful to Joseph Kispal-Kovacs for sharing this project, his friendship, and his archival knowledge of TV shows. He thanks all of the Ryerson University, York University, and University of Guelph-Humber students he has taught over the past five years for teaching him what and how "TV" means to them. Finally, he thanks Colin Mooers and Scott Forsyth for being great peers, and Lauren Kirshner, who he will always love much more than TV.

And finally, both authors are grateful to the wonderful supportive staff at Oxford University Press, in particular Tamara Capar and Stephen Kotowych for all their assistance and support.

The authors, along with Oxford University Press, would like to acknowledge the reviewers whose thoughtful comments and suggestions have helped to shape this text:

Blaine Allan, Queen's University
Paul Babiak, University of Toronto
Jody Baker, Simon Fraser University
Stan Beeler, University of Northern British Columbia
Marusya Bociurkiw, Ryerson University
Yasmin Jiwani, Concordia University
Kevin Schut, Trinity Western University
Ian Steinberg, Wilfrid Laurier University

Contributors

Mark Andrejevic
University of Iowa

Paul Attallah
Carleton University

Doris Baltruschat
Carleton University

Geoffrey Baym
University of North Carolina

Sandra Cañas
University of Texas

Gray Cavender
Arizona State University

Sue Collins
New York University

Dean Defino
Iona College

Sarah K. Deutsch
University of Wisconsin

Zoë Druick
Simon Fraser University

J. Matt Giglio
Virginia Polytechnic Institute and State University

Mark Goodman
Mississippi State University

Jonathan Gray
Fordham University

Mark Gring
University of Texas of the Permian Basin

Lucas Hilderbrand
University of California, Irvine

Marsha Kinder
University of Southern California

Elana Levine
University of Wisconsin-Milwaukee

Matthew P. McAllister
Pennsylvania State University

Mark A. McCutcheon
Athabasca University

Daniel S. Mason
University of Maryland, College Park

Eileen R. Meehan
Louisiana State University

Marc Raboy
McGill University

Lynn Spigel
Northwestern University

Serra Tinic
University of Alberta

Elspeth Van Veeren
University of Bristol

Silvio Waisbord
Academy for Educational Development

Introduction

Making Critical TV Studies "Visible"

The Television Reader is about TV in Canada and the United States, two countries that share the largest border in the world and are economically, politically, and culturally proximate. Television is a tremendously important part of their economies, politics, and cultures. Television is big business. Media corporations develop, produce, sell, and schedule TV shows to maximize profits. Advertising companies buy ad space from TV networks to spark demand for their goods and services. Television is politics. Governments view TV as a national culture industry and an important contributor to the Gross Domestic Product (GDP). State agencies regulate, promote, and protect national TV systems on behalf of public and private interests. Political parties use TV to persuade citizens to vote for leaders and support policies. Television is communication and culture. Television networks transmit images and messages over vast distances that represent "ways of life" to people who rely on TV as a source of entertainment and information. Television is everywhere and millions of people are watching it right now.

Television's pervasiveness makes it difficult to analyze, though many generations of scholars have tried. In the late 1960s, Marshall McLuhan (1989)—a maverick Canadian media theorist—argued that "the electric media constitute a total and near instantaneous transformation of culture, values and attitudes" (107). McLuhan saw North American society being changed by TV and worried that TV viewers were "as unaware of the psychic and social effects of [t]his new technology as a fish of the water it swims"(105). McLuhan believed that TV's psychological and societal impacts were "invisible"(105), and he strove to make TV's impacts "visible" by encouraging people to study TV: "If we understand the revolutionary transformations caused by the new media," declared McLuhan, "we can anticipate and control them"(106). Since McLuhan's time, "TV studies" has become an established field of scholarly inquiry in Canadian and American universities. Television studies scholars seek to understand the history, economy, politics, and cultures of TV. Students enroll in communication studies, media studies, and cultural studies programs to take courses in which they examine TV (and perhaps enjoy a few episodes of *Family Guy*). Journals circulate peer-reviewed articles about TV industries, policies, texts, and viewers. The mainstream news media feature "popular criticism" of TV shows by entertainment journalists. TV show fan-books entail detailed plot synopses. Using social media, viewers chat about and interpret their favourite TV shows. An academic, commercial, and popular discourse about TV in society grows larger each day.

Television studies scholars focus on many facets of TV, including the TV industry, the cultural policies that govern TV, the social meaning of TV shows, and the reception of TV shows by viewers. "Television scholars today enjoy the sometimes perplexing privilege of addressing an object of study that is undergoing fundamental revisions," says William Boddy (2005: 82). They address TV using many methodological and theoretical perspectives, including political economy of communication, cultural studies, history, feminism, and more. The study of TV is an interdisciplinary project. *The Television Reader* makes some of the most salient parts of the study of TV palpable by presenting articles about Canadian and American TV that help "make visible" the ways TV shapes and is shaped by society.

The Television Reader presents critical perspectives in Canadian and American TV studies. A "critical" perspective is not necessarily a negative view of TV, despite how the word might sound. Being "critical" does not mean making a knee-jerk moral value-judgment about TV (as either bad or good). For example, without even studying TV industries, policies, texts, or viewers, some "armchair" critics might jump to the conclusion that TV is bad and bad for society. "TV is bad because it is dumbing society down," says person A, who believes he or she is smarter or more analytical than everyone else when watching TV sitcoms each night for hours. Equally problematic is the assumption that TV is essentially good and good for society. "TV entertainment is good because it reflects what people want," says person B, who does not understand how the actual TV industry works. When not supported by a discussion of what a "good society" is or by rigorous analysis, moral criticism impedes rather than enhances our understanding of TV in society. In *The Television Reader*, being "critical" does not necessarily mean being moralistic, though readers may eventually develop a moral critique of TV through their studies. Neil Postman (1985), an important American TV scholar, claims that "television is our culture's principal mode of knowing about itself"(92). A central task of critical TV studies is to contribute to and deepen public knowledge about the role and impact of TV in society. Critical TV studies requires an examination of the economic, political, and cultural forces that shape TV in society; an analysis of the dominant assumptions, values, and views surrounding TV; and a consideration of how power is exercised, reinforced, and contested by media owners, advertisers, cultural policy-makers, viewers, and even activists through TV.

Canadian and American TV: A Binational View

While *The Television Reader* is customized to suit the TV viewing habits of English-speaking Canadian media studies instructors and their students, it is not a Canadian cultural nationalist book. A cultural nationalist TV studies book would likely include essays by Canadian scholars about Canada's distinctive TV broadcasting system (its history, industry, policies) and Canadian TV shows (defined as TV shows produced by Canadian cultural workers that represent significant Canadian themes, issues, and settings). However, *The Television Reader* is a "binationalist" book. It entails articles about Canadian *and* American TV histories, industries, policies, texts, and viewers written by Canadian *and* US scholars. Our rationale for the *Television Reader*'s binational view is twofold. We include articles that represent what English-speaking Canadian viewers are watching (a mix of Canadian and American TV shows). We also focus on the economic, cultural, and technological proximity and growing convergence of Canadian and American TV systems.

Canada and the United States are distinct nation-states, but they share economic trade relations, political alliances, and popular entertainment, including TV shows. Even the negotiations that led to the 1988 Canada–US Free Trade Agreement (CAFTA) and the 1994 North American Free Trade Agreement (NAFTA), which turned Canada and the United States into a massive trading bloc, were watched on TV. Huge numbers of goods advertised on TV by giant US corporations and their Canadian subsidiaries cross the Canada–US border every day. Television ads promote **consumerism** as a dominant "way of life" in both countries. US presidential campaigns are regularly broadcast on Canadian TV networks with patriotic fanfare (Canadian politics has yet to attract a mass audience in the United States). Both countries belong to multilateral organizations of "global governance," including the G-8, the G-20, the International Monetary Fund (IMF), the North Atlantic Treaty Organization (NATO), the Security and Prosperity Partnership of North America (SPP), the World Trade Organization (WTO), the World Bank (WB), and the United Nations (UN). Private TV networks provide a partial and often parochial window to Canadian–US foreign relations. Canada and the United States are also culturally proximate nations. Prime-time network TV shows remind viewers that English is the most spoken language in both countries. Many TV news and entertainment shows are slowly beginning to represent the multicultural diversity of Canada and the United States, two countries that annually receive hundreds of thousands of new immigrants. Television visually ties Canadian and American economies, polities, and cultures together.

There are many points of convergence between the Canadian and American TV systems. In the twenty-first century, Canada and the United States both have capitalist culture industries that produce TV shows as commodities for circulation within domestic markets and for export to transnational markets. Television networks, private and public, are largely supported by advertising revenue. Canadian and American TV industries interact in interesting ways. Canadian and American TV production studios engage in a variety of treaty co-production agreements. They share creative talent, resources, and places to shoot (and often Canadian state subsidies). Canadian and American TV studios deliberately co-produce TV shows that intend to cross borders and enter many markets. American TV studios regularly "runaway" from Los Angeles, California, to shoot TV shows in Canadian creative cities such as Toronto, Vancouver, and Montreal. For example, ABC's *A Raisin in the Sun* was shot in Toronto; NBC's *Aliens in America* was shot in Vancouver; and SyFy's *Being Human* was shot in Montreal. Canadian actors move to Los Angeles in hopes of becoming global Hollywood celebrities. Pamela Anderson (*Baywatch*), John Candy (*Saturday Night Live*), Kim Cattrall (*Sex in the City*), Michael Cera (*Arrested Development*), Tom Green (*Tom Green Show*), Ryan Gosling (*Young Hercules*), Michael J. Fox (*Family Ties*), Mike Myers (*Saturday Night Live*), Mia Kirshner (*The L Word*), Jason Priestly (*Beverly Hills 90210*), and Kiefer Sutherland (*24*) are a few of the Canadian actors featured in American TV.

American TV has long been central to the growth and profitability of private and public Canadian TV networks. Canada is one of the only nation-states in the world where most of its citizens watch more foreign TV shows (imported from the United States) than home-grown ones. The English-Canadian experience of watching scheduled TV began with the United States. Before the Canadian Broadcasting Corporation (CBC) had a TV division or Canadian private TV networks existed, Canadian viewers were consuming American TV programs. The English-language CBC began broadcasting TV in 1952. Despite CBC's public mandate to defend high-cultural Canadian values against low-cultural Americanization, it started filling up its prime-time schedule with American TV shows. This helped CBC build an audience for Canadian TV shows. In the late 1950s, American TV shows made up more than half of the CBC schedule. Canadians watched made-in-Canada TV shows such as *Down Yonder, U.N. Dateline,* and *Dancing Storybook* alongside *The Perry Como Show, The Howdy Doody Show,* and *The Ed Sullivan Show* (Filion 1996: 467). In 2010, more than 25 per cent of CBC's prime-time schedule featured American TV shows, including popular game shows such as *Wheel of Fortune* and *Jeopardy!* (Sturgeon 2010).

Private TV networks including CTV, Global, satellite, and specialty pay-per-view cable stations purchase and re-transmit American TV shows to Canadian viewers. In 1986, the six top-rated TV shows in English-audience Canada were imported from the United States. Four of these TV shows were re-transmitted by CTV and the other two US shows were broadcast by the CBC (Filion 1996: 462).

In 2007–2008, Canada's private TV broadcasters spent a record $775.2 million acquiring US TV shows (up 7.4 per cent from $721.9 million in 2006–2007) (CCA 2009). In 2009–2010, the top five most-watched TV shows in Canada were *Survivor: Samoa & Heroes vs. Villains* (Global), *Grey's Anatomy* (CTV), *Criminal Minds* (CTV), *American Idol – Performance* (CTV), and *American Idol – Results* (CTV). The ratio of US imports to English-language Canadian TV drama was five to one in 2000. By 2008, the ratio was nine to one. In 2009, CTV was the top re-broadcaster of American TV shows, scheduling eight of the ten most-watched American TV programs in prime time.

Scheduling American TV shows is big business for Canadian TV networks. It costs less to acquire American TV shows than to produce a Canadian TV show that Canadian viewers might not want to watch. Since US media corporations usually recover production costs associated with TV shows in the US market (which is at least ten times the size of Canada's market), they can afford to offer Canadian TV networks TV shows "made for America" at a substantial discount. By scheduling American TV programs, Canadian TV networks usually attract a large audience, which advertising clients pay to reach. Canadian TV networks "simulcast" or simultaneously re-broadcast American TV shows. Thus, when American sports fans in Los Angeles watch the Super Bowl, so too do Canadian fans in Calgary, Charlottetown, and Gatineau. Canadian TV networks profit-maximize by simulcasting American TV shows but removing the US ads and replacing them with ads paid for by Canadian ad firms.

Many Canadian viewers want to watch TV shows about Canada, made by Canadian TV networks. Canadian TV sitcoms like *18 to Life*, *Little Mosque on the Prairie*, *Hiccups*, and *Dan for Mayor* attract a large Canadian audience and are very popular. Canadians also like watching American TV shows, which have been part of English-Canadian culture for a long time. The English-Canadian and American audience are culturally proximate—they share the same language and many similar cultural referent points. Canadian viewers are not forced to watch imported American TV shows and are certainly not "Americanized" dupes for doing so. Canadians are no less "Canadian" when they consume *Sons of Anarchy* reruns. They are entirely capable of engaging in meaningful forms of political activism nationally and internationally (sometimes against the policies of the Canadian and US state) while enjoying *The Wire*. Canadians watched *The Family Guy* in 2003, but this did not deter them from pre-emptively marching for peace in protest of the US invasion of Iraq. Many Canadians enjoy American TV shows because they are good (exciting, entertaining, thought-provoking, and edgy), not because they are "American." The reason why Canadian viewers like or dislike US TV shows perhaps has little to do with "nation-ness."

The Canadian and American TV systems are also converging due to the state-mandated transition from analog TV to digital TV. In 1997, the United States initiated a transition to fully digital broadcasting. In that same year, Canada chose to adopt the American **Advanced Television Systems Committee (ATSC)** standard. In 2009, the United States transitioned from analog to digital. Canada switched to digital TV in 2011. This switch compelled TV viewers who once captured signals with "rabbit ears" to buy a digital convertor box or a new digital-tuner-equipped TV. Today, digital TV is the new standard for Canadian and US broadcast TV, as it frees up spectrum space and enables transmission of high-definition (HD) video and surround-sound audio. The analog shutdown is "a product of a bilateral Canada/U.S. agreement"(Bowman 2009). The public interest implications of the digital transition were debated in the United States. But in Canada, the digital TV transition was mainly handled by industry and "designed to protect industry interests first and foremost"(Taylor 2010: 20). The digital transition has generated a lot of revenue for the US and Canadian states. The US Federal Communications Commission (FCC) got bids for spectrum space totalling about $19 billion. Industry Canada got bids for $4.3 billion from media firms.

Though the Canadian and American TV systems are converging in important economic and technological ways, *The Television Reader* also accounts for how significant cultural and political differences between the two countries persist, especially in the governmental sphere of "cultural policy."

Canadian TV Studies: Beyond Cultural Imperialism Anxiety and the Cultural Nationalist Policy Reflex?

The Television Reader's recognition of the points of convergence between the Canadian and Ameican TV systems might be interpreted as lending tacit support to US cultural imperialism in Canada. However, we are not apologists for global Hollywood's economic and cultural dominance or the active role that the US government plays in supporting its interests. Television is an integral part of the US "Empire," no doubt. It is a major US culture industry export, serves the economic interests of transnational corporations by promoting commercialism to the world, and shores up support for US foreign policy as a source of "soft power." In the twenty-first century, the American TV industry is larger, wealthier, and more culturally powerful than Canada's. There is an asymmetrical power relationship between the Canadian and American TV industries. There is no audiovisual trade reciprocity between Canada and the United States. We don't dispute these points. But in response, we do not take up a defensive cultural-nationalist position and call for state cultural policy actors to stave off "Americanization." *The Television Reader* does not posit the existence of a fledgling Canadian TV industry struggling to survive the economic and cultural incursions of the US media empire. In the twenty-first century, Canada possesses a large and profitable TV industry. US media dominance in Canada was not achieved by coercive domination, but by invitation. Canadian corporate actors have long sought to capitalize on the TV industry's proximity to the United States while maintaining a governmental system of subsidies and protections.

The Television Reader's binational focus reflects the spirit of Paul Attalah (2007; 2009), Bart Beaty and Rebecca Sullivan (2006), Serra Tinic (2005), Ira Wagman (2010), and other scholars who put critical pressure on and attempt to complicate cultural-nationalist TV studies. Twenty-first century "critical" Canadian TV studies can be done without consolidating Canadian essentialist cultural nationalist myths and perpetuating anxieties about the threat of US cultural imperialism to Canada's "whole way of life." In an era when TV industries in the US, Canada, and many other countries are being integrated, networked together, and corporatized by global capitalism and neo-liberal policies, is it possible to identify distinctive "national" TV systems and national cultures? How are Canadian and American TV systems similar and different? What characteristics are particular and which ones are universal? How are "distinctive" national TV systems and cultures constructed and differentiated? What interest groups have a stake in making, maintaining, and managing national distinctions? Why?

The Television Reader's binational focus also complicates policy-oriented Canadian TV studies. For a very long time, "The critical-ness of Canadian communication [and media] studies has been mapped onto discourses of the ongoing search for a unique Canadian national identity"(Hamilton 2010: 21). This search has led to a cultural "policy reflex"(Wagman 2010) by many TV studies scholars who engage with cultural policy issues even when "policy analysis" is not their goal. The cultural policy reflex draws professors and students into simplistic nationalist discussions "where media consumption is an expression of national identity or where the success or failure of a given piece of culture reflects the essence of Canadianness or the efforts of bureaucrats to structure it into existence"(Wagman 2010: 627). The policy reflex has major consequences for critical TV studies in Canada. As Attalah (2009) states: "We have no strong tradition of television study in this country. Instead, we have royal commissions, Senate inquiries and bureaucratic investigations with all their wooden compromises, unexpurgated agendas, political meanness, and incumbent posturing"(170). The cultural policy reflex does not always lead to greater knowledge about cultural policy, democratic policy-making, progressive policy proposals, or outcomes. We encourage students to analyze Canadian and American TV without taking up cultural policy functions or mimicking a cultural policy discourse that is not of their own making. That being said, the cultural-nationalist policy reflex of Canadian TV studies is not inherently disagreeable. Nor is it always "uncritical." More critical TV scholars should participate in the cultural policy debating, analyzing, and shaping process, shouting at and within the bureaucracy, where powerful media firms try to control most of the analysts, regulators, and politicians that do the public talking. They can do so without appealing to nationalist clichés. Research on communication rights and the right to communicate (Raboy and Schtern 2010) and alternative and community media (Kozolanka, Mazepa, and Skinner, 2012) represents the best of Canada's critical cultural policy tradition. In the United States, Robert McChesney (2007; 2008) and other policy researchers spearheaded a vibrant public struggle against media concentration and for media democracy. Research that connects with democratic cultural policy-making can do a lot of good.

The Methodological "Bias": Cultural Materialism

The Television Reader entails many articles that represent "political economy of the media" and "**cultural studies**" methodological and theoretical approaches to the study of TV. According to Robert Babe (2009): "*Cultural studies* may be loosely defined as the multidisciplinary study of culture across various social strata, where culture refers to arts, knowledge, beliefs, customs, practices, and norms of social interaction. *Studies in political economy of media*, in contrast, focus on the economic, financial, and political causes and consequences of culture"(4; italics in original). Throughout the late 1980s and 1990s, advocates of the political economy of the media and proponents of cultural studies described their respective approaches as radically different. A seminal debate in the late 1990s between Nicholas Garnham (representing "political economy of the media") and Lawrence Grossberg (representing "cultural studies") represented a seemingly irresolvable methodological clash.

In "Political Economy and Cultural Studies," Garnham (1999) criticizes "cultural studies" for focusing on the consumption of TV rather than its production (495), the politics of diverse cultural identities rather than working-class struggles (496), viewer pleasure and agency rather than corporate power (499), and the meanings of TV shows rather than the "structures of corporate domination" and state policy-making (502). Garnham presses cultural studies scholars to develop a more "critical" and politically committed study of the material realities of late capitalism, "the world we actually inhabit"(503). In "Cultural Studies vs. Political Economy: Is Anybody Else Bored with This Debate?" Grossberg (1999) responds to Garnham's criticisms of cultural studies. Grossberg fears that political economy entails a reductionist and vulgar economistic approach to TV. From Grossberg's perspective, a political-economy approach reduces TV to "a commodity and an ideological tool of manipulation"(619), views "the market as the site of commodified and alienated exchange"(623), and relies on an "ahistorical and consequently oversimplified notion of capitalism"(623). Grossberg concludes by stating that the political-economy approach "fails to take culture [...] and capitalism seriously enough"(622), and thus "has little room for complexity and contradiction"(619). The debate between Garnham and Grossberg resulted in a stalemate, not a synthesis of approaches.

The Television Reader employs "political economy" and "cultural studies" as complementary approaches, not antagonistic ones engaged in a futile academic turf war for pedagogical supremacy. We feel that the division of labour between political economy of the media and cultural studies approaches to TV is counterproductive and superficial. The best practitioners of political economy are those who integrate the insights of cultural studies, and the best practitioners of cultural studies are those who are firmly grounded in political economy. In fact, Babe (2009) argues that in the formative years of the political economy of the media and cultural studies, these approaches "were fully integrated, consistent, and mutually supportive"(4). *The Television Reader* agrees with this assessment. Raymond Williams (1981) once called for a "cultural materialist" approach to the media: "the analysis of all forms of signification [...] within the actual means and conditions of their production" (64–65). *The Television Reader* presents numerous articles that analyze the significations of TV shows within the actual political and economic means and conditions of their production. In support of this cultural materialist approach to TV, selected articles examine (1) the economy of TV industries; (2) the state policies governing TV; (3) the messages and imagery, systems of representation, and social meanings of TV texts; and (4) the interpretation of TV shows by viewers in reception contexts.

The Sections

The Television Reader is divided into four thematic sections: "Theorizing Television"; "History and Characteristics of TV Broadcasting in Canada and the United States: A Political Economy"; "Television Genre: Contexts and Textual Analysis"; and "Emerging Trends in TV Studies: Commercialism, Globalization, and Post-network TV." Each section is introduced by an original essay that summarizes and discusses the most significant scholarly perspectives in the field of TV studies and contextualizes the articles that follow.

The first section, "Theorizing Television," entails a new essay by the editors that reviews and synthesizes different critical approaches to the study of TV as culture and mass-mediated communication, texts, audiences and contexts, and communication technology. The essay surveys classic and contemporary contributions to the study of TV in society. The purpose of this section is to introduce students to the different ways TV scholars tend to conceptualize, understand, and analyze the role and effect of TV in society. We had originally planned to include in this section a number of seminal articles on TV theory by iconic Canadian, British, and American communication scholars such as Harold Innis, Marshall McLuhan, Neil Postman, Stuart Hall, Horace Newcomb, Raymond Williams, and others. But due to lack of space and our hope that students will have already encountered these key thinkers in a foundational "Introduction to Mass Communications" or "Media Studies 101" course, we decided to write a compact and accessible essay. This provided space to include newer and more pertinent articles in other sections.

The second section, "History and Characteristics of TV Broadcasting in Canada and the United States: A Political Economy," is about the political economy of Canadian and American TV. The articles in this section outline the political and economic forces that shape TV, providing a "big picture" comparison of the similarities and differences of Canadian and American TV industries and policy structures. They explore how markets, the profit-interests of media firms, and cultural policy shape the content, production, and distribution of TV in both national contexts. The articles introduce students to the history of TV in Canada and the United States and help them to understand how forces that operate "behind TV screens" shape in significant ways what they see when they watch TV.

The third section, "Television Genre: Contexts and Textual Analysis," includes a number of contemporary articles about TV genre. The articles combine political-economy and cultural studies approaches and do textual analysis of specific TV shows. The articles introduce students to the study of TV as a commercially produced genre and powerful medium of social representation. Television genres don't simply "reflect" the world, but play an active role in constructing and shaping it. Liz Czach (2010) says: "The analysis of actual television shows [in Canada] has seriously lagged behind that of American or British television studies, and this new 'turn' toward textual analysis acts as a necessary corrective"(175). We encourage students to contribute to the recent "textual turn" in Canadian TV studies by examining the production contexts, specific formal characteristics, and social messages of TV genres. Articles in this section provide good starting points.

The fourth section, "Emerging Trends in TV Studies: Commercialism, Globalization and Post-network TV," examines continuity and change in twenty-first-century TV. The articles in this section focus on the new media audience, TV advertising and commercialism, TV globalization, and post-network TV. At the end of each section is a "Suggestions for Further Reading" list that entails important articles and books about TV and "Discussion Questions."

What's "In" and What's "Out"?

Putting together *The Television Reader* entailed a rigorous selection process. *The Television Reader* does not attempt to represent everything that is occurring in Canadian and American TV studies because that would be impossible given the breadth of the subject and size of the field. *The Television Reader* does not include work by all of the excellent TV studies scholars, though it does highlight works by some of the most important contributors to TV studies in the "Suggestions for Further Reading" lists. Some articles that we originally sought to include were removed due to lack of space. Others were replaced by more contemporary and relevant articles as they became available. We considered including a section that *explicitly* examined TV's representation of race, class, gender, and sexuality. Many excellent books and articles on this topic are referred to in Part I, "Suggestions for Further Reading," and numerous articles in Part III, "Television Genre: Contexts and Textual Analysis," deal with this topic indirectly. Overall, *The Television Reader* includes challenging but accessible articles that reflect some of the most interesting currents in the field.

The Television Reader includes articles on commercially successful and popular English-language Canadian and American TV shows for pedagogical and practical reasons. Excluded are articles that examine Francophone TV, indigenous TV (Miller 2000; Roth 2005), regional TV (Varga 2009), community TV (Kozolenko, Mazepa, and Skinner, forthcoming), and diaspora TV (Naficy 1993; Thussu 2007). These are all important parts of the twenty-first-century contemporary Canadian, American, and transnational TV landscape, but we wanted to include scholarship on TV shows that readers would likely be familiar with and that are available. Sadly, DVDs of many older Canadian TV shows are hard to find and newer Canadian TV shows are irregularly rerun. Tinic (2009) refers to Canada as a "no-rerun nation." All of the TV shows discussed in *The Television Reader* are available on DVD (and are often rerun). We hope that you will find the introductory essays and articles presented by *The Television Reader* a stimulating and useful guide to the critical study of TV in Canada and the United States.

Tanner Mirrlees and Joseph Kispal-Kovacs *August 2011*

Works Cited

Attalah, P. (2007). "A Usable History for the Study of Television." *Canadian Review of American Studies*, Vol. 30(3): 325–45.

———. (2009). "Review Essay: Reading Television." *Canadian Journal of Communication*, Vol. 34: 163–70.

Babe, R. (2009). *Cultural Studies and Political Economy: Toward a New Integration.* Lanham, MD: Lexington Books.

Beaty, B., and Sullivan, R. (2006). *Canadian Television Today.* Calgary, AB: University of Calgary Press.

Boddy, W. (2005). "In Focus: The Place of Television Studies." *Cinema Journal*, Vol. 45: 79–82.

Bowman, J. (12 June 2009). "Canadian Over-the-air TV Following U.S. Down Digital Path." www.cbc.ca/news/canada/story/2009/06/01/f-digital-tv-transition.html

CCA Bulletin (9 April 2009). "Canadian Cultural Exports: A Growing Success Worth Investing In." www.ccarts.ca/en/advocacy/bulletins/2009/1109.htm

Czach, L. (2010). "The 'Turn' in Canadian Television Studies." *Journal of Canadian Studies*, 44(3): 174–88.

Filion, M. (1996). "Broadcasting and Cultural Identity: The Canadian Experience." *Media, Culture & Society*, Vol. 18(1): 447–67.

Garnham, N. (1999). "Political Economy and Cultural Studies." In S. During (Ed.), *The Cultural Studies Reader* (pp. 492–503). New York: Routledge.

Grossberg, L. (1999). "Cultural Studies vs. Political Economy: Is Anybody Else Bored with This Debate?" In J. Storey (Ed.), *Cultural Theory and Popular Culture* (pp. 614–24). New York: Routledge.

Hamilton, S.H. (2010). "Considering Critical Communication Studies in Canada." In L.R. Shade (Ed.), *Mediascapes: New Patterns in Canadian Communication* (pp. 9–26). Toronto: Nelson.

Kozolanka, K., Mazepa, P., and Skinner, D. (Eds). (2012). *Alternative Media in Canada.* Vancouver: UBC Press.

McChesney, R.M. (2007). *Communication Revolution: Critical Junctures and the Future of Media.* New York: The New Press.

———. (2008). *The Political Economy of Media: Enduring Issues, Emerging Dilemmas.* New York: Monthly Review Press.

McLuhan, M. (1989). "Playboy Interview with Marshall McLuhan: A Candid Conversation with the High Priest of Popcult and Metaphysician of the Media." *Canadian Journal of Communication*, Vol. 14(101): 104–19.

Miller, M.J. (2000). *Outside Looking In: Viewing First Nations People in Canadian Dramatic Television Series.* Montreal: McGill-Queen's University Press.

Naficy, H. (1993). *The Making of Exile Cultures: Iranian Television in Los Angeles.* Minneapolis: University of Minnesota Press.

Postman, N. (1985). *Amusing Ourselves to Death.* New York: Penguin.

Roth, L.F. (2005). *Something New in the Air: The Story of First Peoples Television Broadcasting n Canada.* Canada: McGill-Queen's University Press.

Raboy, M., and Schtern, J. (2010). *Media Divides: Communication Rights and the Right to Communicate in Canada.* Vancouver: UBC Press.

Sturgeon, J. (21 June 2010). "CBC Runs Fewer Canadian Shows in Prime Time." www.friends.ca/news-item/9552

Taylor, G. (2010). "Shut-Off: The Digital Television Transition in the United States and Canada." *Canadian Journal of Communication*, Vol. 35(1): 7–25.

Thussu, D.K. (2007). *Media on the Move: Global Flow and Contra-flow.* New York: Routledge.

Tinic, S. (2005). *On Location: Canada's Television Industry in a Global Market.* Toronto: University of Toronto Press.

———. (2009). "No ReRun Nation: Canadian Television and Cultural Amnesia." http://flowtv.org/2009/06/no-rerun-nation-canadian-television-and-cultural-amnesia-serra-tinic-university-of-alberta/

Varga, D. (Ed.) (2009). *Rain/Drizzle/Fog: Film and Television in Atlantic Canada.* Calgary: University of Calgary Press.

Wagman, I. (2010). "On the Policy Reflex in Canadian Communication Studies." *Canadian Journal of Communication*, Vol. 35: 619–30.

Williams, R. (1981). *Culture.* London: Fontana.

THE Television READER

Theorizing Television

Critical Approaches to the Study of "TV": An Introduction

Tanner Mirrlees and Joseph Kispal-Kovacs

What is television? That flat-screen 40-inch LCD screen used to watch TV shows each day? The TV series stored in digital files (legally or illegally downloaded) on a laptop computer or mobile phone? The TV program streamed from a TV network's website on a tablet at your local coffee shop? The stories and characters that comprise the text of a prime-time TV show? Business relationships among TV production companies, TV networks, adverting corporations, and **ratings** firms? The **copyright** to a TV show, which is controlled by a vertically integrated media corporation? Orbiting satellites? The pleasure or boredom felt while watching a TV show? The effect TV has on society? The concept of "television" encompasses all of the above. This introductory chapter reviews some of the main ways of conceptualizing and studying TV. In this chapter, TV is expressed and analyzed in the four following ways: (1) as culture and mass-mediated communication; (2) as texts; (3) as audiences and contexts; and (4) as communication technology.

Television as "Culture" and Mass-mediated Communication

Television is an integral part of Canadian and American "cultures." Raymond Williams (1976) says culture is "one of the two or three most complicated words in the English language"(87). Culture originally meant the tending or cultivation of something (animals and crops in particular). Since the eighteenth century, culture has often been described in the following two ways: (1) as "a particular way of life, whether of a people, a period or a group or humanity in general"(90); and (2) as "the works and practices of intellectual and especially artistic activity"(90). In Canada and the United States, TV is "culture" in both of Williams' uses of the term. Television is interwoven with the "customs, beliefs and practices which constitute the way of life of a specific group" of people (Eagleton 2000: 34). It is also a significant cultural product (part of the works and practices of intellectual and artistic activity) that the culture industries of Canada and the United States produce and distribute as a commodity in a marketplace. The introductory essay in Part II of *The Television Reader*, "History and Characteristics of TV Broadcasting in Canada and the United States: A Political Economy," discusses TV as a culture industry product. In what follows, we discuss TV as part of North America's "way of life."

Television ownership is customary. North American homes are expected to have TV sets. Most do. In 1950, TV penetration in US households was only 9.0 per cent. In 1965, TV penetration reached 92.6 per cent. By 2010, 98.9 per cent of homes had TV sets. Each US household has about three TV sets (Editorial 2010). Few people live without TV. In the late 1970s, Jerry Mander (1978) argued for the elimination of TV. Mander believed that TV made viewers susceptible to ideological manipulation by elites and threatened democracy. Since 1994, TV-Free America (TVFA; now called Center for SCREEN-TIME Awareness or CSTA) has encouraged citizens to reduce the amount of TV they watch in order to promote richer, healthier, and more productive lives, families, and communities. With the support of *Adbusters*, CSTA annually organizes a "TV Turn Off" week. Many people do turn off their TV for a week each year, but for the remaining 51 weeks, TV sets tend to be on. Buying a TV set, placing it in the household, and watching TV shows are customary acts. Television is also on people's minds. People talk with friends, family members, and co-workers about the TV shows they watch; have conversations about whether to buy LCD or LED TV sets; and discuss the effects of TV in society. Watching TV is something the majority of people ritualistically do every day. Television is a routinized cultural practice: "Wake up, turn on the television, get ready, leave for work/school, go home, turn on the television, sleep: [this is] a fairly standard day in the life of the average person"(Gray 2007: 2). Nielsen—a ratings firm—claims that the average North American TV viewer watches a little more than 34 hours of TV each week (Stelter 2011). People are differentiated by their socio-economic class, political views, gender, ethnicity, and religion. But what many people share in common in North America is their consumption of TV. Embedded in custom, belief, and practice, TV is an integral part of Canadian and American cultures.

Television is also a form of mass-mediated communication. The word *communication* comes from the Latin word *comminicare*. This means to impart, share, or make common information or ideas. At its best, communication is a dialogue between two or more people that involves interaction and reciprocity. At its worst, communication is a one-way monologue by a person who strives to impose their ideas upon others. Face-to-face communication happens with our partners, local grocery clerks, and co-workers. Mediated communication occurs between two or more people that while physically separate or set apart are connected together by communication technology. Talking with a friend using Skype or participating in a Facebook-enabled discussion with family members are examples of mediated communication. Unlike face-to-face communication, mass-mediated communication reaches many people that are not located in the same physical place, *simultaneously*. Television **broadcasting** is an important form of mass-mediated communication; it involves the transmission or carriage of TV shows from one point to another, over vast distances (Carey 1989). Television transmission entails a source or *sender* (a TV network, a cable service, Netflix) that distributes a message (a TV show) to a *receiver* (a TV viewer or audience). Technological screens (TV sets, laptop computers, mobile phones) come between TV senders and receivers. Message distortion or interference—poor picture reception, an Internet connection timeout, loss of sound—are called "noise." Viewers may give TV networks "feedback" through ratings, blogging about TV shows, sending emails to TV networks, or changing the channel. Feedback helps TV networks adjust their scheduling strategies in response to TV viewers.

Television viewers may also interpret TV shows in a range of different ways. Stuart Hall (2000) argues that corporate TV networks strive to gain the consent of TV viewers to "preferred" meanings in TV shows in hopes of bringing about a predictable "effect." Viewers, on the other hand, decode TV shows in their own and often unpredictable ways. He further states that there is a "relatively autonomous" relationship between the production context of TV shows (in which TV firms encode TV shows for specific purposes) and the consumption context of TV shows (in which viewers decode TV shows). Hall (2000) distinguishes between three types of viewer decoding: (1) a *dominant hegemonic decoding* (TV viewers passively and uncritically accept the TV message's preferred meaning); (2) a *negotiated decoding* (TV viewers understand the TV message's preferred meaning, but slightly dissent from it); and (3) an *oppositional decoding* (TV viewers understand the dominant or preferred meaning of the TV show message but reformulate, criticize, and reconstitute it in a different and sometimes politically subversive way). Though TV viewers can decode TV shows in a range of ways, they cannot construct whatever meanings they like. As Hall (2000) clarifies:

> encoding will have the effect of constructing some of the limits and parameters within which decodings

> will operate. If there were no limits, audiences could simply read whatever they liked into any message. No doubt some total misunderstandings of this kind do exist. But the vast range must contain some degree of reciprocity between encoding and decoding moments, otherwise we could not speak of an effective communicative strategy at all. Nevertheless, the correspondence is not given but constructed. It is not natural but the product of an articulation between two distinct moments. And the former cannot guarantee or determine, in simple sense, which decoding codes will be employed. (173)

Television Shows as Texts: Ideology and Identity

Television shows can be studied as "texts" (Abercrombie 1996; Burns and Thompson 1989). A TV show is an encoded text and can convey meaning for a specific purpose. Television sitcoms convey meaning that intends to entertain; TV news clips communicate meaning to inform; TV ads impart meaning to persuade. As texts, TV shows can be "read." Critical TV studies scholars interpret the texts of TV shows, examining what TV shows mean and how they mean. Television shows do not "reflect" real life. They do not "hold a mirror" to society. Television show texts entail partial and selective representations of society. Their meanings are *constructed*. Homer, Marge, Bart, Lisa, and Maggie of *The Simpsons*, for example, are not real people. The plots dramatized by *The Simpsons* do not reflect real situations. *The Simpsons* stands in for reality as a partial and selective representation of it. All TV shows entail constructed representations of reality. These representations both reveal and conceal. While watching *Hockey Night in Canada*, Canadians only see the parts of the rink the Canadian Broadcasting Corporation (CBC) camerapeople focus on. Much is left out of the picture. *Glee* gives its viewers a limited view of American high school. Some teenage issues are dealt with, while others are ignored. TV shows therefore re-represent reality, depicting and framing it in partial and selective ways.

Television shows convey a wide number of competing representations of society. Many of TV's representations of society shape, in often profound ways, how people perceive themselves and the world. Television establishes "standards for deciding what is, standards for deciding what can be, standards for deciding how one feels about it, standards for deciding what to do about it and standards for deciding how to go about doing it"(Goodenough 1971: 22). In fact, TV is often a significant instrument of influence that shapes public consciousness, perceptions, and viewpoints. Public relations guru Walter Lippmann (1922) famously described a division between the world outside and the pictures of the world in people's minds, the actual environment and the pseudo-environment of representations (15). Lippmann worried that there was a big gap between the objective world and people's subjective perceptions of it. How big was the gap? Did people suffer a false consciousness about the actual world? Could people be misled as result? In the twenty-first century, TV representations emerge between the objective world and people's subjective perceptions of it. They frame the world outside of people's immediate and local experiences. But they are often mistaken as reflections of the way things are and always will be in society.

Critical TV studies scholars examine TV shows as influential participants in the social construction and representation of reality. They examine whether or not TV shows correspond to the reality they claim to represent or fundamentally distort reality on behalf of powerful interests in society. They also explore how and why TV shows might represent the world from the point of view of dominant groups at the expense of others. Television shows represent a "sense of reality" to viewers that is never value-neutral (Williams 1977). Whose sense of reality do commercial TV shows most often privilege?

Marxist, feminist, and anti-racist TV studies scholars present provocative responses to this question. They argue that TV shows are not apolitical, harmless, or value-free forms of "entertainment." Rather, TV shows are carriers of "**ideology**," defined here as a system of ideas characteristic of a dominant class or group in society, or illusory, false, or distorted ideas that may be contrasted with true or objective knowledge (Williams 1977).

Classical Marxist TV scholars argue that TV's representations of reality promote capitalist ideology. Capitalist society is unequal. It is divided between the financial and industrial owners of the means of production ("the ruling class") and people that must sell their labour in exchange for a wage ("the working class"). Marxists argue that capitalism leads to conflicts between owners and workers, the rich and the poor. The ruling class minority struggles to maintain its power over society and the working class majority by instilling in people's consciousness a "dominant ideology." Ideology represents the world from the point of view of the ruling class while claiming to reflect everyone's point of view; it encourages working people to take ruling class ideas as their own. Capitalist ideology presents rugged individualism, extreme self-interest, and competition as good for everyone; private property as sacrosanct, and public goods as waste; the myth that North America is a vast, upwardly mobile, and ever-expanding middle-class society with no unequal social class structure; identity as a thing to be defined, possessed, and owned through rituals of commodity consumption and display; rich people as innately better than poor people and deserving of their wealth due to their hard work (not their inheritance); and the interests of corporations as the same as society's ("What's good for business is good for North America"). Classical Marxists argue that commercial TV is an instrument of ideological indoctrination. They analyze how TV shows convey, legitimize, and normalize capitalist ideology, promote "false consciousness," and represent and misrepresent the experience of the "working class."

Cultural Marxists present a more nuanced approach to the study of ideological power in society (Hall 2002). They argue that the lived and felt experience of subordinated social groups constantly comes into conflict with and often contradicts the dominant ideology. In response, ruling political blocs (coalitions of dominant class interests) must constantly struggle to build and rebuild their hegemony in society. The concept of "**hegemony**" describes the ruling class's struggle to exert moral leadership in society using strategies of coercion and ideological persuasion, brute force, and consent building (Gramsci 1968). In this context, cultural Marxists view TV as an instrument of ideological persuasion used to *organize the consent* of people to the goals of a ruling bloc. Television viewers are sometimes lied to by pundits dispatched to TV networks from corporate-financed think-tanks, advertising firms, and government-sponsored spin agencies (Ewen 1996; Gutstein 2009; Herman and Chomsky 1988). But not all TV shows communicate a single dominant ideology that serves one dominant class (Hall 2002). Rather, TV shows participate in political struggles for hegemony, legitimizing and de-legitimizing different ideologies. Television is a "terrain of struggle" over what people take (or refuse to take) for granted as "common sense." TV networks (and TV shows) stage struggles for "hegemony" between rival political blocs. Rupert Murdoch's Fox News, for example, promotes conservative ideology while attacking social democratic ideologies. Canada's Sun TV—branded as "Fox News North"—promotes the views of Canada's "New Right." Classic and cultural Marxists present a useful critical approach to the study of how commercial TV participates in the ideological reproduction of capitalism and class dominance.

Feminist TV studies scholars make a tremendously important contribution to the critical study of TV (Arthurs 2003; Baehr and Dyer 1987; Brunsdon, D'Acci, and Spigel 2007; Dow 1996; Hollows 2000; Johnson 2007). Early feminist TV scholars argued that TV's representations of reality promoted the ideology of patriarchy or "male dominance." Women are treated in a range of oppressive ways by men. In Canada and the United States, men control more wealth than women. Men often get paid a higher wage than women for doing similar jobs. Men have more political power than women in government. Many men and women work full-time jobs, but women are often expected to do unpaid domestic work like cooking, cleaning, and tending to the needs of children. Men abuse women. Feminists argue that patriarchy is maintained through a conjunction of institutions (the home, the state, the corporation, and the university) and representations (of women and men in society). Feminist TV studies scholars examine how TV (as an institution and a powerful means of producing and circulating representations) both support and challenge patriarchy. Television representations of gender can have very real effects; they shape perceptions, behaviours, and bodies. Feminists ask the following questions: do TV representations of women help or hamper gender equality? Does TV play a role in maintaining inequitable gender relations between men and women in society or is it an instrument for promoting greater gender equality between them?

Feminist TV studies scholars argue that TV shows represent negative stereotypes of women that perpetuate negative stereotypes of women in society, hindering their equality and opportunity. Many TV shows represent women in stereotypical gender roles that distort the complexity, independence, and diversity of women. Television shows often represent women as innately domestic beings, emotionally unstable and infantile, dependent on men, one-dimensional beauties, and dehumanized sex objects. Yet, TV represents a variety of images of women too, some regressive and others progressive. Shows such as *The Cosby Show* (1984–1992) and *Growing Pains* (1985–1992) represent "superwomen" who amazingly work full-time jobs out of the home and do full-time domestic work within it. Shows including *Mary Tyler Moore* (1970–1977), *Ally McBeal* (1997– 2002), and *Sex and the City* (1998–2004) represent women as independent professionals, pursuing careers and going shopping. Post-feminist TV shows promote the idea that the feminist goals of equal opportunity, equal pay, and equal rights in the workplace have been attained by women. They emphasize women's individual freedom as being achieved through depoliticized consumerism (partaking in cosmetic surgery makeovers or shopping for new clothing, houses, or experiences). The twenty-first-century TV landscape entails many competing representations of women in society that provide a rich site for feminist TV studies. Critical TV studies scholars also analyze how TV shows represent men and masculinity (M&M) and challenge the hetero-normativity of the field by exploring TV's representation of lesbian, gay, bisexual, and transgendered (LGBT) individuals and communities.

Anti-racist TV studies scholars argue that TV's representations of reality often promote the ideology of racism: the idea that there are inherent, essential, and unchanging differences in a group of people's physical and psychological traits and capacities due to their "race" and, as a consequence, forms of racist oppression and discrimination against the racialized group in society are okay. Racist ideology represents certain groups of people as innately superior and other groups as inferior. Racist ideology normalizes hateful practices. Specific social groups are subjected to physical violence and symbolic violence because they are deemed racially "other." Racism also works through acts of discrimination, exclusionary practices or acts of bias toward social groups. Despite liberal multicultural policies and the politics of cultural recognition, racist ideology continues to oppress many people, discriminating against them on the basis of their skin colour, which continues to signify as the chief marker of racial identity in North America.

Anti-racist TV scholars examine how TV participates in the construction of race and racial identities, and how TV shows may support or contest racist ideology in North American society. This line of inquiry focuses on how TV shows under-represent, represent, and misrepresent racialized groups in society. For most of TV's history, prime-time TV shows often represented middle-class whiteness as a racially superior norm. Television networks privileged the representation of white middle-class identities in TV shows while excluding the experiences and struggles of people of colour. Gray (1995) argues that contemporary TV shows do represent racialized groups, but in partial and selective ways. *Assimilationist TV shows* "are distinguished by the complete elimination or, at best, marginalization of social and cultural differences in the interest of shared and universal similarity"(85). These TV shows promote a vision of racial equality that conceals racism. People of colour are represented as living middle-class North American dreams and as having achieved economic, political, and cultural equality relative to white people. Assimilationist TV shows represent a post-racist colour-blind world, an idealized or utopian vision of society. *Pluralist TV shows* emphasize differences between white and non-white people. Though differences are represented, "the social and historical contexts in which these acknowledged differences are expressed, sustained, and meaningful are absent"(87). Pluralist TV shows usually focus on individual relationships between white and non-white characters and deploy "racial difference" as a source of dramatic tension or comedy. *Multicultural TV* shows try to represent the lives, experiences, and struggles of non-white peoples and groups from their own vantage point. They represent the complex and contradictory experiences of people of colour.

Critical studies of TV's ideological representations of class, gender, and race demonstrate that commercially popular TV shows don't reflect everyone in society but often privilege the representation of some people (Dines and Humez 2002). Television shows often overrepresent middle- to upper-class white people while under-representing the majority working poor and various minority groups (indigenous people, people of colour, immigrants, and anti-capitalists). Yet, TV shows do not always represent class, gender, and racialized identities in a one-dimensional way. Demographic shifts combined with targeted TV **narrowcasting** and multichannel niche market programming have opened up and expanded TV's archive of representable and represented identities in society. Certainly, negative representations and harmful stereotypes of specific groups continue to circulate, but they do so within a business model that increasingly profit-maximizes by recognizing, commodifying, and representing diversity. Twenty-first-century TV shows do not always or necessarily enforce culturally homogeneous images of society upon a mass audience. Rather, media corporations package multicultural and lifestyle TV shows and deliver them to viewers so as to profit-maximize. For every lifestyle TV program, there is a corresponding audience niche that TV networks and advertisers have targeted. A neo-liberal identity politic based on demands for cultural recognition and positive multicultural representation is advanced by the commercial logics of the neo-network TV model (Curtin 1999). That being said, TV's representations of a culturally diverse society should not be mistaken for a systematic transformation of society; classism, patriarchy, racism, and homophobia persist. Yet, if TV was only a capitalist-racist-sexist ideology machine that served elite power interests, it would likely not be so "popular" among so many diverse people.

Television studies scholars examine TV show texts as "popular culture." Williams (1976) says that the word *popular* has four meanings: "well liked by many people"; "inferior kinds of work'; "work deliberately setting out to win favour with the people"; and "culture actually made by the people for themselves"(198–99). Many TV shows are well liked by many people; some TV shows are considered aesthetically inferior by cultural critics who make value-judgements (or cultural distinctions) about good TV and bad TV to legitimize their own elite tastes; most TV shows are designed to resonate with a specific audience demographic that is targeted by advertisers; TV shows are not made by viewers, but viewers do actively interpret TV shows. In the late 1970s, cultural studies scholars called for the study of TV as "popular culture"(Fiske and Hartley 1978; Newcomb 1974). Until then, many scholars refused to take the study of TV shows seriously. They denounced TV shows as tools of mass brainwashing or perceived popular TV shows as a threat to established high cultural forms. The Marxist view that TV shows were transmission belts of a dominant ideology that legitimized the capitalist status quo and the cultural-elitist notion that TV shows were dumbed down and aesthetically depraved mass-cultural forms precluded complex analyses of the meanings of TV shows and a deeper understanding of why people enjoyed them. Cultural studies scholars provide a number of useful approaches to TV as popular culture.

Cultural studies scholars examine the complex and sometimes contradictory meanings about society conveyed by TV shows. Horace Newcomb and Paul Hirsch (1983) argued that TV shows represent a "cultural forum" that offers a multiplicity of representations of society that are as complex, contradictory, and confused as the society itself. For these scholars, TV shows represent a "multiplicity of meanings rather than a monolithic dominant point of view" and often focus "on our most prevalent concerns or deepest dilemmas"(Newcomb and Hirsch 1983: 564). On television, society's "most traditional views, those that are repressive and reactionary, as well as those that are subversive and emancipatory, are upheld, examined, maintained and transformed"(Newcomb and Hirsch 1983: 564). For example, *Weeds* contemplates mainstream assumptions about living in the suburbs and smoking (and dealing) marijuana. *The Wire* takes up critical questions about policing, the educational system, and poverty. In the twenty-first-century era of niche narrowcasting and audience segmentation, TV offers many competing "cultural forums" that represent many contending cultural identities.

Cultural studies scholars try to understand why the texts of certain TV shows "win favour with the people." According to John Fiske (1989), TV shows become popular when they entail a "producerly text." Building on the work of Roland Barthes (1974), an important French semiotician, Fiske (1989) employs the concept of "polysemy" to delineate between "open" and "closed" texts. An open text encourages the viewer to interpret a wide range of meanings, while a closed text does not. Popular TV texts are "polysemic": they have many levels of encoded meaning and, as such, lend themselves to a range of interpretations by viewers. Fiske (1989) says "producerly texts" combine elements of the readerly text ("low" cultural forms: formulaic, closed, and easy to understand) and elements of the writerly text ("high" cultural forms: avant-garde, open, and difficult to grasp). Popular TV shows are not as "closed" as the readerly text and not as "difficult" as the writerly text. According to Fiske (1994), viewers to derive pleasure from the process of actively decoding the many layers and levels of meaning encoded in the producerly TV text (254).

To become popular, TV shows must resonate with the fears and hopes, anxieties and desires, experiences and attitudes of the particular viewers they address as their "audience." As Stuart Hall (1981) writes, "if the forms of provided commercial popular culture are not purely manipulative, then it is because, alongside the false appeals, the foreshortenings, the trivialization and short circuits, there are also elements of recognition and identification, something approaching a recreation of recognizable experiences and attitudes, to which people are responding"(233–4). Popular TV shows "win favour" when they invite viewers to identify with the stories they tell and the characters they script. Through narrative, these shows acknowledge and then imaginatively resolve existing social conflicts as they are perceived or actually felt by large groups of people. Some of the most popular TV shows "transcode" the most hotly debated and conflicted issues from the main faultlines of society into consumable forms of entertainment (Kellner 1995).

By analyzing why and how TV shows are popular, cultural studies scholars reject the view that TV is "escapist" entertainment. The notion that TV shows are forms of escapism is a tired cliché. People who claim TV shows provide the audience with an escape tend not to contemplate what people are imprisoned by. If TV shows are escapist, reality must be a cage of some kind. Some argue that TV shows offer to viewers a temporary escape from work in capitalism. They might be the capitalist system's way of symbolically compensating millions of people for the alienating, exploitative, and routinized waged work they endure each day (Jameson 1979; 1981). TV show consumption is a compensatory exchange; viewers are offered targeted TV pleasures in return for their continued acquiescence and subordination to the capitalist status quo (Horkheimer and Adorno 1972). If TV shows are daily participating in a process of capitalist reproduction whereby otherwise rebellious societal energies are managed and defused, then it ought to be asked: how are these potentially explosive energies initially galvanized or enlivened by popular TV shows? How are they contained? Here, cultural studies scholars seek to illuminate a TV show's redemptive moments and utopian appeals. Shane Gunster (2004) argues that "the utopian moments in mass culture can only be accessed through a relentless form of negative critique that frees them, however fleetingly, from the suffocating embrace of the culture industry's false pleasures"(276).

Some TV commentators aren't interested in doing negative critique. Postmodernist TV scholars say that the line between TV's escapist gratifications and the prison-like reality they compensate for no longer exists (Baudrillard 1983a; 1983b; 1988). They say we live in a culture of images and surfaces with nothing beneath or behind them. Postmodernists believe that in earlier times, people could distinguish between true and false, reality and its false copy ("the **simulacra**"). Television viewers were aware of the constructed, false, or distorted "representations of reality" transmitted by TV shows. They knew the American Dream really wasn't as easy to achieve as TV shows often made it seem. They could recognize the digital makeover of Cindy Crawford's face in the TV ad for *Cover Girl*. But in the realm of TV's "hyper-reality," all is image. Postmodernist TV theorists believe that TV is now experienced by people who can't distinguish between fact and fiction, actuality and virtuality, TV representation and the "real world." For them, there is no difference between TV representation and reality. Television *is* reality for millions of people. TV's representation of the "war on terror" in the hit series *24* is the "real war on terror" for viewers. TV's representation of the "middle class" is the middle class for viewers. TV's representations of reality sometimes do displace and often stand in as "reality" for many people. But that does not mean there is no difference between reality (as it is lived and experienced) and its idealized TV image. Illuminating the gap between the actual world and TV's world of representation is the goal of media literacy educators and critical TV studies teachers and students.

The Television Audience

Television studies scholars examine the TV audience. The many people who watch TV shows are sometimes referred to as a "mass audience." The mass audience can be distinguished from small groups and crowds of people. In a small group, people know each other, share the same physical space, and are aware of their common membership. Small groups include McDonald's co-workers assembling burgers or university students in a TV studies seminar. The crowd is bigger than a small group, but it is limited to a single physical space and is temporary in its existence. A crowd is a bunch of protestors gathered in a public place or fans at a hockey game. Members of a crowd come together in one place for a set period of time and then disband. The "mass" audience is different from the small group and the crowd. Members of TV's mass audience are physically separated from each other, don't know each other, and don't regularly communicate with each other.

Many prime-time network TV shows gather a mass audience, but the concept of the "mass audience" has fallen out of favour (Williams 1977). Cultural studies scholars argue that the "mass audience" is a negative or pejorative concept that obscures the complexity and diversity of the actual viewers who actually comprise a TV show's audience. Television's "audience" is not singular or unified, but composed of many different people whose TV watching and decoding practices are shaped by location, class, age, gender, race, and ethnicity (Ang 1994). The "mass audience" concept obscures these differences. When discussed by scholars as active or passive, resistant or controlled, sovereign or dominated, "the audience" often only exists as the construction of scholarly discourse. The audience does not speak; it is spoken for by scholars. **Reception studies** represent a methodological alternative to abstract discussions of the audience. Reception studies scholars attempt to understand the members of a specific TV show audience on their own terms. They explore how different viewers, located in different reception contexts, decode the meanings of TV shows in many ways. Reception studies scholars say that the meaning of TV shows is not just "in the text," but emerges through a relationship between TV viewers, TV texts, and reception contexts. Reception studies scholars examine who watches a specific TV show, what people think and feel while watching, where people watch, why people watch, and how people actually decode the TV shows they watch.

Television as Communication Technology

The cultural forum of TV is not weightless.

> TV is an object produced in a factory that is distributed physically (via transportation) and virtual (via advertising). [. . .] In short, television has a physical existence, a history of material production and consumption, in addition to its renown as a site for making meaning (Miller 2010: 2).

The TV shows we watch rely on grounded and concrete technological systems (TV sets, satellites, computers, mobile phones, fibre optic cables, transmitters, wires, plugs, and electricity). Television sets are the main interface between TV networks and TV audiences. They include a screen for relaying images, a sound processor and speaker system, and usually a bunch of other gadgetry: DVD players, DVRs, video game consoles, and so on. In 2010, nearly 2.5 million TV sets were sold worldwide.

The invention of the TV occurred over many years and was made possible by many people. Throughout the 1920s and 1930s, a number of major US corporations including General Electric (GE), the Columbia Broadcasting System (CBS), American Telephone & Telegraph (AT&T), the Radio Corporation of America (RCA), and Westinghouse undertook intensive TV research and development. US electronics firms once had near-market dominance over the production and distribution of TV sets, selling them to consumers in the United States and other countries. In the 1970s, many US electronics companies were acquired by foreign firms. At present, no major Canadian or American TV set manufacturers exist. Most TV sets are made by electronics corporations including Sony, Panasonic, Toshiba, JVC, Sharp, and Mitsubishi (based in Japan); Samsung and LG (based in South Korea); and Philips based in the Netherlands). The actual production of most TV sets, however, doesn't occur in these firms' base countries, but in the sweatshop factories in the export-processing zones of poor and developing countries. Sony's Bravia TV sets, for example, are produced by Foxconn. This gigantic Taiwanese manufacturing company has TV factories in China, Mexico, and Slovakia. Foxconn has a bad reputation because it pays $1–2 hourly wages to workers, fires workers without giving them advance notice, and physically and emotionally abuses workers. Most of Foxconn's workers must monthly pay a portion of their miniscule wage back to Foxconn so they can rent a small room to sleep in and eat a daily meal (Barbazoa 2010).

The "blow-out" sale advertised by the Best Buy or Future Shop flyer doesn't show North American consumers the material conditions of TV production. Consumers encounter TV sets in finished commodity form, with a price tag attached to them. They are invited by electronics manufacturers, retailers, and marketers to participate in planned obsolescence. Black and white TV sets were replaced by colour TV sets, then high-definition TV sets. LED replaced LCD and plasma. The 27-inch screen size standard became 40 inches. New TV sets become old very quickly. They get consumed, used, and thrown away. They rot in landfills. The new technical standard of digital TV sent thousands of analog TV sets to garbage dumps. The digital switch rendered millions of TV sets non-functional and compelled people to purchase new TV sets that they didn't initially need or want. As Sam Grobart (2011) notes, "The rise of flat-panel television technologies like plasma and LCD almost perfectly coincided with a government-mandated switchover to digital broadcasting and the availability of high-definition TV shows and movies." Now, 3D TV is being promoted as the "must have" commodity of the future. But, over time, this too will likely be rendered obsolete.

Do the TV sets we make, use, and break determine our behaviour? Do we influence our TV sets or do they influence us? Is the TV simply a tool that we use or is it an autonomous entity that gets us to do what it wants? **Technological instrumentalists** say that TV is just a tool that rational humans use for a variety of purposes based on their own decisions. From this point of view, humans are rational choosers and users of TV. We are "in control of TV"; it is a means to an end of our choosing. We use TV to obtain useful information that will help us make decisions. We check the Weather Network to determine whether or not to wear a T-shirt or a winter jacket. We watch TV to figure out what the latest fashion trends are so that we can try to fit in with society. From the instrumentalist perspective, we make the decisions about TV and its uses. We design the set. We change the channel. We watch what we want. We record the TV shows that we like. TV is a tool that we use. It has little power over us. Since we are in control of TV, TV doesn't change us; it doesn't influence our society or way of life. We have power over TV. We influence and change it. An instrumentalist says: "Don't blame TV for the problems of society; blame society."

Technological determinists disagree with instrumentalists. For them, technology is the primary agent of social change. Technology is an "autonomous" agent. Technology, not social relations between people, determines what happens in society. Human factors (i.e., power blocs, state policies, corporate interests) are secondary. A sub-argument of technological determinism is called "media determinism." This posits the power of the communications media to influence, change, and sometimes control society. New media technologies—from the printing press to the telegraph to the TV to the Internet—bring about fundamental changes in society. When the TV emerged, everything changed, at every level of the society, from family life to work to sex. An influential media determinist was Marshall McLuhan (1994), who is remembered for his famous phrase: "The medium is the message"(26). For McLuhan, a medium is "any new technology" that extends the human sensorium. All new communication technologies shape how we perceive and understand the world around us. Thus for McLuhan, the "message" of TV is not a specific TV show's "content" (themes, stories, characters), but rather, the total way that TV has impacted and transformed society.

Like McLuhan, Neil Postman (1985) is a technological determinist, though a much more pessimistic one. Postman's main argument is that "Television turns everything it touches, even the most profound and serious matters, into entertainment"(87). Postman issues a warning:

"Whether politics, religion, news, war, sexuality, teaching or learning, television so alters them that they have no other quality or substance than entertainment value. In doing so, TV transforms even the most important things—life and death, war and peace, hate and love, for example—into mere trifles and trivia, packaged to amuse us to death"(87). For Postman, TV is responsible for the "dissolution of public discourse in [North] America and its conversion into the art of show business." Technological pessimists tend to view TV negatively. For them, TV causes society's problems. It causes obesity and laziness, destroys the family, and creates stupid and violent teenagers. Religious techno-pessimists believe that TV's crass secular content is a threat to religious doctrine. Appearing on Saudi Arabia's government-run Saudi TV on 14 September 2008, Sheik Saleh al-Lihedan of Saudi Arabia's Supreme Judiciary Council, issued a fatwa against Western satellite TV shows (Abu-Nasr 2008). Some Christians make similarly extreme arguments against TV. A Christian website called "Evangelical Outreach" features an article entitled "TV—Could It Be . . . One of the Devil's Chief Weapons to Damn Your Soul?" Expressing disgust at the sex, violence, and profanity displayed in each hour of prime-time TV viewing, the author of the post asks: "Be honest with yourself. If Jesus came to your house to spend a day, would you be ashamed and quickly change the channel, or leave it off altogether for the time?"(Corner n.d.).

Television's message in society has been massive. And its impacts—positive or negative—are hotly debated. Williams (1992) encourages critical TV studies scholars to move beyond a purely instrumentalist or determinist view of TV. Williams says that TV's technological form, function, use, and impact in society are shaped by the choices of society's large-scale structures and organizations. Television is shaped in profound ways by capitalism and the nation-state; it represents the powerful interests of corporate and state actors. The next section in *The Television Reader* introduces the political-economy approach to TV and examines how corporations and nation-states shape TV in society.

Works Cited

Abercrombie, N. (1996). *Television as Text.* Cambridge: Polity Press.

Abu-Nasr, D. (15 September 2008). "Saudi Fatwa Pans 'Immoral' TV." www.thestar.com/printartcile/499265

Ang, I. (1994). "Understanding Television Audiencehood." In H. Newcomb (Ed.), *Television: The Critical View* (pp. 367–86). New York: Oxford University Press.

Arthurs, J. (2003). "Sex and the City and Consumer Culture: Remediating Postfeminist Drama." *Feminist Media Studies*, Vol. 3(1): 83–98.

Baehr, H., and Dyer, G. (Eds.). (1987). *Boxed In: Women and Television.* New York and London: Pandora.

Barboza, D. (19 June 2010). "A Night at the Electronics Factory." www.nytimes.com/2010/06/20/weekinreview/20barboza.html?ref=foxconntechnology

Barthes, R. (1974). *S/Z.* New York: Noonday Press.

Baudrillard, J. (1983a). *Simulations.* New York: Semiotext(e).

———. (1983b). *In the Shadow of the Silent Majorities.* New York: Semiotext(e).

———. (1988). "Symbolic Exchange and Death." In M. Poster (Ed.), *Jean Baudrillard: Selected Writings* (pp. 119–49). California: Stanford University Press.

Brunsdon, C., D'Acci, J., and Spigel, L. (Eds). (2007). *Feminist Television Criticism: A Reader.* New York: Open University Press.

Burns, G., and Thompson, R.J. (Eds). (1989). *Television Studies: Textual Analysis.* New York: Praeger.

Carey, J. (1989). *Communication as Culture: Essays on Media and Society.* Boston: Unwin Hyman.

Corner, D. (n.d.). "TV—Could It Be . . . One of the Devil's Chief Weapons to Damn Your Soul?" www.evangelicaloutreach.org/tv.htm

Curtin, M. (1999). "Feminine Desire in the Age of Satellite Television." *Journal of Communication*, Vol. 49(2): 55–70.

Dines, G., and Humez, J.M. (Eds). (2002). *Gender, Race and Class in Media: a Text Reader.* Thousand Oaks, CA: Sage Publications.

Dow, B.J. (1996). *Prime-Time Feminism: Television, Media Culture, and the Women's Movement Since 1970.* Philadelphia, PA: University of Pennsylvania Press.

Eagleton, T. (2000). *The Idea of Culture.* Malden, MA: Blackwell.

Editorial (19 October 2010). "TV Viewing: Dominates Many Lives." http://sports.tmcnet.com/news/2010/10/19/5075957.htm

Ewen, S. (1996). *PR! A Social History of Spin.* New York: Basic Books.

Fiske, J. (1987). *Television Culture.* London: Metheun.

———. (1989). *Understanding Popular Culture.* London and New York: Unwin Hyman.

———. (1994). "Television pleasures." In D. Graddol and O. Boyd-Barrett (Eds), *Media Texts: Authors and Readers* (pp. 239–55). London: Multilingual Matters.

Fiske, J., and Hartlely, I. (1978). *Reading Television.* London: Methuen.

Goodenough, W.H. (1971). *Culture, Language and Society.* Reading, MA: Addison: Wesley.

Gramsci, A. (1968). *Prison Notebooks.* London: Lawrence and Wishart.

Gray, H. (1995). *Watching Race: Television and the Struggle for "Blackness."* Minneapolis: University of Minnesota Press.

Gray, J. (2007). *Television Entertainment.* New York: Routledge.

Grobart, S. (5 January 2011). "A Bonanza in TV Sales Fades Away." www.nytimes.com/2011/01/06/technology/06sets.html

Gunster, S. (2004). *Capitalizing on Culture: Critical Theory for Cultural Studies.* Toronto: University of Toronto Press.

Gutstein, D. (2009). *Not a Conspiracy Theory: How Business Propaganda Hijacks Democracy.* Toronto: Key Porter Books.

Hall, S. (1981). "Notes on Deconstructing the Popular." In R. Samuel (Ed.), *People's History and Socialist Theory* (pp. 227–43). New York: Routledge and Kegan Paul.

———. (2000). "Encoding/Decoding." In M.G. Durham and D.M. Kellner (Eds), *Media and Cultural Studies: Keyworks* (pp. 116–76). Blackwell: New York.

———. (2002). "The Whites of Their Eyes: Racist Ideologies and the Media." In G. Dines and J.M. Humez, (Eds), *Gender, Race and Class in Media: A Text Reader* (pp. 89–93). Thousand Oaks, CA: Sage Publications.

Herman, E., and Chomsky, N. (1988). *Manufacturing Consent: The Political Economy of the Mass Media.* New York: Pantheon Books.

Hollows, J. (2000). *Feminism, Femininity and Popular Culture.* Manchester and New York: Manchester University Press.

Horkheimer, M., and Adorno, T.W. (1972). "The Culture Industry: Enlightenment as Mass Deception." In *Dialectic of Enlightenment.* New York: 120–67. Herder and Herder.

Jameson, F. (1979). "Reification and Utopia in Mass Culture." *Social Text,* Vol. 1(1): 130–48.

———. (1981). *The Political Unconscious.* New York: Cornell University Press.

Johnson, M.L. (Ed.). (2007). *Third Wave Feminism and Television: Jane Puts It in a Box.* New York: I.B. Tauris.

Kellner, D. (1995). *Media Culture.* New York: Routledge.

Lippmann, W. (1922). *Public Opinion.* New York: MacMillan.

McLuhan, M. (1994). *Understanding Media: The Extensions of Man.* Cambridge, MA: MIT Press.

Mander, J. (1978). *Four Arguments for the Elimination of Television.* New York: HarperCollins.

Miller, T. (2010). *Television Studies: The Basics.* New York: Routledge.

Newcomb, H. (1974). *TV: The Most Popular Art.* New York: Anchor Press.

Newcomb, H., and Hirsch, P.M. (1983). "Television as a Cultural Forum." *Quarterly Review of Film Studies,* Vol. 8(3): 45–55.

Postman, N. (1985). *Amusing Ourselves to Death.* New York: Penguin.

Stelter, B. (2 January 2011). "TV Viewing Continues to Edge Up." www.nytimes.com/2011/01/03/business/media/03ratings.html?_r=3&ref=media

Williams, R. (1976). *Keywords: A Vocabulary of Culture and Society.* London: Fontana.

———. (1977). *Marxism and Literature.* London: Oxford University Press.

———. (1992). *Television: Technology and Cultural Form.* Hanover and London: University Press of New England and Wesleyan University Press.

Part I | Discussion Questions

1 | Critical Approaches to the Study of "TV": An Introduction

1. What is the difference between "encoding" and "decoding"? Provide an example of how a viewer might "decode" the meaning of a TV show in the reception context. How might the meaning decoded be different than the meaning encoded in the production context? Why?
2. Why do TV studies scholars distinguish between "reflection" and "representation" when examining the relationship between TV shows and "reality"? What partial and selective representation of the social world does your favourite TV show entail? What is included? What is excluded? What is represented? What is not?
3. What is ideology? How does a TV show represent class, gender, or race in society? Does the representation support or contest ideologies of capitalism, patriarchy, or racism? What is hegemony? Provide an example of how a TV show (fictional or non-fictional) might participate in the struggle of a political group for leadership in society. How does it "organize the consent" of viewers to a specific ideology?
4. How is a popular TV show a "cultural forum" for addressing and discussing important social issues? Provide an example of a contemporary TV show that is a "cultural forum." What are the cultural reasons for the TV show's "popularity" in society? What hopes and fears does it address, examine, or resonate with?
5. What is the "TV audience"? How do critics, journalists, teachers, and friends talk about the TV audience of a particular show? How is the TV audience represented? Do you feel that it is an accurate portrayal of the TV audience? What is Reception Studies and how might it help TV studies scholars "get to know" actual viewers?

Suggestions for Further Reading

Television as Culture, Mass-Mediated Communication, and Technology

Abercrombie, N. (1996). *Television and Society.* Cambridge: Polity.

Adorno, T. (1991). "How to Look at Television." In J.M. Bernstein (Ed.), *The Culture Industry* (pp. 136–54). London: Routledge.

Allen, R. (Ed.). (1987). *Channels of Discourse.* London: Methuen.

Allen, R.C. (Ed.). (1992). *Channels of Discourse, Reassembled.* Chapel Hill and London: The University of North Carolina Press.

Baudrillard, J. (1983). *Simulations.* New York: Semiotext(e).

Bourdieu, P. (2001). "Television." *European Review,* Vol. 9(3): 245–56.

Chaffee, S.H., and Metzger, M.J. (2001). "The End of Mass Communication?" *Mass Communication and Society,* Vol. 4(4): 365–79.

Curran, J., Gurevitch, M., and Woollacott, J. (Eds). (1977). *Mass Communications and Society.* London: Edward Arnold.

Fiske, J. (1982). *Introduction to Communication Studies.* New York: Routledge

———. (1986). "Television: Polysemy and Popularity." *Critical Studies in Mass Communication,* Vol. 3(4): 391–408.

———. (1998). *Television Culture.* New York: Routledge.

———. (2003). *Reading Television.* New York: Routledge.

———. (2010). *The John Fiske Collection: Understanding Popular Culture.* New York: Routledge.

Fiske, J., and Hartley, J. (1978). *Reading Television.* London: Routledge.

Gauntlett, D., and Hill, A. (1999). *TV Living: Television, Culture and Everyday Life.* London: Routledge.

Gripsrud, J. (1998). "Television, Broadcasting, Flow: Key Metaphors in TV Theory." In C. Geraghty and D. Lusted (Eds.), *The Television Studies Book* (pp. 17–32). London: Arnold.

Gurevitch, M., Bennet, T., Curran, J., and Woollacott, J. (Eds). (1982). *Culture, Society and the Media.* London: Methuen.

Hall, S. (1977). "Culture, the Media and the Ideological Effect." In J. Curran, M. Gurevitch, and J. Woollacot (Eds), *Mass Communication and Society.* London: Edward Arnold.

———. (1997). *Representation: Cultural Representations and Signifying Practices.* New York: Sage Publications.
Hilmes, M. (2005). "The Bad Object: Television in the American Academy." *Cinema Journal*, Vol. 45(1): 111–17.
Johnson, R. (1986). "What Is Cultural Studies Anyway?' *Social Text*, Vol. 16: 38–80.
Kellner, D. (1982). "Television, Mythology and Ritual." *Praxis*, Vol. 6: 133–55.
Lotz, A.D. and Gray, J. (2011). *Television Studies.* New York: Polity.
McLuhan, M., Fiore, Q., and Agel, J. (2001). *War and Peace in the Global Village.* Berkeley, CA: Gingko Press.
———. (2005). *The Medium Is the Massage.* Berkeley, CA: Gingko Press.
McQuail, D., and Windahl, S. (1993). *Communication Models for the Study of Mass Communication.* London: Longman.
Magoun, A.B. (2009). *Television: The Life Story of a Technology.* Baltimore: The John Hopkins University Press.
Merrin, W. (1999). "Television Is Killing the Art of Symbolic Exchange: Baudrillard's Theory of Communication." *Theory, Culture & Society*, Vol. 16(3): 119–40.
Mosco, V. (2004). *The Digital Sublime: Myth, Power & Cyberspace.* Cambridge, MA: The MIT Press.
Newcomb, H. (1974). *TV: The Most Popular Art.* Garden City: Anchor Press/Doubleday.
———. (2009). "Studying Television: Same Questions, Different Contexts." *Cinema Journal*, Vol. 45(1): 107–11.
O'Donnell, V. (2007). *Television Criticism.* Thousand Oaks, CA: Sage Publications.
Uricchio, W. (2008). "Television's First Seventy-Five Years: The Interpretive Flexibility of a Medium in Transition." In R. Kolker (Ed.), *The Oxford Handbook of Film and Media Studies* (pp. 286–305). New York: Oxford University Press.
Wasko, J. (Ed.). (2005). *A Companion to Television.* Malden: Blackwell.

Television, Ideology, and the Representation of Class, Race, Gender, and Sexualities

Alturi, T. (2010). "Lighten Up?! Humour, Race, and Da off colour joke of Ali G." *Media, Culture & Society*, Vol. 21(2): 197–214.
Arthurs, J. (2004). *Television and Sexuality: Regulation and the Politics of Taste.* Maidenhead: Open University Press.
Barbazon, T. (2005). "What Have You Ever Done on the Telly? *The Office*, (Post) Reality Television and (Post) Work." *International Journal of Cultural Studies*, Vol. 8(1): 101–17.
Becker, R. (2006). *Gay TV and Straight America.* Rutgers University Press.
———. (2006). "Gay-Themed Television and the Slumpy Class: The Affordable, Multicultural Politics of the Gay Nineties." *Television & New Media*, Vol. 7(1): 184–215.
Bettie, J. (1995). "Class Dismissed? Roseanne and the Changing Face of Working-Class Iconography." *Social Text*, Vol. 45(1): 125–49.
Bogle, D. (2002). *Primetime Blues: African Americans on Network Television.* New York: Douglas & McIntyre.
Butsch, R. (1992). "Class and Gender in Four Decades of Television Situation Comedy: Plus ca Change . . . " *Critical Studies in Mass Communication*, Vol. 9(1): 387–99.
Butsch, R., and Glennon, L.M. (1983). "Social Class: Frequency Trends in Domestic Situation Comedy, 1946–1978." *Journal of Broadcasting*, Vol. 27(1): 77–81.
Carroll, H. (2008). "Men's Soaps: Automotive Television Programming and Contemporary Working-Class Masculinities." *Television & New Media*, Vol. 9(4): 263–83.
Cloud, D. (1996). "Hegemony or Concordance? The Rhetoric of Tokenism in 'Oprah' Winfrey's Rags-to-Riches Biography." *Critical Studies in Mass Communication*, Vol. 13(1): 115–37.
Coleman, R. (2000). *African American Viewers and the Black Situation Comedy: Situating Racial Humour.* New York: Garland.
Condit, C.M. (1989). "The Rhetorical Limits of Polysemy." *Critical Studies in Mass Communication*, Vol. 6(1): 103–22.
Curtin, M. (1999). "Feminine Desire in the Age of Satellite Television." *Journal of Communication*, Vol. 44(2): 55–70.
Dow, B.J. (2001). "Ellen, Television, and the Politics of Gay and Lesbian Visibility." *Critical Studies in Mass Communication*, Vol. 18(1): 123–40.
Dubrofsky, R.E. (2006). "*The Bachelor*: Whiteness in the Harem." *Critical Studies in Media Communication*, Vol. 21(1): 39–56.
Dyer, R. (1997). *White.* London: Routledge.
Entman, R.M., and Rojecki, A. (2001). *The Black Image in the White Mind: Media and Race in America.* Chicago: University of Chicago Press.
Fuller, J. (2010). "Branding Blackness on US Cable Television." *Media, Culture & Society*, Vol. 32(2): 285–305.
Gandy, O.H. (1998). *Communication and Race: A Structural Perspective.* Oxford: Oxford University Press.
Gray, H. (1989). "Television, Black Americans, and the American Dream." *Critical Studies in Mass Communication*, Vol. 6(4): 376–86.
Haralovich, M.B., and Rabinovitz, L. (Eds). (1999). *Television, History, and American Culture: Feminist Critical Essays.* Durham, NC: Duke University Press.
Havens, T. (2000). "'The Biggest Show in the World': Race and the Global Popularity of *The Cosby Show*." *Media, Culture & Society*, Vol. 22: 371–91.
Heinecken, D. (2003). *The Warrior Women of Television: A Feminist Cultural Analysis of the New Female Body in Popular Media.* New York: Peter Lang.
hooks, bell. (1992). *Black Looks: Race and Representation.* Boston: South End Press.
Hunt, D.M. (Ed). (2004). *Channelling Blackness: Studies on Television and Race in America.* New York: Oxford University Press.
Hussain, A. (2010). "(Re)presenting Muslims on North American TV." *Contemporary Islam*, Vol. 4(1): 55–75.
Jermyn, D. (2009). *Sex and the City.* Detroit, MA: Wayne State University Press.
Jhally, S., and Lewis, J. (1992). *Enlightened Racism: The Cosby Show, Audiences, and the Myth of the American Dream.* Boulder: Westview Press.

Jiwani, Y. (2006). *Discourse of Denial: Mediations of Race, Gender, and Violence.* Vancouver, BC: UBC Press.

Kellner, D. (1995). *Media Culture: Culture Studies, Identity, and Politics between the Modern and the Postmodern.* New York: Routledge.

Kendall, D. (2005). *Framing Class: Media Representations of Wealth and Poverty in America.* Lanham, MD: Rowman & Littlefield.

Langley, S. (2003). "Gender Talk, TV, Hockey and 'Canadian Identity': Feminist Takes on Television Rejection." *Canadian Journal of Communication*, Vol. 28: 413–32.

Levine, E., and Parks, L.A. (Eds). (2007). *Undead TV: Essays on Buffy the Vampire Slayer.* Durham, NC: Duke University Press.

Lotz, A. (2006). *Redesigning Women: Television after the Network Era.* University of Illinois Press.

Mahtani, M. (2009). "Report: Critiquing the Critiques about Media and Minority Research in Canada." *Canadian Journal of Communication*, Vol. 34(1): 715–19.

Mercer, K. (1994). *Welcome to the Jungle.* New York: Routledge.

Miller. T. (2006). *Cultural Citizenship: Cosmopolitanism, Consumerism, and Television in a Neoliberal Age.* Philadelphia, PA: Temple University Press.

Moseley, R., and Read, J. (2002). "'Having It Ally': Popular Television (Post)Feminism. *Feminist Media Studies*, Vol. 2(2): 231–49.

Peck, J. (2008). *The Age of Oprah: Cultural Icon for the Neoliberal Age.* Boulder: Paradigm Publishers.

Perks, L.G. (2001). "The Nouveau Reach: Ideologies of Class and Consumerism in Reality-Based Television." *Studies in Language & Capitalism*, Vol. 2(1): 101–18.

Projansky, S. (2001). *Watching Rape: Film and Television in Postfeminist Culture.* New York: New York University Press.

Rivera-Perez, L. (1996). "Rethinking Ideology: Polysemy, Pleasure and Hegemony in Television Culture." *Journal of Communication Inquiry*, Vol. 20(2): 37–56.

Ross, K. (1996). *Black and White Media.* Cambridge, UK: Polity Press.

Shohat, E., and Stam, R. (1995). *Unthinking Eurocentrism: Multiculturalism and the Media.* London: Routledge.

Smith-Shomade, B.E. (2008). *Pimpin' Ain't Easy: Selling Black Entertainment Television.* New York: Routledge.

Smythe, D. (1954). "Reality as Presented by Television." *Public Opinion Quarterly*, Vol. 18(2): 143–56.

Spigel, L., and Mann, D. (Eds). (1992). *Private Screenings: Television and the Female Consumer.* University of Minnesota Press.

Tait, S. (2007). "Television and the Domestication of Cosmetic Surgery." *Feminist Media Studies*, Vol. 7(2): 119–35.

Tasker, Y., and Negra, D. (Eds). (2007). *Interrogating Postfeminism: Gender and the Politics of Popular Culture.* Durham, NC: Duke University Press.

Torres, S. (Ed.). (1998). *Living Color: Race and Television in the United States.* Durham: Duke University Press.

Wilson, C.C., Gutierrez, F., and Chao, L.M. (2003). *Racism, Sexism, and the Media: The Rise of Class Communication in Multicultural America.* New York: Sage Publications.

Wood, H. (2009). *Talking with Television: Women, Talk Shows and Modern Self-Reflexivity.* Urbana: University of Illinois Press.

Zook, K.B. (1999). *Color by Fox: The Fox Network and the Revolution in Black Television.* New York: Oxford University Press.

Television Audiences and Reception Studies

Abercrombie, N., and Longhurst, B. (1998). Audiences: A Sociological Theory of Performance and Imagination. London: Sage.

Ang, I. (1985). Watching Dallas: Soap Opera and the Melodramatic Imagination. London: Metheun.

———. (1991). Desperately Seeking the Audience. New York: Routledge.

Bird, S.E. (2003). The Audience in Everyday Life: Living in a Media World. New York: Routledge.

Gillespie, M. (1995). Television, Ethnicity and Cultural Change. London: Routledge.

Gray, A. (1999). "Audience and Reception Research in Retrospect: The Trouble with Audiences." In P. Alasuutari (Ed.), Rethinking the Media Audience: The New Agenda (pp. 22–37). Thousand Oaks, CA: Sage Publications.

Hartley, J. (1999). Uses of Television, New York: Routledge.

Kline, S. (2003). "Media Effects: Redux or Reductive?' Particip@tions: International Journal of Audience Research, Vol. 1(1): n.p.

Lewis, J. (1991). The Ideological Octopus: An Exploration of Television and Its Audience. New York: Routledge.

Livingstone, S. (1992). "Audience Reception: The Role of the Viewer in Retelling Romantic Drama." In J. Curran and M. Gurevitch (Eds), Mass Media and Society (pp. 285–306). New York: Edward Arnold.

———. (1993). "The Rise and Fall of Audience Research: An Old Story with a New Ending." Journal of Communication, Vol. 43(4): 5–12.

McQuail, D. (1997). Audience Analysis. Thousand Oaks, CA: Sage.

Maxwell, R. (2000). "Picturing the Audience." Television & New Media, Vol. 1(2): 133–57.

Morley, D. (1980). The "Nationwide"Audience. London: British Film Institute.

———. (1992). Television, Audiences and Cultural Studies. New York: Routledge.

Murray, C. (2003). Researching Audiences: A Practice Guide to Methods in Media Audience Analysis. New York: Bloomsbury.

Seaman, W. (1992). "Active Audience Theory: Pointless Populism." Media, Culture & Society, Vol. 14(2): 301–11.

Seiter, E. (2002). Television and New Media Audiences. Oxford: Clarendon Press.

Staiger, J. (2005). Media Reception Studies. New York: New York University Press.

History and Characteristics of TV Broadcasting in Canada and the United States: A Political Economy

Introduction: A Political Economy of TV Broadcasting in Canada and the United States

The articles in this section of *The Television Reader* examine the history and characteristics of television broadcasting in Canada and the United States. They represent useful political-economic studies of the structures, organizations, and institutions that shape Canadian and American TV broadcasting systems, focusing on how these groups emerged, where they converged, and why they diverged, and on key debates surrounding each system. Before introducing the articles, we present a short essay on the **political economy** of Canadian and American TV systems, which is foundational to this book.

Most people encounter TV shows as consumers. Seated in front of TV sets in their homes or plugged in to mobile screens (laptop computers, tablets, or cell phones) as they travel from home to work or school, millions of people watch TV shows every day. In face-to-face and online communication environments, they comment on the happenings of fictional characters and recount the twists and turns of TV plotlines. They talk with friends about how a TV show's content relates to their everyday lives. At times they may feel that the show was specially "made for them" (or groupings of niche audiences that share their personal tastes and preferences). While viewers watch TV shows and talk about them, they often do not see or discuss the social relations between the people that make the shows. The imagery and messages conveyed by each TV show hides the material conditions of its making. Shows are produced as commodities in industrial production contexts that are shaped by economic and political agents, capitalism, and the state.

A political-economy approach to TV focuses on how economic and political forces shape what viewers see on TV (Garnham 1990, 2000; Mosco 1996). According to Eileen Meehan (2007), the "political economy [of communication] contextualizes the objects and practices under study within the larger industrial systems that originate them [. . .] to trace market and corporate structures as well as relevant legal and regulatory strictures that set the parameters for [creative] expression"(161). Political economists pose a number of important questions: how are TV broadcasting systems shaped by economic and political forces? Who controls the national TV broadcasting system? Should TV broadcasting systems be treated as publicly owned goods or as private ventures? Which is best for democracy? Are the profit interests of media corporations promoted and protected or, alternately, hindered and hampered by the state's media and cultural policies? Do TV broadcasting policies represent the interests of all citizens or powerful interest groups? Does TV broadcasting facilitate or undermine the public sphere, democracy, and the diversity of cultural expressions? What alternatives to the current system are currently offered or politically imaginable?

Political economists attempt to answer these and many more questions through historically informed and empirical studies of TV broadcasting systems and the production, distribution, and exhibition of TV shows in society. The political-economy approach complicates the view that every TV show that is produced and scheduled by TV networks "gives the audience what it wants." The notion that what TV networks schedule in any given time slot reflects the tastes and preferences of everyone in society is incredibly simplistic. Political economists acknowledge that people certainly select which TV shows they want to watch (from thousands upon thousands of available selections). They do not believe, however, that viewers have the power to decide what TV shows are made. The TV production companies that choose to make TV shows and the TV networks that choose to schedule TV shows are shaped by capitalism and the state. In what follows, we describe the main ways that capitalism and the state shape TV as a culture industry.

Television and Capitalism: The Culture Industry

Television is an important part of the culture industry. David Throsby (2008) defines the cultural industry as the means by which "a society's culture is formed and transmitted [...] via the industrial production, dissemination, and consumption of symbolic texts or messages, which are conveyed by means of various media such as film, TV broadcasting and the press"(220). Advertising, film, the Internet, music, publishing, radio, video and computer games, and television are all part of the culture industry. The culture industry is owned and controlled by media corporations, which create, produce, distribute, broadcast, and sell copyrighted TV shows as commodities in the marketplace. To make TV shows, media corporations buy technology and hire the skills and talents of cultural workers. Cultural workers sell their labour to media firms for set periods of time in exchange for a wage or salary. By doing so, they contractually accept the media corporation's right to use their labour to make TV shows. To get a wage, they also must accept the firm's right to control the end product of their creativity (the TV show). By paying cultural workers less than the total amount of money they accumulate through the sale of TV shows, media corporations maximize profit. The labour of cultural workers is exploited for private gain.

Political economists focus on how TV is part of the culture industry in general. In particular, political economists analyze how specific business practices and processes including competition and control, ownership concentration, and market structure (relations among TV production companies, TV distribution firms, advertising firms, and ratings corporations) all shape why TV shows are made, how TV shows are produced, and what TV shows ultimately get scheduled.

Competition and Control

In the North American TV market, competition and control are two sides of the same coin. Media corporations compete to control audience **share**. They want to sell their TV shows to as many consumers as possible (TV networks, cable distributors, pay-per-view channels, individual consumers). Media firms also compete to control the use of TV shows. They fill massive intellectual property portfolios with copyrighted TV shows and license, sell, rent, and even spin-off these TV shows into additional products such as clothing, toys, magazines, and games. Media firms compete to control the means of producing TV shows (the production studios and cultural workers) and the means of distributing them (TV networks, cable companies, websites).

Ownership Concentration and Convergence

Corporate competitions to maximize control of TV audiences, copyrights, and production and distribution systems lead to media concentration. In 1983, 50 corporations controlled the US market; in 1997, there were approximately 10 (Bagdikian 2004: xi–xxi). At present, the US culture industry is controlled by a few vertically and horizontally integrated ("converged") US-based **transnational media corporations** (TNMCs). Time Warner, News Corporation, Walt Disney Company, Comcast NBC-Universal, Viacom, CBS Corporation, and a few other TNMCs control the lion's share of the means of producing media content (newspapers, book and magazine publishing houses, film and TV production studios, music labels) and the means of content distribution (TV and radio broadcasting networks, cinema chains, cable operators, specialty channels, satellite services, and websites) in the United States and elsewhere. Canada's culture industry is ruled by "converged" media firms including

Bell (owner of CTV), Rogers (owner of Citytv), Shaw (owner of Global) and Quebecor (owner of TVA). Dwayne Winseck (2008) says that the image of a multichannel TV world (lots of TV shows and stations to select) masks the reality of shrinking source diversity (fewer owners of TV). Due to convergence, the culture industry is developing a "new vision of television built largely on faith in a modern version of synergy"(Holt 2003: 12). Media corporations distribute the TV shows they own through all of the media platforms they control and exploit cross-promotional opportunities. Convergence supports the culture industry's new vision of TV well.

Market Structure

The classical network structure of TV has four principal actors: (1) TV production studios (which make TV shows), (2) TV networks (which buy the rights to distribute TV shows to an audience), (3) TV advertisers (which buy time and space from TV networks in hopes of reaching an audience), and (4) Nielsen (which sells ratings information to TV networks about the number of people watching what TV shows and when). Here is how the TV market structure functions: TV production studios create TV shows and sell them to TV networks. TV networks license TV shows from TV production companies, schedule them at various times and broadcast them. Viewers turn on their TV sets, channel surf, and select a scheduled TV show to watch. Advertising companies buy space and time from the TV networks, which air their commercials. Networks use TV shows sanctioned by advertising clients to attract an "audience" to advertisements for goods and services. They pay ratings corporations to measure the number of people watching TV shows. They then use ratings information to prove to advertising clients that the ads they place are reaching the audience. This structure is undergoing important transformations in the post-network era (Lotz 2007), but still provides the major foundation for most TV broadcasting in North America. In what follows, each part of this market structure will be discussed in greater detail.

TV Production Companies and TV Networks

Television production companies create TV shows and license them to TV networks, which broadcast them to viewers. A variety of TV networks license TV shows from production companies and distribute them to viewers. Some TV production firms are owned by networks; others are affiliated to them. TV is art for industry's sake. TV shows are not autonomous cultural works. They are the outcome of collaborative work routines and standardized production rituals by hundreds of waged cultural workers. A TV episode's rapid-fire closing credit roll reveals a complex division of TV labour comprised of numerous specialized roles—director, writer, cast, editor, production designer, costume department, make-up, sound editor, grip 1 & 2, and so on. TV shows are produced in a number of stages. A TV production company first develops a TV show concept (the situation, the story, the plots, the characters, the crew, and the various actors). In this stage, the TV production company attempts to anticipate what kinds of TV shows TV networks may want to schedule. This compels cultural workers to imagine what kinds of TV shows viewers might want to watch and what kinds of viewers TV networks may want to attract on behalf of their advertising clients. The attempt to anticipate and reflect what viewers, TV networks, and advertisers want shapes the creative process, leading cultural workers to produce and reproduce standardized TV shows. In the TV industry, creating TV shows "involves both repetition and difference, which in turn can discourage taking risks, curbing costly newness with cheap formulae"(Miller 2010: 83).

Television shows are expensive to make. TV production firms require financing. Distribution firms (i.e., TV broadcast networks, cable stations, pay TV, and specialty channels) usually provide financing to TV production firms if they can be convinced a TV show will be a hit. Convincing is usually referred to as a "pitch." Production firms pitch a TV show concept to many TV networks. If a TV network is interested, it will commission the TV production firm to write a full-length script for a few episodes and possibly assemble a TV pilot (a taped episode of the show). If the TV network likes the pilot, it will negotiate a "deal" with the TV production studio. The deal covers: (1) the right to shape the textual content of the TV show (the story, plot, cast, and crew); (2) the time it will take to shoot the TV show and deliver it to the TV network; (3) the control of the TV show's copyright; (4) the financing arrangements for the TV show; and (5) the licensing-distribution agreement. There are two kinds of licensing agreements: "first-run syndication" (production studios license TV episodes directly to the network that they are affiliated with) and "off-network syndication" (TV production studios license episodes to non-affiliated TV distributors) (Gray 2008: 21). TV networks shape the TV shows that TV production firms make; but they are influenced by advertising firms, which pay them to schedule TV shows that attract audience attention.

TV Advertising and TV Schedules

Advertising firms—the primary source of revenue for TV networks—often shape what TV shows are conceptualized, produced, licensed, and watched by viewers. Large corporations pay TV networks to air advertisements for their goods and services. Networks schedule TV shows, organizing their transmission to viewers into units of time over the course of a day, week, or entire season. Viewers who watch TV without time-shifting devices or digital video recorders (DVRs) are bound by the TV network's schedule. To see show X, the viewer must turn on the TV and tune in at time Y. Networks use schedules to attract, capture, sort, and deliver an audience to the ad firms that pay to advertise between TV shows. The TV schedule is where viewer demand for TV shows and advertising demand for viewer attention converge. Advertisers want a particular audience to be exposed to an ad for a particular kind of product, so a particular kind of TV show is scheduled by the TV network to meet that demand. Television schedules remain a dominant feature of the twenty-first-century TV landscape, especially for the generations of viewers who grew up with and find comfort in their regularity and predictability.

The Audience Commodity

Television networks treat their audience as commodities (things that are bought and sold) (Napoli 2003). Dallas Smythe (2001) argues that TV is too often studied in terms of what it puts into viewers' minds (messages and images), and not what it makes of viewers (exchange-values). For Smythe, a "blind spot" in TV studies was an account of what TV networks actually did with viewer attention (commodify it and sell it to advertising firms in return for money). Smythe claims that the principal commodity produced and exchanged by TV networks is the "audience," or more specifically, the predisposition of viewers to devote time to TV. By watching TV, viewers inadvertently "worked" for TV networks: "what [advertisers] buy [from television networks] are the services of audiences with predictable specifications who will pay attention in predictable numbers and at particular times to particular means of communication. As collectivities these audiences are commodities"(270). Advertisers pay TV networks to run their ads because they believe TV networks attract an audience and channel that audience's attention to advertisements. To draw revenue, TV networks must convince advertising corporations that a collective "audience" (a certain number of people with specific demographic characteristics) are watching their TV shows. They do so with audience ratings.

Television Ratings

A rating is information about the number of people who watch a particular TV show at a specific point in time. Ratings firms emerged in response to the need of TV networks and TV advertisers for a supposedly neutral research mechanism that could generate "objective" information about the TV audience they exchanged. Networks pay ratings corporations such as Nielsen and BBM Canada to measure who is watching TV, what TV shows are being watched, and how long they are watched for to set and justify the price of the ad space and time they sell to advertising firms. Advertising firms use ratings to determine when and where to place their ads and give them—and their larger industrial clients—some assurance that the ads they place reach an audience. Core to the business transaction between TV networks and TV advertisers is a belief that ratings corporations provide a relatively accurate picture of the audience. But this is questionable.

Ratings firms use diaries, surveys, people-meters, and other measurement technologies to determine who is watching what TV shows and when. They don't count everyone (Meehan 1990). Most TV viewers aren't counted as members of the "audience" represented by ratings. The only TV viewers who are considered are those counted by ratings firms. Ratings firms extrapolate the "TV audience" from the small audience sample group they measure; the audience is made synonymous with the few hundred or thousand viewers selected by ratings corporations to be measured, and thus millions of TV viewers are not counted. Ratings firms therefore do not reflect the "audience." They manufacture a partial and selective image of the audience to serve the business needs of TV networks and TV advertisers. Ratings firms assemble an audience and deliver it to TV networks and advertisers as a commodity. They tell us very little about the lives of the actual viewers who watch TV. There is thus a disparity separating the audience objectified by ratings and the actual viewers who watch specific TV shows. The advertising industry is most interested in reaching TV viewers who have a disposable income to spend on goods and services. The tastes and preferences of this "audience" are privileged by TV networks and significantly shape the kinds of TV shows they order and schedule.

In sum, political economists examine the market structure of TV and show how capitalism shapes the production, distribution, and scheduling of TV shows (and audiences) as commodities.

Television and the Nation-State: Cultural Policy

Television is not confined to the sphere of business. While TV is certainly organized as a business, state cultural policies, regulations, and forms of funding significantly shape the business of TV. In the twenty-first century, "cultural sovereignty" refers to the right and ability of a state to develop and enact cultural policies that protect and promote a distinctive culture (the "way of life" of a population) and culture industry (mode of producing and distributing cultural products to a population). Policy connotes the actions, goals, and decisions of states. Tony Bennett and Colin Mercer (1996) define *cultural policy* as "those policies which have a bearing on the conduct of those institutions and organizations which make up the cultural sector. This includes all those organizations, whether public or private, which are involved in the production and distribution of cultural goods and services"(8). TV is a cultural good. Philip Napoli (2006) argues, "When the parameters of cultural policy expand to include the full breadth of cultural industries, the rest of the regulated commercial media sector (broadcast television, cable television, radio, satellite, and, to a lesser extent, the Internet) involved in the production and distribution of cultural products falls within its boundaries as well"(9).

Culture—as a way of life and as an industry that produces cultural goods—is governed. Cultural policy represents the state administrative means and techniques for doing so.

At no point in history has a full-fledged TV industry emerged as result of the "invisible hand" of the "free market." In the United States, Canada, and elsewhere, states have played a central role in facilitating and legitimizing the emergence of TV industries. Political economists challenge the narrow economistic view that TV is only part of a capitalist culture industry by highlighting how state cultural policies, regulations, and funding entities intersect with and shape the economics of the TV industry in many ways. TV production industries, TV broadcasters, and TV shows are influenced by the territorial, political, and cultural ambitions of states. Paul Nesbitt-Larking (2001) says that the state uses its power to influence TV broadcasting: "in shaping, conditioning and influencing the media, both intentionally and unintentionally, the state can be regarded as a proprietor, custodian, regulator, censor, patron, catalyst, actor, masseur, ideologue and conspirator"(161). In what follows, we discuss the main ways that states shape—and support—the TV industry.

Ownership: Public, Private, and Mixed

National TV broadcasting systems are owned. The form ownership takes is not pre-given but the outcome of state policy. The moment of TV's historical emergence in the United Kingdom, the United States, and Canada involved a political choice about whether or not the system would be publicly or privately owned. Canada's broadcasting system emerged between two diametrically opposed systems: the British *public* broadcasting system and the American *private* broadcasting system. We will briefly distinguish between public and private broadcasting models.

Established in 1927, the British Broadcasting Corporation (BBC) was the world's first and largest public service broadcaster. The public service model treats the airwaves as public property and has the public interest as its goal. It is financially supported by citizens; all households owning TV sets pay a small licence fee each year. In the public service model, the purpose of TV broadcasting is primarily to serve the "public interest" by informing, educating, and enlightening citizens. Accordingly, TV broadcasting serves the "public good" not by giving citizens the TV shows they may want (popular entertainment) but the kinds of TV shows they ostensibly need (educational TV shows). Free from corporate control and at an "arm's length" from direct state interference, public service TV ideally encourages a "public sphere." It represents the interests and concerns of all citizens within a territory, regardless of their social class position, race, or creed. Television is a forum for audiences to learn about and reflect upon serious matters so that they may participate as informed citizens in a democracy. Public broadcasting is sometimes criticized as being an elitist state instrument for the nationalist integration and homogenization of citizens. This leads us to ask: what particular public's "interest" is represented by "the public interest"? Whom specifically does public broadcasting serve? Which "public" and whose "service"? These are relevant questions in the critical study of public broadcasting (Hall 1993).

Distinct from the public service model of TV is the commercial model, which treats TV as a for-profit industry. Since the passing of the Communications Act of 1934, American public airwaves have been primarily treated as a capitalist venture. Though the United States has a public broadcasting corporation (PBS), the American TV system is mainly owned and controlled by profit-seeking firms and funded by a combination of advertising revenue and subscriptions. In this model, the first priority of TV broadcasting is to make profit by keeping production costs low and maximizing audience share. TV's function is to sate the preferences of advertising clients by making TV shows that capture the attention of select audience niches. In the United States, TV does not intentionally seek to enlighten intellectually lacking masses or integrate diverse citizens into a mythical national community (though it may in fact do this governmental work). The commercial model assumes that if an identifiable audience wants a certain type of TV show, then the TV industry will provide it. In practice, this model's TV shows often privilege the tastes and preferences of affluent audience groups that advertising firms demand while excluding everyone else's.

At present, there are very few countries that have a completely publicly owned or privately owned TV system. The British public service model was normative in many countries throughout the twentieth century. In the twenty-first century, the US private system is the dominant TV model. Though the United States won the global battle of broadcasting paradigms (Hilmes 2003), many states combine public and private models. In the United States and Canada, we find both capitalist media corporations (NBC and CTV, for example,) and publicly owned media corporations (PBS and CBC, for example). Canada's TV system is a "single system" because it exhibits a mix of public and private ownership and fusion of public and private interests in state policy and regulation.

Television Regulators

Television industries are regulated by the state. Regulators are state agencies that monitor the actions and interactions of public and private TV broadcasters to make sure that they are operating in accordance with the established broadcasting policies. Regulatory agencies have the power to grant, renew, or revoke a TV broadcaster's licence to broadcast. If a TV network violates a broadcasting policy, it may be fined by the regulator. Though regulatory agencies "regulate" on behalf of the public interest, they are sites of political struggle that can be "captured" by elite interest groups. Regulatory agencies do not always enforce broadcasting policies. When there is widespread public outrage about the conduct of TV broadcasters, the regulatory agency may develop new regulations for TV broadcasting or more aggressively enforce old ones.

Established in 1968, the **Canadian Radio-television and Telecommunications Commission** (CRTC) "is an independent public organization that regulates and supervises the Canadian broadcasting and telecommunications systems"(CRTC 2012). The CRTC attempts to balance between facilitating and legitimizing TV capitalism and ensuring the protection and promotion of Canadian culture. The CRTC claims that it "ensures that all Canadians have access to a wide variety of high-quality Canadian [TV] programming as well as access to employment opportunities in the [TV] broadcasting system"(CRTC 2012). It also asserts that "programming in the Canadian broadcasting system should reflect Canadian creativity and talent, our bilingual nature, our multicultural diversity and the special place of aboriginal peoples in our society"(CRTC 2012). The **Federal Communications Commission** (FCC) is "an independent United States government agency [. . .] established by the Communications Act of 1934 and is charged with regulating interstate and international communications by radio, television, wire, satellite and cable"(FCC 2011a). The FCC's Media Bureau "develops, recommends and administers the policy and licensing programs relating to electronic media, including cable television, broadcast television, and radio in the United States and its territories"(FCC 2011a).

Broadcasting Acts

The state regulators of TV industries attempt to uphold the integrity of broadcasting acts—frameworks of laws and rules that are established to govern a country's TV system. Television broadcasting policy is a state instrument that shapes the actions and interactions of TV broadcasters within a national territory.

The 1991 Canadian Broadcasting Act shapes Canada's TV system. The act demands the following: Canadian TV networks and stations should be effectively owned and operated by Canadian citizens. Broadcasts should be offered in English and French, Canada's two official languages. Canadian TV should safeguard, enrich, and strengthen the cultural life of Canada. It also states that TV broadcasters must air a certain level of Canadian cultural content: TV shows that are made by Canadians, feature Canadians, and represent Canada to Canadians. Accordingly, Canadian TV broadcasters must nurture and develop Canadian TV shows expressive of Canadian visions, ideas, and values to contribute to the promotion of the cultural-, political-, and social-economic fabric of Canada (Government of Canada 1991). The CRTC is responsible for ensuring that TV networks do this.

The most important broadcasting policy of the United States since the Communications Act of 1934 is the 1996 Telecommunications Act. This act is perhaps the most important US legislation pertaining to all electronic communication forms—radio, telephony, TV, and the Internet. The act enabled the convergence of telecommunications and broadcasting in the United States by overturning longstanding cross-ownership restrictions. It led to a number of acquisitions, takeovers, and mergers (Herman and McChesney 1997; Schiller 2000). The act had consequences for American TV. In 1970, the FCC instituted the **Financial Interest and Syndication Rules (Fin-Syn Rules)** to prohibit the Big Three TV networks from owning the means of TV content production (and **syndication** rights to TV shows). The 1996 Act overturned the Fin-Syn Rules, enabling large media conglomerates to acquire and integrate the means of TV content production, distribution, and broadcasting. Since the repeal of the Fin-Syn Rules, TV networks have broadcast as much in-house programming as they want and retained the lucrative syndication rights to the TV shows they produce as well (Holt 2003).

Television broadcasting policy is not made in a value-neutral fashion, nor does it necessarily represent everyone's interests. Marc Raboy (2006) states, "the terrain of media policy—is hotly contested; it is a battleground, a field of tension and struggle rooted in social history and the natural law that technologies are not neutral but emerge out of particular historical circumstances"(298). Television policy often represents specific values that belong to particular interest groups in society. Private-sector lobbies, media unions, consumer advocates, and citizen watchdog groups struggle to determine the broadcasting policies that shape the national TV system. Those who shape broadcasting policy have greater power to shape TV in society than those who don't. In Canada and the United States, broadcasting policy often supports the interest of corporations. When faced with a legitimacy crisis, the state makes some concessions to the "public interest."

Regulating Cultural Content

In Canada, the CRTC regulates TV networks to make sure that a proportion of the TV shows they broadcast in Canada to a Canadian audience is "Canadian." The 1991 Broadcasting Act gives the CRTC the power to decide what constitutes a Canadian TV show and the amount of time that TV networks must devote to Canadian content. What is the "Canadian" of Canadian content? The CRTC uses a point system to determine the "Canadianness" of TV shows. The point system is based on the number of Canadians involved in the production of a TV program. To qualify as "Canadian content," TV shows do not need to represent Canadian culture (identity, geography, themes). But they must display Canadian talent (i.e., actors), maximize the use of Canadian creativity (i.e., cultural workers), and be made by the Canadian TV and film production sector (i.e., be manufactured by Canadian-owned media companies). The CRTC also compels TV networks to fill 50 to 60 per cent of their daily schedule with Canadian TV programs.

Are Canadian content quota regulations for TV broadcasting an effective way of ensuring that Canadian viewers watch Canadian TV shows? Lawson Hunter, Edward Iacobucci, and Michael Trebilcock (2010) don't think so. They argue that content quota regulations represent an era when the spectrum was limited, when a few Canadian TV networks—protected from foreign competition by the state—dominated the market, and when the state had the capacity to ensure that these TV networks scheduled Canadian TV shows and contributed a portion of their profit to making them. In an era of technological change, this regulatory model is becoming less effective. Due to the Internet and new media, "the media universe has evolved to a point where consumers have almost infinite choices of what to view, when to view it and on what medium to view it." Hunter, Iacobucci, and Trebilcock (2010) further argue that Canadian content quotas should be abolished and replaced with direct subsidies to TV companies producing Canadian content and the Canadian Broadcasting Corporation (CBC). Other commentators believe the old regulatory model still works. Kate Taylor (2010) argues that TV networks still make money by airing licensed American TV shows in their protected market and can allocate a portion of their profit to the production of Canadian TV shows that Canadians watch. The old content quota system should be preserved because it still enables Canadian TV to be produced. Taylor (2010) argues, "To remove content regulation from Canadian television would destroy a system of Canadian production the country has worked for decades to build, and would either suddenly enrich broadcasters by freeing them from previous obligations or drive them under by also eliminating the protections they currently enjoy in return for those obligations."

The United States does not have an official cultural-nationalist policy for domestic TV broadcasting. The FCC does not regulate TV broadcasters to make sure that a proportion of the TV shows they daily broadcast will represent the "American Way of Life" or employ US media workers. The US federal state does not compel private TV networks to allocate a portion of their profit to the TV production sector. Official cultural regulations are not needed in the United States. The sheer size of the American TV market and the hypernationalism of its viewers ensure that TV shows that represent "America" will be produced and aired. In foreign relations, the US government did have an official cultural-nationalist policy. The 1948 Smith-Mundt Act authorized state agencies to "sell the American Way" abroad, legislating "the preparation, and dissemination abroad, of information about the U.S., its people and its policies, through press, publications, radio, motion pictures and other information media [. . .] to provide a better understanding of the U.S. in other countries and to increase mutual understanding"(cited in Coombs 1964). Throughout the Cold War, the United States Information Agency (USIA), the Central Intelligence Agency (CIA), and the Department of Defense (DOD) worked with private TV networks to co-produce TV shows that promoted positive images of America to viewers worldwide. TV shows are instruments of US "soft power"(Fraser 2004).

Censorship

States also regulate TV content through censorship. In Canada, the CRTC and the **Canadian Broadcast Standards Council** (CBSC) are responsible for monitoring and censoring objectionable TV content. In Canada, TV shows featuring sex, nudity, coarse language, and violence tend not to be censored. CTV regularly airs unedited episodes of possibly offensive TV series such as *The Sopranos* and *Nip/Tuck*. Before a potentially objectionable TV show begins, Canadian TV networks issue "viewer discretion advisories." Advisories intend to inform viewers about the content of the TV show to assist them in making reasonable viewing choices.

The United States' TV censorship regime is much less liberal than Canada's. As Toby Miller (2010) notes: "In the U.S., the First Amendment to the Constitution supposedly guarantees freedom of speech against government censorship. But the hyper-religious sexual obsessions of the U.S. population [. . .] give the FCC an incentive to stop people watching and listening to what they want"(130). Since the Communications Act of 1934, the US state has prohibited "indecency" on the airwaves. The FCC defines *indecency* as "language or material that, in context, depicts or describes, in terms patently offensive as measured by contemporary community standards for the broadcast medium, sexual or excretory organs or activities"(FCC 2011b). *Profane* broadcasts include "language so grossly offensive to members of the public who actually hear it as to amount to a nuisance"(FCC 2011b). There are many instances in the history of American TV when TV networks self-censored so as not to offend US viewers (as legislated by the FCC). In 1952, the word *pregnancy* was not allowed to be spoken by characters in *I Love Lucy* (despite the fact that star Lucille Ball was pregnant!). Between 1964 and 1966, Mary Ann from *Gilligan's Island* and Jeannie from *I Dream of Jeannie* were not allowed to show their belly buttons. In 2004, Janet Jackson's one-second nipple exposure during Super Bowl XXXVIII's half-time show resulted in calls for firmer FCC regulation.

Television Subsidies

States directly and indirectly subsidize—or financially assist—the TV industry. A direct subsidy is a transfer of public wealth by the government to the culture industry. An indirect subsidy is money created when government encourages the production of cultural goods by establishing an environment that supports business (Cowen 2006). The Department of Canadian Heritage and its various agencies encourage the production of cultural goods. The National Film Board's mission is "to reflect Canada, and matters of interest to Canadians, to Canada and the rest of the world through creating and distributing innovative and distinctive audiovisual works based on Canadian points of view and values"(National Film Board 2010). Telefilm Canada is "dedicated to the development and promotion of the Canadian audiovisual industry" and provides "strategic leverage to the private sector, supplying the film, television and new media industries with financial and strategic support"(Telefilm Canada 2012). These and other Canadian state agencies subsidize the TV industry.

The Canadian state directly subsidizes TV production in a variety of ways. Since 1996, the CRTC has compelled private TV broadcast networks to contribute 1.5 to 5 per cent of their annual revenue to the **Canadian Television Fund (CTF)**, which subsidizes Canadian TV production firms. To qualify for CTF support, a TV production company must demonstrate that (1) the TV show will represent Canadian themes and subject matter; (2) the TV show meets point criteria (points are given to TV productions whose directors, screenwriters, actors, photographers, musical composers, picture editors, and so on are Canadian citizens); (3) the TV show will not be based on foreign TV productions, foreign TV format buys, or completed foreign TV scripts; (4) the intellectual property right to the completed TV show will remain the property of a Canadian firm; and (5) the TV show must be shot on location and primarily set somewhere in Canada. In 1998, the **Canada New Media Fund (CNMF)** was created to encourage the development of Canadian digital media products. In 2007–2008, the CNMF provided $11.5 million in financial assistance to 71 projects. In 2009, the CRTC established a $100-million Local Programming Improvement Fund (LPIF), which is financed by 1 per cent of the annual gross revenue of Canadian cable TV and satellite TV firms. This fund was established to "ensure that viewers in smaller Canadian markets continue to receive a diversity of local programming, particularly local news programming; to improve the quality and diversity of local programming broadcast in these markets; and to ensure that viewers in French-language markets are not disadvantaged by the smaller size of those markets" (CRTC 2009). On 1 April 2010, the Canadian state combined the CTF and the CNMF into a $35-million **Canadian Media Fund** (**CMF**). "The Canada Media Fund will help our producers and broadcasters to do what they do best: create, entertain, and connect with Canadians," said Canadian Heritage Minister James Moore. "We are confident that the broadcasting and interactive digital media sectors will continue to contribute to Canada's economic well-being and will benefit Canadians from all regions of the country" (Canadian Heritage 2009). The CMF supports the development of TV shows, video games, podcasts, and streaming video for social media platforms and mobile devices. The Canadian state also encourages TV production by granting tax credits to TV production companies. The Canadian Film or Video Production Tax Credit provides a fully refundable tax credit of up to 12 per cent of the cost of production to Canadian media firms. The Income Tax Act allows Canadian advertising corporations to claim expenses for ads placed on TV stations that are 80 per cent owned by Canadians. This act gives ad firms a financial incentive to advertise on Canadian TV networks and brings ad revenue into the TV system, which may be later allocated to the production of Canadian TV shows.

The American federal government and state-level governments use subsidies and tax breaks to economically support the American TV industry. Toby Miller (2010) states that if a TV show is shot in the United States, "the credits generally thank regional and municipal film commissions from subsidizing everything from hotels to hamburgers. State, regional and municipal commissions reduce local taxes, provide police services, and block public way-fares" (151). In 2006, Louisiana and New Mexico offered a combination of direct and indirect subsidies to TV production firms. Since then, other states have followed. As of 2011, almost every state gives subsidizes and tax breaks to TV production companies as a strategy to keep Hollywood in the United States (and stave off "runaway productions" to Canada and other countries that offer cheap labour and generous subsidies).

In sum, the Canadian and American states are powerful enablers and underwriters of the TV industry. State subsidies and tax breaks facilitate and legitimize the growth of the TV industry in both countries.

Cultural Policy Rationalizations

There are many state rationalizations for cultural policy that have little to do with *l'art pour l'art*. In the twenty-first century, states frequently attach cultural policy to other sets of policy concerns—from nation-building to economic development—in an instrumental fashion.

Cultural Policy as Nation-Making

Cultural policy is a state instrument for nation-making. Jeremy Ahearne (2009) notes: "The links between culture and political power are clear to see. Any political order needs the means to maintain its symbolic legitimacy, and nowhere are those means more prominent than when symbolic legitimacy must first be instituted or salvaged. In this sense, we might say that 'cultural policy' represents a trans-historical imperative for all political orders" (143). Cultural policy is a means of integrating diverse and geographically separated people as citizens into a nation. State actors use cultural policy to overcome society's contending identities and particular interests by representing the nation as a unity or collective essence (Miller and Yudice 2002). "[T]he modern nation-state self-consciously uses language policy, formal education, collective rituals and mass media to integrate citizens and ensure their loyalty" (Schudson 1994: 656). Justin Lewis and Toby Miller (2003) view "cultural policy [as] a site for the production of cultural citizens" (1).

In the context of cultural policy as nation-making, TV production industries and broadcasters are viewed as instruments for building, protecting, and promoting a distinctive and "sovereign" cultural national identity. In Canada, state support for TV is often rationalized as a means of securing, defending, or protecting Canadian culture from "Americanization." Television is also viewed by cultural policy officials as instruments of national unification. Canada has a large geography but a small population. TV unites Canadians, binding diverse and geographically separate citizens together with transmissions of TV shows that convey national myths and symbols. It is a significant site for "imagining" the nation (Anderson 1991). While watching TV shows, individual viewers may feel and perceive themselves to be part of a larger national collective despite the fact that they will never know, meet, or see most of the people that imaginatively belong to this collective. Serra Tinic (2005) contends that Canada is "an example of the ultimate modern imagined community"(16). TV shows convey the symbols of nation to diverse viewers, giving them a sense of being part of a much bigger national Self. Michael Billig (1995) describes mundane, taken-for-granted representations of the nation that remind people that they are part of a bigger national collective as "banal nationalism." TV shows flag viewers, soliciting their identification with a national "I." Banal nationalist TV shows do not reflect the nation. They script the meaning of "Us," a collective national "We." TV shows often tell us who we are and who we are not in a world system of states.

Cultural Policy as Culture Industry-Making

Cultural policy is a state instrument for building, protecting, and promoting a national culture industry. Since the early 1970s, the Canadian state has employed cultural policy to build a profitable and powerful culture industry. The modernist conflict between the values of culture and those of industry was resolved with the "culture industry" concept (Dowler 1996; Milz 2007; Pennee 1999; Throsby 2001). In 2007, the Canadian cultural industry directly contributed about $84.6 billion—or 7.4 per cent—to Canada's Gross Domestic Product (GDP). The Canadian culture industry employs over 500,000 workers and contributes to a total of 1.1 million additional jobs in related sectors. The Alliance of Canadian Cinema, Television and Radio Artists (ACTRA), the Directors Guild of Canada, and the Writers Guild of Canada (2008) say that the TV industry helps Canadians know themselves, see themselves, and tell their own cultural stories. They also say TV is "vital" to Canada's economy. In 2007–2008, the Canadian audiovisual industry (television and film) accumulated $5.2 billion, making it a central sector of Canada's $85-billion culture industry. Cultural policy provides ideological and concrete state support for the growth of the culture industry, helping it to expand and prosper in Canada and in international media markets. Cultural policy for the culture industry shores up the interests of Canadian media corporations by enabling Canadian media owners to carve out a domestic market without being taken over by US media firms. Though we regularly hear about what the state does for "our culture," the actual economic interests served by "our culture" are often concealed. Canadian cultural policy has long been a powerful capitalist support mechanism that protects and promotes the Canadian TV industry.

Cultural Policy as a Solution to Market Failure

Cultural policy is also viewed as a state instrument for protecting and preserving culture from the presumed threat to it posed by the culture industries. In this context, cultural goods such as TV shows are not just exchange values (commodities) with utilitarian properties. TV shows are important communicative vehicles of cultural meanings that may benefit people in non-commercial and non-utilitarian ways. They may give citizens a sense of belonging to a way of life, improve their aesthetic or moral well-being, or resonate with their desire to produce a cultural heritage for future generations in Canada. The cultural value of a TV show (the feelings, experiences, or benefits it adds to society) is very difficult to quantify in purely monetary terms. The cultural value of a TV show is different from what TV networks or consumers pay for it in the marketplace (Cowen 2006; Grant and Wood 2004; Throsby 2008).

Some cultural policy-makers say the state has the responsibility to provide citizens with access to a diverse array of Canadian cultural products. When the market fails to efficiently and effectively provide significant cultural goods to citizens, cultural policy can play an important role in supporting the production of cultural goods in society. If the culture industry is oligopolistic and only features a limited number of producers, distributors, and cultural products, then cultural policy can be used to ensure that a *diversity* of producers, distributors, and cultural products will be available to citizens. If the culture industry only enables some citizens to enjoy cultural products (and excludes other citizens because they cannot pay or are not targeted by media corporations as a desirable niche audience), then cultural policy can be used to ensure that all citizens, regardless of their social class or location, get universal *access* to cultural products.

Cultural Policy Debates

Cultural policy is not value-neutral. The existence and functions of cultural policy is fought over by a variety of political groups with often clashing ideologies and agendas. Who decides what "Canada" is or is not? Who gets included and excluded from the definition of "Canadian"? Should Canadian citizens be compelled to watch Canadian TV shows or should "sovereign" Canadian consumers decide? Would the Canadian industry—and Canadian culture—cease to exist if Canadian cultural policy's TV support systems were eliminated? These questions lead to vibrant and heated debates between fiscal conservatives and cultural nationalists.

Fiscal conservatives demand "laissez-faire" cultural markets. They argue that the state should stop supporting the TV industry with subsidies and eliminate Canadian content quotas. They believe the market, not the state, should determine whether or not the Canadian culture industry grows and prospers. They portray state cultural policies that support the Canadian culture industry as a waste of public expenditure and a coercive means of redistributing wealth from Canadian taxpayers to media firms. They say the state supports media firms and cultural products that could not survive in a competitive marketplace. They argue Canadian citizens don't really watch much Canadian TV and don't want to. Canadian viewers prefer US prime-time TV shows. When given a choice between state support for the Canadian culture industry or Hollywood's dominance, Canadian consumers choose Hollywood. Conservative journalists and policy wonks from conservative think-tanks call for the complete dismantling of state subsidies, content quotas, and protections of the TV industry. They view cultural policy as a distortion of the "free market."

Cultural nationalists say fiscal conservatives are wrong. In the past, Canadians wanted to watch Canadian TV, but quality Canadian TV shows were not offered to the Canadian public and were rejected. High quality Canadian TV shows were in limited supply (because Canada did not have a large TV production industry), had minimal financing available (due to lack of state subsidies and the private sector's aversion to financial risk), and received inadequate exhibition (because private TV broadcast networks loaded their schedules with cheap but often attractive American TV shows). The market failed to provide Canadian citizens with Canadian TV shows. The choice was between state cultural policy or American TV dominance; Canadians chose cultural policy. Without cultural policy, Canada's TV industry would likely not have developed. Very few Canadian TV shows would be available. Cultural nationalists demand continued state cultural policy subvention. They believe the state can help the Canadian culture industry grow and prosper by encouraging the production of Canadian TV shows that Canadian viewers (and international viewers) want to watch. Peter Grant and Chris Wood (2004) argue that cultural policies provide a means by which nation-states that are smaller than the United States can manage the "curious economics" of cultural production to promote and protect national identity. They believe that in the absence of cultural policy support for local culture industries, there would be an eventual and overall reduction in cultural diversity worldwide due to the unrivalled power and influence of US-based global Hollywood. Grant and Wood (2004) claim that "any government prepared to support its own creators without limiting their freedom of expression surely then deserves the gratitude of other nations, not their criticism"(317).Would Canadian viewers be more willing to consume "Canadian" TV shows if more of these shows were supplied or made available by TV networks? (Collins 1990). According to Ira Wagman and Ezra Winton (2010), the "cultural policy caused the growth of the Canadian TV industry" argument overlooks exogenous explanations for the popular success of TV shows, including the creative vision of screenwriters and directors, the talents of actors, TV network scheduling and marketing practices, and audiences. Canadian cultural policy's relationship to TV broadcasting and its role, function, administration, and impact continue to be debated.

The Articles

The articles included in this section examine the history of broadcasting in Canada and the United States. The first article in this section examines the formation of radio broadcasting in the US. Mark Goodman and Mark Gring (2000) examine the formation of the 1927 Radio Act, the cornerstone of US broadcasting legislation. A progressive ideology influenced the way the US Congress wrote the Radio Act. Against arguments that view US broadcasting in essentially market terms, Goodman and Gring demonstrate that the US Congress never intended broadcasting to be part of an unregulated marketplace. It proposed a broadcasting system free of direct state control, but predicated on state surveillance. Free speech was to be protected only for those who used it responsibly.

Lynn Spigel (1992) explores how TV networks, advertisers, and women's magazines constructed an ideal audience type of women in the 1950s (the classical era of network TV). By scheduling soap operas, TV networks mobilized "Mrs Daytime Consumer"—a white, suburban, middle-class, and unpaid but happy domestic labourer—and delivered her attention to ads for domestic products. Matching the rhythms of women's unpaid domestic workday, TV flowed from soap-opera serials to advertisements for laundry detergent, to beauty tip TV shows and commercials for beauty products.

Marc Raboy (1998) traces the Canadian broadcasting system's development from the early days of radio broadcasting to the emergence of CBC TV in Canada in 1952, to the multi- and specialty-channel TV market of the late 1990s. Raboy contends that Canadian TV has developed from the principle that communication is central to nation-building and national representation. In Raboy's view, the state must carefully balance between the cultural and economic priorities of TV broadcasting, "defending" Canadian culture against an ostensibly threatening US media juggernaut while ensuring that cultural-nationalist public interests (and the profit interests of Canadian TV networks) are served.

Paul Attalah (2007) presents a refreshing critique of the cultural-nationalist argument and the "standard story of television" in Canada, which pits a struggling Canadian TV industry and benevolent federal state against the United States. For Attalah, the study of television in Canada "has been hampered by its absorption into the narrative of cultural defense and into the rationale of the policy apparatus justified by that narrative"(325). For too long, Canadian scholars have uncritically adopted the policy discourse of the state, and, as a result, possessed inadequate knowledge of Canadian TV history. Attalah presents a methodologically useful and alternative history of TV in Canada, focusing on the interplay of audiences, communication technologies, and the TV industry itself.

Works Cited

Ahearne, J. (2009). "Cultural Policy Explicit and Implicit: A Distinction and Some Uses." *International Journal of Cultural Policy*, Vol. 15(2): 141–53.

Anderson, B. (1991). *Imagined Communities*. New York: Verso.

Attalah, P. (2007). "A Usable History for the Study of Television." *Canadian Review of American Studies*, Vol. 30(3): 325–45.

Bagdikian, B. (2004). *The New Media Monopoly*. Boston, MA: Beacon Press.

Bennett, T., and Mercer, C. (1996). "Improving Research and International Cooperation for Cultural Policy." Paper prepared for UNESCO on behalf of the Australian Key Center for Cultural and Media Policy.

Billig, M. (1995). *Banal Nationalism*. London: Sage Publications.

Canadian Heritage. (2009). "Minister Moore Announces Canada Media Fund to Give Viewers What They Want, When They Want It." www.pch.gc.ca/eng/1294862439605

Collins, R. (1990). *Culture, Communication and National Identity: The Case of Canadian Television*. Toronto: University of Toronto Press.

Coombs, P.H. (1964). *The Fourth Dimension of Foreign Policy: Educational and Cultural Affairs*. New York: Harper and Row.

Cowen, T. (2006). *Good & Plenty: The Creative Success of American Arts Funding*. Princeton and Oxford: Princeton University Press.

CRTC. (2009). "Broadcasting Regulatory Policy CRTC 2009-406." http://www.crtc.gc.ca/eng/archive/2009/2009-406.htm

———. (2012). "About the CRTC." http://www.crtc.gc.ca/eng/backgrnd/brochures/b29903.htm

Dowler, K. (1996). "The Cultural Industries Policy Apparatus." In M. Dorland (Ed.), *The Cultural Industries in Canada: Problems, Policies, Prospects* (pp. 328–46). Toronto: Lorimer.

Federal Communications Commission (FCC). (2011a). "About the FCC." http://transition.fcc.gov/aboutus.html

———. (2011b). "Obscene, Indecent, and Profane Broadcasts." www.fcc.gov/cgb/consumerfacts/obscene.pdf

Fraser, M. (2004). *Weapons of Mass Distraction: American Empire and Soft Power*. Toronto: Key Porter Books.

Garnham, N. (1990). *Capitalism and Communication: Global Culture and the Economics of Information*. London: Sage Publications.

———. (2000). "Contribution to a Political Economy of Mass Communication." In M.M. Durham and D. Kellner (Eds), *Media and Cultural Studies: Keyworks* (pp. 219–25). Malden, MA: Blackwell.

Goodman, M., and Gring, M. (2000). "The Radio Act of 1927: Progressive Ideology, Epistemology and Praxis." *Rhetoric and Public Affairs*, Vol. 3(3): 397–418.

Government of Canada. (1991). "Broadcasting Act." http://laws.justice/gc.ca/en/B-9.01/

Grant, P.S., and Wood, C. (2004). *Blockbusters and Trade Wars: Popular Culture in a Globalized World*. Toronto: Douglas & McIntyre.

Gray, J. (2008). *Television Entertainment*. New York: Routledge.

Hall, S. (1993). "Which Public, Whose Service?" In W. Stevenson (Ed.), *All Our Futures: The Changing Role and Purpose of the BBC* (pp. 28–37). BBC Charter Review Series. London: British Film Institute.

Herman, E., and McChesney, R. (1997). *The Global Media: The New Missionaries of Global Capitalism*. London and Washington: Cassel.

Hilmes, M. (2003). "Who We Are and Who We Are Not: Battle of the Global Paradigms." In S. Kumar and L. Parks (Eds), *Planet TV: A Global Television Reader* (pp. 53–73). New York: New York University Press.

Holt, J. (2003). "Vertical Vision: Deregulation, Industrial Economy and Prime-Time Design." In M. Jancovich and J. Lyons (Eds), *Quality Popular Television: Cult TV, The Industry and Fans* (pp. 11–31). London: The British Film Institute.

Hunter, L.A.W., Iacobucci, E., and Trebilcock, M. (12 February 2010). "Let's Join the Digital Broadcasting Revolution." www.theglobeandmail.com/news/opinions/

lets-join-the-digital-broadcasting-revolution/article1465142/

Lewis, J., and Miller, T. (2003). *Critical Cultural Policy Studies: A Reader.* Malden, MA: Blackwell.

Lotz, A.D. (2007). *Beyond Prime Time: Television Programming in the Post-network Era.* Routledge: New York.

Meehan, E.R. (1990). "Why We Don't Count: The Commodity Audience." In P. Mellencamp (Ed.), *Logics of Television: Essays on Cultural Criticism* (pp. 117–37). Indiana: Indiana University Press.

———. (2007). "Understanding How the Popular Becomes Popular: The Role of Political Economy in the Study of Popular Communication." *Popular Communication*, Vol. 5(3): 161–70.

Miller, T. (2010). *Television Studies: The Basics.* New York: Routledge.

Miller, T., and Yudice, G. (2002). *Cultural Policy.* London: Sage Publications.

Milz, S. (2007). "Canadian Cultural Policy-making at a Time of Neoliberal Globalization." *ESC: English Studies in Canada*, Vol. 33(1–2): 85–107.

Mosco, V. (1996). *The Political Economy of Communication.* London: Sage Publications.

Napoli, P.M. (2003). *Audience Economics: Media Institutions and the Audience Marketplace.* New York: Columbia University Press.

———. (2006). "Bridging Cultural Policy and Media Policy in the US: Challenges and Opportunities." Working paper, The Donald McGannon Communication Research Centre, 6 September 2006.

National Film Board. (2010). "Mandate." www.onf-nfb.gc.ca/eng/about-us/organization.php

Nesbitt-Larking, P. (2001). *Politics, Society and the Media: Canadian Perspectives.* Peterborough: Broadview Press.

Pennee, D. (1999). "Culture as Security: Canadian Foreign Policy and International Relations from the Cold War to the Market Wars." *International Journal of Canadian Studies*, Vol. 20(1): 191–213.

Raboy, M. (1998). "Canada." In Anthony Smith (Ed.), *Television: An International History* (pp. 161–8). Oxford: Oxford University Press.

———. (2006). "The 2005 Graham Spry Memorial Lecture Making/Making Media: Creating Conditions for Communication in the Public Good." *Canadian Journal of Communication*, Vol. 31(1): 289–306.

Schiller, H. (2000). *Living in the Number One Country: Reflections of a Critic of American Empire.* New York: Seven Stories Press.

Schudson, M. (1994). "Culture and the Integration of National Societies." *International Social Science Journal*, Vol. 46(1): 63–81.

Smythe, D. (2001). "On the Audience Commodity and Its Work." In M. Durham and D. Kellner (Eds), *Media and Cultural Studies: Keyworks* (pp. 253–79). Malden, MA: Blackwell.

Spigel, L. (1992). "Women's Work." In *Make Room for TV: Television and the Family Ideal in Postwar America* (pp. 73–8, 206–11). Chicago: Chicago University Press.

Taylor, K. (30 September 2010). "Digital Waterloo for Cancon Rules?" www.thestar.com/article/868298-digital-waterloo-for-cancon-rules

Telefilm Canada. (2012). "Mandate." www.appointments.gc.ca/prflOrg.asp?OrgID=FDC&lang=eng

Throsby, D. (2008). "Modelling the Cultural Industries." *International Journal of Cultural Policy*, Vol. 14(3): 217–32.

Tinic, S. (2005). *On Location: Canada's Television Industry in a Global Market.* Toronto: University of Toronto Press.

Wagman, I., and Winton, E. (2010). "Canadian Cultural Policy in the Age of Media Abdundance: Old Challenges, New Technologies." In L. Shade (Ed.), *Mediascapes: New Patterns in Canadian Communication* (pp. 61–77). Toronto: Nelson.

Winseck, D. (2008). "The State of Media Ownership and Media Markets: Competition or Concentration and Why Should We Care?" *Sociology Compass*, Vol. 2(1): 34–47.

The Radio Act of 1927: Progressive Ideology, Epistemology, and Praxis

Mark Goodman and Mark Gring

> The Progressive movement, and the propaganda analysis that grew out of it, remains among our most worthy traditions of scholarship and one from which there remains much to be learned.[1]

The Radio Act of 1927 is one of the most influential pieces of legislation in US history. This bill was the first law that regulated radio broadcasting as a mass medium; therefore, the Radio Act became the legal foundation for the development of the broadcasting industry. Further, the Radio Act was incorporated almost word for word into the Communications Act of 1934, extending the reach of the law into television and telephone. The Telecommunications Act of 1996, despite adding sections dealing with newer forms of telecommunications, was a series of amendments to that 1934 law. When the 1996 Act was graphed onto the language of the old, the new law incorporated many past assumptions. In effect, The Radio Act of 1927 remains the legislative cornerstone governing broadcasting in the United States today.

Our goal in this paper is to understand the Progressive mindset which influenced the way Congress wrote the Radio Act. Our approach casts a rhetorical light on this law to illuminate the ideological influences on the people who created the cause and effect relationships. Yet, we do not seek to perform a traditional rhetorical criticism of the text, because we do not believe that the words or structure of the law (the codification of the ideas) provide much new insight unless the ideological framework of Congress in 1927 is understood. Ideological analyses such as this one lend themselves to cultural studies approaches, but our scope is more limited. Our historical, rhetorical, cultural approach pries open this law in search of its Progressivist assumptions.

In light of the current communication revolution and the continued influence of the Radio Act on current regulation, a reconsideration of the epistemological and ontological assumptions within the Radio Act of 1927 is in order, particularly since this act redefined "free speech" along ideological lines. We argue that a prima facie definition of free speech inadequately explains the intent of Congress in 1927. Instead, a Progressive sense of the meaning of free speech in 1927 needs to be understood, to clarify the Radio Act. By understanding the "subtle, ambiguous, nuanced, retrospective, and/or suggestive" use of power,[2] we can go beyond the words of the law or the lawmakers to uncover a more comprehensive intent inherent in the law.

We contend that the interaction among epistemology, power, and praxis expresses the cultural understanding of what Progressives meant in 1927 by the concept of "free speech." Congress in 1927 never intended for radio to become an unregulated part of the marketplace of ideas. In an unregulated marketplace, all voices would be heard and through unimpeded discussion and debate the truth would be discovered. We argue that what Congress had in mind for the radio industry was a system free of direct government interference, but predicated on continual governmental surveillance. Congress intended radio to be the voice for the dominant values in American culture as those values were understood by the Progressives and by much of middle-class America.

In some ways, the tasks we have set for ourselves are hopelessly complex. To "prove" our contention that Congress sought to use radio to present the dominant values of the middle class would require us to do the following: (1) prove what values the middle class held (as if cultural solidarity existed); and (2) prove that all members of Congress who voted or debated radio legislation knew what these values were, agreed with them, and wrote specific provisions to achieve those ideological ends. Even thousands of interviews, all of which included a "smoking gun" statement that supported our thesis, would not prove our contentions. Instead, we make a circumstantial case that supports our contention, not necessarily proving we are "right," but rather that our contentions are worthy of consideration because they do shed additional light on the Radio Act of 1927.

Specifically, we will present the following arguments:

1. The principal players in writing the legislation—Representative Wallace White, Senator Clarence Dill, and Secretary of Commerce Herbert Hoover—were either Progressives or influenced by Progressive ideology, as were the two strongest congressional opponents, Representative Edwin Davis and Senator Key Pittman.
2. The language of the act had its precedents in Progressive legislation, particularly the legal cornerstone of "public interest, convenience, and necessity."
3. Parts of the congressional debate dealing with free speech issues for broadcasters expressed Progressive concepts of epistemology and ideology. The language of the act put into praxis Progressive concepts of epistemology and ideology; as a result, the solutions contained within the Radio Act to resolve points of contention likewise reflect Progressive concepts of epistemology and ideology.
4. Members of the public interested in radio legislation accepted a Progressive concept of regulation based on a "public interest" standard.
5. A Progressive concept of free speech coincided with contemporary rulings of the US Supreme Court, which sought to define free speech rights.

Once we have presented our evidence on these five points, we believe we will have made a prima facie case that *radio was intended to be the voice for the dominant values in American culture as those values were understood by the Progressives and by many middle-class Americans.* Therefore, it is reasonable to conclude that Congress never intended for radio broadcasting to be an unfettered marketplace of ideas.

The Progressives

Progressivism is a controversial term in American history because it describes a wide range of people who frequently disagreed with each other.[3] On one extreme of the movement were Midwestern and Southern farmers (the old populists). On the other were the immigrants who came to the United States by the millions after 1880 to work in the factories and live in the urban slums of America. A third social and economic force were the "captains of capitalism," pushing America into the twentieth century through technology and industrialism. Progressivism began as a grassroots reform movement in the 1800s, alternatively identified with the aspirations of farmers, immigrants, and industrialists but also members of the middle class threatened by the corruption and immorality of changing social systems.

The Progressive members of the middle class sought to define their place in this new order. Oscar Handlin describes them as holding the traditional Protestant values of the agrarian populists; yet, they staked their economic future on the business values of the wealthy industrialists by going to work for and investing in their operations. As the middle class joined the factory force and business classes as managers, they were brought into contact with an immigrant labour force frequently composed of Jews and Catholics from eastern Europe.[4] These non-Protestants held on to their ethnic identities, creating inner-city neighbourhoods where, from the perspective of the middle class, crime, poverty, and sin flourished.

In the competition for control of this social order, Robert H. Wiebe argues, the middle class led the way in a shift from rural, agricultural, small-town thinking to urban, industrial, big-government solutions. Middle-class Progressives placed power and authority in government bureaucracy, which was to manage the new order by limiting the power of corporations in the business marketplace. Only government could conceivably protect what Progressives perceived to be the public welfare, which was permitting individuals to manage their own affairs by freeing them from the abuses of monopolies.[5] That individualism, to David Danbom, was a product of the Victorian age in which the Progressives had grown up and of the Victorian faith in individualism. Explains Danbom, "The individual . . . was the shaper of his own destiny. His economic success was dependent upon his own efforts, as was his social position."[6] Yet, as David N. Rabban notes, Progressives found that too much individualism and too much freedom threatened social harmony:

> More broadly, the shared Progressive commitment to social harmony implied limitations on free speech. Many Progressives appreciated free speech and even dissent as qualities that contributed to, and should be nurtured by, a Progressive democratic society. But they saw no value in, and occasionally expressed hostility toward, dissent that was not directed at positive social reconstruction.[7]

By the 1920s, conflicts between "urban life and rural sentiments" made the creation of a broad-based Progressive coalition impossible.[8] Some senators remained Progressive activists, such as Robert La Follette of Wisconsin, who ran a credible third-party candidacy in 1924. La Follette and Senators George Norris, William Borah, Hiram Johnson, Burton Wheeler, and Fiorello La Guardia earned the nickname "Sons of the Wild Jackass"[9] for their insurgent, Progressive positions.

These senators, however, did not reflect the totality of Progressivism in the 1920s. The movement had changed after World War I. John Chamberlain says Progressivism "ceased to be critical; it contented itself with following the drift of events" and then satisfied itself by "calling the drift decision."[10] Richard Hofstadter contends that World War I led to the "liquidation of the Progressive spirit," allowing the dark side of the movement to flourish in the 1920s.[11] Progressives were no longer the reformers they had been in the early part of the century; however, in many ways they were more powerful. After 50 years of public debate, the Progressive ideal of societal control through federal power was accepted—and still is. McCraw calls "the bureaucratization of American life" one of the continuing legacies of the Progressives.[12] In relationship to the Radio Act of 1927, what is crucial is that congressmen, regardless of party, accepted a Progressive way of thinking about the role and mechanisms of government.[13]

The Praxis of Ideology

Progressivism was one of the competing/emerging ideologies within the hegemony of the 1920s. Antonio Gramsci defines hegemony as the societal interplay of groups which compete for dominance.[14] His emphasis is on the progression of the development of those who are in power and those who are on the fringes of power. This perspective recognizes a dominant group whose ideas maintain the dominant position within the social system while acknowledging the existence of competing ideologies (some of which are "coming into power" while others are "waning in power").

Raymond Williams, building on Gramsci, claims that hegemony "is a concept which at once includes and goes beyond the terms 'culture' and 'ideology.'"[15] One way in which hegemony goes beyond "culture" and "ideology" is in its recognition of process. There is no assumption of a culture or an ideology as static because "hegemony is always a process."[16]

As a process, hegemony does not just passively exist as a form of dominance. It has continually to be renewed, recreated, defended, and modified. It is also continually resisted, limited, altered, and challenged by pressures not at all its own. We have then to add to the concept of hegemony the concepts of counter-hegemony and alternative hegemony which are real and persistent elements of practice.[17] The absence of a singular, dominant hegemony does not mean that there is not a "dominant hegemony"; it only means that an hegemonic dominance is "never either total or exclusive."[18]

Just as Progressivism was one of several competing political movements within its social milieu, so, too, were there competing positions under the rubric "Progressivism." Despite these competing perspectives, commonality existed among Progressives. They argued for societal regulation exerted by the combined forces of the federal government, "experts" from the area, and business. By the 1920s, these regulatory agencies were accepted. Fights over the nature of the regulation and the radio commission nearly wrecked the chances for legislation in 1926, but both houses of Congress, the listening public, and the industry accepted the concept of regulation through commission. Only a handful of amateur radio operators protested.

Through governmental regulation, Progressives had found ways to bring those outside the morality of Progressive ideology under surveillance, even silencing some voices. The US Supreme Court found convictions under the Espionage Act of 1917 constitutional during World War I, even though the justices recognized that the state was silencing voices of protest. Later the Supreme Court extended to the states the authority to silence other radicals.

The forces of silence and surveillance were unified when the Progressives codified their assumptions into the Radio Act of 1927. Our concern is with this legal codification of the Progressive ideology as praxis. This is the actual proposal of law, not just the words used to justify why the law is needed, but the actual working out of the law. It is in the "working out of the law" with which we are intrigued, because here we find the "performance of ideology." Within any ideology there must be the carrying out of one's ideas, the attempt to implement one's epistemological and power assumptions upon the rest of the socio-political system. As Nikolaus Lobkowicz, Jacques Ellul, Kenneth Minogue, and Clodovis Boff argue, it is within the praxis, the socio-political implementation of the ideas, that one becomes ideological and where the actual *doing* begins to inform the philosophical assumptions.[19]

We contend that the Radio Act's "public interest, convenience, and necessity" standard and the creation of the Federal Radio Commission performed ideological functions for the Progressives. Broadcasters and the listening public were told in 1927 that the Radio Act guaranteed "free speech."[20] Everyone could listen to radio programming as they chose and no government agency would create programming. Monopolies would be prevented from controlling the airwaves. Radio seemed to benefit everyone, but in reality only those voices fitting into the framework of the dominant ideology, as defined by the Progressives, were granted easy access to the media. Our critical analysis of the discourse which brought about the Radio Act of 1927 reveals the ideological assumptions of the Progressives, who were the primary promoters of this act and the dominant force behind the ensuing Federal Radio Commission (FRC).

The Principal Players

The four principal players in writing the Radio Act of 1927 reflected the diversity among those falling under the rubric of Progressive. Clarence Dill had aligned himself with the insurgents in the Senate.[21] Herbert Hoover, an engineer by training and profession, believed in the power of disinterested experts to work for and achieve the public good.[22] During the 1920s, Hoover used his position as Secretary of Commerce to nurture the growth of radio. President Coolidge[23] and Congressman

Wallace White both opposed the creation of another regulatory commission.[24] However, both listened to the concerns of the "captains" of the radio industry and were anxious for some kind of governmental regulation.

Dill had been a Progressive before World War I, serving one term in the House of Representatives before losing his seat because he voted against the declaration of war against Germany. Washington voters sent him to the Senate in 1922 on the promise he would join the farm bloc directed by Senator George Norris of Nebraska.

Dill's first radio bill generally copied White's bill introduced in the House. White's 1926 bill and Dill's Senate version derive from other bills introduced that date back to 1922. William Borah, however, introduced competing legislation, labelled an "anti-administration bill" by the *New York Times*, because Borah wanted a new radio commission to assume the authority being exercised by Hoover. Dill reintroduced his bill with the Borah provisions. This was the bill passed by the Senate in the spring of 1926.

Hoover opposed Dill's commission because he considered control of radio important to the functioning of the federal government. In naming individuals to the radio conferences of 1922–1925, Hoover always asked representatives from several governmental agencies to attend. H.C. Smither, chief coordinator of the Interdepartment Radio Advisory, wrote in a 1925 memo to Hoover that radio policy directly affected the following government agencies and cabinet offices: State Department, Treasury, War, Department of Justice, Post Office, Navy Department, Interior, Department of Agriculture, Bureau of Standards, Department of Labor, ICC, Shipping Board, "dissemination of information by the federal government and potential for national defense."[25] While the interest of the listening public may have focused on entertainment, to Hoover, the federal government needed radio to be effective, and that would require direct government control over some aspects of broadcasting. Hoover sought to explain this concept to the participants of the third radio conference: "Through these policies we have established, the Government, and therefore the people, have to-day the control of the channels through the ether just as we have control of our channels of navigation; but outside this fundamental reservation radio activities are largely free."[26] Now Dill and the insurgent Progressives in the Senate sought to remove the administration of radio from the executive branch and place it under five commissioners who were answerable to no one. Hoover needed to prevent that from happening.

Another factor to consider in understanding the battle over the commission was Hoover's role in the development of radio. While he was secretary of commerce, radio had boomed. His careful, bipartisan approach to regulation had helped radio grow and evolve. His radio conferences had paved the way for meaningful regulation. If elected president in 1928, Hoover could continue to nurture radio, guiding it with the moral hand so necessary for it to become an instrument of public good. C.M. Jansky argues that Hoover predicated his concept of free speech and public service upon the existence of the moral hand. If radio served the public interest, then programming would not have to be regulated.[27] Hoover explained this point at the Third Radio Conference: "We will maintain them [radio activities] free—free of monopoly, free in program, and free in speech—but we must also maintain them free of malice and unwholesomeness."[28] This is Hoover the Progressive and the engineer speaking. His biographer Joan Hoff Wilson describes Hoover as a "Progressive engineer."[29] Richard Hofstadter calls Hoover a self-described "independent Progressive" who identified with "efficiency, enterprise, opportunity, individualism, substantial laissez-faire, personal success, and material welfare."[30]

As a Progressive, Hoover believed that engineers should not just be designers, but should seek to maximize opportunities and efficiency for the cooperative good. In 1926, radio was literally and figuratively an engineering project. Its structure needed to be built; its utility needed to be maximized for the greatest good, which would be serving the needs of the listeners. Hoover raised this issue often. One example was in November 1925: "The ether is a public medium, and its use must be for the public benefit. The use of a radio channel is justified only if there is public benefit." Those listeners needed government to protect them from the immoral, the indecent, the lies, and the propaganda that unscrupulous people could broadcast. If radio regulation was in the hands of the secretary of commerce, then Hoover, the engineer, could continue to build radio and ensure that it was a quality product for the public. Under an independent commission such responsibility would rest with individuals who would not have Hoover's background and training, or perhaps even the right moral fibre. Hoover would solve this problem in 1927 by sending commissioners names to Coolidge. In his *Memoirs*, Hoover describes his choices: "They were all men of technical and legal experience in the art, and none of them were politicians."[31]

If Hoover believed so much depended on the proper administration of radio, then why did he agree to a compromise with Senator Dill in January 1927? A consideration to Hoover could have been the one-year expiration placed on the Federal Radio Commission (FRC). Within a year, Hoover planned to be president-elect. When the FRC expired, he would be in a position to influence what would replace it. Meanwhile, the main task of the FRC was to assign broadcasting licences, a task Hoover planned all along to give to his administrative commission, since he did not believe that one person should make those decisions.[32] Nor should the intense lobbying from the radio industry for almost any regulation be forgotten. In a few months, the RCA/GE chief executive officer Owen Young, his protégé, David Sarnoff, and others would create the National Broadcasting Corporation, the first major permanent radio network and a project worth millions. Chaos threatened that economic future in ways that a commission did not, and radio chaos had only increased since a state court decision (*United States v. Zenith*) had undercut Hoover's authority.[33] A decision by acting Attorney General William J. Donovan stated that the court's decision limited Hoover's power to assigning licences, that he had no authority to assign wavelengths, hours of operation, or put limits on power.[34] If Hoover accepted Dill's compromise, a mechanism existed to restore order to the airwaves, please the radio corporations, let the commission accomplish a task he wanted the commission to do, and position himself to guide radio's future. He could outsmart the Progressive senators in the end.

Hoover's influence extended beyond that of commerce secretary. White and Coolidge relied heavily on Hoover's radio expertise. Coolidge looked to Hoover to develop radio policy. Although Coolidge would speak out often on radio legislation, on at least one occasion Hoover wrote Coolidge's speech.[35] White also looked to Hoover.[36] White had conferred with Hoover on radio legislation as early as 1921.[37] During the 1926 debate over the Radio Act, Hoover marked up a copy of the Senate bill[38] and a copy of the legislation labelled "Confidential Conference Draft."[39] It requires little stretch to presume Hoover shared with White his comments in the margins of the draft.

While Congressman E.L. Davis and Senator Key Pittman presented the populist side of Progressivism, White and Hoover preferred to work with the captains of the radio industry. During the Radio Act debate, RCA kept its views known to both Hoover and White. The Radio Corporation of America had been founded in 1919 when General Electric, Westinghouse, American Telephone and Telegraph, and United Fruit took over the assets of American Marconi. Each corporation took shares in RCA and divided the marketing of products.[40] The president of RCA was J.G. Harbord, who corresponded with both Hoover and White on radio legislation.[41] In addition, David Sarnoff, the rising star at RCA, met with White to discuss radio legislation.[42]

Publicly, AT&T, General Electric, and the National Association of Broadcasters stated their support for the White bill.[43]

From these interconnections, meetings, and correspondences, a conclusion can be drawn that the White bill not only reflected the congressman's thinking, but also the influence of RCA and Hoover, with the agreement of President Coolidge.

Even though passage of the Radio Act would pit the insurgent Republicans like Dill against the populists like Key and Davis and against the Coolidge administration, the key point is that Hoover, Coolidge, the senators, and White agreed on what federal regulation could achieve and sought similar goals for radio; the disagreement was over what mechanism of government to use to achieve those goals. The arguments among the principal players were between different shades of Progressive thought.

The Need for Legislation

By 1927, the technology and growth of radio had outpaced existing congressional regulation, written in 1912 when radio meant ship-to-shore communication. Radio was loosely regulated through its growth years in the 1920s. By mailing a postcard to Secretary of Commerce Herbert Hoover, anyone with a radio transmitter—ranging from college students experimenting in science classes, to amateur inventors who ordered kits, to newspaper-operated stations—could broadcast on the frequency chosen by Hoover. The airwaves by 1927 were an open forum for anyone with the expertise and equipment[44] to reach an audience with 25 million potential listeners.[45]

Radio's open forum, however, became unmanageable in 1926 after an Attorney General's decision said the Radio Act of 1912 did not give the secretary of commerce authority to assign specific wave lengths.[46] By 1926, radio in the United States included 15,111 amateur stations, 1,902 ship stations, 553 land stations for maritime use, and 536 broadcasting stations.[47] Geographical separation and power restrictions would make it possible to place six stations per broadcasting channel for a total of 534 stations. In addition, 425 more licensing applications were under consideration by the department of commerce, which had no legal authority to reject any request for a licence. White warned his colleagues in 1926 that radio stations were jamming the airwaves, causing interference between stations in many locations. In the words of the *New York Times*, the radio signal almost anywhere on the dial sounded like "the whistle of the peanut stand."[48] Radio had become what Erik Barnouw calls "A Tower of Babel."[49] The "babel" threatened the emerging economics of radio. The undisciplined and unregulated voice of the public interfered with corporate goals of delivering programming and advertising on a dependable schedule to a mass audience.

Congress faced many difficulties in trying to write legislation. No precedent existed for managing broadcasting except the powerless Radio Act of 1912. No one knew in 1926 v the technology was going nor what radio would be like even the next year, so Congress was trying to write law to cover potentialities. Senator Key Pittman of Nevada expressed his frustration to the Senate chair:

> I do not think, sir, that in the 14 years I have been here there has ever been a question before the Senate that in the very nature of the thing Senators can know so little about as this subject.[50]

Nor was the public much better informed, Pittman noted, even though he received telegrams daily urging passage.

> I am receiving many telegrams from my State urging me to vote for this conference report, and informing me that things will go to pieces, that there will be a terrible situation in this country that cannot be coped with unless this report is adopted. Those telegrams come from people, most of whom, I know, know nothing on earth about this bill.[51]

Offering to bring order out of this chaos were White and Dill. These two congressional radio experts led the year-long fight in 1926 to pass legislation to regulate radio, leading to the Radio Act, signed by Calvin Coolidge in February 1927.

The Historical Argument

Other historians have considered congressional intent in the Radio Act and evaluated Progressive influences, most notably Louise Benjamin and Donald Godfrey. Benjamin's dissertation on free speech in the Radio Act considered the issues of censorship, creation of a regulatory agency, monopoly, and the right of broadcasters to use the medium. In trying to resolve who should be allowed to broadcast, Benjamin argues, Congress placed itself into a larger social debate. A free speech debate existed within American society over those who "saw 'abuses' of free speech as intolerable and those who wished to use speech to further social and economic goals."[52] As Benjamin would later argue, these conflicts were resolved by Secretary of Commerce Herbert Hoover and the radio industry during the 1920s radio conferences conducted by Hoover prior to passage of the Radio Act. The end result of these agreements was "to transform the industry from amateur communication to nationwide broadcasting," which met the economic needs of the major radio corporations.[53]

Godfrey spent some time in his dissertation looking at Progressive influence on the Radio Act. He makes particular note of the Progressive roots of Senator Dill and his identification with Progressive Senators James Watson, William Borah, Robert La Follette, Hiram Johnson, and Burton Wheeler. According to Godfrey, one of the areas of Progressive influence was in the selection of the language "public interest, convenience, and necessity." These words were a way of balancing industrial control of radio against the potential for government censorship. To Godfrey, "The founders of the legislation sought to provide a degree of regulation that would preserve industrial freedom and the public interest."[54] Another way that Progressive senators specifically shaped the Radio Act was in the creation of the Federal Radio Commission, contends Godfrey in a later article.[55] Influenced by Borah and Watson, Dill rewrote his first draft of the 1926 Senate version of the bill to create the FRC. Borah and Watson objected to putting radio control into the hands of the secretary of commerce, for fear that person would use radio for political purposes. Kerry Irish notes that these Progressive senators were not happy with the final version of the Radio Act. George Norris, for example, wanted governmental control of radio. Despite getting the FRC and the public interest standard, Irish claims that Dill, Norris, Borah, and others would not have called the Radio Act a Progressive victory, because White and Coolidge refused to permit government ownership.[56] To an extent, Irish is correct. Coolidge told Hoover to turn to the "successful elements of the industry" for advice.[57] White discussed regulation with representatives from the National Association of Broadcasters, RCA, and even David Sarnoff.[58] In the final analysis, however, whether Borah and other Progressive senators were happy, the fact remains that the Radio Act includes many provisions, particularly the creation of an independent commission and the public interest standard, borrowed from the Progressive model of federal regulation.

White and Dill agreed that the public interest standard was the heart of the Radio Act.[59] The FRC, armed with the "hidden teeth" of the public interest standard, had all the authority it needed to create the machinery for censorship.[60] Public interest provided a criterion for the commission to determine who was fit to broadcast, notes C.B. Rose, but without creating specific guidelines. Without guidelines to follow, the commission could favour large "capital interests."[61] Ultimately, the public interest standard represented "prior restraint" of broadcasters, argues Fred H. Cate, and, therefore, "The First Amendment is nowhere to be found" in the Radio Act of 1927.[62]

However, Progressives would not have seen themselves as violators of free speech. Rabban notes that free speech carried with it moral obligations that were to keep free speech checked. For Goodman these unspoken moral obligations are as much a part of understanding the free speech issues of the Radio Act as are the free speech statements in the language of the law.[63] The congressional goal in the Radio Act was not government censorship, but many in Congress feared the power of radio, Goodman argues. If the FRC licensed the right kind of people with the right moral values, then Congress would have nothing to fear.

The Free Speech Debate

Before radio legislation could be passed, competing Progressive factions debated who would control radio. Senator Pittman and Representative E.L. Davis of Tennessee represented the voice of the common man of rural America. Pittman and Davis believed that RCA was conspiring to turn radio into a monopoly. The monopoly would not only be worth millions, but to Pittman and Davis, RCA would use the voice of radio to gain great political power and to shape thought in America.

RCA was not the first corporation to be targeted by Progressives. Monopolies had long been a principal target of rural Progressives, dating back to their populist roots. This eventually led to the Sherman Antitrust Act of 1890, which sought to prevent the destruction of "free capitalism and restraint of trade."[64]

Dill and White were spokesmen for those who believed progress and technology needed to move forward and that regulation would prevent the evils predicted by Davis and Pittman. White considered the public interest standard to be one of the seven key elements in the law to prevent monopolies.[65]

Free speech under the First Amendment had traditionally meant that everyone had the right to express opinion, creating an uninhibited marketplace of ideas. However, the limited number of radio channels made the old definition obsolete from the viewpoint of Congress. Noting that free speech needed to be "inviolate," White argued that a new concept of free speech was required.

> We [Radio Conference of 1924] have reached the definite conclusion that the right of all of our people to enjoy this means of communication can be preserved only by the repudiation of the idea underlying the 1912 law that anyone who will may transmit and *by the assertion in its stead of the doctrine that the right of the public to service is superior to the right of any individual to use the ether* [emphasis added].[66]

In effect, White was creating a right to listen and equating it with freedom of speech. Such an equation would work, Dill argued,[67] because of the "public interest, convenience, or necessity" standard written into the act.[68]

Proper use of the radio was a second free speech issue debated. The power of the FRC would become the instrument for ensuring that radio was not used for improper speech. Specifically, the Radio Act banned "obscene, indecent, or profane language."[69] In addition, those who would use radio for radical change also could be silenced, White and Dill told their colleagues.

Attempts were made in writing the bill to guarantee that only the "right" kind of material was communicated to the audience. Senator Hiram Bingham of Connecticut thought the commerce department should handle the technical aspects of radio while the Post Office could handle "improper" communication of thought, since it already had expertise.[70] Senator Coleman L. Blease of South Carolina was willing to create the FRC as long as he knew what the politics and religion of the commissioners were. Blease wanted to know if someone could go on the air and say "he came from a monkey."[71] Blease's amendment to prohibit all radio discussion of evolution failed.

At one point during congressional debate, Senator Earle B. Mayfield of Texas wanted to know what was going to keep "bolshevism or communism" off the air.[72] Dill believed that radicals could be excluded from the airwaves since the law[73] only discussed air time for legally qualified candidates.[74] Congressional intent was to give voice to the political parties supported by the middle class while the candidates of immigrants, many of whom supported unions or radical political change, would have limited access to the airwaves.

As praxis in the Radio Act, regulated free speech meant that the only discussions to be heard over the radio would be those consistent with the ideology of the Progressives. In this way, the Progressive agenda could be presented to the public. Unions, socialists, communists, evolutionists, improper thinkers, non-Christians, and immigrants, could be marginalized by keeping these ideas off radio, outside of "public interest, convenience, and necessity." Progressives silenced opposition during World War I with the Espionage Act, and the Supreme Court extended the law during the 1920s through its rulings to control the voice of radicals. Within such an historical and ideological context, the Radio Act of 1927 becomes a performance of Progressive ideology.

The Radio Act put the mechanism in place for control of the airwaves through surveillance and silence. The FRC would review all station logs and programming to determine if each broadcaster was acting in the "public interest, convenience, and necessity." That determination would be based on the assumptions that listeners did not have a right to speak, only a right to hear. Through regulatory agencies, Rabban explains, controls on individualism could be instituted that "would permit a benevolent government to participate actively in creating a society in which all citizens have the resources to exercise effective freedom and to develop their individual capacities for the common good."[75]

The "benevolent" efforts of White and Dill had been successful. They had given both the public and the corporations essentially what they wanted, but the real control of radio would be in the hands of the Progressives' representative: the FRC. The people would be guaranteed access to radio programs that would be entertaining, but they were effectively denied access to the airwaves. Radio station owners had lost the right to speak for themselves, but in return they could use the electromagnetic spectrum to make money through advertising. For Progressives such as Dill, White, and Hoover, technology and progress could go forward, controlled by the moralistic hand of the middle class and the power of "public interest, convenience, and necessity."

Public Interest, Convenience, and Necessity

Dill claims the language "public interest, convenience, and necessity" was a late addition to the Radio Act, that the term resulted from his meetings with White to write the final version of the bill.[76] Yet, the concept of radio operating in the public interest dates back at least to the first radio conference of 1922 when Hoover, in his opening comments, stated that radio should be for presenting information of the "public interest." In 1925, he described "the ether" as "a public medium, and its use must be for public benefit."[77]

Dill acknowledged that the public interest concept was not original but was borrowed from the Interstate Commerce Commission (ICC).[78] White, in a letter, credited parts of the Radio Act to the ICC.[79] Dill served on the Senate's ICC committee while White served on the House committee overseeing railroad regulation. Since Hoover was secretary of commerce, he worked extensively with the ICC and railroad regulation. All three were familiar with the traditions of regulation under a public interest standard before writing the Radio Act.

All three also shared a presumption that a public interest standard conferred on the government the right to limit who spoke. Dill went so far as to admit that the public interest standard created a "twilight zone" between serving the public interest and permitting the federal government the right to censor radio, although he did not believe that public interest, convenience, and necessity gave the government the right to control programming.[80] Rather, the goal of public interest was to "empower the Commission to limit the amount of advertising, prohibit programs that it decided were harmful to the public as a whole, and to refuse to renew licenses of those who disregarded its rulings."[81] To Dill, such use of the language by the FRC did not violate the First Amendment because it protected the listeners. White told the House that the free speech provisions of the Radio Act of 1912 had to be repudiated to be replaced by "the right of the public to service."[82] White also did not believe that protecting the public interest was censorship but that it was "about as far as we can go in permanent legislation" to regulate broadcasters.[83]

Like White and Dill, Hoover did not try to explain apparent free speech restrictions created by implementing a public interest standard. Hoover described the state of radio before the 1927 Act as "a policy of absolute freedom and untrammelled operation, a field open to all who wished to broadcast for whatever purpose desired." However, the only way to end radio chaos was "to keep the best stations." Freedom of speech had two parties, Hoover explained, the speaker and the listener. "Certainly in radio I believe in freedom for the listener," Hoover told the 1924 radio conference. "The greatest public interest must be the deciding factor."[84]

Willard D. Rowland's essay on the public interest standard of broadcasting further explains the perspectives of Hoover, White, and Dill. Rowland points out that a public interest standard dated back nearly a century by 1927. State regulatory agencies had been created early in the 1800s to regulate railroads, and many of these agencies used a public interest standard. The US Supreme Court upheld the standard in 1837.[85] "Convenience and necessity" became associated with the public interest as a provision for the granting of licences to railroads and utilities, Rowland explains. The federal government adopted a public interest standard for the first time in the Interstate Commerce Act of 1887. Congress also relied on public interest in creating the Federal Reserve Board in 1912 and the Federal Trade Commission in 1927. As Rowland explains, "Having become an integral part of the state regulatory philosophy and having been sustained in the courts, the public interest standard readily migrated into the new federal policy."[86]

Rowland disagrees with those historians who have labelled public interest as a vague standard. "In fact, however, it turns out that the public interest standard was neither vague nor undetermined in meaning or practice when introduced into broadcasting legislation," writes Rowland. Its long use as regulatory language provided the writers of the Radio Act a "well-rehearsed doctrine," which was widely understood as the authority for a regulatory agency. Regulators liked the way the standard finessed the balance between the interests of the public in protection and the need for corporate profits. On the surface, public interest language placed regulators on the side of the public. In practice, regulators protected the profits of corporations, since the public interest would not be served if those who served the public failed to survive. This regulatory approach created a need for commission experts to meet regularly with corporate leaders to discuss their needs.

The finesse worked well in creating support for the Radio Act. Dill had his commission which would serve the public interest by protecting the public from an RCA monopoly. Meanwhile, Hoover and White conferred with Sarnoff and other radio industry leaders to discuss their needs. The Radio Act protected profits, which in the long run served the public's demand for entertainment. The public interest standard of the Radio Act symbolizes the Progressive experience, writes Rowland, because it accomplishes the "social and legal compromises" of Progressive "reform and the appeal to public service and welfare."[87]

The Public Perspective

Despite the limitations placed on free speech by the Radio Act, most of the listening public and those in radio accepted the Progressive concept of free speech. A typical example of Progressive thinking was J.H. Morecraft, who wrote a regular column, "The March of Radio," in the industry magazine *Radio Broadcast.* "We need to protect freedom of speech," Morecraft argued, "but our rights cannot interfere with the rights of others."[88] Congestion on the airwaves was a bigger problem than free speech concerns, Morecraft held. "At this writing, we fear more no legislation at all, than the harmful effects of any particular bill or method of control."[89] Radio offered an easy solution to any legislative limitations on the speaking public. "If you have something to say," he told his readers, "go to an existing broadcaster and buy time."[90] Later, Morecraft wrote: "Freedom of the air does not require that everyone who wishes to impress himself on the radio audience need have his private microphone to do so."[91] He reiterated the point in a later column. "Radio waves cannot be freely used by everyone," Morecraft wrote. "Unlimited use will lead to its destruction."[92]

Many others concerned with radio also believed that radio could not be an unfettered marketplace of ideas. As *The Literary Digest* stated in 1924, "[T]he power of one man through a broadcasting station must be curbed if that man persists in affronting the sensibilities of a large or a small part of the population." While censorship was not appealing, the article continued, radio should not appeal to "vulgarities" or morbid affairs. Therefore, broadcasters should be businessmen of the highest class so that radio would remain "clean and fit for the common consumption."[93] When the wrong people were allowed to broadcast, then the listening public suffered, *The Literary Digest* noted in another article. "Propagandists, religious zealots, and unprincipled persons" are using radio to "grind their own axes."[94] Once the Radio Act passed, *The Literary Digest* called upon the new radio commission to assign licences only to the "high type" that would operate the station for public service by providing "well-rounded" programming.[95]

Free Speech: The US Supreme Court Concept

A congressional concept of limited free speech was consistent with several contemporary US Supreme Court rulings, including opinions written by Justices Oliver Wendell Holmes and Louis Brandeis, two Progressives on the Court. Beginning in 1919, the US Supreme Court upheld the constitutionality of the Espionage Act as a tool to quiet discontent against the US effort in World War I, first in *Schenck v. United States* and later in *Frohwerk v. United States* and *Debs v. United States.* Eventually, the Supreme Court extended limitations on free speech beyond the context of World War I to include radicalism and anarchy (*Gitlow v. New York; Whitney v. California*).

Rabban argues that the Espionage Act under which Frohwerk, Schenck, and Debs were convicted held similar ideological assumptions as those we ascribe to the Radio Act. Rabban based his conclusions on a review of the writings of John Dewey, Herbert Croly, and Roscoe Pound, three Progressive intellectuals. Rabban notes that Progressives found that too much individualism and too much freedom threatened social harmony.

> More broadly, the shared Progressive commitment to social harmony implied limitations on free speech. Many Progressives appreciated free speech and even dissent as qualities that contributed to, and should be nurtured by, a Progressive democratic society. But they saw no value in, and occasionally expressed hostility toward, dissent that was not directed at positive social reconstruction.[96]

In light of the writings of Progressive leaders, Supreme Court decisions, and the actions of the federal government during the Red Scare, the concept of free speech as understood in 1927 did not include a marketplace of robust debate and extremist views. Free speech was protected for those who used it responsibly, in ways consistent with the dominant ideology. Therefore, a discussion of radical political change would not only seem to violate the Radio Act's standard of "public interest, convenience, and necessity," but could also be illegal.

Conclusions

We have laid out our circumstantial case. The three people most responsible for writing the Radio Act of 1927 approached radio regulation from a Progressive perspective. White and Hoover sought to balance the profit needs of the radio industry against the entertainment requirements of the public. They relied on the Progressive concept of public interest, convenience, and necessity to achieve and maintain that balance. Dill, the third major player, took a more insurgent approach, forcing Hoover and White to accept the Federal Radio Commission, which Dill hoped would protect the public interest from the monopolist designs of RCA, while encouraging the development of the art of radio. Despite the firm opposition of Hoover and White to Dill's FRC, they both also wanted a commission to play a role in radio regulation. More fundamentally, the difference was over *which branch of the federal government* should provide surveillance over the radio voices, not *if* there should be surveillance. None of the three designers of the law envisioned a free and uninhibited marketplace of ideas over the airwaves. They did not consider surveillance as being a restriction on free speech. Nor did they object to the silencing of radical or immoral voices.

From a Progressive perspective, free speech meant the freedom to behave in a responsible manner. This was the argument made by the US Supreme Court in several contemporary decisions. Further, it was a definition of free speech accepted by the listening public as represented by magazine and newspaper writers of the time. Progressive epistemological and ideological assumptions were put into praxis through public interest, convenience, and necessity and the creation of the FRC. The radio industry accepted limitations because it was given a free hand in developing networks and making radio a profitable industry driven by advertising sales. The public was satisfied as long as it could listen nightly to its favourite programs without the "whistles of the peanut stand" created by station interference.

Since the Radio Act of 1927 remains the cornerstone of broadcasting regulation in America, a fair presumption is that some of the Progressive ideological and epistemological assumptions continue to influence regulation today. The challenge remains for scholars to review the Telecommunications Act of 1996, the US Supreme Court decision in *ACLU v. Reno*, as well as other recent regulatory decisions to discover how Progressivism continues to influence broadcasting today.

Notes

1. James Carey, "Communications and the Progressives," in *Critical Perspectives on Media and Society*, ed. Robert K. Avery and David Eason (New York: Guilford Press, 1991), 28–48.
2. Ronald F. Wendt, "Answers to the Gaze: A Genealogical Poaching of Resistances," *Quarterly Journal of Speech* 82 (1996): 251–73.
3. Many historians make note of the conflicts within Progressivism, including Arthur Link and Richard McCormick, Robert Wiebe, Richard Hofstadter, Robert Murray, Joan Hoff Wilson, LeRoy Ashby, and Kenneth MacKay.
4. Oscar Handlin in the foreword of David P. Thelen, *Robert La Follette and the Insurgent Spirit* (Boston: Little, Brown and Co., 1976), v.
5. Robert H. Wiebe, *The Search for Order 1877–1920* (New York: Hill and Wang, 1967), 297.
6. David B. Danbom, *The World of Hope: Progressives and the Struggle for an Ethical Public Life* (Philadelphia: Temple University Press, 1987), 5–6.

7. David N. Rabban, "Free Speech in Progressive Social Thought," *Texas Law Review* 74 (1996): 955.
8. LeRoy Ashby, *The Spearless Leader: Senator Borah and the Progressive Movement in the 1920s* (Urbana: University of Illinois Press, 1972), 8.
9. Ray Tucker and Frederick R. Barkley, *Sons of the Wild Jackass* (Seattle: University of Washington Press, 1932).
10. John Chamberlain, *The Rise, Life and Decay of the Progressive Mind in America*, 2nd edn, (New York: John Day Co., 1933), 305.
11. Richard Hofstadter, *The Age of Reform: From Bryan to F.D.R.* (New York: Knopf, 1955), 273.
12. Thomas K. McCraw, "The Progressive Legacy," in *The Progressive Era*, ed. Lewis L. Gould (Syracuse, NY: Syracuse University Press, 1974), 182.
13. Key Pittman, for example, was always identified as a party line Democrat, but in 1925 and 1926 he pushed for passage of a Progressive-like piece of governmental regulation, the Long and Short Haul amendment to the Interstate Commerce Act with the help of Progressive leader William Borah. Betty Glad, *Key Pittman: The Tragedy of a Senate Insider* (New York: Columbia University Press, 1986), 139.
14. Antonio Gramsci, *Selections from the Prison Notebook*, ed. and trans, by Quintin Hoare and Geoffrey Nowell Smith (New York: International Publishers, 1971).
15. Raymond Williams, *Marxism and Literature* (New York: Oxford University Press, 1985), 108.
16. Williams, 112.
17. Williams, 112–13.
18. Williams, 113.
19. Nikolaus Lobkowicz, *Theory and Practice: History of a Concept from Aristotle to Marx* (Notre Dame, IN: University of Notre Dame Press, 1967). Jacques Ellul, *Jesus and Marx: From Gospel to Ideology* (Grand Rapids, MI: Eerdman Publishing, 1988). Kenneth Minogue, *Alien Powers: The Pure Theory of Ideology* (London: Weidenfeld and Nicholson Ltd., 1985). Clodovis Boff, *Theology and Praxis: Epistemological Foundations* (Maryknoll, NY: Orbis Books, 1987).
20. Radio Act of 1927, Sec. 29. *Congressional Record*, 1927, 1173.
21. Clarence Dill, *Where the Water Falls* (Spokane: C.W. Hill, 1970), 74.
22. Joan Hoff Wilson, *Herbert Hoover: Forgotten Progressive* (Boston: Little, Brown and Co., 1975), 31.
23. "Coolidge Opposes More Commissions," *The New York Times*, 28 April 1926, 24.
24. "Hoover Backs Radio Bill," *The New York Times*, 7 January 1926, 41.
25. H.C. Smither, Chief Coordinator, Interdepartment Radio Advisory Committee to Herbert Hoover, Secretary of Commerce. 20 May 1925. Box 501: Radio—Interdepartmental Problems, 1923–27. Herbert Hoover Papers; Herbert Hoover Library, West Branch, Iowa (hereafter HHL).
26. "Recommendations For Regulation of Radio, Adopted by the Third National Radio Conference, October 6–10, 1924," p. 2. Box 496: Radio—Conferences; Folder: Radio—Conferences, National—third (6 October 1924), Herbert Hoover Papers, HHL.
27. C.M. Jansky, "The Contribution of Herbert Hoover to Broadcasting," *Journal of Broadcasting* 1 (1957): 241–9.
28. Hoover, Third Radio Conference, 2, Herbert Hoover Papers, HHL.
29. Wilson, 31.
30. Hofstadter, 286.
31. Herbert Hoover, *The Memoirs of Herbert Hoover: The Cabinet and The Presidency 1920–1933*, vol. 2 (New York: Macmillan, 1952), 144.
32. Hoover, *Memoirs*, 145.
33. *United States v. Zenith*, No. 14257, District Court of the U.S., Northern District of Illinois, Eastern Division. Box 502: Radio—Zenith Radio Corporation 1925. Hoover Papers, HHL.
34. Decision by William J. Donovan, Acting Attorney General, 9 July 1926. Box 501: Radio—Legislation, 1926. Herbert Hoover Papers, HHL.
35. See Box 478: President Coolidge 1926, August–November. Herbert Hoover Papers, HHL. On 20 Nov. 1926, Hoover sent a draft of a speech on radio legislation to Coolidge. Coolidge delivered that speech in December 1926 without modification.
36. Hoover and White apparently met socially, since the Hoover files include a handwritten note inviting Mr and Mrs Hoover to the Whites' home. Box 501: Radio—Legislation, 1926. Folder—Radio: Federal Radio Commission Legislation, 1925–1928 & Undated. Herbert Hoover Papers, HHL.
37. To Herbert Hoover from Wallace White, 12 April 1921. Box 283: House of Representatives—White, Wallace H., 1921–28 and undated. Herbert Hoover Papers, HHL.
38. S. 4156, 3 May 1926. Box 501: Radio—Interdepartmental Problems, 1923–27. Herbert Hoover Papers, HHL.
39. Confidential Draft, Radio Act. Box 501: Radio—Interdepartmental Problems, 1923–27. Herbert Hoover Papers, HHL.
40. Erik Barnouw, *Tower of Babel: A History of Broadcasting in the United States*, vol. 1 (New York: Oxford University Press, 1966), 59.
41. Harbord letters to White and Hoover. J.G. Harbord to Herbert Hoover, 4 April 1923. Box 496: Radio—Conferences, National—second (20–24 March 1923). Herbert Hoover Papers, HHL. J.G. Harbord to Wallace White, 26 July 1926. Box 651: Folder—Radio, Miscellaneous #2. Wallace H. White Collection, Library of Congress.
42. From William Brown to Wallace White, 26 October 1926. Box 54: Folder—Radio, Miscellaneous #2. Wallace H. White Collection, Library of Congress, Washington, DC.
43. "Bill Provides for Control of Radio Motion Pictures," *The New York Times*, 17 January 1926, 41.

44. An indication of this is the following numbers reported in *New York Times*, 25 February 1927. In 1927, there were 733 public entertainment stations and 18,119 amateur radio sending stations.
45. Dill, "A Traffic Cop for the Air," *The American Review of Reviews*, February 1927, 183.
46. Herbert Hoover, perhaps to force Congress to pass legislation, asked for an opinion ending his authority to regulate radio after the Zenith court decision undermined his authority. See C.C. Dill, "Hope to Stretch Ether Channels," *New York Times*, 12 September 1926: sec. R, 2.
47. *Congressional Record*, 1927, 5478.
48. "Expect New Radio Law To Be Shaped This Month," *New York Times*, 7 November 1926, sec. XX, 18.
49. Barnouw's title for Volume One of his history of broadcasting.
50. *Congressional Record*, 1927, 3027. Another indicator of the complexity of the issues is that Clarence Dill and Wallace White were ultimately assigned the task of writing the final version of the Radio Act because no others in Congress understood the issues. See *New York Times*, 17 December 1926, 44. Dill referred to himself as a "one-eyed man among the blind." See Dill, *Water Falls*, 114.
51. *Congressional Record*, 1927, 3570.
52. Louise Benjamin, "Radio Regulation in the 1920s: Free Speech Issues in the Development of Radio and the Radio Act of 1927" (Ph.D. diss., University of Iowa, 1985), 116–17.
53. Louise Benjamin, "Working It Out Together: Radio Policy from Hoover to the Radio Act of 1927," *Journal of Broadcasting & Electronic Media* 42 (1998): 233.
54. Donald G. Godfrey, "A Rhetorical Analysis of the Congressional Debates on Broadcast Regulation in the United States, 1927" (Ph.D. diss., University of Washington, 1975), 33.
55. Donald G. Godfrey, "Senator Dill and the 1927 Radio Act," *Journal of Broadcasting* 23 (1979): 477–89.
56. Kerry Irish, "Clarence Dill: The Life of a Western Politician" (Ph.D. diss., University of Washington, 1994), 168.
57. Barnouw, 178.
58. Wallace H. White to L.S. Baker, managing director, National Association of Broadcasters, 2 December 1927, Box 50: Folder—Radio, Miscellaneous, Wallace H. White Collection, Library of Congress.

    Wallace H. White to William Brown, vice president and general attorney, RCA, 24 November 1926, Box 51: Folder—Radio, Miscellaneous, Wallace H. White Collection, Library of Congress.

    Wallace H. White to H. G. Harbord, president, RCA, 22 September 1926, Box 5: Folder-Radio, Miscellaneous, Wallace H. White Collection, Library of Congress.

    Wallace H. White to Paul B. Klugh, ex-chairman, National Association of Broadcasters, 2 September 1926, Box 651: Folder—Radio, Miscellaneous #2, Wallace H. White Collection, Library of Congress.

    Telegram from William Brown to Wallace White, arranging meeting with "SARNOFF," 26 October 1926, Box 651: Folder—Radio, Miscellaneous #2, Wallace H. White Collection, Library of Congress.
59. Frederick W. Ford, "The Meaning of Public Interest, Convenience, or Necessity," *Journal of Broadcasting* 5 (1961): 207.
60. Francis Chase, Jr, *Sound Fury: An Informal History of Broadcasting* (New York: Harper, 1942), 233.
61. C.B. Rose, Jr, *National Policy for Radio Broadcasting: 1940* (reprint, New York: Arno Press, 1971), 6.
62. Fred H. Cate, "A Law Antecedent and Paramount," *Federal Communications Law Journal* 47 (1994): 207.
63. Mark Goodman, "The Radio Act of 1927 as a Product of Progressivism," *Mass Media Monographs* 2 (1999): 1.
64. John Braeman, "The Square Deal in Action: A Case Study in the Growth of the 'National Police Power,'" in *Change and Continuity in Twentieth-Century America*, ed. John Braeman, Robert H. Bremner, and David Brody (Columbus: Ohio State University Press, 1964, 41).
65. Wallace H. White. "Monopoly," undated handwritten notes. Box 64: Folder—Federal Control or Radio, undated. Wallace H. White Collection, Library of Congress.
66. *Congressional Record*, 1926, 5479.
67. *Congressional Record*, 1927,4111.
68. Barnouw, 305–6.
69. *Congressional Record*, 1927, 1173.
70. *Congressional Record*, 1926, 12357.
71. *Congressional Record*, 1926, 12615.
72. *Congressional Record*, 1926, 12502.
73. *Congressional Record*, 1927, 1170.
74. *Congressional Record*, 1926, 12502.
75. David M. Rabban, "Free Speech in Progressive Social Thought," *Texas Law Review* 74 (1996): 967.
76. Dill, *Radio Law: Practice and Procedure* (Washington, DC: National Law Book Co., 1938), 110.
77. Hoover, *Memoirs*, vol. 2, 140, 144.
78. Dill, *Water Falls*, 109.
79. Wallace H. White to W.C. Alley, managing editor, Radio Retailing (25 October 1926), Box 51: File—Radio, Miscellaneous. Wallace H. White Collection, Library of Congress.
80. Dill, *Radio Law*, 85, 92.
81. Dill, *Water Falls*, 110.
82. Wallace H. White. "Radio Communications." House of Representatives (12 March 1926). Box 67: Folder—Speeches, Articles, Remarks. Wallace H. White Collection, Library of Congress.
83. Wallace H. White to Willis Kingsley Wing, editor, *Radio Broadcast* (28 December 1926). Box 50: File—Radio, Miscellaneous. Wallace H. White Collection, Library of Congress.
84. Hoover, *Memoirs*, 6–8.
85. William D. Rowland, Jr, "The Meaning of 'The Public Interest' in Communications Policy, Part I: Its Origins in State and Federal Regulation," *Communication Law & Policy* 2 (1997): 318.
86. Rowland, 323.

87. Rowland, 324.
88. J.H. Morecraft, "March of Radio," *Radio Broadcast*, July 1926, 118.
89. Morecraft, "The March of Radio," *Radio Broadcast*, August 1926, 296.
90. Morecraft, "The March of Radio," *Radio Broadcast*, May 1926, 24.
91. Morecraft, "March of Radio," *Radio Broadcast*, April 1926, 555.
92. Morecraft, "March of Radio," *Radio Broadcast*, October 1926, 475.
93. "Radio Censorship," *The Literary Digest*, 4 October 1924, 28.
94. "The Fight for 'Freedom of the Air,'" *The Literary Digest*, 22 March 1924, 9.
95. "To Kill Off Broadcasting 'Pirates,'" 7 May 1927, *The Literary Digest*, 13–14.
96. Rabban, 955.

Women's Work

Lynn Spigel

The Western-Holly Company in 1952 marketed a new design in domestic technology, the TV-stove. The oven included a window through which the housewife could watch her chicken roast. Above the oven window was a TV screen that presented an even more spectacular sight. With the aid of this machine the housewife would be able to prepare her meal, but at the same time she could watch TV. Although it was clearly an odd object, the TV-stove was not simply a historical fluke. Rather, its invention should remind us of the concrete social, economic, and ideological conditions that made this contraption possible. Indeed, the TV-stove was a response to the conflation of labour and leisure time at home. If we now find it strange, this has as much to do with the way in which our society has conceptualized work and leisure as it does with the machine's bizarre technological form.[1]

Since the nineteenth century, middle-class ideals of domesticity had been predicated on divisions of leisure time and work time. The doctrine of two spheres represented human activity in spatial terms: the public world came to be conceived of as a place of productive labour, while the home was seen as a site of rejuvenation and consumption. By the 1920s, the public world was still a sphere of work, but it was also opened up to a host of commercial pleasures such as movies and amusement parks that were incorporated into middle-class lifestyles. The ideal home, however, remained a place of revitalization and, with the expansion of convenience products that promised to reduce household chores, domesticity was even less associated with production.

As feminists have argued, this separation has justified the exploitation of the housewife whose work at home simply does not count. Along these lines, Nancy Folbre claims that classical economics considers women's work as voluntary labour and therefore outside the realm of exploitation. In addition, she argues, even Marxist critics neglect the issue of domestic exploitation since they assume that the labour theory of value can be applied only to efficiency-oriented production for the market and not to "inefficient" and "idiosyncratic" household chores.[2]

As feminist critics and historians have shown, however, the home is indeed a site of labour. Not only do women do physical chores, but also the basic relations of our economy and society are reproduced at home, including the literal reproduction of workers through childrearing labour. Once the home is considered a workplace, the divisions between public/work and domestic/leisure become less clear. The way in which work and leisure are connected, however, remains a complex question.

Henri Lefebvre's studies of everyday life offer ways to consider the general interrelations between work, leisure, and family life in modern society. In his foreword to the 1958 edition of *Critique de la Vie Quotidienne,* Lefebvre argues:

> Leisure . . . cannot be separated from work. It is the same man who, after work, rests or relaxes or does whatever he chooses. Every day, at the same time, the worker leaves the factory, and the employee, the office. Every week, Saturday and Sunday are spent on leisure activities, with the same regularity as that of the weekdays' work. Thus we must think in terms of the unity "work-leisure," because that unity exists, and everyone tries to program his own available time according to what his work is—and what it is not.[3]

While Lefebvre concentrated on the "working man," the case of the housewife presents an even more pronounced example of the integration of work and leisure in everyday life.

In recent years, media scholars have begun to demonstrate the impact that patterns of domestic leisure and labour have on television spectatorship. British ethnographic research has suggested that men and women tend to use television according to their specific position within the distribution of leisure and labour activities inside and outside the home.[4] In the American context, two of the most serious examinations come from Tania Modleski (1983) and Nick Browne (1984), who have both theorized the way TV watching fits into a general pattern of everyday life where work and leisure are intertwined. Modleski has suggested that the soap opera might be understood in terms of the "rhythms of reception," or the way women working at home relate to the text within a specific milieu of distraction—cleaning, cooking, childrearing, and so on.[5] Browne concentrates not on the individual text, but rather on the entire TV schedule, which he claims is ordered according to the logic of the workday of both men and women. "[T]he position of the programs in the television schedule reflects and is determined by the work-structured order of the real social world. The patterns of position and flow imply the question of who is home, and through complicated social relays and temporal mediations, link television to the modes, processes, and scheduling of production characteristic of the general population."[6]

The fluid interconnection between leisure and labour at home presents a context in which to understand representations of the female audience during the postwar years. Above all, women's leisure time was shown to be coterminous with their work time. Representations of television continually addressed women as housewives and presented them with a notion of spectatorship that was inextricably intertwined with their useful labour at home. Certainly, this model of female spectatorship was based on previous notions about radio listeners, and we can assume that women were able to adapt some of their listening habits to television viewing without much difficulty. However, the added impact of visual images ushered in new dilemmas that were the subject of profound concern, both within the broadcast industry and within the popular culture at large.

The Industry's Ideal Viewer

The idea that female spectators were also workers in the home was, by the postwar period, a truism for broadcasting and advertising executives. For some 20 years, radio programmers had grappled with ways to address a group of spectators whose attention wasn't focused primarily on the medium (as in the cinema), but instead moved constantly between radio entertainment and a host of daily chores. As William Boddy has argued, early broadcasters were particularly reluctant to feature daytime radio shows, fearing that women's household work would be fundamentally incompatible with the medium.[7] Overcoming its initial reluctance, the industry successfully developed daytime radio in the 1930s, and by the 1940s housewives constituted a faithful audience for soap operas and advice programs.

During the postwar years, advertisers and networks once more viewed the daytime market with skepticism, fearing that their loyal radio audiences would not be able to make the transition to television. The industry assumed that, unlike radio, television might require the housewife's complete attention and thus disrupt her work in the home.[8] Indeed, while network prime-time schedules were well worked out in 1948, networks and national advertisers were reluctant to feature regular daytime programs. Thus, in the earliest years, morning and afternoon hours were typically left to the discretion of local stations, which filled the time with low budget versions of familiar radio formats and old Hollywood films.

The first network to offer a regular daytime schedule was DuMont, which began operations on its owned and operated station WABD in New York in November of 1948. As a newly formed network which had severe problems competing with CBS and NBC, DuMont entered the daytime market to offset its economic losses in prime time at a time when even the major networks were losing money on television.[9] Explaining the economic strategy behind the move into daytime, one DuMont executive claimed, "WABD is starting daytime programming because it is not economically feasible to do otherwise. Night time programming alone could not support radio, nor can it support television."[10] Increasingly in 1949, DuMont offered daytime programming to its affiliate stations. By December, it transmitting the first commercially sponsored daytime network show, *Okay Mother,* to three affiliates and also airing a two-hour afternoon program on a full network basis. DuMont director Commander Mortimer W. Loewi reasoned that the move into daytime would attract small ticket advertisers who wanted to buy "small segments of time at a low, daytime rate."[11]

DuMont's venture into the daytime market was a thorn in the side of the other networks. While CBS, NBC, and ABC had experimented with individual daytime television programs on their flagship stations, they were reluctant to feature full daytime schedules. With huge investments in daytime radio, they weren't likely to find the prospects of daytime television appealing, especially since they were using their radio profits to offset initial losses in prime-time programming. As *Variety* reported when DuMont began its broadcasts on WABD, the major networks "must protect their AM [radio] investment at all costs—and the infiltration of daytime TV may conceivably cut into daytime radio advertising."[12] In this context, DuMont's competition in the daytime market posed a particularly grave threat to advertising revenues. In response, the other networks gradually began expanding the daytime lineups for their flagship stations.[13]

It was in 1951 that CBS, NBC, and, to a lesser extent, ABC first aggressively attempted to colonize the housewife's workday with regularly scheduled network programs. One of the central reasons for the networks' move into daytime that year was the fact that prime-time hours were fully booked by advertisers and that, by this point, there was more demand for TV advertising in general. As the advertising agency BBDO claimed in a report on daytime TV in the fall of 1950, "To all intents and purposes, the opportunity to purchase good night-time periods of TV is almost a thing of the past and the advertiser hoping to enter television now . . . better start looking at Daytime TV while it is still here to look at."[14] Daytime might have been more risky than prime time, but it had the advantage of being available—and at a cheaper network cost. Confident of its move into daytime, CBS claimed, "We aren't risking our reputation by predicting that daytime television will be a solid sell-out a year from today . . . and that once again there will be some sad advertisers who didn't read the tea leaves right."[15] ABC Vice-President Alexander Stronach Jr was just as certain about the daytime market, and having just taken the plunge with the *Frances Langford-Don Ameche Show* (a variety program budgeted at the then steep $40,000 a week), Stronach told *Newsweek,* "It's a good thing electric dishwashers and washing machines were invented. The housewives will need them."[16]

The networks' confidence carried through to advertisers who began to test the waters of the daytime schedule. In September of 1951, the trade journal *Televiser* reported that "forty-seven big advertisers have used daytime network television during the past season or are starting this Fall." Included were such well-known companies as American Home Products, Best Foods, Procter and Gamble, General Foods, Hazel Bishop Lipsticks, Minute Maid, Hotpoint, and the woman's magazine *Ladies' Home Journal.*[17]

Despite these inroads, the early daytime market remained highly unstable, and at least until 1955 the competition for sponsors was fierce.[18] Indeed, even while the aggregate size of the daytime audience rose in the early 1950s, sponsors and broadcasters were uncertain about the extent to which housewives actually paid attention to the programs and advertisements. In response to such concerns, the industry aggressively tailored programs to fit the daily habits of the female audience. When it began operations in 1948, DuMont's WABD planned shows that could "be appreciated just as much from listening to them as from watching them."[19] Following this trend in 1950, Detroit's WXYX aired *Pat 'n' Johnny,* a program that solved the housework-TV conflict in less than subtle ways. At the beginning of the three-hour show, host Johnny Slagle instructed housewives, "Don't stop whatever you're doing. When we think we have something interesting I'll blow this whistle or Pat will ring her bell."[20]

The major networks were also intent upon designing programs to suit the content and organization of the housewife's day. The format that has received the most critical attention is the soap opera, which first came to network television in December of 1950. As Robert Allen has demonstrated, early soap opera producers like Irna Philips of *Guiding Light* were skeptical of moving their shows from radio to TV. However, by 1954 the Nielson Company reported that soaps had a substantial following; *Search For Tomorrow* was the second most popular daytime show while *Guiding Light* was in fourth place. The early soaps, with their minimum of action and visual interest, allowed housewives to listen to dialogue while working in another room. Moreover, their segmented storylines (usually two a day), as well as their repetition and constant explanation of previous plots, allowed women to divide their attention between viewing and household work.[21]

Another popular solution to the daytime dilemma was the segmented variety show that allowed women to enter and exit the text according to its discrete narrative units. One of DuMont's first programs, for example, was a shopping show (alternatively called *At Your Service* and *Shoppers Matinee)* that consisted of 21 entertainment segments, all of which revolved around different types of "women's issues." For instance, the "Bite Shop" presented fashion tips while "Kitchen Fare" gave culinary advice. Interspersed with these segments were 12 one-minute "store bulletins" (news and service announcements) that could be replaced at individual stations by local commercials.[22] While DuMont's program was short-lived, the basic principles survived in the daytime shows at the major networks. Programs like *The Garry Moore Show* (CBS), *The Kate Smith Show* (NBC), and *The Arthur Godfrey Show* (CBS) catered to housewife audiences with their segmented variety of entertainment and advice.[23]

Indeed, the networks put enormous amounts of money and effort into variety shows when they first began to compose daytime program schedules. Daytime ratings continually confirmed the importance of the variety format, with hosts like Smith and Godfrey drawing big audiences. Since daytime stars were often taken from nighttime radio shows, the variety programs were immediately marked as being different from and more spectacular than daytime radio. *Variety* reported in October of 1951:

> The daytime television picture represents a radical departure from radio. The application of "nighttime thinking" into daytime TV in regards to big-league variety-slanted programs and projection of personalities becomes more and more important. If the housewife has a craving for visual soap operas, it is neither reflected in the present day Nielsens nor in the ambitious programming formulas being blueprinted by the video entrepreneurs. . . . The housewife with her multiple chores, it would seem, wants her TV distractions on a "catch as catch can" basis, and the single-minded concentration on sight-and- sound weepers doesn't jibe with her household schedule. . . . [Variety shows] are all geared to the "take it awhile leave it awhile" school of entertainment projection and practically all are reaping a bonanza for the networks.[24]

Television thus introduced itself to the housewife not only by repeating tried and true daytime radio formulas, but also by creating a distinct product tailored to what the industry assumed were the television audiences' specific needs and desires.

Initially uncertain about the degree to which daytime programs from an audio medium would suit the housewife's routine, many television broadcasters turned their attention to the visual medium of the popular press. Variety shows often modelled themselves on print conventions, particularly borrowing narrative techniques from women's magazines and the women's pages. Much as housewives might flip through the pages of a magazine as they went about their daily chores, they could tune in and out of the magazine program without the kind of disorientation that they might experience when disrupted from a continuous drama. To ensure coherence, such programs included "women's editors" or "femcees" who provided a narrational thread for a series of "departments" on gardening, homemaking, fashion, and the like. These shows often went to extreme lengths to make the connection between print media and television programming foremost in the viewer's mind. *Women's Magazine of the Air*, a local program aired in Chicago on WGN, presented a "potpourri theme with magazine pages being turned to indicate new sections."[25] On its locally owned station, the *Seattle Post* presented *Women's Page*, starring *Post* book and music editor Suzanne Martin. The networks also used the popular press as a model for daytime programs. As early as 1948, CBS's New York station aired *Vanity Fair*, a segmented format that was tied together by "managing editor" Dorothy Dean, an experienced newspaper reporter. By the end of 1949, *Vanity Fair* was boasting a large list of sponsors, and in the 1950s it continued to be part of the daytime schedule. Nevertheless, despite its success with *Vanity Fair*, CBS still tended to rely more heavily on well-known radio stars and formats, adapting these to the television medium. Instead, it was NBC that developed the print media model most aggressively in the early 1950s.

Faced with daytime ratings that were consistently behind those of CBS and troubled by severe sponsorship problems, NBC saw the variety/magazine format as a particularly apt vehicle for small ticket advertisers who could purchase brief participation spots between program segments for relatively low cost.[26] Under the direction of programming vice-president Sylvester "Pat" Weaver (who became NBC president in 1953), the network developed its "magazine concept" of advertising. Unlike the single sponsor series, which was usually produced through the advertising agency, the magazine concept allowed the network to retain control and ownership of programs. Although this form of multiple sponsor participation had become a common daytime practice by the early 1950s, Weaver's scheme differed from other participation plans because it allowed sponsors to purchase segments on a one-shot basis, with no ongoing commitment to the series. Even if this meant greater financial risks at the outset, in the long run a successful program based on spot sales would garner large amounts of revenue for the network.[27]

Weaver applied the magazine concept to two of the most highly successful daytime programs, *Today* and *Home*. Aired between 7:00 and 9:00 AM, *Today* was NBC's self-proclaimed "television newspaper, covering not only the latest news, weather, and time signals, but special features on everything from fashions to the hydrogen bomb."[28] On its premier episode in January 1952, *Today* made the print media connections firm in viewers' minds by showing telephoto machines grinding out pictures and front page facsimiles of the *San Francisco Chronicle*.[29] Aimed at a family audience, the program attempted to lure men, women, and children with discrete program segments that addressed their different interests and meshed with their separate schedules. One NBC confidential report stated that, on the one hand, men rushing off to take a train would not be likely to watch fashion segments. On the other hand, it suggested, "men might be willing to catch the next train" if they included an "almost sexy gal as part of the show." This, the report concluded, would be like "subtle, early morning sex."[30]

Although it was aimed at the entire family, the lion's share of the audience was female. (In 1954, for example, the network calculated that the audience was composed of 52 per cent women, 26 per cent men, and 22 per cent children.)[31] *Today* appealed to housewives with "women's pages" news stories such as Hollywood gossip segments, fashion shows, and humanistic features. In August 1952, NBC's New York outlet inserted "Today's Woman" into the program, a special women's magazine feature that was produced in co-operation with *Look* and *Quick* magazines.[32] Enthused with *Today's* success, NBC developed *Home* with similar premises in mind, but this time aimed the program specifically at women. First aired in 1954 during the 11:00 AM to noon time slot, *Home* borrowed its narrative techniques from women's magazines, featuring segments on topics like gardening, child psychology, food, fashion, health, and interior decor. As *Newsweek* wrote, "The program is planned to do for women on the screen what the women's magazines have long done in print."[33]

In fashioning daytime shows on familiar models of the popular press, television executives and advertisers were guided by the implicit assumption that the female audience had much in common with the typical magazine reader. When promoting *Today* and *Home,* NBC used magazines such as *Ladies' Home Journal, Good Housekeeping,* and *Collier's* (which also had a large female readership) as major venues. When *Home* first appeared it even offered women copies of its own monthly magazine, *How To Do It.*[34] Magazine publishers also must have seen the potential profits in the crossover audience; the first sponsor for *Today* was Kiplinger's magazine *Changing Times,* and *Life* and Curtis magazines were soon to follow.[35]

The fluid transactions between magazine publishers and daytime producers were based on widely held notions about the demographic composition of the female audience. In 1954, the same year that *Home* premiered, NBC hired W.R. Simmons and Associates to conduct the first nationwide qualitative survey of daytime viewers. In a promotional report based on the survey, Dr. Tom Coffin, manager of NBC research, told advertisers and manufacturers, "In analyzing the findings, we have felt a growing sense of excitement at the qualitative picture emerging: an audience with the *size* of a mass medium but the *quality* of a class medium." When compared to non-viewers, daytime viewers were at the "age of acquisition," with many in the 25- to 34-year-old category; their families were larger with more children under 18; they had higher incomes; and they lived in larger and "better" market areas. In addition, Coffin characterized the average viewer as a "modern active woman" with a kitchen full of "labour-saving devices," an interest in her house, clothes, and "the way she looks." She is "the kind of woman most advertisers are most interested in; she's a good customer."[36] Coffin's focus on the "class versus mass" audience bears striking resemblance to the readership statistics of middle-class women's magazines. Like the magazine reader, "Mrs Daytime Consumer" was an upscale, if only moderately affluent housewife whose daily life consisted not only of chores, but also, and perhaps even more importantly, shopping for her family.

With this picture of the housewife in mind, the media producer had one primary job—teaching her how to buy products. Again, the magazine format was perfect for this because each discrete narrative segment could portray an integrated sales message. Hollywood gossip columns gave way to motion picture endorsements; cooking segments sold sleek new ranges; fashion shows promoted Macy's finest evening wear. By integrating sales messages, with advice on housekeeping and luxury lifestyles, the magazine format skillfully suggested to housewives that their time spent viewing television was indeed part of their work time. In other words, the programs promised viewers not just entertainment, but also lessons on how to make consumer choices for their families. One production handbook claimed: "Women's daytime programs have tended toward the practical—providing shopping information, marketing tips, cooking, sewing, interior decoration, etc., with a dash of fashion and beauty hints. . . . The theory is that the housewife will be more likely to take time from her household duties if she feels that her television viewing will make her housekeeping more efficient and help her provide more gracious living for her family."[37] In the case of *Home*, this implicit integration of housework, consumerism, and TV entertainment materialized in the form of a circular stage that the network promoted as a "machine for selling."[38] The stage was equipped with a complete kitchen, a workshop area, and a small garden—all of which functioned as settings for different program segments and, of course, the different sponsor products that accompanied them. Thus, *Home's* magazine format provided a unique arena for the presentation of a series of fragmented consumer fantasies that women might tune into and out of, according to the logic of their daily schedules.

Even if the structure of this narrative format was the ideal vehicle for "Mrs Daytime Consumer," the content of the consumer fantasies still had to be carefully planned. Like the woman's magazine before it, the magazine show needed to maintain the subtle balance of its "class address." In order to appeal to the average middle-class housewife, it had to make its consumer fantasies fit with the more practical concerns of female viewers. The degree to which network executives attempted to strike this balance is well illustrated in the case of *Home*. After the program's first airing, NBC executive Charles Barry was particularly concerned about the amount of "polish" that it contained. Using "polish" as a euphemism for highbrow tastes, Barry went on to observe the problems with *Home's* class address: "I hope you will keep in mind that the average gal looking at the show is either living in a small suburban house or in an apartment and is not very likely to have heard of Paul McCobb; she is more likely to be at a Macy's buying traditionally." After observing other episodes, Barry had similar complaints: the precocious stage children weren't "average" enough, the furniture segment featured impractical items, and the cooking segment showcased high-class foods such as vichyssoise and pot-de-crème. "Maybe you can improve tastes," Barry conceded, "but gosh would somebody please tell me how to cook corned beef and cabbage without any smell?"[39] The television producer could educate the housewife beyond her means, but only through mixing upper-class fantasy with tropes of averageness.

The figure of the female hostess was also fashioned to strike this delicate balance. In order to appeal to the typical housewife, the hostess would ideally speak on her level. As one producer argued, "Those who give an impression of superiority or 'talking down' to the audience, who treasure the manner of speaking over naturalness and meaningful communication . . . or who are overly formal in attire and manners, do not survive in the broadcasting industry. . . . The personality should fit right into your living room. The super-sophisticate or the squealing life of the party might be all right on occasion, but a daily association with this girl is apt to get a little tiresome."[40] In addition, the ideal hostess was decidedly not a glamour girl, but rather a pleasingly attractive, middle-aged woman—Hollywood's answer to the home economics teacher. When first planning *Home*, one NBC executive considered using the celebrity couple Van and Evie Johnson for hosts, claiming that Evie was "a sensible woman, not a glamour struck movie star's wife, but a wholesome girl from a wholesome background. . . . She works hard at being a housewife and mother who runs a not elaborate household in Beverly Hills with *no swimming pool*."Although Evie didn't get the part, her competitor, Arlene Francis, was clearly cut from the same cloth. In a 1957 fanzine, Francis highlighted her ordinariness when she admitted, "My nose is too long and I'm too skinny, but maybe that won't make any difference if I'm fun to be with."[41] Francis was also a calming mother figure who appealed to children. In a fan letter, one mother wrote that her little boy took a magazine to bed with him that had Arlene's picture on the cover.[42] Unlike the "almost sexy" fantasy woman on the *Today* show who was perfect for "morning sex," *Home's* femcee appealed to less erotic instincts. Francis and other daytime hostesses were designed to provide a role model for ordinary housewives, educating them on the "good life," while still appearing down to earth.

In assuming the role of "consumer educator," the networks went beyond just teaching housewives how to buy advertisers' products. Much more crucially in this early period, the networks attempted to teach women and their families how to consume television itself. Indeed, the whole system pivoted on the singular problem of how to make the daytime audience watch more programming. Since it adapted itself to the family's daily routine, the magazine show was particularly suited for this purpose. When describing the habits of *Today's* morning audience, Weaver acknowledged that the "show, of course, does not hold the same audience throughout the time period, but actually is a service fitting with the family's own habit pattern in the morning."[43] Importantly, however, NBC continually tried to channel the movements of the audience. Not merely content to fit its programming into the viewer's rhythms of reception, the network aggressively sought to change those rhythms by making the activity of television viewing into a new daily habit. One NBC report made this point quite explicit, suggesting that producers "establish definite show patterns at regular times; do everything you can to capitalize on the great habit of habit listening."[44] Proud of his accomplishments on this front, Weaver bragged about fan mail that demonstrated how *Today* changed viewers' daily routines. According to Weaver, one woman claimed, "My husband said I should put casters on the TV set so I can roll it around and see it from the kitchen." Another admitted, "I used to get all the dishes washed by 8:30—now I don't do a thing until 10 o'clock." Still another confessed, "My husband now dresses in the living room." Weaver boastfully promised, "We will change the habits of millions."[45]

The concept of habitual viewing also governed NBC's scheduling techniques. The network devised promotional strategies designed to maintain systems of flow, as each program ideally would form a "lead in" for the next, tailored to punctuate intervals of the family's daily routine. In 1954, for example, an NBC report on daytime stated that *Today* was perfect for the early morning time slot because it "has a family audience . . . and reaches them just before they go out to shop." With shopping done, mothers might return home to find *Ding Dong School,* "a nursery school on television" that allowed them to do housework while educator Frances Horwich helped raise the preschoolers. Daytime dramas were scheduled throughout the day, each lasting only 15 minutes, probably because the network assumed that the drama would require more of the housewife's attention than the segmented variety formats like *Home.* At 5 PM, when mothers were likely to be preparing dinner, *The Pinky Lee Show* presented a mixed bag of musical acts, dance routines, parlour games, and talk aimed both at women and their children who were now home from school.[46]

NBC aggressively promoted this kind of routinized viewership, buying space in major market newspapers and national periodicals for advertisements that instructed women how to watch television while doing household chores. In 1955, *Ladies' Home Journal* and *Good Housekeeping* carried advertisements for NBC's daytime lineup that suggested that not only the programs, but also the scheduling of the programs, would suit the housewife's daily routine. The ads evoked a sense of fragmented leisure time and suggested that television viewing could be conducted in a state of distraction. This was not the kind of critical contemplative distraction that Walter Benjamin suggested in his seminal essay, "The Work of Art in the Age of Mechanical Reproduction."[47] Rather, the ads implied that the housewife could accomplish her chores in a state of "utopian forgetfulness" as she moved freely between her work and the act of watching television.

One advertisement, which is particularly striking in this regard, includes a sketch of a housewife and her little daughter at the top of the page. Below this, the graphic layout is divided into eight boxes composed of television screens, each representing a different program in NBC's daytime lineup. The caption functions as the housewife's testimony to her distracted state. She asks, "Where Did the Morning Go, The house is tidy . . . but it hasn't seemed like a terribly tiring morning. . . . I think I started ironing while I watched the *Sheila Graham Show.*" The housewife goes on to register each detail of the programs, but she cannot with certainty account for her productive activities in the home. Furthermore, as the ad's layout suggests, the woman's daily activities are literally fragmented according to the pattern of the daytime television schedule, to the extent that her everyday experiences become imbricated in a kind of serial narrative. Significantly, her child pictured at the top of the advertisement appears within the contours of a television screen so that the labour of childrearing is itself made part of the narrative pleasures offered by the network's daytime lineup.[48]

Negotiating with the Industry's Ideal Viewer

The program types, schedules, and promotional materials devised at the networks were based upon ideal images of female viewers and, consequently, they were rooted in abstract conceptions about women's lives. These ideals weren't always commensurate with the heterogeneous experiences and situations of real women and, for this reason, industrial strategies didn't always form a perfect fit with the audience's needs and desires. Although it is impossible to reconstruct fully the actual activities of female viewers at home, we can better understand their concerns and practices by examining the ways in which their viewing experiences were explained to them at the time. Popular media, particularly women's magazines, presented women with opportunities to negotiate with the modes of spectatorship that the television industry tried to construct. It is in these texts that we see the gaps and inconsistencies—the unexpected twists and turns—that were not foreseen by networks and advertisers. Indeed, it is in the magazines, rather than in the highrise buildings of NBC, CBS, and ABC, where female audiences were given the chance to enter into a popular dialogue about their own relations to the medium.

While the networks were busy attempting to tailor daytime programming to the patterns of domestic labour, popular media often completely rejected the idea that television could be compatible with women's work and showed instead how it would threaten the efficient functioning of the household. The TV-addict housewife became a stock character during the period, particularly in texts aimed at a general audience where the mode of address was characterized by an implicit male narrator who clearly blamed women—not television—for the untidy house. In 1950, for example, *The New Yorker* ran a cartoon that showed a slovenly looking woman ironing a shirt while blankly staring at the television screen. Unfortunately, in her state of distraction, the woman burned a hole in the garment.[49] Women's magazines also deliberated upon television's thoroughly negative effect on household chores, but rather than poking fun at the housewife, they offered sympathetic advice, usually suggesting that a careful management of domestic space might solve the problem. In 1950, *House Beautiful* warned of television: "It delivers about five times as much wallop as radio and requires in return five times as much attention. . . . It's impossible to get anything accomplished in the same room while it's on." The magazine offered a spatial solution, telling women "to get the darn thing out of the living room," and into the TV room, cellar, library, "or as a last resort stick it in the dining room."[50]

In *The Honeymooners*, a working-class situation comedy, television's obstruction of household work was related to marital strife. The first episode of the series, "TV or Not TV" (1955), revolves around the purchase of a television set and begins with an establishing shot of the sparsely decorated Kramden kitchen where a clothes basket filled with wet wash sits on the table. Entering from the bedroom in her hausfrau garb, Alice Kramden approaches the kitchen sink and puts a plunger over the drain, apparently attempting to unclog it. As pictured in this opening scene, Alice is, to say the least, a victim of household drudgery. Not surprisingly, Alice begs Ralph for a television set, hoping that it will make her life more pleasant.

In a later scene, after the Kramdens purchase their TV set, this situation changes, but not for the better. Ralph returns home from work while Alice sits before her television set. Here is the exchange between the couple:

> *Ralph:* Would you mind telling me where my supper is?
>
> *Alice:* I didn't make it yet. . . . I sat down to watch the four o'clock movie and I got so interested I . . . uh what time is it anyway?
>
> *Ralph:* I knew this would happen Alice. We've had that set three days now, and I haven't had a hot meal since we got it.

Thus, television is the source of a dispute between the couple, a dispute that arises from the housewife's inability to perform her productive function while enjoying an afternoon program.

A 1955 ad for Drano provided a solution to television's obstruction of household chores. Here the housewife is shown watching her afternoon soap opera, but this unproductive activity is sanctioned only insofar as her servant does the housework. As the maid exclaims, "Shucks, I'll never know if she gets her man 'cause this is the day of the week I put Drano in all the drains!" The Drano Company thus attempted to sell its product by giving women a glamorous vision of themselves enjoying an afternoon of television. But it could do so only by splitting the functions of relaxation and work across two representational figures—the lady of leisure and the domestic servant.[51]

If the domestic servant was a fantasy solution to the conflict between work and television, the women's magazines suggested more practical ways to manage the problem. *Better Homes and Gardens* advised in 1949 that the television set should be placed in an area where it could be viewed, "while you're doing things up in the kitchen." Similarly in 1954, *American Home* told readers to put the TV set in the kitchen so that "Mama sees her pet programs . . . ." Via such spatial remedies, labour would not be affected by the leisure of viewing nor would viewing be denied by household chores.[52] In fact, household labour and television were continually condensed into one space designed to accommodate both activities. In a 1955 issue of *American Home,* this labour-leisure viewing condensation provided the terms of a joke. A cartoon showed a housewife tediously hanging her laundry on the outdoor clothesline. The drudgery of this work is miraculously solved as the housewife brings her laundry into her home and sits before her television set, while letting the laundry dry on the television antenna.[53]

The spatial condensation of labour and viewing was part of a well-entrenched functionalist discourse. The home had to provide rooms that would allow for a practical orchestration of "modern living activities" that now included watching television. Functionalism was particularly useful for advertisers, who used it to promote not just one household item but an entire product line. In 1952, for example, the Crane Company displayed its appliance ensemble, complete with ironing, laundering, and cooking facilities. Here the housewife could do multiple tasks at once because all the fixtures were "matched together as a complete chore unit." One particularly attractive component of this "chore unit" was a television set built into the wall above the washer/dryer.[54]

While spatial condensations of labour and leisure helped to soothe tensions about television's obstruction of household chores, other problems still existed. The magazine suggested that television would cause increasing workloads. Considering the cleanliness of the living room, *House Beautiful* told its readers in 1948: "Then the men move in for boxing, wrestling, basketball, hockey. They get excited. Ashes on the floor. Pretzel crumbs. Beer stains." The remedy was again spatial: "Lots of sets after a few months have been moved into dens and recreation rooms."[55] In a slight twist of terms, the activity of eating was said to be moving out of the dining area and into the television-sitting area. Food stains soiling upholstery, floors, and other surfaces meant extra work for women. Vinyl upholstery, linoleum floors, tiling, and other spill-proof surfaces were recommended. Advertisers for all kinds of cleaning products found television especially useful in their sales pitches. In 1953, the Bissell Carpet Sweeper Company asked housewives, "What do you do when the TV crowd leaves popcorn and crumbs on your rug? You could leave the mess till morning—or drag out the vacuum. But if you're on the beam, you slick it up with a handy Bissell Sweeper."[56] In addition to the mess generated by television, the set itself called for maintenance. In 1955, *House Beautiful* asked if a "misty haze dims your TV screen" and recommended the use of "wipe-on liquids and impregnated wiping cloths to remedy the problem." The Drackett Company, producer of Windex Spray, quickly saw the advantage that television held for its product; in 1948 it advertised the cleaner as a perfect solution for a dirty screen.[57]

Besides the extra cleaning, television also kept housewives busy in the kitchen. The magazines showed women how to be gracious hostesses, always prepared to serve family and friends special TV treats. These snacktime chores created a lucrative market for manufacturers. For example, in 1952 *American Home* presented a special china collection for "Early Tea and Late TV," while other companies promoted TV snack trays and TV tables.[58] The most exaggerated manifestation appeared in 1954. The TV dinner was the perfect remedy for the extra work entailed by television, and it also allowed children to eat their toss-away meals while watching *Hopalong Cassidy.*

While magazines presented readers with a host of television-related tasks, they also suggested ways for housewives to ration their labour. Time-motion studies, which were integral to the discourses of feminism and domestic science since the Progressive era, were rigorously applied to the problem of increasing workloads. All unnecessary human movement that the television set might demand had to be minimized. Again, this called for a careful management of space. The magazines suggested that chairs and sofas be placed so that they need not be moved for watching television. Alternatively, furniture could be made mobile. By placing wheels on a couch, it was possible to exert minimal energy while converting a sitting space into a viewing space. Similarly, casters and lazy Susans could be placed on television sets so that housewives might easily move the screen to face the direction of the viewers.[59] More radically, space between rooms could be made continuous. In 1952, *House Beautiful* suggested a "continuity" of living, dining, and television areas wherein "a curved sofa and a folding screen mark off [the] television corner from the living and dining room." Via this carefully managed spatial continuum, "it takes no more than an extra ten steps or so to serve the TV fans."[60]

Continuous space was also a response to the more general problem of television and family relationships. Women's household work presented a dilemma for the twin ideals of family unity and social divisions, since housewives were ideally meant to perform their distinctive productive functions but, at the same time, take part in the family's leisure-time pursuits. This conflict between female isolation from and integration into the family group was rooted in Victorian domestic ideology with its elaborate social and spatial hierarchies; it became even more pronounced as twentieth-century lifestyles and housing contexts changed in ways that could no longer contain the formalized spatial distinctions of the Victorian ideal.

The problems became particularly significant in the early decades of the century when middle-class women found themselves increasingly isolated in their kitchens due to a radical reduction in the number of domestic servants. As Gwendolyn Wright has observed, women were now cut off from the family group as they worked in kitchens designed to resemble scientific laboratories, far removed from the family activities in the central areas of the home. Architects did little to respond to the problem of isolation, but continued instead to build kitchens fully separated from communal living spaces, suggesting that labour-saving kitchen appliances would solve the servant shortage.[61] In the postwar era when the continuous spaces of ranch-style architecture became a cultural ideal, the small suburban home placed a greater emphasis on interaction between family members. The "open plan" eliminated some of the walls between dining room, living room, and kitchen. However, even in the continuous ranch-style homes, the woman's work area was "zoned off" from the activity area, and the woman's role as homemaker still worked to separate her from the leisure activities of her family.

Women's magazines suggested intricately balanced spatial arrangements that would mediate the tensions between female integration and isolation. Television viewing became a special topic of consideration. In 1951, *House Beautiful* placed a television set in its remodelled kitchen, which combined "such varied functions as cooking, storage, laundry, flower arranging, dining and TV viewing." In this case, as elsewhere, the call for functionalism was related to the woman's ability to work among a group engaged in leisure activities. A graphic showed a television placed in a "special area" devoted to "eating" and "relaxing" which was "not shut off by a partition." In continuous space, "the worker . . . is always part of the group, can share in the conversation and fun while work is in progress."[62]

While this example presents a harmonious solution, often the ideals of integration and isolation resulted in highly contradictory representations of domestic life. Typically, illustrations that depicted continuous spaces show the housewife to be oddly disconnected from the general flow of activities. In 1951, for example, *American Home* showed a woman in a continuous dining-living area who supposedly is allowed to accomplish her housework among a group of television viewers. However, rather than being integrated into the group, the woman is actually isolated from the television crowd as she sets the dining room table. The TV viewers are depicted in the background while the housewife stands to the extreme front-right border of the composition, far away from her family and friends. In fact, she is literally positioned off-frame, straddling between the photograph and the negative (or unused) space of the layout.[63]

The family circle motif was also riddled with contradictions of this sort. In particular, Sentinel's advertising campaign showed women who were spatially distanced from their families. In 1952, one ad depicted a housewife holding a tray of beverages and standing off to the side of her family, who were clustered around the television set. The following year, another ad showed a housewife cradling her baby in her arms and standing at a window far away from the rest of her family, who were gathered around the Sentinel console.[64] In a 1948 ad for Magnavox Television, the housewife's chores separated her from her circle of friends. The ad was organized around a U-shaped sofa that provided a quite literal manifestation of the semicircle visual cliché. A group of adult couples sat on the sofa watching the new Magnavox set, but the hostess stood at the kitchen door, holding a tray of snacks.

Spatially removed from the television viewers, the housewife appeared to be sneaking a look at the set as she went about her hostess chores.[65]

This problem of female spatial isolation gave way to what can be called a "corrective cycle of commodity purchases." A 1949 article in *American Home* about the joys of the electric dishwasher is typical here. A picture of a family gathered around the living room console included the caption, "No martyr banished to kitchen, she never misses television programs. Lunch, dinner dishes are in an electric dishwasher." In 1950, an advertisement for Hotpoint dishwashers used the same discursive strategy. The illustration showed a wall of dishes that separated a housewife in the kitchen from her family, who sat huddled around the television set in the living room. The caption read, "Please . . . Let Your Wife Come Out Into the Livingroom! Don't let dirty dishes make your wife a kitchen exile! She loses the most precious hours of her life shut off from pleasures of the family circle by the never-ending chore of old-fashioned dishwashing!"[66]

This ideal version of female integration in a unified family space was contested by the competing discourse on divided spaces. Distinctions between work and leisure space remained an important principle of household efficiency. Here, room dividers presented a perfect balance of integration and isolation. In 1952, *Better Homes and Gardens* displayed a room divider that separated a kitchen work area from its dining area. The cut-off point was a television set built into the wall just to the right of the room divider. Thus, the room divider separated the woman's work space from the television space, but as a partial wall that still allowed for continuous space, it reached the perfect compromise between the housewife's isolation from and integration into the family. It was in the sense of this compromise that *American Home's* "discrete" room divider separated a wife's work space from her husband's television space in a house that, nevertheless, was designed for "family living." As the magazine reported in 1954, "Mr Peterson . . . retired behind his newspaper in the TV end of the living kitchen. Mrs P. quietly made a great stack of sandwiches for us behind the discrete screen of greens in the efficient kitchen end of the same room."[67]

This bifurcation of sexual roles, of male (leisure) and female (productive) activities, served as an occasion for a full consideration of power dynamics among men and women in the home. Typically, the magazines extended their categories of feminine and masculine viewing practices into representations of the body. For men, television viewing was most often represented in terms of a posture of repose. Men were usually shown to be sprawled out on easy chairs as they watched the set. Remote controls allowed the father to watch in undisturbed passive comfort. In many ways, this representation of the male body was based on Victorian notions of rejuvenation for the working man. Relaxation was condoned for men because it served a revitalizing function, preparing them for the struggles for the workaday world. For women, the passive calm of television viewing was never so simple. As we have seen, even when women were shown watching television, they often appeared as productive workers.

Sometimes, representations of married couples became excessively literal about the gendered patterns of television leisure. In 1954, when the Cleavelander Company advertised its new "T-Vue" chair, it told consumers, "Once you sink into the softness of Cleavelander's cloud-like contours, cares seem to float away." Thus, not only the body, but also the spirit would be revitalized by the TV chair. But while the chair allowed Father "to stretch out with his feet on the ottoman," Mother's TV leisure was nevertheless productive. As the caption states, "Mother likes to gently rock as she sews."[68] Similarly, a 1952 advertisement for Airfoam furniture cushions showed a husband dozing in his foam rubber cushioned chair as he sits before a television set. Meanwhile, his wife clears away his TV snack. The text reads, "Man's pleasure is the body coddling comfort" of the cushioned chair while

"Woman's treasure is a home lovely to look at, easy to keep perfectly tidy and neat" with cushioning that "never needs fluffing."[69] In such cases, the man's pleasure in television is associated with passive relaxation. The woman's pleasure, however, is derived from the aesthetics of a well-kept home and labour-saving devices that promise to minimize the extra household work that television brings to domestic space. In addition, the Airfoam ad is typical as it depicts a female body that finds no viewing pleasures of its but instead functions to assist with the viewing comforts of others.

As numerous feminist film theorists have demonstrated, spectatorship and the pleasures entailed by it are culturally organized according to categories of sexual difference. In her groundbreaking article on the subject of Hollywood film, Laura Mulvey showed how narrative cinema (her examples were Von Sternberg and Hitchcock) is organized around voyeuristic and fetishistic scenarios in which women are the "to-be-looked-at" object of male desire.[70] In such a scheme, it becomes difficult to pinpoint how women can have subjective experiences in a cinema that systematically objectifies them. In the case of television, it seems clear that women's visual pleasure was associated with interior decor and not with viewing programs. In 1948, *House Beautiful* made this explicit when it claimed, "Most men want only an adequate screen. But women alone with the thing in the house all day have to eye it as a piece of furniture."[71] In addition, while these discussions of television were addressed to female readers, the woman's spectatorial pleasure was less associated with her enjoyment of the medium than it was with her own objectification, her desire to be looked at by the gaze of another.

On one level here, television was depicted as a threat to the visual appeal of the female body in domestic space. Specifically, there was something visually unpleasurable about the sight of a woman operating the technology of the receiver. In 1955, Sparton Television proclaimed that "the sight of a woman tuning a TV set with dials near the floor" was "most unattractive." The Sparton TV, with its tuning knob located at the top of the set, promised to maintain the visual appeal of the woman.[72] Beyond this specific case, there was a distinct set of aesthetic conventions formed in these years for male and female viewing postures. A 1953 advertisement for CBS-Columbia Television illustrates this well. Three alternative viewing postures are taken up by family members. A little boy stretches out on the floor, a father slumps in his easy chair, and the lower portion of a mother's outstretched body is gracefully lifted in a sleek modern chair with a seat that tilts upward. Here as elsewhere, masculine viewing is characterized by slovenly body posture. Conversely, feminine viewing posture takes on a certain visual appeal even as the female body passively reclines.[73]

As this advertisement indicates, the graphic representation of the female body viewing television had to be carefully controlled. It had to be made appealing to the eye of the observer, for in a fundamental sense, there was something taboo about the sight of a woman watching television. In fact, the housewife was almost never shown watching television by herself. Instead, she typically lounged on a chair (perhaps reading a book) while the television set remained turned off in the room. In 1952, *Better Homes and Gardens* stated one quite practical reason for the taboo. The article gave suggestions for methods of covering windows that would keep neighbours from peering into the home. It related this interest in privacy to women's work and television: "You should be able to have big, big windows to let in light and view, windows that let you watch the stars on a summer night without feeling exposed and naked. In good conscience, you should be able to leave the dinner dishes on the table while you catch a favourite TV or radio program, without sensing derogatory comments on your housekeeping."[74] Thus, for the housewife, being caught in the act of enjoying a broadcast is ultimately degrading because it threatens to reveal the signs of her slovenly behaviour to the observer. More generally, we might say that the magazines showed women that their subjective pleasure in watching television was at odds with their own status as efficient and visually attractive housewives.

Although these representations are compatible with traditional gender roles, subtle reversals of power ran through the magazines as a whole. Even if there was a certain degree of privilege attached to the man's position of total relaxation—his right to rule from the easy chair throne—his power was in no way absolute, nor was it stable. Although such representations held to the standard conception of women as visually pleasing spectacles—as passive objects of male desire—these representations also contradicted such notions by presenting women as active producers in control of domestic affairs. For this reason, it seems that the most striking thing about this gendered representation of the body is that it inverted—or at least complicated—normative conceptions of masculinity and femininity. Whereas Western society associates activity with maleness, representations of television often attributed this trait to the woman. Conversely, the notion of feminine passivity was typically transferred over to the man of the house.[75] It could well be concluded that the cultural ideals that demanded women be shown as productive workers in the home also had the peculiar side effect of "feminizing" the father.

Perhaps for this reason, popular media presented tongue-in-cheek versions of the situation, showing how television had turned men into passive homebodies. In the last scene of *The Honeymooners'* episode "TV or Not TV," for example, the marital dispute between Alice and Ralph is inverted, with Alice apparently the "woman on top." [76] After Ralph scolds Alice about her delinquent housekeeping, Alice's TV addiction is transferred over to her husband and his friend Ed Norton, who quickly become passive viewers. Ralph sits before the television set with a smorgasbord of snacks, which he deliberately places within his reach so that he needn't move a muscle while watching his program. Norton's regressive state becomes the centre of the comedic situation as he is turned into a child viewer addicted to a science-fiction serial. Wearing a club-member space helmet, Norton tunes into his favourite television host, Captain Video, and recites the space scout pledge. After arguing over program preferences, Ralph and Norton finally settle down for the *Late, Late, Late Show* and, exhausted, fall asleep in front of the set. Alice then enters the room and, with a look of motherly condescension, covers Ralph and Norton with a blanket, tucking them in for the night.

Men's magazines such as *Esquire* and *Popular Science* also presented wry commentary on male viewers. In 1951, for example, *Esquire* showed the stereotypical husband relaxing with his shoes off and a beer in his hand, smiling idiotically while seated before a television set. Two years later, the same magazine referred to television fans as "televidiots."[77] Nonetheless, while these magazines provided a humorous look at the man of leisure, they also presented men with alternatives. In very much the same way that Catharine Beecher attempted to elevate the woman by making her the centre of domestic affairs, the men's magazines suggested that fathers could regain authority through increased participation in family life.

Indeed, the "masculine domesticity" that Margaret Marsh sees as central to Progressive era lifestyles also pervaded the popular advice disseminated to men in the 1950s. According to Marsh, masculine domesticity has historically provided men with a way to assert their dominion at home. Faced with their shrinking authority in the new corporate world of white-collar desk jobs, the middle-class men of the early 1900s turned inward to the home where their increased participation in and control over the family served to compensate for feelings of powerlessness in the public sphere. Moreover, Marsh argues that masculine domesticity actually undermined women's growing desire for equal rights because it contained that desire within the safe sphere of the home. In other words, while masculine domesticity presented a more "compassionate" model of marriage where men supposedly shared domestic responsibilities with women, it did nothing to encourage women's equal participation in the public sphere.[78]

Given such historical precedents, it is not surprising that the postwar advice to men on this account took on explicitly misogynistic tones. As early as 1940, Sydnie Greenbie called for the reinstitution of manhood in his book, *Leisure for Living*. Greenbie reasoned that the popular figure of the male "boob" could be counteracted if the father cultivated his mechanical skills. As he wrote, "At last man has found something more in keeping with his nature, the workshop, with its lathe and mechanical saws, something he has kept as yet his own against the predacious female. . . . And [it becomes] more natural . . . for the man to be a homemaker as well as the woman."[79]

After the war the reintegration of the father became a popular ideal. As *Esquire* told its male readers, "Your place, Mister, is in the home, too, and if you'll make a few thoughtful improvements to it, you'll build yourself a happier, more comfortable, less back breaking world. . . ."[80] From this perspective, the men's magazines suggested ways for fathers to take an active and productive attitude in relation to television. Even if men were passive spectators, when not watching they could learn to repair the set or else produce television carts, built-ins, and stylish cabinets.[81] Articles with step-by-step instructions circulated in *Popular Science*, and the *Home Craftsman* even had a special "TV: Improve Your Home Show" column featuring a husband and wife, Thelma and Vince, and their adventures in home repairs. *Popular Science* suggested hobbies through which men could use television in an active, productive way. The magazine ran several articles on a new fad—TV photography. Men were shown how to take still pictures of their television sets, and in 1950 the magazine even conducted a readership contest for prize-winning photos that were published in the December issue.[82]

The gendered division of domestic labour and the complex relations of power entailed by it were thus shown to organize the experience of watching television. These popular representations begin to disclose the social construction of television as it was rooted in a mode of thought based on categories of sexual difference. Indeed, sexual difference, and the corresponding dynamics of domestic labour and leisure, framed television's introduction to the public in significant ways. The television industry struggled to produce programming forms that might appeal to what they assumed to be the typical housewife, and in so doing they drew an abstract portrait of "Mrs Daytime Consumer." By tailoring programs to suit the content and organization of her day, the industry hoped to capture her divided attention. Through developing schedules that mimicked the pattern of her daily activities, network executives aspired to make television a routine habit. This "ideal" female spectator was thus the very foundation of the daytime programs the industry produced. But like all texts, these programs didn't simply turn viewers into ideal spectators; they didn't simply "affect" women. Instead, they were used and interpreted within the context of everyday life at home. It is this everyday context that women's magazines addressed, providing a cultural space through which housewives might negotiate their peculiar relationship to a new media form.

Women's magazines engaged their readers in a dialogue about the concrete problems that television posed for productive labour in the home. They depicted the subtle interplay between labour and leisure at home, and they offered women ways to deal with—or else resist—television in their daily lives. If our culture has systematically relegated domestic leisure to the realm of nonproduction, these discourses remind us of the tenuousness of such notions. Indeed, at least for the housewife, television was not represented as a passive activity; rather, it was incorporated into a pattern of everyday life where work is never done.

Notes

1. This stove was mentioned in *Sponsor,* 4 June 1951, p. 19. It was also illustrated and discussed in *Popular Science,* May 1952, p. 132. The *Popular Science* reference is interesting because this men's magazine did not discuss the TV component of the stove as a vehicle for leisure, but rather showed how "a housewife can follow telecast cooking instructions step-by-step on the TV set built into this electric oven." Perhaps in this way, the magazine allayed men's fears that their wives would use the new technology for diversion as opposed to useful labour.
2. Nancy Folbre, "Exploitation Comes Home: A Critique of the Marxist Theory of Family Labour," *Cambridge Journal of Economics* 6 (1982), pp. 317–29.
3. Henri Lefebvre, foreword, *Critique de la Vie Quotidienne* (Paris, L'Arche, 1958), reprinted in *Communication and Class Struggle,* ed. Armond Mattelarund and Seth Siegelaub, trans. Mary C. Axtmann (New York: International General, 1979), p. 136.
4. See David Morley, *Family Television: Cultural Power and Domestic Leisure* (London: Comedia, 1986); and Ann Gray, "Behind Closed Doors: Video Recorders in the Home," *Boxed In: Women and Television,* ed. H. Baehr and G. Dyer (New York: Pandora, 1987), pp. 38–54.
5. Tania Modleski, "The Rhythms of Reception: Daytime Television and Women's Work," *Regarding Television: Critical Approaches,* ed. E. Ann Kaplan (Frederick, Md.: University Publications of America, 1983), pp. 67–75. See also fourth chapter in Modleski, *Loving with a Vengeance: Mass-Produced Fantasies for Women* (New York: Methuen, 1984).
6. Nick Browne, "The Political Economy of the Television (Super) Text," *Quarterly Review of Film Studies* 9 (3) (Summer 1984), p. 176.
7. William Boddy, "The Rhetoric and Economic Roots of the American Broadcasting Industry," *Cinetracts* 6 (2) (Spring 1979), pp. 37–54.
8. William Boddy, "The Shining Centre of the Home: Ontologies of Television in the 'Golden Age,'" *Television in Transition,* ed. Phillip Drummond and Richard Paterson (London: British Film Institute, 1985), pp. 125–33.
9. For a detailed analysis of the rise and fall of the DuMont Network, see Gary Newton Hess, *An Historical Study of the DuMont Television Network* (New York: Arno Press, 1979).
10. Cited in "DuMont Expansion Continues," *Radio Daily,* 12 April 1949, p. 23. See also "DuMont Skeds 7 AM to 11 PM," *Variety,* 22 September 1948, p. 34; "Daytime Tele as Profit Maker," *Variety,* 27 October 1948, pp. 25, 33; "Round-Clock Schedule Here to Stay as DuMont Programming Makes Good," *Variety,* 10 November 1948, pp. 29, 38.
11. Cited in "Daytime Video: DuMont Plans Afternoon Programming," *Broadcasting-Telecasting,* 28 November 1949, p. 3. See also "WTTG Gives Washington Regular Daytime Video with New Program Setup," *Variety,* 19 January 1949, p. 30; "Video Schedule on Coax Time," *Variety,* 12 January 1949, p. 27; "DuMont's 'Mother' Goes Network in Daytime Spread," *Variety,* 27 November 1949, p. 27.
12. "ABC, CBS, NBC Cold to Full Daytime Schedule; DuMont to Go It Alone," *Variety,* 6 October 1948, p. 27.
13. "CBS All-Day TV Programming," *Variety,* 26 January 1949, p. 34; "Video Schedule on Co-Ax Time," *Variety,* 12 January 1949, p. 27; "WNBT, N.Y., Swinging into Line as Daytime Video Airing Gains Momentum," *Variety,* 19 January 1949, p. 24; Bob Stahl, "WNBT Daytime Preem Has Hausfrau Pull but Is Otherwise Below Par," *Variety,* 9 February 1949, p. 34; "Full CBS Airing Soon," *Variety,* 2 March 1949, p. 29; "Kathi Norris Switch to WNBT Cues Daytime Expansion for Flagship," *Variety,* 1 March 1950, p. 31.
14. Cited in "Daytime TV," *Broadcasting-Telecasting,* 11 December 1950, p. 74.
15. *Sponsor,* 4 June 1951, p. 19.
16. *Newsweek,* 24 September 1951, p. 56.
17. *Televiser,* September 1951, p. 20.
18. In the early 1950s, many of the shows were sustaining vehicles—that is, programs that were aired in order to attract and maintain audiences, but that had no sponsors.
19. "DuMont Skeds 7 AM to 11 PM," *Variety,* 22 September 1948, p. 25.
20. "Pat 'N' Johnny," *Variety,* 1 March 1950, p. 35. This example bears interesting connections to Rick Altman's more general theoretical arguments about the aesthetics of sound on television. Altman argues that television uses sound to signal moments of interest, claiming that "the sound track serves better than the image itself the parts of the image that are sufficiently spectacular to merit closer attention on the part, of the intermittent viewer." See Altman, "Television/Sound," *Studies in Entertainment: Critical Approaches to Mass Culture,* ed. Tania Modleski (Bloomington and Indianapolis: Indiana University Press, 1986), p. 47.
21. Robert C. Allen, *Speaking of Soap Operas* (Chapel Hill: University of North Carolina Press, 1985).
22. See "Daytime Video: DuMont Plans Afternoon Program" and "DuMont Daytime 'Shoppers' Series Starts," *Broadcasting-Telecasting,* 12 December 1949, p. 5.
23. Some variety programs included 15-minute sitcoms and soap operas.
24. "TV's 'Stars in the Afternoon,'" *Variety,* 3 October 1951, p. 29.
25. "Women's Magazine of the Air," *Variety,* 9 March 1949, p. 33; "Women's Page," *Variety,* 1 June 1949, p. 34.

26. NBC had particular problems securing sponsors and, especially during 1951 and 1952, many of its shows were sustaining programs. So critical had this problem become that in fall of 1952 NBC temporarily cut back its schedule, giving afternoon hours back to affiliates. Affiliates, however, complained that this put them at a competitive disadvantage with CBS affiliates. See "NBC-TV's 'What's the Use?' Slant May Give Daytime Back to Affiliates," *Variety,* 3 September 1952, p. 20; "Daytime TV—No. 1 Dilemma," *Variety,* 24 September 1952, pp. 1, 56; "NBC-TV to Focus Prime Attention on Daytime Schedule," *Variety,* 24 December 1952, p. 22; "NBC-TV Affiliates in Flareup," *Variety,* 6 May 1953, p. 23.
27. Weaver's concept was adopted by CBS executives who in 1952 instituted the "12 plan" that gave sponsors a discount for buying 12 participations during the daytime schedule. "Day TV Impact," *Broadcasting,* 3 November 1952, p. 73; Bob Stahl, "CBS-TV's Answer to "Today,"" *Variety,* 12 November 1952, pp. 23, 58.
28. John H. Porter, memo to TV network salesmen, 11 June 1954, NBC Records, Box 183: Folder 5, Wisconsin Center Historical Archives, State Historical Society, Madison.
29. George Rosen, "Garroway 'Today' Off to Boff Start as Revolutionary News Concept," *Variety,* 16 January 1952, p. 29.
30. Joe Meyers and Bob Graff, cited in William R. McAndrew, confidential memo to John K. Herbert, 23 March 1953, NBC Records, Box 370: Folder 22, Wisconsin Center Historical Archives, State Historical Society, Madison.
31. *Daytime Availabilities: Program Descriptions and Estimates,* 1 June 1954, NBC Records, Box 183: Folder 5, Wisconsin Center Historical Archives, State Historical Society, Madison.
32. "Early Morning Inserts Get WNBT Dress-Up," *Variety,* 13 August 1952, p. 26.
33. "For the Girls at Home," *Newsweek,* 15 March 1954, p. 92. NBC's advertising campaign for *Home* was unprecedented for daytime programming promotion, costing $976,029.00 in print, on-air promotion, outdoor advertising, and novelty gimmicks. See Jacob A. Evans, letter to Charles Barry, 28 January 1954, NBC Records, Box 369: Folder 5, Wisconsin Center Historical Archives, State Historical Society, Madison.
34. Jacob A. Evans, letter to Charles Barry, 28 January 1954, NBC Records, Box 369: Folder 5, Wisconsin Center Historical Archives, State Historical Society, Madison.
35. In a promotional report, NBC boasted that on *Today's* first broadcast, Kiplinger received 20,000 requests for a free copy of the magazine. Matthew J. Culligan, sales letter, 27 January 1953, NBC Records, Box 378: Folder 9, Wisconsin Center Historical Archives, State Historical Society, Madison.
36. The report cited here was commentary for a slide presentation given by Coffin to about 50 researchers from ad agencies and manufacturing companies in the New York area. *Commentary for Television's Daytime Profile: Buying Habits and Characteristics of the Audience,* 10 June 1954, NBC Records, Box 183: Folder 5, Wisconsin Center Historical Archives, State Historical Society, Madison. For the actual survey, see W.R. Simmons and Associates Research, Inc., *Television's Daytime Profile: Buying Habits and Characteristics of the Audience,* 15 September 1954, NBC Records, Box 183: Folder 8, Wisconsin Center Historical Archives, State Historical Society, Madison. A short booklet reviewing the findings was sent to all prospective advertisers; *Television's Daytime Profile: An Intimate Portrait of the Ideal Market for Most Advertisers,* 1 September 1954, NBC Records, Box 183: Folder 5, Wisconsin Center Historical Archives, State Historical Society, Madison. For NBC's exploitation of the survey, see also Ed Vane, letter to Mr Edward A. Amonili, 7 December 1954, NBC Records, Box 183: Folder 5, Wisconsin Center Historical Archives, State Historical Society, Madison; Hugh M. Beville, Jr., letter to Robert Sarnoff, 27 July 1954, NBC Records, Box 183: Folder 5, Wisconsin Center Historical Archives, State Historical Society, Madison; Thomas Coffin, letter to H.M. Beville, Jr, 21 July 1954, NBC Records, Box 183: Folder 5, Wisconsin Center Historical Archives, State Historical Society, Madison. The survey also made headlines in numerous trade journals, newspapers, and magazines. For press coverage, see NBC's *clipping file,* NBC Records, Box 183: Folder 5, Wisconsin Center Historical Archives, State Historical Society, Madison.
37. Edward Stasheff, *The Television Program: Its Writing, Direction, and Production* (New York: A.A. Wyn, 1951), p. 47.
38. Consumer spectacles were further achieved through rear-screen projection, an "aerial" camera that captured action with a "telescoping arm," and mechanical devices such as a weather machine that adorned products in a mist of rain, fog, sleet, or hail. *Daytime Availabilities: Program Descriptions and Cost Estimates,* 1 June 1954, NBC Records, Box 183: Folder 5, Wisconsin Center Historical Archives, State Historical Society, Madison.
39. Charles C. Barry, memos to Richard Pinkham, 2 March 1954, 3 March 1954, and 4 March 1954, NBC Records, Box 369: Folder 5, Wisconsin Center Historical Archives, State Historical Society, Madison.
40. Franklin Sisson, *Thirty Television Talks* (New York: n.p., 1955), p. 144. Cited in Giraud Chester and Garnet R. Garrison, *Television and Radio* (New York: Appleton-Century-Crofts, Inc., 1956), p. 414.
41. Caroline Burke, memo to Ted Mills, 20 November 1953, NBC Records, Box 377: Folder 6, Wisconsin Center Historical Archives, State Historical Society, Madison; Arlene Francis, cited in Earl Wilson, *The NBC Book of Stars* (New York: Pocket Books, 1957), p. 92.
42. Cited in Wilson, *The NBC Book,* p. 94.

43. Sylvester L. Weaver, memo to Harry Bannister, 10 October 1952, NBC Records, Box 378: Folder 9, Wisconsin Center Historical Archives, State Historical Society, Madison.
44. Joe Meyer cited in William R. McAndrew, confidential memo to John K. Herbert, 23 March 1953, NBC Records, Box 370; Folder 22, Wisconsin Center Historical Archives, State Historical Society, Madison.
45. A.A. Schechter, "'Today' as an Experiment Bodes Encouraging Manana," *Variety,* 16 July 1952, p. 46. NBC also advertised *Today* by claiming that "people are actually changing their living habits to watch 'Today.'" See *Sponsor,* 25 February 1952, pp. 44–45.
46. *Daytime Availabilities: Program Descriptions and Cost Estimates,* 1 June 1954, NBC Records, Box 183: Folder 5, Wisconsin Center Historical Archives, State Historical Society, Madison.
47. Walter Benjamin, "The Work of Art in the Age of Mechanical Reproduction," *Illuminations: Essays and Reflections,* ed. Hannah Arendt (New York: Schocken, 1969), pp. 217–51.
48. *Ladies' Home Journal,* April 1955, p. 130. See also *Ladies' Home Journal,* February 1955, p. 95; *Good Housekeeping,* July 1955, p. 135.
49. *The New Yorker,* 3 June 1950, p. 22.
50. Crosby, "What's Television Going to Do to Your Life?" *House Beautiful,* February 1950, p. 125.
51. *American Home,* October 1955, p. 14.
52. Walter Adams and E.A. Hungerford, Jr, "Television: Buying and Installing It Is Fun; These Ideas Will Help," *Better Homes and Gardens,* September 1949, p. 38; *American Home,* December 1954, p. 39.
53. *American Home,* May 1955, p. 138. The cartoon was part of an advertisement for the *Yellow Pages.*
54. *House Beautiful,* June 1952, p. 59.
55. W.W. Ward, "Is It Time To Buy Television?" *House Beautiful,* October 1948, p. 220.
56. *Ladies' Home Journal,* May 1953, p. 148.
57. "The Wonderful Anti-Statics," *House Beautiful,* January 1955, p. 89; *Ladies' Home Journal,* November 1948, p. 90.
58. Gertrude Brassard, "For Early Tea and Late TV," *American Home,* July 1952, p. 88.
59. In August 1949, for example, *House Beautiful* suggested that a swivelling cabinet would allow women to "move the screen, not the audience" (p. 69). Although portable sets were not heavily marketed in the early 1950s, they were sometimes presented as the ideal solution to the problem of moving the heavy console set.
60. *House Beautiful,* May 1952, p. 138.
61. Wright, *Building the Dream,* p. 172.
62. *House Beautiful,* June 1951, p. 121.
63. Vivian Grigsby Bender, "Please a Dining Room!" *American Home,* September 1951, p. 27.
64. *Better Homes and Gardens,* December 1952, p. 144; *Better Homes and Gardens,* February 1953, p. 169; see also *American Home,* September 1953, p. 102.
65. *House Beautiful,* November 1948, p. 5.
66. Edith Ramsay, "How to Stretch a Day," *American Home,* September 1949, p. 66; *House Beautiful,* December 1950, p. 77.
67. *American Home,* February 1954, p. 32.
68. *House Beautiful,* November 1954, p. 158. For additional examples, see *American Home,* November 1953, p. 60; *Better Homes and Gardens,* December 1951, p. 7; *TV Guide,* 18 December 1953, p. 18.
69. *Better Homes and Gardens,* October 1952, p. 177.
70. Laura Mulvey, "Visual Pleasure and Narrative Cinema," *Screen* 16 (3) (1975), pp. 6–18. Since the publication of Mulvey's article, numerous feminists—including Mulvey—have theorized ways that women might find subjective pleasures in classical cinema, and feminists have also challenged the idea that pleasure in the cinema is organized entirely around scenarios of "male" desire. For a bibliography on this literature and a forum on contemporary views on female spectatorship in the cinema, see *Camera Obscura* 20–21 (May–September 1989).
71. W.W. Ward, "Is It Time to Buy Television?" *House Beautiful,* October 1948, p. 172.
72. *House Beautiful,* May 1955, p. 131.
73. *Better Homes and Gardens,* October 1953, p. 151. There is one exception to this rule of male body posture, which I have found in the fashionable men's magazine *Esquire.* While *Esquire* depicted the slovenly male viewer, it also showed men how to watch television in fashion by wearing clothes tailored specifically for TV viewing. In these cases, the male body was relaxed, and the men still smoked and drank liquor, but they were posed in more aesthetically appealing ways. See "Town-Talk Tables and Television," *Esquire,* January 1951, pp. 92–93; and "Easy Does It Leisure Wear," *Esquire,* November 1953, p. 74. The figure of the fashionable male television viewer was taken up by at least one male clothing company, The Rose Brothers, who advertised their men's wear by showing well-dressed men watching television and by promising, "You Can Tele-Wise Man by His Surretwill Suit." See *Colliers,* 1 October 1949, p. 54.
74. Robert M. Jones, "Privacy Is Worth All That It Costs," *Better Homes and Gardens,* March 1952, p. 57.
75. This is not to say that television was the only domestic machine to disrupt representations of gender. Roland Marchand, for example, has argued that advertisements for radio sets and phonographs reversed traditional pictorial conventions for the depiction of men and women. Family-circle ads typically showed husbands seated while their wives were perched on the arm of the chair or sofa. In most of the ads for radios and phonographs in his sample, the opposite is true. Marchand argues that "in the presence of culturally uplifting music, the woman more often gained the right of reposed concentration while the (more technologically inclined) man stood prepared to change the records or adjust the radio dials." See *Advertising the American Dream,*

pp. 252–53. When applied to television, Marchand's analysis of radio does not seem to adhere since men were often shown seated and blatantly unable to control the technology.

76. I am borrowing Natalie Zemon Davis's phrase with which she describes how women in preindustrial France were able to invert gender hierarchies during carnival festivities and even, at times, in everyday life. See "Women on Top," *Society and Culture in Early Modern France* (Stanford, CA: Stanford University Press, 1975), pp. 124–51.
77. *Popular Science,* May 1954, p. 177; *Esquire,* March 1951, p. 10; Jack O'Brien, "Offsides in Sports," *Esquire,* November 1953, p. 24.
78. Marsh, *Suburban Lives,* p. 82.
79. Greenbie, *Leisure for Living,* p. 210. Greenbie, in fact, presented a quite contradictory account of mechanization in the home, at times seeing it as the man's ally, at other times claiming that modern machines actually took away male authority.
80. "Home Is for Husbands Too," *Esquire,* June 1951, p. 88.
81. In addition, companies that produced home-improvement products and workshop tools continually used television sets in their illustrations of remodelled rooms. Typically here, the Masonite Corporation promoted its do-it- your self panelling in an advertisement that displayed a television set in a "male room" just for Dad. See *Better Homes and Gardens,* August 1951, p. 110. For similar ads, see *American Home,* June 1955, p. 3; *Better Homes and Gardens,* February 1953, p. 195; *American Home,* November 1952, p. 105. It should be noted that some of these ads also showed women doing the remodelling work.
82. "From Readers' Albums of Television Photos," *Popular Science,* December 1950, p. 166. See also "TV's Images Can Be Photographed," *Popular Science,* August 1950, pp. 184–5; R.P. Stevenson, "How You Can Photograph the Fights Via Television," *Popular Science,* February 1951, pp. 214–16.

Canada

Marc Raboy

The story of television in Canada is totally intertwined with the story of Canada itself. One hundred and thirty years after Confederation, Canada is still essentially a work-in-progress, an experiment in communication, which on its better days exhibits many of the characteristics of a post-modern nation-state. The problem is that, perched on the rump of the United States as it is, Canada suffers from a lack of critical mass. It has been said that Canada is a place with too much geography and not enough history, but the main point is that Canada has no common political culture. In Canada, communication technology is the only tie that binds.

This is also the situation of Canadian television. Where, in the nineteenth century, the railroad was central to the project of creating Canada, in the twentieth, broadcasting was essential to maintaining it. (In the twenty-first century, the information highway may result in a plethora of Canadas, or Canada-like states, but that is a different story.) But where the railroad linked a string of disparate colonies together—at least until bankruptcy put an end to that—television has shone the spotlight on some of the most flagrant contradictions of the Canadian project. Canadian television has been preoccupied with issues of distribution over issues of content, and in Canada, the conflicting imperatives of economics and culture that have dominated the evolution of television everywhere else are constantly cancelling each other out in deference to the higher national interest of self-preservation.

Canadians, perhaps more than many others, viscerally understand what Philip Schlesinger has called the "relevance of communication for analyzing the formation of a collective identity." This understanding is, for example, one of the features which most dearly distinguishes Canadians from Americans. It is reflected, first of all, in the political framework of television.

Broadcasting in Canada is, by law, "a public service essential to the maintenance and enhancement of national identity and cultural sovereignty." Canadian broadcasting is then deemed to be a single system comprising public, private, and community elements. It is to be effectively owned and controlled by Canadians (foreign ownership is restricted to 33 per cent in any single broadcasting undertaking), is to make maximum use of Canadian creative and other resources, and is to serve the needs and interests, and reflect the circumstances and aspirations, of Canadian men, women, and children. These circumstances, the law states, include equal rights, linguistic duality, the multicultural and multiracial nature of Canadian society, as well as the special place of Aboriginal peoples within that society. In the event of conflicting interest between public and private sector elements of the system, the objectives of the public sector are supposed to prevail. Overseeing and implementing all of this is an independent public authority for the regulation and supervision of the Canadian broadcasting system, the Canadian Radio-television and Telecommunications Commission (CRTC).

However, reality is such that the promises enshrined in this generous policy have more often than not been a pious wish-list.

Before Television, There Was Radio

To a remarkable extent, the major issues that define Canadian television have remained unchanged since the early days of radio.

Throughout the 1920s, Canadian commercial radio developed essentially in the private sector, with stations operating in either English or French, some of them affiliated with the emerging networks in the United States, and all of them filling the air with a large proportion of American programming. During the same period, the publicly owned Canadian National Railways set up the first national radio network, whose basic purpose was to entertain passengers on the long transcontinental journey from Halifax to Vancouver. In western Canada the Manitoba telephone system and the University of Alberta each operated non-commercial radio stations, and the province of Quebec adopted the country's first broadcasting legislation, authorizing the government to own and operate stations as well as to produce programs for broadcast by private stations.

The only requirement for broadcasters at that time was to obtain a licence from the national Department of the Marine, which limited its role to the distribution of radio frequencies. But in 1928, faced with an accumulation of difficult problems, the national government mandated a Royal Commission to study all aspects of broadcasting and make proposals for organizing the system. The commissioners travelled the length and breadth of the country and even ventured to New York and London to study the leading broadcasting models of the day, before recommending that all broadcasting in Canada be organized on the basis of public service, and that a national, publicly owned corporation be created to produce and acquire programs, own and administer stations in English and in French, eventually absorb the existing private-sector stations, and in the interim, act as the regulatory authority of all broadcasting in Canada. The Royal Commission was motivated by its findings that "Canadian listeners want Canadian radio programming," and by the conviction that broadcasting was too important a social and educational force to be left to function according to business criteria. In the particular cultural and political context of Canada, it recommended that the national corporation be run by a board made up of commissioners from each province, and that each province have authority over the content broadcast within its territory.

This culturally nationalist, socially progressive, and politically astute report was widely debated for four years after its 1928 publication. Before acting at all, the national government obtained a court ruling declaring that jurisdiction over broadcasting was exclusively *its* own, and need not be shared with the provinces (which had claimed legal competence on the constitutional grounds that broadcasting was a cultural and educational activity). The young and dynamic commercial broadcasting industry and its supporters strongly lobbied against the idea of a public service monopoly. A popular coalition of unions, voluntary associations, educational groups, patriotic organizations, and progressive business leaders formed the Canadian Radio League which, under the slogan "The State or the United States," argued for adopting the proposals of the Royal Commission report. Finally, in 1932, a Conservative government adopted Canada's first national broadcasting legislation, creating the Canadian Radio Broadcasting Commission (CRBC), which became the Canadian Broadcasting Corporation (CBC) in 1936.

However, the system that emerged was rather different than the one proposed by the Royal Commission. While the legislation did provide for the public broadcaster to establish a national public service monopoly, no move was ever made to limit the expansion of private, commercial radio. Provincial authorities were completely excluded from playing any official role and, indeed, would be explicitly prohibited from operating broadcasting stations until the introduction of educational television in the 1970s. While official policy documents emphasized the importance of a publicly owned national corporation, funded by a licence fee, advertising (and therefore competition with the private sector) was to play an important part in funding its activities from the beginning. And while the entire strategy was centred on the goal of creating an authentic, autonomous Canadian broadcasting system on the periphery of the United States, that system would become a vehicle for introducing American broadcasting content into Canada.

Even before the introduction of television, the major themes that characterize Canadian broadcasting today had already been established. These can be summarized by three sets of tensions: *(a)* between private capital and the state, over the economic basis of television; *(b)* between the state and the public, over the socio-cultural mission of television; and *(c)* between dominant and alternative visions of the state, over the relationship of television to the politics of nationhood. Overriding these are the constant pressures of North American continentalism—and, increasingly, globalization—against the desire for Canadian television to be *Canadian* and the tendency of each succeeding wave of technological change to make matters worse rather than better.

The Origins . . .

In 1951 the CBC was mandated to develop and introduce television as a public service monopoly, following the report of another, more wide-ranging Royal Commission on the arts, letters, and sciences. Broadcasting began in 1952 with the launching of bilingual French–English broadcasts in Montreal. Within a year the CBC was well on its way to establishing two national television networks. The 1950s were critical in setting the tone for Canadian television, in English and in French. Distinctive Canadian news and current affairs formats were developed and, in French particularly, popular dramatic serials known as "télé-romans." *Hockey Night in Canada* became a national ritual, in both official languages, which continues to this day.

It soon became clear, however, that television could not be supported by the licence fee, even with advertising. During the 1950s the licence fee was abolished and an annual grant from Parliament became the norm for balancing the CBC's budget. This funding approach remains in effect to this day, despite repeated calls for a more stable, multi-year funding formula. Also for financial reasons, private companies were allowed to own "affiliated" stations, enabling the CBC to complete its two national networks (in English and French) at lower cost.

A major shift occurred in 1958 following a change of government. The private sector finally got the independent regulatory authority it had been arguing for since the end of the war: the Board of Broadcast Governors (BBG). One of the first activities of the BBG was to authorize the introduction of private commercially driven television, which began operating in major cities in 1960, and on a national network basis in English in 1961. As CBC television is dependent for an important part of its revenue on advertising, public and private competition in television has been an important factor ever since.

Meanwhile, CBC faced a series of political crises. On the English side, attempts by the government to interfere with programming led to massive resignations among current affairs staff in 1959. In the same year, a strike by French-language Radio-Canada producers paralyzed the French television service for over two months, and became an important symbolic reference point for the emerging Quebec nationalist movement.

During the 1960s, news and information programming continued to be a source of friction both within the CBC and in the corporation's relationship with the government. The unorthodox current affairs program *This Hour Has Seven Days*, which rated the highest audience "enjoyment index" ever achieved by a CBC show, provoked an internal management and authority crisis that eventually toppled CBC's senior management while redefining Canadian television journalism. During the same period, French service news programs infuriated the government by paying serious attention to Quebec separatist politicians and issues, and in 1968 the law was rewritten obliging CBC to "contribute to national unity," albeit with little concrete effect.

Commercial television flourished in the 1960s, due in no small measure to the political problems that plagued CBC during that stormy decade. Through the late 1960s and 1970s, the government continuously threatened to reduce the CBC's funding level if it did not begin to toe the line, but actually permitted significant expansion as long as it believed the public broadcaster had a political role to play. By the late 1970s, however, this belief was undermined, as the introduction of more and more competing signals ate away at the CBC's audience share, and as government advisers began to realize that using a public broadcaster for propaganda purposes would fail anyway. In the 1980 Quebec referendum on sovereignty, the CBC was basically left alone and all sides relied on television advertising to reach their constituencies. But the CBC's fortunes as the centrepiece of the Canadian broadcasting system began to seriously decline soon after that.

The 1968 Broadcasting Act also enshrined the basic principles and structures of Canadian broadcasting and created a new regulatory authority, the CRTC. On the margins of the system, meanwhile, social pressure from the youth and oppositional movements that grew up in the 1960s led to a range of community broadcasting initiatives in radio, video, and television. At the same time, political pressure to redefine the nature of the Canadian federation finally led to the first provincial incursions into public broadcasting, in the guise of educational television networks set up, first in Quebec and Ontario, later in Alberta and British Columbia, and eventually in Saskatchewan and the north. By 1992 educational television accounted for some Canadian $233 million in public spending.

Meanwhile, while CBC led the way in Canadian programming, private television was slowly and steadily carving a place for itself, building an audience by consistently offering the most popular American programs, competing with CBC for the broadcasting rights to Canadian sports classics such as football's annual Grey Cup Game, and emulating the CBC's successes in news and current affairs. By the late 1980s the CBC's share of the Canadian television audience was down to around 20 per cent in English and 30 per cent in French.

The issue of maintaining a balance between Canadian and American programs was tackled by the regulatory authority early on. Beginning in 1960, Canadian television broadcasters were required to offer 55 per cent Canadian programs. In 1970 this was stiffened to 60 per cent in prime time. Canadian content regulations would be a controversial and ongoing issue in Canadian television. Apart from the philosophical question surrounding the legitimacy of intervening in audience "choice," the effectiveness of content quotas in bringing Canadian programs to the screen and getting Canadians to watch them has been a subject of continual debate. Since the 1960s, however, there has been a general consensus that without Canadian content requirements commercial broadcasters would have no incentive to produce Canadian programs when they could acquire American exports for as little as one-tenth of the cost.

The CRTC spent most of the 1970s developing a regulatory framework for the rapidly expanding cable industry, which had emerged in television's early days as community antenna services to remote areas. By retransmitting signals picked out of the air from US border-town transmitters (for which they paid no licence fees until 1989), the cable industry built an attractive product for the Canadian television audience, which quickly developed a taste for the best of both worlds. To extend the dictum of the 1929 Royal Commission on broadcasting, Canadians wanted Canadian television, but they wanted American television too.

Aware that the increasingly widespread cable model was undermining its policy to support and promote Canadian content, the CRTC moved to ensure that cable, as well, contributed to the overriding policy objective of delivering Canadian television to Canadians. Must-carry provisions ensure that every available Canadian over-the-air signal in any area is offered as basic service, along with a local community channel. But in exchange, cable companies are authorized to distribute the three American commercial networks plus PBS. This was, for many years, the basic cable package available to Canadian cable subscribers, and on this basis, 76 per cent of Canadian homes subscribed to cable by 1995.

The CRTC was also charged with putting in place Canadian ownership regulations, limiting foreign participation in Canadian broadcasting companies to 20 per cent, up until 1995. This policy has resulted in the fact that Canadian television is still entirely Canadian controlled, with only a handful of operations having any proportion of foreign ownership at all. It has not prevented the rise of Canadian media conglomerates along the lines of those known elsewhere, however, and the Canadian television industry is characterized by a high degree of concentration of ownership. The trend since the mid-1980s is toward the takeover of private television outfits by cable companies, creating multimedia conglomerates which, in some cases, verge on monopoly. The best-known examples are the Quebec cable enterprise Vidéotron, which also owns Canada's main French-language network, TVA; and Rogers Communications, Canada's largest cable company, which acquired the Maclean-Hunter publishing, television, and cable conglomerate in 1994.

Development . . .

An important shift in the ecology of Canadian television occurred in the 1970s, as the CRTC began to license second private stations in large metropolitan markets. Regional networks such as Global (in southern Ontario) and Quatre saisons (in Quebec) grew out of this policy, which also saw the establishment of independent stations in many cities, including Toronto's highly successful Citytv. The resulting audience fragmentation contributed to further eating away at the CBC's audience share, and consequently, at an important basis for legitimating the spiralling cost of public broadcasting to the public purse.

After two lucrative decades, private television also began to experience the financial doldrums of a weak market in the 1980s as a period of stagnating advertising revenues followed the earlier licensing boom. But the private sector received an important boost in 1983, with the creation of the Broadcast Program Development Fund, publicly funded and administered by Telefilm Canada. This fund has been responsible for injecting about Canadian $140 million a year into independent production of programs destined for broadcast on both public and private television as well as for export. The result has been to create a new independent production sector and increase the visibility of publicly funded Canadian programs on private television, while diminishing the role of the CBC as the principal producer of Canadian programs. The CBC is still by far the largest distributor of Canadian programs, however. In 1994 Canadian content on CBC television was about 85 per cent in prime time, while the total across the entire system was about 75 per cent foreign. Viewing patterns, meanwhile, corresponded closely to the total offer.

The situation of conventional broadcasters faced another challenge with the introduction, in 1982, of pay-TV and later, in 1987, of a series of Canadian speciality channels. The CRTC had resisted pressure from the cable industry to allow it to import the new US services such as HBO that came on the market in the mid-1970s, opting instead to promote the development of Canadian services along the same lines. In most cases, such as movies, sports, and rock videos, the Canadian services provide a similar range of programs to their American counterparts, but they are Canadian-owned, subject to

CRTC licensing, and they do offer at least a window for Canadian programs. In some cases, such as the CBC's 24-hour news service, *Newsworld,* or the international francophone channel, TV5, the first generation of Canadian speciality services licensed in 1987 represented a distinctive addition to the program offer.

The financing of Canadian pay-TV and speciality channels provides an instructive example in the problems of competing with global television products in a small domestic market. The regulatory justification for creating Canadian pay-TV in 1982 was to provide an additional vehicle for Canadian feature films but the actual percentage of Canadian films offered has never been statistically significant. At the same time, the film channels' weak penetration of cabled households made them commercially unviable. When it decided to license a new series of speciality channels in 1987, the CRTC therefore chose a different formula. This time, cable operators were authorized to provide the new range of services to all subscribers in their territory, and charge accordingly. The discretionary aspect was thus shifted from the consumer to the cable operator, who could calculate the economics of the deal with great precision. The cost to the consumer for each additional service was relatively low, and as rates were regulated, the market mechanism was essentially removed. At the same time, cable operators could still offer the traditional discretionary pay-TV channels which they were by now packaging along with a range of authorized American services not considered to be competitors of the Canadian ones.

Since 1987 Canadian cable subscribers in most markets received a package which includes the 24-hour CBC news channels, channels featuring music videos, sports, weather, and children's programming (in either English or French), and TV5. In addition, they can choose to subscribe to pay-TV movie channels, specialized channels in the other official language, and, depending on where they live, a range of American channels including CNN (but not, for example, MTV, which is considered a direct competitor of its Canadian equivalent).

By the early 1990s all of these services combined accounted for somewhat under 20 per cent of overall viewing. But pressure to establish even more Canadian services continued, in the light of the anticipated "500-channel universe" and the perceived need to maintain the attractiveness of cable subscription to Canadian viewers as a means of forestalling their defection to US direct broadcast satellites. Thus, as of 1 January 1995, a cabled Canadian household could receive, in addition to everything mentioned previously, a French-language CBC news channel, arts and entertainment channels in English or French (depending on the market), a science channel, a women's channel, a lifestyle channel, a Canadian country-music channel, and a channel featuring old programs. The specific offer and funding formulas have become extremely complicated, and vary from territory to territory according to the leeway provided by the CRTC to each cable operator. The initial response from consumers has been laced with confusion and frustration as, despite the slogan of "consumer sovereignty" that is supposed to accompany increased channel capacity, the consumer finds that he or she is not really the one who has the choice.

In the mid-1990s Canadian television was struggling to adjust to the new technological and economic environment characterized by the metaphor of the "information highway." The CRTC's regulatory regime was under review, the CBC faced increasingly radical budgetary restrictions, private broadcasters were competing for dwindling advertising revenue. As in other western countries, the conventional model of generalist television was increasingly under a state of siege. However, Canadian distribution undertakings—still protected from US dominance under the cultural industries exemption of the North American Free Trade Agreement—were well-positioned in the Canadian market. And across the range of channels available, Canadian independent productions were finding an audience.

In this context, the government initiated a series of reviews of the mandate and funding arrangement of the CBC in the autumn of 1994. Debate focused on whether the CBC should continue to be a generalist broadcaster and even branch out aggressively into a whole range of new speciality services, or limit itself to being a single, highly distinctive service among many. For the government, cost was the main consideration. The CBC's annual grant from Parliament was still nearly Canadian$1,100 million in 1994–95 (for television and radio combined), despite accumulated cutbacks. This represented one-third of all federal spending in the sphere of culture. But the CBC was still dependent on its annual advertising revenue of Canadian$30 million—enough to be an important consideration in every programming decision, but not nearly enough to take the pressure off the public treasury.

While critics argued that this dependency gave CBC television the look of a commercial broadcaster, the strongest pleas for getting the CBC out of advertising came from the private sector, which desperately wanted the extra revenue (private television earned $1,300m from advertising in 1992). The CBC's dilemma, particularly in English, has been how to maintain a distinctive television profile while competing commercially, and how to respond to the vast demands of an encompassing mandate in a context of government cutbacks. The government, meanwhile, irritated by what it has perceived as a negative CBC role in failing to promote Canadian national unity in the face of the threat of Quebec secession, has continued to cut the CBC's annual parliamentary appropriation. By 1996 total projected budget cuts for the period 1984–98 had reached a summit of Canadian$414 million, or 47 per cent in per capita funding terms.

But regardless how one slices it, maintaining the traditional policy objective of a strong Canadian screen presence means finding more money, not less, for public television. Access for and to Canadian content also requires public subsidy. Even assuming maintaining government funding and advertising revenue at existing levels, more money needed to be found simply to maintain the existing level of Canadian screen content.

Indeed, by 1997 it was clear that the only way to meet the goals set for Canadian broadcasting was to take the Broadcasting Act at its word and adopt a holistic approach to the economics and policy expectations of the system as a whole: to stop treating a distribution franchise as a licence to print money, to stop agonizing over the fiscal "bellyaching" of both private broadcasters and the CBC and insist they meet their respective mandate requirements, and to open up new windows of public service in the expanding media environment.

Conclusion

Public debate over communication has been one of the dominant themes of Canadian social discourse since the early days of radio broadcasting. Communication, in Canada, has been seen variously as a binding force for national unity, as a vehicle for social development, and as an instrument of cultural affirmation.

Canadian television, then, has developed from the principle that communication is central to nation-building. The Canadian system has developed ways of promoting this: an emphasis on publicly owned and operated national institutions, carriage rules for distribution systems, public support for production of Canadian content, licensing of services to ensure that products reach their markets.

Canadian television industries have flourished within this framework, by providing services designed to meet national policy objectives. At the same time, the public-service basis of television has kept social preoccupations on the policy agenda. In this respect, more so than in Europe or the United States, where one or the other pole has conventionally dominated, television in Canada has evolved according to the push and pull of the tension between economics and culture.

Because of its historic concerns in the areas of culture and communication, Canada has developed a set of established institutional practices which may be particularly appropriate for understanding the role of television in a variety of settings. Among these particularities are the principles that communication infrastructures constitute a cornerstone of national cultural heritage, that the way to realizing national goals in culture and communication is a mixed system of publicly owned and publicly regulated public and private industries, and that social and cultural objectives should be the locomotive of the system.

A Usable History for the Study of Television

Paul Attallah

The story of the relationship between film and television is usually told from the point of view of the Hollywood majors and the US networks. There are good reasons for doing so, given the canonical status of those industries, but the same story could not easily be told for most other countries, and certainly not for Canada. Nonetheless, the story is valuable for both its aporias and its details. Together, they provide a history as well as hints on how to rewrite it.

In the beginning, Hollywood loathed television. Legend holds that Jack Warner would not permit a television set to appear in his films and that David Selznick believed people would quickly tire of watching a wooden box. Television's impact, however, soon required a more sophisticated response. In 1946, Hollywood's peak year, weekly film attendance was 100 million out of a population of 140 million. In 2005, weekly film attendance was only 25 million out of a population of 295 million (Menand). By 1949, movie attendance had already dropped 25 per cent and unemployment in Hollywood was on the rise. These trends were only magnified as television entered more and more homes.[1]

However, the relationship between film and television began even earlier than usually acknowledged. The Nipkow disk, which forms the basis of all television scanning systems, was patented in 1874 by Paul Nipkow at the very time that Marey, Muybridge, and others were experimenting with motion pictures. C. Francis Jenkins, co-inventor with Thomas Armat of the most widely used movie projector of the silent era, was also one of the earliest American pioneers of mechanical television. In the 1920s, he coined the term "radiomovies" for what we now call "television." Even as late as 1936, John Logie Baird, the British pioneer of the mechanical era, urged the BBC to adopt his film-based scanning system as the basis of its television service.

These origins make it plain that film and television have not always been opponents or competitors, but were, rather, technologies that could be mixed and matched. Furthermore, they were sometimes championed by the same people. For them to become opposing technologies and to struggle over the same audiences, they had first to become industries. In that respect, the film industry developed earlier because its technical infrastructure was less complex and because television came under the control of corporations primarily interested in radio. The major studios had invested in television throughout the 1930s and 1940s. Between 1933 and 1947, radio mogul Don Lee ran Los Angeles television station W6XAO (later KTSL) on which he regularly aired feature-length Hollywood films. By the late 1940s, Paramount, Warner Brothers, Loew's-MGM and 20th Century Fox had all launched television stations or applied for broadcast licences. Paramount was the most active, and in 1941, it established one of the dominant television stations in Los Angeles, W6XYZ (KTLA after 1946). By the late 1940s, it undertook experiments using the Phonevision, Skiatron, and Telemeter systems to deliver films to the homes of paying subscribers. The dream of a pay-movie network came to fruition in 1972 when another studio, Warner Bros., now part of Time Warner Entertainment, launched HBO.[2] In a sense, the flirtation with television merely extended Hollywood's relationship with radio.

Another way in which the two industries co-operate is in sharing expertise. Many writers, directors, technicians, actors, and other industry professionals get their initial training in one medium before moving on to the other. From different ends of the time spectrum, Alfred Hitchcock and Ridley Scott are emblematic of this back-and-forth movement.[3]

Hollywood eventually responded to the challenge of television with several strategies. The first was to withhold its product. Some hoped that, without Hollywood films, television would simply wither and die. Instead, television developed its own forms and stars, frequently borrowed from radio and vaudeville or from the back rows of Hollywood itself. In this way, Jack Benny (*The Jack Benny Show*, CBS, 1950–1965), Bob Hope (NBC, various specials), and Groucho Marx (*You Bet Your Life*, NBC, 1950–1961) simply transferred their hugely successful radio programs to hugely successful television programs. Lucille Ball transformed a moderately successful radio show (*My Favorite Husband*, CBS, 1948–1951) into the definitive sitcom of the 1950s (*I Love Lucy*, CBS, 1951–1961), and Jack Webb turned a minor showbiz career into the iconic crime drama of its day (*Dragnet*, NBC, 1951–1970). Arthur Godfrey (*The Arthur Godfrey Show*, CBS, 1948–1958) and Ed Sullivan (*Toast of the Town* and *The Ed Sullivan Show*, CBS, 1948–1971) became celebrities in their own right and reinvigorated vaudeville. William Boyd (*Hopalong Cassidy*, NBC, 1952–1954) had retained ownership of his films and found an excellent aftermarket in television, even as the film industry collapsed. Television even created its own stars, like George Wagner, a.k.a. Gorgeous George (*Wrestling*, various networks), Dagmar (*Broadway Open House*, NBC, 1950–1951), and Jack Paar (*The Tonight Show*, NBC, 1957–1962). Withholding product failed to win back the audience.

The second strategy used by the film industry was to highlight the intensity and impact of the film image through colour, 3D, Cinerama, and Cinemascope. Not until 1966 did the three US networks adopt full-colour schedules, and not until 1972 did more than 50 per cent of American homes own a colour television set. The filmic experience, therefore, would be superlative by comparison, and it would use an aspect ratio that television could not accommodate. As such, television would be seen as an inferior medium that degraded the image and subjected the narrative to unnatural rhythms. However, the intensity of the image also failed to win back film audiences.

The third strategy was to underscore the grandeur of film narrative. *Cleopatra* (1963) is the iconic example, but numerous other spectacles attest to the same impulse. Film would provide a special experience which television, with its tiny budgets and high turnover, could never duplicate. Still audiences stayed away.

Eventually, Hollywood targeted and segmented its audience. Horror films, sci-fi, beach blanket films, and anything starring Elvis Presley were aimed at the audience that least watched TV and most went out: teenagers. This eventually turned into the wave of "pornographic" films of the late 1960s and early 1970s (*I Am Curious [Yellow]*, 1969; *Carnal Knowledge*, 1971; *Deep Throat*, 1972; *Bob & Carol and Ted & Alice*, 1973).

The final and most fruitful strategy was to cooperate with television. Columbia Pictures was the first studio to produce for television (*The Adventures of Rin Tin Tin*, ABC, 1954–1959, and *Father Knows Best*, CBS, 1954–1963) but Walt Disney had the greater impact. Disney provided ABC with its first genuine hits (*Disneyland*, 1954–1961; *The Mickey Mouse Club*, 1955–1959; *Zorro*, 1957–1959). Indeed, Disney's *Davy Crockett* trilogy (1954) may have been the first film/TV crossover. The three-part series was shot in Technicolor, but broadcast in black and white. It was subsequently released to theatres as a 90-minute colour feature. It also drove the first large-scale, cross-promotional, tie-in campaign in the form of Davy Crockett hats, toy guns, lunch boxes, colouring books, pajamas, and other merchandise. Other studios followed suit, and by the end of the 1950s, they were the main providers of filmed entertainment for television. Throughout the 1960s and most of the 1970s, Hollywood provided the prototypes of stories and styles, which television imitated. These films included westerns such as *Wagon Train* (NBC/ABC, 1957–1963) and *The Virginian* (NBC, 1962–1971); situation comedies such as *Please Don't Eat the Daisies* (NBC, 1965–1967), *The Ghost and Mrs. Muir* (NBC, 1968–1970), and *M*A*S*H* (CBS, 1972–1983); science fiction such as *Voyage to the Bottom of the Sea* (ABC, 1964–1968); and crime drama such as *Naked City* (ABC, 1958–1963). In this era, television aspired to the status of film.

By the late 1970s, however, the situation had reversed. Prototypical stories and styles were now provided just as frequently by television, with Hollywood doing the imitation. The best known examples are the nine *Star Trek* films, beginning in 1979, but Hollywood has also remade *The Jetsons* (1990), *Car 54, Where Are You?* (1994), *Sergeant Bilko* (1996), *Mission: Impossible* (1996, 2000, 2006), *The X Files* (1998), *Lost in Space* (1998), *My Favorite Martian* (1999), *South Park* (1999), *Charlie's Angels* (2000, 2003), *Jackass* (2002), *Starsky and Hutch* (2004), *Bewitched* (2005), *The Dukes of Hazzard* (2005), *The A-Team* (2006), and others. By the early 1990s, film aspired to the status of television.

Along the way, beginning roughly with *Jaws* (1975), Hollywood also discovered the blockbuster, which represented a new attitude toward the audience and film distribution. The blockbuster is a film whose advertising budget typically equals or exceeds its production cost. Rather than compete with television, it uses television as part of a saturation advertising campaign in order to build up expectations for its opening weekend, where it typically earns 50 per cent or more of its entire revenue in the two days following its opening. To achieve that feat, the blockbuster is distributed simultaneously to 2,000 or more screens. Blockbusters also typically depend on spectacular special effects and offer an almost visceral experience. Their primary targets are males aged 14–25, who on average will return to the theatre to see the same film 2.5 times. Significantly though, as Epstein reports, most blockbusters fail to earn back their advertising, production, and other costs at the box office. This hardly matters, however, since their real goal is to create "intellectual property," often in the form of characters and storylines, that can be licensed to a broad range of industries and recycled in sequels, DVDs, novelizations, websites, video games, children's clothing, toy give-aways, ring tones, and other merchandising. It is in merchandising where the real money now lies, and the blockbuster should be understood principally as an expensive advertisement for a full range of cross-promotional tie-ins.

Nonetheless, two quintessentially televisual technologies, the VCR and pay-cable, proved to be Hollywood's revenge on television in the 1980s and 1990s. Both wrested control of television schedules—including the flow of images, their periodicity, and timing—from the networks and vested it in individuals. Additionally, while originally intended as a television time-shifting device, the VCR proved more attractive as a movie playback device, a characteristic since fully realized in the DVD, whose player generally possesses no recording capability. So attractive was the control afforded by the VCR over the speed, duration, and frequency of viewed material that its functionality has been integrated into the latest generation of television services. Television on-demand (TVOD) has VCR-like capability; virtually all cable and satellite suppliers offer time-shifting via multiple broadcast windows; electronic program guides (EPG) take the guesswork out of setting timers; and the list goes on. Pay-cable likewise affords multiple viewing windows, which allow the individual control over the timing, duration, and frequency of viewing. Likewise, it incorporates VCR-like controls and is the driver behind TVOD. In short, television technologies now conspire to give viewers greater control over the viewing experience. The culmination of these efforts can be found in the sudden popularity of personal and digital video recorders (PVR/DVR) such as TiVo.

Since the 1980s, audiences have also flocked to specialty channels, causing network television's audience to undergo the same precipitous decline as film audiences in the 1940s. From 1976, television's peak year, to 2005, the US network share of all television viewers has dwindled from 92 per cent to barely 45 per cent.

Now television must fight to retain its audience and is borrowing some of Hollywood's old tactics. First, though, rather than withhold product, television has chosen to flood the market. As a result, the DVD has emerged within the last five years as a privileged medium for the distribution of old television shows. Likewise, numerous specialty channels devoted to recycling television archives have come into existence.

This aftermarket produces two contradictory effects. On the one hand, it reinforces the notion that the US networks are the main, standard, or normal providers of television content. On the other hand, it also creates a market for "hard-to- see" television that frequently is not produced by the networks. Canada provides a case in point. The government forbids Canadians access to HBO, and many Canadians choose not to subscribe to TMN, its CRTC-mandated substitute. These viewers, therefore, cannot watch such highly acclaimed programs like *The Sopranos, Six Feet Under, Deadwood,* or *Rome.* However, they can purchase DVDs of the programs. As a result, the DVD has become a preferred means to access this content. However, the very nature of the DVD also removes the desired content from the rhythms and scheduling prerogatives of television itself, tending to make the experience more "cinematic" and less "televisual." It may even be logical that HBO, which began as an outlet for Hollywood studios, should now produce television content according to a filmic model. Its shows are limited-run features characterized by high production values and the type of artistic freedom usually associated with art cinema. The DVD, therefore, both reinforces network television and undermines the nature of its experience. The HBO slogan "It's not TV. It's HBO." amply captures this ambiguous process.

Television content also floods the market through the Internet, mainly via BitTorrent sites but also through Usenet and real-time streaming. The television industry has responded to downloading in the same way as the film and music industries have, though perhaps with less vigour. As broadcast television has always been given away for free, it may be somewhat counterfactual to clamp down on its equally free distribution via the Internet. Nonetheless, the Internet does create a zone of exchange beyond the control of copyright holders and such a situation is bound to attract attention.[4] Furthermore, the US Digital Millennium Copyright Act authorizes the prosecution of online file sharing, including TV files.[5]

Also unlike Hollywood, television has decided, up front, to co-operate with its competitors. It is doing so by altering both its technological characteristics and its content. From a technological point of view, television is undergoing the greatest upheaval since the current NTSC[6] standards were finalized in 1953. They are being replaced by ATSC,[7] a new set of digital standards which permits high definition broadcasts. To that end, the television set itself is being redesigned. No longer based solely on cathode-ray scanning, the new generation of fixed-pixel displays (plasma, LCD, LCoS, DLP, D-ILA) uses a high-definition, 16:9 aspect ratio that just happens to suit many feature films. Furthermore, the new generation of sets is becoming the centre of a "home theatre" experience involving multi-speaker surround sound or Dolby Digital (AC-3) systems. When computers are attached to the system, it can also become an "information hub."[8]

Consequently, convergence is occurring not just between television and film but also between television and computers. Software designers, led by Microsoft's Windows XP Home Edition, increasingly are designing interfaces that make the flat screen TV the centre of the entertainment, information, and home automation experience. This creates yet another link between television and the Internet and heightens the desire for and ease of downloading in ways uncongenial to rights holders.

These technological changes are mirrored by content changes. If the blockbuster was Hollywood's way of recapturing its audience in the 1970s, then reality TV is television's way of achieving the same outcome in the new millennium. Reality programming may be the most visible television event since *Survivor* aired as a CBS summer replacement in 2000. Reality programming serves networks in several ways. First, it brings back to TV the audience that had already abandoned it, teenagers and young adults, by tying into the Internet. Every reality TV show has a website, listserv, or forum where viewers discuss the show and producers lurk in order to gauge audience reaction. In many cases, the show's "story" is actually extended, amplified, or otherwise augmented online so that the full experience can only be enjoyed by Internet-savvy viewers: that is, to say, precisely the audience segment whose use of computers takes it away from television. The same phenomenon recurs when reality shows invite viewers to vote by cell phone or text messaging. Again, the point is to link new communication technologies to the habit of television viewing, a strategy likeliest to work with young viewers who are the earliest adopters of new technologies.

While reality TV generates huge ratings, it also manufactures celebrities who have no clout. The celebrities of reality shows need TV more than it needs them. As a result, they can never use their power to aggrandize themselves at television's expense. Indeed, the ultimate value of reality TV is to reassert television's ability to manufacture fame. Reality TV can take the truly unknown and genuinely ordinary and turn it into momentary fame. It feeds the seductive fantasy, most potent among the young, that anybody can become an American idol.

We are, therefore, confronted with television's new disposition. No longer simply an "idiot box" or "boob tube," television is, increasingly, an information hub that provides a cinematic experience with content that specifically appeals to the emergent world of gadgetry and digitization. The result is not the devaluation of the television experience but its overvaluation. The reality TV viewer who text-messages and trades views online is spending not less time with television but more. "Home theatre," therefore, encourages greater involvement in television.

Finally, of course, television and film have tended to merge as manufacturing processes, management structures, and technological infrastructures. Film is now almost wholly a digital medium, and film and television companies are now single corporate entities.[9] The spat over audience control and cultural authority has been resolved by an agreement to share in order to concentrate attention on the new threats, the Internet and video games.

Meanwhile, Back in Canada . . .

The same story could hardly be told of Canada. To be sure, American film and television—and American culture generally—exercise a significant amount of pressure upon Canadian culture. Canadians are intimately acquainted with the forms and genres of American television and the medium's technological transformations are equally important here. However, in Canada, the industries were institutionalized differently and produced different outcomes.

First, Canada possessed no equivalent of Hollywood, and no strong theatrical, acting, or literary traditions upon which the nascent medium of television could draw for its stars, technicians, producers, directors, and narratives. Next, there was no phalanx of private radio networks anxious to make the transition to television. Instead, there was the CBC, created in 1936, which then rapidly expanded to meet the requirements of war coverage in the 1940s, giving it significant expertise in news and public affairs. Hence, when it entered into television in 1952, the CBC retained not only its managerial structures and production habits but also its propensity to the factual, the documentary, and the didactic. Finally, an important segment of public opinion was distrustful of television because it disliked American culture and linked the one to the other. This cultural nationalist segment was well represented in the Massey Commission Report of 1951, which contains the blueprint for television in Canada. The Massey commissioners self-consciously wished for a television system that would be the opposite of the US system. If American television was popular and entertaining, then Canadian television would be didactic and enlightening. They rejected popular taste and sought to contain or reform it.

Canadian television was born, therefore, into a paternalistic atmosphere that sought to wean the public from its own preferences. Unfortunately, in 1951, one full year before the launch of Canadian television, there were already about 150,000 television sets in Canada. Plainly, Canadians were watching American television. In Canada, therefore, film and television did not conflict over control of the audience. Rather, television's need for a steady stream of content created the opportunity for the emergence of a production sector within Canada. However, the story of how the content was provided falls into two major time periods: (a) 1952 to 1982 and (b) 1982 to the present.

From 1952 to 1982, the CBC was the dominant producer. After 1982, however, three important events occurred: (1) Telefilm Canada was created to fund both film and television production; (2) part of the CBC's budget was transferred to Telefilm Canada for disbursal to independent production companies; (3) the CBC was instructed to acquire 50 per cent of its entertainment content from independent producers. The change transformed the CBC, after 1982, from a major in-house *producer* of Canadian content to a major *purchaser* of externally produced Canadian content, and the Canadian audiovisual landscape has come to resemble a mini-Hollywood. Nonetheless, all Canadian networks—the CBC from 1952, CTV from 1961, Global from 1975—sought to meet the need for a steady stream of content via certain characteristic strategies.

The first and most important strategy was in-house production. This had been standard practice in radio and, given the absence of independent television producers, it was an obvious response. Virtually all types of content—news, sports, children's, drama, comedy, etc.—were manufactured by consistent teams of technicians, directors, writers, producers, and other production people, who frequently were borrowed from radio. As a result, networks and television stations developed recognizable "house styles," equivalent to a Hollywood "studio style." The Canadian style has often been described as deliberate and expository. In-house production also reduced the opportunities for the emergence of an independent production sector since in-house producers acquired only from themselves. Without lucrative network sales, the few independent producers who did exist were often confined to more modest fare such as *The Littlest Hobo* (McGowan-Canamac Productions, 1963–1965), *The Forest Rangers* (CBC/ASP Productions, 1963–1965), *Adventures in Rainbow Country* (Manitou Productions Ltd./CBC/ABC Films Ltd. of Britain/Australian Broadcasting Corporation, 1970–1971), *The Starlost* (Glen-Warren Productions/CTV, 1973–1974), and *Dr. Simon Locke* (Chester Krumholz, 1971–1974). In-house production was also relatively insulated from market pressures and tended to result in very long runs. *Front Page Challenge* ran on the CBC for 25 years (1957–1983), and *The Beachcombers* ran for 18 years (1972–1990). *Reach for the Top* has been in production since 1961, and *The Nature of Things* since 1956.[10]

The second strategy was to acquire ready-made content on the international market. As the United States was the world's leading television producer, most purchases occurred there although some British content (*Dr. Who, The Avengers, Coronation Street*) and the occasional Australian program (*Skippy the Bush Kangaroo, The Terrible Ten, The Magic Boomerang*) also made it to Canadian screens. However, the global television market did not assume its current shape until European public broadcasters were hit with a wave of privatization in the mid-1980s. This phenomenon created a series of strong independent production companies driven, like the US networks, by audience ratings rather than national mandates. They were, therefore, able to rival the US networks in terms of output, market reach, and production values not because they would suddenly break into the US market—they generally have not—but because they were able to create a parallel European market within which American content became relatively less desirable. Indeed, the creation of Telefilm may be seen as part of the privatization logic which swept Europe.

The third and most recent strategy, spawned essentially after 1982, was to co-produce with other countries whose situations were similar to Canada's. Co-productions are official state-to-state treaties, and co-producing partners have access to each other's markets and resources while continuing to enjoy the full range of regulatory protection and benefits that their national situations grant. Consequently, if a Canadian production company enters into an official co-production agreement with, for example, a Spanish production company, several advantages accrue. First, both partners need only put up half the cost of the project. Both are guaranteed access to the other's market, and furthermore, in their own national market, the project will count as 100 per cent "national content." For Canadian production companies, the joint program which they co-produce will count as 100 per cent Canadian content and the production company will be eligible for the full range of financial assistance, fiscal incentives, and other benefits that apply to any fully Canadian television project. If several partners are involved, it may be possible to manufacture a 100 per cent Canadian program by investing perhaps as little as 10 per cent of the total cost. Co-productions, therefore, typically involve countries with (a) relatively small populations, (b) relatively weak or underdeveloped cultural industries, (c) similar regulatory structures, and (d) a desire or mandate to promote indigenous or national culture. Canada and France are the world's leading co-producers. Canada and the United States do not co-produce because the United States does not have a similar regulatory regime, its broadcasters and producers are governed by no national or regulatory mandate, and no benefits accrue from increased access to the Canadian market. However, Canadian and American companies can engage in *co-ventures*. These are standard business deals to manufacture a television program or series in which the partners share the costs and benefits. As in all such deals, the greatest benefit and the greatest amount of creative control go to the partner who assumes the greatest risk.

It is within the context of *co-ventures* that the infamous "point system" for establishing eligibility for government funding becomes important.[11] In order to be eligible for financial assistance, tax write-offs, and other benefits, any television production must earn at least six points on the scale. Points are awarded depending on the nationality of key creative personnel, so a project can earn points for a Canadian director (2 points), scriptwriter (2 points), lead performer (1 point), second lead performer (1 point), and so on. In contrast, *co-productions* automatically achieve the required number of points since they are governed by state-sanctioned treaties which guarantee the "nationality" of the product. Furthermore, *because* their nationality is guaranteed and *because* they are guaranteed access to markets and resources, co-producing partners are typically relieved of the pressures of the marketplace. They are free to manufacture content which may be difficult, experimental, uncommercial, or otherwise not mainstream. Co-productions, therefore, effectively *internationalize* the mandate of "national broadcasting." However, while they may be free of commercial pressures, their products may also have relatively short lifespans.[12]

It is more difficult for *co-ventures* to achieve the required points since they are merely business arrangements ungoverned by state treaties without guaranteed access to markets and resources.

Co-ventures, therefore, involve "creative negotiation" intended to achieve two objectives: (a) manufacture a product that will enjoy international success and (b) manufacture a product which does not run afoul of the point system and may therefore access governmental assistance. As such, co-ventures typically result in projects that are commercial but not *too* commercial.

Finally, so powerful is the draw of international success that even many official co-productions are structured in such a way as to include a US co-venture. The point is not only for the official co-producers to gain access to each other's markets and resources or to manufacture "national content," but also, and more crucially, to gain access to the immensely rewarding US market. A classic example is *Bordertown* (1989–1991), a Canada/France co-production with co-venture participation from the US Family Channel. The plot concerns a town located on the border between Canada and the US policed by both a Mountie and a sheriff, whose mutual love interest is a female doctor from France. The setup is plainly intended to appeal to various national audiences as well as to national regulators while gaining a US window. *Katts and Dog* (1989–1991) followed a similar strategy. Set in a generic North American city, this Canada/France co-production, which aired on CTV and the US Family Channel (the co-venturer), also included a French policewoman who regularly flew her fellow officers to Paris to solve crime in that city.

While Canadian and other producers are strongly motivated to break into the US market, American producers are rarely motivated to break into the Canadian market. They already have access, their product is already highly valued, and the Canadian market represents but a fraction of their overall business. Were they suddenly to be shut out of the Canadian market, the Canadian networks who depend on them, not the American producers themselves, would suffer the most. There is, consequently, no business case for the exclusion of American content from Canadian television.

The true advantage to US producers lies in the cheap Canadian dollar,[13] the availability of well-trained crews who speak English and know American television, and the proximity of Vancouver to Los Angeles. For these reasons, many American shows are shot in Canada and governments extend fiscal benefits to the production companies in order to buoy local economies. From the American perspective, these shoots are called "runaway productions," and from the Canadian perspective, they are often called "industrial" or "inauthentic" Canadian content. They also constitute an employment policy typical of many countries.

What may be striking about the industrial development of Canadian television outlined above is how unrelated it is to the standard story of television in this country. That story is too well known to warrant detailed repetition here, but it may be briefly summarized as "a small culture struggles heroically to 'tell its own stories' over and against a predatory presence from the South." That struggle produces some fine moments (*Wayne and Shuster, The National Dream, Canada: A People's History*) but is consistently betrayed by indolent politicians, unfair markets, and the inexplicable preference of audiences for American content. This last fact is attributed to the sheer frequency of exposure to American culture, which results in an ideological misrecognition whereby Canadians mistake American television for what they really like while simultaneously neglecting the Canadian television that they ought to like. Its most pathological manifestations occur in those people who belong to the grey and black satellite markets, who demand access to HBO, ESPN, and other US pay-cable channels, and who download TV from the Internet. From the perspective of the standard story told, they are engaged in criminal behaviour: they divert resources from Canadian industry, they steal, they fail to display the requisite markers of citizenship—they should be punished. The logical response in the standard story, therefore, is to wean Canadians from their mistaken preferences through a complex set of regulatory structures that will channel them toward approved choices and impose cost or entry barriers to some types of content (linkage and tiering rules), prohibit access to various content providers (the approved channel distribution list), and systematically substitute Canadian equivalents for US originals (simultaneous substitution and CRTC licensing policies). Failure to embrace this structure becomes itself further evidence of the very pathology it is intended to cure.

Clearly, our knowledge of the history of television is still very underdeveloped. This is even more so in Canada where the story of its development has been entirely absorbed into the narrative of cultural defence. As a result, most scholars can parrot some version of the heroic struggle for national broadcasting but almost no one knows about developments in private broadcasting, the pragmatic questions which affect all production companies, the types of debates they arouse, the relationships they entertain with audiences, the content which typifies them, and so on.

This should cause us to study the way we study television.

Television Study

Television did not undergo the transformation that affected film studies, when, at some point in the 1950s or 1960s, film became an art form, or at least a non-pathological activity, worthy of academic attention. This was greatly assisted by the arrival of television itself, which assumed the mantle of "phobic social object" from the movies. Now, all the fears that had once belonged to film—juvenile delinquency, illicit sexual knowledge, unhealthy relationships, bad habits, violence, and other social evils—could be projected onto television. Consequently, film came to be housed in film departments at universities across North America, whereas television remained a problem: an object of sociological and psychological inquiry.

Indeed, the most salient feature of the study of television may be its institutional dispersal. Psychologists, sociologists, film scholars, physicians, criminologists, political scientists, communication scholars, industry analysts, columnists, TV commentators, and others have all had something to say about it. No discipline has claimed television exclusively as its own nor has television generated its own stable set of questions or methods. It has not marked out its "field" or acquired disciplinary autonomy, and no common problematic unites its researchers. It is, instead, an object—usually a bad one—upon which anyone may produce a discourse. The resultant cacophony is deafening.

For example, between June 2004 and June 2005, television was implicated in childhood obesity, the early onset of puberty, a propensity toward bullying, and a net gain in intelligence. That this list should be neither believable nor coherent indicates the distance which separates the study of film from that of television. Indeed, every year, the TV Turnoff Network (www.tvturnoff.org) organizes "TV Turn Off Week." In 2005, the theme was "More Reading, Less TV" in the classroom. One can barely imagine a similar campaign to boycott film or newspapers or popular music for one week every year, with the enthusiastic support of the usual cast of reformers, concerned parents, citizens groups, and watchdog organizations. Naturally, in 2002, the classic crackpot denunciation of television, Marie Winn's *The Plug-in Drug,* was reissued in a special 25th anniversary edition.

Clearly, to many, television is a social problem to be solved, not an expressive form to be appreciated. It is an industry driven by base motives and low regard for its audience, not an intellectual or artistic enterprise. It produces effects, outcomes, and impacts to be diagnosed, neutralized, and guarded against, not meanings to be shared or circulated. It is an excellent scapegoat for all manners of unhappiness.

But is this bad? Why *should* television have a particular domain in which only those with the requisite knowledge are invited to play? For example, movie theatres admit anyone with the price of admission and everyone can have an opinion about movies, even the ones they have not seen. No prior knowledge is required. This is surely the function of the perennial debate on television violence: It permits people who otherwise would be shut out to enter the field of public debate. People who have no standing in industry discussions, who can not enter the policy discourse, who do not understand statistics, who are not part of the world of celebrity, or who find their aesthetic preferences dismissed can nonetheless produce a discourse that creates a discourse of alarm and concern over television violence that resounds in the public sphere.

The problem, of course, is not whether everyone should or should not be allowed to express an opinion. There is likely no good way to prevent it. The problem is whether, from an intellectual point of view, we should be satisfied with the mere republic of views or should, rather, strive to produce a specialized discourse, which at least claims to generate new knowledge and new questions.

One of the most influential attempts was made by Raymond Williams, with his concept of "flow." However, ever the moralist, Williams was actually referring to the "single irresponsible flow of images and feelings" typical of American television which mixed the program itself with commercials, station breaks, news updates, promos, and so on.[14] Williams found it all very confusing and downright . . . irresponsible. He did not want people to watch *television,* but to watch *programs.* He hoped that television might aspire to the status of film and valued the "one-off" play or presentation. His volume of television criticism (see O'Connor) is very eloquent in this regard.

One of the things that the concept of flow underscores is the sheer quantity of television. There is just so much of it! Its production cycle is so tight that it is very difficult to compass all of it, and someone who did would immediately fall suspect to the judgment of others ("You watch *how much* TV?"). There are 431 episodes of *Bonanza,* 73 hours of *Star Trek,* 248 hours (so far) of *ER,* 255 episodes of *M*A*S*H,* and so on. No wonder people watch DVDs. Furthermore, the "text" of study is highly elusive. It is bound up in strange temporalities, which include the original air dates, summer reruns, syndication, late afternoon stripping, revivals on rerun channels, spin-offs, reunion shows, "the making of" documentaries, and so on. What is the object of the study? A particular episode of an ongoing series? The series itself? With or without commercials? Within the network schedule or in syndication? The experience of watching the show? The answer, of course, is all of these. Together, they make up the institution of television: its products, its modes of production and distribution, the rhythms of their circulation, the discourses surrounding them. Basically, we want to know how *that* program, mediated through *those* structures, produced *this* feeling in *that* audience, a slight transformation of Lasswell's famous approach to communication as the study of "who says what, in which channel, to whom, with what effect?"

Nonetheless, the enduring value of the concept of flow was to get us to think of television *not* as film but as *broadcasting,* as an endless stream of content washing over us. Of course, the only people who needed such encouragement were those who persisted in seeing it as a subspecies of film. People who had always thought of television as an extension of radio needed much less encouragement. This may be why *The Burns and Allen Show* (CBS, 1950–1958) generated so much talk. Anyone who has seen the show knows that it possesses certain apparently unique characteristics: George Burns frequently interrupts the narrative flow in order to comment, directly to the camera, on the events of the show so far; announcer Harry Von Zell slips in and out of the narrative as both announcer and character; the sets are clearly presented as sets; commercials are folded into the dialogue; and so on. For scholars who approached television from the perspective of film, attending to the uniqueness of the image and the semiotic coherence of the text, this approach was postmodern, or at the very least late modern, as it shattered the conventions of the fourth wall, and confronted viewers with the materiality—or at least the artifice—of what they were watching. The argument is well known and need hardly be repeated here. What this says about the audience—were they upset by George's shenanigans and the show's failure to adhere to conventions, simply confused and disoriented, enthusiastic endorsers of irony?—is a question rarely broached.

However, it may be worth noting that for scholars who approached television from the perspective of broadcasting, it was just business as usual. They attended to the strategy of contact implicit in the show, to the way in which it addressed its audience, and included it in the very construction of the narrative. Burns and Allen had transferred their act from radio, and radio, like television, had always mixed the sound of the program with advertising, news updates, and promos. Indeed, the most characteristic of radio forms, the soap opera, was so named in recognition of the mutual imbrication of commerce and narrative, and of advertising with storytelling. Consequently, a late successor such as *Seinfeld* could be either the herald of postmodern television or the extension of virtually any radio comedy of the 1930s and 1940s.

Whatever status we may wish to assign various sitcoms, the very desire to do so underscores one of our most pressing needs: the construction of a usable television history. To that extent, the standard story of the struggle between Hollywood and the US networks may do more harm than good. While it gets many facts right, it also ignores others which do not fit its paradigm. Indeed, its unspoken presupposition is that we should understand television as the interloper in the garden of filmic Eden rather than see film, for example, as an imperfect attempt to create television: that we should value the historical experience of film (our nostalgia for a lost "language of film") over the evolving reconstruction of the television experience.

Likewise the standard Canadian story, which links television to cultural defence, systematically substitutes its version of "good" culture to the observable behaviour and preferences of audiences. It, too, gets many facts right but it also virtually eliminates the possibility of studying audiences on their own terms. In linking television to cultural defence, it imagines audiences as imperilled—the garrison mentality—and audience preferences as errors in need of correction. Its unspoken presupposition is its narrow definition of culture.

Like all histories, these standard stories should be treated as invitations to rewrite them, but rewriting history requires that we investigate it. Our knowledge of television history remains inadequate. We have not asked questions about production, distribution, exhibition, and audiences, which would supply us with pragmatic knowledge on the basis of which fruitful speculation could occur. This is especially true in the case of Canada, where such pragmatic knowledge is almost totally non-existent but where disquisitions on the role and meaning of policy abound. Indeed, in Canada, the discourse of cultural defence and its attendant policy manifestations have substituted themselves for pragmatic knowledge.

A usable history would necessarily raise the question of the audience. There is no television without an audience to which it is addressed. One of the great classics of broadcasting research, Merton's *Mass Persuasion: The Social Psychology of a War Bond Drive* (1946) is subtitled "a study in convergence" precisely in order to underscore the mutual imbrication of audience with message. Unfortunately, the audience is usually left out of discussions of television, except inasmuch as it can be characterized as unintelligent or victimized. Television itself usually includes the audience only as statistics or as the appreciative background to talk shows, quiz shows, and contest shows. However, most of our statements about television are also statements about the audience. To condemn television as a "vast wasteland" is to take a very dim view of the audience that attends to it. To praise *Seinfeld* as ironic is to presume knowledge on the part of the audience.

This is not a call to revisit Fiske's (or other) work on the "active" or "resistant" audience; that work exists in tension with, and in response to, the contrary tendency to view audiences as manipulated or victimized by-products of a capitalist system. It is, rather, a wish to undertake fundamental research on the historical constitution and evolution of television audiences. Here again, Canada provides an excellent case in point. As we have seen, Canadian television, in its English-language version, emerged as a self-distant medium dedicated to a socially meliorative project. However, in its French-language version, it emerged as a hugely popular, demotic medium dedicated to the celebration of self. As a result, French-language television, with its popularity, star system, flurry of celebratory publications and spin-offs, talk and quiz shows, prime-time dramas, *téléromans,* appreciation of particular shows, advertising industry, and feverish anticipation of the new season, resembles nothing so much as American television. Not only is this state virtually unimaginable in English-language television, it also highlights certain persistent distortions in our study of television. As well, the state of French-language television should greatly distress all technological determinists. Canada is the textbook example of how a single technology, housed within identical structures, nonetheless produces wildly divergent outcomes. Furthermore, to the extent that the wild success of French-language television underscores the modesty of English-language television, it poses a fundamental question: How did one version reach an audience while another did not? This points us firmly in the direction of attempting to understand how strategies of contact are implemented. Finally, it further highlights the shortcomings of our standard history of Canadian television. The story writes out entirely the experience of French-language television, which obviously fails to conform to the narrative. It is a thoroughly cultural nationalist story that disqualifies what audiences *really* watch in favour of prescriptions for what audiences *should* watch. It is exclusively condemnatory of the role of private broadcasting, and espouses the agenda of the state and regulatory agencies uncritically.

The audience is a significant blind spot in the study of television, especially in Canada. There are good reasons for this blind spot. To study audience behaviour is to recognize that Canadian audiences have expressed a range of attitudes and opinions that frequently fall outside the bounds of the official story of television. Audiences like the wrong things, and often in very great quantity. To study audiences is to recognize that they have happily consumed vast amounts of American television with no apparent concern for their enduring national identity. It may even force us to recognize the audience's sophistication as cultural consumers, something which flatly contradicts the standard narrative whose preferred audience is weak, victimized, and imperilled. To study the audience, therefore, underscores the inadequacy of the standard television history and the failure of the policies and structures which it justified.

In this context, the history of television is not the history of successful shows, the unveiling of a new season, the celebration of stars, famous moments, or breakthrough formats; it is the history of regulation and of attempts to reform audience tastes, to protect market incumbents, and to shore up the legitimacy of the regulator. In Canada, no one studies television more than the government, and the types of knowledge useful to governments have tended to pass over into the common sense of everyday television talk.

That Canadian television should have failed to connect with popular audiences is hardly surprising when it deprived itself of the tools to do so and when it construed such connection as evidence of cultural degeneracy. As a result, with few exceptions, English-language television failed to develop the habit of regular tuning; it failed to create a star system; and it failed to draw to itself a loyal and popular audience.[15]

Of course, this failure does not belong to television alone. It is symptomatic of the general weakness of civil society. The autonomous spheres of individual action, which could form a public, tend to be colonized by the state and its agencies, and so it is of television. In short, English speakers viewed television with suspicion, as a Trojan horse of Americanization, rather than ask themselves why they were attracted to American culture. They declined to investigate their own civil society. French speakers, however, looked upon television with delight, as the medium that would finally allow all to speak to all. They viewed it as an extension of civil society.

As a result, Canadians are preoccupied with CRTC regulations, licensing hearings, the rules of simultaneous substitution, grey and black market satellite systems, and other legal and regulatory issues, and the intellectuals who study television have tended to adopt this policy discourse uncritically. They have tended to assume the role of those who would *explain* policy choices to recalcitrant audiences: of those who would *defend* the imperilled culture, not least against those who failed to appreciate it. The problem with policy discourse is that it sees audience preferences as a problem to be solved. Rather than take audience preferences as reliable indicators of what markets should produce, policy discourse takes them as errors to be corrected through the application of access controls, import substitutions, the development of a discourse of guilt and shame, and an intricate web of interlocking regulations, amongst other methods.

Besides constructing a usable history and examining the constitution of audiences, then, the third major task we may wish to undertake is one of detachment from the policy discourse of governments. This does not mean an outright condemnation of policy discourse or a systematic refusal to accept some of its terms. It means the refusal to adopt its point of view systematically, as the principal or necessary or natural starting point. It means returning policy discourse to its genuine status of one discourse amongst many.

Significantly, by rejecting the primacy of policy discourse, we may find ourselves freer to undertake historical investigation and to treat audience constitution seriously.

Conclusion

A spectre haunts television studies: the Internet. We already know that computer use has significantly displaced television viewing time, especially among the young. We also know that the Internet is already surrounded by a discourse of outrageous alarm and denunciation. It is, apparently, the playground of international criminals, pornographers, privacy thieves, hackers, spammers, and all manner of undesirables. In short, it may be poised to assume the mantle of phobic object and to relieve television of that burden.

Perhaps television is about to be transformed into a non-pathological activity. Just as likely, though, is the possibility that television as we know it is about to disappear as an object altogether as it is absorbed into other technological systems and experiences. Film and television may even achieve a common destiny as versions of each other.

Notes

1. See Sterling and Kittross, 337–8, 398.
2. Phonevision was run by the Zenith Radio Corporation in Chicago in 1951. Skiatron Electronics and Television Corporation launched "Subscriber-Vision" in New York in 1953. International Telemeter Corporation operated in Palm Springs, California, from 1953 to 1955. Video Independent Theaters operated "Telemovies" in Bartlesville, Oklahoma, in 1957 and 1958. From 1960 to 1965, International Telemeter Corporation operated a coin-box pay-TV system in Etobicoke, Ontario. From 1962 to 1968, Phonevision, now jointly owned by RKO and Zenith, operated a pay-TV system in Hartford, Connecticut. In 1964, Subscription Television Inc. (STV) was launched in San Francisco and Los Angeles. Several other pay-TV systems were also attempted.
3. Hitchcock is best remembered for *Alfred Hitchcock Presents* (CBS/NBC, 1955–1965) of which he directed the first episode of every season. However, he also directed episodes of *Suspicion* (NBC, 1957–1958), *Ford Startime* (NBC, 1959–1960), and *The Alfred Hitchcock Hour* (CBS/NBC,

1962–1965). Ridley Scott is currently the executive producer of *Numb3rs* (CBS, 2005–present) but also directed episodes of *R3* (BBC, 1964–1965), *Reluctant Bandit* (BBC, 1965), *Out of the Unknown* (BBC, 1965–1971), and *Z Cars* (BBC, 1962–1978), and is planning a television mini-series based on *The Andromeda Strain* (1971).

4. Indeed, in a 2002 interview with Cableworld, Jamie Kellner, president and CEO of Turner Broadcasting, described people who use PVRs or other devices to watch television without the commercials as actually stealing from the copyright holders!
5. Significantly, though, in a refreshingly forward-looking move, the BBC has decided not to withhold its television content from the Internet but to use the Internet as a new distribution medium. This decision was announced by BBC Director General Mark Thompson in August 2005 at the Edinburgh Film Festival. Mr Thompson even added that, unless the BBC undertook to do so, "we won't deserve or get licence-fee funding beyond 2016" (BBC News).
6. NTSC stands for National Television System Committee and is the name given to the set of technical standards adopted in North America and certain other parts of the world for television broadcasting. It resulted from an extended series of meetings amongst television set manufacturers, broadcasters, and regulators in the United States between 1941 and 1953.
7. ATSC stands for Advanced Television Systems Committee and is the name given to the set of technical standards adopted in North America and some other parts of the world for digital and high-definition television broadcasting. It resulted from an extended series of talks amongst television set manufacturers, patent rights holders, inventors, regulators, universities, and international partners in the United States between 1986 and 1994. See Brinkley.
8. The ATSC broadcast standard requires high-definition broadcasts to incorporate digital Dolby or AC-3 surround sound. The boom in home theatre is therefore part of the technical standards of the new generation of television receivers. Likewise, virtually all ATSC sets come equipped with connectors for computer hookup.
9. Sony acquired Columbia, Disney acquired ABC, Viacom Paramount acquired CBS, Fox acquired Fox, and so on.
10. *Reach for the Top* began local production in 1961, and went national in 1966. The CBC stopped production in 1984, and the show was syndicated to private broadcasters across Canada in the same year.
11. The point system for radio, film, and television is available online at http://news.bbc.co.uk/2/hi/entertainment/default.stm.
12. An official list of co-productions for both film and television may be accessed from the Telefilm Canada website at http://www.telefilm.gc.ca/04/48/482.asp.
13. This article was written before the rise in the value of the Canadian dollar in 2007 that has brought the two currencies to near parity. It is too early to tell what the impact of parity will be on "runaway" production but if historical precedent holds, it will not be good.
14. Williams's comment about "irresponsible flow" occurs on page 94 of *Television: Technology and Cultural Form*. The Department of Radio, Television and Film at the University of Texas has named its recent online television publication *Flow*. See http://idg.communication.utexas.edu/flow/links.php.
15. The exceptions may be worth noting. The CBC, in particular, has had considerable success in manufacturing an audience for sport, especially hockey. It has also earned a well-deserved reputation for daring to air "difficult" programming; this runs the gamut from ballet and opera to narratively challenging content and documentaries. In short, then, the attempt to use regulation to create an audience relationship not based exclusively on commercial motives is neither an unmitigated disaster nor an unworthy undertaking.

Works Cited

Anderson, Christopher. *Hollywood TV: The Studio System in the Fifties*. Austin: U of Texas P, 1994.

BBC News. "BBC TV Channels to be Put on Net." 27 August 2005. 7 November 2007 <http://news.bbc.co.uk/2/hi/entertainment/4187036.stm>.

Brinkley, Joel. *Defining Vision: The Battle for the Future of Television*. New York: Harcourt Brace, 1997.

Department of Canadian Heritage. "Canadian Content Rules." Winter 2001. 6 November 2007 <http://www.pch.gc.ca/progs/ac-ca/pubs/can-con/can_con.html>.

CTV News. "Kids' Obesity Linked to Watching TV in New Study." 16 July 2004. 7 November 2007 <http://www.ctv.ca/servlet/ArticleNews/story/CTVNews/1089982726139_85391926?hub=Health>.

Epstein, Edward Jay. *The Big Picture: The New Logic of Money and Power in Hollywood*. New York: Random House, 2005.

Jenkins, C. Francis. *Radiomovies, Radiovision, Television*. Washington: Jenkins Laboratories, 1929.

Johnson, Steven. "Watching TV Makes You Smarter." *The New York Times Magazine* 24 April 2005: 55–59.

Journal of the American Medical Association. "Early Home Environment and Television Watching Influence Bullying Behavior." *ScienceDaily* 21 April 2005. 6 November 2007 <http://www.sciencedaily.com/releases/2005/04/050420091955.htm>.

Kenter, Peter, with notes by Martin Levin. *TV North*. Vancouver: Whitecap, 2001.

Menand, Louis. "Gross Points. Is the Blockbuster the End of Cinema?" *The New Yorker* 7 February 2005. 7 November 2007 <http://www.newyorker.com/archive/2005/02/07/050207crat_atlarge>.

Merton, Robert. *Mass Persuasion: The Social Psychology of a War Bond Drive*. New York: Harper, 1946.

Newcomb, Horace, ed. *The Encyclopedia of Television*. Chicago: Fitzroy Dearborn, 1997.

O'Connor, Alan, ed. *Raymond Williams on Television: Selected Writings*. New York: Routledge, 1989.

Ritchie, Michael. *Please Stand By: A Prehistory of Television, 1920–1947*. Woodstock, NY: The Overlook Press, 1994.

Sterling, Christopher H., and John Michael Kittross. *Stay Tuned: A History of American Broadcasting*. 3rd edn. Mahwah, NJ: Lawrence Erlbaum, 2002.

Telefilm Canada. "Coproductions officielles." 2004. <http://www.telefilm.gc.ca/04/48.asp>.

Vince, Gaia. "Television Watching May Hasten Puberty." *New Scientist* 28 June 2004. 7 November 2007 <http://www.newscientist.com/article.ns?id=dn6081>.

Williams, Raymond. *Television: Technology and Cultural Form*. London: Fontana, 1974.

Part II | Discussion Questions

Introduction: A Political Economy of TV Broadcasting in Canada and the United States

1. What business or economic factors determined the existence of your favourite TV show?
2. What is a TV schedule? How does advertising shape what kinds of TV shows are scheduled by TV networks?
3. What is cultural policy? How does cultural policy shape the activities of the TV network you watch most? What are the most important contemporary cultural policy issues that shape TV?
4. What is the difference between private TV broadcasting and public TV broadcasting? Is public TV broadcasting relevant in the twenty-first century? Why?
5. What is Canadian content? Select a specific Canadian TV show and discuss what makes it distinctly "Canadian." Must a TV show satisfy "Canadian content" regulations to be considered by viewers as "Canadian"? Why or why not? Do you think Canadian content regulations are needed to protect and promote distinctly Canadian TV shows?

2 | The Radio Act of 1927: Progressive Ideology, Epistemology, and Praxis

1. What is progressivism? Are the values of progressivism represented by *contemporary* US broadcasting policy? Do you think the values of progressivism are relevant today?
2. How did the Radio Act of 1927 limit the parameters of free speech? Do you feel that speech on TV should be limited in certain ways? Which kinds of speech? Why?
3. What were some of the practical reasons for limiting the number of radio stations on the airwaves in the United States in the 1920s? In the era of digital broadcasting, do these limits still exist?
4. What is the "public interest"? Select a contemporary broadcasting policy document, speech, or related news article. Examine how the "public interest" is constructed. According to the document or speech, what is the "public interest"? Does the "public interest" reflect your interest? If not, whose "public interest" is represented?
5. How did the commercial radio industry benefit from the Radio Act of 1927? How specifically? What contemporary policies benefit the contemporary TV industry? How specifically?

3 | Women's Work

1. What does Spigel mean by women's "unpaid labour" in the home? Do twenty-first-century women do unpaid domestic work? Do you think the representation of gender by TV shows encourages or discourages women's unpaid labour in the home? Provide examples.
2. Why did early American TV networks target women? Do contemporary TV networks target women as their viewers? Which ones? How does a specific TV network construct women as its "ideal consumer"? What particular kind of woman is targeted by the TV network?
3. Are contemporary TV networks that target women as consumers motivated by the same economic imperatives that motivated TV networks to target women 60 years ago? Why? How? What is the same? What has changed? Discuss with reference to a particular TV network.

4. Why was the soap opera such an important TV genre? Are soap operas still important to TV networks? Are any soap operas ever made for a male audience demographic? Discuss with reference to contemporary examples.
5. How was consumerism and domesticity promoted by early network TV shows? Select a current TV show about women. Does the TV show promote "old-fashioned" domestic-consumerism to women or are alternative visions of femininity available?

4 | Canada

1. Why was the establishment of a distribution system important to Canada's early broadcasters?
2. Why was early broadcasting established and perceived as a "public service" in Canada?
3. What is the CBC's funding model? What funding models for TV does Canada draw on?
4. What is the significance of the Broadcasting Act of 1968 and the Broadcasting Act of 1991?
5. What is the function and mandate of the Canadian Radio-television and Telecommunications Commission (CRTC)?

5 | A Usable History for the Study of Television

1. How did the US film industry respond to the emergence of TV? How did this response change over time?
2. In the era of globalization and technological convergence, what are some of the main economic and cultural challenges facing Canada's film and TV production and distribution industries?
3. Why are the TV and film industries in Canada different than those in the United States? Compare and contrast the TV and film industries of Canada and the United States. How are these two industries similar and different? In the twenty-first century, are these industries converging?
4. Select a Canadian TV show. How does the TV show "imagine" Canadian national identity? Who is represented as belonging to Canada and who is not? Do you think the TV show reflects Canada or contributes to the construction of Canada? Do you feel more or less Canadian when watching the TV show? Do you think people rely on TV shows to get a sense of what it means to be a citizen of the Canadian state?
5. How does Attallah criticize the "nationalist paradigm" in Canadian television studies?

Suggestions for Further Reading

Political Economy, Production, and Culture Industry Studies

Babe, R. (1995). *On Political Economy. Communication and the Transformation of Economics.* Boulder, CO: Westview Press.

———. (2009). *Cultural Studies and Political Economy: Toward a New Integration.* Lanham, MD: Lexington Books.

Baker, C.E. (2001). *Media, Markets and Democracy.* New York: Cambridge University Press.

Banks, M., and Hesmondhalgh, D. (2009). "Looking for Work in Creative Industries Policy." *International Journal of Cultural Policy,* Vol. 15(4): 415–30.

Betting, R.V., and Hall, J.L. (2003). *Big Money, Big Media: Cultural Texts and Political Economics.* Lanham, MD: Rowman & Littlefield.

Calabrese, A., and Sparks, C. (Eds). (2004). *Toward a Political Economy of Culture: Capitalism and Communication in the Twenty-first Century.* Lanham, MD: Rowman & Littlefield.

Caldwell, J.T. (2008). *Production Culture: Industrial Reflexivity and Critical Practice in Film and Television*. Durham: Duke University Press.

Cowen, T. (1998). *In Praise of Commercial Culture*. Cambridge, MA: Harvard University Press.

Curtin, M. (1997). "On Edge: Culture Industries in the Neo-Network Era." In R. Ohmann (Ed.), *Making and Selling Culture* (pp. 181–202). Hanover, NH: Wesleyan University Press.

Curtin, M., and Shattuc, J. (2009). *The American Television Industry*. London: British Film Institute.

Deuze, M. (2007). *Media Work*. New York: Polity.

Dorland, M. (Ed.). (1996). *The Cultural Industries in Canada*. Toronto: James Lorimer & Company.

Garnham, N. (1999). "Political Economy and Cultural Studies." In S. During (Ed.), The Cultural Studies Reader (pp. 492–503). New York: Routledge.

———. (2005). "From Cultural to Creative Industries." *International Journal of Cultural Policy*, Vol. 11(1): 15–29.

Gomery, D., and Hockley, L. (Eds). (2006). *Television Industries*. London: British Film Institute.

Grossberg, L. (1999). "Cultural Studies vs. Political Economy: Is Anybody Else Bored with this Debate?" In J. Storey (Ed.), *Cultural Theory and Popular Culture* (pp. 614–24). New York: Routledge.

Hall, S. (1993). "Which Public, Whose Service?" In W. Stevenson (Ed.), *All Our Futures: The Changing Role and Purpose of the BBC*. London: British Film Institute.

Hartley, J. (Ed.). (2005). Creative Industries. Malden, MA: Blackwell.

Havens, T., Lotz, A.D., and Tinic, S. (2009). "Critical Media Industry Studies: A Research Approach." Communication, Culture & Critique, Vol. 2(2): 234–53.

Hesmondhalgh, D. (2007). *The Cultural Industries*. Thousand Oaks, CA: Sage Publications.

Hesmondhalgh, D., and Pratt, A.C. (2005). "Cultural Industries and Cultural Policy." *International Journal of Cultural Policy*, Vol. 11(1): 1–13.

Holt, J., and Perren, A. (Eds). (2009). *Media Industries: History, Theory and Method*. Malden, MA: Wiley-Blackwell.

Howkins, J. (2007). *The Creative Economy: How People Make Money from Ideas*. New York: Penguin.

Innis, H.A. (1972). *Empire and Communication*. Toronto: University of Toronto Press.

McChesney, R.W. (2004). *The Problem with the U.S. Media: Communication Politics in the 21st Century*. London: Monthly Review Press.

———. (2007). *Communication Revolution: Critical Junctures and the Future of Media*. New York: The New Press.

———. (2008). *The Political Economy of Media: Enduring Issues, Emerging Dilemmas*. New York: Monthly Review Press.

Mayer, V., Banks, M., and Caldwell, J. (Eds). (2009). *Production Studies: Cultural Studies of Media Industries*. New York: Routledge.

Mosco, V. (2008). "Current Trends in the Political Economy of Communication." *Global Media Journal: Canadian Edition*, Vol. 1(1): 45–63.

Murdock, G., and Wasko, J. (Eds). (2007). *Media in the Age of Marketization*. Creskill, NJ: Hampton Press.

Schiller, H.I. (1989). *Culture, Inc.: The Corporate Takeover of Public Expression*. New York: Oxford University Press.

Smythe, D. (1981). *Dependency Road: Communications, Capitalism, Consciousness and Canada*. Norwood, NJ: Ablex.

Sparks, R. (1992). "Delivering the Male: Sports, Canadian Television, and the Making of TSN." *Canadian Journal of Communication*, Vol. 17(1): 319–42.

Tinic, S. (2010). "The Global Economic Meltdown: A Crisotunity for Canada's Private Sector Broadcasters?" *Popular Communication*, Vol. 8(3): 193–97.

Ursell, G. (2000). "Television Production: Issues of Exploitation, Commodification and Subjectivity in UK Television Labour Markets." *Media, Culture & Society*, Vol. 22(1): 805–25.

Winseck, D. (2002). "Netscapes of Power: Convergence, Consolidation and Power in the Canadian Mediascape." *Media, Culture & Society*, Vol. 24(6): 795–819.

———. (2010). "Financialization and the 'Crisis of the Media': The Rise and Fall of (Some) Media Conglomerates in Canada." *Canadian Journal of Communication*, Vol. 35(3): 365–93.

Cultural Policy

Armstrong, R. (2010). *Broadcasting Policy in Canada*. Toronto: University of Toronto Press.

Bennet, T. (1992). "Putting Policy into Cultural Studies." In L. Grossberg, C. Nelson, and P. Reichler (Eds), *Cultural Studies* (pp. 23–37). New York: Routledge.

Bennet, T., and Mercer, C. (1996). "Improving Research and International Cooperation for Cultural Policy." Paper prepared for UNESCO on behalf of the Australian Key Center for Cultural and Media Policy.

Cunningham, S. (2009). "Creative Industries as a Globally Contestable Policy Field." *Chinese Journal of Communication*, Vol. 2(1): 13–24.

Demers, F. (2003). "Canadian Television: The Exhaustion of a Domestic Paradigm?" *Journal of Broadcasting and Electronic Media*, Vol. 1: 656–61.

Edwardson, R. (2008). *Canadian Content: Culture and the Quest for Nationhood*. Toronto: University of Toronto Press.

Flew, T. (2005). "Sovereignty and Software: Rethinking Cultural Policy in a Global Creative Economy." *International Journal of Cultural Policy*, Vol. 11(3): 243–60.

Freedman, D. (2008). *The Politics of Media Policy*. Cambridge: Polity Press.

Livingstone, S., Lunt, P., and Miller, L. (2007). "Citizens and Consumers: Discursive Debates during and after the Communications Act 2003." *Media, Culture & Society*, Vol. 29(4): 613–38.

McGuigan, J. (2004). *Rethinking Cultural Policy.* Maidenhead: Open University Press.

———. (2005). "Neo-Liberalism, Culture and Policy." *International Journal of Cultural Policy*, Vol. 11(3): 229–41.

Milz, S. (2007). "Canadian Cultural Policy-making at a Time of Neoliberal Globalization." *ESC: English Studies in Canada*, Vol. 33(1–2): 85–107.

Pennee, D. (1999). "Culture as Security: Canadian Foreign Policy and International Relations from the Cold War to the Market Wars." *International Journal of Canadian Studies*, Vol. 20(1): 191–213.

Raboy, M., and Shtern, J. (2010). *Media Divides: Communication Rights and the Right to Communicate in Canada.* Vancouver: UBC Press.

Rintels, J. (2006). "Big Chill: How the FCC's Indecency Decisions Stifle Free Expression, Threaten Quality Television and Harm America's Children." www.creativevoices.us/cgi-upload/news/news_article/CVPaperFINAL092106.pdf

Taras, D. (2001). *Power and Betrayal in the Canadian Media.* Peterborough: Broadview Press.

Throsby, D. (2001). *Economics and Culture.* Cambridge: Cambridge University Press.

———. (2010). *The Economics of Cultural Policy.* Cambridge: Cambridge University Press.

Vaidhyanathan, S. (2005). "Remote Control: The Rise of Electronic Cultural Policy." *The Annals of the American Academy*, Vol. 597: 122–33.

Wagman, I. (2001). "Rock the Nation: MuchMusic, Cultural Policy, and the Development of English Canadian Music Video Programming, 1979–1984." *Canadian Journal of Communication*, Vol. 26: 47–62.

———. (2007). "The B Side: Why Content Regulations Aren't Necessary for the Survival of Canadian Music." In J. Greenberg and C. Elliot (Eds), *Communication in Question* (pp. 223–29). Toronto: ITP Nelson.

———. (2010). "On the Policy Reflex in Canadian Communication Studies." *Canadian Journal of Communication*, Vol. 35: 619–30.

Wagman, I., and Winton, E. (2010). "Canadian Cultural Policy in the Age of Media Abundance: Old Challenges, New Technologies." In L.R. Shade (Ed.), *Canadian Mediascapes* (pp. 61–77). Toronto: Nelson Education.

Canadian and American TV Broadcasting History

Balas, G.R. (2003). *Recovering a Public Vision for Public Television.* Lanham: Rowman & Littlefield.

Barnouw, R. (1990). *Tube of Plenty: The Evolution of American Television.* New York: Oxford University Press.

Blevins, D. (2011). *Television Networks: More than 750 American and Canadian Broadcasters and Cable Networks.* New York: McFarland Press.

Boddy, W. (1990). *Fifties Television: The Industry and its Critics.* Urbana: University of Illinois Press.

Castleman, H., and Podrazik, W.J. (2010). *Watching TV: Six Decades of American Television.* Syracuse, NY: Syracuse University Press.

Charland, M. (1986). "Technological Nationalism." *Canadian Journal of Political and Social Theory*, Vol. 10(1–2): 196–220.

Collins, R., Finn, A., McFaydyen, S., and Hoskins, C. (2001). "Editorial: Public Service Broadcasting Beyond 2000: Is There a Future for Public Service Broadcasting?" *Canadian Journal of Communication*, Vol. 26(1): 3–15.

Conway, K. (2009). "Public Service Broadcasting and the Failure of Political Representation." *The Velvet Light Trap*, Vol. 64(1): 64–75.

Edgerton, G. (2009). *The Columbia History of American Television.* New York: Columbia University Press.

Fremeth, H. (2011). "Television." *The Canadian Encyclopedia.* www.thecanadianencyclopedia.com/index.cfm?PgNm=TCE&Params=A1ARTA0007905

Gitlin, T. (2000). *Inside Prime Time.* Berkeley, CA: University of California Press.

Gomery, D. (2007). *A History of Broadcasting in the United States.* London: Blackwell.

Hoynes, W. (1994). *Public Television for Sale: Media, the Market, and the Public Sphere.* Boulder: Westview Press.

Kellner, D. (1990). *Television and the Crisis of Democracy.* Boulder: Westview Press.

McCarthy, A. (2010). *The Citizen Machine: Governing Television in 1950s America.* New York: The New Press.

McChesney, R. (1999). "Graham Spry and Public Broadcasting." *Canadian Journal of Communication*, Vol. 24(1): 25–47.

Mazepa, P. (2005). "Democracy of, in and through Communication: Struggles around Public Service in Canada in the First Half of the Twentieth Century." *Info*, Vol. 9(2/3): 45–56.

Minow, N. (1971). "The Broadcasters Are Public Trustees." In A. Kirschener and L. Kirschener (Eds), *Radio & Television: Readings in the Mass Media* (pp. 207–17). New York: Odyssey Press.

Minow, N., and Cate., F.H. (2003). "Revisiting the Vast Wasteland." *Federal Communication Law Journal*, Vol. 55: 407–40.

Mittel, J. (2009). *Television and American Culture.* New York: Oxford University Press.

Nesbitt-Larking, P. (2001). *Politics, Society and the Media: Canadian Perspectives.* Peterborough: Broadview Press.

Ouellette, L. (1999). "TV Viewing as Good Citizenship? Political Rationality, Enlightened Democracy and PBS." *Cultural Studies*, Vol. 13(1): 62–90.

———. (2002). *Viewers Like You? How Public TV Failed the People.* New York: Columbia University Press.

Ouellette, L., and Lewis, J. (2000). "Moving beyond the 'Vast Wasteland': Cultural Policy and Television in the United States." *Television & New Media*, 1(1): 95–115.

Peers, F. (1969). *The Politics of Canadian Broadcasting, 1920–1951.* Toronto: University of Toronto Press.

———. (1979). *The Public Eye: Television and the Politics of Canadian Broadcasting, 1952–1968.* Toronto: University of Toronto Press.

Price, M. (1996). *Television, the Public Sphere, and National Identity.* New York: Oxford University Press.

Raboy, M. (1992). *Missed Opportunities: The Story of Canada's Broadcasting Policy.* Montreal: McGill-Queen's University Press.

———. (1998). "Public Broadcasting and the Global Framework of Media Democratization." *Gazette,* Vol. 60(2): 167–80.

———. (2005). "The 2005 Graham Spry Memorial Lecture Making Media: Creating the Conditions for Communication in the Public Good." *Canadian Journal of Communication,* Vol. 31(1): 389–6.

Raboy, M., and Taras, D. (2004). "The Politics of Neglect of Canadian Broadcasting Policy." *Policy Options,* Vol. 25(3): 63–8.

Rutherford, P. (1990). *When Television Was Young: Primetime Canada, 1952–1967.* Toronto: University of Toronto Press.

Scannel, P. (1989). "Public Service Broadcasting and Modern Life." *Media, Culture & Society,* Vol. 11(2): 135–66.

———. (1990). "Public Service Broadcasting: The History of a Concept." In A. Goodwin and G. Whannel (Eds), *Understanding Television.* New York: Routledge.

Spigel, L. (1992). *Make Room for TV: Television and the Family Ideal in Post-war America.* Chicago: University of Chicago Press.

Starr, P. (2004). *The Creation of the Media: Political Origins of Modern Communications.* New York: Basic Books.

Streeter, T. (1996). *Selling the Air: A Critique of the Policy of Commercial Broadcasting in the United States.* Chicago: University of Chicago Press.

Vipond, M. (2000). *The Mass Media in Canada.* Toronto: James Lorimer.

West, E. (2002). "Selling Canada to Canadians: Collective Memory, National Identity, and Popular Culture." *Critical Studies in Media Communication,* Vol. 19(2): 212–29.

Television Genre: Contexts and Textual Analysis

Introduction: Television Genre and Textual Analysis

In the second section of *The Television Reader*, we examined how TV shows are shaped by economics and politics, the profit interests of media companies, and the political interests of states. Television shows, however, are much more than commodities and state instruments of cultural nationalism. Every TV show relies on "genre," which will be discussed in this section.

The word *genre* is derived from a French (and originally Latin) word for "a class" or "a kind of text." In general, genre studies divide the world of texts (literature, film, TV, and even video games) into specific categorical types. Television genre studies classify types of TV texts according to their common codes and conventions (e.g., sitcom, science fiction, western, horror). This practice of organizing and classifying texts according to genre categories is part of an analytic heritage that goes back more than 2000 years. Aristotle's *Poetics*, for example, classified literature according to genre categories such as "comedy"' or "tragedy."

Genre analysis of other media forms were later derived from Aristotle's studies. Among Aristotle's insights was that the medium in which a genre operates is an important part of its effectiveness. Hence, genre analysis cannot simply be transferred from one medium to another. Literary genres and film genres, for example, are not easily interchangeable. While there may be some important similarities between literature and film, and they may influence each other, the circumstances of their construction and reception differ.

The division of the world of TV shows into discrete genre categories often leads to considerable dispute. Genres are not fortified semantic walls. Television texts do not exist in isolation, but in relation to other TV texts. It is often difficult to make clear-cut distinctions between one TV genre and another because many of them entail mixtures of textual elements from pre-existing genres. Genres are therefore "intertextual"; *intertextuality* refers to "the process by which [TV] texts communicate meaning to audiences through references to other [TV] texts" and how "our understanding of any one [TV] text will be informed, in part, by our experience of other texts"(Casey et al. 2002: 127–8). Many TV shows often exhibit the codes and conventions of more than one genre and are hybrid texts. Nonetheless, a TV genre is a socially constructed category that enables scholars to compare TV shows (in terms of subject matter, narrative structure, characterization, setting, aesthetics, and so on). The concept of genre helps us to identify similarities and differences between TV shows circulating at any given time.

In addition to classifying TV texts, scholars who study TV genres examine their industrial uses. All TV genres are shaped by the economic imperatives of TV production firms, broadcasters, and advertisers. Paul Attalah (1984) says that "the entire television industry is organized around the production of specific genres [. . .]. Television could be said not to exist outside of its genres"(227). For this reason, some scholars have proposed "[u]sing the terminology of 'program forms' rather than 'genres' [. . .] to signal the industrial focus, as genre is a classification more common when emphasizing textual features and norms"(Lotz 5). Television genres (or program forms) have many industrial uses. They help to routinize and standardize TV production, make TV scheduling decisions, and attract TV advertisers.

For the most part, TV production firms make TV shows that adhere to established or time-tested genre categories to create efficiencies in the production stage. Television genres provide a template to follow, an easily understood and easily explained way of making TV shows. Television workers that are familiar with the codes and conventions of specific TV genres will be able to produce TV shows more efficiently than those who are not. Genre also helps TV production firms market TV shows to TV networks, which want to know what they are receiving from TV production companies so that they can make scheduling decisions. TV networks also license and schedule TV genres to attract and organize an audience on behalf of their advertising clients. Genres help TV networks convince advertisers to buy time/space. Genres are important to TV viewers too. Genres help viewers to orient themselves to different kinds of TV shows while providing a level of standardization and predictability. Genres are comforting to TV viewers because they provide an important frame of reference, which helps viewers to identify, select, and interpret TV shows that are scheduled. Consumers of TV shows have certain expectations about what they will see, read, or hear. Genres represent a promise to please and meet specific viewer expectations. They make TV series recognizable to viewers and tell them what to expect from TV shows.

How do TV scholars study genre? Jason Mittell (2004, 2010) addresses the many debates and challenges involved in TV genre study and provides a methodologically useful framework. Mittell (2001) reviews common approaches to TV genre studies, noting that some scholars start with a pre-existing formalistic notion of a TV genre (e.g., a crime show). They then select a specific show and examine how it entails all the qualities and conventions of that genre. Here, the scholar slots a TV show to a pre-existing genre category. By hastily reducing the TV text to a pre-given TV genre, they risk missing what might be novel or unique about the TV show. Other scholars undertake a more difficult approach to genre studies. They watch several TV shows that seem to have similar codes and conventions. In this approach, the scholars might collect every single episode of every single vampire TV series produced in the past five years, watch them all, and make extensive notes about what codes and conventions the shows have in common. The result would be a genre study of vampire TV shows.

A third approach—advocated by Mittell—is to study genres as socially constructed "discursive formations." A genre is not an intrinsic property of a TV text. Rather, TV texts are given meaning as distinct genres by a number of different actors in society, from TV networks to TV viewers. This methodological approach to genres asks us to examine what people—creators, business, critics, audiences—are saying about a TV show. How do they give specific TV shows meaning as distinct genres? Mittell wants TV studies scholars to explore the material ways in which genres are socially defined, interpreted, and evaluated. Instead of trying to figure out an inherent genre, we should examine how a specific TV show is given meaning as a distinct or essential genre by TV production companies, networks, advertisers, and viewers. While many TV genre studies originated as textual analysis, industrial, historical, and social constructivist approaches have supplemented narrowly textual analysis of TV genres more recently.

What are the characteristics associated with specific TV genres? Why do TV networks schedule certain TV genres? How do viewers define and relate to specific TV genres? This section of *The Television Reader* entails articles that analyze a number of popular and influential TV genres in Canada and the United States. Although the following articles are organized thematically according to the TV show genres they examine, the articles should not be read exclusively as text-specific "genre studies." In addition to focusing on TV show texts, the articles in this section examine the industrial and social contexts in which TV genres circulate.

Sitcoms

The **situation comedy** (or sitcom) was a regular genre broadcast by commercial radio in the United States in the 1930s and 1940s. When American TV broadcasting took off after World War II, sitcoms made for radio and many sitcom codes and conventions started to appear in TV shows. In a study of the American TV sitcom, Gerald Jones (1992) discusses the sitcom as an ideal TV commodity:

> The sitcom is a corporate product. It is a mass consumption commodity, designed, like a sedan, to be constructed decade after decade on the same safe, reliable pattern, yet allowing enough surface variations to be resold as a new product every few years. On a conscious level, it is an expression of the underlying assumptions of the corporate culture that has come to dominate American society.(4)

Sitcom conventions have developed slowly over time. Mike Eaton (1981) argues that most sitcoms focus on the trials and tribulations of a family and their home life, the relationships between employees in a workplace, and tensions between people as they navigate home life and work. The setting of many "classic" sitcoms of the 1950s was the home. In the fictional world of these sitcoms, women are expected to function as homemakers while men work to support their families. Whether situated in an apartment in Manhattan (*I Love Lucy*) or a suburban home in a fictitious town (*Leave It to Beaver*), female and male gender roles were more structured on TV sitcoms than they were in US society, where women were actually entering the workforce in significant numbers. For example, Lucile Ball was a successful film and TV actress and producer. But the character she played in her sitcom was woefully incapable of making it in the working world despite her frequent efforts to enter it.

Like the traditional comic form, the sitcom features anti-heroic characters in everyday situations. Many sitcoms are about unexceptional people that do not desire or hope for a better or different way of life. Week in and week out, the characters that inhabit the specific location(s) of the TV sitcom remain trapped in the same place whether it is a living room couch (*Married . . . With Children*), the bar stool at the local watering hole (*Cheers*), or the barracks at a military base (*The Phil Silvers Show, M*A*S*H*). The narrative structure of the sitcom is standardized. In the beginning, the characters in a presumably "normal" domestic or work situation face a conflict of some kind; in the middle, they try to resolve the conflict through a series of actions; the sitcom ends with the conflict being resolved and "normalcy" re-established. Conflicts are neatly resolved after each episode only to reappear in a slightly different form in the following episode. There are no radical transformations in the fictional worlds represented by sitcoms. Each episode reproduces the routine of everyday life at home, at work, and in between. David McQueen (1998) says that the essential feature of the TV sitcom is that nothing ever changes.

Sitcoms sometimes raise important issues that represent social changes, although the sponsored nature of commercial TV shows in the network era ensured that these issues were dealt with in a timid way. Consider, for example, network TV's representation of sexual orientation. Despite the valiant efforts of lesbians and gays (and their supporters) to end discrimination based on sexual orientation, and the successes they achieved, it took until 1997 to have a sitcom feature an out-of-the-closet main character on broadcast television (*Ellen*). **Post-network era** sitcoms, particularly those on premium cable and some of the cable networks, can be more provocative in their representation of contentious social issues. The move away from advertising-supported TV programming has much to do with this recent phenomenon. The Showtime premium cable network's *Weeds* (about a marijuana-selling suburban mother) and *Californication* (about a sexually promiscuous writer) are good examples of sitcoms that wouldn't have appeared on TV in the network era.

The two sitcoms discussed in *The Television Reader—Trailer Park Boys* and *Little Mosque on the Prairie*—are recent manifestations of the sitcom genre. Both of these TV sitcoms were made in Canada but have had some success as a cultural export. Both are among the most popular cable and network sitcoms in Canadian television history.

Trailer Park Boys has not been able to find a regular spot on American TV (it ran briefly on BBC America), but it has a large cult following in Canada. *Trailer Park Boys* is one of the most successful cable shows in the history of Canadian television and its DVD sales were among the best for any Canadian TV show, comparable to those of many big American films (Neilson Soundscan 2006). The first theatrical movie spun off from the show, *Trailer Park Boys: The Movie,* had the highest gross of any Canadian film for an opening weekend (Adams 2006). Dean Defino's (2009) article on the *Boys* situates the series in the long tradition of comedies about the lives of the poor, specifically within a tradition of situation comedies about the poor. The series also grafts a mock documentary or **mockumentary** aesthetic onto the traditional sitcom form. This allows the shows creators to skewer the whole tradition of reality-based and ideologically conservative TV programs like *COPS*.

Little Mosque on the Prairie has had a much larger audience than *Trailer Park Boys* because of its airing by a broadcast network rather than cable. Its premiere on CBC in January 2007 drew 2.1 million people, a very large audience for Canadian TV (Canadian Press 2007). The show's producers recently signed a deal with the US network FOX, which plans to make an American version of the TV program (Ryan 2008). In 2008, *Little Mosque on the Prairie* was viewed in 80 different TV markets globally (Canadian Press 2008). Sandra Cañas' (2008) essay about *Little Mosque on the Prairie* draws on the work of cultural theorists such as Edward Said and Fredric Jameson to situate the show within the context of the widespread xenophobia in North America toward its Muslim citizens. Drawing on the conventions of the sitcom form, *Little Mosque on the Prairie* uses humour to demonstrate how ridiculous some people's ideas about others are. Set in the fictional prairie town of Mercy, *Little Mosque on the Prairie* also uses humour to show viewers the diversity of opinion and discussion within the small Muslim community in the town.

Science Fiction

Science fiction is a newer genre, one generally associated with modernity. Science fiction's ur-text, Mary Shelley's *Frankenstein* (1818), combines a number of genres, most notably the Gothic. Among the many mythical and literary sources that Shelley draws on is the Greek myth of Prometheus. In Greek mythology, Prometheus is a master craftsman who steals fire from the gods and gives it to humanity as a gift. The gods punish both Prometheus and humans as a consequence. In Shelley's adaptation of this tale, the character Dr Victor Frankenstein is punished for acquiring the power of the gods and engineering life. Dr Frankenstein uses science to create something that becomes uncontrollable, destroys life, and eventually kills its creator. Science fiction TV shows draw from this important novel's key theme and Frankenstein is an archetype for many scientists represented by science fiction TV shows. Scientists—and societies—push the boundaries of the possible and then are punished, harmed, or killed by their new inventions. Technology is the outcome of scientific advances but is often represented as a destructive force that fundamentally changes the world. Technology designed to serve humanity eventually dominates it. Many science fiction books, films, and TV shows represent this theme. Shows such as *Battlestar Galactica*, for example, posit a dystopian future universe where the technological products of human science become humanity's most deadly enemy.

Science fiction is "a cultural expression of public attitudes toward technology" that "oscillates between hope and despair, between celebration and warning, in its depiction of technological change" (Murphie and Potts 2004: 95). Science fiction often expresses public attitudes toward science and technology, but sets them in a futuristic setting. It extrapolates from present-day scientific and technological developments to explore the ways these developments might impact, positively or negatively, the imagined worlds of the future. Set in distant environments and different periods, science fiction explores utopian hopes and dystopian fears about science and technology in highly creative and fantastical ways. Many science fiction texts have elements of the horror and fantasy genres. US science fiction films and TV shows even graft the qualities of the western into their narrative structures. Space is depicted as a frontier in which other civilizations are encountered, colonized, or befriended. The most influential of all the science fiction TV series, *Star Trek* (1966–1969), was pitched to TV networks by writer Gene Roddenberry as "Wagon Train to the Stars." Like *Wagon Train*, a popular western TV show, *Star Trek* focused on "individuals who traveled to promote the expansion of our horizons" (cited in Gibberman 2011).

Science fiction TV shows were somewhat popular in the 1960s and 1970s. However, expensive productions costs and the inability to make the top tier in ratings made networks cautious about embracing them. For example, the original *Star Trek* TV series was the most expensive show on the NBC-TV network in the late 1960s. The show's low ratings caused NBC-TV to try to cancel it after two seasons. Its few but dedicated fans undertook a letter campaign that convinced NBC-TV to renew it for another season, but it was nonetheless cancelled after its third season. However, its long life in syndication eventually gave it a large legion of devoted "trekkie" fans and enabled its owner, Paramount, to develop a successful film and TV franchise out of it in the 1980s. The rise of specialty channels like SyFy in the United States and Space in Canada has encouraged the production and consumption of more science fiction TV shows.

Canadian TV companies have not produced any immensely popular and profitable science fiction TV series. Curiously, though, Canada has been the place of production for many of the most successful US science fiction TV shows in recent years: *The X-Files*, *Stargate: SG1*, *Stargate: Atlantis*, and *Battlestar Galactica* to name just a few. Other shows are international co-productions: *Highlander: The Series* was shot in Canada, the United States, France, and Scotland. This type of runaway production from Los Angeles to Hollywood North has been a great source of employment for Canadian cultural workers, particularly in British Columbia.

The Television Reader entails an article by Mark McCutcheon (2009), which examines the most recent version of *Battlestar Gallactica* (2004–2009). McCutcheon's case study examines this Canadian-produced but US-distributed science fiction TV show, which can be interpreted as a geopolitical allegory of the post-9/11 US national security state and the widespread anxieties about US foreign policy "blowback." The Cylons (a race of cybernetic worker-soldiers that, while engineered by humans, ultimately destroy them) are read as stand-ins for Islamic terrorists (which were originally developed as part of a US foreign policy strategy in the 1970s and 1980s to fight the Soviet Union in Afghanistan) (McCutcheon 2009: 5). Tiffany Potter and C.W. Marshall (2008) provide an excellent anthology of critical essays about the production, meaning, and reception of *Battlestar Gallactica*'s first three seasons.

Cop/Crime Shows

The **police procedural** is derived from early twentieth-century Hollywood cinema. Its ideological function was to rehabilitate the largely negative attitude many people felt toward the police during that time. This film genre was eventually transformed into a TV genre, but it did not become a large part of prime-time TV network schedules until the 1970s. That decade proved pivotal in the development of the genre in both film and TV. Following the immense popularity of films like *Dirty Harry* (1971), theatre and TV screens were filled with stories about cops. Two factors shaped this development: (1) the attempt by the US federal government, through the President's Commission on Law Enforcement and Administration of Justice Report, to make policing a profession rather than just a job (Rafter 2000: 71); and (2) the profound social and economic crisis of the 1970s (characterized by rising crime and extreme anxiety on the part of many North Americans). Stories about heroic cops, even mavericks, proved comforting and continue to thrive on TV today.

Since the late 1970s, the political landscapes of Canada and the United States have been transformed by the rise of "**neo-liberalism**." This ideology and policy repudiates the idea that the nation-state should be the guarantor of its citizens' health and welfare and embraces the idea that the role of the state should be limited to serving the interests of business and providing internal and external security. In a sense, the Keynesian "welfare state" has been replaced by a "police state." In the US, this represented by the more than four-fold increase in the number of people incarcerated as prisoners in an expanding prison-industrial complex since 1980 (Parenti 1999). The US has the highest rate of incarceration in the world. It has more prisoners in jails or on parole than even China, which is often characterized by the US as an authoritarian police state and which has a population three times larger. In Canada, a growing police-state mentality has been expressed by the rise of the neo-conservative "law-and-order" agenda, which sends the police into poor and immigrant communities to terrify their inhabitants (Gordon 2006). Cop shows attempt to reaffirm public confidence in the state and its armed protectors even as the citizens who are targeted by the security apparatus increasingly see the police as a hostile, invading force.

One of the most popular TV series in the last 10 years is *CSI: Crime Scene Investigation*. This TV show combines elements of the police procedural with the scientific detective story (e.g., Sherlock Holmes). Police laboratory equipment manufacturers place their products in *CSI*. Some viewers believe *CSI* is a documentary and others presume that new-fangled technology, to the chagrin of criminologists, always solves crime. Gray Cavender and Sarah Deutsch (2007) examine the first season of *CSI* and draw out its socially resonant meanings, particularly its assertion of the moral authority of both scientific investigation and policing. They also discuss how *CSI* and other cop shows represent groups of police officers as members of a family, much like most people in society are members of families (73). By doing so, *CSI* makes cops appear to be "just like us" with the same family quarrels and the same ability to negotiate a way of resolving them.

The HBO television show, *The Wire* (2002–2008), has received significant critical acclaim by academics. It was the subject of a special issue of the prestigious film journal, *Film Quarterly* (Winter 2008/09) and the subject of an anthology edited by Tiffany Potter and C.W. Marshall (2009). Marsha Kinder's (2009) article, published in the special issue of *Film Quarterly*, analyzes how *The Wire*'s producers use the seriality of television narrative to its full potential while also offering viewers a critical examination of all kinds of media representations of crime—from "TV, cinema, literature, theater, and journalism" (Kinder 2009: 50). Of all the crime dramas to have appeared on US and Canadian TV networks, this show most accurately represents the consequences of the neo-conservative police-state's war on North America's poor, marginalized, and ethnic communities.

Reality TV

Reality TV shows are among the most popular of TV genres. They combine elements of other genres, including game shows and talent shows. Some reality shows mimic athletic competitions. Still others offer advice on anything from home renovation to improving your looks. What constitutes reality TV's "reality"? Unlike most fictional TV shows, reality TV shows feature people that are not paid professional actors and action that is unscripted and filmed in real-time, as it unfolds. Yet, despite its "reality" claim, the genre of reality TV is just as manufactured as other TV shows. Reality TV shows put "ordinary people" (as opposed to trained actors) in loosely scripted situations to heighten drama, and are encouraged to improvise. However, their actions and interactions are not entirely spontaneous or authentic. Reality TV shows entail live action, but live action that is derived from thousands of hours of material that has been edited into a few exciting hours of entertainment. Furthermore, the "ordinary people" on reality TV shows are profiled and auditioned. Sometimes, they are aspiring actors, trying to get their first break by appearing on reality TV.

Laurie Ouellette and James Hay's (2008) path-breaking study of the reality TV genre links the rise of these various subtypes of the reality TV genre to the impact of neo-liberal ideology on the cultural imaginary of many citizen-consumers living in the United States and elsewhere. At a time when the pillars of the welfare state and its social programs are being dismantled systematically as result of neo-liberal policy, it is not surprising to see the widespread presence of TV shows that promote rugged individualism over group values and volunteerism, personal responsibility, and charity over social and economic entitlement.

As an industrial program format, reality TV largely emerged in response to the economic imperatives of TV networks to fill their schedules with cheap, easy-to-produce and anti-union TV shows. Reality TV has also been employed by TV networks to challenge labour disputes. The Fox TV network responded to the 1988 Writer's Guild of America (WGA) strike by commencing the production of low-end first-generation reality TV shows such as *America's Most Wanted* and *COPS* by non-unionized cultural workers. During the 2007–2008 Screen Writers Guild (SWG) strike, TV networks filled their schedules will many reality TV shows. Why? Reality TV shows are classified as an "unscripted" as opposed to "scripted" TV genre. This genre classification allowed numerous TV networks to successfully provide "scab" TV programming for the duration of the walkout. It saved them a lot of money in unpaid wages to the writers of "scripted" programming. Reality TV also undermines the struggles of the Screen Actors Guild (SAG) to win high wages for professional actors. Wages for non-unionized contestants—recruited from amateur actor labour pools—are generally far lower than those paid to SAG members. A small number of contestants may make some money in prizes, but this is not guaranteed.

The Television Reader entails articles on some of the economic and political characteristics of reality TV shows. Sue Collins (2008) discusses the union-busting aspect of the reality TV genre and also examines how reality TV shows commodify and trade on pseudo-celebrity. Contestants spend countless hours preparing themselves for reality TV show competitions and swarm to reality TV show auditions motivated by the hope that an appearance will turn them into actual celebrities. Doris Baltruschat (2009) examines reality TV format imitation in a global TV marketplace. Popular talent shows like *Pop Idol* (UK) are part of a global franchise with local variations in 35 countries including Canada and the United States. Baltruschat (2009) explores *Canadian Idol* as a globally popular yet localized TV format.

TV News Production and News Parody

In the United States, TV news grew out of two other media traditions: the theatrical newsreel and radio news broadcasting. Television news entails a combination of the short visual clips that made up the segments of theatrical newsreel programs and the authoritative voices of radio news readers and anchors that were featured in radio broadcasting's sound newsreels. News was not a major part of early TV broadcasting, but it took on increasing importance in the 1950s and 1960s as the major commercial networks, especially NBC and CBS, competed for the loyalty of viewers. It was a "loss leader" for a long time (a TV form produced at high price and used to attract viewers to other TV shows). Television networks employed TV news to give "prestige" to the burgeoning TV networks, but commercial imperatives pulled TV news in two, sometimes incompatible, directions. The TV news is primarily organized as a business that, in order to profit-maximize, must aggressively compete for viewers, advertising revenue, and ratings. Fuelled by ad dollars, TV news reporting is often cautious, careful not to challenge the status quo. Yet, the TV news is more than any ordinary business. It plays a significant role in democracy. News networks have a responsibility to inform the public about current issues, expose the machinations of power (state and corporate), and provide citizens with comprehensive information about the world they live in so they can act rationally and participate in the democratic life of their community and country. The desire of journalists to tell important stories and the quest for professional respectability by TV networks does allow some excellent and sometimes critical news reporting to take place.

At its best, TV news would support a "**public sphere**." In *The Structural Transformation of the Public Sphere*, Jürgen Habermas (1989) argues that during the seventeenth and eighteenth centuries, struggles by bourgeois individuals against the absolutist monarchical state and the arbitrary authority of the Church for basic civil freedoms before the law (speech, press, assembly, association, no arrest without a trial and so on), combined with the printing press and new mass-distributed print media (the free press), heralded the emergence of a public sphere. Though the public sphere excluded the working poor, women, and other "rabble," it was considered by Habermas as an "ideal speech" situation. A public sphere would free speech from the coercive power of the state and market, ensure the equality of access to the media, enable the expression of a diversity of points of view, facilitate rational discussion, and provide a space to address issues of collective importance.

The public sphere was to be a kind of informational feedback loop between citizens and the state in a democratic society. Through deliberative discussion and debate, citizens would arrive at a rational consensus about the common good; the state would reflect this consensus and govern accordingly. Habermas bemoaned the transformation of the public sphere by state and corporate forces. Over the course of the late nineteenth century and throughout the twentieth century, the public sphere was "re-feudalized" and administered by state propagandists, corporate spin doctors, and the dominance of commercial TV news. The prestige of TV networks as a trusted source of news programming has been in decline for a number of years. With advertising-driven, pundit-occupied, and overly emotional transmissions in a 24/7 format, TV news regularly fails to support the public sphere and democracy. The number of viewers who use the nightly network news broadcast as their main source of information is shrinking. Young people often ignore TV news completely. Others are increasingly drawn to the niche market TV news programming available on cable networks and the Internet. This is all a part of the general crisis in commercial journalism that has affected a number of different media (McChesney and Nichols 2010).

The context of news journalism in crisis helps us understand the popularity of comic or parodic news and public affairs TV programs. The crisis of TV news is both an economic one (rooted in the proliferation of new media sites that allow people to produce and consume news, leading to declining TV news network revenues) and one of public legitimacy (rooted in a timid, docile, and uncritical approach that makes contemporary journalism seem like a joke). If TV news reporting today is in fact a joke, why not watch the comedians instead?

The Television Reader features two articles on news parody TV shows. Zoë Druick (2008) examines news parody TV shows and explores why these kinds of TV shows are favoured by the Canadian Broadcasting Corporation (CBC), which has a long and successful tradition of airing them. Geoffrey Baym (2005) ties the crisis in US journalism to the positive appeal of *The Daily Show,* a widely popular news parody TV show, which is broadcast in both the US and Canada. The show's host, Jon Stewart, seems to command more respect as a source of political information and opinion than many of the anchors that regularly appear on mainstream TV news programs, particularly among young and skeptical viewers.

TV War

Television news journalists in the United States, like their predecessors in film, radio, and print, often play an uncritical, even cheerleading role in their support of US foreign wars and empire-building. When war breaks out, two wars take place: the actual war, in which real people kill, suffer, and die, and the media war, in which the actualities of war are distanced from the civilian audiences comfortably seated in front of various screens (Taylor 1997). In the 24/7 real-time global TV age, viewers are regularly presented with an image of war that obscures its actuality. War is constructed by TV networks as entertainment to attract a mass audience into the ad flow. Since the 9/11 terrorist attack on the World Trade Center, the commercial TV news has done a poor job of offering a critical perspective of why the attacks happened. Lynn Spiegel (2004) examines the ways commercial TV news programs, talk shows, documentaries, dramas, and even comedies attempted to construct a nationalist narrative about US unity following the 9/11 attack.

The lead up and aftermath of the US invasions of Afghanistan in 2001 ("Operation Enduring Freedom") and Iraq in 2003 ('"Operation Iraqi Freedom") were heavily promoted by TV news networks. Critical media scholars have examined TV news' irresponsible representation of these invasions and its contribution to the manufacture of public consent to elite US foreign policy goals (Calabrese 2004; Kamalipour and Snow 2004; Kumar 2006; Rutherford 2004). Commercial TV news failed utterly to explain why Afghanistan and Iraq—countries which did not threaten the United States—were invaded in response to terrorist attacks on the US by Al Qaeda. The architects of the attacks appear to be able to continue to operate under the protection and financial support of the elite of two other countries, Saudi Arabia and Pakistan, which are said to be "loyal" allies of the US.

In the aftermath of 9/11, the manufacture of consent to US military and imperial goals in central Asia and the Middle East was supported by many action-adventure TV dramas about US military and intelligence agencies. Among the most popular of these TV shows is the recently concluded *24* (2001–2010). Elspeth Van Veeren's (2009) article examines this hybrid espionage, reality TV, and Hollywood blockbuster–like TV show. Ideologically, *24* "(re)produces keys elements of the Bush administration's discourse of the 'global war on terrorism' (including the exceptional and pervasive nature of the threat posed by terrorism, and the corresponding need for a militarized and repressive form of counter-terrorism)"(Van Veeren 2009: 363). As a popular support for the elite fears and fantasies of the US national security state, *24* sanctions "practices such as rendition, detention without charge, and torture"(Van Veeren 2009: 362). *24* also cleverly incorporates elements of the conspiracy genre by representing sinister US business and state elite working hand-in-hand with terrorists behind the public's back to enrich themselves.

TV Sports

The final part in this section of *The Television Reader* examines TV sports in North America. In 1993, Gary Bettman became Commissioner of the National Hockey League (NHL; the smallest of the major team sports leagues—after football, baseball, and basketball). Bettman undertook a strategy of expanding the number of American teams in the league. Prior to this, the NHL was concentrated in a number of large Canadian cities and a number of northern US cities (with a few outliers in the South). Bettman increased the number of teams in the US south, which, while having no history of support for the sport, represented untapped potential. To increase the wealth of the NHL team owners (new and old), Bettman tried to land a lucrative broadcasting contract with a major American TV network. Fox was the first to bite and signed a contract with the NHL in 1994. Daniel Mason's (2002) article examines Fox TV network's attempt to win a larger audience in the US by introducing a gimmick called the FoxTrax puck. This made-for-TV puck was supposed to be easier for viewers to follow because it glowed. This promotional experiment highlighted the conflict between hockey traditionalists in Canada and US newcomers to the sport.

Joseph Kispal-Kovacs's article provides a general historical account of the relationship between TV and team sports in North America. Kispal-Kovacs examines the role that various mass media have played in shaping the popular appeal and economic underpinning of professional and US college team sports. Sports are now an important part of TV network programming schedules and are also crucial to the economic survival of various team sport leagues. The 2011 lockout of NFL players by NFL owners, for example, was precipitated largely by a disagreement over how the enormous sums of money in the NFL's contract with TV networks should be divided up and allocated between the two sides.

Works Cited

Adams, J. (2006). "Payday in the Trailer Park." *The Globe and Mail*, 11 October 2006, p. R2.

Aristotle. (c330 BCE). *Poetics*. S.H. Butcher, trans. Mineola, NY: Dover Publications, 1997.

Attalah, P. (1984). "The Unworthy Discourse: Situation Comedy in Television." In W. Rowland and B. Watkins (Eds), *Interpreting Television: Current Research Perspectives* (pp. 222–49). Beverly Hills: Sage.

Baltruschat, D. (2009). "Reality TV Formats: The Case of *Canadian Idol*." *Canadian Journal of Communication*, Vol. 34(2): 41–59.

Baym, G. (2005). "The Daily Show: Discursive Integration and Reinvention of Political Journalism." *Political Communication*, Vol. 22(2): 259–76.

Calabrese, A. (2005). "Casus Belli: U.S. Media and the Justification of the Iraq War." *Television & New Media*, Vol. 6(2): 153–75.

Canadian Press. (2007). "Record Debut for CBC with Little Mosque." *The Globe and Mail*, 11 January 2007, p. R1.

———. (2008). "CBC's Mosque Picked up by More European Networks." *The Globe and Mail*, 20 February 2008, p. R2.

Cañas, S. (2008). "The *Little Mosque on the Prairie*: Examining (Multi) Cultural Spaces of Nation and Religion." *Cultural Dynamics*, Vol. 20(3): 195–211.

Casey, B., Casey, N., Calvert, B., French, L., and Lewis, J. (2002). *Television Studies: The Key Concepts*. New York: Routledge.

Cavender, G., and Deutsch, S. (2007). "*CSI* and Moral Authority: The Police and Science." *Crime, Media, Culture: An International Journal*, Vol. 3(1): 67–81.

Collins, S. (2008). "Making the Most of 15 Minutes: Reality TV's Dispensable Celebrity." *Television & New Media*, Vol. 9(2): 87–110.

Defino, D. (2009). "From Trailer Trash to *Trailer Park Boys*." *Post Script*, Vol. 28(3): 47–57.

Druick, Z. (2008). "Laughing at Authority or Authorized Laughter? Canadian News Parodies." In Z. Druick and A. Kotsopoulos (Eds), *Programming Reality: Perspectives on English-Canadian Television* (pp. 107–28). Waterloo: Wilfred Laurier University Press.

Eaton, M. (1981). "Television Situation Comedy." In T. Bennet, S. Body-Bowman, C. Mercer, and J. Woollacott (Eds), *Popular Television and Film* (pp. 26–52). London: British Film Institute.

Gibberman, S. (2011). "Gene Roddenberry." Museum of Broadcast Communications. www.museum.tv/eotvsection.php?entrycode=roddenberry

Gordon, T. (2006). *Cops, Crime, and Capitalism: The Law-and-Order Agenda in Canada*. Halifax: Fernwood Publishing.

Habermas, J. (1989). *The Structural Transformation of the Public Sphere: An Inquiry into a Category of Bourgeois Society*. Cambridge: Polity.

Jones, G. (1992). *Honey, I'm Home! Sitcoms: Selling the American Dream*. New York: St. Martin's Press.

Kamalipour, Y.R., and Snow, N. (Eds). (2004). *War, Media and Propaganda: A Global Perspective*. Lanham, MD: Rowman & Littlefield.

Kinder, M. (2009). "Re-Wiring Baltimore: The Emotive Power of Systemics, Seriality, and the City." *Film Quarterly*, Vol. 62(2): 50–7.

Kumar, D. (2006). "Media, War, and Propaganda: Strategies of Information Management During the 2003 Iraq War." *Communication and Critical/Cultural Studies*, Vol. 3(1): 48–69.

Mason, D. (2002). "'Get the Puck Outta Here!': Media Transnationalism and Canadian Identity." *Journal of Sport & Social Issues*, Vol. 26(20): 140–67.

McChesney, R.W., and Nichols, J. (2010). *The Death and Life of American Journalism: The Media Revolution that Will Begin the World Again*. New York: Nation Books.

McCutcheon, M. (2009). "Downloading Doppelgängers: New Media Anxieties and Transnational Ironies in *Battlestar Galactica*." *Science Fiction Film and Television*, Vol. 2(1): 1–24.

McQueen, D. (1998). *Television: A Media Student's Guide*. London: Arnold.

Mittell, J. (2004). *Genre and Television: From Cop Shows to Cartoons in American Culture*. New York: Routledge.

———. (2010). "Television Genres." In *A Number of Works* (pp. 234–68). Oxford: Oxford University Press.

Murphie, A., and Potts, J. (2003). *Culture and Technology*. New York: Palgrave Macmillan.

Neilsen Soundscan. (2006). "Top DVDs." *The Globe and Mail*, 30 May 2006, p. R3.

Ouellette, L., and Hay, J. (2008). *Better Living through Reality TV: Television and Post-welfare Citizenship*. Oxford, UK: Blackwell.

Parenti, M. (1999). *Lockdown America: Police and Prisons in the Age of Crisis*. New York: Verso.

Potter, T., and Marshall, C.W. (Eds). (2008). *Cylons in America: Critical Studies in Battlestar Galactica*. New York: Continuum.

———. (2009). *The Wire: Urban Decay and American Television*. New York: Continuum.

Rafter, N. (2000). *Shots in the Mirror: Crime Films and Society*. Oxford: Oxford University Press.

Rutherford, P. (2004). *Weapons of Mass Persuasion: Marketing the Case Against Iraq*. University of Toronto Press: Toronto.

Ryan, A. (2008). "Popular CBC Series Gets Second Life South of the Border." *The Globe and Mail*, 10 June 2008, p. R3.

Spiegel, L. (2004). "Entertainment Wars: Television Culture after 9/11." *American Quarterly*, Vol. 56(2): 235–70.

Taylor, Philip M. (1997) *Global Communications, International Affairs and the Media Since 1945*. London: Routledge.

Van Veeren, E. (2009). "Interrogating *24*: Making Sense of U.S. Counter-terrorism in the Global War on Terrorism." *New Political Science*, Vol. 3(3): 361–84.

From Trailer Trash to *Trailer Park Boys*

Dean Defino

Though little-known in the United States, *Trailer Park Boys* is one of the most popular programs in the history of Canadian television. Over seven seasons and two feature films,[1] the show has offered a mockumentary window into the lives of a group of petty criminals in a Nova Scotia trailer park. As one series character explains, the program is "kinda like *COPS*, but from a criminal's point of view" ("Fuck Community College, Let's Get Drunk and Eat Chicken Fingers," Season 1: Episode 2). But where *COPS* and similar reality shows hide their schadenfreude ethos behind a pose of verite objectivity, *Trailer Park Boys* clearly plays the absurd criminal schemes and quotidian adventures of Sunnyvale Trailer Park's loser heroes—Julian, Ricky, and Bubbles—for laughs. They subsist on a diet of cheap booze, pepperoni, and chicken fingers and speak in a vernacular that is equal parts malapropism ("cubic zarcarbian," "supply and command', "get two birds stoned at once") and obscenity (in one episode, the word "fuck"' is spoken 91 times), but while some critics of *Trailer Park Boys* deride the show for "laughing at the poor," its out-sized characters are drawn with remarkable affection. "The idea isn't to make trailer parks look bad or have fun at their expense," series creator and director Mike Clattenberg claims. "It's about the people on the show playing the cards they're dealt."[2]

While *Trailer Park Boys* draws easy comparisons to other situation comedies having to do with socio-economic class, from *The Honeymooners*, to *The Jeffersons*, to *My Name Is Earl*, it differs from them in two significant ways. The first is its mockumentary realism. Where the typical sitcom plays its thin plots and relentless gags on a state-of-the-art studio sound stage before a live audience, *Trailer Park Boys* was, until Season Six, shot entirely on location at three different Nova Scotia trailer parks, in a coarse documentary style that is partly a matter of budget, and partly a matter of design. The show looks and feels remarkably like what it is supposed to be: a cheap documentary of trailer park life compiled by amateur filmmakers, for reasons that are never made clear. The second difference between *Trailer Park Boys* and these other programs is the characters' tightly circumscribed world view. Where Ralph Kramden indulges fantasies of an upper-class existence funded by prize money from The $64,000 Question, and George Jefferson dreams of "moving on up" to the East Side, and Earl Hickey hopes to balance his cosmic books by righting all of the wrongs he has done, the boys of Sunnyvale want nothing more than to stay precisely where they are, and to have just enough money to "hang out and get drunk with friends."

Sunnyvale Trailer Park is a fully realized community with a clearly defined social hierarchy. Its owner, Barb Lahey, rules almost invisibly through cunning manipulation of her ex-husband and Park Supervisor, Jim Lahey, an ex-cop who was thrown off of the force for being drunk on duty, and thrown out of his trailer for taking up with a pot-bellied, cheeseburger-addicted male prostitute named Randy. As Assistant Trailer Park Supervisor, Randy shares not only Jim Lahey's bed, but also his draconian schemes to destroy Lahey's nemesis, Ricky. Randy's tragic affection for "Mr Lahey," as he calls him, is the result of his having known the prelapsarian Jim, a man of kindness and genuine passion who saved the ever-shirtless, hirsute young hustler from a life on the street.

Barb, Jim, and Randy represent the legitimate governing structure of the park, but the true seat of power is Julian's trailer. Julian, the gun-toting park stud in black T-shirt and jeans who continually sips rum-and-coke and plots early retirement around unlikely criminal schemes, is the patriarch of the community: arbiter of disputes, diffuser of tensions between Lahey and Ricky, benevolent despot and Robin Hood. The series begins with his and Ricky's return to Sunnyvale after 18 months of incarceration, only to find Cyrus, a 9-mm-wielding would-be thug, has taken over the Park and moved into Julian's trailer. Julian's first task is to eject the alien presence and restore his own de facto authority. His method is simple: He challenges Cyrus to shoot him in the head. When Cyrus turns tale and runs, Julian reconfirms his own Ubermensch status. But Julian is a benevolent leader: his criminal schemes are all about protecting the integrity of the park. In Season Four, he and Ricky parlay an enormous crop of marijuana into enough cash to buy, as Ricky suggests, "an island with a Ferris Wheel," but Julian has other plans: to buy the trailer park and end Jim Lahey's drunken reign of terror ("A Man's Gotta Eat," 4:2). Their plan is foiled when Barb tricks their brainless accomplices, Trevor and Cory, into signing a worthless contract, but Julian never abandons his mission. In Season Six, he uses money from yet another improbable drug deal to buy the trailers of several evicted residents, fixes them up and returns them to their rightful owners.

If Julian is the great stabilizer, Ricky is an erratic man-child with a pompadour to shame Elvis, who would have perished long ago were it not for Julian's vigilant care and his own ability to grow what everyone admits is "amazing dope." An idiot savant in track pants and a battered Martin Luther King T-shirt, he has lived off and on in Julian's grandmother's abandoned car—a doorless 1978 Chrysler New Yorker dubbed "the Shitmobile"—for the entire run of the series. Though his intellect barely exceeds Trevor's and Cory's (in "The Winds of Shit," 5:7, he boasts of being smarter than a plastic potted plant, but admits that a clock radio probably has him beat "cause it has a battery"), his love for family and friends is boundless. And though that love is almost always expressed in inappropriate ways—like teaching a group of Junior Achievers how to steal barbeque grills ("Where the Fuck Is Randy's Barbeque?" 3:6) and fixing the brake hoses in the doorless Shitmobile before allowing his nine-year-old daughter, Trinity, to drive it ("Dressed All Over and Zesty Mordant," 5:8)—his desire to do right is unmistakable, if ill conceived. "I don't want her driving around in an unsafe car," he says in a facsimile of reason that is at once convincing, hilarious, and chilling. Having recently taught her to drive, his ultimate goal is to sell enough hashish that he can give her the car. But his benevolence goes beyond caring for Trinity. "I try to be a role model for kids around the park," he explains in "Where the Fuck Is Randy's Barbeque?" (3:6). "If some kid wants to grow dope, they can come talk to me. Instead of growing dope six or seven times through denial and error [sic], they're going to get it right the first time and have some good dope."

Filling out the power trio, Bubbles is roundly considered "the sharpest guy in the park," though most outsiders take him for "retarded" because of his thick glasses, jutting lower lip, and Simian vocal inflections. Bubbles was abandoned by his parents at age four and forced to live (as he continues to do, now in his 30s) in Julian's tool shed. A frequent caution to Julian and Ricky, he dispenses baubles of moral wisdom from the proverbial ("If you love something, set it free. . . . and if it doesn't come back you're an arsehole") to the erudite (he convinces Julian to trick Ricky into asking his girlfriend to marrying him by discoursing on Plato's notion of the "Noble Lie"). But Bubbles is no mere Jiminy Cricket. Whatever the scheme, and with full knowledge of its inevitable outcome, he willingly ties his own destiny to that of the boys, even if it means going to prison, as he does at the end of Season Four.

As a comic arena, Sunnyvale Trailer Park might be lumped together with any number of impoverished comedic settings, from the Kramdens' tenement building in *The Honeymooners,* to the Queens row houses of *All in the Family,* to the Evans' rundown apartment in the Chicago projects of *Good Times:* narrowly defined narrative spaces inhabited by broad comic types whose nebulous adventures give rise to the program's self-contained gags. Contrary to the claims of the creators of *Seinfeld,* there is nothing original about a sitcom where "nothing happens." The sitcom story is never more than the thinnest pretense for a series of jokes, anchored, not by the sweep of events, but by the invariable situation that gives the genre its name. For shows like *Good Times* and *Trailer Park Boys,* poverty is that situation, the foundation of the gags. Comedy writers since Chaucer have known that poverty breeds its own particular varieties of humour, from the humanist paeans of Charlie Chaplin to the thinly veiled shit jokes and barroom double entendres of Archie Bunker's cronies. Most successful comedies attempt to strike a balance between these modes, if only to offset the potential offence of one and the saccharine tendency of the other. *All in the Family,* for example, inevitably follows the familiar "whoosh" of Archie's toilet with a speech by Gloria or Mike advertising their evolving social consciousness, or Edith confirming Archie's basic decency with a fond recollection of their younger days: all of this surgically undercut by an Archie one-liner as he descends the stairs adjusting his trousers.

Trailer Park Boys is particularly adept at achieving a balance between the higher and lower registers of humour, such as when Ricky's father, Ray—an alcoholic Calvinist who is working a disability scam by pretending to be crippled from the waist down—professes his love for Ricky while the two get sloppy drunk in a strip club ("Who the Hell Invited All These Idiots to My Wedding?" 1:6), or when Ricky, recently busted for siphoning and reselling gas at a makeshift gas station, asks the judge that he be allowed to use profanities in order effectively defend himself, citing the "People's Freedom of Choices and Voices Act" ("If I Can't Smoke and Swear I'm Fucked," 3:3). The humour in these scenes is evident, but no more so than the pathos we feel when the characters acknowledge the gap between their desires and their personal limitations.

Perhaps the best example of striking a balance between profane and ennobling humour is a scene from "A Man's Gotta Eat" (4:2), where Randy bathes in a makeshift outdoor shower he has constructed from a garden hose, shredded plastic bags, and the remnants of an old lawn chair. Thrown out of their trailer by Ricky, who has risen to the rank of Trailer Park Supervisor, Randy and Jim Lahey are forced to live in their own car and plot their revenge. In the meantime, they adapt to circumstance: Lahey fries bacon and eggs on the engine block, and Randy makes his morning ablution. When Ricky arrives to take the car from them (as it technically belongs to whomever holds the title of park supervisor), he spots Randy showering and protests: "Randy, I can see you through all those goddamn liquor bags and lawn chair strapping, fucksakes!" To which Randy responds simply, "Well, stop friggin' looking, Rick!" Ricky is so disgusted by the scene that all he can do is drive away, taking Randy and Lahey's breakfast, half of their belongings, and the cord holding up Randy's ersatz shower with him, leaving Randy and Lahey completely exposed. Conspicuously absent from this hilarious scene is any malicious laughter. Though Ricky literally strips them of their dignity and privacy, he takes little pleasure in doing so. Despite the deep well of hatred between the three men, and Lahey's oft-sworn pledge to kill Ricky, their battles are, for them, tragic and of great consequence.

At the end of Season Four, Lahey tries to murder Ricky in a shootout that will eventually land both in jail, but he is too drunk to shoot straight. When the two are paroled at the beginning of Season Five, Ricky plots Lahey's murder, but his plan is spoiled when Lahey offers him what seems a sincere apology and a sobriety pledge. The truce is broken when Ray reveals that Jim has been secretly drinking, and Lahey responds by exposing Ray's disability fraud, then tipping off a gang of gun-crazy drug dealers that Ricky and Julian stole their stash ("Jim Lahey Is a Fucking Drunk and He Always Will Be," 5:5). The characters' exaggerated sense of scale—their typically disproportionate response to threats, implied and real—fuels the humour in each of these scenes, but it also speaks to the charm and purpose of the show's realism. If Sunnyvale Trailer Park seems at first a remarkably banal narrative arena, the petty dramas that play out there make what I think is a profound social statement about the objectification of poverty. Poverty is not a crucible to try men's souls, nor a social problem to be corrected by ambition and government funding, nor merely a world of liquor-bag-thin walls, where the private lives—and private functions—of one's neighbours become the stuff of crass humour. It is a state of being and belonging, with its own unique set of social pressures and problems, and a narrative arena as viable as any other. For Dickens and Horatio Alger, poverty is a smithy of the soul, but for the trailer park boys, it is simply where their stories begin and end, more or less peaceably and to good effect.

In an elaborate sequence from the series' second episode, "Fuck Community College, Let's Get Drunk and Eat Chicken Fingers," Ricky acclimates himself to his new home—the derelict car in Julian's side yard—by tricking it out with domestic comforts: Julian's stolen toaster oven on the roof, a dish rack on the trunk, various cutlery spread out on the hood, and a garden hose lashed to the window pillar with lengths of duct tape, in lieu of indoor plumbing. Over time, the collection will grow to include a television, a hot plate, a microwave oven, a clothesline, a lazy Susan, an elaborate pantry and—after he gets the car running again—a hockey stick to "clear all that shit off" when he needs to go somewhere. Swelling with home pride, he invites Ray and Julian over for a meal, but while the promise of free booze and blues music blasting from the car stereo is enough to entice Ray to roll by in his stolen wheelchair, Julian will have none of it. At the first whiff of chicken fingers, he storms out of his trailer, tosses the contents of the toaster oven on the ground, serves Ricky a handwritten eviction notice and threatens to leave the park and enroll in community college to become "an electrician, a meat cutter, or a television and radio broadcaster." As Julian huffs off, Ricky turns to the camera and launches into a monologue about Julian's ingratitude and lack of perspective. Gesturing toward Julian's trailer, which Ricky describes as a "fuckin' palace," Ricky notes that he is happy simply to live in a car, where he is provided with "everything I need."

Though the scene is certainly humorous, it avoids absurdity, partly due to the sincerity of the characters, and partly due to the matter-of-fact manner of its presentation. In their seminal study of mock documentary, *Faking It*, Jane Roscoe and Craig Hight argue that the genre frequently uses the documentary camera as a sort of straight man to amplify the comedic affect of absurd material by pretending to take it seriously.[3] We see this especially in the films of Christopher Guest: *Waiting for Guffman* (1996), *Best in Show* (2000), and *A Mighty Wind* (2003), which at once ridicule and celebrate the petty dramas and victories of their community theatre actors, washed up musicians, and dog fanciers by using the camera as an earnest and sympathetic observer, bridging the ironic distance between the audience and the subject. But the mockumentary format also opens up a unique critical dialogue between the viewer, the "straight" camera and the subject that becomes apparent at moments of circumspection like the one described above. Though Ricky's Panglossian response to his and Julian's living situation suggests a witless optimism, his interpretation of the events—his narration—forces us to consider potential gaps in our own perception. Sure, it is funny, but doesn't Ricky have a point? Moreover, because the documentarians themselves do not explicitly contribute to that narration, the characters are at times able to commandeer the narrative and make of it a diary of their thoughts, opinions, and unashamed self-reflection.

Like Guest's films and the two television versions of *The Office, Trailer Park Boys* eschews the narrator/interviewer convention of mockumentaries like *Take the Money and Run* (1969), *This Is Spinal Tap* (1984), and *C.S.A.: The Confederate States of the America* (2004), for a seeming monologic form not unlike what we find in the documentaries of Errol Morris. Morris' Interrotron device, which compels his subjects to look directly into the camera while answering questions the audience does not hear—nor in most cases might guess—creates an experience both immediate and uncanny, where the audience becomes keenly aware of any cracks in the subject's facade. The effect is not unlike that of Kurosawa's clever device for framing the testimonies in *Rashomon* (1950). Absent any sensible avatar of the questioner, subjects' remarks seem far less structured, more associational, immediate, and contingent. But the willful subject can use this exposure to advantage by appropriating the camera's gaze, leaving the viewer to wonder who exactly is the straight man after all. Sasha Baron Cohen's mockumentary, *Borat: Cultural Learnings of America for Make Benefit Glorious Nation of Kazakhstan* (2006), offers a brilliant variation on this narrative strategy, where Borat Sagdiyev—an extraordinary amalgam of hateful stereotypes unconcealed by his grey serge suit and exuberant gestures of affection—plays straight man and stooge by way of revealing the true butt of the joke, the audience. For we cannot laugh at Borat's monstrous prejudices and those of the people he meets on his journey through America without reflecting upon our own. Of course, the film is also self-reflexive. As a mockumentary that is also a documentary—a film that uses the devices of documentary for comic effect, but also documents that effect—Borat blurs the line between text and metatext. Clearly Cohen is the one driving the ice cream truck—in costume—through the American South, and clearly the resolution of that journey—Pamela Anderson in a "wedding sack"—is pre-scripted. But each time "Borat" introduces himself to another citizen of his documentary version of America, we ask ourselves, "Who is walking into whose frame?"

Similar, though less ontologically complicated, questions arise in *Trailer Park Boys* when the fake documentary crew intrudes upon the narrative space. Two examples come to mind from the Season One, because they are the first times we catch a glimpse of the people behind the camera. In Episode 4, "Mrs. Peterson's Dog Gets Fucked Up," Ricky grabs the boom mike and drags the soundman into the frame because he and Julian are having difficulty moving a lawn tractor they intend to steal from a farmer's barn. "I don't mind you guys following us around," he demurs, "but you could at least give us a hand here." Later in the scene, the soundman is wounded in a shootout between Ricky, Julian, and the farmer, and Ricky and Julian drop him at the curb in front of a hospital emergency room before fleeing, to have their own wounds tended by a veterinarian. Later that evening, the soundman leaves a message on Julian's answering machine, thanking him for saving his life and explaining the situation to his employers, helping him to keep his job, which the soundman claims is "the best one I've ever had." The second instance occurs in the final episode of Season One, "Who the Hell Invited All These Idiots to My Wedding?" when the same soundman and his partner with the digital video camera unwittingly walk in front of a supermarket surveillance camera as they document the boys' holding up the store. Later, footage of this and other of the boys' crimes is used to throw them back in jail, but what we see is very telling: a tiny crew of eager young filmmakers so earnest in their desire to accurately document their subjects that they unwittingly conspire not only in their crimes but their conviction. Significantly, we witness this scene not through the probing, investigative lens of the dedicated straight man, but through the passive, clinical eye of the security camera: one more view of the complex relationship between subject and object.

More important than the earnest tone of such scenes is the remarkably realistic backdrop against which they are played. While Christopher Guest's dramas culminate in theatres, dog show arenas, and sound stages—"play" spaces that intentionally undercut the emotional impact of the action—the diegesis of *Trailer Park Boys* is presented using a comic facsimile of the observational, direct cinema approach of Frederick Wiseman, where characters are observed in situ, their dramas organic outgrowths of their environment. In Wiseman's films, the dramatic space is also tightly circumscribed: the Massachusetts Correctional Institution at Bridgewater in *Titicut Follies* (1967); Philadelphia's Northeast High in *High School* (1968); the ICU at Boston's Beth Israel Hospital in *Near Death* (1989); The Spring, a Tampa battered women's shelter in *Domestic Violence* (2001). This specificity not only establishes an authenticity of place, but also amplifies the cathartic force of their dramas and tragedies, because they happen to these people in—and largely because of—these environments. While most fiction and non-fiction film narratives lend themselves to universal application—we identify with the stories because the characters and settings seem generically familiar—Wiseman's documentaries are not about shared experience, so they require a far more detailed rendering of narrative space in order to produce the empathy required for catharsis. The viewer must get to know the place before entering it.

Many dramatic television programs make claims to a documentary realism, particularly crime dramas like *NYPD Blue* and *Law and Order.* But in most cases this is merely a debased style, having about as much to do with the empathetic ontology of Wiseman as the fast-paced cutting of the so-called "MTV style" has to do with the Romantic sensibilities of the avant garde filmmakers who invented that style in the 30s, 40s, and 50s. The rare exception is HBO's *The Wire,* a show that splits its crime-and-corruption narrative cleanly in half along the thin blue line and takes the viewer—with equal intimacy and attention to detail—from the Mayor's office, to the precinct house, to the crack house and, perhaps most importantly, to the street corners where Baltimore's drug trade lives and dies. In a recent interview with novelist Nick Hornby, the show's creator and principal writer, David Simon, addresses the show's remarkable authenticity:

> My standard for verisimilitude is simple and I came to it when I started to write prose narrative: fuck the average reader. . . . I decided to write for the people living the event, the people in that very world. . . . I would consider [the show] a failure if people in these worlds took in my story and felt that I did not get their existence, that I had not captured their world in any way that they would respect.[4]

More than the hope of gaining himself "street cred" among drug dealers and corrupt cops, Simon needs that authenticity to give real substance to his story. In the same interview, he compares the two models of tragedy: the classical, where the hero is confronted by unknowable external forces and, though he strikes back valiantly, is finally crushed by them without knowing why (Oedipus, for example), and the modern, where the hero is confronted with a problem that challenges his sense of identity and forces him to undergo an internal transformation (Hamlet, for example). Though most contemporary narratives follow the second model, *The Wire* clearly follows the first, where the inscrutable external forces are not gods or fates, but the endlessly labyrinthine social codes of contemporary America, which are all but hidden from the racially and economically marginalized—hence, the insistent realism of the show. Like Wiseman's films, whose subjects are also at the mercy of the unknowable gods and monsters, *The Wire* demands authenticity in order to create dramatic empathy.

Much of what David Simon says could easily be applied to *Trailer Park Boys* (or Balzac, for that matter), and the two programs share much in common: both are about poverty, crime, and drugs; both develop elaborate plots around complex criminal schemes using a large ensemble cast; and both feature a character named Bubbles (in *The Wire,* he is a homeless heroin addict who sells information to cops; in *Trailer Park Boys,* he is a cat lover who lives in a tool shed and gives advice to thieves). But, as any comedy writer will tell you, realism is much more difficult to sustain in a genre that is nearly always about exaggerated perceptions. The more realistic the diegesis, the more mean-spirited the humour appears: it simply cuts too close to the bone. This can, of course, be used to brilliant effect. *Curb Your Enthusiasm,* for example, adopts the mockumentary pose to amplify the level of existential discomfort in Larry David's escalating scenarios of miscommunication and social ostracism. The pleasure of the show owes mostly to the exquisite pain of watching the events unfold in a "real" narrative space. But if this cruel humour is acceptable in a show about ultra-rich celebrities in that simulacrum of reality known as Hollywood (*Curb* is a fish-out-of-water story, but the fish is worth $500 million and surrounds himself with celebrity friends), nearly all comedies about the poor avoid documentary realism, perhaps because layers of aesthetic artifice shield the audience from the charge of "laughing at the poor," or because realistic depictions of poverty awaken antipathies that spoil our delusions of humanistic concern for the less fortunate. Yet *Trailer Park Boys* offers a remarkably rich diegesis that rings far truer to life than the fantasies of yuppie prosperity that have so long been the staple of American television comedy in shows like *Friends, Seinfeld,* and *Sex in the City,* with their hermetically sealed worlds photographed like mail-order catalogues, where the twin consumer aspirations of security and plenty are implicitly met. The nearest parallel to *Trailer Park Boys*' aesthetic in contemporary television is *The Office,* which renders the all-too-familiar environment of corporate park culture in loving detail. But shows explicitly about class like *The Beverly Hillbillies, Roseanne, Married . . . With Children,* and *The King of Queens* play their comic versions of social commentary on stage sets, and even those that occasionally leave the studio sound stage create alternative universes: the post-card Manhattan of *Sex and the City,* the Martha Stewart fantasia of *Desperate Housewives.* This is equally true of the opposite end of the social scale. *My Name Is Earl,* for example, combines the visual crassness of John Waters and the jocular pacing of the Coen brothers to create a cartoon backdrop for its running commentary on commonality and karma. But the denizens of Sunnyvale Trailer Park live among the foot-high grass, old tires and engine blocks, raccoon-ravaged trashcans, and stolen shopping carts familiar to anyone who has spent time in a trailer park. Where dramatic series like *The Wire* might use this authenticity to serve the socio-political ends of neo-realism, *Trailer Park Boys* presents poverty, not as ennobling or degrading, nor as a metaphor for the shared human condition, but merely as a precondition of its characters' lives.

Mockumentary is by definition ironic, yet the combination of authenticity and specificity in *Trailer Park Boys* produces a level of empathy for characters equivalent to that in *The Wire* and Wiseman's films. The only difference is the manner of catharsis each seeks, tears or laughter. One cannot help but feel compassion for the absurd causes and trials of Sunnyvale's residents, nor resist embracing their ethos, best expressed in the title of the second episode of the series, "Fuck Community College, Let's Get Drunk and Eat Chicken Fingers": to cast off ambition for the nobler virtue of friendship. Far from mocking them, we soon see that they are, in the words of Robb Wells, who plays Ricky and co-writes the show, "better than most people in the real world. They'd do anything for their family . . . and friends." Sunnyvale's resident white rapper, J-Roc, has a more poetic way of expressing the same sentiment: "In this park it's one mafucka for all and all mafuckas for all mafuckas." And he does mean all mafuckas, including the villains. In "Jim Lahey Is a Drunken Bastard" (2:2), Lahey caps his campaign for Trailer Park Supervisor against interloper, Sam Losco, with a drunken speech that borders on Chaplinesque humanism:

> Who in this park, or even in the whole world, doesn't have problems? Who doesn't have a drink too many times once in a while and maybe even winds up passed out in their own driveway, pissing themselves? Who doesn't drink too much sometimes or who doesn't have a puff from time to time? And who doesn't have problems with the people they love? This is our home. This is our community.

The notion of the community built upon mutual fallibility and boorishness is the cornerstone of many successful comedies, not least of which the greatest of all class based American sitcoms, *The Simpsons.* This acceptance—this inclusive spirit—owes much to the classical fatalism that undergirds the humour in each show. While Homer Simpson may be oblivious—and so strangely immune—to his terrible parental and environmental legacy, we and Marge and Lisa and Karl and Lenny must all admit to ourselves, in moments of sober contemplation, that the apocalyptic meltdown is inevitable. Our affectionate laughter is ever tinged with perverse irony. And Ricky knows it, too. "I'm like a frog running along the highway," he tells Julian as the police start closing in at the end of Season One: "Eventually some car is gonna hit you, and this is the fuckin' car" ("Who the Hell Invited All These Idiots to My Wedding?" 1:6). Or, as his Calvinist father, Ray, explains after he blows all of the boys' savings on video lottery games, "That's the way she goes, boys. Sometimes she goes, sometimes she doesn't. Cause that's the fuckin' way she goes" ("The Fuckin' Way She Goes," 5:3). Few—if any—of Springfield's or Sunnyvale's residents could claim to be among Calvin's elect, but at very least they can laugh at the cosmic joke.

One could, of course, find a valuable class commentary at the centre of *Trailer Park Boys,* where the damned state of these characters affects something between marginalization and rebellion. In his essay, "From Back Bacon to Chicken Fingers: Recontextualizing the 'Hoser' Archetype," Ryan Diduck highlights the program's "counter commodity culture."[5] Sunnyvale residents aspire, but merely to better trailers and more liberty to hang out and get drunk with friends. They trade, but only in illegal goods: hydroponic marijuana, pirated rap CDs, amateur porn, bootleg vodka, and stolen groceries, barbeque grills, Christmas trees, cable television, and propane. For Diduck, they are outlaws of capitalism, refusing to recognize the legitimacy of corporate culture. Perhaps the most glaring statement of the show's critique of this culture is the fact that all brand names—be they cola logos on cans, raised white letters on tires, or insignias on T-shirts—all branding is blurred out in post-production. This commentary is less the biting Marxist wit of a Bunuel or Godard film than the feckless tag of a drunken graffiti artist—a smudge on the ordinary barely noticed by any but intimates of the program—but, by denying the hegemony of the brand, the objects per se are restored to their original position of primacy. Almost invisibly, they are transformed from emblems of consumer culture into precisely what they always were: the detritus of modern life, the trash and the soon-to-be trash. In place of the rows of General Mills cereals on Jerry Seinfeld's kitchen shelf and the carefully posed hand of Elaine holding (albeit with winking acknowledgment) a pristine bottle of Snapple with its logo turned to the camera, *Trailer Park Boys* gives us a shredded bag of salt and vinegar potato chips and a soda can stuffed with cigarette butts.

No doubt, the boys are outlaws, but unlike corporate raiders and gangsters, whose grand ambitions elevate them to the level of anti-heroes, the narrow circumscription that constitutes the boys' worldview renders their schemes ridiculous. Where Gordon Gekko builds an empire from insider trading and his "Greed is good" mantra (*Wall Street,* 1987) and Tony Soprano lords over the New Jersey crime syndicate with a Machiavellian will and a business paradigm that includes web fraud and bogus HUD loans (*The Sopranos*), Julian and Ricky's plans are not only ludicrous, but doomed to fail: smuggling marijuana across the US/Canadian border using a model railroad and hashish in the handles of stolen shopping carts; operating a night club out of J-Roc's Mom's trailer and a "Convenients Store" of stolen goods from Cory's Mom's shed. The central narrative structure of the show varies little from season to season: the boys leave jail, set a criminal scheme of idiotic complexity into motion, get caught and go back to jail. Each season is prefaced by a short interview with Ricky and Julian—just before or after their release—where Julian discourses on lessons learned during their incarceration. But as soon as the boys leave the prison grounds, it is back to business. Season Two, for example, begins with Julian laying out the plans for "Freedom 35," an early retirement program that requires them to grow enough marijuana for 20 pounds of hashish. In order to grow the hash, they need money for plants and hydroponic equipment, which they hope to raise by a bit of petty larceny. "I picked you up at jail ten minutes ago," Bubbles protests after Julian lays out the plan, "and now you're telling me we're going to steal car stereos" ("What the Fuck Happened to Our Trailer Park?" 2:1). The season ends with a police chase: a helicopter and a half-dozen squad cars in hot pursuit of the boys hauling their Airstream trailer grow house through Nova Scotia farmland. Season Three begins with a plan to supplement their illegal income with "semi-legit" businesses until they can raise enough money to take a cruise, and ends with Julian taking the fall for a stolen ATM machine while Bubbles, Trevor, and Cory quaff umbrella drinks on the high seas.

Key to their relentless optimism, as well as their invariable pattern of behaviour, is the notion that bleak circumstances can be transformed through "the power of positive thinking." But theirs is at best a gross misreading of Norman Vincent Peale, and at worst a hallucination. Ricky's version is clearly the latter: "You can either pretend you're in jail, or right now I'm pretending I'm in university" ("Who the Hell Invited All of These Idiots to My Wedding?" 1:6). With Julian, the matter is a bit more remote. Though he claims to be an avid reader in prison, the only time we actually see him with a book is in "Give Peace a Chance" (5:1). His pre-release interview takes place in his prison cell, and in the foreground we see an unopened tome entitled *Triumph of the Salmon.* A pure invention of the show, the title of the text nonetheless offers a pretty clear notion of Julian's life philosophy: his poetics, if you will. As a symbol of eternal determination, the salmon is an ideal role model for Julian. The "triumph" of the salmon isn't that it reaches the spawning ground upstream, but that it does so year after year, relentlessly pursuing the path of greatest resistance. Like Julian, it swims against the current of conventional wisdom, out of instinct, not principled rebellion.

Of course, rebellion is a necessary mark of the hero, classical or modem. Achilles is merely the best of the Greek warriors until Agamemnon's insult compels him to do something truly willful: he refuses to fight. Satan is God's minion until he leads a rebellion against His tyranny and is cast into chaos. Each may be playing a part divinely ordained for him, but his actions run counter to everything that once defined him. The soldier uses his sword, not passive resistance, and angels of God obey Divine Will, they don't question it. While it is true that Ricky, Julian, and Bubbles rebel against the law, the petty tyrannies of Jim and Barb Lahey, and common sense, their actions are as predictable as if written in their DNA or, in Ray's Calvinistic view, simply preordained. In Sunnyvale Trailer Park, you are who you are, and nothing can change that. Or, as Ricky explains to Julian after he suggests Ricky give up growing marijuana in "The Bare Pimp Project," "It's like telling NWA to stop being black" (2:7). He will not stop, cannot stop. Nor will Julian leave Sunnyvale, nor Bubbles move out of his shed, nor Jim Lahey stop pursuing his revenge upon Ricky because, as Jim says of Ricky, "A shit-leopard can't change his spots" ("A Shit Leopard Can't Change His Spots," 3:8). Perhaps this is what Mike Clattenberg means when he says that the show is about the characters playing the cards they are dealt. If the cards do not change, the hand plays out the same. That is, unless one of them learns to bluff.

This endlessly repeating narrative of instinctual resistance combines with the ontological instability of the show's mockumentary format to create the sort of giddy anxiety one feels when watching a drunken pal list toward the bathroom. We know that he will get there eventually, and we laugh as he stumbles and bumps into the coffee table, but we also cross our fingers and hope he doesn't get too badly hurt or make too much of a mess along the way. In place of symbols and social commentary, cheap laughter at the expense of those who can afford it, or the somewhat illogical notion that nothing of merit happens in a culturally devalued landscape, *Trailer Park Boys* offers the willing viewer more than just a comic glance into its rusted-rivet counterculture. It offers us a sort of temporary membership. Like the soundman who has to beg for his job back even after having taken a bullet for the boys, we are happy to be invited into their generous company, if only to watch them list through our living room week after week, stumbling over the coffee table and stopping to urinate in the fichus, for it is in this teetering world of the absurd and the all-too-real that we come to know the true meaning of empathy.

Notes

1. The series was developed from a feature-length film, *Trailer Park Boys* (1999), and has run on Canada's Showtime Network since 2001. A second feature film, *Trailer Park Boys: The Movie* (a.k.a. *Trailer Park Boys: The Big Dirty*) was released in 2006, and quickly became the highest-grossing English-language Canadian film. Following the recent first run of Season Seven, the show announced an indefinite hiatus.
2. Durbin, Jonathan. "Canadian Crude." *Macleans,* 116.47 (24 November 2003): 60.
3. Roscoe, Jane, and Craig Hight. *Faking It: Mock-documentary and the Subversion of Factuality.* New York: Palgrave, 2001.
4. Nick Hornby. "David Simon" (interview). *The Believer* 5.6 (August 2007): 72.
5. Diduck, Ryan. "From Back Bacon to Chicken Fingers: Recontextualizing the 'Hoser' Archetype." *Offscreen* 10.1 (31 January 2006). http://www.offscreen.com/biblio/phile/essays/hoser_archetype/

Works Cited

Diduck, Ryan. "From Back Bacon to Chicken Fingers: Recontextualizing the 'Hoser' Archetype." *Offscreen* 10.1 (31January2006).http://www.offscreen.com/biblio/phile/essays/hoser_archetype/

Durbin, Jonathan. "Canadian Crude." *Macleans* 116.47 24 November 2003): 60.

Hornby, Nick. "David Simon" (interview). *The Believer* 5.6 (August 2007). 70–8.

Roscoe, Jane, and Craig Hight. *Faking It: Mock-documentary and the Subversion of Factuality.* New York: Palgrave, 2001.

Sibiga, Matthew, and Don Winninger. *The Complete* Trailer Park Boys. Toronto: Random House Canada, 2007.

The *Little Mosque on the Prairie*: Examining (Multi) Cultural Spaces of Nation and Religion

Sandra Cañas

Introduction

Arabs and Muslims have a long, often dark history of representation by dominant western media. Jack Shaheen (2001) has studied stereotypes of Arabs and Muslims in films and television, arguing that Muslim men have been portrayed as fanatics and, more recently, as terrorists. Muslim women, in particular, have also been at the centre of media representations. However, as Mernissi (2001) illustrates, their images seem more contradictory compared to the representation of Muslim men. Muslim women have long been represented either as exotic and voluptuous belly dancers closeted in harems, always ready to please men's desires, or as submissive victims of a patriarchal religion.

These forms of representation follow a discursive logic of what Edward Said (1978) calls "orientalism," that is, the exoticization and colonization of the Other by means of discourse and representation. Orientalist discourses portray Muslims as inferior, premodern, and violent, unlike the West, which emerges as superior, modern, and enlightened. And oftentimes, orientalist discursive formations are crosscut by gender. Meyda Yegenoglu's (1998) work offers a critical departure from Said's orientalism. In her *Colonial Fantasies*, Yegenoglu insists on Said's failure to acknowledge how gender and sexuality (the latent or unconscious feature of orientalism) have been at the very centre of orientalist discursive formations. Beyond the mere addition of women and gender to Said's argument, Yegenoglu borrows from Lacanian psychoanalytical approach to examine the veil as prototypical orientalist fantasy—a site for colonial desire and sexuality. Several other postcolonial feminist critics have underlined the persistence of colonial images about Muslim woman in the imaginaries of western feminist scholarship (Hoodfar, 1993; Kahf, 1999; Moallem, 2005; Mohanty 1988). Western representations of so-called "Third World women" portray them as traditionalist, religious, and submissive, in contradistinction to their western sisters who are regarded as modern, liberated, and thus capable of liberating their allegedly oppressed sisters. These types of colonial discourses on women create or reinforce fixed and monolithic representations that effectively obliterate the real complexities and contradictions that permeate such communities' everyday lives.

While within a post-9/11 geopolitical context, orientalist discourses on Muslims have been greatly reinforced and spread by media. A challenge to this orientalist orthodoxy cultivated and nurtured by hegemonic media discourse has emerged from within this very media space itself. It is a relatively new Canadian TV series, called *Little Mosque on the Prairie.*

Since it first aired on 9 January 2007, the Canadian comedy *Little Mosque on the Prairie* has been a focus of public attention. Transmitted through Canadian Broadcasting Corporation (CBC) on Monday nights, the series revolves around a Muslim community settled in a fictional Canadian prairie town called Mercy. The show's creator, Zarqa Nawaz, is a 39-year-old Muslim woman born in England and raised in Toronto.

According to Nawaz, *Little Mosque on the Prairie* is based on her own experiences as a Muslim in the West: "I grew up in a mosque, I got married in a mosque, I spend a lot of time in a mosque—the mosque is a really important part of my life" (Goodman, 2006). Indeed, as we will see, the series focuses on the contradictory space of a mosque located inside a Christian parish, which metaphorically stands for an ethical vision of the post-9/11 multicultural nation.

This article seeks to develop a cultural analysis of *Little Mosque on the Prairie*. I will approach the show both as a *cultural text* rich in complex symbolic meanings that demand decoding, and as a *cultural practice* situated in a broader political terrain of signification.[1] Inspired by the approaches of Richard Flores (1998), Kamran Ali (2004, 2005), and Jafari Allen (n.d.), I analyze *Little Mosque* not only as a cultural text laden with symbolic meanings, but also as a cultural practice rooted in a cultural-political field of struggle. In his work, Allen analyzes how erotic subjectivities are performed in Cuba, underlining how national politics inform this performance. Through an analysis of Pakistani pulp fiction and TV serials, Ali illustrates how media is a means to produce narratives that call into question universal representations generated within a conservative society. And, finally, Flores's analysis of the Alamo helps us to think how the production of spaces and meaning is linked to economic and political processes of the modern nation.

These approaches, especially that of Flores, take seriously the need to situate cultural texts within broader fields of struggle, a departure famously and systematically articulated by Fredric Jameson's classic work *The Political Unconscious: Narrative as a Socially Symbolic Act* (1981). In this work, Jameson seeks to place cultural texts—such as, in his examples, the novels of Balzac, Gissing, and Conrad—in relation to wider fields of signification, or "semantic horizons." For Jameson, cultural criticism is urged to move across several overlapping scales of meaning production: these proceed from (1) the individual text (the novel, the film, a TV series) understood as a symbolic act; (2) to the level of the "ideologeme" (the individual text situated within a broader social field); and finally, to the intersection of the "ideology of form" (which Jameson describes in terms of "the symbolic messages transmitted to us by the co-existence of various sign systems" and the "mode of production": 1981: 76). While I will not discuss the strengths and limitations of Jameson's approach here, I do find his methodological movement essential to understanding the force fields of signification within *Little Mosque on the Prairie*. In this sense, Jameson's model of cultural criticism inspires the organization of my analysis.

First, I examine several of the prominent cultural symbols within the show considered as a cultural text, with particular attention to how the Muslim community settled in the prairie town of "Mercy" struggles to build spaces of its own. Central to this process is the role of the media and public institutions within the show. How do the people struggle over this space? How is this space a central site for questions of identity, both within the Muslim community, and between the Muslims and the broader society? Next, I begin to examine how the show situates itself within a broader terrain of cultural-political struggle. I analyze how the series seeks to contest hegemonic, orientalist representations vis-à-vis the emphasis upon tensions and differences within the Muslim community of Mercy. What messages are conveyed through the show? What kind of narrative, if any, emerges out of the articulation and sequencing of individual episodes? How might this narrative be understood within the wider geopolitical terrain of the cultural politics of meaning around nation and Islam? That is, I explore how representation works in tandem with narrative to produce socially symbolic acts whose meanings must be grasped within a historically specific field of cultural politics around Islam, gender, and the nation. In the conclusion, I consider some of the strengths and weaknesses of the ambivalent dynamics of multiculturalism operationalized in the series, broaching the contradictions of the very "ideology of form" around which *Little Mosque* is constructed.

Negotiating Contested Spaces in *Little Mosque*

Little Mosque on the Prairie takes place almost entirely within a mosque-within-a-parish-hall—a fact of great significance to how the cultural politics of nation and religion are dealt with by the series. The first episode is particularly significant, for it is there that the audience is introduced to the series as a whole, as well as to the individual characters and their dilemmas. The entire episode is preoccupied—but in a hilarious way—with the xenophobia and alarmism of non-Muslim understandings of Islamic practice and culture.

But the first episode is also, as with each succeeding episode, an irruption into the public imaginary of the Muslim presence, an encounter, unfolding from the creative imagination of Nawaz, which seeks to expose western viewers to the everyday lives of Muslims living in the West. The series begins here strategically for a reason, namely, to start the process of calling into question the orientalist "political unconscious" of the western imaginary and its construction of the figure of the threatening Muslim Other.

How this first episode unfolds, how it constitutes a "socially symbolic act" in the lexicon of Jameson, is key to the broader narrative of the series. The first encounter between the Muslim community and western Canadian society takes place when a white man wanders in on a prayer session. He immediately leaves the place, making all kind of assumptions, and calls the "terrorist hotline." The man was looking for the construction company owned by Yasir; instead, he found the community praying. Completely disturbed, he exclaims: "Osama bin Laden also ran a construction company." Another illustrative scene takes place in the airport where a Muslim is detained and interrogated by the police guards. This Muslim is the new Imam for the mosque. When interrogated in an office, all his movements and words are considered suspicious. The Imam is released and when he finally arrives in Mercy, a journalist is waiting for him, and immediately questions him as a terrorist, inquires into his connections to Saudi Arabia, Al Qaeda, and a sleeper cell. Later, the Imam holds an interview with the local conservative radio pundit, who immediately asks him whether he is a terrorist, referring to him as "Johnny Jihad" and a "Bedouin Buckaroo." Throughout the series, this conservative media talk show host plays an important role, and it is through his character, as with such media forms, that the prejudices and stereotypes about Muslims are recreated and spread. Indeed, the radio pundit shows how the media operates as a site of production of orientalist imaginaries, which are later disseminated throughout and internalized by groups in society, such as the disturbed white man who calls the "terrorist hotline" after having come across people praying.

The first episode of *Little Mosque on the Prairie* is thus important because it shows some of the most common prejudices and assumptions associated with Islam and Muslims, propagated through and reinforced by media and public institutions. It shows the institutional channels that help produce public imaginaries about Muslims and Islam in western societies, including dominant media discourse (the journalist and the radio pundit), and policing institutions such as the airport security officers. However, as we will see, this episode also starts to break the homogeneity of representations constructed and deployed by dominant institutional and media channels.

Contested Spaces: Mosque in a Church, the Public Pool

Particularly relevant in the first episode is the establishment of the mosque within a parish, and the relationship that develops between the Imam and the Priest. Both the existence of such contradictory space and the friendship between two local religious leaders call into question the theory that Muslims tend to belong to isolated communities, showing instead that interfaith dialogue is desirable and possible, especially in a geopolitical context that exacerbates xenophobia.

The first episode of *Little Mosque on the Prairie* begins with Arabic music overlaying the visual sequences. The camera frame narrows in upon what appears to be a church, whose sign reads "Mercy Anglican," rather than a mosque. After the opening sequence, the episode begins as the Muslims, one by one, enter their new mosque. Viewers later learn about each of the different characters. There is Baber, a Pakistani economics professor, who is the most conservative member of the Mercy Muslim community. He is the father of Layla, a teenager, who constantly challenges his traditionalism with such comments as: "You're looking fresh off the boat today!" We also encounter Yasir, a Lebanese secular Muslim who runs a construction company out of the Mercy Mosque, who is married to Sarah, a white woman and former Christian who converted to Islam when she married. Sarah and Yasir have a daughter, Rayyan, a 25-year-old doctor, who considers herself a Muslim feminist. We also learn of Amaar, the new Imam[2] of the community, a young lawyer of Pakistani descent who quit the law to study Islam in Egypt. And finally we encounter Fatima, an African Muslim from Nigeria, who owns a diner where Muslims and non-Muslims hang out. At the door, Yasir salutes the group with a warm "Salam Alaykum."[3] The last man to get inside is Baber, who exclaims: "Alhamdo-lillah[4]! Finally our own Mosque! No more shuffling from one basement to another! Well done Yasir!" The door closes, and above it the viewer discerns the words "Parish Hall." Beyond the Mercy Muslim community, viewers also find Reverend Duncan, the priest of the Anglican church; Fred, a radio pundit who leads a talk show called *Wake-up People*; and Mayor Ann, who runs the town.

After this first scene, one wonders why the mosque is inside an Anglican parish hall? Why is it disguised under the rubric of the construction company owned by Yasir, the businessman of the Muslim community? The mosque emerges as a contradictory cultural space where a variety of social struggles unfold within and over it. In this sense, the mosque functions, in part, as an allegory of the marginality of the Muslim community in a western society and the struggles they face to build spaces of their own in a non-Muslim country such as Canada—while trying to establish a mosque, the community is compelled to settle it in a Christian parish. Alternatively, a Christian space is becoming a Muslim one.

In a similar vein, the fourth episode focuses upon how the Mercy Muslim community struggles to win public spaces and, at the same time, to integrate into the broader Canadian society. This time the contested space is a public pool. Due to her medical condition, Rayyan, the young doctor, prescribes a swimming routine for Fatima. At the public pool, both of them seem really disappointed when they find out that the lifeguard is a male. As Muslims, they are not allowed to show themselves in the presence of men who are not their relatives. They decide to talk to the Mayor to request the hiring of a female lifeguard. In response the Mayor asks them to gather some signatures from the rest of the people. While Fatima and Rayyan succeed in collecting signatures, the Mayor later tells them there is no money available to pay an extra female lifeguard. As a result, they end up wearing Islamic swimming suits in order to attend the public pool.

This episode gives an example of how public spaces are negotiated. It also shows the complexities that underlie Muslim integration into Canadian society. As illustrated by the pool incident, Mercy Muslims want a distinct form of integration, one that does not take away their religious beliefs and practices, but rather respects their right to practice Islam. The process of Muslim integration into western societies has only recently begun to be discussed by some scholars (Haddad et al., 2006; Halim, 2006; Ramadan, 2004). Despite the important differences in the form and degree of integration by different Muslim groups, these scholars have drawn attention to the many shared challenges that Muslims in the West face and how these challenges are complicated by the diversity of Islamic cultural backgrounds and religious ideologies, to which we now turn.

Nation-Religion-Community: Contradictions and Differences within a Muslim Community

The presence of a young Imam generates different responses that underline the diversity within the Muslim community. For example, when Fatima, the Black African Muslim woman, first meets him, she says "You don't even look like an Imam," suggesting Imams should be old and have beards. In contrast to Fatima, Rayyan, the feminist Muslim, who belongs to a younger generation, states that the new Imam is what a spiritual leader of a community is supposed to be: progressive and born in Canada. However, the opposition between tradition and modernity is not always clear. It is interesting to see how two people belonging to a young generation oppose their parents. The Imam's parents never fasted, and Rayyan's parents are progressive Muslims within the Mercy community. This younger generation desires to retain a deep connection to Islamic tradition. However, as we will see shortly, the manner in which this connection is established is not without contradictions.

Between Tradition and Modernity

Several scenes and encounters bring out the social differences between tradition and modernity that are at the centre of the Mercy Muslim community. Take the problematic relation between the secular Yasir and the orthodox Baber. One scene that illustrates this relationship is the discussion around how to determine the beginning of Ramadan more exactly. While Baber wants to identify the beginning of Ramadan as the Prophet did—by observing the moon directly—Yasir is trying to do it using a telescope he purchased at COSTCO. The dispute is only resolved when the Imam intervenes and decides to climb to the roof and look at the moon. In another situation, Baber, the most traditionalist member of the community, is challenged to renegotiate his fundamentalist position. When his daughter has her period for the first time, she is supposed to cover her hair with a *hijab*. But after some heated discussions, Baber gives in to his daughter's wish to not wear the *hijab*, a stance which contrasts sharply with his apparently inflexible orthodoxy.

In a similar way, another episode shows how Hallowe'en is appropriated in a Muslim fashion, thus creating "Halal-oween."[5] What we see in this episode is a critical appropriation of certain aspects of western culture. Baber dresses in his traditional garb, and on Hallowe'en night, the children and parents mistakenly congratulate him for his disguise, saying he looks "just like a Taliban." The Muslim kids Baber escorts are, in contrast, actually dressed in costume, but in a manner that does not violate Islamic customs: the boy wears an olive suit, and the girl dresses like a *jinn*.[6] In this negotiated engagement with Hallowe'en, Baber, his daughter Layla, and her Muslim friend shed light on one of the most salient challenges that Muslim families face when living in the West: how to raise their children so that they can be good Muslims and at the same time adapt to the new environment. Such creative adaptations are a central strategy within the series, which seek, through satire, humour, and other comedic means, to break apart the homogenizing, western representations of the threatening Muslim Other.

Contesting such hegemonic representations occurs by other means as well. Within the series, religious debate on food and clothes also helps to mark the tension between tradition and modernity, especially the discussions among Fatima and Sarah as to what food is better—curry or cucumber sandwiches— to break the fast during the holy month of Ramadan. Sarah, the convert married to the Lebanese Yasir, identifies herself as a Muslim. However, the rest of the community, particularly the most traditionalist members, regard her as less Muslim and, even, an unauthentic Muslim. This image is reinforced by the fact that she does not dress with Muslim clothes like the rest of the women. However, throughout the show Sarah struggles to become a "good Muslim." Sarah represents the bridge between two faiths and two different worlds: she functions as a kind of mediator or cultural broker, the community member that helps her brothers and sisters understand her former religion, Christianity. But more generally, Sarah illustrates some of the major challenges converts face in western societies, where most of the Muslims are immigrants born into the religion and who tend to exclude recent converts, or to be critical of their efforts to adopt Islam. And in terms of gender, the character of Sarah sheds light on how women married to Muslim men have to struggle to be accepted in the Muslim community, and the challenges—such as being criticized not only by men, but by other Muslim women—they have to confront. In fact, the dilemmas around gender and religion are at the centre of the multicultural narrative that emerges out of *Little Mosque.*

Negotiating Gender Relations

Islam has constantly been associated with greater gender inequality. *Little Mosque on the Prairie* seeks to break down the erroneous ideas about the position that Muslim women hold within Islam by showing the complexities, tensions, and contradictions inherent in gender relations within a specific western context. One of the most contentious aspects of Islam is the segregation imposed between women and men. The second episode of *Little Mosque* engages with this issue. The first scene shows how some Muslim men are trying to set a barrier inside of the mosque to prevent men from being distracted by watching women when they pray. Baber, the orthodox Muslim, is the most interested in establishing this barrier. Rayyan, the young feminist, is the first one to oppose Baber's idea, saying: "the women already pray behind the men, isn't that enough?" Unlike Rayyan, Fatima, the African Muslim woman, wants the barrier, because "it gives privacy to the women too." However, according to Islamic practice, only the Imam can decide on such an issue. The Imam says the barrier doesn't have a theological foundation. Later, the discussion around the establishment of the barrier goes beyond the mosque, becoming an issue of marital disagreement. Sarah is against the barrier and asks her husband to convince the Imam and the other men not to set the barrier. Indeed, she stops having sex with him until he takes down the barrier. The barrier debate also becomes a public matter when the conservative radio pundit hears of the issue and lambasts the idea through his radio program. Immediately, western feminist women organize a protest outside the mosque in support of their sisters against oppression. Sarah, the community mediator, negotiates with the women, convincing them to stop the demonstration. After a big fight between supporters and opponents to the barrier, the Imam finally takes a decision: "the barrier stays *and* goes." After the Imam goes back to history and stumbles upon an episode of Suleyman, he decides to keep half of the barrier, forging a compromise between the warring factions of the Muslim community. This episode discusses how sex segregation is negotiated within the Muslim community. It also underlines the diverse opinions around the barrier, including those of both men and women. An interesting point is how the western women reacted: by organizing a demonstration against oppression, a collective action that reveals the ethnocentric grounding of western feminist notions of sisterhood (Mohanty, 1988). What the demonstration exemplifies is the ignorance about the multiplicity of opinions and feelings of what oppression is, erasing particular experiences such as the one illustrated by Fatima, who views the barrier as a positive thing rather than as a symbol of oppression.

Another aspect of Islam strongly criticized and poorly understood in the West is polygamy. Through humour and satire, episode 7 of *Little Mosque* illustrates the complexities involved when Muslim men attempt to take a second wife. Mother Hamoudi, Yasir's mom, comes to visit from Lebanon. The reason of the visit is her decision to have Yasir marry his cousin Samira, whose husband recently passed away. Mother Hamoudi insists on what a wonderful woman Samira is, her couscous being "heavenly tastes like angel droppings." In the eyes of Mother Hamoudi, compared to Sarah, the allegedly unauthentic Muslim convert, Samira is a *real* Muslim woman of Lebanese descent. Frightened to contradict his mother's decision, Yasir does not do anything at all. Mother Hamoudi looks for the Imam—and, like Fatima before, she cannot believe he is the Imam because he looks too young and does not have a beard. She asks the Imam to perform a second marriage, but he argues that polygamy is illegal in Canada. She insists, arguing that the marriage can be kept secret. Furious, Sarah asks Yasir to end the second marriage issue and she leaves the household, threatening to return only when Yasir faces up to his mother. Yasir fails in his first attempt to tell Mother Hamoudi he will not marry his cousin Samira when his mother manipulatively pretends to have a heart attack.

Later, an interesting conversation showing the different perspectives women have about polygamy takes place at Fatima's diner. Fatima, apparently a traditional Muslim, says polygamy is a dying tradition. Rayyan adds that even in Muslim countries very few men take a second wife. Mother Hamoudi insists Yasir needs a "real wife." But when she is asked if her husband took a second wife, she answers: "I was enough for my husband." Fatima adds that, even though Sarah is not her favourite person, because she is a bad Muslim, she is the only wife for Yasir. Mother Hamoudi gets upset and asks them: "What's wrong with you? Are you feminists?" In a different scene, the Imam advises Yasir to say "No!" to his mother. He asks Yasir if he has a prenuptial agreement excluding polygamy. Not having one, Yasir thinks a prenuptial agreement will dissuade his mother. Finally, showing a false prenuptial agreement to Mother Hamoudi, Yasir states he cannot marry his cousin and Sarah returns home.

Episodes 2 and 7 call into question the common assumption that associate women with oppression and men with domination, and which thereby create a static dichotomy of gender relations within Islam. Both episodes dismantle this representation by showing all the tensions, nuances, and contradictions generated when issues such as polygamy and sexual segregation are discussed. The traditional woman is not always so traditional and, in the same way, the modern woman is not always modern. Moreover, men do not always impose their decisions on women. And they are not the only ones that have power. In other words, the episodes seek to emphasize how polygamy and sexual segregation are experienced differently by each woman. Both of them are contentious issues, contested in multiple ways by both men and women, and in these episodes, women appear as agents of their own histories and lives, challenging implicitly colonial representations. The series is particularly adept in employing this critical approach to rethinking representation in two further episodes.

Contested Representations I: The Open House

With the purpose of inviting outsiders and generating an opportunity to improve the image of the Muslim community, the Mercy Muslim community celebrates an Open House, or "a celebration of diversity," as the Imam says. However, at first not everyone agrees with the Imam's plan. Baber, for example, thinks the mosque is not a tourist attraction. Other members of the community seem more enthusiastic: Rayyan, the Muslim feminist, is interested in giving the right impression about the status of women within Islam; Fatima, the African

Muslim, is more interested in telling the story of her ancestors from an African perspective, not "the missionary position," she jokes. Finally, agreeing to participate in the Open House, Baber is trying to decide what to teach to the largely Christian attendees, to whom he refers as "infidels," "crusaders," "heathens," "faithless," and "barbarians." Initially, everyone wants to speak during the Open House. However, the Imam insists that he is the only one who will speak. In response, many of the community members threaten to boycott the Open House. After being advised by the Reverend, the Imam lets the rest of the people speak.

Baber's categorization of westerners as barbarians, infidels, crusaders, etc. underlines another important aspect of orientalist discursive practices: a reverse orientalism. As this scene shows, not only the powerful produce orientalist imaginaries of the other, but also the subaltern. Baber's character is important because it satirizes Islamic fundamentalism, and, in the process, calls into question the idea that men have all the authority within the Muslim community and that such authority cannot be challenged. This is clear when some of the members of the community disagree with the Imam's decision to represent the whole community during the Open House. They do not want to be represented but want, rather, to represent themselves, questioning the Imam: "What do you know about being a Muslim *woman*?" "Or what do you know about being a *Black* Muslim woman?" These questions underline a common trend present throughout the series: the diversity existing in the community, especially the different experiences of what it means to be Muslim.

Contested Representations II: The First Convert

Episode 5 shows how hegemonic discourses on Islam and Muslims are enacted and contested, in this case, through the revealing experience of the first white convert in the Muslim community of Mercy. The episode starts with the end of the sermon or *khutbah*,[7] when all Muslims are exchanging their impressions. Strangely, a white man called Marlon is wandering around, observing and talking to some of the Muslims. When meeting the Imam he expresses his interest in Islam and his desire to become a Muslim. Close to them, Baber listens to the conversation and exclaims, "What a blessing! Our first real convert!"—unlike Sarah who, in Baber's opinion, is not a real convert and is thus a bad Muslim. Marlon visits Fatima's diner where he meets Baber and Layla (Baber's daughter). After salutation he immediately poses his eyes on Layla asking Baber why she is not wearing a *hijab*. Interestingly, Baber laughs nervously, replying: "the wind was very strong today and it must have blown off," and the daughter responds angrily: "I'm not wearing it," overtly defying her father's authority. After *Shahadah*[8] takes places, Marlon starts screaming *Allahu Akbar! Allahu Akbar! Allahu Akbar!* (God is great! God is great! God is great!), each time louder. The rest of the community seems happy, but after a while they look uncomfortable and start to worry. Trying to be what he thinks is a good Muslim, Marlon continues to criticize other community members.

At the cafeteria, he wants to make sure that all the food is *halal* and gets disappointed when Fatima tells him there is no *halal* store at Mercy and that, instead, she has to buy kosher. When he meets Rayyan, the convert exclaims: "Finally, a real Muslim! You'll make an obedient wife." Later, Baber invites the convert to his place. He shows up wearing Muslim clothes and immediately asks Baber's daughter: "Still no *hijab*?" And in return she answers: "Still no life?" Baber laughs embarrassed but does nothing else. Then, the convert asks him: "Have you tried beating her? It worked for the Taliban." Baber suggests he "find a model a little bit closer to home." Suddenly loud music is heard and the convert asks: "Do you permit that decadent music?" Baber tries to stop it, but his daughter answers: "Dad, you bought it for me!" Even more disappointed, Marlon adds that perhaps Allah is punishing Baber with this evil child. The convert even criticizes the fact that Yasir's business is inside of the mosque, threatening to talk with the Regional Islamic Council. Worried about his behaviour, some of the members of the community wonder what to do with this "white fool." The Imam offers to talk to him but Baber says: "You can't talk to fanatics." Yasir comes up with a plan, which consists of having a meeting where they will act inappropriately in order to scare away the convert: loud music, alcohol, dance, and inappropriate clothes. Indeed, the convert is completely disappointed about his Muslim brothers not being Muslim enough and leaves the community. The last scene of this episode shows Marlon in an event organized by the Anglican Church. When the Imam asks the Reverend about him the Reverend shrugs his shoulders and says some people like "spiritual shopping." This episode sheds light on some of the most common assumptions about Islam and Muslims. In particular, it examines how hegemonic discourse constantly seeks to homogenize, demonize, and exclude an Other rendered as a threat. The experience of the new convert helps to show how Islam is thought about and how Muslims are represented in the field of imagination. Marlon, for example, associates Islam with the Taliban, with punishing, with having an obedient wife, with beating women and/or with women wearing *hijab*. All these hegemonic ideas have been produced and spread widely by the media, and Marlon is simply enacting this "manufactured authenticity."

Conclusion: An Ambivalent Cultural Politics of the Multicultural

Islam can no longer be conceived as an outside to the West since it has become an inextricable presence in society. *Little Mosque on the Prairie* engages this reality in a humorous way, revealing some of the major challenges Muslims face in non-Muslim societies. One of the major challenges Muslims seem to struggle with is the construction of a space of their own, one that is flexible enough to allow the practice of their beliefs, while also making possible a degree of integration. The representations of identity and community in *Little Mosque* operate as counter-hegemonic symbolic acts that seek to illustrate the divergences and fissures that permeate the process of building a community. Much of my analysis has sought to highlight some of the primary contours of this first level of critique—identification of the structures of meaning permeating the cultural text. But, as Jameson's analysis emphasizes, texts and the meanings produced by them are part of a broader discursive and material field. As a cultural practice, *Little Mosque* might be conceptualized as an intervention into the contested cultural politics of post-9/11 nation formation. Through different characters that live diverse experiences, this Canadian serial shows that the Islamic world is multifaceted and contradictory, calling into question static, monolithic ideas of this religion and its practitioners. However, the Muslim community of *Little Mosque* does not live isolated from the rest of the world, and the series emphasizes the complex encounters between the Muslims and the often ignorant and xenophobic Canadian.

Abu-Lughod (1993) and Ali (2004) have analyzed how Egyptian and Pakistani television are used to promote certain cultural-political agendas. Similarly, *Little Mosque* exemplifies how the media are used to promote certain cultural politics. Apparently, this show seeks to provide a counter-hegemonic narrative through different strategies such as satire, mimicry, and personalization, which question stereotypes and prejudices of Muslims and Islam. This is particularly relevant in the post-9/11 context, where media have been used precisely in the opposite way, that is, to reinforce the idea that all Muslim men are terrorists and all Muslim women are oppressed. In direct opposition to the dominant media's orientalizing logics, one might think about *Little Mosque* as part of a more general Gramscian "war of position," which seeks to redefine what

Jameson calls the cultural "semantic horizons" which shape the public imagination. Kamran Ali's point about *Umrao Jan Ada* is here very relevant. As he writes, "Unlike the modest reach of academic works, Geo's production brought courtesan life into domestic spaces as it also intervened into a debate on morality, sexuality, and gender politics in present day Pakistan"(2004). The same can be argued for *Little Mosque* in its Canadian context.

Moreover, *Little Mosque on the Prairie* also seems to promote a particular national narrative. Scholars like Ali (2004), Abu-Lughod (1993), and Jirattikorn (2003) have focused on how media draw upon the past to produce specific narratives of the nation. *Little Mosque* is part of a national project as well, but, in contrast to the former, it does not re-imagine the past but instead explores the dilemmas lived in the present and, through this, seeks to create alternative imaginaries for the future. In this sense, *Little Mosque on the Prairie* can be thought of as a metaphor of a new, multicultural, and tolerant Canadian nation.

But herein lies the crux of the series and we might ask, as anthropologist Charlie Hale (2002) has queried, "Does multiculturalism menace?" In answering this question, analysis must shift from the first and second epistemological fields Jameson delimits, to the third: the intersection of the "ideology of form" and the "mode of production." It is important to note that the connection here is not deterministic in the manner of orthodox Marxism, where the base (the mode of production in the abstract) determines the superstructure (in this case the cultural sign systems). Rather, it is a question of exploring the connecting filaments between a formal meaning system and a broader historical horizon, where the nature of this connection is contradictory and marked by social conflict. In the case of *Little Mosque*, it means examining the striations suturing together the logics of multiculturalism, nation formation, and global capitalism. The work of Elizabeth Povinelli is suggestive. Povinelli's (2002) research on the production of multicultural Australia reveals how modern nations are subjected to international scrutiny through the pressure exerted by national indigenous struggles and social movements that increasingly demand recognition of localized cultural and economic claims. Such nations are often forced to comply with the exigencies of the global market and, to this extent, modern nations often have to appear as multicultural and tolerant, but within a framework determined not just by humanitarian concerns but also by the dictates of commercial capitalism. In Povinelli's work, cultural tolerance becomes a market dynamic, a central factor influencing global investment practices. This raises one of the key issues of international governance within late capitalism: in the global market, powerful countries are often unwilling to establish commercial relations with non-democratic countries hostile to a multicultural agenda.

As both Povinelli (2002) and Hale (2002) have shown in different contexts, multiculturalism has important limitations. One of them is its limited definition of diversity grounded in a perspective that takes away any practice and belief that would disturb the liberal vision of the multicultural nation. Multiculturalism, in other words, can "menace" (Hale) to the degree that it can be co-opted and redefined by the hegemonic powers producing sanitized versions that exclude so-called extreme cultural forms. In terms of *Little Mosque*, this has arguably involved a selective emphasis upon certain types of diversity. The complexity of Islam is only partly emphasized, with no mention made of cleavages between Sunnis, Sufis, and Shiites. The show emphasizes the forging of national unity through the resolution of conflict; little attention is given to the complexities of the cultural backgrounds of some of the characters: Fatima the Nigerian woman, Baber the Pakistani, and Yasir the Lebanese. This is what *Little Mosque* leaves out. Perhaps this is the political limitation of the professed multiculturalism of the series: the form of the cultural text—a television comedy—can only use satire, parody, and mimicry in comedic ways that, while challenging the orientalist discourse of the Muslim Other, produces its own silences.

Jameson has signalled a key challenge involved here, writing that

> . . . the affirmation of such nonhegemonic cultural voices remains ineffective if it is limited to the merely "sociological" perspective of the pluralistic rediscovery of other isolated social groups: only an ultimate rewriting of these utterances in terms of their essentially polemic and subversive strategies restores them to their proper place in the dialogical system of the social classes.(1981: 86)

The "ideology of form" that over determines such counter-hegemonic utterances within *Little Mosque* limits the oppositional potential and the range of resistance available within the contradictory, post-9/11 multicultural semantic horizon. For it is through the very process of critique that animates each show in the series that a final, if unstable, resolution of conflict is achieved on the basis of a totalizing sublation, one which effects a reconfiguration of the nation as a multicultural national unity.

Notes

1. This distinction—cultural text versus cultural practice—is inspired by Jameson's (1981) work on narrative as well as by Pierre Bourdieu's sociology of practice (1977). Rather than constituting an ontological division between mutually exclusive spheres, this distinction is analytical and seeks to highlight how textual representation is both a product (an assemblage of relatively stable meanings) and a process of production (a signifying practice whose meanings are subject to change, appropriation, and contestation). In terms of cultural analysis, this distinction therefore requires considering the interrelations of two epistemological fields: the "text" and its associated bundle of meanings, and the broader semantic horizons that overcode and recode the meanings of any given text.
2. The leader of the community.
3. Peace be with you.
4. Praise be to Allah.
5. Halal means legally permissible.
6. Mischievous spirit.
7. Sermon delivered at the Friday congregational prayer.
8. Affirmation of the oneness of God and the prophethood of Muhammad.

References

Abu-Lughod, L. (1993). "Islam and Public Culture: The Politics of Egyptian Television Serials," *Middle East Report*, 180: "Power, Mass Media and the Middle East" (Jan.–Feb.): 25–30.

Ali, K. (2004). "Pulp Fictions: Reading Pakistani Domesticity," *Social Text* 78(22/1): 123–45.

———. (2005). "Courtesans in the Living Room," *International Institute for the Study of Islam in the Modern World (ISIM) Review* 15 (Spring): 32–3.

Allen, J. (n.d.). "Uses of the Erotic: From Transgression, ¡Adelante! [Onward!]," introduction to "¿Venceremos? Sexuality, Gender and Black Self-Making in Cuba" (unpublished manuscript).

Bourdieu, P. (1977). *Outline of a Theory of Practice*. Cambridge: Cambridge University Press.

Flores, R.R. (1998). "Memory-Place, Meaning, and the Alamo," *American Literary History* 10(3): 428–45.

Goodman, L.-A. (2006). "CBC has High Hopes for 'Little Mosque' But Creator Hoping it Gets Laughs," *National Post* (Canada, 18 Dec.).

Haddad, Y., J.I. Smith, and K.M. Moore. (2006). *Muslim Women in America: The Challenge of Islamic Identity Today*. Oxford: Oxford University Press.

Hale, C. (2002). "Does Multiculturalism Menace? Cultural Rights and the Politics of Identity in Guatemala," *Journal of Latin American Studies* 34: 485–524.

Halim, F. (2006). "Pluralism of American Muslims and the Challenge of Assimilation," *Journal of Muslim Minority Affairs* 26(2): 235–44.

Hoodfar, H. (1993). "The Veil in Their Minds and in Our Heads: The Persistence of 0 of Muslim Women," *Colonialism, Imperialism and Gender: Resources for Feminist Research* 22(3–4, fall/winter): 5–16.

Jameson, F. (1981). *The Political Unconscious: Narrative as a Socially Symbolic Act*. Ithaca, NY: Cornell UP.

Jirattikorn, A. (2003). "Suriyothai: Hybridizing Thai National Identity through Film," *Inter-Asia Cultural Studies* 4(2): 296–308.

Kahf, M. (1999). *Western Representations of the Muslim Woman: From Termagant to Odalisque*. Austin, TX: University of Texas Press.

Mernissi, F. (2001). *Scheherazade Goes West: Different Cultures, Different Harems*. New York: Washington Square Press.

Moallem, M. (2005). *Between Warrior Brother and Veiled Sister: Islamic Fundamentalism and the Politics of Patriarchy in Iran*. Berkeley, CA: University of California Press.

Mohanty, C. (1988). "Under Western Eyes: Feminist Scholarship and Colonial Discourses," *Feminist Review* 30 (autumn): 61–88.

Povinelli, E.A. (2002). *The Cunning for Recognition: Indigenous Alterities and the Making of Australian Multiculturalism*. Durham, NC: Duke University Press.

Ramadan, T. (2004). *Western Muslims and the Future of Islam*. Oxford: Oxford University Press.

Said, E. (1978). *Orientalism*. New York: Pantheon Books.

Shaheen, J.G. (2001). *Reel Bad Arabs: How Hollywood Vilifies a People*. North Hampton, MA: Interlink Publishing Book.

Yegenoglu, M. (1998). *Colonial Fantasies: Towards a Feminist Reading of Orientalism*. Cambridge: Cambridge University Press.

Downloading Doppelgängers: New Media Anxieties and Transnational Ironies in *Battlestar Galactica*

Mark A. McCutcheon

Battlestar Galactica (US 2004–2009) has become a phenomenally popular fictional show in an age of "reality" programs. A pointedly post-9/11 updating of Glen A. Larson's 1970s broadcast series of the same name, the new *Battlestar* has produced ardent fan communities across the US. Thanks to its international circulation, it has also generated a strong global audience. Much of its popularity derives from the creative liberties that executive producers Ronald D. Moore and David Eick have taken with Larson's series. Far from being a niche SF program, it reworks the original with more and stronger female characters, and has season-spanning serial drama storylines every bit as soap as they are space operatic. It consistently and creatively elaborates on its premise as an allegory of the US's twenty-first-century "war on terror."

There is, however, another war being fought in the remade *Battlestar*, a guerrilla-style culture war that is, in its articulation of cultural economic problems in intellectual property (IP) and transnational productions, as timely as the show's post-9/11 theme. In this article I will triangulate *Battlestar*'s storyline, especially its characterization of the Cylon antagonists, to the Canadian contexts of the show's production and the globalized contexts of its distribution—both formal (on cable TV) and informal (on the Internet). While the series speaks strongly to US and UK audiences about homeland security and "home-grown" terrorism, it speaks less obviously but just as compellingly to global debates over new media and IP law. In Canada, which provides *Battlestar* with several of its star actors and its outdoor scene locations, these debates have been recently galvanized by the conservative Harper regime's introduction, in June 2008, of Bill C-61: IP legislation that has been widely criticized as Canada's answer to the Digital Millennium Copyright Act (DMCA)—complete with allegations that it answers not to Canadian media consumers but to US entertainment interests. In this context, the new media anxieties that drive *Battlestar*'s narrative produce interesting transnational ironies of nationalist ideology and cultural economy between the US and Canada. These ironies—and *Battlestar*'s thematization of current globalized debates over new media and cultural trade wars—become apparent in reviewing its adaptation of the original series and its production history from the perspective of the Canadian experience of media imperialism.

A Twenty-first-century *Frankenstein*

Battlestar Galactica (US 1978–1979) originated as a prime-time network television series one year after the box-office success of *Star Wars IV: A New Hope* (Lucas US 1977). The story begins as the Cylons break a 40-year truce and devastate all 12 human worlds. Only one military spaceship—a "Battlestar"—and a few thousand civilians escape. The Canadian actor Lorne Greene starred as

Commander William Adama, who leads the "ragtag fugitive fleet" in its quest for humanity's fabled "thirteenth tribe" on a planet called Earth. It was a short-lived series, ridiculed for campy acting and recycled special effects footage; but it built a hard-core fan base, periodically reinvigorated by the efforts of Richard Hatch (who played pilot Lee "Apollo" Adama) to remake the series. When the series was re-branded and re-cast for a new decade as the even shorter-lived *Galactica 1980* (US 1980), it descended into farcical self-parody. The *Galactica* found Earth, only to occupy it covertly and continue its cat-and-mouse war games with the Cylons, and the plots became little more than extended gags about US popular culture, with cameos from celebrities such as Wolfman Jack. The series' heavy biblical borrowing from Genesis and Exodus has also provoked speculations about its religious and ethnic subtexts: some critics read *Battlestar*'s story of the search for a thirteenth tribe as a link to Mormon theology; others read in the original series' adoption of classical and Egyptian tropes an extension of Nazi Aryan ideology.[1]

More germane to this article, though, is the fact that *Battlestar* was also embroiled in a legal skirmish over IP, with George Lucas promptly charging that Universal Studios had plagiarized *Star Wars*. SF writer and critic Brian Aldiss recalls that the case was never brought to trial; he advised Universal's lawyers at the time that *both* texts drew so heavily on prior SF that trying to prove originality for either one would be absurd. "The lawyers' first formal question to me was this: 'What was your initial response to *Star Wars*?' I replied, 'I experienced the delights of recognition.' They thought about it. Then they smiled" (Aldiss and Wingrove 274). As I will argue, the original series' cultural quotations and alleged plagiarism have been self-reflexively woven into the remake; however, a closer look at the remake's adaptation strategies is required first.

Premiering as a cable mini-series in 2003, *Battlestar* became a fascinatingly anachronistic and transnational curiosity—a 1978 concept that could only make sense after 9/11—and a pointedly American allegory about disaster, diaspora, and deregulation, that would only be produced with pivotal Canadian resource contributions. It reproduces the premise of the 1978 series, but through a realist aesthetic shared by other post-9/11 action series such as *24* (US 2001–). As the remake's developer Ron Moore (a former writer-producer for the *Star Trek* film and TV franchises, as well as of *Roswell* (US 1999–2002) reflects: "I knew that if you did 'Battlestar Galactica' again, the audience is going to feel a resonance with what happened on 9/11. . . . And it felt like there was an obligation to ... tell it *truthfully* as best we can through this prism" (qtd in Hodgman, my emphasis). Following Frederic Jameson, Jason McCullough notes how Hollywood's post-9/11 action productions trade heavily in both realism and conspiracy plots; in this connection, the realist mode privileges the associations of metonymy over the substitutions of metaphor (a point worth noting in relation to the associations and connotations of *Battlestar*'s cast, sets, and themes I discuss below). If the realism of *24* is produced through its multiple-frame shots and "real-time" plotting, *Battlestar*'s realism emerges through its combination of "military-journalism" shooting (e.g., handheld-style footage, quick zooms), state-of-the-art CGI effects and adaptation strategies for script, costume, and set that model the imagery and story of the remake very closely on actual US military and government institutions, as well as contemporary fashion and media. An early memo by Moore describes the remake's realism:

> We take as a given the idea that the traditional space opera, with its stock characters, techno-double-talk, bumpy-headed aliens, thespian histrionics and empty heroics has run its course, and a new approach is required. Call it "naturalistic science fiction." There would be no time travel or parallel universes or cute robot dogs. There would not be "photon torpedoes" but instead nuclear missiles, because nukes are real and thus are frightening. (qtd Hodgman 21)

The general chain of command replicates that of the US military, including its ultimate subordination to a democratically elected president as commander-in-chief. Whereas Lorne Greene's Adama wore a silver-trimmed blue jumper and cape, the remake's Adama (Edward James Olmos) wears a decorated military uniform. Greene's Adama was the sole leader of the fleet, with a nominal council of robed patriarchs far in the background to provide some mild drama, whereas the remake foregrounds the fleet's internal conflict, thanks to the presence of President Laura Roslin (Mary MacDonnell),[2] who drives subplots in gender politics (she has breast cancer) and, predictably, romance (she and the Commander develop a love interest). This re-imagining of the fleet's social structure makes for a wide variety of other subplots about the politics and ethics of a postapocalyptic—and postcolonial—society, poised precariously among liberal democracy, martial law, and radical deregulation. By modelling the culture of an imagined remainder of all humankind on that of the contemporary US, the remake not only lends critical urgency to its allegory but also reproduces the universalizing tendency of US national ideology to imagine itself (as that '80s charity single put it) as "the world." The nationalist synecdoche of US as world must be given special emphasis here so as to fully appreciate the transnational ironies arising from the remake's Canadian contexts of production.

The remake's major adaptation strategies give the concept not only a timely realism, but also a fundamentally Frankensteinian premise, as both a cautionary tale of technology run amok (Baldick 7) and as a trope of geopolitical rhetoric (60). Central to this is the antagonistic role of the Cylons. In the original series, a back story attributed their creation to a vanished race of reptilian aliens; in the remake, they are products of human technological instrumentalism who rebelled against their makers. In *Battlestar Galactica: The Miniseries* (US 2003), which functioned as the new series' pilot, Adama, speaking at the *Galactica*'s decommissioning ceremony, extemporizes on the Cylons in terms that echo Victor Frankenstein's relationship with his creature:

> You know when we fought the Cylons, we did it to save ourselves from extinction. But we never answered the question why. Why are we as a people worth saving? We still commit murder because of greed, spite, jealousy. And we still visit all of our sins upon our children. We refuse to accept responsibility for anything that we've done. Like we did with the Cylons. We decided to play God. Create life. When that life turned against us, we comforted ourselves with the knowledge that it really wasn't our fault, not really. You cannot play God then wash your hands of the things that you've created. Sooner or later, the day comes when you can't hide from the things that you've done anymore.

Attributing the Cylon threat to human agency, the remake casts human–Cylon antagonism in much more ambiguous terms than did the original, weaving together the problems of technological determinism and political backfire to make US foreign policy, especially "the war on terror," its chief allegorical object. For example, Saddam Hussein and Islamic extremism have been referred to as the Frankensteinian progeny of US foreign policy (Roy 4).

From the mini-series forward, Adama frames the difference between human and Cylon in a binary opposition between the organic and the mechanic, even as Cylon technology gradually reveals itself as viscerally organic in many respects. A kind of neo-Luddite discourse, articulated by Adama and his crew, configures as asymmetrical the main conflict between the Cylons (as cyborgs characterized by sublime and uncanny technological power) and the human fleet (defended by a Battlestar whose very low-tech obsolescence is its saving grace).[3] Early dialogue between Adama and Roslin sets the stage for the series' overarching problematization of technology through new media discourse. Roslin, prior to assuming the presidency, is aboard *Galactica* for its decommissioning and transformation into a public museum; flanked by Aaron Doral (Matthew Bennett), a PR agent who is later discovered to be a Cylon infiltrator, Roslin tries to persuade Adama to network the ship's systems:

> *Roslin:* ... it could tell people things like where the restroom is—
>
> *Adama:* It's an integrated computer network and I will not have it aboard this ship.
>
> *Roslin:* I heard you're one of those people—you're actually afraid of computers.
>
> *Adama:* No, there are many computers on this ship. But they're not networked.
>
> *Roslin:* A computerized network would simply make it faster and easier for the teachers to be able to teach—
>
> *Adama:* Let me explain something to you: many good men and women aboard this ship lost their lives because someone wanted a faster computer to make life easier.

The remake complicates the problematic of technology and the ambiguities of responsibility by characterizing the Cylons as a more complex and diverse society than the original series' chrome-plated Centurion soldier-drones who spoke in Casio-chip monotone and were led by a caped robot conehead. The remake's Cylons consist not only of Centurions (nicknamed "toasters" by *Galactica*'s personnel) but also of 12 human-simulacrum models, distinguishable from humans only by a blood test—or when more than one copy of a given model appears.[4] Exacerbating the Cylons' Baudrillardian scandal of simulation, the 12 Cylon models are also technically immortal: dying individuals download their consciousness into new bodies produced by a distributed network of "resurrection ships." Furthermore, these replicant Cylons are also proselytizing, monotheistic fundamentalists who ridicule the humans' explicitly classical pantheism. The re-imagined Cylons thus embody a metonymic chain of enemy figures and security threats: spies, sleeper agents, hackers, "home-grown" terrorists, the so-called "clash of civilizations," and "synthetic" alien "skin jobs."[5]

As the series progresses, questions of human responsibility for the Cylon "machines" deepen and overlap, set in the confines of sombrely appointed spaceships that offer Gothic, carceral settings for paranoia, violence, and romance. As self-styled "children of men," the Cylons routinely blame humanity for its own annihilation. One major subplot focuses on the internal conflict of Gaius Baltar (James Callis), a self-absorbed, Faustian race traitor who gave defence secrets to his lover—unbeknownst to him, a Cylon spy who engineered the attack;[6] while a third-season episode, "Hero" (17 November 2006), suggests that the human military, not the Cylons, violated the truce with a "black op" mission in Cylon territory which provoked the Cylons to attack. Far from simplistic, *Battlestar*'s "war on terror" allegory is deeply ambiguous in blurring the lines between good and evil, friend and enemy, human and inhuman. As producer David Eick comments, "the bad guys are all beautiful and believe in God, and the good guys all [fuck] each other over" (qtd in Hodgman). This ambiguity has helped *Battlestar* to find both liberal and conservative audiences. In this respect, *Battlestar* (not unlike *24*, or, for that matter, *Star Wars* before it) continues the Hollywood tradition of "Reaganite" entertainment, which privileges military action as a vehicle for mobilizing liberal and conservative tropes, and for resolving these ideological oppositions through personal dramas and family romances (see Forsythe). *Battlestar* must also be situated as a *critical* product of what Henry Jenkins identifies as an emerging "military/entertainment complex" (75)—*critical* in its allegorical emphasis on military culture as a synecdoche for US culture, in its popular adoption by audiences across the US political spectrum and in its marked ambivalence towards controversial security topics.

That *Battlestar* responds with imaginative sophistication to such current concerns as biological weaponry, military discipline, torture, ethnic profiling, and suicide bombing partially explains its wide appeal. However, as its cybernetic-simulacral version of the Cylons suggests, its global popularity also results from the widespread downloading of episodes across a distributed network of file-sharing computers and programs. Between its security-minded content and its insecurely distributed context, the dependence of *Battlestar* on Canadian production resources opens up a range of mutually articulating transnational ironies and new media anxieties—ironies and anxieties localized by the longstanding perception, shared (for different reasons) by Americans and Canadians alike, that Canada is a slightly off-kilter reproduction or mimic of the US. If the fleet, as the balance of all humankind, stands for the contemporary US, then the Cylon enemy that is virtually indistinguishable from it—*except in the uncanny identity of its reproduction*—stands, suggestively (because invisibly), for Canada.

Rethinking Media Imperialism in Canada

Battlestar's outdoor scenes are shot on various locations in and around Vancouver, British Columbia (BC), and several of its stars (as well as many of its production crew) are Canadian. The use of BC locations as extraterrestrial settings and—more importantly—the casting of Canadian actors in key roles are extremely suggestive when considering the transnational implications of the series' major themes. To understand these implications, it is first necessary to outline the relationship between US and Canadian cultural production in terms of media imperialism.

As theorized by Oliver Boyd-Barrett in 1977, the media imperialism thesis "characterize[s] the unidirectional nature of international media flows from a small number of source countries" (Lorimer et al. 287). Although the thesis was subsequently challenged for its deterministic model of unilateral cultural power (which neglects the uses and appropriations of "imperial" media products by its target audience "colonies"), I would argue from a postcolonial perspective that the present, high-pressure state of US–Canadian trade relations and their implications for Canadian sovereignty warrant not the dismissal but the critical retrieval of the idea that cultural exportation is closely connected to "territorial annexation" (287). In contrast to media scholars who abandoned the media imperialism thesis because it identified cultural export with political takeover, a postcolonial perspective recognizes: the hegemonic power of cultural production as a tool of empire; the adoption of imperial structures and strategies by transnational conglomerates; and the constant, increasing pressure by US corporate lobby groups to liberalize trade with (i.e., exploit) Canada in everything from cultural products (viewed by corporate lobbies as multiplatform intellectual property), to health care (viewed as a market, not a public service), to water (viewed as a commodity, not a human right). Since dominant US ideology has enshrined "the idea of the marketplace as the fullest expression of democracy" (Schlosser 219)—an idea promoted incessantly by major US media corporations—the difference between media and political imperialism seems to collapse when viewed from a Canadian perspective.

Anglophone Canadians consume far more US media products than Canadian ones. For example, in mid-October 2006, the top ten most-watched television shows in Anglophone Canada were all US imports (Lorimer et al. 71).[7] This is not only because the US cultural industries can appeal to global audiences with superior production values, but also because they can export their products for a fraction of the cost they charge in their domestic market (Grant and Wood 54). It is thus cheaper for Canadian broadcasters and distributors to buy foreign programmes (like *Battlestar*) than to produce domestic ones, however popular the domestic products may be (17). In light of these market- and mindset-dominating realities of US media imperialism, and in recognition of the "curious economics" (44–5) of the cultural market, Canada has developed a complex policy toolkit to promote the development of its cultural industries and thereby protect Canada's cultural (and political) sovereignty. This toolkit includes federal and provincial arts and culture funding agencies, Canadian content quotas for broadcasters, production tax credits and initiatives such as the Canadian-led UN plan to develop a New International Instrument on Cultural Diversity (NIICD) (386–8).

The priorities and efficacy of Canada's cultural policy toolkit, which first took shape during the early Cold War as a militaristic response to the domination of Canadian culture by US interests (Pennee 197), shift according to different times, regions, governments, and international pressures. Federal arts funding rises or falls depending on how left- or right-leaning is the government of the day; tensions persist between federal and provincial arts funding bodies; the cultural exemption clause Canada negotiated for NAFTA perennially comes up for renegotiation as US entertainment interests seek a greater share of Canada's media market. And so Stephen Harper's current minority-conservative regime's introduction of new copyright legislation has become widely understood as a response to US corporate and government pressures. The government minister responsible for Bill C-61 has consulted with US media and entertainment companies, but not the Canadian public; and the introduction of this Bill in June 2008 seemed specifically timed as a response to the US Congressional International Anti-Piracy Caucus's announcement, in May, that it had placed Canada on an "anti-piracy watch list"—in third place, after China and Russia ("Co-chairs"). This Caucus's main problem with Canada, it seems, is online IP enforcement: "We remain deeply concerned that Canada has failed to update its copyright laws to provide for online enforcement, making it a safe haven for Internet pirates" ("2008 Country Watch List"). Canadian critics of this manoeuvre and of the Canadian government's response of appeasement suggest that this Caucus may be motivated less by legal than by venal interests, noting that career total contributions made to its members' campaigns by the US TV, film, and music industries have exceeded $19 million ("Canadian Bill").

The widespread public protest over Bill C-61—a protest fittingly mobilized through online social network sites and blogs—repeatedly targeted the bill's evident "made in the USA" privileging of US media companies over Canadian media consumers (see Geist, "How the U.S."). As such, it demonstrates something of the efficacy of Canada's post-war, nation-building cultural policy in connection with Canadians' abiding assertion of cultural difference from the US. Recent research suggests that Canadian media consumers demonstrably read US media texts "through a special lens made in Canada" (Rutherford 113), a lens variably focused not only through national but also through regional and cultural priorities. (The circulation of "culture" as a keyword in Canadian policy is itself substantially different from that of "entertainment" in the US.) Noting that Canada has provided media scholars with "a paradigm case of media imperialism," Aniko Bodroghkozy claims that

> there is one experience all residents of the True North Strong and Free [i.e., Canada] share (if diversely): an ambivalent relationship to a fictive American Other ... a continual working and reworking of the irresolvable dilemma of how Canadians can construct their imagined community as ultimately different from an intensively desired, but just as deeply loathed made-in-Canada construction of America. (568–70)

In this context of conflicts, colonizations and collaborations between US and Canadian media and culture, questions of national identity centre on overall likeness and devilish detail—that is, on a kind of cross-border identity crisis, a crisis of replication and simulacrum. Paul Rutherford characterizes the historical relationship between US and Canadian media as the latter's colonization by and mimicry of the former in "home-grown imitations" (108). He quotes a 1907 study, *The Americanization of Canada*, which articulates a perennial symptom of Canada's problematic nationalism, one as familiar during Confederation as in today's debates over "deep integration": "The English-speaking Canadians protest that they will never become Americans—they are already Americans without knowing it" (105).

From the slightly different perspective of dual US–Canadian citizenship, Laura Marks explores the flipside of American images in Canada, noting an equally robust perception of what she calls the "'little bit off' quality in Canadian images, seen from a U.S. perspective" (198). For Marks, Canada's identity-with-a-difference, in metonymic terms, poses a "subversive potential" in "American contexts," with "the detail" of Canadian difference making "it possible to question the whole" ideological apparatus of US nationalist identity (198). Citing a wealth of audience research on how Canadians appropriate US cultural products, Bodroghkozy makes a similar claim: "It is a foundation of fine details, *typically unnoticed by non-Canadians*, upon which Canadians have built their shaky edifice of national identity" (579, my emphasis).[8] Both the British Columbia setting and Canadian casting of *Battlestar* trade heavily in such fine details, the implications of which, in connection with the show's theme, hinge precisely on their not being noticed.

On Location: *Battlestar*'s British Columbia

Perhaps the transnationally mediatized image of Canada as not-quite-America finds its fullest expression in the BC media industry that has hosted the production of *Battlestar Galactica*. Mike Gasher detaches the BC film industry from any simplistic role in a national cinema, arguing instead that it emphasises industry over culture (103) and depends heavily on foreign location production, not collaborating but *competing* with other Canadian film centres (Toronto and Montreal) for the title of "Hollywood North" (i.e., the preferred foreign location for "externalized" Hollywood productions) (140–2). For the longer shooting schedules of TV production, Vancouver competes less with other Canadian cities for US business than with American cities like San Francisco and San Diego (109).

The BC film industry's strategy for attracting foreign location production has been to promote "the province's protean nature" (112): "what is noteworthy in British Columbia's case is the degree to which the province has built an industry based on its malleability, selling itself to Hollywood as a place that is willing to stand in for anywhere or nowhere" (106). In *Battlestar*, BC settings, buildings, and landscapes are used to represent an intergalactic array of cities, settlements, and planets (many of which thus share uncannily similar redwood forests and mountainous terrain). Vancouver provides the locations for urban settings, especially Caprica, the capital city of the human colonies, a postapocalyptic cityscape occupied by the Cylon army but otherwise devoid of people—not unlike the photos used by the BC Film Commission to promote its locations to Hollywood (Gasher 113–14), or, for that matter, the perennial self-promotion of Canada more generally as a prime site for colonization, "a largely unpopulated place full of scenic wonders and infinite resources" (Rutherford 106). In light of these promotions, media imperialism in Canada also encompasses how various governments and policies actively invite foreign colonization and investment.

For Canadian and especially BC audiences of *Battlestar*, the viewing is richly strewn with local landmarks abstracted into generic SF topoi (for longer-term fans of SF television, BC and Vancouver landmarks also evoke their own earlier appearances in series such as *The X-Files* (US/Canada 1993–2002)). The Vancouver public library provides a suitably futuristic background for several early scenes in which the Cylons take over the wasted capital. Simon Fraser University supplies a bleak, institutional setting for the first season's finale. In a series so insistently grounded at Ground Zero, the colonial capital, Caprica, evokes New York, making Vancouver, through these allegorical associations, a "landscape double" for one of the most symbolically charged cities in post-9/11 America. Yet as such, it is "less ... a distinct geographical location than ... a social class" (Gasher 120)—that is, it is still just a "little bit off."

As Gasher argues, "place"—understood as a specific intersection of particular social relations (136), even just as background setting—does contribute (whether intentionally or not) "to the story's tone, atmosphere, and possibly its central themes" (106). Like Toronto and Montreal, Vancouver is one of Canada's biggest cities and quite close to the US border; Vancouver is also of particular interest to the US Drug Enforcement Agency as a heroin hub (it has been called the Baltimore of the west coast) and—more importantly—as a city receptive to harm-reducing and decriminalizing drug policy initiatives, such as safe injection sites and medical-use marijuana distribution. Marijuana mail-order entrepreneur and former Vancouver mayoral candidate Marc Emery has been fighting extradition to the US for three years now, facing felony charges for seed distribution that have made him one of the DEA's most wanted ("Prince of Pot"). The formulaically bellicose rhetoric of US policy colours its representation of black-market and legitimate trade issues alike. Take, for instance, film and audiovisual production. Gasher quotes from reports commissioned in 1998 and 2001 by US lobby groups to rein in "runaway" foreign location production; the 1998 report describes it as "a grave threat to the future of [domestic US] film and television production," while the 2001 report calls it "a serious threat" to the US positive trade balance (103). As Pennee observes, Canada and the US may have exchanged the Cold War for a trade war, but culture remains a question of national security (191). And since Vancouver is a Canadian hot spot on the US map of northern-border security issues, its filmic milieu carries with it the residue of some very fraught border politics in Fortress North America.

"They Look Just Like Us": *Battlestar*'s Canadian Conspirators

The perception by US cultural industries of Canada as a threat—as a rival for production spending—seems to focus more on state borders than agents. As the casting of Lorne Greene in the original *Battlestar* exemplifies, generations of Canadian actors since Mary Pickford have been able to make very comfortable second homes for themselves in Hollywood. The absorption of Canadian bodies by Hollywood seems more tolerable to US producers and audiences than the decampment of Hollywood productions to Canada (which puts such runaway productions in the stereotypical company of job-stealing "foreigners" and unpatriotic draft dodgers), even providing occasional material for self-reflexive commentary on Canada–US relations as played out in the US entertainment industry. For example, in 1985 Greene hosted a mockumentary that exposed a "Canadian conspiracy" to take control of the US by infiltrating and occupying its media industry, and which satirized how Hollywood routinely erases the Canadian nationality of actors such as Leslie Nielsen, William Shatner, and Greene himself.

Admittedly, the fact that the dominant discourse of Canadian citizenship is itself an exercise in self-effacing, postcolonial diffidence makes it easy for the citizenship of Canadians in US media to get erased. In the 1970s, a CBC contest to find a Canadian equivalent of the expression "as American as apple pie" awarded its prize to a teenager who completed the sentence "as Canadian as ... "

with "possible under the circumstances." Using a computing metaphor that will resonate with my argument below, Marshall McLuhan claimed: "Canadians live at the *interface* where borderlines clash. *We have, therefore, no recognizable identity*, and are suspicious of those who think they have" (qtd in Pevere 132, my emphasis). Adding some political nuance to this common self-deprecation, Richard Collins suggests that Canadians' weak nationalism in fact drives our nation-state's efficacy as a global model: "Political institutions are more important than television and culture, or even language, in producing and reproducing a solid sentiment of national identity among Canadians" (qtd in Bodroghkozy 570). In the light of these images of Canadian citizenship (self-effacing, non- or anti-nationalist, American doppelgängers—whether unwitting or scheming), it is hard to imagine that *Battlestar*'s casting is not in fact some kind of deliberate in-joke for Canadian audiences about Canadian identity, conspiracy, and camouflage in the ideoscape of North American popular culture. In looking at the Canadian cast, two patterns of characterization become apparent.

Five of the twelve Cylon models represent the series' leading antagonists, and they are all played by Canadian actors. Alberta model Tricia Helfer takes the star villain's role as Six, the love spy lauded as a "hero of the Cylons" for her leadership of the attack on the colonies. The romance between Six and Baltar figures them as quarrelling lovers; Six travels with Baltar, in an ambiguous role as a spectral advisor, his absent but tangible beloved, the Cylon version of a devil's voice in his ear, speaking of God's love. With Six's help, Baltar escapes the attack, joins the fleet, and wins the presidency; but she also helps him to survive torture by the Cylons, to win his case in a war-crimes trial, and (halfway through the final season) to become a messianic spokesperson for the Cylons' "one true God." By repeatedly blurring the line between lover and foe, good and evil, Six's involvement with Baltar becomes an exemplar for several other major relationship subplots.

Korean-Canadian actor Grace Park plays the Cylon Eight. One of her copies is the "sleeper agent" Boomer, whose assassination attempt on Commander Adama closes season one. The other, Athena, is impregnated by the *Galactica* officer Helo while they are stranded on Caprica; they later marry, and she becomes a *Galactica* officer, while their child Hera becomes an object of Cylon–human power struggles and an iconic harbinger of "the shape of things to come." Helo is played by BC actor Tahmoh Penikett, a rebellious officer who takes flak from his mates for being a Cylon collaborator, a "toaster lover." In one third-season episode, "A Measure of Salvation" (10 November 2006), he subverts a plan to exterminate the Cylons with biological weaponry; and in another, "Rapture" (21 January 2007), he reluctantly agrees to kill Athena so she can download herself to a nearby Cylon ship in order to steal back their child. Like the relationship between Six and Baltar, that between Helo and Athena blurs ethical lines of good and evil, but on balance the story tends to figure this pair as renegade protagonists rather than as antagonists.

Boomer, the doomed Eight, is also romantically involved, at the start of the series at least, when she is covertly dating the hangar crew chief, Tyrol. Tyrol, played by BC actor Aaron Douglas, eventually discovers, in seasons three and four, that he himself is a Cylon sleeper agent, a discomfiting discovery he shares with no less pivotal an officer than the Commander's right-hand man, Executive Officer Saul Tigh, played by Canadian stage and radio veteran Michael Hogan (whose northern Ontario accent is perhaps the only conspicuously "Canadian" detail in the series). Tigh is one of the show's most conflicted characters, a grizzled alcoholic whose despair deepens as the series develops, to the point that he deploys suicide bombers against Cylon targets and even kills his own wife for collaborating with the enemy. Ironically, his discovery of his own Cylon identity gives him the mettle to precipitate a new truce between Cylons and humans, a truce that helps lead humans and Cylons together to

Earth, on which cliff-hanging plot point the fourth and final season ended its first half.

Another of the four "sleeper" Cylons disclosed at the end of season three is the president's advisor Tory Foster, played by Vancouver actor Rekha Sharma. Unlike the other three awakened sleepers, Tory embraces her newfound Cylon identity, initiating a relationship with Baltar and killing Tyrol's wife, Cally, played by fellow Vancouverite Nicki Clyne. The fourth "sleeper" Cylon is the erstwhile athlete and guerrilla leader Sam Anders (Michael Trucco), husband to the pilot Starbuck, a lead character from the original series whose drinking-and-smoking machismo (as played then by Dirk Benedict) has been creatively gender-bent by the casting of Katee Sackhoff. An archetypal and self-destructive maverick, Starbuck also develops a mysterious connection with the oracular, trickster-like Cylon Leoben Conoy, played by Canadian screen regular Callum Keith Rennie. Leoben alternately stalks and woos Starbuck, who repeatedly kills his copies, amidst conflicting suggestions that she is the "final" Cylon, a "harbinger of death" and a human whose unique destiny is to discover the way to Earth. In addition, Leoben's appearance in the pilot mini-series first alerts the military command that the Cylons are human replicants, as Rennie's character fights Adama in a grisly showdown:

> *Adama:* What you got is silica pathways to the brain or whatever it is you call that thing you pretend to think with. It's decomposing as we speak. . . . you'll be dead in a few minutes. How does that make you feel? If you can feel?
>
> *Leoben:* Oh, I can feel more than you can ever conceive, Adama. But I won't die. When this body dies my consciousness will be transferred to another one. And when that happens, I think I'll tell the others exactly where you are, and I think that they'll come and kill all of you, and I'll be here watching it happen.

Lastly, Torontonian Matthew Bennett plays Aaron Doral, the PR agent who, in "Litmus" (22 November 2004), becomes the civilian fleet's first clue that "the Cylons look like us now."

As the casting of Penikett and Clyne suggests, Canadian actors do not exclusively play Cylons or their collaborators. Winnipeg-born-and-trained actor Donnelly Rhodes plays the *Galactica*'s harried, hard-boiled doctor—a chain-smoking straight-talker who gets involved in dubious stratagems, such as delivering Athena's hybrid baby then telling her it died so that it can be hidden anonymously in the fleet for security reasons. Alessandro Juliani plays Lieutenant Gaeta, plotting the *Galactica*'s journey and jerry-rigging its crude ICT. Luciana Carro and Leah Cairns play minor pilots Kat and Racetrack; and Paul Campbell played Billy, the president's first advisor, killed in a second-season hostage-taking incident.

But Canadians predominate in the antagonists' roles; of eleven known Cylon models, only four are not played by Canadians (but by US actors Trucco, Rick Worthy, Dean Stockwell, and New Zealander Lucy Lawless). This preponderance of Canadian actors in antagonist and especially Cylon roles is largely invisible and unremarked, at least among *Battlestar*'s various online fan sites and networks. "Speaking as an American," writes one participant at *Battlestar Forum* in response to a survey posted as part of the research for this paper, "the nationality of the casting and where scenes were shot doesn't matter to me at all" (qtd in sonicfiction, "A question"). Another respondent finds the Canadian production contexts "amusing" but unimportant.[9] According to the peculiar transnational dynamic of identity-with-a-difference described above, it is significant here that the question of Canadian contributions has generated barely any discussion—the very *invisibility* and *unremarkableness* of Canadian labour and imagery in fact consolidates the nationalist metonymies at work in the show's cast, locations, and theme.

In Cylon roles, Canadian actors simultaneously *embody* the exposure of national difference while *enacting* its erasure. Furthermore, these transnational metonymies add timely significance to the discourse of new media and computer networks that *Battlestar*'s dialogue uses to describe the Cylons' technology of reproduction. Throughout the series, tropes of programming, software, drives, kill switches, and viruses accompany those of networks and downloading; for example, in "Flight of the Phoenix" (16 September 2005), Athena identifies "a Cylon virus [that has] been learning your system, testing, adapting, finding weak spots ... so they can turn *Galactica*'s systems against you: crash you into other ships, detonate your weapon stores, suffocate the crews." This discourse of the Cylons as downloadable transgressors, in turn, prefigures the official US government view of Canadians as new media offenders. Through the characterization and Canadian casting of Cylons as a technologically superior enemy, *Battlestar* stages a specific current issue in Canadian–US border tensions, and connects these connotations and associations to its formal and thematic grounding in the "convergence culture" theorized by Henry Jenkins as a globally distributed network of transmedia franchises, online fan communities and collisions and collusions between old and new media, between creative consumers and controlling corporations (18).

As the Congressional Caucus quoted above suggests, it is not only pot seeds but digital seeders that have made the Canadian border a multifaceted security concern for American interests. The US Trade Representative's Office has "made veiled threats about 'thickening the border' between Canada and the U.S. if Canada refused to put copyright reform on the legislative agenda" (Geist, "How the U.S."). And this is a border already thickening for Canadians, who are now required to present passports to US customs officials[10]—as well as their digital devices, which may now be searched by said officials, *without cause* (see Singel).[11]

The perception of Canada as a "safe haven for Internet pirates" seems based on the *fair dealing* provision of Canadian copyright law (which is in ways quite different from, but not necessarily better than, US fair *use*), which "grants Canadians the right to make personal, non-commercial copies of music without requiring permission from the copyright holder. Both the Copyright Board of Canada and the Federal Court of Canada have ruled that private copying may include peer-to-peer music downloads" (Geist, "Piercing" 25). One consequence of this ruling is that downloading music—for private, non-commercial use—is technically legal in Canada, while uploading music is not (Lorimer et al. 175). As suggested by the spectrum of cultural industry interests lobbying for copyright reform, this legal situation has clear implications for other media. The proliferation of increasingly rhizomorphic torrent networks, which orchestrate the transfer of *parts* of files from arrays of "seeder" sources, has not only muddied the waters of accountability in more punitive jurisdictions of copyright enforcement, such as the UK and US, but it has also combined with improved bandwidth infrastructures to facilitate the sharing of other cultural products such as video games, television programs, and films, which represent exponentially larger file sizes.

In this context, the government publicizes Bill C-61 to Canadians as a clarification and entrenchment of users' rights under fair dealing, but its fine print—the controversial "anti-circumvention" clause—effectively neutralizes those rights by imposing harsh penalties for media consumers who work around, disable, or otherwise hack the technological protection measures like Digital Rights Management and DVD region codes that producers increasingly build into the cultural commodities themselves. "The bill essentially says that technology trumps whatever rights consumers or competitors might have otherwise had," writes law professor Jeremy de Beer. "So the law no longer matters. People only have whatever rights content owners choose for them."

These contours of the present Canada–US debate over intellectual property, its digital insecurity, and the legacy of the "Napster wars" (see Marshall) produce another transnational irony in *Battlestar*'s

Canadian production context—a temporal irony of the show's distribution and broadcast schedule.

Battlestar Galactica: The Miniseries was co-produced by Universal, USA Cable, the British cable channel Sky One, and the US Sci Fi channel. It first aired on Sky in the UK in late 2003. Positive response from the UK audience led to the weekly series, again airing first in Britain, in the fall of 2004. In January 2005, NBC broadcast an edited version of the mini-series and a few episodes from the first season already underway in the UK. NBC's subsidiary Sci Fi channel then began airing the first season in January 2005, followed by the second in July. As of spring 2006, the series was airing simultaneously in both the UK and US. While Canada's Space Channel began airing first-season episodes in January 2005, it did not air the mini-series until October of that year. Space subsequently aired the second season in January 2006, and the third that October. The point here is that for most of the series' broadcast history, the Canadian cable audience has had to settle for third place in line, half a year (or in the case of the crucial, scene-setting pilot mini-series, nine months) behind UK and US airings, in order to watch a show shot in Canada with numerous Canadian actors.[12] Only with the third season, which began in October 2006, did *Battlestar* air simultaneously in all three national markets (Space Communications).

However, the debut of *Battlestar* on UK cable in 2003 coincided with the networked spread of advances in online file-sharing, which began to shift industry attention from music sharing to video and film sharing. 2003 saw a massive surge in the popularity of peer-to-peer applications that use BitTorrent technologies to choreograph multiple sources, thus accelerating the upload and download of very large files. And in Canada, 2003 also saw the launch of the CA*net 4 high-bandwidth network (Lorimer et al. 72). In short, new file-sharing technologies popularized in 2003 meant that *Battlestar* gained popularity with a global audience in the informal digital sector almost as soon as it aired in Britain's formal broadcast sector—a global popularity assisted by the decidedly tech-savvy profile of the show's target audience. *Battlestar* is far from being the only show to find a huge transnational audience in the online informal sector, but it was an early instance of the "shape of things to come" in the convergence of broadcast and online media (Pesce 5–6). For audiences like these, particularly those participating in online "knowledge communities" (Jenkins 27–8) to interpret and decode plot mysteries like the *Survivor*-esque hidden identity of the "final five" (see Jenkins 25), even the one or two days between US and UK air times in otherwise synchronized screening schedules is sufficient to drive significant file-sharing traffic.

If the Cylon discourse of new media anticipates something of *Battlestar*'s online popularity and suggests something of how it constructs a tech-savvy target audience, the episode "Black Market" (27 January 2006) explicitly thematizes the underground milieu in which much file-sharing takes place. Apollo (Jamie Bamber) tracks the fleet's black-market supply chain back to the conspicuously racialized black kingpin, Phelan (Bill Duke), whom Apollo summarily executes. True to the series' overall ambiguity (and perhaps in a nod to the promotional value of online file-sharing), the military then permits the black market to continue operating, but only on condition of tighter surveillance and a non-negotiable prohibition of using children as collateral (which practice contributes centrally to the kingpin's characterization). This political-economic subplot allegorizes the US as a market society where the line between privatization from above and informalization from below is as blurry as *Battlestar*'s Canadian-based line between good guys and villains (see Sassen 266 n. 11).

In this respect, *Battlestar* belongs to a recent trend in speciality cable programs about the US as an increasingly deregulated and/or underground market society—such as Showtime's *Dead Like Me* (Canada/US 2003–2004), in which the grim reaper's work is all outsourced to undead subcontractors; Showtime's *Weeds* (US 2005–), in which a single mother tries to maintain her gated-community lifestyle by dealing drugs; and HBO's *Deadwood* (US 2004–2006), a western which, like *Battlestar*, works as a frontier allegory of diasporic migration, militarized public space, technologized security threats, and unregulated enterprise in a society characterized less by democracy than "adhocracy" (Doctorow qtd in Jenkins 251). Among these series, *Battlestar* most stridently articulates questions of market-society culture, technologies of reproduction and political-economic ethics to a military problematic. Just as the Bush administration attempted to link recreational drug use with terrorism in the public imagination, *Battlestar* embeds processes of recording and reproduction technologies in its themes of market culture, militarization, and diasporic displacement and re-territorialization. That Canadian involvement is so materially central but symbolically marginal to this series provides grounds not only for reading the ironies between its text and its context, but, moreover, for speculating on what these ironies imply for Canada, as a site for the increasing investments of SF capital.

Canada: SF Capital?

Whether coincidentally, conspiratorially or just uncannily, *Battlestar* has kept a thematic finger on the pulse of Canadian–US trade relations, especially in the vexingly un-public domain of intellectual property. In 2008, the fourth season (only the second one to air simultaneously in the US and Canada) saw the humans reaching a new diplomatic accord with a Cylon faction that has emerged as the victor in a Cylon civil war, and the long-awaited arrival of both these parties at Earth. Meanwhile, Canada's minority Conservative government, on the cusp of parliamentary suspension, tabled Bill C-61, received across the board as a new economic accord with the US entertainment industry lobby. Bill C-61 is a salutary symptom of cross-border initiatives in "deep integration": legislation that aligns Canadian political, economic, and cultural structures ever closer to US models, under pressure or open threat from US politicians, government bodies, and trade representatives. Like the Liberal government it narrowly succeeded, the present Conservative regime represents its policies and platforms on behalf of Canadian sovereignty, although they tend ultimately not to serve it. For example, Prime Minister Stephen Harper's recent campaign to bolster Arctic sovereignty seems like a nationalist assertion of the Canadian state's northern border, but increasing military spending to do so—and to intensify the Afghanistan operation—was more in step with Bush administration spending priorities. Likewise, Bill C-61 pays lip service to cultural sovereignty, but would facilitate further cross-border colonization of media use and control.

Kodwo Eshun summarizes "SF capital" as "the synergy, the positive feedback between future-oriented media and capital" (290). As such, the post-nuclear Vancouver and the "scandalous bodies" (see Kamboureli) of Canadian-played replicants that have been deeply integrated into *Battlestar Galactica* project a troubling image of what deep integration could mean for Canada's cultural economy, when justified by a sense of the "Canadian conspiracy" as a cons' piracy: a piracy of American national identity, run (and overrun) by Canadians as the cons. In their very unmarked quality, the integration of Canadian actors, crew members, landscapes, and industry facilities into the production of *Battlestar* position Canada as a site of anxious uncertainty over national identity and the security of intellectual property, and as a reservoir of future (and futuristic) resource extraction (Rutherford 106–11). If *Battlestar* episodes that depict the gleaning of water ("Water" (25 October 2004)) and harvesting of food ("The Eye of Jupiter" (15 December 2006)) amid locations shot in the BC interior prove as uncannily pertinent to Canada–US relations as the series' thematization of cross-border identity crises and new media trade wars, then Canada's role as a source of SF capital augurs ominous implications for Canada's more basic ecological sovereignty.

Notes

1. I am indebted to Julie Rak and to the peer reviewers of an early version of this paper for alerting me to these fascinating cultural subtexts.
2. In the kind of irony I will detail later, Canadian actor Colm Feore cameos as president of the colonies prior to their destruction.
3. Attacked by Cylon viruses and kill switches, the networked computing systems of the other, more up-to-date Battlestars proved their Achilles' heel.
4. *Battlestar* self-reflexively alludes to *Blade Runner* (Scott US/Singapore 1982) in several ways, not least by the casting of Olmos as Adama. In *Blade Runner*, he played the cop Gaff, a character whose origami unicorn implied that the protagonist, Deckard (Harrison Ford), was himself a replicant; early in *Battlestar*, Adama is suspected of being a Cylon.
5. Another *Blade Runner* allusion: see the season 2 episode "Downloaded" (24 February 2006).
6. In "Six Degrees of Separation" (29 November 2004), this Cylon infiltrates the *Galactica* under the name of Shelley Godfrey, in a nod to *Frankenstein*'s author.
7. CTV's *Evening News* was the top Canadian program, in eleventh place.
8. Since Marks and Bodroghkozy wrote their essays, Canada's legalization of medical marijuana (Schlosser 226) and gay marriage—which pushed that issue to the forefront of the 2004 US election—have undoubtedly only exaggerated the perversity of Canadian difference in the US imagination.
9. My thanks go to the *Battlestar Forum* moderator and participants for fielding this research question. An interesting related thread that I read there, worthy of more detailed discussion than I can give it here, concerns the Orientalist depiction of model Eight Cylons (those played by Park) in groups; see cylon_democrat, "Disturbing depiction." I concur with this participant that the recurring depiction of Eights in large groups is conspicuous; it activates many of the stereotypical images theorized in Smaro Kamboureli's *Scandalous Bodies*, an analysis of multiculturalism in Canadian English literature.
10. Until recently, Canadians have required only a birth certificate or other proof of Canadian citizenship to cross into the US.
11. I wish to thank the Society for Socialist Studies, and especially June Madeley, for hosting productive presentations on trans-mediatized popular culture at the 2008 Congress; it was Carolyn Guertin's paper "Remixing Participation" that alerted me to this US Customs development, among numerous other hot topics in contemporary "pirate capital."
12. The complexities of the relationship between US and Canadian culture and markets, here, also mean that many Canadians have direct access to the major American networks (ABC, NBC, CBS, FOX, UPN) through satellite or cable television packages marketed within Canada. Thus some of the Canadian audience relied neither on the first Canadian-owned broadcast of the series nor on uploaded sources, but rather were able to watch at the same time as could American audiences by tuning in to an American station.

Works Cited

"2008 Country Watch List." USA Congressional International Anti-Piracy Caucus. 15 May 2008 <http://schiff.house.gov/antipiracycaucus/pdf/IAPC_2008_Watch_List.pdf>.

Aldiss, Brian, and David Wingrove. *Trillion Year Spree: The History of Science Fiction*. New York: Atheneum, 1986.

Baldick, Chris. *In Frankenstein's Shadow: Myth, Monstrosity, and Nineteenth-century Writing*. Oxford: Clarendon Press, 1987.

Bodroghkozy, Aniko. "As Canadian as ... Possible: Canadian Popular Culture and the American Other." *Hop on Pop: The Politics and Pleasures of Popular Culture*. Eds Henry Jenkins, Tara McPherson, and Jane Shattuc. Durham: Duke UP, 2002. 566–89.

"Canadian Bill Made in the USA" Appropriation Art: A Coalition of Art Professionals. 28 May 2008 <http://www.appropriationart.ca/212.htm>.

"Co-chairs Announce 2008 Caucus 'Watch List' and Introduction of Legislation." USA Congressional International Anti-Piracy Caucus. 15 May 2008 <http://schiff.house.gov/antipiracycaucus/news.html>.

cylon_democrat. "Disturbing Depiction of the Eight Groupies." Posting to *Battlestar Forum*, 11 May 2008 <http://www.battlestarforum.com/showthread.php?t=1065>.

de Beer, Jeremy. "Canada's New Copyright Bill: More Spin than 'Win-Win.'" *National Post* 16 June 2008 <http://www.nationalpost.com/todays_paper/story.html?id=590280& p=2>.

Eshun, Kodwo. "Further Considerations on Afrofuturism." *New Centennial Review* 3.2 (2003): 287–302.

Forsythe, Scott. "Liberalism, Neo-Liberalism and Imperialism: Hollywood's New Left?" Society for Socialist Studies conference. U of British Columbia. 4 June 2008.

Gasher, Mike. *Hollywood North: The Feature Film Industry in British Columbia*. Vancouver: U of British Columbia P, 2002.

Geist, Michael. "How the U.S. Got its Canadian Copyright Bill." *Toronto Star* 16 June 2008 <http://www.thestar.com/sciencetech/article/443867>.

———. "Piercing the Peer-to-Peer Myths: An Examination of the Canadian Experience." *First Monday* 10.4 (2005) <http://firstmonday.org/issues/issue10_4/geist/>.

Grant, Peter, and Chris Wood. *Blockbusters and Trade Wars: Popular Culture in a Globalized World.* Vancouver: Douglas & McIntyre, 2004.

Guertin, Carolyn. "Remixing Participation: User-Generated Culture and the Politics of Creation." Society for Socialist Studies conference. U of British Columbia. 4 June 2008.

Hodgman, John. "Ron Moore's Deep Space Journey." *New York Times* 17 July 2006 <http://www.nytimes.com/2005/07/17/magazine/17GALACTICA.html?ex=1279252800&en=59af86a6d662986b&ei=5090&partner=rssuserland&emc=rss>.

Jenkins, Henry. *Convergence Culture: Where Old and New Media Collide.* New York: New York UP, 2006.

Kamboureli, Smaro. *Scandalous Bodies: Canadian Diasporic Literature.* Oxford: Oxford UP, 1999.

Lorimer, Rowland, Mike Gasher, and David Skinner. *Mass Communication in Canada.* 6th edn. Oxford: Oxford UP, 2007.

Marks, Laura. "Packaged for Export, Contents under Pressure: Canadian Film and Video in a U.S. Context." *Cultural Subjects: A Popular Culture Reader.* Eds Allan J. Gedalof, Jonathan Boulter, Joel Faflak, and Cameron McFarlane. Toronto: Thomson Nelson, 2005. 189–201.

Marshall, Lee. "Metallica and Morality: The Rhetorical Battleground of the Napster Wars." *Entertainment Law* 1.1 (2002): 1–18.

McCullough, Jason. "*24* and Post-9/11 Culture." Society for Socialist Studies conference. U of British Columbia. 4 June 2008.

Pennee, Donna Palmateer. "Culture as Security: Canadian Foreign Policy and International Relations from the Cold War to the Market Wars." *International Journal of Canadian Studies/Revue internationale d'études canadiennes* 20 (1999): 191–213.

Pesce, Mark. "Piracy Is Good? How *Battlestar Galactica* Killed Broadcast TV." *Mindjack: The Beat of Digital Culture* 13 May 2005 <http://www.mindjack.com/feature/piracy051305. html>.

Pevere, Geoff. *Mondo Canuck: A Canadian Pop Culture Odyssey.* Toronto: Prentice Hall, 1996.

"Prince of Pot: The USA vs. Marc Emery." CBC Newsworld. 23 October 2007.

Roy, Arundhati. "9 Is Not 11 (And November Isn't September)." *Outlook India* 12 December 2008 <http://www.outlookindia.com/full.asp?fodname=20081222&fname=ARoy+(F)&sid=1>.

Rutherford, Paul. "Made in America: The Problem of Mass Culture in Canada." *Cultural Subjects: A Popular Culture Reader.* Eds Allan J. Gedalof, Jonathan Boulter, Joel Faflak, and Cameron McFarlane. Toronto: Thomson Nelson, 2005. 101–14.

Sassen, Saskia. "Spatialities and Temporalities of the Global: Elements for a Theorization." *Globalization.* Ed. Arjun Appadurai. Durham: Duke UP, 2001. 260–78.

Schlosser, Eric. *Reefer Madness: Sex, Drugs, and Cheap Labor in the American Black Market.* New York: Houghton Mifflin Mariner, 2004.

Singel, Ryan. "Border Agents Can Search Laptops without Cause, Appeals Court Rules." *Threat Level: Privacy, Security, Politics and Crime Online.* Wired Blog Network, 22 April 2008 <http://blog.wired.com/27bstroke6/2008/04/border-agents-c.html>.

sonicfiction [Mark McCutcheon]. "A Question about Canadian Production Details." Posting to *Battlestar Forum,* 9 August 2008 <http://www.battlestarforum.com/showthread.php?t=1691>.

Space Communications. Email to author. 23 October 2007.

CSI and Moral Authority: The Police and Science

Gray Cavender and Sarah K. Deutsch

Introduction

On Friday, 6 October 2000, the pilot episode of *CSI: Crime Scene Investigation (CSI)* premiered on CBS. It debuted to 17.3 million television viewers and was ranked eighth on Nielsen's weekly top 10 television programs (Armstrong, 10 October 2000). That debut signalled the beginning of a very long and successful run. Now beginning its seventh season, *CSI* remains among the top 10, and frequently is the number one program on television (see Nielsen Ratings, 2005; Arthur, 2006). Its popularity has led to two successful spin-off series, *CSI: Miami* and *CSI: NY.*

CSI's consistently high ratings are interesting and ironic. The series foregrounds science and yet many in its audience lack a science background. It is a successful police drama at a time when there are many challenges to the legitimacy of law enforcement. Indeed, some of these challenges actually come from science in the form of DNA evidence. The focus of our research is to understand how *CSI* circulates images and proffers cultural meanings that assert the moral authority of the police and science.

Two important institutions—policing and science—stand somewhat discredited today. As a result of continuing revelations about wrongful convictions or the FBI's failure to process evidence that might have prevented the attacks on September 11, 2001 the police have lost some of the moral authority that is necessary for their legitimacy in a democratic society. And the certainty that science traditionally has been promised as a solution to problems caused by ignorance or disease is lacking today. Science seems to be less certain, even contradictory, for example when knowledgeable scientific experts like the FDA and the National Academy of Sciences disagree about the medical benefits of marijuana (Harris, 2006). In other cases, science seems to be implicated in the problems that threaten us, for instance global warming. The police and science now add to life's uncertainties and they seem to be at odds with each other. When we read about issues of science and justice, as often as not the story is about an innocent person who is exonerated by DNA evidence after years in prison or on death row. We suggest that in this situation where the moral authority of policing and science seems to be lacking, *CSI* offers surety and certainty, and that this, in part, is why the program is so successful. Our research focuses on how *CSI* combines the traditions of the crime genre with a new forensic realism to fuse the police and science with a convergent moral authority.

A skillful combination of old and new programming techniques contributes to *CSI*'s popularity, but also circulates a series of cultural images about crime. Because they stand at the intersection of crime, media, and culture, these forensic programs are a worthy site for analysis. Accordingly, in this article we analyze the content and tactics of *CSI*'s first season along with new data from its 2006 season and from its two spin-offs, *CSI: NY* and *CSI: Miami.*

Television Crime Drama

According to one well-known formulation, culture consists of the stories we tell ourselves about ourselves (Geertz, 1973). The stories provide an interpretative framework through which we are encouraged to understand various aspects of culture (McCullagh, 2002). This framework draws upon shared symbols and meanings, and uses these cultural elements even as it reinforces them. Such stories, then, both reflect and shape our culture. Today, these stories are told on television. Television circulates the cultural images through which we understand aspects of our social world ranging from our own identities to our concepts of right and wrong (Wilson, 2000; Wittebols, 2004; Wykes and Gunter, 2005).

Since television's inception, one of its most prevalent genres has been the crime drama (Mawby, 2004). Crime dramas provide interpretative perspectives that shape our thought, in this case about crime (Jewkes, 2004). Crime dramas are morality plays which feature struggles between good and evil, between heroes who stand for moral authority and villains who challenge that authority (Rafter, 2006). The crime genre exhibits stable elements, for example a focus on crime, usually violent crime, and the quest for justice, but it also reflects social change. Over the past 50 years television crime drama has shifted from storylines in which private detectives or criminal defence lawyers protected their innocent clients, to programs in which police officers apprehend the guilty (Cavender, 2004). Today, the police are the heroes and lawyers are the villains who impede their quest for justice (Rapping, 2003).

To a significant degree, the frameworks of understanding that the crime genre circulates go unnoticed. There are several reasons for this. First, because the producers of television crime dramas seek to attract a large audience, they tend to offer programs that reflect the cultural beliefs and sentiments about crime shared by the audience (Rapping, 2003). Similarly, crime genre plots are comfortably situated within dominant socio-political ideologies (Cavender, 2004). Finally, crime dramas provide an understanding of crime and criminals that is consistent with the criminological theories that are in vogue (Rafter, 2006). The frameworks of understanding about crime are unnoticed then, because they reflect dominant, taken-for-granted assumptions, but they, in turn, perpetuate those assumptions and, in so doing, perpetuate cultural views about crime and criminals. The crime genre also circulates cultural images of gender. These images go largely unnoticed because they also conform to cultural assumptions (Roberts and Inderman, 2005). These cultural ideals about gender influence notions of heroism (Rafter, 2006). In the earlier crime dramas, the hero was a man, usually macho, and likely to be an iconoclastic loner. Thus, gendered identity, the nature of work, and the hero's moral authority were stitched nicely into the narratives of television crime dramas. But times change and so do the narratives. Today, women are featured more in crime dramas, and notions of the ideal cop focus less on macho displays of strength and more on technical competence, what Messerschmidt (1993) calls *techno-masculinity*. The hero is less likely to be a loner and more likely to work in the police organization. These genre changes reflect larger cultural changes such as changes in the nature of masculinity (Messerschmidt, 1993), what it means to be a hero (Cavender, 1999), or the fact that there are more women in the criminal justice workplace (Martin and Jurik, 2006).

Similarly, the crime genre circulates shifting representations of race. Years ago, the genre often was racist: black characters, for example, were colourful "extras" or menacing figures, but, in either case, were portrayed as "the other" and juxtaposed against the usually white protagonist. The situation has changed today, especially on television. When black characters appear, they are more likely to be depicted as members of a legitimate profession like police officers than as a criminal (Hunt, 2005). However, the nature of the representation remains problematic.

In what Gray (2005) calls an assimilationist style of presentation, black characters typically are in a largely white world where race is not a concern.

The shift toward more dramas about the police organization entails other changes in the crime genre. The narratives in the contemporary dramas not only deal with crime and the efforts to capture the criminal, they also include more details about the police subculture and about the personal lives of the police (Wittebols, 2004). These personal lives may be portrayed as home life (McLaughlin, 2005); at other times, the members of the police organization are portrayed as a "police family" (Joyrich, 1996: 48–9). These narratives often have a melodramatic quality, complete with plots that are motivated by the characters' personal backstories (Mittell, 2004). Stories that utilize these plot devices, for example personal involvement or police family, make the characters seem like "real people," which attracts an audience but also reinforces the cultural meanings that are conveyed through the characters (Wittebols, 2004; also see Jermyn, 2003).

Notwithstanding its melodramatic nature, contemporary crime drama is linked with crime news and reality television; indeed, crime fact and crime fiction blur on television in representing the spectacle of crime (Altheide, 2002; Jewkes, 2004). Crime news, reality programs like *America's Most Wanted*, and crime drama all emphasize violent crime (Cavender et al., 1999; Chadee and Ditton, 2005; Roberts and Inderman, 2005). Their presentations are couched in notions of good and evil, and these binary opposites act as emotional, moralistic hooks that draw an audience for news or drama (Jewkes, 2005; McLaughlin, 2005; Roberts and Inderman, 2005). Television's various depictions of crime weave together realism and melodrama. The result is a forensic style of journalism that dwells on the minutiae of the crime scene (Websdale and Alvarez, 1998) and the forensic realism of television crime dramas like *CSI*. These factual and fictional depictions of crime are compelling because they offer mutually validating cultural images of crime and the police.

In our analysis of *CSI*, we adopt the perspective of cultural criminology which sees the media portrayal of crime and the efforts to solve it as entertaining (Ferrell and Websdale, 1999), but which works through a symbolism that reflects a series of cultural meanings, in this case, about crime, policing, and science. We argue that *CSI* provides an interpretative framework for understanding the moral authority of the police and of science. After a brief synopsis of the program and a description of our methodology, we turn to our analysis.

CSI Synopsis

Most episodes open with a shot of the Las Vegas strip, which identifies and locates the upcoming crime scenarios within a landscape that is familiar to the television audience. The camera then zooms in and travels across Las Vegas to what will be the opening scene of the episode. Then, opening credits roll over stock shots of the *CSI* cast in action: Gil Grissom, the head of the *CSI* unit, and investigators Catherine Willows, Sara Sidle, Warrick Brown, and Nick Stokes. There are similar establishing shots at the opening of *CSI: NY* and *CSI: Miami*.

During the program, the *CSI* team is depicted examining crime scenes, securing evidence, conducting lab experiments, interviewing witnesses and suspects, and, ultimately, using forensic science to solve crimes. In a week's episode the *CSI* team solves several cases, controls the threat to society that crime occasions, and brings closure to victims. This gives each episode an interesting flavour of crime, melodrama, and the seeming authenticity of science. This format is repeated in the two spin-off series.

Methodology

To understand more about the cultural meanings of the police and science as conveyed in *CSI*, we conducted a content analysis of its first season. We wanted to consider that season in close detail because *CSI*'s initial popularity ushered in an era of television forensic crime drama. Today, *CSI*, its reruns, and its two spin-offs air five nights a week in our television market. We updated the original data with observations of eight episodes from the 2006 season: three *CSI* episodes, three *CSI: NY* episodes, and two *CSI: Miami* episodes. They were the first eight episodes to air (between 22 February and 6 April 2006) after our decision to update the data from the first season.

CSI's first season was available in a DVD compilation. We watched and coded the 23 episodes which originally aired between 6 October 2000 and 17 May 2001. Our referencing system begins with the number 100, the pilot episode, and continues consecutively through the episodes as they appear in the DVD compilation. Initially, we watched four episodes, and, based upon this preview, formulated a code sheet.

The code sheet was organized around three aspects of *CSI*: (1) crime statistics, for example types of offences and demographic details about offenders and victims; (2) crime genre, for example elements typical of the genre such as the nature of plot development (such as personal involvement narratives); and (3) forensic science, that is, how *CSI* employs dialogue, narrative, or other programming features to present science. Our interest here is not the accuracy of presentation but rather in how *CSI* dramatically constructs a sense of science and interweaves police themes with representations of science in culturally significant ways.

With the eight current episodes, our observations are provided as qualitative, thematic comparisons with the first season rather than the quantitative coding that we initially employed. We were interested in how *CSI* (2006), *CSI: NY*, and *CSI: Miami* were similar to, or differed from, the programs in that initial season. We taped the episodes, and our referencing system for them begins with number 200.

We present our analysis in three sections. The first section addresses how *CSI* relies on the conventions of television's crime genre and presents the police as a moral authority. In the second section, we consider how *CSI* evokes a sense of science and how it rehabilitates science such that it stands as a moral authority. In the third section, we show how its combination of melodrama and realism converge with police themes to enhance the cultural meanings that *CSI* conveys.

Analysis

The Television Crime Genre

The team treats me like family. (Episode 202)

CSI's focus on forensics makes it unique, but the success of the program and its spin-offs also reflects the long-term popularity of the crime genre. The programs exemplify both the stability and the change that are common to the genre. These features are central to the cultural meanings that the program circulates, especially that of the police as a moral authority.

Among the genre's more stable features is the emphasis on violent crime. Our coding reveals that 72 percent of the crimes depicted during *CSI*'s first season were violent crimes; 64 per cent of the crimes involved murder. Although these are the type of crimes that would involve forensic investigations, the focus on murder is a crime genre staple. Murder was prominent in *CSI*'s current season and in the two spin-off series. Murder serves as an emotional hook in the crime genre: it entails the loss of a life, which in itself is important, and it symbolizes a threat to the social order (see Wilson, 2000).

CSI employs other emotional hooks as well. These include the pain of loss to a victim's family. In Episode 111, Catherine cries because, as a mother, she shares the grief of another mother who must identify her dead son. This episode demonstrates a frequent pattern in the first season: emotional hooks are constructed around personal involvement narratives. Catherine has an emotional connection on cases that involve parents or victimized children. The spin-offs also employ this technique. *CSI: Miami*'s lead character, Horatio, befriends a boy whose dad murdered his mother; Horatio suffered a similar fate as a boy (Episode 205). These narrative devices circulate cultural meanings that are common to the crime genre, for example, crime as a threat to ourselves, to our families, and to fundamental moral values (Rapping, 2003). But they also create characters with whom the audience can identify.

CSI also circulates images of gender. These images reflect cultural changes but they also perpetuate the notion of the investigators as "the good guys" and of the police as a moral authority. During *CSI*'s first season, Gil Grissom is depicted as a father figure who heads the unit. He demonstrates a vast amount of forensic knowledge and offers sage advice to his younger subordinates. William Peterson who plays Gil was the series' best-known actor during that first season. This cemented his status as the lead character, and also reinforced the gendered images: he is a man and he is the boss (see Cavender, 1999). The spin-offs also have well-known male actors in lead roles: David Caruso (formerly of *NYPD: Blue*) in *CSI: Miami* and Gary Sinese in *CSI: NY*. These men display a techno-masculinity (see Messerschmidt, 1993) that both updates the portrayal of masculinity and reaffirms the notion of men as heroes (Rafter, 2006).

As women have increased their presence in the criminal justice workplace, they appear more frequently in crime dramas like *CSI*. *CSI*'s female characters have essentially the same duties and abilities as their male counterparts. This depiction persists across the episodes in our analysis. A female investigator adeptly uses a jack hammer to open a chimney where a body is hidden, demonstrates agility while working on a roof, and is shown to be competent in the lab (Episode 204). In a series that foregrounds competency in science, intelligence is as important as physical strength. Sometimes, however, these programs reaffirm extant stereotypes about women. A woman may supply the key element that solves a crime, but does so with "special women's insights." An investigator who had been a victim of domestic violence realizes that such abuse is important in a case, and she mobilizes a secret network of female victims to discover key facts (*CSI: Miami*, Episode 205). *CSI* and its spin-offs are not sexist, but in their presentations of who is in charge and in their portrayal of women investigators, they reinforce some notions of patriarchy, for example, men are the boss and women are stereotypically feminine (see Joyrich, 1996).

CSI is one of the ten most popular programs among African-American viewers (Hunt, 2005). During the initial season, one of the five investigators is an African-American man. Only occasionally, however, is race a relevant plot issue (see Episode 103). For the most part, *CSI* represents race in the assimilationist style (Gray, 2005), that is, Warrick, the African-American character, exists in a white world and racial issues are rare in the plots.

In the past, a tension between a protagonist and others, even other police agencies, was a standard plot device. It set the protagonist off from others and established his (usually a man's) moral authority. *CSI* employed this plot device during its first season. It served to establish the forensic investigators as unique, as different from other police (Episode 100). We saw less of this plot device in the current season or with the spin-offs. Perhaps the series writers felt that, after many successful seasons, such tensions were no longer needed to demonstrate the uniqueness of the forensic team. *CSI* makes this point when a reporter asks an investigator, formerly in forensics but now a detective, "Which side of the fence do you prefer?" She answers, "It's the same side" (Episode 207). Forensic science blends with policing to promote the legitimacy of both spheres.

Tensions still occur but they are more like disagreements among friends or family members. In a *CSI: Miami* episode, two investigators argue about whether it was a mistake for a colleague to put up posters that call attention to a pedophile. Later, they argue about the appropriate sentence of a man who killed the pedophile. These disagreements reflect the "police family" dimension of the programs. The characters are respectful of each other, and, at the episode's end, agree to continue the discussion over a beer after work. When the investigator who made the posters is offered a reassignment because her actions have possibly hurt her career, she declines with the statement that opened this section: "The team treats me like family" (Episode 202).

The police family device may resonate with the audience because it normalizes the characters who are like our own families, but it also circulates an image of the police as a moral authority. Across these programs, the forensic units are portrayed as smooth-running organizations. The investigators work together as a team, and, as a result, they usually solve the case. Indeed, in only four episodes during *CSI*'s first season do the investigators fail to apprehend the criminal, and in two of these (Episodes 103 and 109) they have an idea about the criminals' identity but not enough information for an arrest. *CSI* circulates a set of cultural meanings about the police: they are competent, they are a team, and they are a moral authority that stands against social disorder (see Wilson, 2000).

CSI's villains also circulate cultural meanings. Occasionally criminals are sympathetic characters. In Episode 204, a father, bereft because the police never found his missing daughter, undertakes a form of vigilante justice against the man he suspects of murdering his daughter. Catherine sympathizes with the father's grief. More often however, *CSI*'s villains are unsympathetic characters who lack moral values. First, they are usually murderers. In the current *CSI* season and in the spin-offs the criminals rarely show remorse for their crimes. Some even blame the victim. An abusive ex-husband who murders his wife berates her for having an empty gun and being unable to defend herself against him (*CSI: Miami*, Episode 205). In the eight current programs, many witnesses are unwilling to assist the police. This may be a plot device that is designed to misdirect the audience's suspicions, although the witnesses seem to be nasty characters who rely on a twisted sense of the law to avoid civic responsibility. Indeed, law is portrayed as being problematic in some episodes. In the vigilante justice case, Catherine apologizes to the bereaved father because the law failed him and he had to take matters into his own hands (Episode 204). And if the law is problematic, lawyers are worse. The detectives worry that an "aggressive attorney" will file a civil suit against them (Episode 202) or file motions to exclude incriminating evidence they have uncovered (Episode 204). The cultural meanings are clear. *CSI*, like the crime genre generally, reinforces stereotypes about who is and who is not deserving of our moral sympathy (Rapping, 2003; Jewkes, 2004).

These genre elements, both traditional and contemporary, are standard features in *CSI*'s first season, its current season, and in its spin-offs. At the same time, science sells these programs. Therefore, it is essential that they construct a sense of science that appears to be accurate and decisive, thus convincing viewers of the show's forensic realism.

CSI's Forensic Science

King Solomon didn't have a DNA lab. (Episode 201)

Genres are identified by, among other markers, iconographic signs and symbols which include settings, costumes, and props. *CSI* exhibits an iconography which is marked by the accoutrement of science. These accoutrement include markers such as "scientific" dress and language, and importantly, narrative and cinematographic techniques that make a claim of scientific verisimilitude. These markers separate *CSI* from other television crime genre dramas but also circulate a series of cultural meanings which suggest that science solves problems. The accuracy of the scientific equipment and techniques is less important than the meanings about science that *CSI* conveys: the program essentially rehabilitates science by making it appear less equivocal, less contradictory. Science stands for truth on *CSI*, truth in a deeper philosophical sense, and in terms of the case at hand, that is, proving who is the criminal. But, because this is television, science must also be entertaining and accessible. The programs in our updated sample are consistent in their treatment of science.

Iconography and Accoutrement

CSI characters look the part of forensic investigators at the crime scene and in the crime lab. At a crime scene, they display the markers of the police such as identification badges, but they also wear clothing which visually marks their special status such as jackets and caps labelled "forensics." Gloves and booties complete the crime scene ensemble. As befitting scientists, in the crime lab characters wear lab coats, smocks, or lab aprons.

The characters use specialized equipment which validates their scientific status. Crime scene equipment ranges from adhesives and plasters to lift finger and footprints, to chemicals like luminol which, when illuminated with a special blue light, causes invisible blood traces to glow (Episodes 110 and 120). In a *CSI: NY* episode (203), they use a plastic tent which they inflate with a special gas to reveal fingerprints on a corpse. The crime laboratory set is stocked with microscopes, beakers, and test tube trays which are designed to lend credibility to *CSI*'s forensic science.

As the characters use this specialized scientific equipment, they explain its purposes. This dialogue acts as a primer that helps to make science accessible for the audience. The use of scientific jargon also makes the characters seem to be knowledgeable forensic specialists. Their language covers a vast array of scientific specializations, including forensic medicine, ballistics, toxicology, and chemistry. During a fire investigation, Gil is conversant with such terms as "spalling" and "alligatoring"; these refer to burn patterns which suggest that an accelerant was used to start a fire (Episode 111). The characters are knowledgeable in other ways as well. They are knowledgeable about crime and criminal careers (Episode 207), and possess non-science information which is relevant in their investigations such as how automobile windshields are made (*CSI: Miami*, Episode 205).

Forensic databases are frequently referenced on *CSI*. These include the Forensic Medical Journal, the Dental Society Database, and the Combined DNA Index System (CODIS). These databases often reveal key information. As the investigators painstakingly restructure a skeleton, they post images of the jaw on the Dental Society Database. A dentist compares his records with that image and identifies the victim (Episode 113). In a *CSI: Miami* episode (202), the investigators use a special camera to photograph under a man's skin; it reveals an unformed bruise, which, in turn, reveals the design of the gun barrel that caused the bruise. They then use a gun ownership database to locate the gun's owner. These databases not only help solve crimes, equally important, they convey the idea that science has the answers, and that they are even computerized. *CSI* and its spin-offs thereby circulate cultural meanings about the infallibility of science.

Verisimilitude

The crime genre has long been characterized by a sense of realism. *CSI* maintains this tradition, but in a unique sense: it privileges the accuracy of physical evidence, and, by extension, of science. The verisimilitude of physical evidence surfaces through recurrent dialogue, dead-on experiments, and accompanying visualizations. The evidence solves the case and elevates the credibility of the forensic sciences.

In most episodes, someone declares the evidence to be the absolute truth. A definitive example occurs in the pilot (Episode 100) when Gil urges them to "concentrate on what cannot lie, the evidence." He reinforces the point in another episode: "The evidence only knows one thing: the truth. It is what it is" (Episode 105). The dialogue consistently asserts that physical evidence is superior to all other proof, and insinuates that it is completely accurate.

Gil's formulation of this position is that they "chase the lie 'til it leads to the truth" (Episode 111). Again, truth on *CSI* seems to refer to the notion that there are answers to the unknowns that confront the investigators. The King Solomon reference at the start of this section makes this point in a *CSI* episode. The investigators encounter a dilemma: two women claim to be a boy's mother. When a detective references the Bible story wherein Solomon confronted such a problem, another responds, "King Solomon didn't have a DNA lab" (Episode 201). Science can supply the answers. The current programs maintain this notion. When the *CSI: NY* investigators are temporarily stymied, one mentions Max's (Gary Sinese) mantra, "Dig deeper" (Episode 200). The reference presumes that if one does this, the truth is there and will be unearthed.

The investigators dig deeper by conducting experiments or re-enactments of the crime. Experiments are routine in *CSI* episodes, and they serve to substantiate the notion that there are answers and that forensic science can and will reveal them. However, because most viewers lack a science background, *CSI* uses cinematographic effects to explain these scientific techniques, that is, to visually supplement the complicated forensic language, and to make them more entertaining. Visualizations include close-ups of microscopic evidence. As Catherine peers into a microscope, enlarged images of the physical evidence appear on the screen allowing the viewers to feel as if they, too, are looking through the microscope (Episode 112). These visualizations combine with the dialogue to convey a sense that the audience understands forensic science and can do this job and also can see the truth. Such techniques continue in the current programs. Moreover, as an investigator conducts an experiment that reveals some important fact, visuals confirm it with a flashback to that portion of the crime. Near the end of a program when the investigators have solved the crime, more complete flashbacks confirm their theory (e.g., *CSI: NY*, Episode 200). Science provides the police and the audience with an understanding of the crime and the criminal (Wilson, 2000).

Police and Science

Everyone learns from science; it all depends on how you use the knowledge. (Episode 207)

The cultural images that *CSI* and its spin-offs circulate about the police and about science are bolstered by the long-term popularity of the crime genre and by the esteem of science. The police and science are mutually reinforcing. Moreover, *CSI* fits into other television programming trends that also enhance the cultural meanings that the programs disseminate.

Earlier, we noted that the boundaries between fact and fiction are blurring on television. This blurring is evident on *CSI* and its spin-off series. *CSI* is informed by many elements popularized by reality television. It uses the sights and sounds of seemingly real police at work to suggest its own realism in the manner of *America's Most Wanted*. When the forensic investigators first appear at a crime scene, background effects includes squawking police radios and the flashing of police car blue lights; yellow police tape and milling extras in police uniform complete the effect: this is a crime scene. In one current *CSI* episode, the forensic detectives are even the subject of a fictional reality television program.

Reality television enhances its own realism by citing official crime data. *CSI* and its spin-offs work such data into the dialogue. For example, as he conducts an autopsy of a murdered sexual assault victim, a coroner states, "Women are four times as likely as men to be victims in sexual-related murders, and men are ten times as likely to be the murderer" (*CSI*, Episode 207). Such factually based dialogue adds authenticity to the program's forensic science claims by making it seem more news-like.

Although we did not code for these news-like aspects in our analysis of *CSI*'s first season, we did see them in the updated data, especially with the spin-off series. In our television market, *CSI: NY* and *CSI: Miami* precede the 10 p.m. local news, and teasers for the local news appear during commercial breaks in these programs. In one *CSI: NY* episode (200), the teaser notes that the news will feature an interview with Gary Sinese, the program's lead actor. In other episodes, the teasers mention crimes that will be the lead news story. Following a *CSI: Miami* program about the murder of a child molester, the news opened with a story about technology developed by the military that can trace sex offenders (Episode 202). Another news broadcast opened with a reporter in a helicopter hovering over a crime scene. Below, we could see yellow police tape and crime scene investigators at work just as in the preceding crime drama (*CSI: NY*, Episode 203).

The relationship among a crime drama like *CSI*, reality television, and the news is important because of its impact on the cultural meanings circulated by television. For cultural historian Raymond Williams (1974), the individual program is not as important as the *flow* of television programs over the course of an evening. The cultural images that television circulates in this flow are mutually reinforcing, unnoticed, and therefore more compelling. With *CSI*, there is an image of the police and science as absolute authorities. Williams's observation is all the more relevant with crime dramas which, as we noted earlier, also square with widely held views about crime, with dominant ideologies, and even with extant criminological theory.

CSI and its spin-offs, consistent with reality television and the news, depict the modern world as a mean and scary place. People already fear crime and the programs reinforce these fears. Crime is random, the characters tell us, and you never know when you will be victimized. As one investigator puts it, "Juries want explanations, nice and neat. They don't want to know that we live in a random world" (*CSI*, Episode 207). People are angry at criminals and the characters in the programs reflect those sentiments as they express their indignation at criminals (Rapping, 2003). *CSI* is consistent with current themes of individual responsibility for social problems, and also reinforces contemporary criminological theory, for example, routine activities theory: criminals are irresponsible people (Rafter, 2006). Crime is usually motivated by selfishness, as with the New Yorker who murdered a woman to get her apartment (*CSI: NY*, Episode 200). The crimes and the motivations for these criminals are without social context. The programs circulate a cultural meaning about crime: crime is normal and opportunistic (Jewkes, 2004). For example, in the episode about sexually related murders, when the coroner gives his statistical litany about men killing women, he adds, "That's just the way it is" (*CSI*, Episode 207). Nothing is said about how sexism or patriarchy might help us to understand why it is this way (see Websdale and Alvarez, 1998). Contextual comments that might address a criminal's motivation are lampooned. Such a presentation privileges reliance on the police and science, and offers little hope for collective social change.

Plots may be complicated on these programs, but right and wrong usually are portrayed as straightforward matters. When asked if there is a danger that criminals might learn to avoid detection by watching forensic crime programs, Gil Grissom responds with the piece of dialogue that opened this section: "Everyone learns from science; it all depends on how you use the knowledge" (*CSI*, Episode 207). *CSI* suggests that the police use science to set things right. The result is a powerful legitimation of the union of police and science.

Conclusion

Television circulates images which convey cultural meanings about many facets of social life, including crime. At the outset, we suggested that *CSI* is an interesting site for analyzing the intersection of crime, media, and culture. Perhaps they are only crime dramas, but *CSI* and its progeny traffic in cultural meanings on matters as diverse as gender, race, family, work, and of course, crime and policing. As we have argued, chief among the meanings that these programs convey is the view that the police, aligned against crime and criminals, stand as a moral authority. In part, this view is accomplished through adherence to the traditions of the crime genre: violent crime, especially murder, represents a threat to the social order which the police, here the forensic detectives, contain by apprehending the criminal.

At the same time, *CSI* stakes out new territory in television crime drama. *CSI*, *CSI: NY*, and *CSI: Miami* circulate cultural images which validate scientific evidence and science itself. *CSI*'s mantra—that physical evidence cannot lie, that evidence is a truth that science will reveal—suggests that the police have harnessed science. And more, they have rehabilitated science by reducing any contradictions it might exhibit in the real world, for example, competing expert opinions in a court case. If we see justice as reaching the correct answer as the program suggests, the *CSI* team almost always produces justice. And, they never enter a courthouse. Indeed, lawyers, and, to a degree, even the law, are problematic. Cases are solved in the crime lab which renders a jury unnecessary: there is no better judge than science.

CSI circulates these cultural meanings through narratives that reflect and reproduce popular beliefs about crime. Crime is a random, routine event on these programs. Criminals typically are selfish, venal, remorseless people, so no causal explanation of criminality is needed. The idea that there is a social context in which crime occurs is not an issue or is depicted as a farcical one. The proper response to the criminal event may be predicated on the rationality of science, but it also takes for granted a strong measure of punitiveness, what Jewkes (2004: 180) calls an "authoritarian populism," which plays as indignation against the criminals by the investigators. Many episodes end with the investigators confronting the criminals and engaging in status degradation ceremonies (Garfinkel, 1956).

Ironically, however, the very success of *CSI* and its spin-offs raises new challenges, to them as television programs, and to the meanings they circulate. Some commentators claim that not all of *CSI*'s science is valid. One forensics expert calls some of it, for instance, using a knife wound to make a mould of a knife, "blatant hokum" (Roane, 2005). What is interesting is not so much the accuracy of the scientific procedures as the fact that *CSI* presents them in such a realistic fashion that fans (and experts) try to find fault with them. There is a further irony as well: *CSI*'s mantra about scientific evidence may have produced another dilemma, the so-called "*CSI* Effect." Members of the television audience, convinced that they understand forensic science, maintain these beliefs as jurors. One prosecutor says that because of programs like *CSI*, jurors now have unreasonable expectations about scientific technology (Walsh, 2004). According to another attorney, *CSI* "projects the image that all cases are solvable by highly technical science, and if you offer less than that, it is viewed as reasonable doubt" (Roane, 2005: 50). It is difficult to make definite judgments about *CSI*'s accuracy or the *CSI* Effect. Some experts claim that the program is fairly accurate, but modified to be entertaining. Others note that the *CSI* Effect is, for now, mainly anecdotal (Tyler, 2006).

In any case, *CSI* has brought forensic science into the popular discourse. All of this is occurring in a country that is not known for a scientific culture. Our analysis of *CSI*'s first season and the updated observations from its 2006 season and from *CSI: NY* and *CSI: Miami* suggest that their careful blend of melodrama, which attracts an audience, combines with the form of realism that is characteristic of television which today blurs the boundaries between fact and fiction. In these programs, crimes are solved, the guilty get their come-uppance, and order is restored (at least until the next episode). Members of the audience believe that they understand forensic science and that they could be forensic detectives, so they side with them. Perhaps such a belief brings a sense of closure or certainty in an uncertain world. If the police sometimes fail at their tasks in the real world, *CSI* provides a new and legitimate way of catching the bad guys. At a time when so many problems are intractable, *CSI*'s stock-in-trade is dependable and untarnished: science united with the police. Comforting though that may be, it is a media construction of science; it is television.

References

Altheide, D. (2002). *Creating Fear: News and the Construction of Crisis.* New York: Aldine de Gruyter.

Armstrong, M. (2000). "Premiere Week Ratings: Everybody Loves CBS?" Available at: http://www.eonline.com (10 October).

Arthur, K. (2006). "Survivor vs. Idol," *New York Times*, 11 March.

Cavender, G. (1999). "Detecting Masculinity," in J. Ferrell and Neil Websdale (eds) *Making Trouble: Cultural Constructions of Crime, Deviance, and Control*, pp. 157–75. New York: Aldine De Gruyter.

———. (2004). "Media and Crime Policy: A Reconsideration of David Garland's *The Culture of Control*," *Punishment & Society* 6(3): 335–48.

Cavender, G., L. Bond-Maupin, and N. Jurik (1999). "The Construction of Gender in Reality Crime TV," *Gender & Society* 13(5): 644–63.

Chadee, D., and J. Ditton (2005). "Fear of Crime and the Media: Assessing the Lack of Relationship," *Crime Media Culture* 1(3): 322–32.

Ferrell, J., and N. Websdale (eds). (1999). *Making Trouble: Cultural Constructions of Crime, Deviance and Control.* New York: Aldine De Gruyter.

Garfinkel, H. (1956). "Conditions of Successful Degradation Ceremonies," *American Journal of Sociology* 61: 420–42.

Geertz, C. (1973). *The Interpretation of Culture.* New York: Basic Books.

Gray, H. (2005). "The Politics of Representation in Network Television," in D. Hunt (ed.) *Channeling Blackness: Studies on Television and Race in America*, pp. 155–74. New York: Oxford University Press.

Harris, G. (2006). "F.D.A. Dismisses Medical Benefit of Marijuana," *New York Times*, 21 April.

Hunt, D. (ed.) (2005). *Channeling Blackness: Studies on Television and Race in America.* New York: Oxford University Press.

Jermyn, D. (2004). "Photo Stories and Family Albums: Imagining Criminals and Victims on Crimewatch UK," in P. Mason (ed.) *Criminal Visions: Media Representations of Crime and Justice*, pp. 174 – 91. Cullompton: Willan.

Jewkes, Y. (2004). *Media and Crime.* London: SAGE Publications.

Joyrich, L. (1996). *Re-viewing Reception: Television, Gender, and Postmodern Culture.* Bloomington, IN: Indiana University Press.

McCullagh, C. (2002). *Media Power: A Sociological Introduction.* Basingstoke: Palgrave.

McLaughlin, E. (2005). "From Reel to Ideal: *The Blue Lamp* and the Popular Construction of the English Bobby," *Crime Media Culture* 1(1): 11–30.

Martin, S., and N. Jurik. (2006). *Doing Justice, Doing Gender: Women in Legal and Criminal Justice Occupations*, 2nd edn. Thousand Oaks, CA: SAGE Publications.

Mawby, R. (2004). "Completing the Half-formed Picture? Media Images of Policing," in P. Mason (ed.) *Criminal Visions: Media Representations of Crime and Justice*, pp. 214–37. Cullompton: Willan.

Messerschmidt, J. (1993). *Masculinities and Crime: Critique and Reconceptualization of Theory.* Lanham: Rowan & Littlefield.

Mittell, J. (2004). *Genre and Television: From Cop Shows to Cartoons in American Culture.* London: Routledge.

Nielsen Ratings. (2005). "Top Ten Primetime Broadcast TV Programs." Available at: http://www.nielsenmedia.com/ratings/broadcast_programs.html (26 June).

Rafter, N. (2006). *Shots in the Mirror: Crime Films and Society*, 2nd edn. New York: Oxford University Press.

Rapping, E. (2003). *Law and Justice as Seen on TV.* New York: New York University Press.

Roane, K. (2005). "The CSI Effect," *U.S. News & World Report*, 25 April.

Roberts, L., and D. Inderman. (2005). "Social Issues as Media Constructions: The Case of Road Rage," *Crime Media Culture* 1(3): 301–21.

Tyler, T. (2006). "Viewing CSI and the Threshold of Guilt: Managing Truth and Justice in Reality and Fiction," *Yale Law Journal* 115: 1050–85.

Walsh, J. (2004). "Prosecutors: Crime Shows Blur Reality," *Arizona Republic*, 29 August.

Websdale, N., and A. Alvarez. (1998). "Forensic Journalism as Patriarchal Ideology: The Newspaper Construction of Homicide–Suicide," in F. Bailey and D. Hale (eds) *Popular Culture, Crime and Justice*, pp. 123–41. Belmont, CA: West/Wadsworth.

Williams, R. (1974). *Television: Technology and Cultural Form.* New York: Schocken Books.

Wilson, C. (2000). *Cop Knowledge: Police Power and Cultural Narrative in Twentieth Century America.* Chicago: University of Chicago Press.

Wittebols, J. (2004). *The Soap Opera Paradigm: Television Programming and Corporate Priorities.* Lanham, MD: Rowman & Littlefield.

Wykes, M., and B. Gunter. (2005). *The Media and Body Image: If Looks Could Kill.* London: SAGE Publications.

Re-Wiring Baltimore: The Emotive Power of Systemics, Seriality, and the City

Marsha Kinder

The Networked City as Intertext

Through its network of intertextual allusions (to TV, cinema, literature, theatre, and journalism), which continues growing through the final episode (with its pointed references to Shakespeare, Kafka, and H.L. Mencken), *The Wire* explicitly mentions both precursors and foils, with which it should be compared, training us how to remix or resist what we previously have been encouraged to admire. In season 5, metro editor Gus Haynes (Clark Johnson) tells his staff of writers at the *Baltimore Sun* (the paper where series creator David Simon was a crime reporter for 12 years): "There are a million stories in this naked city, but you mooks only have to bring in two or three." When Simon came to visit TV critic Howard Rosenberg's class at USC on 3 March 2008, he acknowledged *Naked City* as an important influence on *The Wire*. (Unless otherwise noted, quotations from Simon in this article are taken from this visit.) Running from 1958 to 1963 on ABC, this classic TV cop series broke new ground with its gritty realism and its narrative focus on New York City. Yet an urban focus doesn't guarantee systemic analysis, as demonstrated not only by *Naked City* but also by one of *The Wire's* primary foils, *CSI: Crime Scene Investigation*, the most popular crime series currently on TV. In the final season of *The Wire*, a glib psychologist offers his services as a criminal profiler, citing his previous work for *CSI*, and is summarily rejected. Set in glamorous Las Vegas, the city where no one is held accountable for their actions and where chance rules supreme, *CSI* uses its location as ironic backdrop for its optimistic depiction of infallible scientific police work, which spares no expense. But *CSI* never illuminates its urban context—either its actual setting of Las Vegas or the city of Los Angeles, whose race-based trials of O.J. Simpson and the cops who battered Rodney King and their disturbing outcomes help explain the popular appeal of this escapist procedural series. As strategic sites for its formulaic spin-offs, *CSI* chose Miami and New York, cities associated thematically with international drug wars and the terrorist disaster of 9/11, and commercially with popular precursors like *Miami Vice*, *NYPD Blue*, and *New York Undercover*.

In contrast, *The Wire* is committed to a systemic analysis of Baltimore, combining narrative strategies from two earlier TV Baltimore crime series, with which Simon was personally connected. *Homicide: Life on the Street* (1993–99), a realistic TV police series based on Simon's non-fiction book, *Homicide: A Year on the Killing Streets*, focused primarily on cops rather than criminals who changed from week to week; and Simon's own 2000 HBO mini-series, *The Corner*, based on a non-fiction book he co-wrote with Ed Burns (*The Corner: A Year in the Life of an Inner-City Neighborhood*), had a narrower narrative field (one year in the life, on one corner, in one season comprised of six episodes). This series was better suited to the family as the basic unit of analysis, for it lacked the broad canvas of *The Wire*, whose first season combined cops from homicide with drug dealers on the corner. (The casting of Clark Johnson, one of the cops from *Homicide*, in *The Wire* emphasizes the connection between the two series.) Simon says when he first proposed

The Wire series to HBO, he mentioned only the drug war—not his goal of building a city and performing a systemic analysis that would dramatize the dire need for policy reform.

Yet this narrative focus on the city distinguishes both *The Wire* and *Naked City* from other successful serial crime fiction structured around the family—like the HBO series *The Sopranos* (1999–2007) and Francis Ford Coppola's cinematic *Godfather* trilogy (1972, 1974, and 1990), neither of whose systemic analyses rivals the breadth of that found in *The Wire*. Instead, their focus on the multi-generational crime family brings a strong dimension of melodrama into the gangster genre. The Corleones may stand in for America, but it is the family's ups and downs and internecine betrayals that raise the story to tragedy, and Coppola's casting of Robert De Niro, Marlon Brando, and Al Pacino that keeps us sutured into who's in charge. *The Sopranos* (which ran for six seasons) used its enlarged canvas to go into greater emotional depth for its array of complex characters. But, despite the breadth and high-quality acting of its ensemble cast, there was never any doubt over who was the protagonist: it was Tony Soprano's family that was being investigated and his memories, phobias, and dreams that were being subjected to depth analysis.

Systemic Suture

While *The Wire* is not the first work of crime fiction to perform such a systemic analysis of corruption, it may be the most successful in making it emotionally compelling; for systemics usually demand a critical distance that is incompatible with most forms of character identification. I am arguing that the uniqueness of the series depends on this combination, whose most interesting precedents (both precursors and foils) come from cinema rather than television. As foils, I'm thinking of the emotional distance in political films like Francesco Rosi's *Salvatore Giuliano* (1960), a dialectic reconstruction of the famous bandit's relationship to political and economic power, or in most of Jean-Luc Godard's reflexive works from the late 1960s and early 1970s, including *Weekend* and *Two or Three Things I Know About Her* (both 1967), which reject realism and emotional suture altogether. Significantly, Simon cites Stanley Kubrick's *Paths of Glory* (1957) as his primary cinematic model and "the most important political film in history," a war film that succeeds in combining systemic analysis with more traditional forms of realism and emotional identification. Yet one can also find this combination in other cinematic precursors *within* the crime film genre, like Fritz Lang's *M* (1931) and John Mackenzie's *The Long Good Friday* (1980). In moving their focus from a fascinating individual criminal to a broader analysis of the culture that creates and destroys him, they design narrative strategies that are expanded in *The Wire*.

M moves from the compulsive pedophile (played by Peter Lorre) to the police and criminals pursuing him, who increasingly become mirror images of each other. This reflective relationship (like the one between drug dealers and cops in *The Wire*'s first season) proves more terrifying than the irrational acts of the child-killer (however heinous his uncontrollable urges and crimes). The relationship becomes central to the film's systemic analysis of Germany, which prefigured the rise of the Third Reich. This kind of reflective relationship between both sides of the law can also be found in later serial crime fiction like the *Godfather* trilogy, but nowhere is it developed more expansively than in *The Wire*.

The Long Good Friday focuses on an ambitious London gangster, Harold Shand (Bob Hoskins) who, like *The Wire*'s equally charismatic drug dealer Stringer Bell (Idris Elba), tries to go legit by investing in his city's docklands as a future site for the Olympics. Describing himself as, "not a politician, but a businessman with an historical sense and global perspective," he fails to understand how the emergent power of the IRA challenges his old-fashioned conception of empire. His political naivety prevents him from seeing beyond the gangster paradigm. In the final close-up when Harold is about to be whacked, he finally realizes his opponents are international terrorists rather than local mobsters, that this movie is a European political thriller rather than an Anglicized Hollywood gangster film, and that he has misunderstood the power dynamics both of the genre and of globalism. If we can't read this close-up, then we misunderstand the movie and its prophetic analysis of Thatcherism in the 1980s. Similarly, despite Stringer's intelligence and driving ambitions, he is still too naive to understand the power dynamics that drive the so-called legitimate worlds of business, law, and politics (dynamics that his young successor Marlo Stanfield [Jamie Hector] will also have to fathom). In both crime narratives, this last-minute gain in systemic understanding helps reconcile these gangsters to their premature death, as if it's a fitting tragic payoff for their respective transformations.

Despite the deep pessimism of *The Wire*'s systemic analysis of our crumbling cities and pervasive corruption, unlike these precursors, it achieves a delicate emotional balance, for it is not merely one charismatic outlaw who must be transcended, but several promising yet vulnerable characters who generate a series of transformative moments season after season. As actor Jamie Hector put it in an article titled "*Wire* Leaves a Legacy of Hope," which appeared in the Sunday *Los Angeles Times* on the night the final episode was aired, "I believe he [David Simon] is saying there is hope through the people in the institutions" (9 March 2008, E1). Not restricted to any single family, race, class, gender, sexual persuasion, or generation (though the youngsters from season four are the most poignant), these promising characters keep emerging on both sides of the law. The emotional power of the series depends on this dynamic tension between, on the one hand, having so many vibrant characters with enormous potential and, on the other hand, seeing how the culture is wired to destroy them. What results is serial tragedy with a systemic form of suture, which inspires awe and pity week after week and makes it difficult for viewers to turn away.

Although Simon claims that *The Wire* is more about class rather than race ("I just happened to be doing a series about a city that's 65 per cent black . . . *Homicide* already covered race"), the fact that most of these complex characters are African American and most of them brilliantly played by actors we've never previously seen—these facts alone create a sense of hope. As actress Sonja Sohn, who plays Kima Greggs, puts it in the same *Los Angeles Times* feature: "This cast might not be here if there was no hope in the ghetto" (E22). *The Wire*'s emphasis on black characters marks an important departure from successful serial crime precursors like the *Godfather* trilogy and *The Sopranos*, whose more traditional Italian American characters share middle America's racism against African Americans, a dimension that might regrettably make it easier for white viewers to identify with them. Aware that this emphasis on race might reduce the size of his audience but determined to pursue it as part of his systemic analysis, Simon acknowledges: "We have more working black actors in key roles than pretty much all the other shows on the air. And yet you still hear people claim they can't find good African-American actors." It is this "richness of the black community," as actor Lance Reddick (who plays Cedric Daniels) calls it, that makes the series "so different from anything that's been on television" (E22).

Yet we also are aware that every character in the ensemble cast (whether black or white, and no matter how seemingly central) can be killed off at any moment, as in real life, without threatening the systemic level of the series. Nowhere is this awareness more painful than in the murder of the courageous black homosexual assassin Omar Little (brilliantly played by Michael K. Williams), one of the most powerful characters in the series. This chilling event catches us off-guard as much as it does Omar, for he is gunned down not by Marlo's "muscle," Chris (Gbenga Akinnagbe) and

Snoop (Felicia Pearson) who are doggedly hunting him down, but by the vicious little street-corner kid, Kenard (Thuliso Dingwall). In Rosenberg's class, Simon reminded us that midway through season 3, there's a shot of Kenard playing in the street with other kids and picking up a stick and shouting, "It's my turn to play Omar." *The Wire* presents three generations of street killers (Kenard, Marlo, and Omar) as victims of the city, whose failed institutions waste their potential. That's why the *Baltimore Sun*'s failure to cover Omar's death, and the dysfunctional police lab's misidentification of his corpse, are almost as chilling as his murder. As Simon says, the series is all about subtext (what's omitted) and the need to change policy. Yet we care deeply about these issues because of our emotional engagement with these characters who emerge from the ensemble cast.

Seriality and the Ensemble Cast

As a mini-series spread over five seasons, *The Wire* has been structured to take full advantage of television's expanded narrative field. It doesn't merely track the longitudinal history of a police investigation or repeat formulaic situations. Each season *The Wire* shifts the focus to a different segment of society: the drug wars, the docks, city politics, education, and the media. It thereby avoids the endgame of the ordinary TV series, as described by Janet Murray in *Hamlet on the Holodeck: The Future of Narrative in Cyberspace* (Free Press, 1997): "When every variation of the situation has been played out, as in the final season of a long-running series, the underlying fantasy comes to the surface . . . We can look at it directly, with less anxiety, but we also find it less compelling" (169–70).

Despite its hyper-realism and its array of black characters, the first season is the most conventional segment, for the drug war is a typical topic for crime fiction. Though the series transforms the genre, it first hooks us with the traditional lures of what is being transformed. Like the *Godfather* trilogy, *The Wire* begins with a compelling narrative segment (season 1) that is firmly positioned within the genre, and lets the second segment perform the dramatic rupture. Titled "The Port," season 2 focuses on the loss of blue-collar jobs at the docks, the weakening of unions, and the rise of global capitalism—a dramatic shift that felt like it was introducing an entirely new series. Not only is a new set of characters introduced, but their networked crimes go global. The mysterious bad guy (played by Bill Raymond) is called "the Greek," though his "muscle" is Ukrainian and Israeli, and the new crime family is East European, as are the prostitutes being illegally imported and victimized. This move evokes another cinematic precursor about dock workers (made by a Greek)—Elia Kazan's Oscar-winning *On the Waterfront* (1954). The evocation encourages us to compare what has happened in the interim not only to the unions but also to the rivalries between movies and television for hyper-realistic representation and systemic analysis, as if the narrative format of cinema is now insufficiently expansive for covering the complex networked society. The tragic ending of season 2 was even bleaker than that of its cinematic precursor, with two generations of the Sobotka family totally wiped out and with the only survivors being the cops, the female love interest Beadie Russell (Amy Ryan), who hooks up with Jimmy McNulty (Dominic West) in season 3, and the mysterious Greeks. This allusion also underscores Simon's claim that his primary dramatic model is Greek tragedy, where characters with potential are doomed by larger forces (in this case failing institutions rather than fickle gods). This is the season that feels most unified and self-contained. According to Simon, they got it right and had nothing more to say on this subject. This season performed its function of raising the series to a systemic level of tragedy.

The Conflict between Systemic Analysis and Emotional Suture

In season 2 we also begin to experience a conflict between this systemic analysis of Baltimore and our emotional engagement with the characters with whom we choose to identify. Although in season 1 it's the combination of these two dimensions that define the uniqueness of *The Wire*, over the arc of the series the conflict between them keeps building until it reaches a climax in season 5, with the storyline of the fake serial killer. Significantly, this scheme is concocted by McNulty as a "creative" way of getting the funding Homicide needs to take down the reigning drug lord, Marlo Stanfield. But by the end of the series, viewers are forced to choose between their commitment to a sympathetic character like McNulty or to the truth, which, as in tragedy, is made to seem an absolute value, only because characters are willing to sacrifice anything for it.

Despite the emphasis on black characters, from the very first episode *The Wire* tempts us into thinking that Jimmy McNulty might be the protagonist of the series. Not only is he one of the cops who provide continuity across all five seasons, but he gets the first credit in the opening titles and his face was prominently featured on the posters and on the cover of season 1's DVD. Although Simon claims he cast British actor Dominic West because all the American actors who read for the part had seen too many American cop series and were unable to go beyond the stereotypes, McNulty evokes Al Pacino's Serpico (who is mentioned in one of the episodes)—a self-destructive, white anti-hero who has trouble with authority and whom many female characters find appealing. The fact that he fits this stereotype becomes ironic in season 5 when an FBI psychologist profiling the alleged serial killer comes up with a description that perfectly evokes McNulty. The show continues to monitor McNulty's ups and downs (on the job, on and off the wagon, and in and out of relationships with women), perhaps because, like the black, gay drug addict Bubbles (one of the most likeable characters in the series, played by Andre Royo), he is willing to accept blame for his own actions and their impact on other underdogs.

Since no single individual can solve all of the systemic problems raised in the series, we soon realize that it's the relations that count. From the beginning we are led to compare McNulty with at least three other sets of characters. First, he is compared with his former black partners in the Homicide Division: Bunk Moreland (Wendell Pierce), who is more reliable and less flashy, and his subsequent partner, Kima Greggs, a lesbian who shares similar domestic problems with her partner that McNulty experiences with his ex-wife. Despite McNulty's close emotional ties to both, they harshly condemn his "fake serial killer" plot. Secondly, McNulty is compared to two brainy black cops who share his antagonism toward authority and his passion for inventing creative ways of fighting crime. Yet their schemes (unlike McNulty's) are *not* based on lies. Lester Freamon (Clarke Peters) designs the original plan for wire-tapping the Barksdale gang, and thus is willing to use resources from the fake serial killer plot to revive his own scheme. Bunny Colvin (Robert Wisdom) sets up an unauthorized buffer zone called "Hamsterdam" where dealers and addicts are not arrested, a scheme (like McNulty's) that enables cops to focus on other more important crimes. Although this plan brings down Baltimore's crime rate, Bunny is forced to retire. The schemes of all three characters prove successful, yet once the authorities discover them, the outcomes are reversed, which demonstrates there's something terribly wrong with public policy. All three schemes demonstrate that individuals *can* make a difference, even if they can't single-handedly solve all of Baltimore's systemic problems.

McNulty is also compared with two deceptive white men from other sectors, who at first seem to have enormous potential. In season 3, Thomas Carcetti (Aiden Gillen) wins the electoral race for mayor as "the great white hope," but by the end of the season proves to be just as corrupt as the black politicians he replaced. Carcetti's connection to McNulty is strengthened by their boyish good looks and their sexual involvement with the same powerful woman (Carcetti's abrasive campaign manager, Theresa D'Agostino, played by Brandy Burre). In season 5, McNulty's compared to the ambitious journalist Scott Templeton (Tom McCarthy), who also fabricates stories. Early in the season, McNulty says, "I wonder what it feels like to work in a real fucking police department," a line later echoed by Scott: "I wonder what it's like to work at a real newspaper." Although it's easy to condemn both Carcetti and Templeton as self-centred careerists with their eyes on the prize (the governor's mansion or a Pulitzer), it's harder to condemn a self-destructive figure like McNulty, whose motives are rarely self-serving. He plays Huck Finn to their Tom Sawyers, yet all three schemers become (as McNulty puts it in the final episode) "trapped in the same lie." The plot of the fake serial killer violates the commitment to truth and realism that *The Wire* demands throughout the series. In the final season we are forced to choose between our commitment to a truthful systemic analysis and our emotional engagement with McNulty, a painful choice already made by his former partners—by Russell (who was ready to leave him), Bunk (who continually condemns him), and Greggs (who exposes the plot to Commissioner Daniels, played by Lance Reddick).

Without betraying McNulty, Bunk chooses the truth, which is hardly surprising. In the first episode of the final season, one of Bunk's lines of dialogue is chosen as an epigraph: "The bigger the lie, the more they believe." Though Bunk was referring to standard interrogation methods found on most conventional cop series, *The Wire* makes us read it (like the other epigraphs) systemically—emphasizing its resonance across the entire series. Like Bunk, the series ultimately chooses truth over emotion, a priority that distinguishes *The Wire* from other TV crime series, yet it acknowledges that many of its careerist characters still stick with the lie. When his fake plot is exposed and he's still not arrested, McNulty rewrites Bunk's line: "The lie's so big, people can't live with it."

That's why *The Wire* ends with the media and focuses on the city newspaper, an institution whose mission is to discover and disseminate the truth. Yet city newspapers across America are rapidly disappearing. Forced to compete with the Internet as a primary source of news, they can no longer afford to retain expensive international bureaus (which are supposed to gather rather than merely remix the news). And their local coverage is forced to compete with the entertainment model of television journalism. According to Simon, in some ways papers like the *Baltimore Sun* may *deserve* to disappear because they have failed to cover the most important stories in their city, a journalistic task that has been taken over by his own fictional TV series. *The Wire* clearly blames these failed institutions more than the individual criminals they create and destroy. As Snoop puts it, just before she is whacked, "Deserve got nothin' to do with it."

Before the first episode of this final season had been broadcast, some critics were already claiming that its analysis of the media would be less complex and more Manichean than that found in earlier seasons, perhaps anticipating the usual endgame for a series. Or maybe it was because the final season was focusing on Simon's former home base, the *Baltimore Sun*, where he had worked several years as a crime reporter (and might have personal scores to settle). But no matter how thorough the show's indictment against the media might be, *The Wire* itself is still a powerful counter-example—even though it attracted a relatively small audience (around four million viewers per episode, less than half of what *The Sopranos* normally drew). Despite all the critical praise (for its innovative structure, hyper-realism, and brilliant array of black characters), *The Wire* never won an Emmy (whereas *The Sopranos* won 22). Maybe its cast was too black and its analysis too systemic for middle America. Yet, *The Wire* still stands out as a subversive alternative—one that maintains the delicate balance between hope and desperation and makes Snoop's dying words reflexive: "Deserve got nothin' to do with it."

The Final Episode: Systemic Closure

The final 90-minute episode leverages a number of *The Wire*'s earlier strategies to deliver narrative closure while still maintaining systemic suture. The system of rewards and punishments remains consistent with Snoop's realistic analysis. Corrupt careerists like Templeton, Carcetti, Commissioner Bill Rawls (John Doman), and double-dealing Herc Hauk (Domenisk Lombardozzi) are rewarded for their dishonesty with big prizes or promotions. In contrast, those with integrity who tried to improve the system—Daniels, McNulty, Freamon, and honest reporter Alma Gutierrez (Michelle Paress)—are shut out of their institutions where their commitment could (or should) have made a difference. Yet the systemic analysis also enables us to perceive a generational pattern of replacements that might leave us with a glimmer of hope. Michael (Tristan Wilds) steps up to replace Omar; Marlo is forced to follow the path pioneered by Stringer; and (if he's lucky and honest) Dukie (Jermaine Crawford), whose parents were junkies, begins the painful cycle of addiction and recovery that was earlier pursued by Bubbles. As the only character in the series who deserves the modest reward he receives, Bubbles is the one exception to this corrupt system of injustice: for, he is finally welcomed upstairs and allowed to dine with his sister and nephew. Unlike the others, he can go home again. As actress Sonja Sohn puts it, "Bubbles is the only character on the whole show that represents hope, and hope that has succeeded at the end of the series" (*Los Angeles Times*, E22).

Yet McNulty also reaps both rewards and punishments. Once his fake serial killer plot is exposed by his former partner Greggs, he has to relinquish his job as detective, which has been the centre of his life. Like Freamon, Alma, and Marlo, he can't go home again. Yet his refusal to blame all the fake murders on the copycat killer helps him regain other positions that easily could have been lost. He is allowed to stay at home in the relationship with Russell; he is paired with Freamon as "partners in crime"; he is eulogized by Sergeant Jay Landsman (Delaney Williams) in his "fake wake" as "the black sheep" who is "natural po-lice"); and, perhaps most important, he re-emerges as potential protagonist. In the process, our emotional engagement with him is restored. Besides being the centre of attention at the wake, McNulty is singled out from the ensemble cast in several long takes. These singular moments with McNulty are followed by montage sequences either of Baltimore's cityscape, the fates of other characters, or the city's ordinary citizens, sequences that use the ensemble to reaffirm systemic analysis. Thus the combination of emotional engagement and systemic analysis is restored, and we are left having it both ways: the protagonist is both McNulty and the city of Baltimore, both the individual and the ensemble.

The interplay between individuals and ensemble is also emphasized by a series of key words and phrases that recur throughout the episode like a musical refrain. Some of the phrases express fear ("keep my name out of it"); other words are more hopeful—like the recuperation of "clean" (as in Gus's "I remember clean" and Daniels's insistence on "clean stats"), and the reaffirmation of "home" (which reasserts *The Wire*'s commitment to Baltimore). In this final episode, although several characters refer to the many meanings of home, it is McNulty who gets the last word. As he stands at the side of the freeway, looking at the cityscape, he turns to the homeless man he has brought back to Baltimore, and says: "Let's go home."

Making the Most out of 15 Minutes: Reality TV's Dispensable Celebrity

Sue Collins

In February 2004, Bunim/Murray Productions bestowed on Philadelphia's civic tourism and marketing officials the kind of "cool" publicity that can't be bought: they decided to shoot the fifteenth season of the MTV reality series *The Real World* in Philly's Old City neighbourhood. In their efforts to remodel the former Seamen's Church Institute, the show's producers hired non-union labour, a practice they had been following in 13 *Real World* cities since 1992. But this time, the producers encountered the unbridled wrath of a union town's organized labour, which after two weeks of picketing effectively prompted producers to pull out with 70 per cent of construction complete and three weeks left before taping was scheduled to begin (Klein 2004b). It took a fan-based, tech-savvy grassroots movement, civic sycophancy, and a secret unprecedented agreement to include union workers along with non-union at the job site to get MTV back (Anderson 2004; Klein 2004a, 2004b; Tkacik 2004). In this case, however, Philly's trade unions claimed the job site as their turf, and not as a television "set" that would normally employ the International Alliance of Theatrical Stage Employees (IATSE; Klein 2004b).

Reality TV's production principles have triggered widespread displacement for Hollywood's unionized labour. Challenges to the genre's encroaching colonization of prime time have been mildly successful, as in the case of IATSE winning unionization for *Big Brother*[1] and the Writers Guild of America[2] securing union work for some host introductions and voice-over scripts (Rendon 2004). Because of the enormous popularity of network reality shows such as *Survivor*, *American Idol*, *Joe Millionaire*, and *The Apprentice*, among others, reality TV has precipitated a "radical restructuring of the network business" (Carter 2003), which calls attention to the new industry practice of bypassing costly unionized actors. The American Federation of Television and Radio Artists (AFTRA) and the Screen Actors Guild (SAG) have been unable to contest the hiring of ordinary people, the staple of unscripted reality formats, because these shows, in general, do not fall outside of pre-existing rules of AFTRA coverage. The fact that reality formats are popular with producers and audiences alike, however, is reducing the opportunities for scripted work on broadcast space across union membership. With employment dropping 1.6 per cent in 2003, 6.5 per cent in 2002, 9.3 per cent in 2001,[3] and 15 per cent from the high point of employment in 1998, SAG claims to be taking a hit for the popularity of reality shows too, over which it has no jurisdiction, alongside the ever-present threat of American productions shot on foreign soil without SAG contracts (Brodesser 2004; Kiefer 2002; McNary 2002; Screen Actors Guild 2005a). With some 40 reality shows occupying broadcast and cable space in the spring of 2003 (Groves 2003), and 20.5 prime-time hours allotted to reality programming in Fall 2004, SAG and AFTRA projected a loss of over 9,000 union jobs between Spring 2004 and 2005 (Screen Actors Guild 2005b).[4]

Although the industry's trades warn of continuing unrest and the unions confer with each on how to combat the displacement of actors, this is not to say that celebrity as a cultural commodity will suffer under the new economic logic of reality programming. On the contrary, reality TV invites new considerations for theorizing production strategies of celebrity, particularly with respect to formats that do not deal in "talent" per se, but with the "performance of the everyday" (Roscoe 2001). Recent scholarship has engaged theoretically with reality TV's promise to democratize celebrity as a way to explain the genre's widespread appeal, but the question of how reality TV alters celebrity production within the cultural industries warrants more exploration. In particular, I ask: What happens when an influx of reality TV's cast members try to enter the celebrity field? To what extent are they absorbed and how does this affect the larger system of celebrity valorization?

The Real World cast members left the first season in 1992 to be greeted by the "immediate buzz" of the celebrity infrastructure: talk show guest appearances, profile articles, commercial endorsements, mall openings appearances, lectures, and the like. After the first *Survivor* finale, which attracted 51.7 million viewers, reality TV veterans were "showered with interview requests, sitcom cameos, and managers and agents pleading to represent them" (Wolk 2002, 33). While some go on to bigger and better celebrity valorization, such as original *Survivor* contestant Colleen Haskell, who managed to land a part in Rob Schneider's film *The Animal* and an appearance on *That '70s Show*, others such as George Boswell, a 43-year-old commercial roofer who was voted out of the *Big Brother* house, give up their day job believing they are destined for show business. Most of these reality TV vets find that in the sixteenth minute, they are not absorbed into the celebrity system; rather, their celebrity currency runs out and they are channelled back into obscurity. Yet, this D-level reality TV celebrity has very real benefits for cultural producers,[5] broadcasters, advertisers, and a host of related cottage industries borne out of reality TV's system of production.

The making of celebrity, as with most cultural products, is configured around what has worked before. Reality TV's recombinant nature proves the point that new cultural products are structured to standardize them, and the genre's production of celebrity is no exception. With this in mind, Mark Andrejevic's (2003) claim that "reality programming has, paradoxically, undermined the uniqueness of celebrity," and rendered star quality "fungible" (11), needs to be modified to account for the system of stratified production in which the economic value of celebrity is a function of potential exchange.[6] In other words, what needs to be emphasized in an understanding of the production of celebrity is the degree to which celebrity's intertextual property, as a function of symbolic valorization through which audiences derive meaning, pleasure, or distaste, determines its economic value. Although celebrity success is located in its distribution, that is, in the creation of sustained audiences for its consumption, what is new with reality TV is the construction of a new category of celebrity—what I am calling *dispensable celebrity*—that generates novelty out of audience self-reflexivity with minimal risk and temporal flexibility. This lower stratum of celebrity value affords both surplus for cultural industries and the maintenance of the larger system of celebrity valorization, which, as with other commodities, is based on scarcity.

Ostensibly, reality shows featuring ordinary, real people demonstrate that the genesis of celebrity as a top-down production of the cultural industries is being challenged by the audience's attention to itself. The talent shows such as *American Idol* and *Last Comic Standing*, recombinant forms from old pop talent show formats such as *Star Search*, openly mine celebrity from talented contestants. In this format, audiences are "interpellated" into "a discourse of care" as they engage in the "fantasy of participatory democracy" by casting their vote for their new idol or star (Cowell 2003), and at the same time, virtually guaranteeing producers surplus, for example in record sales, when they contract both winners and losers. Through the use of personal "backstage" narrative constructed by a visual aesthetic characteristic of reality TV, the pop shows also promise to reveal "the internal workings of the music industry, and crucially, its manufacture of fame and stardom" (Holmes 2004, 148). Many of the high ratings reality TV shows, however, while competition based, do not place the cultivation of celebrity at their centre.[7] Rather, shows such as the "gamedoc" (*Survivor, Big Brother, The Apprentice*, etc.), purport to represent ordinary, real individuals in competitive situations that require astute manipulation and resiliency, while the "docusoap" (*Real World, High School Reunion, My Life as a Sitcom*, etc.) places them in "natural" settings, and uses documentary style production values to focus on their everyday lives but with the intervention of soap opera structuring techniques (Murray 2004). As Murray and Ouellette (2004) put it, the reality show works by promising viewers "revelatory insight into the lives of others as it withholds and subverts full access to it" (6).

The reality gamedoc and docusoap formats, in particular, highlight the utility of celebrity stratification for cultural producers. Within the production of reality TV, celebrity operates out of an expanded field of labour stock to include non-union low-cost workers, the risk of celebrity production is minimized, the temporal boundaries for celebrity's success are flexible, and celebrity itself undergoes a new form of dispensable synergy that shelters the larger system of celebrity valorization from the dual problems of scarcity and clutter.

Celebrity Is a Commodity

To understand the system of reality TV celebrity production and how its operations complement the organizational restructuring of the television industry currently underway, celebrity needs to be situated as a commodity form meaningful to media theory. Celebrity, understood in modern terms, is a product of the nineteenth century "graphic revolution," in which image reproduction facilitated by advances in print technology enabled the "manufacture" of fame (Boorstin 1987) and subsequent human interest journalism (Ponce de Leon 2002; Schickel 1985). But a celebrity's reproduction, while a necessary condition, is not a sufficient one.[8] Celebrity should also be conceptually differentiated from fame, a precapitalist conception of visibility, which while having carried over to modernity had been restricted by precapitalist technology, time and space contingencies, and the designations of the heroic by the ruling class to the "great men" of royalty, aristocracy, nobility, and the church. Only after the invention of the printing press and the rise of early forms of capitalist production did an economics of publicity emerge to augment the visibility of self-proclaimed and celebrated authors as well as to protect the ownership of their work (Braudy 1986; Eisenstein 1979; Ong 1982). Celebrity is distinctly a capitalist phenomenon coinciding with changes in communication technology that enabled news forms of social mobility, the democratization of the consumption of cultural goods, and the production of secular notions of popular culture (Benjamin 1969; Ewen 1988; Gabler 1998). Celebrity is the democratization of fame, but more importantly, it is fame *commodified*. That is, it is a symbolic form whose transmission and reception within a commercial media system renders it a cultural commodity.[9] Celebrity is established by its visibility as a function of its reproducibility, or by its exposure to audiences, who subjectively participate in the discursive construction and maintenance of celebrity through their reception. Graeme Turner (2004) argues that celebrity is not produced uniformly within the cultural industries nor without (for example, in business, politics, journalism, etc). It exists as "a genre of representation and a discursive effect," but also as a commodity produced and distributed by the promotions, publicity, and media industries, and it is a "cultural formation" whose social functions involves forms of pleasure and constructions of identity (9). These generic and intertextual properties, together with the fluctuations in the marketplace for celebrity consumption, enable entertainment celebrity to act as an audience-gathering mechanism whose properties as labour power and capital represent stratified value to cultural producers.[10]

The Political Economy of Entertainment Celebrity

Similar to other cultural goods, celebrity is the outcome of complex interplay among processes of production, mediation, and reception. Foremost, it is dependent on strategies of capitalist production that try to predict the capriciousness of audiences' preferences and tastes. But celebrity is complicated as a cultural commodity because it is both part of a cultural product, such as a film or TV show, and a commodity itself. Richard Dyer (1986), whose work has been predominately concerned with the production of film stars and the "star image," points out the complex market function of stars. They are a category of property in the form of brand name and image that can be used to raise capital for a film; they are part of how films get sold to audiences who expect certain meanings from the star's presence in the film; they are an asset to the star him or herself and to the studio and professionals involved in their promotion; they are a major expense in the production of a film; and they are a part of the labour that goes into the film as a commodity. In short, stars are "both labor and the thing that labor produces" (Dyer 1986, 5). Once the "raw material" of the person has been fashioned into the star by a host of professionals who perform labour onto the star (hairdressers, coaches, dietitians, make-up artists, etc.) and by the professionals involved in the making of the film as well as the performances of the star , the "star image" can be seen as "congealed labor," that is, "something that is used with further labor (scripting, acting, directing, managing, filming, editing) to produce another commodity, the film" (6).

Since the beginning of the film star system in the second decade of the twentieth century, star value has been managed as a form of product differentiation to satisfy audience demand (Kindem 1985; Klaprat 1985), but also as meaning that could be distributed throughout extrafilmic texts such as popular, trade, and fan magazines (deCordova 1990).[11] "Cultural producers" of stars were limited to film studio heads and their producers and directors. In the post-studio era, star management and control over access to stars was taken up by a new set of "players" such as talent agents and personal managers (Litwak 1986; Wasko 2003). More recently, celebrity production is thought about in broader terms such as a "promotional culture," which involves media professionals who make decisions about hiring talent, agents and managers who negotiate with these producers on behalf of their clients, and other intermediaries such as publicists who work between producers and agents on the one side, and various media outlets on the other (Turner, Bonner, and Marshall 2000).

In contemporary terms, celebrity autonomy has enhanced the potential value a celebrity can claim, or perhaps more accurately, what agents or managers can negotiate, but it has also increased the risk for unstable meaning when celebrity moves among other spheres of activity besides entertainment. For example, an increase in symbolic value (more visibility and therefore more meaning) may not increase economic value, such as in the case of celebrity personal scandal or high involvement with controversial socio-political issues. On the other hand, as Thompson (1990) argues, "the symbolic value of a good may be inversely related to its economic value, in the sense that, the less 'commercial' it is, the more worthy it is seen to be" (156), which, of course, does not negate real commercial value.[12] In any case, strategies of production surely take into account and monitor celebrity's dynamic symbolic meanings as a direct function of its profitability. In this sense, celebrity should be seen as a kind of intertextually fluid "capital" that gets "deployed with the intention of gaining advantage in the entertainment market and making profits" for cultural producers and the celebrity him or herself (McDonald 2000, 5).

Given the unstable and unpredictable nature of celebrity value, key objectives for the production of celebrity are to manage the problem of novelty and the problem of scarcity vis-à-vis media reproduction. Aside from marketing studies on the value of celebrity endorsements and economic analyses that try to account for market values of film stars or predict their box office appeal or marketing cachet, there are few studies in cultural studies or the political economy of the cultural industries that make the production of celebrity as a *commodity* their focal point. A few scholars, however, have done important work on the "cultural industries" in general that is useful for thinking about dispensable celebrity.[13]

In his analysis of cultural production, Bernard Miège (1989) argues that producers must concern themselves with the risks and uncertainty that characterizes cultural products and so they become an intervening factor in the production of the text.[14] To spread the risks associated with uniqueness and to militate against the demands of cultural labour, the producer intervenes to ensure the product is "marked by the stamp of the unique, of genius, in order to be standardized" (Miège 1989, 29). In other words, reproducibility both standardizes types (e.g., "rat pack," "brat pack," etc.) and facilitates the potential for intertextual meanings that potentially increase symbolic value. However, these constructions are no easy matter to predict, evident by the fact that both large and small production companies meet with success and failure.[15] Miège explains that because producers need to spread the risks, they construct "catalogues," operating by a policy that "requires direct access to cultural workers and implies their rapid renewal and rotation according to the swings of fashion" (30).[16] Thus, celebrity needs to be seen as a cultural product that is born out of a vast "reservoir" of cultural workers who are ready to work without wage retainers in which very few "make it" and whose success is not predictable nor necessarily sustainable. The entertainment industry, in fact, is characterized by a massive earnings disparity and high unemployment for up to 90 per cent of its union membership on any given day (Gray and Seeber 1996). Only about three-quarters of SAG members earn the $9,000 yearly minimum to qualify for health and pension benefits, while 8 to 10 per cent earn a middle class standing and only 2 per cent enjoy superstar earnings (Bloom 2002).[17] While a few of these stars use their capital to enhance their power as directors or producers themselves, most actors are in constant competition for work in a field with excess supply, and they experience little autonomy or creative freedom in their work (Peters and Cantor 1982). Indeed, David Hesmondhalgh (2002) observes, "The poor working conditions and rewards for creative cultural work have been obscured by the fact that, in a complex professional era, very generous rewards are available for symbol creators who achieve name recognition in the minds of audience members" (58). The star system, which gives the highest marketing priority to "star symbol creators," in Hesmondhalgh's terms, is employed by producers as a type of "formatting" that links stars with privileged texts (hits) to offset misses. Additionally, stars can be seen as brands that act as guarantors of meaning across a variety of texts with which audiences can identify, including the capture of a star's image as a type-set for the purposes of endorsing goods and services outside of the entertainment industry.

Nicholas Garnham (1990) also underscores the importance of what he calls the "editorial" function: that is, the commensurate matching of the "cultural repertoire" and its production costs with audience taste and spending power. Because demand for cultural products is unpredictable, the cultural industries offer audiences a cultural repertoire of goods to spread the risks. Increased productivity in this context takes the form of expanding the audience for the product by offering symbolic values in the form of novelty or difference. There is a "constant need to create new products which are all in a sense prototypes" while, at the same time, commodities produced are "not destroyed in the process of consumption" (160). Scarcity, on which price or value is based for most commodities, must be artificially created by using strategies of vertical integration such as monopoly control over distribution to limit access to the reproduction of cultural products. These factors lead Garnham (1990) to argue that it is "cultural distribution, not cultural production, that is the key locus of power and profit" (162).

Borrowing from Miège (1989), Garnham (1990), Ryan (1992), and Hesmondhalgh (2002) outlines four "stages" of cultural production: creation, reproduction, circulation, and retailing/exhibition/broadcast.[18] In response to the unique problems facing the cultural production (high risk and unpredictability, high "first copy costs" and low reproduction costs, and the need to create artificial scarcity), the cultural industries organize with respect to a number of practices: misses offsetting hits, concentration and integration, creation of artificial scarcity, and formatting strategies using stars, genres, and serials. Given these dynamic conditions, Hesmondhalgh concludes that the principal organizing response of the cultural industries since the 1980s and 1990s[19] to their distinctive problems has been to oversee creative input of cultural products with loose control while tightening control over reproduction and distribution—two distinct stages, the latter of which he refers to as "circulation" (55–6) . Circulation signifies a more comprehensive process than distribution and wholesaling; it also includes marketing and promotions, which are critical processes for the reproducing of celebrity as a commodity in and of itself (56).

More specifically, there are two key ways these analyses inform celebrity. First, it is clear that celebrity's symbolic value is a function of its novelty or difference within its class as a cultural product (both part of a product and a product itself), yet its production as a commodity is generally similar for any single celebrity. Efforts to market, publicize, and cross-promote a new celebrity or to sustain a celebrity's audience base are undertaken in ways that are commensurate with a celebrity's potential or projected value. For example, arrangements for celebrities to appear in various media formats and at PR events are often written directly into the celebrity contract.[20] However, an analysis of celebrity's reproduction is problematic because unlike the material production process (in which the cost of materials and scale wage, or below-the-line cultural labour, is generally fixed), or cultural production in which celebrity is an input of fixed creative cost, celebrity's reproduction cost is complicated when by *reproduction* we now mean *reproducing a single celebrity in subsequent cultural products*. Celebrity value from a political economic perspective, as I have been arguing, is best understood as a function of visibility based on potential reproducibility and the subsequent sustaining of an audience base. Its economic valorization, then, is constantly shifting as celebrity intertextuality accumulates as a function of exposure within texts and around them (i.e., marketing, publicity, and cross-promotion in relation to specific texts, celebrity self-promotion, and celebrity exposure outside of the entertainment sphere). Stable intertextual meanings from the perspective of cultural producers may constitute surplus value or loss in the case of overexposure until celebrity renegotiates its value in relation to the production of some text, but novelty implies some shift in celebrity meaning, or the introduction of new celebrity.

Second, when Garnham argues that distribution is the key factor of power and profit, we can infer that celebrity's success is located in the creation of audiences for its consumption. Distribution in this sense for celebrity means the degree to which celebrity's intertextual property (a function of its symbolic value for audiences) determines its economic value, in terms of box office draw for a particular text and in terms of gathering audiences for advertisers.[21] As Horkheimer and Adorno ([1944] 1997) noted, the logic of cultural production, while an interdependent process, is much less about the differentiation of content of cultural products, than it is about how consumers are classified, organized, and labelled to receive cultural commodities. In more contemporary terms, Magder (2004) argues that the logic of commercial broadcasting is not to give audiences what they need or say they want to watch but to "give people what they are willing to watch, or at the very least, programming from which they will not turn away" (143). To amass a public that can be sold somewhat reliably to advertisers, cultural producers try to reduce uncertainty by offering a range of mass-produced products that vary in quality, while "triangulating" between "the wants and needs of advertisers and the wants and needs of viewers" (142). With respect to celebrity production, the cultural industries recruit talent, manage and control the construction and reproduction of their personae, and execute diffusion processes as strategies dictate what will secure a reliable audience base. How celebrity gets reproduced across various texts depends on the processes of circulation that work to distribute celebrity beyond broadcasting and film distribution. Marketing and publicity are key to celebrity's accumulation of symbolic value that, in turn, determines its reproducibility. In this way, the "producers" of celebrity, which is a form of congealed labour, include not only the owners and executives who exhibit loose control over creative decisions, but also the "creative managers"[22] who intervene in the ways Miège (1989) and Garnham (1990) suggest, as well as the host of people involved in the promotions business who distribute celebrity among the texts that feature celebrity as a commodity itself.

But the processes of celebrity reproduction and circulation are largely predictions made by cultural producers, and at the same time, they are vulnerable to the problem of clutter. In conventional economic theory, more celebrity (as a class of cultural products) would suggest the value of each member would diminish. However, the system of celebrity valorization seems to defy this law. A "unit" of celebrity can increase in value (both symbolic and economic) with the increase in its reproduction and its access by audiences. The celebrity system as a whole has not suffered from diminishing returns, if the burgeoning celebrity journalism industry is any indication. The system of stratification seems to profit from the traversing play of celebrity as abstract value among the strata. Celebrity value at lower levels of stratification valorizes the star system because it serves as points of lesser comparison with A-list celebrities, while the existence of a star system stimulates the continuing production of aspiring celebrity. The celebrity system as stratified value transcends the laws of the market economy in that its reproduction at some point within the strata assures its larger reception as a system. Moreover, as distinct living human beings, celebrities bring idiosyncrasies to the equation that are not fully controllable, or even explainable for that matter, and it is this potential instability in celebrity meaning combined with shifting audience tastes that makes celebrity value particularly difficult to pin down. Still, reproduction and circulation processes work to "create" celebrity scarcity. For the production of television celebrity, this implies variously limiting access to higher values of celebrity while also maintaining some optimal degree of celebrity circulation as an audience-gathering mechanism for advertisers.

Herein lies the economic beauty of reality TV for cultural producers: a new level of celebrity stratification produces novelty that is easily and cheaply produced, while circulation, the key to creating scarcity as a measure of value, intrinsically limits access to higher values of celebrity because ordinary people in reality television, ironically, are not "real" actors with accumulated intertextual capital. They do not have access to wider circulation by which to accrue sustained symbolic and economic value. They do earn value, however, as a form of dispensable celebrity that pleases audiences for its novelty and self-reflexivity, and producers for its financial and temporal expediency. Let us look more closely at how reality TV has developed as a production logic and why dispensability is the defining feature of this new mode of celebrity.

The "Real"-ization of Dispensable Celebrity

The success of reality television, particularly its "second wave,"[23] has spawned a great deal of scholarly research that attends to close readings of specific texts, industry perspectives, and audience reception to explain its widespread popularity and cultural significance. Chad Raphael (2004) analyzes the political economy of "reali-TV,"[24] arguing that this mode of television production emerged in the late 1980s as a cost-cutting "fiscal strategy" in response to a new Hollywood economic environment characterized by the rising costs of network program production, competition for advertising revenue among more distributors, greater debt incurred by the networks, media industry deregulation, and new audience measuring techniques designed to measure segmented markets. In addition, reality programming offered producers a way to prepare for potential strikes because these shows did not rely on scripts or acting talent, which also meant bypassing Hollywood agents' commission fees, and because they could be produced more quickly than fictional shows.[25] Reality shows "gained currency in this environment of relative financial scarcity and labor unrest," Raphael suggests, largely doing away with "higher-priced stars and union talent" (124). Moreover, low-end production values were embraced as a cost-cutting strategy, while also operating to make rhetorical claims on representing "the real" (see, for example, Dovey 2000).

Raphael points out that in the early 1990s, reality television was the only category of prime-time programming in most cases not to operate on deficit financing. Today, the average scripted show can cost $1 to $2 million for a prime-time hour, while an hour of reality programming costs about $700,000 to produce (Rendon 2004). The higher the prime-time climb up the celebrity ladder, the higher the price tag. Magder (2004) shows that in the 2001-to-2002 season, for example, NBC's hit drama *ER* cost the network some $13 million, while *Friends* had a production cost of $7 million per episode. CBS's *Survivor*, one of the few game-docs that still captures the coveted 18- to 35-year-old demographic, was the most expensive reality show, costing the network $1.4 million per episode. In this case, savings from above-the-line labour can be used to cross-subsidize higher budgets to pay for insurance premiums that cover increasingly daring stunts as well as the infrastructures to build sets and maintain contestants and crew in exotic places. In fact, Magder argues, the *Survivor* business model represents a larger shift in network programming currently underway. This new business model operates off of preproduction sponsorship to offset the cost of having the show made (which the network would normally pay via a licensing fee and then hope for advertisers' interest), using product placement, merchandizing tie-ins, and subscription website interactivity. Despite the fact that reality programming doesn't lend itself to syndication, it has proven profitable, at least so far, because its reliance on pre-established, successful formats "greatly reduces the risks associated with first-copy costs and the nobody knows principle" (147). Endemol Entertainment's *Big Brother* format, for example, is a "template" complete with a production and marketing "playbook" that can be adapted to a specific locale. "If things go well," as Magder puts it, "a format becomes an international brand with distinctive and carefully modulated local variation—the formula is tweaked, like the sugar content in Coca-Cola" (147). *Pop Idol*, for example, was developed by the UK company Fremantle, who sold the concept to Fox. Similarly, CBS has sold *Amazing Race* to markets in Europe, Southeast Asia, and Israel, and Next Entertainment has sold *The Bachelor* to Scandinavian markets (Albiniak 2002; Internet Movie Database 2005a, 2005b).

Indeed, the logic of the reality TV model serves as a counterprogramming mechanism against the high cost of scripted shows with unionized talent and against the threat of strikes, but, has reality programming become, in Anna McCarthy's (2005) words, "a mode of production?" At the very least, reality TV lends credence to the argument that production organization in the television industry is increasingly characterized by strategies of flexibility and adaptation (Christopherson 1996). In its restructuring of labour relations within the film and television industries generally, "flexible specialization" has created new segmentations within the labour force, redefined skills, and generally increased conflicts between employers and workers throughout the industry (Christopherson and Storper 1989; Paul and Kleingartner 1994). The labour market for talent, in particular, has become increasingly short term, with more entrants competing for fewer union jobs. Although the majority of reality shows are under AFTRA jurisdiction as per the employment of hosts, voice-over narrators, and stunt performers, the labour of reality TV cast members remains untouched by unionization as long as the shows' producers cast people as contestants or as playing themselves, and thus not under any acting directorship. This technicality, coupled with the ever-present need to fill more broadcast time cheaply, complements the industry's movement toward the flexible model of organizational production. The field for ordinary, untalented people vying for potential fame is virtually inexhaustible, and the production of short-term, non-skilled, non-union celebrity generates novelty with minimal financial risk and greater control. As Turner (2004) rightly argues, the manufacture of celebrity as a programming strategy integral to the reality formats works to contain potential conflicts (commercial or personal) between producers or networks and potential celebrities because these relations are structurally accommodated to each other from the start, meaning "these celebrities are especially dependent upon the program that made them visible in the first place; they have virtually no other platform from which to address their audience" (54).

Debora Halbert's (2003) work on reality TV and publicity rights substantiates reality TV celebrity's subordination to the shows' producers, at least insofar as CBS's contractual arrangement with its *Survivor* contestants attests. CBS controls its contestant's access to celebrity status in two ways. First, the contract stipulates that contestants are subject to authorization by CBS for any media contact or appearances for three years after the show airs. Not only does CBS protect the show's "trade secrets" through the confidentiality proviso, but contestants are also prohibited from accepting paid celebrity work not sanctioned by CBS long after the show's winner has been disclosed to the public. A breech in contract entitles CBS to sue the contestants for damages. In addition, the contract includes a "life story rights" section that effectively binds the signatory into relinquishing control over his or her life story and public image. Halbert sums up the extent to which CBS retains control and power over the contestant's labour and image, and thus its circulation:

> Essentially, CBS controls their ability to appear in public and in what type of venue, their ability to talk about the show, and their life stories. CBS owns their public identities and the rights to disclose their private identities. CBS owns the telling of the experiences that made them who they are. Everything a *Survivor* cast member could communicate to the

> public might be construed as the property of CBS. Additionally, CBS owns these rights throughout the universe forever. (45)

In effect, CBS is rationalizing that it is responsible for both transforming the ordinary person as "raw material" into a public personality, and disseminating the image to the public; therefore, since it has invested in the labour of celebrity construction, the result is the property of CBS. As Halbert points out, this "aggressive extension of property rights" over reality celebrities problematizes the distinctions between the rights of "real" celebrities who play fictional characters to control the use of their public image and what should be the rights of reality celebrities who play themselves "living their private lives in public" (Halbert 2003, 45–6). While it is true that potential contestants who sign the contract are ostensibly willing to give up control over their personal lives as a lived story and their public image to take their chances on the show, this contractual arrangement underscores the enormous differential in power relations between producer and cultural worker. "The 'reality' of power," Halbert explains, "is invisible to the public who only sees the spectacle" (51). Confidentiality agreements also obscure the conditions of labour for aspiring reality contestants, as well as for industry analysts, scholars, and cultural critics. We do not know the specifics of other reality show contracts, but if producers operate off "the playbook," then the dispensing of this novel reality celebrity becomes the spectacle itself as the reality model moves into the recombinant stage to reproduce the cultural form and to control the circulation of the celebrity.

The Real World, for example, led the way in reproducing what Caves (2000) calls the "lottery prize phenomena" (57) by offering its "housemates" the possibility of being invited back to show reunions and spin-offs. Although most reality players will not cross over to celebrity status, the fact that a few do get more exposure after their initial reality experience ends, and that fewer still sustain their visibility through exposure in other electronic media texts and celebrity print journalism, ensures that there will always be cheap labour to perform "the real" in hopes of becoming the next Eric Nies. An original *Real World* veteran, Nies has appeared in numerous Viacom holdings including *The Brady Bunch Movie*, VH1's *I Love the 90's*, and over a dozen MTV *Real World* series, specials, or documentaries, as himself, as a host and co-host, and as an actor, since his debut in 1992. Other popular housemates, such as Puck Rainey, Trishelle Cannatella, and Mark Long, have been following Nies's lead, enjoying exposure primarily in other MTV formats, but also landing small parts in films, music videos, and commercials. Once select reality celebrities cross over to media formats involving hosting or acting, AFTRA membership becomes a mandatory ticket to a higher status of celebrity.[26] Appearances on reality formats such as *The Surreal Life* or *I'm a Celebrity Get Me Out of Here*, for example, which feature people hired for their celebrity status, signify the crossover point to professional acting, union wages, health and pension benefits, and AFTRA dues.[27] However, while celebrity may be the real prize many reality players are after, producers' objectives are less about cultivating a star system than to use the promise of celebrity as continuous low-cost bait to gather contestants or players, and ultimately to sell audiences to advertisers. Borrowing from *Real World* and *Survivor* production strategies, *The Apprentice* started its second season by instructing the two remaining apprentices to compile a team out of subordinates who had been fired during the first season. Not only does this strategy eliminate the expense of casting calls, it extends and valorizes compelling narrative structures that keep people watching, and that encourage reality players to self-direct their roles to increase their chances of sustaining visibility through other media formats.[28]

Although it may be the case that reality TV has meant fewer opportunities for talent agents to secure scripted work for their clients, agents are not entirely bypassed by the reality phenomenon.

Aside from the pop idol format, for the most part, the rush to represent reality celebrities is over, but agents keep an eye out for whatever "heat" is generated from after-show exposure. Still, budding reality TV celebrities entering a field with an oversupply of unemployed talent must do the work of seeking out agents, who, as gatekeepers operating out of a glut of talent, screen the amount and quality of talent they can efficiently represent to match talent with jobs. Since reality players are mostly dispensed around other reality formats and short-term media texts, established agents are less inclined to forgo commissions as reality celebrities gain exposure. Perhaps these low-capital celebrities make fodder for a new class of novice agents and managers. More likely, agents are concentrating on placing hosts, anchors, disc jockeys, and other union-covered talent generated by reality shows into other paid media texts.

The political economic perspective explains why the industry has embraced reality TV, but why do audiences watch and why do they want to participate? While much of the popular press has scorned and lamented the public's preoccupation with aspirations of celebrity in Boorstin's (1987) critical sense of the word, as the vapid and trivial state of being known for "well-knownness," scholarly work more carefully deconstructs reality TV to reveal its appeal to audiences in more nuanced, analytically distinct ways. Indeed, the promise of celebrity is one of the motivating factors for audience participation, particularly with respect to the pop show talent format. In general, all of the formats tap into the fetishism of celebrity by suspending the traditional gate-keeping mechanisms of Hollywood's hierarchical structure. At the same time, by claiming to represent "the real," reality TV shows profess to democratize celebrity by demystifying access to it or debunking its aura through the normalization of surveillance techniques to get at the private, intimate, and authentic moments of individuals on display (Andrejevic 2003). Interestingly, Andrejevic (2003) intimates, reality TV tries to capitalize on the extraordinary/ordinary paradox theorized in star studies in a dual sense: by "cultivating the fantasy" of celebrity for the ordinary, it turns real people into celebrities; by "rehabilitating fading stars" in celebrity gamedocs (*I'm a Celebrity Get Me Out of Here*, *Celebrity Big Brother*), it extends the tabloid coverage of celebrities, rendering them "real" through self-disclosure and "authentic" moments captured by surveillance as voyeuristic entertainment. But as I have stated, I am interested in thinking about how celebrity works to entice audience participation, not with pop show formats structured around the talent contest, but with less obvious celebrity-manufacturing formats such as the gamedoc and docusoaps involving ordinary people. Here, audience members become contestants or players whose potential for fame is then contingent on their behaviour under arduous competition or behind-the-scenes challenges, or the spectacle of the "hidden" social experiment (see, for example, Brenton and Cohen 2003; Dovey 2000).

Interestingly, although these formats traffic in potentially embarrassing moments of intimacy, confession, or humiliation captured by the camera and fashioned into dramatic narratives by editors for the audiences' pleasurable voyeurism, casting calls continue to elicit thousands of responses. *Survivor* producers, for example, claim to get something in the neighbourhood of 65,000 self-made audition tapes each season (*The Reality of Reality*, Bravo Networks, 2003). The mass of applicants is then reduced to a small portion of the call and subjected to live audition calls and interviews, which are designed by psychologists to help producers gauge the individual's coping strategies and characteristics that make for interesting drama (Roscoe 2001). The shows' producers, then, "cast" the applicants into predictable "types," and as the series repeat, the new players learn to perform the roles that get media attention (e.g., the *Big Brother* prototypes "Nasty Nick" and "Mistress Andy" in Britain and Australia respectively; *Survivor*'s evil Richard Hatch, villainous Jerri Manthey, conniving "Boston Rob," and sweetheart-in-crime Amber Brkich). Murray and Ouellette (2004) point out, "The fifteen minutes of fame that is the principal reward for participating on the programs limits the selection of 'real people' to those who make good copy for newspaper and magazine articles as well as desirable guests on synergistic talk shows and news specials" (8). Once the numbers are whittled down to the dozen or so players, ordinary people begin "the work of being watched," which in Andrejevic's (2003) analysis, suggests they "invert" the celebrity frame by exposing the intimate details of their lives, and more significantly, invite "the vast majority of noncelebrities" to do the same by normalizing their submission to surveillance as a form of "wage labour" in the online economy (78). Nick Couldry (2002), noting that most contestants are explicit about the goal of attaining celebrity, argues that the transition to celebrity is the culmination of *Big Brother*'s plot. The ritual passage from the ordinary (non-media) person to celebrity (media) person is "the master frame without which the game [makes] no sense" (289). Because real people are constituted as repeat performers for the length of the series, audiences identify with their "media friends" as they come to care about and strategize with them (or against them), and to predict and "know" the behaviour of mediated identities on display, many perhaps imagining their own strategies to win access into the media world.[29] Audiences, by their very watching and more actively by their online and cell phone interactivity, partake in the fantasy of celebrity's democratization, although the form of celebrity that is produced, dispensable celebrity, is an ephemeral level of celebrity's stratification that generates enough value to reproduce itself cheaply as a programming strategy without devaluing the larger celebrity field.

Celebrity Place Dispenses "the Real"

So far, I have argued that celebrity is the commodification of fame, its visibility a function of its reproducibility vis-à-vis a commercial media system. The relationship of celebrity value to cultural production for producers is measured in terms of audience volume and its projected purchasing power. It is in this sense that celebrity's success is located in its circulation, that is, in the creation of sustained audiences for its consumption, and whose attention ultimately deems the reproduction of celebrity status. Yet celebrity is complicated in terms of its analysis as a cultural commodity because it is both part of a cultural product and a product itself whose value is unstable. As configurations of celebrity meaning accumulate, audiences and fans, in particular, take interest in the many ways that they might "read" the celebrity text.

Celebrity value, then, should be seen as a kind of stratified but also fluid intertextual capital that gets constructed in two sites: the cultural products or texts that house celebrity, and the sites of "intertextual circulation" (Holmes 2004), or what I call *celebrity place*—the aggregate of media space devoted to celebrity coverage by all facets of the cultural industries. Celebrity place is the seat next to Leno or Letterman, the guest appearance on *Saturday Night Live*, the lead to *Entertainment Tonight*, and the feature story of *People* or *Entertainment Weekly* that function to signify celebrity, symbolically and materially. For analytical purposes, it is the site in the singular that houses celebrity as a product in and of itself, and it is the infrastructure that gathers audiences for advertisers as it manages the production and promotion of personalities into celebrity status. In other words, celebrity place functions to reconstitute, reproduce, and circulate celebrity, and it is here in contemporary culture that the extraordinary/ordinary paradox theorized in star studies is played out. This dynamic between star performance and the fans' engagement with meaning as pleasurable is key to understanding how reality TV's dispensable celebrity works as a temporally dispensable cultural commodity.

According to predominate theories in star studies, the film "star image" is the multitude of media texts embodying the person/employee/star—whether in film performance or extrafilmic moments—that work to collapse distinctions between the star-as-person and the star-as-performer (Dyer 1979, [1977] 1991; Ellis 1982). The construction of a star image during the studio era was used to entice fans into following the studios' star performers' texts. Knowledge about a star's identity outside of the textuality of her films, for example, in fan magazines published by the industry, was restricted so that fans would be under the illusion that the star's personality in film was consistent with her offscreen life, and that to follow a star's film career would lead to the pleasurable discovery of the authentic personality (deCordova 1990). While the star image may be incoherent and ordinary in extrafilmic discourse, the film performance is thought to offer the promise of its "completeness," which reconstitutes the star as extraordinary, thus repeatedly inviting audiences to re-establish the authentic. It is this paradox of the star as extraordinary and ordinary that continually renews both the star image and the audience's pleasure in their consumption of film stars. In a similar way, King (1991) explains the star performance in terms of creating and sustaining a persona, which is where cinematic technique and filmic and extrafilmic discourses come together to suggest a coherent subjectivity, or unique star personality. Marshall (1997), in summarizing Dyer, explains that the star image works to keep the audience "obsessively and incessantly searching the star persona for the real and the authentic" (17).

The broader phenomenon of celebrity, I am arguing, functions similarly but in differing degrees, depending on celebrity's stratification. Although star studies theorists distinguish between cinema's "photo effect" and television's lack of one, by which Ellis argues that television does not have stars but "TV personalities," Su Holmes (2004) rightly points out that "the considerable increase in celebrity coverage in the popular press and magazines has evinced an appetite for disclosing the off-screen lives of all types of celebrities, thus demanding a reconceptualization of television's intertextual frameworks" (124). Indeed, much of the fun of consuming celebrity for many is making sense of what Turner (2004) highlights as its contradictions: celebrity is deserved and arbitrary, authentic and manufactured, extraordinary and ordinary. In contemporary culture, celebrity place is the site where audiences take pleasure in working through these contradictions, "enjoying the hype," and discovering the authentic, real identities of celebrities. It is also the site of cultural production in which a large share of the negotiation around celebrity's value as a product itself is conducted.

What is particularly noteworthy about reality celebrity is the way these individuals are dispensed through celebrity place along synergistic paths. For example, in addition to appearing on the *Survivor* remakes series *Survivor: All-Stars*, and *Survivor: The Reunion*, as well as providing footage for other *Survivor* productions such as *The Greatest and Most Outrageous Moments* video documentary, popular CBS *Survivor* contestants are effectively cross-promoted through various Viacom holdings, in some cases as actors, but most often as guests, playing themselves. Rupert Boneham, of *Survivor: Pearl Islands*, appeared on *The Early Show* (six times since his *Survivor* debut), *The Saturday Early Show*, the CBS and Eye Productions show *Half & Half*, VH1's *Best Week Ever*, and a CBS's upfront presentation to advertisers at Carnegie Hall. Jerri Manthey's credits are more extensive, but dominated by appearances and cameos in Viacom-owned, or partly owned, and distributed productions such as *The Early Show* (at least five times), *The Late Show with David Letterman*, *The Late Late Show with Craig Kilborn*, *The Young and the Restless*, MTV's *The New Tom Green Show*, Spike TV's *The Joe Schmo Show*, Comedy Central's *The Daily Show*, *Rendez View*, VH1's *The Surreal Life*, and VH1 *Goes Inside*. Similarly, Amber Brkich has appeared on *The Early Show* (at least five times), *The Late Show with David Letterman* (twice), *The Late Late Show with Craig Kilborn*, CBS's *Amazing Race*, and the *Rob and Amber Get Married* two-hour CBS special. Other networks have followed suit. Trista Rehn and Ryan Sutter of ABC's *Bachelor* and *Bachelorette* fame have also appeared or been featured on several ABC distributed talk shows and specials, including *Trista & Ryan's Wedding* and *Trista and Ryan's Honeymoon Hot Spots*. Likewise, Bill Rancic of NBC's *The Apprentice* has been a guest on *The Tonight Show*, *The Tony Danza Show*, MSNBC's *Deborah Norville Tonight*, and CNBC's *The Big Idea* (three times), while Omarosa Manigualt-Stalworth of *The Apprentice 2* became a contestant on NBC's *Fear Factor*, and appeared on *The Apprentice 3*, *The Big Idea* (three times), and Bravo's *Celebrity Poker Showdown*.[30]

Audiences who watch reality shows and partake in celebrity consumption throughout celebrity place are attentive, no doubt, to celebrity's stratification. But, the onscreen and offscreen dynamic particular to stardom, or celebrities high in intertextual value, is distinct from the media "flashpoints" of which reality TV celebrities are the object in predominately two ways. First, these low-capital celebrities provide a one-hit-wonder kind of novelty and timeliness to celebrity place, particularly as the reality shows' publicity apparatuses harvest attention across various media formats. Reality celebrities might make it on *The Tonight Show* or *The Late Show*, which primarily book A-level talent, but they are unlikely to displace stars looking to be booked or to become part of the stable of regular guests needed to sustain the shows. Non-unionized reality celebrities help "fill" the spaces of celebrity bookings on talk and variety shows, which by one estimate requires some 4,500 celebrity guests per year (Spring 1998). It is also worth noting that, in general, non-union reality celebrities do not collect the scale wages nor benefits to which actors are entitled when appearing on shows under AFTRA's jurisdiction, while news shows, such as CBS's *The Early Show*, do not pay their guests.

Second, as audience reception studies on reality TV have shown, a large part of the pleasure for audiences is to look for the "authentic" moments within the tension between the constructed and the real as ordinary people cross over to celebrity (Hill 2002; Johnson-Woods 2002; Jones 2003). When reality TV's contestants and cast members experience the media attention of celebrity status after they finish the shows,[31] that is, when they are effectively cross-promoted or dispensed throughout celebrity place, their actual status as dispensable celebrities blocks their entry into the larger system of celebrity valorization. I have discussed how CBS is able to control its *Survivor* reality players' access to potentially significant media formats. But this is also the case because the reality celebrities' acting "talent" is largely dismissed by the industry; they have not achieved extraordinary status in the conventional sense of stardom, thus they are low in intertextual capital, and audiences have, for the most part, exhausted locating their "authentic" identities in the interstices between their reality texts and celebrity place. In deCordova's (1990) sense, they are "personalities," whose intertextual value is relegated to the real, ephemeral texts of reality TV. They are what Chris Rojek (2001) calls "celetoids," extremely short-lived "accessories of culture organized around mass communication and staged authenticity" (20–1). On the rare occasions when reality celebrities win parts on fictional genres, such as Rupert Boneham did with the sitcoms *Half & Half* and *Yes, Dear*, or when UPN's *America's Next Top Model* contestant Eva Pigford appeared on UPN's *Kevin Hill*, these dispensable celebrities signify the immediacy of the episode in relation to the reality celebrity's success and the recentness of the episode, which soon appears dated during repeats, rather than the "potentially infinitely repeatable aura of stardom" garnered from "real" celebrities.[32] By reminding audiences of what they are not, dispensable celebrities reaffirm the star system.

For cultural producers, the reality TV audience is both the source of unlimited low paid or unpaid labour that displaces union actors from scarce production opportunities, and it is what gets sold to advertisers. The gamedoc format generates a form of celebrity that is new and limited in its circulation. Reality TV celebrity produces novelty while also shielding the larger field of celebrity from excess value. Dispensable celebrity both creates its own scarce value and verifies the upper strata of celebrity value manifest in the star system. With respect to audiences, reality TV keeps viewers watching with its promise to democratize celebrity, while also keeping the boundaries distinct between the "real celebrities" and the wannabes, perhaps, like you or me.

Notes

1. According to Groves (2003), "below-the-line" labour may be shouting the loudest to challenge reality TV's business model because reality programming has been a boon for non-union cameramen and editors.
2. The Writers Guild of America (WGA) continues to address jurisdiction over reality TV in its contract negotiations at the time of this writing.
3. These figures include both television and theatrical productions and exclude commercials and animation.
4. AFTRA reads the situation somewhat differently. According to Chris de Haan, press spokesperson, while reality programming has decreased opportunities for unionized actors on network slots, a multitude of cable channels with scripted programming have created opportunities for dramatic work (personal communications).
5. By the term *cultural producers*, I mean to include a variety of media professionals involved in the production, management, and distribution of celebrity, whose differentiations I discuss presently.
6. I am grateful to David Morley for turning my attention to thinking about celebrity production more specifically as a *process*, which indicates to me that its commodity form from an economic standpoint is best understood in terms of varying degrees of potential economic value. This process is operationalized in the site of production I refer to as *celebrity place* later in this piece.
7. Su Holmes (2004) makes the important point that theoretical approaches to conceptualizing fame in relation to reality TV must take care not to conflate the formats such that significant differences between the programs are neglected in analysis. While her thoughtful analysis examines constructions of fame in the well-received UK programs *Popstars* and *Pop Idols*, I am interested in thinking about how the gamedoc and docusoap afford cultural producers celebrity value.
8. Here I am taking issue with Daniel Boorstin's (1987) assertion that celebrity reproduction is what "overshadows everything else," such that a celebrity is simply anyone who is "known for his well-knownness" (57).
9. John Thompson's (1990) theory of "mediazation," while not specifically addressing celebrity, is useful for understanding how symbolic forms become cultural commodities. In short, Thompson argues that when symbolic forms become cultural forms—that is, when they are constituted as commodities to be bought and sold in the marketplace—symbolic value provides meaning or pleasure for people so that they attend to or consume them, while economic value is a reflection of how producers see the worth of products not based on their form as art or intrinsically valuable as per meaning, but as reliably profitable. The exchange of symbolic form between producers and receivers, or their cultural transmission, takes place through mediazation, a framework that involves considerations of the technical medium of transmission, the phenomenology of space–time distanciation, and the institutional structures of the media industries.
10. The discourses on celebrity, of course, are not restricted to the denizens of Hollywood. For broader historical arguments, see Braudy (1986) and Ponce de Leon (2002); for literary celebrity, see Moran (2000); for political celebrity, see Street (2003); for non-scholarly accounts and do-it-yourself celebrity, see Aronson (1983), Sudjic (1990), and Rein, Kotler, and Stoller (1997).
11. Richard deCordova's (1990) study on the early star system shows how stars, as opposed to "picture personalities," emerged out of the industry's construction of audience knowledge about the actors' lives outside their film work. Serialized stories "disclosing" the private lives of stars were strategically released to suggest that the actor's "real" personality was consistent with the screen image; Jane Gaines (1991) in her discussion of intellectual property law and star contracts also identifies the bifurcation of star images into two "basic zones of utilization—the product and its exploitation" (157).
12. Joshua Gamson (1994) found in his study *Claims to*

Fame that audiences in their consumption of celebrity, by being privy to the commercial process as fabrication, have also learned to transcend the value of belief and disbelief in meaning and simply enjoy the hype. Here the postmodern irony of celebrity is a "combination of exposure of the celebrity-and-image-manufacturing processes and mockery of it" which serves to diffuse a "threat to admiration by offering the audience a position of control" (18) in their use of symbol meaning.

13. Hesmondhalgh (2002) provides a precise definition of the cultural industries: "those institutions (mainly profit-making companies, but also state organizations and non-profit organizations) which are most directly involved in the production of social meaning," or "the primary aim of which is to communicate to an audience, to create texts." The core cultural industries (film, broadcasting, publishing, music, advertising and marketing, and new media) all involve the "industrial production and circulation of texts" (11–12).
14. Because development in the cultural industries is characterized by uncertain and uneven production, Miège (1989) is careful to argue for distinct analysis with respect to cultural products. While he does not consider celebrity in terms of the symbolic structuring of cultural workers who are themselves featured in the texts of cultural products, I argue that the ways in which celebrity is symbolically constructed and negotiated, packaged, and disseminated within media organizations is a function of the complicated interplay among strategies of capital constrained by the "logics" of production Miège identifies, particularly, in the case of reality TV, the "flow logic" by which broadcast audiences are created and sold to advertisers.
15. Gitlin (1983) shows in his study of television production that "recombinant" forms result when broadcasters practise a "logic of safety" by repeating profitable program formulas. Similarly, Caves's (2000) identification of the "nobody knows" principle echoes the sentiment of uncertainty shared by cultural producers.
16. Caves (2000) identifies this practice as the "A list/B list" property, but as Hesmondhalgh (2002) points out, Miège implies that the notion of "catalogue" is highly stratified as per value afforded cultural producers and as an indicator of celebrity success.
17. Gorham Kindem (1985) argues that SAG's classification of members inherited from the studio era and its post-war history of co-operative interaction with producers have functioned largely to benefit its most visible and better-known actors. After the immediate break-up of the studio system, greater competition and uncertainty caused the studios to produce fewer films with the most popular stars, while the 1970s saw a turn by Hollywood toward using stars in other media such as television and the recording industry.
18. Hesmondhalgh (2002) is careful to note that these are not discrete stages. They "overlap, interact and sometime conflict" (55).
19. This period is referred to by Hesmondhalgh (2002) as "the complex professional era."
20. Turner, Bonner, and Marshall (2000), in their study of celebrity production from the Australian promotion industry perspective, highlight the extent to which publicity apparatuses use celebrities as "bait" for general media coverage and cross-promotion, and the occasional "flashpoints" of media saturation in which celebrity dominates most media coverage.
21. It is important to note that the concentration of media ownership and strategies of synergy increasingly blur distinctions between revenue gathered from Miège's distinctions among "publishing," "flow," and "written press" logics. Film and television stars promote their cultural products across a media firm's holdings by appearing in made-for-TV movies, on talk shows, by granting magazine interviews, and appearing at publicized events for photo-ops, etc.
22. Hesmondhalgh (2002) borrows this term from Ryan (1992).
23. Raphael (2004) notes this phase began with the success of *Who Wants to Be a Millionaire* in 1999 and *Survivor* in 2000.
24. Raphael uses the neologism *Reali-TV* in his analysis as a device for emphasizing the political economy of the television industry without neglecting the genre's claims to represent "the real" through distinct formats.
25. The WGA strike in 1988, which had little negative effect on the production of reality shows, also served as an impetus for producers to develop more reality programming during the delay of the season. The same likely applies to the current WGA strike.
26. Although many reality celebrities get agency representation or manage their marketability from personal websites, union membership is less transparent. SAG will not disclose membership but will locate an actor's agency if the actor is listed in their database. AFTRA will indicate membership but not an actor's current status as a member. Nies disclosed that he is currently an AFTRA member and was a SAG member for 10 years. Mark Long is both an AFTRA and SAG member. Trishelle Cannatella and Puck Rainey did not respond to my queries, but AFTRA lists Trishelle Cannatella as a member.
27. Although I am not addressing the format here, it should be noted that reality TV also provides cost-effective opportunities to revitalize C-list celebrities with shows that pit celebrity against celebrity or expose "the real person" behind the fading celebrity. According to an AFTRA representative, all celebrities appearing on *The Surreal Life* are covered by AFTRA because they have been employed on the basis of their celebrity status, so that budding reality celebrities who make it onto this show are at the very least covered under the Taft-Hartley law.
28. It is the case that some neophyte and aspiring actors make their way onto reality shows, but they do so by

claiming to be "ordinary," and without invoking the privilege of union membership or protection of agency representation. CBS *Survivor* villain Jerri Manthey, for example, was both a SAG and AFTRA member, having performed in two music videos and a made-for-TV movie, before her participation on *Survivor.* Despite SAG's strict no non-union work policy and AFTRA's discouragement of non-union employment, the majority of Manthey's involvement on *Survivor* series and specials classified her as a contestant, which, consistent with other game shows, is not covered by union jurisdiction. It is not known how CBS exercises its rights to publicity with respect to Manthey.

29. Joshua Meyrowitz (1985) uses the "media friends" construct to suggest that parasocial interaction (Horton and Wohl 1956) can apply to relations between actors in fictional roles and fans.
30. Of course, reality celebrities are also guests, hosts, and actors on shows distributed by networks other than their home-based network, but combined searches on Internet Movie Data Base Pro and Lexis-Nexis yield credits for reality celebrities predominantly synergized around the holdings of the media company that houses the reality show in which they got their initial exposure.
31. Roscoe (2001), for example, details how eviction from the *Big Brother* house is turned into a spectacle, and Johnson-Woods (2002) documents the post-show mediated activities of some of the popular players.
32. I am grateful to Moya Luckett for providing this insightful example and for her commentary.

References

Albiniak, Paige. 2002. Get Ready for a New, Heavy Dose of Reality: Once a Fad, Unscripted Shows Have Become a Schedule Staple. *Broadcasting and Cable*, December 16.

Anderson, Carla. 2004. "Depressed," "Angry" Yippies Rally in Protest. *Philadelphia Daily News*, March 18, 6.

Andrejevic, Mark. 2003. *Reality TV: The Work of Being Watched, Critical Media Studies.* Lanham, MD: Rowman & Littlefield Publishers.

Aronson, Steven M.L. 1983. *Hype.* 1st edn. New York: Morrow.

Benjamin, Walter. 1969. Art in the Age of Mechanical Reproduction. In *Illuminations*, ed. H. Arendt. New York: Schocken Books.

Bloom, David. 2002. The Money Issue: Showbiz Economy, Employment and Paycheck Levels Are Still Searching for Solid Ground. *Daily Variety*, July 24, A1.

Boorstin, Daniel J. 1987. *The Image: A Guide to Pseudo-events in America.* 25th anniversary edn. New York: Atheneum.

Braudy, Leo. 1986. *The Frenzy of Renown: Fame and Its History.* New York: Oxford University Press.

Brenton, Sam, and Reuben Cohen. 2003. *Shooting People: Adventures in Reality TV.* New York: Verso.

Brodesser, Claude. 2004. Roles Rolling Away. *Daily Variety*, October 7, 5.

Carter, Bill. 2003. Reality Shows Alter the Way TV Does Business. *New York Times*, January 25, A1, C14.

Caves, Richard E. 2000. *Creative Industries: Contracts between Art and Commerce.* Cambridge, MA: Harvard University Press.

Christopherson, Susan. 1996. Flexibility and Adaptation in Industrial Relations: The Exceptional Case of the U.S. Media Entertainment Industries. In *Under the Stars: Essays on Labor Relations in Arts and Entertainment*, ed. L.S. Gray and R.L. Seeber. Ithaca, NY: Cornell University Press.

Christopherson, Susan, and Michael Storper. 1989. The Effects of Flexible Specialization on Industrial Politics and the Labor Market: The Motion Picture Industry. *Industrial and Labor Relations Review* 42(3): 331–47.

Couldry, Nick. 2002. Playing for Celebrity: *Big Brother* as Ritual Event. *Television & New Media* 3(3): 283–93.

Cowell, Simon. 2003. All Together Now! Publics and Participation in *American Idol. Invisible Culture* 6. http://www.rochester.edu/in_visible_culture/Issue_6/cowell/cowell.html.

deCordova, Richard. 1990. *Picture Personalities: The Emergence of the Star System in America.* Urbana: University of Illinois Press.

Dovey, Jon. 2000. *Freakshow: First Person Media and Factual Television.* London: Pluto Press.

Dyer, Richard. 1979. *Stars.* London: Educational Advisory Service British Film Institute.

———. 1986. *Heavenly Bodies: Film Stars and Society.* New York: St. Martin's Press.

———. [1977] 1991. Four Films of Lana Turner. In *Star Texts: Image and Performance in Film and Television*, ed. J. Butler. Detroit, MI: Wayne State University Press.

Eisenstein, Elizabeth L. 1979. *The Printing Press as an Agent of Change: Communications and Cultural Transformations in Early Modern Europe.* Cambridge, UK: Cambridge University Press.

Ellis, John. 1982. *Visible Fictions: Cinema, Television, Video.* London: Routledge & Kegan Paul.

Ewen, Stuart. 1988. *All Consuming Images: The Politics of Style in Contemporary Culture.* New York: Basic Books.

Gabler, Neal. 1998. *Life the Movie: How Entertainment Conquered Reality.* 1st edn. New York: Alfred A. Knopf.

Gaines, Jane M. 1991. *Contested Culture: The Image, the Voice, and the Law.* Chapel Hill: University of North Carolina Press.

Gamson, Joshua. 1994. *Claims to Fame: Celebrity in Contemporary America.* Berkeley: University of California Press.

Garnham, Nicholas. 1990. *Capitalism and Communication: Global Culture and the Economics of Information.* Newbury Park: Sage Publications.

Gitlin, Todd. 1983. *Inside Prime Time.* 1st edn. New York: Pantheon Books.

Gray, Lois S., and Ronald Leroy Seeber. 1996. *Under the Stars: Essays on Labor Relations in Arts and Entertainment.* Ithaca, NY: ILR Press.

Groves, Christopher. 2003. Reality Sets In. *Daily Variety,* April 28, A2.

Halbert, Debora. 2003. Who Owns Your Personality: Reality Television and Publicity Rights. In *Survivor Lessons: Essays on Communication and Reality Television,* ed. M.J. Smith and A.F. Wood. Jefferson, NC: McFarland & Company, Inc., Publishers.

Hesmondhalgh, David. 2002. *The Cultural Industries.* London: Sage Publications.

Hill, Annette. 2002. *Big Brother*: The Real Audience. *Television & New Media* 3(3): 323–40.

Holmes, Su. 2004. "Reality Goes Pop!" Reality TV, Popular Music, and Narratives of Stardom in *Pop Idol. Television & New Media* 5(2): 147–72.

Horkheimer, Max, and Theodor W. Adorno. [1944] 1997. *Dialectic of Enlightenment, Verso Classics: 15.* New York: Verso.

Horton, Donald, and R. Richard Wohl. 1956. Mass Communication and Para-social Interaction. *Psychiatry* 19: 215–29.

Internet Movie Database. 2005a. *The Amazing Race (2001 TV Series Documentary): Release Info.* http://pro.imdb.com/title/tt0285335/releaseinfo.

———. 2005b. *The Bachelor (2002 TV Series Documentary): Release Info.* http://pro.imdb.com/title/tt0313038/releaseinfo.

Johnson-Woods, Toni. 2002. *Big Bother: Why Did that Reality-TV Show become Such a Phenomenon?* St. Lucia, Qld.: University of Queensland Press.

Jones, Janet Megan. 2003. Show Off Your Real Face: A Fan Study of the UK *Big Brother* Transmissions (2000, 2001, 2002). Investigating the Boundaries between Notions of Consumers and Producers of Factual Television. *New Media & Society* 5(3): 400–21.

Kiefer, Peter. 2002. SAG Report: Hollywood Roles Decrease in 2001. *Hollywood Reporter,* July 2, 1–2.

Kindem, Gorham. 1985. Hollywood's Movie Star System during the Studio Era. *Film Reader* (6): 13–26.

King, Barry. 1991. Articulating Stardom. In *Star Texts: Image and Performance in Film and Television,* ed. J.G. Butler. Detroit, MI: Wayne State University Press.

Klaprat, Cathy. 1985. The Star as Market Strategy: Bette Davis in Another Light. In *The American Film Industry,* ed. T. Balio. Madison: University of Wisconsin Press.

Klein, Michael. 2004a. Carpenters Picket "Real World" Site. *Philadelphia Inquirer,* March 30, B2.

———. 2004b. Philadelphia Is Part of the "Real World" Again. *Philadelphia Inquirer,* March 24, B01.

Litwak, Mark. 1986. *Reel Power: The Struggle for Influence and Success in the New Hollywood.* New York: Morrow.

Magder, Ted. 2004. The End of TV 101: Reality Programs, Formats, and the New Business of Television. In *Reality TV: Remaking Television Culture,* ed. S. Murray and L. Ouellette. New York: New York University Press.

Marshall, P. David. 1997. *Celebrity and Power: Fame in Contemporary Culture.* Minneapolis: University of Minnesota Press.

McCarthy, Anna. 2005. Crab People from the Center of the Earth. *GLQ: A Journal of Lesbian and Gay Studies* 11(1): 97–101.

McDonald, Paul. 2000. *The Star System: Hollywood's Production of Popular Identities.* London: Wallflower.

McNary, Dave. 2002. Thesps' Squeeze Play. *Daily Variety,* July 2, 3.

Meyrowitz, Joshua. 1985. *No Sense of Place: The Impact of Electronic Media on Social Behavior.* New York: Oxford University Press.

Miège, Bernard. 1989. *The Capitalization of Cultural Production.* New York: International General.

Moran, Joe. 2000. *Star Authors: Literary Celebrity in America.* London: Pluto Press.

Murray, Susan. 2004. I Think We Need a New Name for It: The Meeting of Documentary and Reality TV. In *Reality TV: Remaking Television Culture,* ed. S. Murray and L. Ouellette. New York: New York University Press.

Murray, Susan, and Laurie Ouellette. 2004. *Reality TV: Remaking Television Culture.* New York: New York University Press.

Ong, Walter J. 1982. *Orality and Literacy: The Technologizing of the Word.* London: Methuen.

Paul, Alan, and Archie Kleingartner. 1994. Flexible Production and the Transformation of Industrial Relations in the Motion Picture and Television Industry. *Industrial and Labor Relations Review* 47(4): 663–78.

Peters, Anne K., and Muriel G. Cantor. 1982. Screen Acting as Work. In *Individuals in Mass Media Organisations: Creativity and Constraint,* ed. J.S. Ettema and D.C. Whitney. Beverly Hills, CA: Sage.

Ponce de Leon, Charles L. 2002. *Self-Exposure: Human-Interest Journalism and the Emergence of Celebrity in America, 1890–1940.* Chapel Hill: University of North Carolina Press.

Raphael, Chad. 2004. The Political Economic Origins of Reali-TV. In *Reality TV: Remaking Television Culture,* ed. S. Murray and L. Ouellette. New York: New York University Press.

Rein, Irving J., Philip Kotler, and Martin R. Stoller. 1997. *High Visibility: The Making and Marketing of Professionals into Celebrities.* 1st edn. New York: Dodd, Mead.

Rendon, Jim. 2004. Unions Aim to Share in Success of Reality TV. *New York Times,* January 25, C4.

Rojek, Chris. 2001. *Celebrity.* London: Reaktion Books, Ltd.

Roscoe, Jane. 2001. *Big Brother* Australia: Performing the "Real" Twenty-Four Seven. *International Journal of Cultural Studies* 4(4): 473–88.

Ryan, Bill. 1992. *Making Capital from Culture: The Corporate Form of Capitalist Cultural Production, De Gruyter Studies in Organization: 35.* Berlin: Walter de Gruyter.

Schickel, Richard. 1985. *Intimate Strangers: The Culture of Celebrity.* Garden City, NY: Doubleday.

Screen Actors Guild. 2005a. Performers Bear Brunt of Reality TV and Runaway Production Trends, 2003 Casting Data Shows. http://www.sag.org/sagWebApp/Content/Public/castingdatareports.htm.

Screen Actors Guild. 2005b. SAG/AFTRA TV/Theatrical Agreement 2005. http://www.sag.org/sagWebApp/application?origin=news_and_events_archives.jsp&event=bea.portal.framework.internal.refresh&pageid=Hidden&contentUrl=/templates/newsLander.jsp&newsUrl=/Content/Public/ratification_summary.htm&cp=NewsAndEventsArchives.

Spring, Greg. 1998. Booking Wars: Talk Shows See Battle for Celebrity Guests. *Electronic Media*, February 23, 1.

Street, John. 2003. The Celebrity Politicians: Political Style and Popular Culture. In *Media and the Restyling of Politics: Consumerism, Celebrity and Cynicism*, ed. J. Corner and D. Pels. London: Sage.

Sudjic, Deyan. 1990. *Cult Heroes: How to Be Famous for More than Fifteen Minutes.* 1st American edn. New York: Norton.

Thompson, John B. 1990. *Ideology and Modern Culture: Critical Social Theory in the Era of Mass Communication.* Stanford, CA: Stanford University Press.

Tkacik, Maureen. 2004. In Philadelphia, Trying to Keep It Real. *New York Times*, March 21, 12.

Turner, Graeme. 2004. *Understanding Celebrity.* London: Sage.

Turner, Graeme, Frances Bonner, and P. David Marshall. 2000. *Fame Games: The Production of Celebrity in Australia.* Cambridge, UK: Cambridge University Press.

Wasko, Janet. 2003. *How Hollywood Works.* London: Sage Publications.

Wolk, Josh. 2002. Fame Factor. *Entertainment Weekly*, August 2, 32–7.

Reality TV Formats: The Case of *Canadian Idol*

Doris Baltruschat

The surge of reality TV programs since 2000 can be traced back to tabloid-style documentaries, which first appeared in the late 1980s. Shows such as *America's Most Wanted* (Heflin & Klein, 1988), *Cops* (Langley & Barbour, 1989), and *Crimewatch* (Gay, 1984) marked a fundamental shift from programming rooted in investigative journalism to documentaries of diversion and display (Corner, 2002). Their development was linked clearly to the emergence of multichannel television in the 1990s, which created the need for provocative programs to attract audiences in an increasingly competitive media environment. The proliferation of reality TV in Canada is also linked to changes in television program development, especially the emergence of "format franchising," which is based on the adaptation of popular program concepts for different markets around the world (for example, *Canadian Idol*, *Canada's Next Top Model*, and *Deal or No Deal*).

This article details how reality TV producers attempt to create all-enveloping experiences that transgress the boundaries of traditional broadcasts. They accomplish this by staging media events and engaging audiences in online environments. One reality format in particular—*Canadian Idol* (Bowlby & Brunton, 2003)—exemplifies how franchise format localization, or "glocalization,"[1] involves the engagement of actual and virtual communities to ensure its successful adaptation for Canadian audiences.

The analysis presents key findings from a three-year research project on international co-productions and TV format franchising. The study highlights the importance of situating reality TV within its production context. In particular, it demonstrates the need to address the complex interplay between producers, interactive audiences, and cross-platform media that underlies the "format franchising" processes of programs such as *Canadian Idol*.

From Documentaries to Docu-soaps and Game-docs

The emergence of reality TV represents a shift from what Kilborn (2003) calls the more "serious" representation of socio-historical events to programming that is produced predominantly for entertainment purposes. Reality programs are linked to different documentary forms, such as documentary journalism, cinéma vérité traditions, and the observational documentary. However, due to elements of popular entertainment programming (e.g., talk shows, game shows, and soap operas), reality TV ultimately creates its own generic map. Hill (2005, p. 50) suggests a fact/fiction continuum, which reflects the sliding scale of factuality in these programs. The continuum covers contemporary documentaries and popular factual entertainment ranging from docu-soaps and game-docs to makeovers and quiz shows.

Similarly to documentaries, reality programs aim for the "articulation of the authentic self" in order to depict "moments of truth" (Holmes, 2004, p. 159). Teleconfessionals in designated video rooms and individual strategies for winning the game provide intimate accounts of unfolding events. Also, slightly off-the-mark camera angles and out-of-focus shots contribute to a sense of immediacy and intimacy with characters and suggest a "fly-on-the-wall" experience for viewers. Reality TV producers aim for this "tele-factuality" (Corner,

2002, p. 257), which is reflected in statements such as "the camera doesn't lie, [e]specially up close" (*Canada's Next Top Model*, Citytv, 2006). Similarly, the executive producer of *Big Brother* states, "I wanted it to look live and exciting. . . . [T]his was not meant to be a polished drama. *We were filming it for real*, and it was a virtue of the programme that viewers understood that" (Ruth Wrigley, cited in Ritchie, 2000, p. 11, italics added). Indeed, Lewis (2004) refers to a "tele-reality" into which people from the "everyday world" are submerged to perform their role. Viewers understand this blurring of boundaries between the public, private, and "adjacent realities" (Lewis, 2004, p. 295). And they find pleasure in looking for moments of "truth" that may shine through improvised performances (Hill, 2005).

Yet a closer look at the production context of reality TV reveals that such programs are highly contrived. Casting decisions and scripts linking locations and circumstances for the purpose of creating action and conflict frame many story lines ("Reality writer-anonymous," 2005). A testimonial from Julia Corrigan, a contestant on the BBC/Lion TV reality series *Castaways* (Mills, 2000), highlights this aspect of the genres:

> I **hate** to admit it, but the television company obviously thought that some people/incidents were a lot more interesting than others in terms of storylines! Yet the darker side of that is that there was a bit of harrying going on to get us to do the things they wanted us to do. In the latter stages, there were lists on the wall about what we should talk about in video diaries. We did feel that events were being manipulated. (Corrigan, cited in Kibble-White, 2003 p. 25, emphasis in the original)

Thus, in spite of claims of "authenticity" and the showcasing of "real people," reality TV programs are underlain by a subtext: the behind-the-scenes production and economic contexts that are not apparent to the viewer. Kilborn (2003) addresses this important aspect when he comments on the production context for *Castaways* (Mills, 2000):

> What was of course *not* shown . . . were the potentially far more revealing discussions between key members of the production team concerning the structuring of the whole event: how the choice of specific participants might generate certain types of dramatic conflict, how the known likes and prejudices of the target audiences might be reflected in a particular mix of characters and how the needs of certain embryonic storylines might be served if certain casting decisions were made. (Kilborn, 2003, p. 86)

Another key characteristic of reality TV production is the incitement of "buzz" around shows in order to extend broadcasts into online environments and conversations outside scheduled air dates (Scannell, 2002). In the late 1990s, reality TV producers in the UK were the first to take advantage of new interactive, cross-platform modes of production with the *Idol* and *Big Brother* formats (Television Research Partnership, 2002; Wrigley, Powers, Green & Jones, 2000). Reality TV producers in the US and Canada (with shows such as *American Idol* and *Canada's Next Top Model*) now also tap into new revenue streams generated from text-message votes, as well as downloadable ringtones and music clips for cell phones.

To create interest in cross-platform inter-activity—from voting for contestants to posting comments in chatrooms—producers use similar techniques to those used in soap opera production: multiple story lines, which focus on human relationships; close-up shots to connote intimacy; and heightened identification with characters through online blogs. In addition, they use "cliffhangers" to entice audiences to return to the program the following week or to discuss potential outcomes with other viewers in chat rooms. Consequently, an important task for reality TV producers is the creation of interesting storylines through casting unusual characters and scripting dramatic narratives. In addition, producers stage media events in the form of open auditions, which transgress the boundaries of regular programming and work intertextually across multiple platforms and contexts. This point will be illustrated in more detail in the case study of *Canadian Idol.*

Stories of Change and Transformation

The typical plot in reality programs involves a "story of change" (Hill, 2005). The transformation of characters is an integral part of most narrative structures, but stories of change in game-docs and talent contests follow a particular formula: they tend to be about attaining success through fame (usually short-lived), in addition to prize monies (or equivalent materials and goods) and contracts with prestigious organizations (e.g., a record company or modelling agency). Transformation processes in these programs therefore reflect predominant values in capitalist societies that place individual achievements above collective goals. The narratives are limited to the portrayal of people entrenched in competitive environments for personal gain and exclude social transformations that benefit society as a whole. Even in programs where alliances between contestants are encouraged, one individual's selfish pursuit is rewarded in the end. According to Foster (2004), "The brand of reality depicted on *Survivor* reinforced the widespread notion that self-interest ultimately trumps self-reliance, just as it coincides with the formula for successful television programming: conflict is compelling and conflict sells" (p. 280). Similarly, reality TV producer Mark Burnett comments about *Survivor* (2000), "Compelling television comes from seeing rather ordinary people put in uncomfortable situations—social interactions, not in the peril of their lives. The best way to describe the show is *social Darwinism*" (as quoted in *USA Today,* 2000; italics added).

A key element in the transformation process in reality TV is the application of consumer products to enhance a character's physical appearance (for example, Cover Girl cosmetics in *America's Next Top Model*). The intertwining of dramatic narratives and product placements links the story of change to patterns of consumption. In addition, this places an emphasis on the exchange value of products rather than their use value (Jhally, 1987). For example, on the website for *Canada's Next Top Model* (Manuel, 2006),[2] each weekly episode is accompanied by a "resource guide" listing sponsors, designers, and vendors that are featured on the show. Stories of change, therefore, extend beyond the diegetic world of the program and signal to viewers and users of interactive media (e.g., Internet, PDAs, and video cell phones) that their own transformation can be achieved through the consumption of featured products, thus closing the circle of viewer identification with characters on the show.

Another narrative device is intervention by experts, often in the form of judging panels, which present obstacles, as well as opportunities, along the character's journey. Their presence as gatekeepers adds drama to the narrative, as they select characters for the next stage of the contest and, ultimately, announce the winner. Part of this admittance to the next (or final) stage is the "reveal" of the "transformed character," signifying the end of the character's journey and the end of the series. According to Scannell (2002), a game-doc such as *Big Brother* has "from the start . . . a powerful drive toward a climactic moment of resolution" (p. 272) to complete its narrative structure of beginning, middle, and end. In programs such as *American Idol* (Fuller, 2002) and *Canadian Idol* (Bowlby & Brunton, 2003), the revelation of the final winner is staged as a special television spectacle, denoting the pinnacle of the series, which tends to draw the highest audience ratings.

Idol finales are broadcast live from special venues such as the Kodak Theatre (used for the Academy Awards) in Los Angeles or Toronto's Roy Thomson

Hall. They are also accompanied by special community events in the "home towns" of contestants. For example, in 2004, 5,000 people gathered in Saskatoon's Credit Union Centre (formerly Saskatchewan Place) for the two-hour *Canadian Idol* finale, which was broadcast on two giant video screens. The community "came together" for the event to celebrate its local contestant Theresa Sokyrka, runner up for the title of *Canadian Idol,* which ultimately went to her competitor, Kalan Porter:

> The sight of Sokyrka on the big screens continually evoked ear-splitting screaming, clapping and cheering and some fans jumped out of their seats to get a better look at the hometown hero. At times, Credit Union Centre took on a New Year's atmosphere as fans carried balloons, blew horns, threw confetti and did the wave. (Kachkowski, 2004)

In this instance, the narrative is intertwined with familiar cultural references and national sentiment to create maximum resonance for viewers. The result is a strong engagement with *Canadian Idol,* which has been referred to as one of the most watched programs in Canada's television history (CTV, 2005).

In the lead-up to the finale, the weekly "television stage" for many reality programs is a "self-contained space" (usually a "house" such as the *Idol* Mansion in Toronto or "The House" on *Canada's Next Top Model*) that is wired for video and sound-recording equipment to capture interactions between contestants. This living space is a "televisual construct" (Kilborn, 2003, p. 80) that signifies the story world in which the competition unfolds. In *Canadian Idol* and *Canada's Next Top Model,* the house is a grand mansion that extends the connotation of the private luxury associated with the life of stars:

> While the Idols were surely enjoying living it up in a swank downtown hotel during the Top 22 phase of the show, it doesn't compare to the star treatment of the Top 10 and a spot in the exclusive Idol Mansion. Located in a posh Toronto neighbourhood surrounded by sprawling estates of the rich and famous, the 7-bedroom mansion has enough luxurious features to entertain even the most distractible Idol on a rare free day. That includes an indoor pool, Jacuzzi, two saunas, racquetball/basketball court, home theatre, fitness room, and tennis court. (CTV, 2006a)

The mansions are depicted on program-related websites through photos and descriptions, which invite comments from users of interactive media. The use of a familial environment such as a house amplifies the blurred boundaries between public and private realms and enhances viewer identification with the characters. However, these houses are also voyeuristic settings and thus raise ethical questions about surveillance and the privacy of contestants (Andrejevic, 2004; Dovey, 2000; Glynn, 2000).[3]

Program-related chatrooms provide additional entry points into the narrative. As a result, interactive media users engage with content in a manner similar to online communities dedicated to soap operas (Baym, 2000). These interactive possibilities *create the impression* that viewers actually influence narrative progression and are part of the transformation process of their favourite characters (for example, through voting for a contestant), as well as by encouraging contestants along their journey (in the form of online commentary such as blogs). Producers of *Canada's Next Top Model* teamed up with Yahoo Entertainment to make extensive use of viewers' commentaries,[4] as exemplified by a blog from "Sarah S." addressed to Andrea, winner of the program's first season:

> Andrea, I think you're gorgeous and *have clearly come a long way in the short time between now and the first day* . . . but it's clear that you're the one who is going to defeat you! Trash-talking Tricia and getting all hacked off that there are cameras on you 24/7 when you had to know that a television reality show was

> going to be just like that (and I'm sure your contract said as much) is just immature. Rise above it all and be beautiful in your strength of character! (2006, italics added).

Similarly, the *Canadian Idol* website dedicates a space for online commentary from contestants, their families, and their friends, exemplified by the entry from the father of Eva Avila, winner of the fourth season:

> I see her more confident on stage and I know she's learning a lot of tricks of the trade. *I've seen a big change.* It feels like she is doing what I wasn't able to do (as a musician). I never had an opportunity like this growing up. I'm very, very proud. (CTV, 2006; italics added)

This engagement with reality programs' online communities contributes to a sense of familiarity with the protagonists of the storylines. It furthermore promotes involvement in virtual environments, which emulate closeness to the "stars" of the programs.

In *Canadian Idol* and *Canada's Next Top Model*, the transformation narrative is clearly linked to the celebrity cult, which has grown in recent years due to extensive cross-referencing of star stories in tabloid-style magazines and TV programs. In many reality programs, the "ordinary" individual is transformed into a star or "celetoid" (a term coined by Rojek [2001] to capture their short-lived public recognition), a process that the viewer witnesses and partakes in at key moments. Holmes (2004a) states that "the emphasis on the ordinariness of the contestants contributes to the deliberate blurring between contestant and viewer and, as a result, a potential invocation of the audience's own aspirations (or fantasies) of success and stardom" (p. 156). Accordingly, *Canadian Idol* and *Canada's Next Top Model* tap into this "success myth," which, as part of the "American dream," creates the illusion that in spite of social stratification, anyone can rise above their rank (Dyer, 1998). These programs, in particular, are paradigmatic of the success myth, with their predominant focus on the "innate" talent of contestants, as well as the contestants' transformation through dedication and professionalism (Holmes, 2004). Within the context of reality TV production, formats such as *Idol* also epitomize the construction of celebrity to maintain control over a program franchise and to manage financial risks by manufacturing multiple celebrities as vehicles for promotion and online engagement (Turner, 2004).

However, stories of change in reality TV programs are limited to individual transformations associated with processes of consumption, thus foreclosing ideas about broader social transformations. Furthermore, programs do not address any significant debates in society or highlight particular issues of concern, because they

> do not have an investigative agenda, but are rather, obsessively concerned with larger-than-life characters, with lively conversational exchanges and with occasional dramatic outbursts which are, however, almost always swiftly and amicably resolved. All docu-soaps have ultimately the same objective: to produce a mildly diverting entertainment more likely to provoke an amused chuckle than to produce new insights into the world and its workings. (Kilborn, 2003, p. 102)

And in spite of increased engagement with reality programs through votes, comments, and blogs, viewer involvement tends to be superficial in its concentration on narrowly defined narratives about personal success, stardom, and consumption.

A Closer Look at *Canadian Idol*

The story of *Canadian Idol* (Bowlby & Brunton, 2003) is linked inevitably to the development of *American Idol* (Fuller, 2002),[5] which is based on the original UK program *Pop Idol* (Fuller, 2001).

The *Idol* format is a reality TV contest with the aim of finding a "pop idol" and recording artist by staging nationwide auditions. From the thousands of hopeful applicants, 500 contestants are selected. After more auditions, this number is reduced to 100, then to 50, and finally to 10. The more "interesting" moments in these auditions are broadcast to showcase "broken dreams and shattered egos" (Schmitt, Bisson & Fey, 2005, p. 147). Each week the public and a group of four judges (or three, in the case of *American Idol*) vote off one contestant—out of the final 10—until the winner is designated "Idol" for that particular television cycle.

The *Idol* format entails elements of universal appeal. It is a family-oriented program that is reminiscent of earlier televised talent contests during the era of broadcasting, such as *The Original Amateur Hour* (Graham, 1948), which aired from 1948 to 1970 (Dederer, 2006), *Star Search* (Banner & Wagner, 1983), and *Tiny Talent Time* (Lawrence, 1957), which aired from 1957 to 1992 on CHCH Television in Hamilton. However, global franchising and format interactivity have made *Idol* a "business changer for all of network television" (Carter, 2006, p. 194), since it exemplifies how to "maximize ancillary exploitation of a format in order to generate maximum revenue" (Schmitt, Bisson & Fey, 2005, p. 147).

By 2008, the *Idol* format had been licensed to over 35 countries, including Belgium, Germany, South Africa, Norway, Australia, Russia, Croatia, Serbia and Montenegro, the US, Kazakhstan, and Canada (FremantleMedia, 2004; FremantleMedia, 2006; Wikipedia, 2006), as well as India, Malaysia, Indonesia, and Vietnam (*FremantleMedia*, 2004a; Le, 2004). As is typical of most format sales, FremantleMedia and 19 Entertainment maintain control over the show's adaptation in local markets. 19 Entertainment also manages the careers of the show's winners and takes a cut of the profits generated through their concerts and record sales (Hearn, 2004). The *Idol* program has generated high audience ratings in England, the US, and Australia (FremantleMedia, 2004b). In Canada, with almost 3.6 million viewers for the closing section and winner announcement on *Canadian Idol* in 2003, the format earned one of the highest ratings in Canada's television history (Edwards, 2003).

According to FremantleMedia's format "bible,"[6] the *Idol* franchise contains four essential components:

- A specific "look" in set design and colours, logos, sequence of events, role of host(s) and judges, lighting and camera angles, et cetera;
- Contracting audience members/contestants for the actual TV program;
- Basing the elimination of contestants on telephone votes; and
- Interactive online forums.

Hence, *Pop Idol* serves as the template for all *Idol* franchises. In the words of *Canadian Idol* host Ben Mulroney, "The great thing about a format like *Canadian Idol* is that it can be adapted to any national context" (Ben Mulroney, host, *Canadian Idol*, personal communication, Vancouver, BC, April 29, 2004). The Canadian franchise also follows the value-added *American Idol* template, since the producers "wanted to mirror the American show, because audiences were familiar with it" (Mark Lysakowski, line producer, Insight Production, personal communication, Toronto, ON, 29 April 2004).

In 2002, CTV licensed the format for the Canadian market and hired Toronto's Insight Production for its local adaptation. During preproduction, Insight producers John Brunton and Mark Lysakowski went to Los Angeles to attend *American Idol* auditions and to "figure out how it works and to get some pointers on the whole operation" (Mark Lysakowski, line producer, Insight Production, personal communication, Toronto, ON, 29 April 2004). The producers also watched the entire seasons of *American Idol* and *Pop Idol* to become familiar with the program and its production matrix. Throughout the first season of *Canadian Idol*, FremantleMedia remained in close contact with its Canadian co-producers, "because it is in their [FremantleMedia's] interest that the show does well in Canada and adheres to the format" (Mark Lysakowski, line producer, Insight Production, personal communication, Toronto, ON, 29 April 2004). Consultations via telephone and face-to-face meetings ensured that the format maintained its recognizability while being adapted to Canada's television culture and viewer sensibilities. FremantleMedia, therefore, checked the rough cuts and premiere tapes of *Canadian Idol* to make sure that production standards were met (Mark Lysakowski, line producer, Insight Production, personal communication, Toronto, ON, 29 April 2004).

Even though *Canadian Idol* is a hybrid of *Pop Idol* and *American Idol*, its fundamental structure and content follows the original *Pop Idol* format. According to Lysakowski, Insight Production, the show therefore adheres to the format bible as closely as possible, in addition to

> the whole philosophy of a single person coming through a door-to audition for a show, to the ultimate winner chosen by the public. It's the journey that the person takes to become the next Idol, an American, British or whatever—that's the underlying theme of the show. The basic structure of the series remains the same. (Mark Lysakowski, line producer, Insight Production, personal communication, Toronto, ON, 29 April 2004)

In some instances, the Canadian producers find the UK show to be closer to Canadian sensibilities, while at other times they utilize elements from the value-added American adaptation (Mark Lysakowski, line producer, Insight Production, personal communication, Toronto, ON, 29 April 2004). In contrast to three judges on *American Idol*, *Canadian Idol* features four, like *Pop Idol* and other *Idol* formats around the world. Also, Simon Cowell's trademark as the "nasty judge" on *Pop Idol* and *American Idol* is copied in Zack Werner in Canada. This "character adaptation" has proven to be more or less successful. Whereas *Canadian Idol* judge Zack Werner (as quoted in Tilley, 2004) denies ironically that he is anything but himself, *Idol* judges in other TV markets have drawn criticism for culturally inappropriate behaviour. For example, in *Vietnam Idol*, the judge was scrutinized by the government for deviating from Communist Party principles of "developing Vietnam's culture into an advanced culture imbued with national identities" because he criticized a contestant for following "too strict a dress code" (as quoted in Le, 2004).

Idol hosts also share characteristics across format adaptations. Since *Pop Idol* features two hosts, the first season of *American Idol* had two presenters (Ryan Seacrest and Brian Dunkelman), which was then copied for the first season of *Canadian Idol*. In later seasons, producers decided to feature only one host in the North American franchises to keep the focus on contestants and judges. Ben Mulroney comments on his role as an *Idol* host:

> THE PERFECT HOST for *Idol* should be slightly more interesting than vanilla . . . Fashionable, but not like he's trying to upstage anyone. Funny, but not necessarily a comedian. Confident, but not necessarily cocky. He should be like a good child: speak when spoken to and recognize his place in the family. This show is first and foremost about the singers, and then about the judges, and maybe if we're lucky after that, and we have time, it should be about the host. (as quoted in Gillis, 2003; emphasis in the original)

Cultural signifiers, national symbols, and local stories are used throughout the *Canadian Idol* season to localize and underscore Canadian aspects of the franchise. For example, the program's opening shots feature ice sculptures in Ottawa and the historic intersection of Main Street and

Portage Avenue in Winnipeg; the Canadian flag is prominently displayed on clothing during audition rounds; and the Canadian anthem is sung before and during the auditions and forms part of the televised programs as well (Read, 2004). According to Mulroney,

> It's a fairly rigid system, the way the performance show goes, followed by the telephone vote. Certain types of songs are sung, and the visual look of the show is pretty much universal. But within the rigid system you build in [the capacity] for each country to tell its own stories. We tell unique Canadian stories from a Canadian perspective, and we tell it to a Canadian audience, using Canadian judges, Canadian kids, Canadian audiences and Canadian songs. (Ben Mulroney, host, *Canadian Idol*, personal communication, Toronto, ON, 29 April 2004)

In order to successfully "glocalize" *Idol*, the producers therefore emphasize certain "Canadianisms," reflected particularly in stories about contestants and their origins. From the young teacher from Saskatchewan who is voted "most popular" by her high school students to the "hometown hero" (such as Theresa Sokyrka), to the best friends from the Maritimes heading for Toronto, local aspects and culturally familiar stories are intertwined with the *Idol* narrative to create viewer identification with the program's characters. Yet the Canadian producers also introduce small changes to meet cultural sensibilities and audience preferences:

> Working with Fremantle was a very collaborative process. Just like other international brands—like a fast food restaurant or a clothing line—not everything translates internationally. So the people that own the trademark work closely with us. There were some things they wanted us to do, and I said "no, that would not play well in Canada." (Mark Lysakowski, line producer, Insight Production, personal communication, Toronto, ON, 29 April 2004)

For example, when contestants from *American Idol* made a guest appearance in Canada in 2003, American producers suggested they perform a rendition of "God Bless the USA." The Canadian producers feared a backlash from Canadian viewers and strongly recommended that the group perform the song "What the World Needs Now Is Love") instead (Mark Lysakowski, line producer, Insight Production, personal communication, Toronto, ON, 29 April 2004).

All changes in format adaptations are only "cosmetic," however, and they have to be approved by the licensor, because the fundamental structure of the format cannot be altered:

> We do the window dressing, some cosmetic changes, to make the show a little different. In the American show, the national auditions generally only show the worst singers. We show the bad singers, and it gives people a chance to laugh. But we also show the good singers and the interesting human stories, which make people far more interested in our show. (Mark Lysakowski, line producer, Insight Production, personal communication, Toronto, ON, 29 April 2004)

The focus is on the interchangeable aspects of the format, namely, the contestants and their local stories, which differ for every TV season. The recruitment of "semi-professional" performers is an important aspect of reality format production, since it reduces costs and adds interactive elements (for example, through blogs, online chats, and so on). Similarly, the staging of media events and national auditions provide entry points for interactive engagement.

Since *Canadian Idol* airs during the summer months, auditions coincide with the final episodes of *American Idol*, which results in additional cross-promotion for the shows. *Canadian Idol* is produced on a seasonal basis. Thus its success—based on audience ratings and advertising rates—determines future production, as well as employment for local producers and crews (Mark

Lysakowski, line producer, Insight Production, personal communication, Toronto, ON, 29 April 2004).

Telus is the official wireless sponsor of *Canadian Idol* and has been so since 2006. This gives Telus clients access to wireless content, as well as the ability to vote by text message. The service provides *Idol* news, video footage, ringtones, and voicetones of the competitors. Clients also have access to biographies and images of the host and judging panel (Telus & CTV, 2006). In 2006, Telus also partnered with Samsung to provide *Idol* finalists with a new Samsung A950 cell phone as a cross-promotional strategy. Similar to other *Idol* programs, the winner signs a recording contract—in the case of *Canadian Idol*, with Sony BMG Canada—and releases a debut album in the months following the show's finale.

In addition to entering a recording contract with a local subsidiary of the Bertelsmann Music Group (or a nominee of 19 Recordings), finalists also have to sign agreements with a management company and promote merchandise from sponsors associated with the format. *All* proceeds from merchandizing and sponsorship arrangements in the UK and the US are retained by 19 Entertainment; in Canada, a 50/50 split between 19 Entertainment and FremantleMedia applies. Finalists are contractually obliged to keep all aspects of the program and the series strictly confidential.

Overall, *Canadian Idol* is an adaptation that resembles the UK version closely, juxtaposed with Canadian stories and overtones from the American version. The glocalization of this reality format is achieved through extensive cross-promotion and insertion of local stories, and as well as by skillfully embedding the production into local communities through media events (such as the finale and nationwide auditions). By tapping into the matrix of familiar national and cultural symbols, *Idol* achieves a proximity to viewers that heightens their potential for identification and engagement with characters on the program, as well as with the consumer products associated with the show.

Staging *Idol* Auditions

Audience interactivity with program content extends the traditional "lean back" experience of television viewing into a more active "lean forward" activity through computer technology. According to Murray (1997), audiences now tend to progress though several stages: first, they move through sequential activities (e.g., watching a program, then interacting with content online); next, they engage in simultaneous interactivity with two media (audience members interact online while watching the program on television); and finally, interactive users engage in a merged experience, watching and interacting in the same medium. Even though the possibilities for interactive narratives and "imaginative engagement" appear endless, the political economy of television and the Internet determines the parameters and extent to which audience members can express themselves in interactive domains. As Murray (1997) rightly points out, "there is a distinction between playing an active role within an authored environment and having authorship of the environment itself" (p. 152). In most cases, media participation and interactivity therefore take place within pre-established frameworks determined by producers and website developers, which delimit the degree of audience engagement to a pre-determined spectrum of choices.

In addition to offering opportunities for online interactivity, reality TV producers source many contestants and semi-professional performers from an audience pool at auditions staged across the country. These auditions are advertised in print media, as well as on television, radio, and websites, and they promise young recruits a slice of the "American dream," as highlighted below in CTV's promotional strategy. In the case of *Canadian Idol*, the format bible stipulates the selection of two groups: those with good singing voices and on-air presence, and those who can easily be ridiculed for the "humour" portion of the program. Producer John Brunton comments on auditions held in Ottawa during the 2004 season:

> There's 1,600 or 1,700 kids out there lining up and I will show the Canadian public what we've seen. . . . I can't necessarily tell you what that's going to be right now or what that mix will be or if we'll have as many eccentric singers coming back . . . There's an element of cineme verite [sic] in this experience. . . . There's a certain awe and lack of self-awareness that is entertaining. (quoted in Cheadle, 2004)

Regional producer Cousineau adds, "We are making a reality TV show and we want to show a range. People are either very good or good for TV, those in the middle don't make it" (as quoted in Winwood, 2004). The growing importance of casting agents in reality TV genres is therefore based on finding the right amateurs, who can be exploited for dramatic situations, comedy, and talent, as well as for the "star" transformation described above.

The ridicule of contestants is part of the original concept of *Idol* and, according to Cowell, is in rebellion against "the terrible political correctness that invaded America and England" (quoted in Carter, 2006, p. 189). However, this objective is not part of the open promotional strategy of *Idol*, which, on the contrary, fuels the hopes and dreams of applicants in recruitment statements such as the following:

> [E]nrich and develop a greater understanding for music and the music business . . . [M]eet music industry players and professionals . . . Meet fans who swarm outside every studio screaming for your autograph . . . Make numerous public appearances in front of thousands of adoring fans. (CTV, 2006c)

Contestants have to be between 16 and 28 years of age, representative of the target demographic of the program. As part of the auditioning process, contestants sign a release form, by which they waive copyright to their performance, moral rights, and integrity rights, as well as personality and privacy rights (CTV, 2006a). Contestants sign their rights to their audition, performance, and program contribution over to the producers, who are entitled to exploit (and license others to use and exploit) such contributions in all media and formats (CTV, 2006a). In addition, producers set the framework for online interactivity with the following stipulation:

> As part of Competitors' contribution to the Program, the Producer may request Competitors to participate in additional activities relating to the Program including without limitation web-casts, pod-casts, blogs, video diaries, chat rooms, SMS chats, as well as various interviews, appearances, promotional, publicity, sponsorship and merchandising activities in any and all media. (CTV, 2006b)

As a result, each contestant has to relate personal experiences through blogs on the show's website. Similarly to *Top Model*, the program also invites viewers to respond and comment via the *Idol* chatroom.

A study about public participation in television programming in the UK reveals that producers generally seek informed consent from participants, but that "[production] pressures will almost inevitably result in some producers behaving less honourably than they should with contributors" (Hibberd, Kilborn, McNair, Marriott & Schlesinger, 2000, p. 67). The authors of the study recognize that public participation in reality programs is an important industry strategy for reducing production costs, even though participants may suffer the consequences of on-air ridicule for years to come. They recommend stringent guidelines for contracting "semi-professional" on-air personalities and propose that informed consent should be based on participants' understanding of a program's format, objectives, and aims.

This is especially important considering the age group that *Idol* targets for recruitment. Questions about ethics are also relevant in light of recent revelations that participants in programs such as *Paradise Hotel* (Ringbakk, 2003), *Real World* (Murray & Bunim, 1992), and *Joe Millionaire* (Cowan & Michenaud, 2003) are frequently provided with free alcohol to manipulate the story plot for comedic effect (Fletcher, 2006).[7]

To summarize, audience interactivity and viewer participation need to be placed within the context of reality TV production processes. In particular, the staging of media events in the form of auditions highlights how the genres have shifted the focus to audience members as a cheap labour pool for program development. Indeed in 2007, over 50 casting calls for semi-professional performers could be accessed on Internet sites such as jobsearch.about.com. The sites also advise on how to audition for reality TV shows on all the major networks, such as NBC, CBS, Fox, ABC, and MTV, as well as smaller ones such as CW, Bravo, SciFi, TLC, VH1, HGTV, and the Food Network (Reality TV World, 2007).

As discussed, stringent contractual agreements curtail audience participation in reality formats such as *Idol*. Consequently, the notion that reality TV programs are "fostering interactive participation in social spaces, releasing everyday voices into the public sphere and challenging established paternalism" (quoted in Dovey, 2000, pp. 83–4) has to be reviewed in light of a specific production context that has a significant impact on content development and program (inter)activities. As this analysis has shown, interactivity is built into reality formats intentionally to increase profit margins through text messaging, enhanced character identification, and immersion in virtual communities (as in the case of *Canadian Idol's* online chatrooms), in which commercial products are often key in resolving the narrative arc. Format producers also extract "work" in the form of viewer creativity from their interactive engagement with media texts. Voting, texting, blogs, actual program participation, and so on augment the overall program format package and allow producers to sell the value-added product to additional markets for higher profits. And finally, the recruitment of semi-professional performers to "star" in reality formats is reflective of the production mandate: to maximize profits by minimizing labour protection.

Summary and Conclusion

Reality TV programs are characterized by their hybridized genres, which range from game-docs and soap-docs to variety contests. Placed within their production context of format franchising, franchises such as the *Idol* programs reveal how concepts are licensed for international markets and adapted to local audience preferences. These "glocalization" processes are based on collaboration between the owners of the program, the licensee, and the contracted production crew, who customize the program for local markets under the supervision of the original producers. In the case of *Canadian Idol*, the combination of the UK and US versions results in a glocalized franchise with the addition of Canadian "stories of change," contestants, and cultural references. The Canadian format therefore works primarily through references to and depictions of "local stories"—represented through contestants' performances and online blogs—national symbols, and cultural signifiers, which are superimposed onto the original template of the show. As discussed, these include using opening shots of historic Canadian sites, performing the national anthem as part of televised auditions, and staging media events, as well as a variety of online interactive elements.

A key difference between reality formats and many other television programs is their "built-in" cross-platform accessibility, which allows for enhanced audience interactivity, on the one hand, and additional revenue streams for producers, on the other. This audience interactivity follows pre-established modes through phone and/or text voting, which generates revenues for participating sponsors such as Cingular in the US and Bell Globemedia and Telus (for mobile phone content) in Canada. Online interactivity in the form of blogs and comments is rapidly becoming standardized across international markets, as are Web stores for wallpaper, ringtones, and *Idol* clothing (T-shirts, hats, et cetera). Due to its international success, *Idol* has become a prototype for the global format trade, especially where game-docs and talent shows are concerned. The popularity of *Idol* is also linked to its genre, the game-doc and talent contest, which appeals to interactive users familiar with peer-to-peer networks for exchanging music and with commentary in the form of blogs. Tie-ins to these formats are sponsors and advertisers, who migrate with the program's narratives across multiple platforms.

Reality TV programs emerged in response to changing industry conditions in the 1990s. Technological convergence, multichannel television, and increased competition provided the backdrop for an increase in reality format franchising. In addition, successful formats such as *Idol* set the bar for a new kind of program development, starting with the recruitment of voluntary participants. The continuing practice of sourcing semi-professionals from an audience pool is linked clearly to reducing program development costs, as well as to circumventing labour standards and union contracts. Yet the stringent contractual conditions under which contestants labour for format producers are not commonly known. On the contrary, "stories of transformation" and "success myths" distort this aspect of reality TV, amplified by the fact that contestants are obliged contractually not to disclose details of their experiences on the shows.

In analyzing a reality format such as *Idol*, it is important to understand the production processes that underlie the adaptation of an international franchise and its narrative development. Many of the key elements are standardized to ensure the successful glocalization of a format. From the basic concept to characters, the role of hosts, logos, sponsors, media events, website layout, and interactive components, licensors (such as Fremantle-Media) stipulate the degree to which a format can be adapted to a new market, yet remain recognizable as an international brand. As a result, reality TV formats reflect a new stage in the globalization of television, which is not defined primarily by programming flows, but by the trade of intellectual property and expertise. The fact that a program such as *Canadian Idol* is referred to as a "local program" by representatives from organizations as diverse as Our Public Airwaves (2006) and PricewaterhouseCoopers (2006)[8] highlights the importance of creating greater awareness of reality TV production processes and labour relations on production sets, as well as the broader context of the international format franchising trade.

Notes

1. According to Robertson (1992), "glocalization" relates to the creation of niche markets for globally distributed products and programs. It therefore represents the extension of international trade, economic networks, and labour.
2. *Canada's Next Top Model* (Manuel, 2006) is based on *America's Next Top Model* (Banks & Mok, 2004). The US has been lagging behind the UK in international format development, but is gaining recognition through formats such as *Top Model*, which has been adapted to 14 international markets. The Canadian format is produced by Temple Street Productions and airs on Citytv/CHUM and on the Living Channel in the UK.
3. This is especially the case with *Big Brother* in the UK, where webcam footage is transmitted over the Internet 24 hours a day, 7 days a week.
4. Most contestants on reality TV programs are contractually obliged to engage with viewers and interactive users online through blogs, chatrooms, video diaries, SMS chats, and podcasts.
5. *American Idol's* worth as a television franchise is estimated at US$2.5 billion. It generates US$500 million in TV advertising revenues, in addition to US$30 to

50 million in sponsorship deals (International Format Lawyers Association [IFLA], 2007).

6. The "bible" contains the "building blocks" for a reality format (plot; sample scripts; role of characters, contestants, and judges; camera and editing work; visual graphics; audience interactivity, et cetera) that ensure "recognizability" and limited copyright with format producers, but at the same time provide "adaptability" to localize a global concept to fit culturally defined audience preferences.
7. Contestants on *America's Next Top Model* have also been shown inebriated. In addition, the application for *Canada's Next Top Model* includes a questionnaire with questions such as "How do you act when you get drunk? . . . Do you get quiet, or are you wild?" (Citytv, 2006a).
8. *Canadian Idol* has also been placed in the same category as home-grown Canadian programs such as *Corner Gas* (Butt & Storey, 2004), *DaVinci's Inquest* (Haddock, 1998), and the *Royal Canadian Air Farce* (Rosemond, 1993).

References

Andrejevic, Mark. (2004). *Reality TV: The work of being watched.* Lanham, MD: Rowman & Littlefield Publishers.

Banks, T., & Mok, K. (Executive producers). (2004). *America's next top model* [Television series]. Los Angeles, CA: CW Network.

Banner, B., & Wagner, T. (Executive Producers). (1983). *Star search* [Television series]. Los Angeles, CA: CBS Television.

Baym, Nancy K. (2000). *Tune in, log on: Soaps, fandom, and online community.* Thousand Oaks, CA: Sage Publications.

Bowlby, B., & Brunton, J. (Executive producers). (2003). *Canadian idol* [Television series]. Toronto, ON: Canadian Television (CTV).

Butt, B., & Storey, D. (Executive Producers). (2004). *Corner gas* [Television series]. Toronto, ON: CTV.

Carter, Bill. (2006). *Desperate networks.* New York, NY: Doubleday Broadway Publishing Group.

Cheadle, B. (2004, 13 February). Audition numbers almost double as second *Canadian idol* opens door in Ottawa. *The National Post.* URL: http://www.canada.com/nationa/nationpost/news/artslife [29 April 2004].

Citytv. (2006). *Canada's next top model: Official website.* URL: http://www.citytv.com/cntm/ [30 November 2006].

———. (2006a). *Citytv presents Canada's next top model: Application rules—2005.* URL: http://www.citytv.com/cntm/ combined.1st.pdf [30 November 2006].

Corner, John. (2002). Performing the real: Documentary diversions. *Television & New Media, 3*(3), 255–68.

Cowan, C., & Michenaud, J.M. (Executive producers). (2003). *Joe millionaire* [Television series]. Beverly Hills, CA: Fox Broadcasting Company.

CTV. (2005). *Canadian idol rocks with star-studded finale as audience peaks at 3.8 million viewers.* URL: http://ctvmedia.ca/ idol05 [12 July 2006].

———. (2006). *Eye on idol: Idols live it up in their swank top 10 mansion.* URL: http://www.ctv.ca/servlet/ArticleNews/story/CTVNews/20060725/idol_mansion_20060725/20060726?s_name=idol2006&no_ads= [15 October 2006].

———. (2006a). *Canadian idol competition rules—2006.* URL: http://www.ctv.ca/servlet/ArticleNews/idol/CTVShows/20060202/idol_rules_regs [18 March 2006].

———. (2006b). *Competitors regional auditions—2006: Competitor's release form.* URL: http://www.ctv.ca/idol/gen2006/Home.html [18 March 2006].

———. (2006c). *Why audition for Canadian idol.* URL: http://www.ctv.ca/servlet/ArticleNews/idol/CTVShows/20060131/idol_why_audition/20060208 [20 October 2006].

———. (2007). *First-ever Canadian idol top 3 tour announced following biggest vote in series' history.* URL: http://www.ctv.ca/servlet/ArticleNews/story/CTVNews/20070911/idol_release_20070911/20070911?s_name=idol2007&no_ads= [15 October 2007].

Dederer, C. (2006, 19 March). More shameless pandering to that over-89 demographic. *The New York Times,* p. AR21.

Dovey, John (2000). *Freakshow: First person media and factual television.* London, UK: Pluto Press.

Dyer, Richard (1998). *Stars* (2nd edn). London, UK: BFI Publishing.

Edwards, I. (2003, 24 November). A year to remember . . . or maybe forget. *Playback Magazine,* p. 17.

Fletcher, H. (2006, 29 October). Drink up. It's not like you have lines to learn. *The New York Times,* p. AR32.

Foster, D. (2004). "Jump in the pool": The competitive culture of *Survivor* fan networks. In S. Holmes & D. Jermyn (Eds), *Understanding reality television* (pp. 270–89). London, UK: Routledge.

FremantleMedia. (2004). *About us: Profile.* URL: http://www.fremantlemedia.com/aboutus/ [18 July 2004].

FremantleMedia announces India, Malaysia, and Indonesia idol competitions. (2004a, March 29). URL: http://www.univox.com/writer/asiaidol.html [18 July 2004].

FremantleMedia. (2004b). *Programmes: Entertainment factual, idols.* URL: http://www.fremantlemedia.com/ourprogrammes/view/Global+Hit+Formats/ [18 July 2004].

———. (2006). *Global hit formats: Idols.* URL: http://www.fremantlemedia.com/our-programmes/view/Global+Hit+Formats/viewprogramme/Idols [16 September 2006].

Fuller, Simon. (Creator). (2001). *Pop idol* [Television series]. London, UK: FremantleMedia Licensing Worldwide.

———. (2002). *American idol: The search for a superstar* [Television series]. London, UK: FremantleMedia Licensing Worldwide.

Gay, O. (Executive producer). (1984). *Crimewatch* [Television series]. London, UK: BBC.

Gillis, C. (2003, 15 September). Ben Mulroney emerges as a star. *Maclean's Magazine.* http://www.canadianencyclopedia.ca/index.cfm?PgNm=TCE&Params=M1SEC761792 [9 June 2006].

Glynn, Kevin. (2000). *Tabloid culture.* London, UK: Duke University Press.

Graham, L. (Executive Producer). (1948). *The original amateur hour* [Television series]. New York: National Broadcasting Company (NBC).

Haddock, Chris. (Creator). (1998). *Da Vinci's inquest* [Television series]. Toronto, ON: Alliance Atlantis Communications.

Hearn, A. (2004, 19 April). *Idol* thoughts. *Toronto Star,* p. A17.

Heflin, L., & Klein, G. (Executive producers). (1988). *America's most wanted* [Television Series]. Beverly Hills, CA: Fox Network.

Hibberd, M., Kilborn, R., McNair, B., Marriott, S., & Schlesinger, P. (2000). *Consenting adults?* London, UK: Broadcasting Standards Commission.

Hill, Annette. (2005). *Reality TV: Audiences and popular factual television.* London, UK, & New York, NY: Routledge.

Holmes, Su. (2004). "All you've got to worry about is the task, having a cup of tea, and doing a bit of sunbathing": Approaching celebrity in *Big brother.* In S. Holmes & D. Jermyn (Eds), *Understanding reality television* (pp. 111–35). New York, NY: Routledge.

———. (2004a). "Reality goes pop!": Reality TV, popular music, and narratives of stardom in *pop idol. Television & New Media, 5*(2), 147–72.

International Format Lawyers Association (IFLA). (2007). *Value of television formats continues to grow despite legal uncertainty.* URL: http://www.ifla.tv/format.html [19 June 2007].

Jhally, Sut. (1987). *The codes of advertising: Fetishism and the political economy of meaning in consumer society.* London, UK: St. Martin's Press.

Kachkowski, A. (2004, 26 September). Theresa is no. 2 in *Canadian idol,* but no. 1 in Saskatoon. *The Ukrainian Weekly, 39*(LXXII). URL: http://www.ukrweekly.com/old/archive/2004/390430.shtml [15 July 2005].

Kibble-White, Jack. (2003). *Spiking the narrative.* Jack Kibble-White interviews David Bodycombe, Simon Goodman and Jerry Glover. Off the Telly/Interviews. URL: http://www.offthetelly.co.uk/interviews/ [12 January 2006].

Kilborn, Richard. (2003). *Staging the real: Factual programming in the age of* big brother. Manchester, UK & New York, NY: Manchester University Press.

Langley, J., & Barbour, M. (Producers). (1989). *Cops* [Television series]. Beverly Hills, CA: Fox Network.

Lawrence, B. (Host). (1957). *Tiny talent time* [Television series]. Hamilton, ON: CHCH-TV.

Le, Quynh. (2004, 15 July). Vietnam unsettled by *pop idol* contest. *BBC News.* URL: http://news.bbc.co.uk/2/hi/asia-pacific/3895265.stm [19 July 2004].

Lewis, J. (2004). The meaning of real life. In S. Murray & L. Ouellette (Eds), *Reality TV: Remaking television culture* (pp. 288–302). New York, NY: New York University Press.

Lysakowski, Mark. (2004, 29 April). Line producer. Insight Production. Toronto, ON: Personal communication.

Manuel, J. (Executive producer). (2006). *Canada's next top model* [Television series]. Toronto, ON: CHUM Television.

Mills, J. (Executive producer). (2000). *Castaway* [Television series]. London, UK: BBC.

Mulroney, Ben. (2004, 29 April). *Host: Canadian idol.* Vancouver BC: Personal communication.

Murray, Janet H. (1997). *Hamlet on the holodeck: The future of narrative in cyberspace.* Cambridge, MA: MIT Press.

Murray, J., & Bunim, M.B. (Executive producers). (1992). *Real world* [Television series]. New York, NY: MTV Networks.

Our Public Airwaves. (2006, 27 September). *Brief to CRTC on TV policy. CRTC Intervention Broadcasting Notice of Public Hearing CRTC 2006-5.* URL: http://www.publicairwaves.ca/index.php?page=1775&PHPSESSID=94e09c9 [9 June 2007].

PricewaterhouseCoopers. (2006). *Global entertainment and media outlook: 2006–2010.* URL: http://troy.lib.sfu.ca:80/record=b5113561a [2 February 2007].

Read, Nicholas (2004, 27 April). Contestants' minds filled with Idol thoughts. *The Vancouver Sun,* p. B1.

Reality TV World. (2007). *Recent show application news.* URL: http://www.realitytvworld.com/index/articles/newssection.php?x=ll4 [1 November 2007].

"Reality writer-anonymous." (2005). URL: http://www.wga.org/content/organizesub.aspx?id=1092 [9 September 2006].

Ringbakk, R. (Supervising producer). (2003). *Paradise hotel* [Television series]. Beverly Hills, CA: Fox Network.

Ritchie, J. (2000). *Big brother: The official unseen story.* London, UK: Channel Four Books.

Robertson, Roland. (1992). *Globalization: Social theory and global culture.* London, UK: Sage Publications.

Rojek, Chris. (2001). *Celebrity.* London, UK: Reaktion Books.

Rosemond, P. (Producer/Director/Writer). (1993). *Royal Canadian air farce* [Television series]. Toronto, ON: CBC.

S., Sarah. (2006, 3 July). *Andrea's blog.* URL: http://ca.blog.360.yahoo.com/blogej8HN8EwdaLwaU0ZNcaJpcUzPfH.nCftCw—?cq=1&p=196 [12 September 2006].

Scannell, Paddy. (2002). *Big brother* as a television event. *Television & New Media, 3*(3), 271–82.

Schmitt, D., Bisson, G., & Fey, C. (2005). *The global trade in television formats.* London, UK: Screen Digest Ltd and FRAPA with the support of the German Federal State of North Rhine-Westphalia.

Slocum, C. B. (2005). *The real history of reality TV or, how Alan Funt won the cold war.* URL: http://www.wga.org/organizesub.aspx?id=1099 [9 September 2006].

Television Research Partnership. (2002, October). *Interaction: Making money from interactive TV.* URL: http://www.trponline.co.uk [15 July 2005].

Telus & CTV. (2006, 22 June). *TELUS named official wireless sponsor of CTV's Canadian idol.* URL: http://www.ctv.ca/servlet/ArticleNews/story/CTVNews/20060622/Idol_media_20060622/20060622?s_name=idol2006&no_ads [15 September 2006].

Tilley, Steve. (2004, 22 April). Zapped by Zack here. *Edmonton Sun.* URL: http://www.ctv.ca/servlet/ArticleNews/show/CTVShows/20040422/CI2-20040422-Press/20040422/ [28 April 2004].

Turner, Graeme. (2004). *Understanding celebrity.* London, UK: Sage Publications.

USA Today. (2000). *"Survivor": Mark Burnett.* URL: http://www.usatoday.com/community/chat/0719burnett.htm [5 October 2006].

Wikipedia. (2006). *Idol series.* URL: http://en.wikipedia.org/wiki/Idol_series [19 November 2006].

Winwood, D. (2004, 23 April). Facing down the real judge. *Saint City News.* URL: http://www.ctv.ca/servlet/ArticleNews/show/CTVShows/20040423/CI2-20040423-Press/20040423/ [20 June 2004].

Wrigley, R., Powers, S., Green, C., & Jones, S. (Executive producers). (2000). *Big brother* [Television series]. London, UK: Channel 4 Television Corporation.

Laughing at Authority or Authorized Laughter?: Canadian News Parodies

Zoë Druick

In Canada, a nation with a television system closely bound to both American politics and American popular culture, news has fulfilled a particularly prominent role in the media landscape. As most Canadian news promotion emphasizes, Canadian news gives not only a view of Canada but, perhaps more importantly, a Canadian perspective on world affairs, inflecting, to use Mary Jane Miller's term, not only the genre of news but also perspectives on the American foreign policy that dominates its content.[1] The imagined Canadian nation is thus well accustomed to the idea of a peripheral perspective on disruptive, disastrous world affairs from the relative safety of the margins of both geopolitics and mediascape.

It is often noted that Canada has achieved some measure of success in sketch comedy in general and news parody in particular, and given television's nation-building role in this country, it seems like no coincidence. In this chapter, I argue that Canadian news parody has proved popular with comedians and audiences alike precisely because it lampoons a sober official discourse with close ties to nation-building on the one hand and American television on the other. The topic of news parody also raises larger questions about the meaning and transformation of televisual texts and genres. I consider the history of news parody as a spin-off of sketch comedy and look at how this genre developed in Canada in shows such as *SCTV*, *CODCO*, *This Hour Has 22 Minutes*, *Royal Canadian Air Farce*, *Double Exposure*, and *The Rick Mercer Report*.[2]

But, first, the news. Since the 1970s, the news has come under attack by media scholars for being a ritualistic exercise in presenting a limited view of reality filtered through the values that organize the rhythms of the visual journalism workplace.[3] The emphasis on binaries—for and against—the almost exclusive reliance on elites, the insistence on concision, and the integrating and ultimately reassuring presence of the news anchor, a trusted "supersubject," to use Margaret Morse's term, not to mention the close, even incestuous relationship between government and news reporting, are just some of the characteristics of television news highlighted by scholars.[4] Rather than distortions of the "real world," these parameters are intrinsic to the materialization of a cultural discourse about the world known as the news.

As all-news channels proliferate, news has sustained itself as one of the most iconic forms of television. Although assigned a privileged relationship to reality and politics, news and current affairs programming has long been affected by the storytelling conventions of entertainment programming—when it comes to televisual strategies, reality and fiction are not necessarily very far apart.[5] Today, along with a proliferation of news parodies, there have appeared a variety of hybrid genres of infotainment, including tabloid news, as well as more legitimate forms of the so-called new news.[6] Emerging in the 1990s, the new news displays a heavy reliance on visuals and a low emphasis on editorial content, much like a tabloid newspaper, and is seen to be targeted at a youth market accustomed to music videos and video games.[7]

In this chapter, I explore some of the ways in which humour is used in news parodies to bring about a rethinking of news as discourse, a topic imbricated with the theory of texts, or genre. Genre if most often defined in television studies as a basis for the industry's categorization of shows—a categorization used by producers and audiences alike.[8] According to this perspective, the television industry organizes audiences according to generic preference as a way of delivering coherent markets to advertisers. This analysis is no less pertinent for news. As news genres multiply, so do the divisions in the news audience.

News as Genre

Although the theory of genres as taxonomy has abundant uses in media studies, I propose that a Bakhtinian notion of genre is more effective for talking about the ongoing process of genre hybridization that is such an essential aspect of television.[9] For Mikhail Bakhtin, a twentieth-century Russian literary theorist, genre represents not just a type of speech but also an essential site of creative expression. According to Bakhtin, all utterances are inevitably responses to previous utterances, a phenomenon that implicates all speech, and therefore all culture and individual psychology, both of which are mediated by signs, in social relations of power.[10] Bakhtin uses the concept of genre, or what he calls "speech genre," to think about expression as a site for social and historical struggle, neither the purview of a dominating system nor a realm of unconstrained creative freedom.[11] As in the dominant notion of genre as taxonomy, speech genres also provide the shared reference points for speakers, listeners, and, by implication, industries involved in the production of media products. This expanded and socially embedded concept of genre introduces a social and historical layer of mediation to all signification. For Bakhtin, "dialogism" is another word for the many voices—social, institutional, and individual—involved in genres. Each utterance, wrote Bakhtin, "is filled with dialogic overtones."[12] These two key concepts, dialogism, or the connection of each utterance to a linguistically mediated social field, and genre as the particular weave of time and space produced by the rules organizing cultural expression, were further elaborated by Julia Kristeva with her development of the concept of "intertextuality."[13]

Humour is a pointed example of dialogism. According to Jerry Palmer, some of the key work of humour is the creative juxtaposition of unlikely terms—repetition that includes difference—not unlike a good metaphor or a parody, and in this sense, humour is a telling example of a multi-voiced discourse.[14] Some of the key work of humour is to make the predictable unpredictable, to defamiliarize the everyday.[15] In new parodies, exactly such an operation occurs: the predictable text signalled by the iconic news set and the stentorian voice and serious demeanour or the anchor is made strange by replacing one of the terms of the news speech genre. If the prevailing news scenario combines a sober-looking person with serious discourse to produce a trusted news source, news mockery needs to replace at least one term to subvert the expectation of the speech genre: silly person delivering serious news; silly person delivering silly news; serious person delivering silly news. Arguably, this mockery implies a dialogue between audience, authority, and comic utterance.

Some clarification should be given on the terms "parody" and "satire." Parody is a double-voiced discourse and as such addresses a sophisticated reader or viewer expected to decode multiple texts in dialogic relation. Parody is, then, by nature a self-reflexive textual manoeuvre. Satire, by contrast, is a commentary not on a text but on the social world. Where parody is a discourse on texts, satire is a discourse on things.[16] Be that as it may, "Satirists choose to use parodies of the most familiar of texts as the vehicle for their satire in order to add to the initial impact and to reinforce the ironic contrast."[17] As a result, satires often use texts as metonyms of the aspects of the social world most deserving of comment. It follows that the objective to satirize the political process, or public discourse on national or international affairs, would choose to parody the vehicle of the news (a similar move has appeared in documentary with the advent of the "mockumentary").[18] As a reality-based speech genre most closely associated with the performance of official positions on topics of social and political import, the news makes a legitimate target for satiric parody.

To deliver the news, the anchor must occupy, in terms of speech, dress, and demeanour, "a zero-degree of deviation from the norm."[19] The anchor's ability to utter legitimate discourse is therefore a tempting starting place for disrupting the chain of normative utterances associated with news. Palmer argues that humour is the process of disturbing "normal usage," of "constructing absurd actants" of statement and/or utterance.[20] In the best cases, this construction can spark in the audience a critical re-assessment—or confirmation—of some alternative vision of reality. "The butt of the absurd," writes Palmer, "is always, inherently, a feature of the real social world in some form or other."[21] Because parody has a parasitic relation to previous texts, its power is often described as limited. "Parody's transgressions ultimately remain authorized—authorized by the very norm it seeks to subvert," writes Linda Hutcheon. "Even in mocking, parody reinforces; in formal terms, it inscribes the mocked conventions onto itself. Thereby guaranteeing their continued existence."[22] Yet the dialogism of all absurdity against an implicit norm presumes a tacitly critical position.

Of course, humour need not be political. In Freud's terms, joke-work is similar to dream-work. Both deal with transgressions of taboos and the play of the unconscious through doubled meanings and a non-logical both/and—what Kristeva calls a double- or dia-logic.[23] For this reason, Palmer argues, much humour, like the unconscious mind itself, is childish, in the sense of playing with rather than by the rules. "What the childish mind demands, what the pleasure principle demands, is the play of the signifier, and this play of the signifier is repressed by the reality principle just as are the other primary processes. Thus the focal point in this process, the point at which subversion occurs in all forms of comic utterance, is the relation of denotation."[24] Humour in all its forms, then, uses surprise to mobilize an absurd logic that contravenes normal logic and asserts instead a playful logic of subversive reversal where each statement is pregnant with its opposite.

News as genre, in the Bakhtinian sense, invites a reading of news parody as an intertext that calls upon the audience both to reflect on the production of television news and, potentially, to question the authority of the news as the official television discourse of the "real."[25] However, there are many ways, with a variety of effects, to engage with the news genre. For example, the double-voiced discourse about the news can become a commentary on television itself. Alternatively, the use of the news idiom can be an attempt to displace the "real" news by a parodic version. In the case of a successful news parody, not only will the parodic text demonstrate its own implausibility, but by troubling the equation between form and content, it will also imply the tenuousness of all news discourse as a genre with limited ability to represent or explain the world. As we will see, however, most news parody doesn't go much further than bringing about surprising, and preferably silly, end to the news syllogism.

Sketch Comedy and the Parodic Newscast

The beginnings of such reversals and absurdities in television about television date from the late 1960s and early 1970s. In his analysis of the ponderance of parody in 1970s American cinema, John G. Cawelti attributed this phenomenon to what he described as the "tendency of genres to exhaust themselves, to our growing historical awareness of modern popular culture, and finally, to the decline of the underlying mythology on which tradition genres have been based."[26] He noted that genres have life cycles, from articulation and discovery to conscious self-awareness on the part of creators and audiences to a moment when conventions become tired and predictable, when "parodic and satiric treatments proliferate and new genres gradually arise."[27] By the 1970s, many classic popular forms were, according to Cawelti, exhausted. Cawelti's prescient analysis of the increasing preponderance of self-reflexive, double-voiced media, not to mention the connection between the exhaustion both of genres and of their founding mythologies, adds an important dimension to the notion of genre put forward by Bakhtin.

British youth-oriented, anarchic sketch comedy shows such as *That Was the Week That Was*, or *TW3* (BBC, 1962–63), *The Ronnies* (BBC-1, 1971–87), and especially *Monty Python's Flying Circus* (BBC, 1969–74) satirized social mores and parodied dominant cultural forms. As media about mass culture, they represented some of the first examples of widespread televisual self-reflexivity. One of the targets of this genre was television itself as a sign of all that was authoritative, over-rehearsed, and serious. In the US, with notable exceptions such as *Rowan and Martin's Laugh In* (George Schlatter–Ed Friendly Productions/ Romart, NBC, 1968–73), sketch comedy was overshadowed by a strong industry system that favoured building situation comedies around stand-up comedians. Late-night celebrity talk shows, beginning with *The Tonight Show* (NBC, 1954–), were genres for commenting on and participating in popular culture, and not only became more self-reflexive over time but also served as one of the templates for television itself: people chatting in front of a studio audience on a set resembling a living room.

In terms of the mocking of news, *Saturday Night Live* (NBC, 1975), produced by Canadian Lorne Michaels, and *SCTV*, which ran on two Canadian networks (Global, 1978–89; CBC, 1980–81) before being picked up to run after *Saturday Night Live* by NBC (1981–83), both featured a range of self-parodying skits about television and popular culture.[28] *SCTV* was built around the antics and products of the television station in the fictional town of Melonville. Unlike *SNL*, which broadcast from New York City and strove to achieve quintessential downtown comedy, *SCTV* mocked its Canadian provenance by making fun of small-town television.

SCTV's newscasters were Earl Camembert and Floyd Robertson, loosely based on Earl Cameron, affectionately known as Mr CBC News for anchoring the flagship CBC show *The National* from 1959 to 1966, and Lloyd Robertson, a CBC journalist who moved to CTV to anchor its national news in 1976 and is still the anchor there.[29] On the *SCTV* news sketch, Camembert, played by Eugene Levy, and Robertson, played by Joe Flaherty, were often distracted from their roles as local and national newscasters, respectively, by their interpersonal relationship and underlying rivalry. In one sketch from 1981, Robertson, returning from an absence prompted by an attempt to control his drinking, reports disinterestedly on a massive May Day parade in Melonville. Using footage obviously taken from postwar Soviet newsreels, the appearance of this event in North America is ludicrous—impossible. By contrast to Robertson's disengagement, Camembert wants to discuss how shocking it is that this many communists are active in town, but Robertson ignores him. The encounter underscores the falsity of most banter between anchors. Here, Camembert is expressing true shock, rather than the banal chat we expect from newscasters. Robertson's refusal to respond highlights the degree to which this "dialogue" is usually inauthentic.

A second, almost incidental comment on the news is made in this sketch by the reversal of expectations. The Soviet May Day Parade was an annual event. Where most planned state events like this would be precisely the kind of thing that the news would be called upon to report, Camembert's shock at the overrunning of Melonville by communists ruptures the collusion between news and the state that we are used to and thus has the potential to defamiliarize the news. Despite the improbability of a May Day parade in North America, the news is recast as a genre in which personal emotions and relationships figure more prominently than reference to external events. Robertson's refusal, as be battles his inner demons, to banter with the eternally sunny Camembert is the emotional core of the sketch.

Chronologically speaking, the next important sketch comedy show on Canadian television was *CODCO* (Salter Street Films/CBC, 1988–93), built around the antics of a theatre group from Newfoundland. The troupe's work was originally based on its members' background in live performance but increasingly came to utilize and lampoon the conventions of television itself. Typical, perhaps, of Canadian culture formed in the 1970s and 1980s, the target of many *CODCO* satirical sketches was American image politics and media. Routines about Ronald Reagan's failing intelligence, American celebrity-watching shows such as *Entertainment Tonight*, and parodies of *Dynasty* were common fare. Sketches about Canadian culture, by contrast, tended to be located in the St. John's context, with particular emphasis on scathing satires of the church—the most extreme of which, "Pleasant Irish Priests in Conversation," was censored by the CBC and led to the indignant resignation of founding member Andy Jones—and small-town rebels. Although "House of Budgell" was ostensibly a parody of soaps like *EastEnders*, the target of its humour was at times no more cutting than a subtle rumination on the vagaries of aging.

CODCO included an ongoing parody of US news, generically titled "American News," in which the complicity of news with dominant ideologies was emphasized. In one piece on terrorism in the Middle East, newscaster Dawn Day, played with impeccable superficiality by Tommy Sexton, parodies both the inscription of gendered roles in newscasting and American insularity: "Dan, when is it going to end, this bizarre, frightening behaviour . . . these acts of terrorism for no apparent reason that we as Americans can comprehend?"[30] By inhabiting and exaggerating the noncritical and jingoistic aspect of American news, the comedians were able to highlight the complicity of news with dominant ideologies.

Cast member Greg Malone developed an imitation of Barbara Frum, at the time a very well-known Canadian news media personality. Her show, *The Journal* (CBC, 1982–92), a current affairs show that aired after *The National*, was renamed *The Jugular*, and Malone encapsulated her characteristically unsympathetic interviewing style with the catch phrase "Are you bitter?" which was asked of everyone who appeared on the show, including, absurdly, a weather system (14 September 1989). Much of the humour in *CODCO*, as well as in *Monty Python* and *Kids in the Hall* (CBC, 1988–94), for that matter, came from male cross-dressing such as this. So not only her catch phrase, but also her big hair and shoulder pads were part of the creation of Frum as an absurd actant.

One of the troupe's most biting news parodies appears on the video *CODCO Uncensored* (1995). Titled "News Breakdown," the sketch builds up the usual expectation for news, a serious set and a serious topic, presented by a sober-looking anchor; the subversion occurs with the mode of expression. The sketch consists of Malone dressed as a well-coiffed male anchor seated behind a desk in front of a map of the world, the most basic setup of the news genre. He gives a report of a typical topic for the news, a recent summit on AIDS in Africa. However, with a straight face, Malone describes the conference, "Blaming Africa for AIDS," in a racist doggerel that ostensibly unearths the unspeakable subtexts of colonialism, economic exploitation, and anal sex subtending the AIDS crisis. The American delegation is quoted as saying: "It's all your fault. It's all your fault. Nah nah nah nah nah nah. You're black, you're black, take your dirty bugs back. You're screwing green monkeys and giving it to our junkies. We give you all our foreign aid, and all we gets back is AIDS, AIDS, AIDS."

This combination of implausible speech and a news context makes for the shocking difference necessary for humour and parody. Rather than focus on sending up Canadian news personalities, the piece succeeds in being a satire of north–south relations that teeters on the edge of offensiveness. Malone's phrase "all we *gets back* is AIDS, AIDS, AIDS" also signals the show's Newfoundland origins, which further distances it from official mainstream Canadian diction. "In order to produce laughter," writes Palmer, "[comedy] must be genuinely surprising, and preferably a little shocking: the contradiction of discursively defused expectations must be as sharp as it possibly can be. But if the shock is too great, it risks either (or both) giving offense or creating embarrassment."[31] With sketches such as this, I believe that *CODCO* treaded the line between humour and offence more dangerously than any other Canadian comedy show.

In 1993, *CODCO* cast members Mary Walsh and Cathy Jones were joined by Greg Tomey and Rick Mercer to create *This Hour Has 22 Minutes* (Salter Street Films/CBC, 1993–). Unlike earlier sketch comedies such as *SNL*, *SCTV*, and even *CODCO*, which incorporated the occasional news parody into an overall variety format taken from their evolution as stage shows, *This Hour* made television its focus and integrated a wide array of sketches into an overall news format. This reversal has a number of significant implications. First and foremost is the indication of an entrenched self-reflexivity relying on television itself as a source.[32] This reliance is signalled in the title of the show, which makes direct reference to an earlier CBC show, *This Hour Has Seven Days* (CBC, 1963–66), as well as indicating the number of content minutes in a typical half-hour television show.[33]

The performers appear at different points throughout the show, including at the beginning and the end, at a highly iconic news desk, to the accompaniment of percussive "news" music. The camera work, zooming in from the audience to the "news" presenters, connects the conventions of TV news with other studio set genres, such as the variety show and the late-night talk show. The show ultimately undercuts the news by combining a highly conventionalized reporting style, in which an anchor is framed in medium close-up behind a desk with a number of monitors behind him or her and next to a video insert, with humorous juxtapositions in order to make a comment on either a major current event, the absurdity of some minor news footage, or something completely unrelated to news. In any of the three cases, the show's format allows for the dialogic connection between unlikely or surprising elements. In one sketch from 1997, a story that starts off talking about finance minister Paul Martin's austerity cuts and comparing the Canadian economy to that of Australia ends up showing a group of Australian consumers stripped of their clothes—the result of austerity measures. The story doesn't go where political reporting usually goes. Instead, we are presented with a surprise ending, nudity that would never be shown on the news, which has the ancillary effect or destabilizing the news by showing how conventional its stories usually are.

In a trope borrowed from investigative journalism and stalkarazzi tabloid reporting, as the 1990s wore on the *22 Minutes* trademark became the ambushing of politicians in media scrums by outlandish fake journalists, such as Marg, Princess Warrior, a bespectacled, middle-aged version of Xena played by Mary Walsh, and Marge Delahunty, her dowdy auntie counterpart. In these ambushes, *22 Minutes* became part of the spectacle of television news production in Canada, drawing attention to its reliance on media routines and the good behaviour of "real" journalists. Marg's excessive behaviour, which often included planting kisses on the cheeks of provincial leaders and telling them how cute and lovable they were, allowed her to skewer their political and economic policies in an era of expanding neoliberalism.

As the show became more and more well-known through the 1990s, however, the ambushes diminished and politicians became co-operative participants on the show, goofing around with the cast in a variety of situations. Prime Minister Jean Chrétien shared a burger at Wendy's with Rick Mercer, shared golf tips with Marg Delahunty, and sprayed breath freshener at Greg Thomey after the Vancouver APEC Conference pepper spray controversy. Although these examples served to highlight issues in the news, they played mostly on personality and the show was accused of providing promotion rather than satire of the Canadian media and political establishment.[34] Still, many saw the show as an important social commentary, and through the 1990s, its ratings remained high, approximately 2.5 million per week for the show and its rebroadcasts.[35]

More recently, *This Hour* has spun off into an occasional series, *Talking to Americans* (2001)—which drew 2.7 million, the highest audience for a TV comedy broadcast on the CBC—and *The Rick Mercer Report* (2004). *Rick Mercer* continues the same mix of commentary on news coverage and bantering with public figures seen in *This Hour* but adds a new commitment to cross-Canada road pieces where Mercer spends time with ordinary folks, such as university students and soldiers, as well as public figures, in different parts of Canada.[36] Doing away with the team of anchors, Mercer, a white man, has greater potential to parody the singular, monologic news host or pundit. However, he tends not to send himself up so much as to use the news desk as a platform to make fun of politicians.

Following on the success of *This Hour,* the CBC moved two shows from radio to television in the 1990s, both of which have been huge hits: *Royal Canadian Air Farce* (CBC, 1993–) and *Double Exposure* (CBC, 1994–96; CTV/Comedy Network, 1997–). At the peak of its popularity, *Air Farce,* a sketch comedy show with an emphasis on political satire that makes regular use of news as a motif, was drawing up to 2.5 million viewers per week.[37] The emphasis of the news sketches is usually, as in *SCTV,* the inappropriate language, class, or emotional expressions of the anchors, including relationships between the presenters—in short, the subversion of the news genre. Recent examples have included presenters reading the news from a trailer park, wearing rain gear and speaking in Newfoundland accents, and a male news reader making direct sexist attacks on a female presenter (*Royal Canadian Air Farce, 4x4,* 2003). In each of these examples, a surprising substitution is made in the news syntagm, but arguably these differences serve to reinforce the rightness of the "real" news by contrast.

Air Farce has also been home to a long-running gag about Peter Mansbridge, *The National's* anchor, that pokes fun at the self-important attitude of the new Mr CBC News, as well as his physical features, such as pursed lips and bald head. This sketch is more or less along the lines of *Air Farce's* political satires, which usually consist of broad imitations of well-known Canadian politicians, especially the prime minister and the leaders of the other political parties. As with all double-voiced discourses, it is hard to know the degree to which this mimicry destabilizes the authority of the original or merely provides a relief valve for authorized laughing at authority. This ambiguity became especially marked as politicians such as Jean Charest, Preston Manning, Joe Clark, Deborah Gray, Mike Harris, Jean Chrétien, and Sheila Copps began to appear regularly on the show's annual New Year's Eve specials.[38]

Double Exposure, which is composed by dubbing in silly soundtracks over video images of news events, particularly the pseudo-events of the news conference or the ceremonial meeting of leaders, as well as the imitation of politicians, news readers, and other public figures, raises a similar question of effectivity. In satirizing the official culture of politics and news through the addition of usually puerile countertexts about sex and other material equally inappropriate for the public sphere, the show laughs at official culture without establishing any kind of sophisticated critique.

The Newsroom (CBC, 1996–97, 2002, 2004–05), one of only a few successful situation comedies in Canadian television history, deserves mention for its self-reflexive parodic satire of Canadian news media. Written by, directed, and starring Ken Finkleman, the show is a behind-the-scenes satire of the people who produce and read the news. Using the CBC building in Toronto as its set and constantly referencing the Canadian media elite, as well as featuring cameos by Canadian pundits such as Linda McQuaig and Naomi Klein, the show travesties the sobriety assumed to be part of the news production process, highlighting the ratings-grabbing choices behind the decisions to air particularly sensationalist stories. In a newsroom composed of a particularly disaffected group of producers, a vain and superficial news reader, and, running it all, a dangerously myopic and self-obsessed producer whose main concerns are the prestige of his parking spot, the flavour of his muffins, and his ability to seduce young women, the show takes cruel pleasure in demonstrating the mundane concerns of the people behind television's most important contribution to democracy.

Conclusions: The Sorry State of Canadian Satire

I've addressed the Canadian aspect of these popular and increasingly omnipresent comedies about news and, by extension, self-reflexive humour about television. By way of conclusion, I want to also consider them in relation to two related non-Canadian shows, the BBC's *Spitting Image* (1984–92) and Comedy Central's *The Daily Show* (1996–). In a recent article on *Spitting Image* Ulrike H. Meinhof and Jonathan Smith point out that the show was equally a satire of British politics and a parody of British television. "*Spitting Image*'s entertainment valve surely derived from the way it pointed up and made play with the things we already half-knew about television itself, and about the ways in which, perhaps increasingly, television programmes are conceived and watched."[39] Using life-size latex puppets to caricature well-known public figures, the show achieved mimetic status of both humans and television genres. By substituting the infinitely malleable puppet signifier for the human referent, the show was able to highlight the semiotic aspect of television, where images of people and events in the world stand in for—represent—those specific people and events while simultaneously representing general categories. The puppets allowed for the burlesque of human life. Placed in recognizable television formats, they also made a stinging critique of television and our reliance on it for knowledge about the public sphere.

Jason Mittell notes a similar process at work in animated series such as *The Simpsons*. "Though parodic conventions such as caricature and hyper-exaggeration that are typical of animation, *The Simpsons* forces us to question the codes of realism associated with live-action systems of representation."[40] It bears noting that both *The Simpsons* (20th Century Fox Film, 1989–) and *Family Guy* (20th Century Fox Film, 1999–) at times contain outrageous parodies of news that use the properties of animation to exceed what is possible in sketches with actors and arguably to import an intensely defamiliarizing experience to the news. As shows organized around the fictional worlds of their characters, however, their news parodies, no matter how intertextual, tend to be about lampooning the pomposity of the news itself rather than about commenting on particular real-world news stories.

When *The Daily Show* (Comedy Central, 1996–) was hosted by Craig Kilborn (1996–99), it ran along the lines similar to *Double Exposure*'s juvenile commentary on figures of authority or political scandals. Since it has been hosted by Jon Stewart (1999–), however, it has surpassed any previous news parody show. Currently, a million people watch *The Daily Show* on a regular basis and there has been a great deal of discussion about how it has filled the role of news for disaffected young people who no longer either watch the news or participate in the democratic process, such as it is.[41]

As with other news parodies, *The Daily Show* features a comedian—stand-up, not sketch—performing a dialogue between the genres of news and comedy. Unlike most other news parodies, however, *The Daily Show* is sufficiently timely, coming at the end of each day and even competing with 11 PM newscasts, to actually provide a specific rather than general rereading of the news. Stewart takes on a newscaster persona, sitting on a set in front of a live studio audience and relating to "field reporters" and experts through monitors even when they're in the studio and commenting ironically on news clips. As with *SCTV* and *Air Farce*, Stewart expresses emotional stakes inappropriate in the news genre, but unlike those shows, his comments are made in the spirit of deflating the real news' parasitic relationship with the government.

Jon Stewart also regularly features interviews on the show, which brings it closer to late-night talk show than parodic newscast. Politicians, writers, and pundits are regularly featured in this section of the show. In these pieces, Stewart's own liberal-left position is often clearly expressed, unlike the diffuse anti-authority or anti-everything position of much Canadian news comedy. Stewart's show does what news never does explicitly and most news parodies obscure: he takes a position, albeit mainly through the parodic satire of official news discourse. Stewart's following among the young, then, may well have to do not only with his parody of the news but also his political views, which are those that young voters and viewers are often sympathetic with.

In this increasing emphasis on comedic forms such as news parody rather than traditional forms of documentary or other sober attempts to intervene in public discourse, a popular left-wing politics, epitomized in the US by the practical-jokey style of someone like Michael Moore, has found a way to sidle onto mainstream TV. These cultural producers have heeded advice given by scholars such as Robert Stam that the left need not lecture to be heard: "An austere, super-egoish left that addresses its audience in moralistic terms—while advertising and mass culture speak to its deepest desires and fantasies—is theoretically and pragmatically handicapped."[42] Nevertheless, despite the fact that this dialogic form of humour does have the potential to introduce a different sort of logic into public discourse, restricting political opposition to the double-voiced or intertextual discourse of parody may well lead to a political and cultural dead end.

Even so, by contrast to the scathing mimesis of *Spitting Image* and the serious left-wing parody of Stewart's show, Canadian news parody has been quite timid. From the character-based skits of *SCTV* to the panparodic character of *This Hour* and its spin-offs, the equal-time parody of *Air Farce*, the facile mimicry of *Double Exposure*, and the cringe-worthy though hilarious navel gazing of *The Newsroom*, Canadian humour in the realm of news parody has actually been a fairly soft touch. The one show that did seem to pack a satirical punch was *CODCO*, which made power the unrelenting target of all its humour. But with the departure of Greg Malone and Andy Jones from TV projects in the early '90s and the untimely death of Tommy Sexton in 1994, the legacy was muted in *This Hour*.

Where the target of *CODCO*'s humour was often the media and politics in America and everyday life in Canada, *This Hour*, *Talking to Americans*, and *The Rick Mercer Report* tend to lampoon Canadian politics and media, as well as the everyday life, or at least everyday opinions, of Americans. Paradoxically, this shift has taken the edge off the satire. The change seems to have occurred as the *CODCO* troupe and its breakaway groups moved from their marginal position in Newfoundland toward Ontario, the centre of both Canadian media and Canadian politics. In *On Location*, Serra

Tinic argues that, because of their position on the margins of Canada, the creators of *This Hour* are able to construct a "counter-narrative" of the nation, a site of resistance to both central Canada and the United States.[43] Although the show's Newfoundland accent allows for subversive expressions, literal and figurative, unavailable to non-regional Canadians, the extent of the show's ultimate challenge to the national narrative is certainly debatable.

The preponderance of news comedies on the CBC in the 1990s may also point to specific policy and cultural contexts during this period. As the CBC was faced with massive cutbacks and the threat of privatization, the corporation and its supporters fought back by emphasizing the role of the public broadcaster as the voice of the nation. Many nationalist programs were made during this period, including *Canada: A People's History* and the *Heritage Minutes*, and a Canadianization of the corporation was undertaken. It bears consideration, then, that the creation of spaces for authorized dissent occurred at the very moment that legitimacy was being shored up by the broadcaster for its authoritative newscasts and other nation-building programming.

By that token, the presence of such shows on the public broadcaster also most likely muted their satire, as the CBC was then and continues to be under scrutiny for any sign of promoting the party in power.[44] The safest route for comics reliant on public funds is to apply the satire thinly and evenly across the political spectrum. Arguably, the less the comic news shows can be seen to take a particular position, the more they paradoxically reinforce the similar tropes of balance and objectivity upheld by the sober news. The non-subversive aspect of *This Hour* and *Air Farce* in particular was underscored when the CBC began airing the shows in rerun on Newsworld in 1996. Baton Broadcasting, which had just been awarded a licence for a comedy channel, contested this move, claiming that the shows did not belong on a news channel. The CBC argued that they operated like political cartoons and therefore had a place alongside the news. Said Slawko Klimkiw, head of Newsworld at the time, "We think a network like ours needs a place where people can sit back and laugh from time to time at the events that transpire around us."[45] But the regulatory body, the Canadian Radio-television and Telecommunications Commission, sided with the private broadcaster and disagreed, finding that the shows were not adequately related to politics to qualify as satire.[46]

The context of news comedy production in Canada, and the debates the shows have spawned, help highlight the role of genre as regulated social text and a site of a creative dialogue constrained by rules and, at times, industry and policy frameworks as well. Although intelligent and often highly amusing, these shows risk restricting political opposition to the double-voiced or intertextual discourse of parody, a parasitic relationship that ultimately reinforces the primacy and authority of news even while it brings authorized discourse into question. However, although news parody may provide nothing more than a safety valve for authorized laughter, its widespread presence, in the Canadian context and elsewhere, is at the very least an indication of an ongoing struggle over official forms of knowledge. Self-reflexive comedy such as news parody has become a particularly typical televisual form, which may well signal the exhaustion of the news and widespread disillusionment with its founding mythology about democratic deliberation and the promise of the electronic public sphere. This disillusionment deserves attention and can teach us something about the role of dialogic cultural forms, of which television is currently one of the most important, for negotiating both culture and politics.

Notes

1. Miller "Inflecting the Formula."
2. *The Kids in the Hall* (CBC, 1988–94), one of Canada's most successful sketch comedy shows, avoided news parody altogether.
3. Tumber, "Introduction."
4. Morse, "The Television News Personality."
5. Hogarth, *Documentary Television in Canada.*
6. Barkin, *American Television News;* Glynn, *Tabloid Culture.*
7. Glynn, *Tabloid Culture.*
8. Creeber, *The Television Genre Book;* Feuer, "Genre Study and Television"; Mittell, *Television and Genre;* Neale, *Genre and Hollywood.*
9. See, for example, Grant, *Film Genre: Reader III.*
10. Volosinov, *Marxism and the Philosophy of Language.*
11. Bakhtin, "The Problem of Speech Genres."
12. Bakhtin, "The Problem of Speech Genres," 92.
13. Although "intertextuality" is widely used to refer to the practice of quotation, its meaning as a translation of "dialogism" is much broader, encompassing the concept of speech genre outlined above. For more on the history of the use of the dialogic and intertextuality concept in media studies, see Zoë Druick, "Dialogic Absurdity: TV News Parody as a Critique of Genre," in *Television and New Media* (forthcoming).
14. Palmer, *The Logic of the Absurd,* 61; Hutcheon, *A Theory of Parody,* 33.
15. Palmer, *The Logic of the Absurd,* 46.
16. Dane, "Parody and Satire."
17. Hutcheon, *A Theory of Parody,* 57.
18. See Roscoe and Hight, *Faking It.*
19. Morse, "The Television News Personality," 57.
20. Palmer, *The Logic of the Absurd,* 218, 90.
21. Palmer, *The Logic of the Absurd,* 90.
22. Hutcheon, *A Theory of Parody,* 75
23. Allen, *Intertextuality,* 44; Freud, *Jokes and Their Relation to the Unconscious;* Kristeva, *The Kristeva Reader,* 42.
24. Palmer, *The Logic of the Absurd,* 221.
25. This gloss on genre connects it with another Bakhtinian concept, that of carnival (Bakhtin, *Rabelais and His World*). Space constraints force me to sideline that discussion in this context.
26. Cawelti, "*Chinatown* and Generic Transformation," 260.
27. Cawelti, "*Chinatown* and Generic Transformation," 260.
28. Although it is outside the parameters of this paper, I would note that one of the original writers for *Saturday Night Live* was Rosie Shuster, at the time Lorne Michaels's wife. Shuster was the daughter of Frank Shuster, one half of the earliest successful sketch comedy team in Canada, Wayne and Shuster (Durden-Smith, "Breaking Up America," 17).
29. Eugene Levy's parody was even mentioned in Cameron's obituary ("Mr. CBC News").
30. Cited in Peters, "From Salt Cod to Cod Filets," 15.
31. Palmer, *The Logic of the Absurd,* 140.
32. The show is produced by Geoff D'Eon, who took the job after working as executive producer of CBC Halifax's television news.
33. *This Hour Has Seven Days* (CBC, 1963–66) was a public affairs show in the form of a variety show. It combined filmed sequences with studio interviews, editorials from the hosts, skits, and even musical synopses of the week's events. The show had a satirical edge and courted controversy, and it was brought to a well-publicized end in 1966 when CBC management fired its young hosts, Patrick Watson and Laurier LaPierre.
34. Cobb, "Willing Victims." In one complex example, during the 2004 federal election, NDP candidate Ed Broadbent used a rap video produced by *This Hour* to promote his campaign (Pilieci, "Broadbent Gets Rapped").
35. In 2000, the *This Hour* team successfully inspired over one million people to sign an online petition supporting the idea of a referendum to force Stockwell Day to change his name to Doris. This gag petition came in the wake of the newly formed Canadian Alliance's attempt to install a model of direct democracy based on referenda supported by 3 per cent of the population, in order to bypass Parliament and the Supreme Court on contentious issues such as abortion and gun control ("Rick Mercer's Referendum"). The success of the absurd petition effectively put the issue to rest (Riley, "*This Hour Has 22 Minutes* Becomes Effective Opposition").
36. D. Grant Black has characterized Rick Mercer as the "Wayne Ronstad of comedy." (Black, "More Offence, Please").
37. Kellogg, "Year of the Farce."
38. Turbide and Ajello, "The Air Farce Is Flying High"; Canadian Press, "Old PMs Yuk It Up"; Honey, "Did You Hear the One about the *Air Farce?*"
39. Meinhof and Smith, "*Spitting Image,*" 60.
40. Mittell, "Cartoon Realism," 24.
41. McKain, "Not Necessarily Not the News"; Feldman, "The News about Comedy."
42. Stam, *Subversive Pleasures,* 238.
43. Tinic, *On Location,* 155, 151.
44. Rebecca Addelman has argued in an article in *The Walrus* that this can be attributed to a chilly climate produced by the omnipresent threat of litigation.
45. Atherton, "Newsworld Is Going for Laughs."
46. Zerbisias, "*Farce* and *This Hour* Ordered Off."

References

Addelman, Rebecca. "The Last Laugh: Why Canadian Satire Can't Measure Up to *Stewart* and *Colbert*." *The Walrus*, May 2007: 34–6.

Allen, Graham. *Intertextuality*. London: Routledge, 2000.

Atherton, Tony. "Newsworld Is Going for Laughs." *Calgary Herald*, 3 June 1996: C10.

Bakhtin, Mikhail M. *Rabelais and His World*. Bloomington: Indiana University Press, 1984.

———. "The Problem of Speech Genres." In *Speech Genres and Other Late Essays*, 60–102. Austin: University of Texas Press, 1986.

Barkin, Steve M. *American Television News: The Media Marketplace and the Public Interest*. Armonk, NY: M.E. Sharpe, 2003.

Black, D. Grant. "More Offence, Please." *Globe and Mail*, 6 October 2007: D15.

Canadian Press. "Old PMs Yuk It Up on New Year's Eve." *Calgary Herald*, 30 December 1998: C1.

Cawelti, John G. "*Chinatown* and Generic Transformation in Recent American Films." In *Film Genre Reader III*, edited by Barry Keith Grant, 243–61. Austin: University of Texas Press, 2003.

Cobb, Chris. "Willing Victims: Politicians Seem Eager to Be Mocked on *This Hour Has* 22 *Minutes*." *Halifax Daily News*, 10 December 1996: 35.

Coulter, Diane. "Yuk Yuk Canuck: Rick Mercer Takes a Poke at Our American Neighbours' Cultural Myopia." *St. John's Telegram*, 30 June 2001: E1.

Creeber, Glen, ed. *The Television Genre Book*. London: British Film Institute, 2000.

Dane, Joseph A. "Parody and Satire: A Theoretical Model." *Genre* 13 (1980): 145–59.

Druick, Zoë. "Dialogic Absurdity: TV News Parody as a Critique of Genre." *Television and New Media* 10(3) (forthcoming).

Durden-Smith, Jo. "Breaking Up America: How One Honorary and Six Real Canadians Create a Weekly Panic called *Saturday Night Live*." *The Canadian*, 29 May 1976: 16–18.

Feldman, Lauren. "The News about Comedy: Young Audiences, *The Daily Show* and Evolving Notions of Journalism." Paper presented at the annual meeting of the International Communication Association, New York, 2005: 1–29. www.allacademic.com/meta/p13125_index.html.Accessed 12 February 2008.

Feuer, Jane. "Genre Study and Television." In *Channels of Discourse Reassembled: Television and Contemporary Criticism*, 2nd edn, edited by Robert C. Allen, 138–60. Chapel Hill: University of North Carolina Press, 1992.

Fiske, John. *Television Culture*. London: Routledge, 1987.

Freud, Sigmund. *Jokes and Their Relation to the Unconscious*, Pelican Freud Library, Vol. 6. Translated by James Strachey. Harmondsworth, UK: Penguin, 1976.

Glynn, Kevin. *Tabloid Culture: Trash Taste, Popular Power, and the Transformation of American Television*. Durham, NC: Duke University Press, 2000.

Grant, Barry Keith, ed. *Film Genre Reader III*. Austin: University of Texas Press, 2003.

Hogarth, David. *Documentary Television in Canada: From National Public Service to Global Marketplace*. Montreal and Kingston: McGill-Queen's University Press, 2002.

Honey, Kim. "Did You Hear the One about the *Air Farce* on CBC?" *Globe and Mail*, 1 January 2002: A1, A4.

Hutcheon, Linda. *A Theory of Parody: The Teachings of Twentieth-Century Art Forms*. Urbana: University of Illinois Press, 1985.

———. "The Politics of Postmodern Parody." In *Intertextuality*, edited by Heinrich F. Plett, 225–36. Berlin: Walter de Gruyter, 1991.

Kellogg, Alan. "Year of the Farce: Pure Canadian Comedy Team Is at the Top of Its Form." *Edmonton Journal*, 16 May 1997: D10.

Kristeva, Julia. *The Kristeva Reader*, edited by T. Moi. New York: Columbia University Press, 1986.

McKay, John. "Canadian Comics Weighing in on Tuesday's U.S. Presidential Election." Canadian Press News Wire, 29 October 2004. Available at http://proquest.umi.com/pqdweb?did + 731907121&Fmt= 3 &clientld=3667&RQT =309&VName+PQD. Accessed 10 January 2008.

McKain, Aaron. "Not Necessarily Not the News: Gatekeeping, Remediation, and *The Daily Show*." *The Journal of American Culture* 28(4): 415–30.

Meinhof, Ulrike H., and Jonathan Smith. "*Spitting Image*: TV Genre and Intertextuality." In *Intertextuality and the Media: From Genre to Everyday Life*, edited by Ulrike H. Meinhof and Jonathan Smith, 43–60. Manchester: Manchester University Press, 2000.

Miller, Mary Jane. "Inflecting the Formula: The First Seasons of *Street Legal* and *L.A. Law*." In *The Beaver Bites Back? American Popular Culture in Canada*, edited by David H. Flaherty and Frank E. Manning, 104–22. Montreal and Kingston: McGill-Queen's University Press, 1993.

Mittell, Jason. "Cartoon Realism: Genre Mixing and the Cultural Life of *The Simpsons*." *The Velvet Light Trap* 47(Spring 2001): 15–28.

———. *Television and Genre: From Cop Shows to Cartoons in American Culture*. New York: Routledge, 2004.

Morse, Margaret. "The Television News Personality and Credibility: Reflections on the News in Transition." In *Studies in Entertainment: Critical Approaches to Mass Culture*, edited by Tania Modleski, 55–79. Bloomington: Indiana University Press, 1986.

"Mr. CBC News Set the Tone for a Generation." *Edmonton Journal*, 15 January 2005: E9.

Neale, Stephen. *Genre and Hollywood*. London: Routledge, 2000.

Palmer, Jerry. *The Logic of the Absurd: On Film and Television Comedy*. London: British Film Institute, 1987.

Peters, Helen. "From Salt Cod to Cod Filets." *Canadian Theatre Review* 64(Fall 1990): 13–17.
Pilieci, Vito. "Broadbent Gets Rapped in Final Debate." *Ottawa Citizen*, 25 June 2004: B3.
"Rick Mercer's Referendum: Hundreds of Thousands of Canadians Log on to the Internet to Support: Direct Democracy Demand Comes Back at Stockwell Day." *Halifax Daily News*, 17 November 2000: 47.
Riley, Susan. "*This Hour Has 22 Minutes* Becomes Effective Opposition." *StarPhoenix* (Saskatoon), 1 March 1997: C1.
Roscoe, Jane, and Craig Hight. *Faking It: Mock-documentary and the Subversion of Factuality*. Manchester: Manchester University Press, 2001.
Stam, Robert. *Subversive Pleasures*. Baltimore: Johns Hopkins University Press, 1989.
Tinic, Serra. *On Location: Canada's Television Industry in a Global Market*. Toronto: University of Toronto Press, 2005.
Tumber, Howard. "Introduction." In *News: A Reader*, edited by Howard Tumber, xv–xix. Oxford: Oxford University Press, 1999.
Turbide, Diane, and Robin Ajello. "The Air Farce Is Flying High." *Maclean's*, 26 February 1997: 52–4.
Volosinov, V.N. *Marxism and the Philosophy of Language*. New York: Semina Press, 1973.
Zerbisias, Antonia, "*Farce* and *This Hour* Ordered Off CBC Newsworld." *Toronto Star*, 7 March 1997: D14.

Filmography

CODCO: Uncensored (Salter Street Films, 1995)
This Hour Has 22 Minutes, Best of 1994–5; Best of 1996–7 (Salter Street Films)
Royal Canadian Air Farce, 4X4 (Air Farce Productions/CBC, 2003)
SCTV: Network 90, Vol. I (NBC, 1981)

The Daily Show: Discursive Integration and the Reinvention of Political Journalism

Geoffrey Baym

There appears to be a crisis in broadcast journalism. In quantitative terms, there is more of it than ever before, but many would suggest its quality has degraded in recent years. The once-authoritative nightly news has been fractured, replaced by a variety of programming strategies ranging from the latest version of network "news lite" to local news happy talk and 24-hour cable news punditry. In the increasingly competitive battle for market shares, some of the basic principles of good journalism—independence, inquiry, and verification—are often sacrificed to meet the demand for eye-catching content (Kovach & Rosenstiel, 1999). Driven by market pressures, the erosion of journalism-as-public-inquiry has only hastened in the post–September 11 environment, in which most commercial news media outlets aligned themselves soundly with the White House and the apparatus of state security (Hutcheson et al., 2004).

To complicate the matter, the public appears to be growing dissatisfied with its broadcast news alternatives. According to a 2002 Pew Research Center study, the audiences for most forms of television news fell considerably between 1993 and 2002, with the audience for nightly network news down 46 per cent, network news magazines down 54 per cent, local news down 26 per cent, and CNN down 28 per cent. Not surprisingly, the sharpest decline came among 18–24-year-olds, but the Pew data also reveal a generation gap across the ages. Among 18–29-year-olds, only 40 per cent reported watching television news at all in the previous day, a number that climbs to only 52 per cent among 30–49-year-olds. These trends come into greater focus in the Pew Center's 2004 study on election coverage. This study shows that even in the four years between the 2000 and 2004 presidential campaigns, 18–29-year-olds increasingly turned away from mainstream sources of broadcast news, with only 23 per cent saying they "regularly learn something" from network news (compared to 39 per cent in 2000), 29 per cent from local news (compared to 42 per cent in 2000), and 37 per cent from cable news (compared to 38 per cent in 2000). It would appear, then, that as the population ages, mainstream broadcast news faces a difficult future.

In the midst of this narrative of decline, however, young people are turning to another form of news and campaign information—late-night television and comedy shows. The 2004 Pew survey found that 21 per cent of people ages 18–29 say they regularly learn about news and politics from comedy shows such as *Saturday Night Live*, and 13 per cent report learning from late-night talk shows such as NBC's *Tonight Show* with Jay Leno and CBS's *Late Show* with David Letterman. Among the programs regularly cited as a rising source of political information is Comedy Central's mock news program *The Daily Show with Jon Stewart*. With the post–September 11 passing of ABC's *Politically Incorrect*, *The Daily Show* has risen to the cutting edge of the genre. Its unique blending of comedy, late-night entertainment, news, and public affairs discussion has resonated with a substantial audience. For the 2004 calendar year, Comedy Central estimates the nightly audience for the show's first run at 1.2 million people, with another 800,000 tuning in to one of the program's subsequent repeats (S. Albani, personal communication, 24 February 2005).

National Annenberg Election Survey (NAES) (2004) research has found that 40 per cent of the audience is between the ages of 18 and 29, but perhaps surprisingly, the show also attracts an older audience, with 27 per cent above the age of 44. The NAES data further reveal that the audience is more educated, follows the news more regularly, and is more politically knowledgeable than the general population.

The show's host, comedian Jon Stewart, and his co-producers label their work as "fake news," and insist that their agenda simply is "to make people laugh" (S. Albani, personal communication, 3 May 2004). The label of "fake" news has provided the primary frame for conversations about the show, both in popular and academic circles. That moniker, however, is problematic on two levels. For one, it fails to acknowledge the increasingly central role the show is playing in the domain of serious political communication. The program has won a Peabody Award and also was nominated as one of television's best newscasts by the TV Critics Association (CBC, 2004). At the start of the 2004 presidential campaign, *Newsday* named Stewart as the single most important newscaster in the country (Gay, 2004). Further, the show's nightly interview segment regularly features members of the national political, legislative, and journalistic establishment. Senator John Edwards chose *The Daily Show* as the media venue from which to announce his candidacy for the 2004 Democratic presidential nomination. Bill Moyers, the dean of American public service television news, may be correct in his assertion that "you simply can't understand American politics in the new millennium without *The Daily Show*" (PBS, 2003).

The label of "fake news" also has a deeper problem. Any notion of "fake" depends upon an equal conception of "real." Fake news necessitates assumptions about some kind of *authentic* or *legitimate* set of news practices, ideals that one rarely hears articulated or necessarily sees as evident today. In the absence of any codified set of professional guidelines, a standardized entrance examination, or a supervisory guild, news instead is defined and constrained by a set of cultural practices, informal and often implicit agreements about proper conduct, style, and form that today are in flux, increasingly multiple, debatable, and open for reconsideration. Thus, in his interview with Jon Stewart, Bill Moyers asks if *The Daily Show* is "an old form of comedy" or a "new kind of journalism" (PBS, 2003). The suspicion here is that it is both—something of the former and much of the latter. Seen against a backdrop of declining audiences, boundary contestation, and textual exploration (e.g., Bishop, 2004), *The Daily Show* can be understood as an experiment in the journalistic, one that this study will argue has much to teach us about the possibilities of political journalism in the twenty-first century.

To better understand these possibilities, this essay first locates *The Daily Show* within an evolving media environment defined by the forces of multiplicity, consolidation, and integration. It then turns to a textual analysis of the program itself, examining its coverage of the 2004 presidential campaign. Based on a daily review of the show from early May through election day, it offers a close reading of the three primary programmatic elements—the daily news segment, parody reports, and studio interviews—and then considers the implications for journalistic practice and political discourse. It concludes that *The Daily Show* can be better understood not as "fake news" but as an alternative journalism, one that uses satire to interrogate power, parody to critique contemporary news, and dialogue to enact a model of deliberative democracy.

The Daily Show is a product of emerging arrangements in the media environment, or what Neuman (1996) has called the "infrastructure" of political communication. We can identify three interrelated, yet distinct, structural transformations, developments on the levels of the technological, economic, and cultural, that are redrawing the boundaries of journalism and the public sphere (see also Bennett & Entman, 2001). In terms of technology, the continuing expansion of cable television and satellite delivery systems has resulted in an ever-increasing number of channels. Similarly, the speed at which information can be transmitted continues to increase. As we saw in the recent Iraq war, broadcasters now can transmit instantly from anywhere in the world. So too does the Internet provide nearly instantaneous global linkages not just to text, but to high-resolution images and video. At the same time, the emergence of hand-held and computer-based video and editing systems fundamentally is lowering the threshold to production, in terms of both required capital and technical skills. Together, these developments are creating an easily accessible and relatively unconstrainable information environment, expanding the boundaries of the public sphere to a "communicative space of infinite size" (McNair, 2000, p. 40).

Of course, the multiplication of media outlets has been countered by the consolidation of ownership (McChesney, 1999). Outside of the Internet, most distribution channels have become the province of a few giant media firms, including Viacom, which owns Comedy Central. Paralleling the trend toward technological convergence, Viacom and other media conglomerates are vertically and horizontally integrated, structured to share resources, personnel, and approaches to content across what were once distinct media outlets (see Murdock, 1990). Conglomeration has been accompanied by commodification, the reconceptualization of all media content not as public service but as products packaged for profit, and of the audience not as citizens but as consumers. At the same time, however, media companies are pursuing strategies of market segmentation, largely abandoning the one-size-fits-all model of earlier network programming in favour of narrowly targeted, demographic-based appeals (Gandy, 2001).

Finally, these trends have been complemented by the wider breakdown in contemporary culture of traditional boundaries and social structures. In an age of cultural diversity, the media environment has become defined by blurred borders. The metaphoric wall between the editorial and business sides of news has dissolved (Underwood, 1993), as have any clear distinctions between the public and private spheres, public affairs and popular culture, and information and entertainment (Bennett & Entman, 2001; Delli Carpini & Williams, 2001; McNair, 2000). Delli Carpini and Williams suggest that current media organization and practice both reflect and contribute to the obscuring of traditional boundaries as the divisions among media types, ownership, and, perhaps most important, genres become increasingly porous. They further suggest that the dissolution of such borders is in part a recognition of the arbitrary nature of those distinctions and a challenge to the structures of political and social power upon which those borders ultimately depend.

This is not simply the move toward "infotainment," although the fundamental blurring of news and entertainment—a conflation that cuts both ways—certainly is a constituent element. Rather, it is a more profound phenomenon of *discursive* integration, a way of speaking about, understanding, and acting within the world defined by the permeability of form and the fluidity of content. Discourses of news, politics, entertainment, and marketing have grown deeply inseparable; the languages and practices of each have lost their distinctiveness and are being melded into previously unimagined combinations. Although some may see this as a dangerous turn in the realm of political communication, it also can be seen as a rethinking of discursive styles and standards that may be opening spaces for significant innovation.

The Daily Show

The Daily Show is the epitome of such discursively integrated media. Its hybrid nature is evident from its opening moments. The show begins each night with a full-screen graphic of the date, an American flag, and the globe, accompanied by a music track serious in tone and suggestive of a network newscast. An unseen announcer then pronounces the date, followed by "From Comedy Central's world news headquarters in New York, this is *The Daily Show with Jon Stewart.*" The initial emphasis on the date borrows a technique from broadcast journalism that seeks textual authority through a claim to immediacy. The phrase "world news headquarters in New York" similarly contains obvious connotations, invoking the power and prestige of the New York–based national news. The connotation, however, quickly is complicated as the graphic gives way to a live camera shot that swings though the studio, a technique of fast motion more common to entertainment than to news. At the same time, the audio cuts to a decidedly more upbeat, rock-and-roll soundtrack, while the live studio audience cheers in the background.

From the start, then, the program interweaves at least two levels of discourse, borrowing equally from traditions of authoritative nightly news and the entertainment talk show. Although the opening may suggest that a discourse of entertainment supersedes a discourse of news, the two are placed not in binary opposition, but in complementary arrangements. The show functions as *both* entertainment *and* news, simultaneously pop culture and public affairs. Its format is built on the familiar structure of late-night talk shows such as Leno's *Tonight Show* and Letterman's *Late Show*, which move from the host's introductory monologue to sketch comedy and conclude with the desk-and-couch interviews with noted personalities (see Timberg, 2002). *The Daily Show* reworks each of these production elements, however, blending humour with a serious concern for current events in ways that render the program difficult to pigeon-hole. Its hybrid combinations defy simple generic taxonomies as well as reductionist labels such as "fake news." It undoubtedly is comedy—often entertaining and at times absurd—but it is also an informative examination of politics and media practices, as well as a forum for the discussion of substantive public affairs. This study now turns to an examination of each of these specific elements, arguing that *The Daily Show* invites us to reconsider journalistic conventions in an age of media multiplicity and discursive integration.

Interrogating Power

The first of the program's three major content elements—the satire news update—represents a significant development in the genre of comedic news, building on the introductory monologue common to the late-night talk show since the 1950s. Still readily apparent on shows such as Letterman and Leno, the host makes brief references to current events to set up a punchline. Although the politically oriented one-liner uses the news for its inspiration, its focus usually falls on the personal foibles and character flaws of the primary political actors (Niven et al., 2003). Thus, the late-night joke appears to contain little relevance to the sphere of policy and debate, what Bennett and Entman (2001) refer to as the *political* public sphere. *The Daily Show*'s approach also can be traced to the more complex style of fake news offered by *Saturday Night Live*'s "Weekend Update" segment, a feature on that program from its inception in the mid-1970s. There, one of the cast members plays the role of news anchor, seated at what appears to be a traditional television news set. The segment complicates the late-night monologue with the addition of visual elements, usually suggestive photographs or newspaper headlines placed in an over-the-shoulder graphic. The "anchor" offers a brief explanation of the image and then the punchline. Again, like the one-liners of late-night talk, the focus of the Weekend Update joke rarely falls on substantive political issues and often turns to the surreal to find its humour.

Both styles of comedic news present "stories" in a rapid-fire fashion, moving (as does most conventional television news) quickly between political references and jokes. This is a version of what

Postman (1986) has called the "now this" format of news, in which no topic is placed in wider context or receives elaboration. Instead, the anchor jumps from story to story, often placing back-to-back stories of wildly different content and significance. In television news, the effect is to reduce the importance of political information to a form of "trivial pursuit"—political information and knowledge become fodder for quiz shows and trivia games, containing little perceivable real-world importance or relevance. Both the talk show monologue and the fake news Weekend Update mimic this approach and thus further reduce any sense of engagement with or connection to the political public sphere. Comedic news so practised would appear to fall outside the frame of legitimate political discourse, and thus scholars of political communication often are surprised (and perhaps dismayed) when empirical studies reveal that, for many people, these forms have become influential sources of political information.

The Daily Show, however, while borrowing from these styles of "fake" news, offers a considerable advancement over them, more deeply melding approaches of news and comedy. To the standard comedic style, *The Daily Show* adds more elements common to news, including video clips, soundbites, and (as considered below) complete reporter packages. The satire news segment does at times focus on the trivial aspects of the political domain, but it more often tackles national and global issues of unquestioned significance. During the shows examined here, recurrent topics included American foreign policy and the Bush administration's war on terrorism, the occupation of Iraq and the Abu Ghraib torture scandal, the search for weapons of mass destruction and the failure of pre-war intelligence, and the presidential election campaigns of both candidates, including the party conventions and debates. In discussing such topics, *The Daily Show* forsakes the "now this" model, often providing single-issue coverage for as long as 8 minutes. The segment also places its topics in wider contexts, often providing background information and drawing historical linkages of the sort uncommon to television news.

Soundbites from the primary political actors provide the grist of the segment. Here the format is reminiscent of an earlier style of network news built around soundbites from lawmakers and other political actors (Baym, 2004). President Bush and his administration earn the main focus of the segment, but considerable attention also is paid to Senate hearings, Congressional debate, and press conferences with various governmental figures. This material is culled from C-SPAN, 24-hour cable news, and other readily available sources. The visuals are complemented with information gained from major newspapers such as the *New York Times*, *USA Today*, and the *Wall Street Journal*.

The Daily Show thus is enabled by the multiplicity and availability of news and information in a hypermediated era. Stewart acknowledges the point during the show's coverage of CIA Director George Tenet's resignation in early June: "Huge breaking news story," Stewart begins, "we're gonna get right to it, because you know when news breaks . . . we may not be the first people on the scene, but we've got televisions, we know what's going on" (6/3/04). Stewart's line appears on the surface to be self-deprecating humour, a reminder that the show refuses to take itself seriously. It also is significant commentary, however, on the volume of informational resources now publicly available and the decreasing role traditional news sources play in filtering the flow of information. It is possible, *The Daily Show* suggests, to construct a newscast simply by mining the raw material available on the average cable television system.

Drawing on live broadcast coverage of public statements and government proceedings, the content of *The Daily Show* resembles much of the mainstream news media. Empowered by the title of "fake news," however, *The Daily Show* routinely violates journalistic conventions in important ways. For one, while it covers the same raw material as does the mainstream news, its choices of soundbites turn contemporary conventions on their head. The unwritten rules of journalism define a good quote as a coherent statement of policy or attitude, ideally containing emotion or character and completed neatly in about 8 to 12 seconds. Professional journalists are trained to ignore long, rambling verbal presentations; quotes with poor grammar or misstatements; and soundbites with long pauses or any significant absence of verbal content. In the effort to package 8 seconds of speech, that which does not conform to conventional expectations is left on the proverbial cutting room floor. *The Daily Show*, however, mines those outtakes for a wealth of informative content.

Consider the coverage of Bush's statement following Tenet's resignation. ABC's *World News Tonight* offered the following soundbite from the president: "I told him I'm sorry he's leaving. He's done a superb job on behalf of the American people" (6/3/04). On the CBS *Evening News*, the only soundbite from Bush showed him proclaiming "He's strong, he's resolute, and I will miss him" (6/3/04). Here, however, is part of *The Daily Show's* selection:

> *Bush*: George Tenet is uh . . . is . . . a . . . the kind of public service, uh, servant, you like to work with. He has been a, a, um . . . a strong and able leader at the agency. He's been a, uh . . . he's been a strong leader in the war on terror. (6/3/04)

In their coverage of Bush's statement, the network newscasts hold to standard conventions, and in so doing reduce Bush's sloppy, pause-saturated speech to a tightly constructed set of words that suggest clarity of thought and purpose. *The Daily Show*, however, reveals a different aspect of Bush's statement, one that calls into question his focus and perhaps his sincerity. Both versions are "accurate" in the strict sense of the word, but each achieves a markedly different textual effect.

In rejecting the standard conventions of quote selection, *The Daily Show* achieves a critical distance that cannot be said of the networks. Mainstream journalism's reliance on predictable conventions can render it susceptible to manipulation by the professional speech writers and media handlers who seed public information with pre-scripted soundbites and spin (Jones, 1995; Underwood, 2001). The Bush administration, especially, has been remarkably adept at playing to journalistic conventions in ways that limit inquiry and encourage the news media to amplify the administration's rhetoric without critical challenge (Fritz et al., 2004). As "fake news," however, *The Daily Show* is not beholden to conventions that arguably have outlived their usefulness. *The Daily Show*'s refusal to abide by standard practices may offer a measure of resistance to manipulation, a counterbalance to the mutual embrace between press and politics.

A second convention *The Daily Show* freely rejects is the mainstream news media's insistence, at least in name, on a dispassionate observation that elides the journalist's subjectivity. If the insistence on objectivity too easily can become amplification, *The Daily Show* instead engages in subjective interrogation. Consider the treatment of the Bush statement quoted above. Here is how it appeared on air:

> *Bush*: George Tenet is uh . . . is . . . a . . .
>
> *Stewart*: Um, a convenient fall guy . . . um . . . liability to our intelligence operation.
>
> *Bush*: the kind of public service, uh, servant, you like to work with.
>
> *Stewart*: I was gonna say that, that was on the tip of my tongue.
>
> *Bush*: He has been a, a, um . . . a . . .
>
> *Stewart*: Uh, uh, an albatross around the neck of your administration, an albatross.
>
> *Bush*: a strong and able leader at the agency. He's been a, uh . . . he's been a . . .
>
> *Stewart*: He's been around too long. No, that's not it.
>
> *Bush*: been a strong leader in the war on terror.
>
> *Stewart*: No, that's not it. It's right here, I don't know what it is . . .

The humour lies in Stewart's interruptions, in his willingness to read Bush's statement against the grain and confront it with his own reactions and responses. Stewart's presentation is explicitly situated; he speaks with the voice, as Douglas (2003) has noted, of the "outraged individual who, comparing official pronouncements with his own basic common sense, simply cannot believe what he—and all of us—are expected to swallow." This kind of juxtaposition, between official pronouncements and Stewart's version of common sense, is the primary strategy of *The Daily Show*'s news updates. Juxtaposition also is a basic principle of the genre of political satire, which pits the "presumptions and pretensions of the politicians" against the "intuitions and instincts of the commonplace" (Street, 2001, p. 69). Like all satire, *The Daily Show* is *dialogic* in the Bakhtinian sense, the playing of multiple voices against each other in a discursive exchange that forces the original statement into revealing contexts (see Griffin, 1994).

One can see the strategy of dialogic confrontation in a lengthy but revealing example from the July 13 program. The day after the Senate had released its report documenting the breakdown in the pre-war intelligence, Bush gave a 32-minute speech addressing the war in Iraq in which, as Stewart notes, he "used a particular phrase eight times." This exchange then follows:

> *Bush*: Because America and our coalition helped to end the violent regime of Saddam Hussein, and because we're helping to raise a peaceful democracy in its place, the American people are safer.
>
> *Stewart*: [surprised and enthusiastic] Oh! Oh good! We're, we're, we're safer! That's why we did this, because American is safer! [changes tone] Granted, some have said that Iraq now is a bigger breeding ground for anti-American groups, and even Tom Ridge has said that Al Qaeda plans on attacking us before the election, uh, so, some might think we're . . . *less safe* . . . but . . .
>
> *Bush*: The American people are safer.
>
> *Stewart*: Oh! So, uh, well he said it again! That was his second time. So, you know, the thing is, even Bush's own State Department released a report that, once that report was *de-f***ed* up, it said that there were more terrorist attacks last year than at almost any point since it's been tracked.

At this point, a clock superimposed on the screen while Bush is talking tracks the time from which his soundbites were drawn.

> *Bush*: [11:37 a.m.] And the American people are safer.
>
> *Stewart*: [hanging head] Oh, oh, OK. But let me ask you this, just for schnicks between the two of us . . . what criteria are you using to prove that? I mean what evidence is there other than you saying it?
>
> *Bush*: [11:39] The American people are safer.
>
> *Bush*: [11:43] And the American people are safer.
>
> *Bush*: [11:45] The American people are safer.
>
> *Bush*: [11:47] And the American people . . . are safer.
>
> *Stewart*: [After a moment of silence] So basically, what it comes down to is this, the Bush administration's strategy to fight terrorism is . . . *repetition.* [pause] You know what, give us one final "America is safer," and this time, give it a flourish that says "stop questioning me about any of this."
>
> *Bush*: [11:50, with his finger pointing] And America and the world are safer.
>
> *Stewart*: Boom! Nicely done.

The treatment of Bush's speech functions on multiple levels. By emphasizing his *rhetorical* strategy of repetition, it lays bare Bush's clear attempt to plant the soundbite "the American people are safer" in that day's news. At the same time, Bush's one-sided, singular-voiced presentation is reworked into dialogue ("let me ask you this, just for schnicks between the two of us"), his certainty forced into critical exchange. Stewart speaks as interlocutor, confronting the president with counterargument and suggesting he lacks both the factual evidence and logical criteria to support his claim. Here Stewart engages in *undermining* humour (Paletz, 2002, p. 13), challenging not just the legitimacy of the president's statement but the wider authority upon which it relies. Finally, Stewart shifts to the voice of choreographer ("this time, give it a flourish") to make the point that Bush's speech is more theatrical spectacle than it is reasoned argument, designed ultimately to shut down avenues of inquiry ("stop questioning me") rather than inform the public.

In contrast to *The Daily Show's* dialogue, conventional news is *monologic*, pretending to "possess a ready-made truth" (Griffin, 1994, p. 42). Satire instead represents a searching for truth through the process of dialogical interaction. Unlike traditional news, which claims an epistemological certainty, satire is a discourse of *inquiry*, a rhetoric of challenge that seeks through the asking of unanswered questions to clarify the underlying morality of a situation. The show's coverage of the Iraqi prisoner abuse scandal is illustrative here. Says Stewart on the May 6 program, the revelation of torture is "difficult for all of us to wrap our heads around. Clearly this is a time for our defense secretary to speak clearly and honestly to the American people about these egregious instances of torture." A soundbite from Donald Rumsfeld follows:

> *Rumsfeld*: Uh, I think that . . . uh [scratches his head] . . . I'm not a lawyer, my impression is that what has been charged thus far is abuse, which I believe, technically, is different from torture [audience groans], and therefore I'm not gonna address the torture word.
>
> *Stewart*: I'm also not a lawyer, so I don't know, technically, if you're *human*, but as a fake news person, I can tell you, what we've been reading about in the newspapers, the pictures we've been seeing . . . it's f***ing torture.

Stewart's response is distinctly subjective ("*I* can tell you"), an approach he suggests he is allowed to pursue because he is not a journalist, but a "fake news person." Conventions of objectivity would disallow comment here: Traditional journalists can reiterate Rumsfeld's troubling quote in hopes it will "speak for itself," but they cannot engage with it as does Stewart. He uses satire to challenge it with a statement of morality, suggesting that both the incidences of torture and Rumsfeld's obfuscation, his refusal to speak "honestly and clearly," are fundamental violations of human decency.

In an age of disconnect between words and actions, *The Daily Show* uses satire to hold the leadership accountable to both. The June 21 program covers the 9/11 Commission report that the Bush administration was wrong in its insistence on a connection between Iraq and Al Qaeda, which in the absence of weapons of mass destruction became the primary justification for the invasion of Iraq. We see a recent clip of a CNBC interview with Vice President Cheney, who aggressively insists, much to the interviewer's surprise, that he "absolutely never said" that the alleged meeting between 9/11 hijacker Mohammed Atta and an agent of the Iraqi government had been "pretty well confirmed." From there we return to Stewart, who merely scratches his chin in puzzlement. A replay immediately follows of Cheney on NBC's *Meet the Press* in which he says, word for word, that the meeting had been "pretty well confirmed." With Cheney's blatant lie thus exposed, Stewart follows simply by saying "Mr. Vice President, your pants are on fire."

The Daily Show's satire news can be understood as a discourse of inquiry that seeks to penetrate a political communication system Stewart himself suggests has become "purposefully obtuse" (Schlosser, 2003). In an age in which few power holders are willing to speak clearly and honestly, *The Daily Show* uses humour as the licence to confront political dissembling and misinformation and to demand a measure of accountability. In so doing, the program is attempting to revive a spirit of critical inquiry and of the press as an agent of public interrogation that largely has been abdicated by the post–September 11 news media. In the frantic competition for ratings, in the fear of appearing "unpatriotic," and in the professional need to avoid alienation from the halls of power, a journalism of supervision and accountability has been replaced by one of conformity and complicity. As Griffin (1994) argues, it is in such times that satire most readily appears:

> It is the limitation on free inquiry and dissent that provokes one to irony—and to satire. If open challenge to orthodoxy is freely permitted, then writers will take the most direct route and debate the ideas and characters of political leaders openly in newspapers, protected by guarantees of free speech. It is difficult, or unnecessary, to satirize our political leaders when the newspapers are filled with open attacks on their integrity and intelligence. But if open challenge is not permitted, writers will turn to irony, indirection, innuendo, allegory, fable—to the fictions of satire. (p. 139)

With its discourse of inquiry, *The Daily Show* thus may be better understood not as "fake" news, but as a new form of critical journalism, one which uses satire to achieve that which the mainstream press is no longer willing to pursue.

Critiquing News

The Daily Show also interrogates the content of the news media, the "real" news that arguably is failing its democratic function. A recurring topic is the media's interest in the trivial at the expense of the consequential. On the June 28 program, Stewart discusses filmmaker Michael Moore's appearance on CBS's *The Early Show*, in which Moore accuses CBS News of functioning as propaganda for refusing to question the Bush administration's rationale for war. After a contentious exchange, anchor Hannah Storm well-illustrates the "now this" approach: "Up next," she says, "the right bug spray this summer. Deet or no?" From there, we return to a chuckling Stewart, who says "Deet or no. And he says the media won't ask the hard questions."

The consistent critique here is of the American media's refusal to engage in the kind of critical inquiry the May 11 program shows a British journalist pursuing. In a clip from a press conference following Prime Minister Tony Blair's meeting with a representative of the Chinese government, the reporter asks:

> Who are we to talk to the Chinese about human rights, when we are an active member of a coalition which has detained, without trial, without access to lawyers, in often inhumane, and we now know degrading conditions, both in Iraq and in other places in the world. What right do we, then, have to question the Chinese about human rights?

Before Blair answers, we cut back to Stewart, who says:

> Dude, where can we get a reporter like that? Seriously, you know what I was wondering? England, I'm just throwing this out there, let me ask you this. We'll trade you one Aaron Brown, two Brit Humes, and a Van Susteren, and I'm not talking about the *old* Van Susteren, I'm talking about the *new* Van Susteren. (5/11/04)

Stewart refers of course to the anchors of CNN and Fox News and to the lawyer-turned-TV-news-personality Greta Van Susteren, who dyed her hair and underwent plastic surgery upon moving from CNN to Fox. Here Van Susteren becomes emblematic of much that is wrong with contemporary news.

If the news updates provide a venue for explicit criticism of the media, such criticism functions more implicitly in *The Daily Show*'s second primary element—its parody news reports. Building on the sketch comedy format familiar to late-night talk, the show's cast of comedians act as news reporters. Often they appear on set with Stewart or in a pretend "live" shot, standing in front of a chroma-key background said to be the scene of the big story. In these, they offer mock versions of the instant analysis common to contemporary news. They also appear in pre-produced news packages, here literally travelling around the country to cover real and sometimes substantive stories from the domain of public affairs. During the presidential campaign, these included Rob Corddry on the appeal of Ralph Nader on college campuses, Ed Helms on the "free speech zone" established in Boston for the Democratic convention, Stephen Colbert on the tenuous coalition of interests that make up the Democratic base, and Samantha Bee on the minimal legal restrictions on the "527" groups and the advertising they produce.

Always silly and at times ridiculous, these stories do offer a measure of insight into topics of significance for the political process. Their greater purposes, however, may be to mock the genre of television news itself. *Parody* can be defined as a relatively polemical imitation of a given cultural practice, an aping that simultaneously reinvokes and challenges the styles and standards of a particular genre (Dentith, 2000). Parody is a moment of criticism, one that employs exaggeration, often to the point of ludicrousness, to invite its audience to examine, evaluate, and re-situate the genre and its practices. The parody pieces may generate a laugh, but their deeper thrust is subversion, an attack on the conventions and pretensions of television news.

For one, the comedians delight in emphasizing that they are playing the role of reporter, suggesting that many of those who posture as "real" journalists likewise are playing a role. They claim a constantly changing list of praise-worthy titles, including "senior Baghdad bureau chief," "senior election/terrorism correspondent," and "senior vice-presidential historian." Targeting the tenuous claim to expertise broadcast journalists so often make, their revolving credentials emphasize the point that in the contemporary media environment, expertise is a conferred rather than an earned status. Like Van Susteren, one becomes an expert by being on television, rather than the reverse (Kovach & Rosenstiel, 1999). Armed with fake credentials, the reporters pretend to travel the globe to cover the big story. Stretching the point to absurdity, Rob Corddry appears "live" from Vietnam, there to report on the controversy over Kerry's 30-year-old war record. Corddry mocks television news's overuse of the live shot, its insistence that the reporter's physical presence is isomorphic with good journalism. Finally, the comedians indulge in self-celebration, often focusing more on themselves than on the subject matter. Samantha Bee begins a fake report from a real fundraiser for John Kerry held by aid workers in Afghanistan by telling Stewart: "It was real exciting. After flying into Karachi by single-engine Piper, my translator Hafuz and I travelled by muleback over the Khyber pass and through the minefilled Tora Bora range before arriving at the Kerry fundraiser" (6/29/04). Bee calls into relief the trend in today's theatrical broadcast news to celebrate the reporter as the central actor in the story (Baym, 2003).

Suggesting that too many "journalists" are only playing the role on TV, the parody pieces further critique television news for the simplicity of its informational content. Reporter Ed Helms acts visibly bored as the legal expert he interviews explains to him the finer points of campaign law (8/11/04). Elsewhere, Corddry asks a California election official to explain, "in a nutshell," the problems facing the state's electoral system. After she gives a thoughtful and lengthy answer, Corddry responds: "Great. Now can you take that long-ass answer and put it in a nutshell, like I asked you?" (6/14/04). These examples call attention to television news's aversion to factual detail and complexity of argument. So too do the parody pieces expose the media's reliance on conventional frames and stock narratives. Reporting the night before the first presidential debate, Helms reads the *prewritten* story he says he intends to file *after* the debate. Stewart interrupts him, asking "Ed, you've written your story already?

In advance?" Helms replies: "Yeah, we all do. We write the narratives in advance based on conventional wisdom, and then whatever happens, we make it fit that story line." When Stewart asks why journalists do this, Helms shrugs his shoulders and suggests "We're lazy?" (9/29/04).

Ultimately, it is this disinterest in fact, the construction of televisual spectacle at the expense of understanding, for which the parody pieces most criticize mainstream television news. As the news media pondered at length who Kerry would pick as his vice presidential candidate, so too did Corddry appear several times to discuss the potential choices. On the day Kerry selected Edwards, Corddry literally holds his hands to his ears to avoid hearing the name. He then explains in a serious tone: "As a journalist, my job is to speculate wildly about these things. I can't let that responsibility be compromised by the facts" (7/16/04). Elsewhere, when discussing the "Swift Boat Veterans" attack on Kerry, Corddry rejects Stewart's suggestion that he has an obligation to determine the factual basis of the allegations. In a highly sarcastic tone, he mocks Stewart's point: "Oh, this allegation is spurious, and upon investigation this claim lacks any basis in reality." Dismissing any responsibility to identify the truth, he explains: "I'm a journalist, Jon. My job is to spend half the time reporting what one side says and half the time reporting the other. A little thing called ob-jec-tivity. You might want to look it up someday" (8/23/04).

The parody pieces ask us to consider just what a reporter's job *should* be. As such, they ultimately play a diagnostic function, identifying much that is wrong with news in its current form. If imitation is the highest form of flattery, *The Daily Show* reminds us we need broadcast journalism. At the same time, it illuminates several contemporary conventions that threaten to render television news irrelevant if not harmful to the democratic process. It asks us to be skeptical of much that passes for news today, but in a time of discursive reinvention, a moment when the conventions of journalism are open to reconsideration, it equally argues that there can, and should, be new alternatives.

Dialogue and Democracy

The daily interview segment that follows offers such an alternative model of public affairs programming. Running as long as 10 minutes, the studio interview can constitute more than half the show's content. While it is modelled in the tradition of the late-night celebrity interview, the discussion segment differs from its predecessors in important ways. Although the guests at times are the familiar movie stars who frequent the late-night circuit to promote their latest films, more often they are politicians, journalists, or commentators. Of the 78 guests who appeared from May through election day, 50 were from the domains of government, news, or politics. Political figures who appeared on the program included John Kerry, Bill Clinton, Ralph Nader, Dan Bartlett, Ed Gillespie, Terry McAullife, Madeline Albright, John McCain, and Joe Biden, among many others. Journalists and commentators included Thomas Friedman, David Brooks, Maureen Dowd, Bill Kristol, Seymour Hirsch, Michael Isikoff, Tim Russert, Wolf Blitzer, Bob Schieffer, Ted Koppel, and even Al Jazeera's Hassan Ibrahim.

In further contrast to the traditional late-night talk show, Stewart's approach is neither purely entertainment oriented nor overly accommodating. The interviews may touch on tales from childhood or other endearing anecdotes, but like the rest of the program, they are a hybrid form that blends laughter and pop culture with a willingness to engage with difficult issues. Although Stewart may insist, as he did to Fox's Bill O'Reilly, that "we literally do these interviews so we don't have to write another five minutes of comedy" (10/17/04), he often engages his guests in heady discussions of public affairs. Speaking of the war in Iraq, John McCain leans toward Stewart and in a sombre voice says "Jon, *this* is serious" (5/10/04). McCain here acknowledges that while Stewart's witty interruptions and responses inject an obvious levity to the tone, the discussion segment can be characterized by an equal seriousness of content and purpose.

The interviews likewise are distinct from the politically oriented talk shows common to cable news such as CNN's *Crossfire* or MSNBC's *Hardball*, which have transformed political discussion into a packaged form of trite verbal combat. Stewart himself has expressed disdain for such programs, sarcastically describing the former as a "nuanced public policy show that is named after the stray bullets that hit innocent bystanders in a gang fight" (10/18/04). That comment came the week after Stewart himself appeared as a guest on *Crossfire*. Much to the dismay of the hosts, Stewart took the opportunity to criticize them for "hurting America"—for failing "miserably" to live up to their "responsibility to the public discourse" by offering only theatre and "partisan hackery" instead of legitimate debate (CNN, 10/15/04).

In place of reductionist polemics, Stewart's politically oriented interviews pursue thoughtful discussions of national problems. The goal of the discussions is not the tearing down of the "other" side (although Stewart never hides his own political preferences) or some banal prediction of the shape of things to come, but rather an effort to gain greater understanding of national problems and their potential solutions. During the presidential campaign, recurrent topics included Bush's record in the White House, the occupation of Iraq, and the vitality of the American democratic process. Taken as a whole, the interview segment pursues these topics through a variety of perspectives. Seymour Hirsch minces no words in arguing that the neo-conservatives who drove the invasion of Iraq must be removed from power (9/29/04), but neo-conservative writer Stephen Hayes insists that Iraq *was* in league with Al Qaeda and the invasion was necessary (6/21/04). Comedian and liberal commentator Janeanne Garofalo argues that support for Bush is "a character flaw" (5/3/04), but former New York mayor and Democrat Ed Koch explains the reasons he says he will vote *for* Bush (10/18/04). Articulating at times contrasting arguments, the interviews further bring a measure of historical and intellectual context to the conversation. In contrast to most mediated political discourse, discussion of political history and references to thinkers such as Marx, Chomsky, or Zinn are not unusual. (Indeed, shortly after the election, Howard Zinn himself was a guest on the program.)

It is noteworthy here that like the movie star promoting a new film, the political guests also appear on the show largely to promote their work or their cause. In this regard, Stewart is happy to play along—he begins and ends each segment with an overt pitch for the product. Obviously, the interview is a marketing device, as is *The Daily Show* to be sure, but it is also the circulation of ideas and argument. The products being promoted usually are some form of political information and commentary—a book, documentary film, television program—and the interview segment provides a portal into this exchange of discourse. Producer Stuart Bailey suggests the goal is to connect to an ongoing national conversation, to make the show's content relevant to a wider political discussion (CBC, 2004). To put it differently, the interviews function as an opening to or an extension of a public sphere in the Habermasian (1989) sense—a forum for the rational-critical discussion of issues of public importance.

Indeed, the well-being of public discourse is a central concern in many of the interviews. Stewart chides DNC Chair Terry McAullife for insulting Bush, and then asks him to explain "the breakdown in civility" that has come to characterize the campaign (6/28/04). Stewart and Bill Clinton have a long discussion about the prevalence of negative campaigning and specifically the Swift Boat attack ads (8/9/04). Speaking of those, John Kerry himself suggests "most Americans would like to have a more intelligent conversation about where the country is going." To that the live audience shows its approval, bursting into applause. Similarly, Stewart says to RNC Chair Ed Gillespie that "we should have a discussion of the issues" (8/25/04). That point is endorsed by Republican Senator Norm Coleman, who says he hopes the country can "have a civilized debate . . . not about Vietnam, what your wife says, what your wife wears" (8/17/04), and also by McCain, who calls on "the American people" to "demand to change the debate" (9/12/04).

More important than the loss of civility, however, is the marginalization of honesty. Stewart chastises Congressman Henry Bonilla for refusing either to budge from his GOP talking points or to seriously discuss the tenuous factual basis behind them. "All I want," Stewart tells the congressman, "is an honest discussion" (8/12/04). Likewise, in concluding his interview with John Kerry, Stewart thanks him for "having a normal conversation" (8/24/04). Here "honest" and "normal" are contrasted with the strict adherence to the talking points and partisan spin that comprise the balance of mediated political talk.

At its core, *The Daily Show* advocates a conversational or deliberative theory of democracy—a notion that only open conversation can provide the legitimate foundation for governance (Bohman & Rehg, 1997). A theory of deliberative democracy can be distinguished from a market theory of politics, which begins from the assumption that the polity is comprised of instrumentally rational individuals who enter the debate with fully formed preferences, intent on maximizing their own self-interest. In such an economic theory of democracy, politics is seen as conflict between divergent interests, while political discourse becomes competition that at best can produce functional compromises (see Elster, 1997). It is this logic that appears to underlie political discussion programs such as *Crossfire* or *Hardball* and their "You're wrong, I'm not" model of political conversation. Such shows reduce political discourse to a zero-sum game, an unreflexive contest in which only one side can win.

In contrast to a market or instrumental understanding of democracy, a theory of deliberative democracy as expressed on *The Daily Show* understands the political system ideally to be comprised of individuals engaged in reasoned discussion, a co-operative discourse that seeks to reach a consensual notion of the common good (see Habermas, 1996). It is a *dialogical* notion of democracy, one that "requires citizens to go beyond private self-interest of the 'market' and orient themselves to public interests of the 'forum'" (Bohman & Rehg, 1997, p. xiv). The forum provides the central metaphor of deliberative democracy, which depends *in the first instance* on active deliberation among citizens. Dialogue here is the locus of democracy, the public process through which citizens determine their preferences and define the public will.

For Habermas and other advocates of a deliberative democracy, reasoned conversation is the defining feature of a democratic system, a feature clearly lacking in much of the reactionary, frenzied, and often unintelligible 24-hour news media. It is this shortcoming of the mainstream news media and politicians alike that motivates *The Daily Show*'s interview segments, and much of the program's criticism of contemporary political communication practices. One sees this well expressed in Stewart's interview with former Treasury Secretary Robert Reich, who pleads for what he describes as a return to reason in political argument. "Irrationality rules the day," Reich insists, "but reason is in the wings." Before Stewart can respond, the audience bursts into applause, at which point Stewart leans toward Reich and says: "By the way, the people clamoring for reason? You hear that? You don't see that too often" (6/14/04). *The Daily Show*, however, regularly offers a model of and resources for political dialogue and reasoned conversation.

Reinventing Political Journalism

The Daily Show represents an important experiment in journalism, one that contains much significance for the ongoing redefinition of news.

Unquestionably, its primary approach is comedy, and much of the show's content is light and, at times, vacuous. Often, however, the silly is interwoven with the serious, resulting in an innovative and potentially powerful form of public information. The blending of news and satire confronts a system of political communication that largely has degenerated into soundbites and spin with critical inquiry. The use of parody unmasks the artifice in much contemporary news practices, while the interview segment endorses and enacts a deliberative model of democracy based on civility of exchange, complexity of argument, and the goal of mutual understanding. Lying just beneath or perhaps imbricated within the laughter is a quite serious demand for fact, accountability, and reason in political discourse.

Both the increasing commercial success and the political significance of *The Daily Show* may be due to its hybrid form, its willingness to blend once-distinct discourses into previously unimagined combinations. Comedy provides its initial appeal; humour assembles the audience. In an age when young people increasingly are abandoning sources of traditional news, *The Daily Show* attracts many of them with its initial discourse of entertainment. But comedy also provides the method to engage in serious political criticism; the label of "fake news" enables *The Daily Show* to say that which the traditional journalist cannot. So too does categorization as comedy grant it immunity from accusations that it violates journalistic standards. Never claiming to be news, it can hardly be charged with being illegitimate journalism, either by the political structure it interrogates or the news media it threatens.

The Daily Show is indeed a threat to the mainstream news media. While the latter have responded to the continual hemorrhaging of audiences with various versions of news lite, happy talk, and political punditry, *The Daily Show* pursues a different path. In a time when most media have turned to shallow infotainment to try to ensure ratings points, *The Daily Show* offers instead a version of *news that entertains*. Entertainment here must be understood as a doubly articulated concept. On one hand, "to entertain" means to interest, to amuse, to give one pleasure. It can also mean, however, to engage with and to consider. *The Daily Show* suggests that that which gives pleasure need not necessarily divert and distract from significant issues. The mainstream news media, however, have been unwilling or unable to learn this lesson. They have tried at times to incorporate the comedy—consider former *Daily Show* comedian Mo Rocca's inane contribution to CNN's convention coverage—but have so far failed to grasp the deeper insight that in an age of discursive integration, it is possible to be entertaining in the sense of both amusement and serious thought, and that each one may have the ability to enhance the other.

It also may be possible for a television newscast to be both profitable and substantive, an argument Stewart himself has made. "For some reason, people think that solid, good, in-depth all equals dull, low ratings, low profitability," he argues. "I don't think that's the case. I think you can make really exciting, interesting television news that could become the medium of record for reasonable, moderate people" (Schlosser, 2003). It is indeed possible, and as news audiences increasingly come of age in a discursively integrated world, it may be absolutely necessary. Graber (2001) has argued that political news must begin to meet the needs of "21st-century Americans" who generally find "the abominable quality of the content and presentation of much of the televised news . . . neither salient nor attractive" (pp. 445–6). The perceived political apathy of younger Americans, she argues, may be due less to their own intellectual shortcomings than to the poor quality and apparent irrelevance of contemporary broadcast news. The increasing success of *The Daily Show* gives weight to that argument.

The suggestion here is not that *The Daily Show* itself should become *the* news of record, the 21st-century, discursively integrated version of Walter Cronkite's

CBS *Evening News.* The program is a product of a specific historical moment, fuelled both by the post–September 11 dissuasion of open inquiry and the particular talents of its current host. Whether its specific approach can withstand the test of time certainly remains to be seen. The greater significance of *The Daily Show,* however, lies in its willingness to experiment, in its opening of a door to a world of discursive possibilities. *The Daily Show* thus offers a lesson in the possible to which all students of journalism, political communication, and public discourse would be wise to pay attention.

References

Baym, G. (2003). Strategies of illumination: U.S. network news, Watergate, and the Clinton affair. *Rhetoric & Public Affairs, 6,* 633–56.

———. (2004). Packaging reality: Structures of form in U.S. network news coverage of Watergate and the Clinton impeachment. *Journalism, 5,* 279–99.

Bennett, W.L., & Entman, R.M. (2001). *Mediated politics: Communication in the future of democracy.* New York: Cambridge University Press.

Bishop, R. (2004). The accidental journalist: Shifting professional boundaries in the wake of Leonardo DiCaprio's interview with former President Clinton. *Journalism Studies, 5,* 31–43.

Bohman, J., & Rehg, W. (1997). *Deliberative democracy: Essays on reason and politics.* Cambridge, MA: MIT Press.

CBC. (2004, February 10). *CBC News: Disclosure.* Retrieved 8 April 2004, from http://www.cbc.ca/disclosure/archives/040210_pop/stewart.html

Delli Carpini, M.X., & Williams, B.A. (2001). Let us infotain you: Politics in the new media environment. In W.L. Bennett & R.M. Entman (Eds), *Mediated politics: Communication in the future of democracy* (pp. 160–81). New York: Cambridge University Press.

Dentith, S. (2000). *Parody.* New York: Routledge.

Douglas, S. (2003, May 5). *Daily Show* does Bush. *The Nation.* Retrieved 8 April 2004, from http://www.thenation.com/doc.mhtml%3Fi=20030505&s=Douglas

Elster, J. (1997). The market and the forum: Three varieties of political theory. In J. Bohmanm & W. Rehg (Eds), *Deliberative democracy: Essays on reason and politics* (pp. 3–34). Cambridge, MA: MIT Press.

Fritz, B., Keefer, B., & Nyhan, B. (2004). *All the president's spin: George W. Bush, the media, and the truth.* New York: Touchstone.

Gandy, O.H., Jr. (2001). Dividing practices: Segmentation and targeting in the emerging public sphere. In W.L. Bennett & R.M. Entman (Eds), *Mediated politics: Communication in the future of democracy* (pp. 141–59). New York: Cambridge University Press.

Gay, V. (2004, January 19). Not necessarily the news: Meet the players who will influence coverage of the 2004 campaign. You might be surprised. *Newsday,* p. B6.

Graber, D. (2001). Adapting political news to the needs of twenty-first century Americans. In W.L. Bennett & R.M. Entman (Eds), *Mediated politics: Communication in the future of democracy* (pp. 433–52). New York: Cambridge University Press.

Griffin, D. (1994). *Satire: A critical reintroduction.* Lexington: The University Press of Kentucky.

Habermas, J. (1989). *The structural transformation of the public sphere: An inquiry into a category of bourgeois society* (T. Burger, Trans.). Cambridge, MA: MIT Press.

———. (1996). Three normative models of democracy. In S. Benhabib (Ed.), *Democracy and difference: Contesting the boundaries of the political* (pp. 21–30). Princeton, NJ: Princeton University Press.

Hutcheson, J., Domke, D., Billeaudeaux, A., & Garland, P. (2004). U.S. national identity, political elites, and a patriotic press following September 11. *Political Communication, 21,* 27–51.

Jones, N. (1995). *Soundbites and spin doctors.* London: Cassell.

Kovach, B., & Rosenstiel, T. (1999). *Warp speed: America in the age of mixed media.* New York: Century Foundation Press.

McChesney, R.W. (1999). *Rich media, poor democracy: Communication politics in dubious times.* New York: New Press.

McNair, B. (2000). *Journalism and democracy: An evaluation of the political public sphere.* New York: Routledge.

Murdock, G. (1990). Redrawing the map of the communications industries: Concentration and ownership in the era of privatization. In M. Ferguson (Ed.), *Public communication—The new imperatives: Future directions for media research* (pp. 1–15). London: Sage.

National Annenberg Election Survey. (2004). Daily Show viewers knowledgeable about presidential campaign. Retrieved 24 February 2005, from http://www.annenbergpublicpolicycenter.org/naes/2004_03_late-night-knowledge-2_9-21_pr.pdf

Neuman, W.R. (1996). Political communications infrastructure. *Annals of the American*

Academy of Political and Social Science, 546, 9–21.

Niven, D.S., Lichter, R., & Amundson, D. (2003). The political content of late night comedy. *Press/Politics, 8,* 118–133.

Paletz, D. (2002). *The media in American politics: Contents and consequences.* New York: Longman.

PBS. (2003, July 11). *NOW with Bill Moyers.* Retrieved 8 April 2004 from http://www.pbs.org/now/transcript/transcript_stewart.html

Pew Research Center for the People and the Press. (2002). *Public's news habits little changed since September 11.*

Retrieved 8 April 2004, from http://people-press.org/reports/display.php3?ReportID=156

———. (2004). *Cable and Internet loom large in fragmented political news universe.* Retrieved 8 April 2004, from http://people-press.org/reports/display.php3?ReportID=200

Postman, N. (1986). *Amusing ourselves to death: Public discourse in the age of show business.* New York: Penguin Books.

Schlosser, E. (2003). The kids are alright. *Columbia Journalism Review, 41,* 27–30.

Street, J. (2001). *Mass media, politics, and democracy.* London: Palgrave.

Timberg, B.M. (2002). *Television talk: A history of the TV talk show.* Austin: University of Texas Press.

Underwood, D. (1993). *When MBAs rule the newsroom: How the marketers and managers are reshaping today's media.* New York: Columbia University Press.

———. (2001). Reporting and the push for market-oriented journalism: Media organizations as business. In W.L. Bennett & R.M. Entman (Eds), *Mediated politics: Communication in the future of democracy* (pp. 99–116). New York: Cambridge University Press.

Entertainment Wars: Television Culture after 9/11

Lynn Spigel

After the attacks of September 11, traditional forms of entertainment had to reinvent their place in US life and culture. The de rigueur violence of mass media—both news and fiction—no longer seemed business as usual. While Hollywood usually defends its mass-destruction ethos with claims to "free speech," constitutional rights, and industry-wide discretion (à la ratings systems), in the weeks following September 11 the industry exhibited (whether for sincere or cynical reasons) a new will toward "tastefulness" as potentially trauma-inducing films like Warner's *Collateral Damage* were pulled from release. On television, violent movies also came under network scrutiny. USA cancelled its prime-time run of *The Siege* (which deals with Arab terrorists who plot to bomb New York). At TBS violence-packed films like *Lethal Weapon* were replaced with family fare like *Look Who's Talking.* TNT replaced its 1970s retro lineup of *Superman, King Kong,* and *Carrie* with *Close Encounters of the Third Kind, Grease,* and *Jaws* (although exactly why the blood-sucking shark in Jaws seemed less disturbing than the menstruating teen in *Carrie* already begs questions about exactly what constitutes "terror" in the minds of Hollywood executives).[1]

But it wasn't just the "hard" realities of violence that came under self-imposed censorship. Light entertainment and "diversions" of all kinds also didn't feel right. Humorists Dave Letterman, Jay Leno, Craig Kilborn, Conan O'Brien, and Jon Stewart met the late-night audience with dead seriousness. While *Saturday Night Live* did return to humour, its jokes were officially sanctioned by an opening act that included a sombre performance by Paul Simon, the entire New York Fire Department, and Mayor Giuliani himself. When producer Lorne Michaels asked the mayor if it was okay to be funny, Giuliani joked, "Why start now?" (implicitly informing viewers that it was, in fact, okay to laugh). In the midst of the new sincerity, numerous critics summarily declared that the attacks on the Pentagon and World Trade Center had brought about the "end of irony."[2]

Despite such bombastic declarations, however, many industry leaders were actually in a profound state of confusion about just what it was that the public wanted. Even while industry leaders were eager to censor trauma-inducing images of any kind, video outlets reported that, when left to their own discretion, consumers were eagerly purchasing terrorist flicks like *The Siege* and *The Towering Inferno.* One video retailer noted an "uneasy" feeling about consumer desire for films like *The Towering Inferno,* and one store owner even "moved such videos so they were arranged with only the spines showing, obscuring the covers."[3] Meanwhile, Internet companies worried about the hundreds of vulgar domain names for which people applied in the hopes of setting up websites. One major domain name reseller halted auctions for several names it considered tasteless, including "NewYorkCarnage.com."[4] As these cases suggest, the media industries had to balance their own public image as discriminating custodians or culture with the vagaries of public taste.

Given its historical status as a regulated private industry ideally meant to operate in the "public interest," television was the medium hardest hit by this conflict between maintaining the image of "public servant" and the need to cater to the public taste (or at least to what advertisers think the public likes). Getting back to the normal balance between its public service and entertainment/commercial functions posed problems for broadcasters and cablers alike.[5] In the midst of the turmoil, the Academy of Television Arts and Sciences and CBS postponed the Emmy Award ceremonies twice.

To be sure, television executives' nervous confusion was rooted in the broader havoc that 9/11 wreaked on television—not just as an industry but also as "a whole way of life."[6] Most fundamentally, on September 11, the everydayness of television itself was suddenly disrupted by news of something completely "alien" to the usual patterns of domestic TV viewing.[7] The nonstop commercial-free coverage, which lasted for a full week on major broadcast networks and cable news networks, contributed to a sense of estrangement from ordinary life, not simply because of the unexpected nature or the attack itself but also because television's normal routines—its everyday schedule and ritualized flow—had been disordered. As Mary Ann Doane has argued about television catastrophes more generally, not only television's temporal flow, but also its central narrational agency breaks down in moments of catastrophe.[8] We are in a world where narrative comes undone and where the "real" seems to have no sense of meaning beyond repetition of the horrifying event itself. This, she claims, in turn threatens to expose the underlying catastrophe of all TV catastrophes—the breakdown of capitalism, the end of the cash flow, the end of the logic of consumption on which US television is predicated.

By the weekend of September 15, television news anchors began to tell us that it was their national duty to return to the "normal" everyday schedule of television entertainment, a return meant to coincide with Washington's call for a return to normalcy (and, hopefully, normal levels of consumerism). Of course, for the television industry, resuming the normal TV schedule also meant a return to commercial breaks and, therefore, TV's very sustenance. Already besieged by declining ad revenues before the attacks, the television industry lost an estimated $320 million in advertising revenue in the week following the attacks.[9] So, even while the media industries initially positioned entertainment and commercials as being "in bad taste," just one week after the attacks the television networks discursively realigned commercial entertainment with the patriotic goals of the nation.[10] In short—and most paradoxically—entertainment and commercialism were rearticulated as television's "public service."

By September 27, Jack Valenti, president and CEO of the Motion Picture Association of America, gave this "commercialism as patriotism" ethos an official stamp of approval. In a column for *Variety*, he wrote: "Here in Hollywood we must continue making our movies and our TV programs. For a time, during this mourning period, we need to be sensitive to how we tell a story. But in time—and that time will surely come—life will go on, must go on. We in Hollywood have to get on with doing our creative work. . . . The country needs what we create."[11] Valenti's message was part of a much older myth of show business—a myth that ran through countless Depression-era and World War II musicals—a myth of transcendence in which showbiz folks put aside their petty differences and join together in patriotic song. If in the 1940s this myth of transcendence emboldened audiences for wartime sacrifice, now, in the twenty-first century, this transcendent myth of show business is oddly conjoined with national mandates for a return to "normal" consumer pleasures. In a bizarrely Baudrillardian moment, President Bush addressed the nation, begging us to return to normal life by getting on planes and taking our families to Disneyland.[12]

In fact, despite the initial tremors, American consumer culture and television in particular did return to normal (or at least a semblance of it) in a remarkably short span of time. Yet, while many people have noted this, the process by which this happened and the extent to which it was achieved beg further consideration. Media scholarship on 9/11 and the US attacks in Afghanistan has focused primarily on print and television news coverage. This important scholarship focuses on the narrative and mythic "framing" of the events; the nationalistic jingoism (for example, the use of flag graphics on news shows); the relative paucity of alternative views in mainstream venues—at least in the immediate weeks following the attacks; the role of alternative news platforms, especially the Internet; competing global news outlets, particularly Al Jazeera; and the institutional and commercial pressure that has led to "infotainment."[13] Despite its significant achievements, however, the scholarly focus on news underestimates (indeed, it barely considers) the way the "reality" of 9/11 was communicated across the now of television's genres, including its so-called entertainment genres.[14] The almost singular focus on news fails to capture the way television worked to process fear (even fear trumped up by the media) and return the public to "ordinary" life (including routine ways of watching TV).

The return to normal has to be seen from this wider view, for it was enacted not just through the narrative frames of news stories but also through the repositioning of audiences back into television's fictive time and places—its familiar series, well-known stars, favourite characters, and ritualized annual events (such as the Emmy Awards).

In the following pages, I explore how an assortment of television genres—dramatic series, talk shows, documentaries, special "event" TV, and even cartoons—channelled the nation back to normalcy—or at least to the normal flows of television and consumer culture. I am particularly interested in how these genres relied on nationalist myths of the American past and the enemy/"Orient." But I also question the degree to which nationalist myths can sustain the "narrowcast" logic or today's multichannel television systems (and the more general movement of audiences across multiple media platforms). In other words, I want to interrogate the limits of nationalist myths in the post-network, multichannel, and increasingly global media systems.

Admittedly, the fate of nationalism in contemporary media systems is a huge question that requires perspectives from more than one field of inquiry. (For example, we would need to explore the impact of deregulation and media conglomeration, the dispersal of audiences across media platforms, competition among global media news/entertainment outlets, relations between local and global media flows, audience and interpretive reception contexts, and larger issues or national identity and subjectivity.) My goal here is not to provide exhaustive answers to all of these questions (obviously no one essay could do so), but rather to open up some points of interrogation by looking at post-9/11 media industry strategies, the discourses of the entertainment trade journals, and especially at the textual and narrative logic of television programs that channelled the nation back to commercial TV "as usual."

History Lessons after 9/11

Numerous critics have commented on the way that the attacks of 9/11 were perceived as an event completely outside of and alien to any other horror that ever happened anywhere. As James Der Derian notes, as a consequence of this rhetoric of American exceptionalism, "9/11 quickly took on an *exception ahistoricity*" as even many of the most astute critics refused to place the events in a political or social context from which they might be understood. Der Derian argues that when history was evoked in nonstop news coverage of destruction and loss, it appeared as nostalgia and analog, "mainly in the sepia tones of the Second World War—to prepare

America for the sacrifice and suffering that lay ahead."[15] But, at least after the initial news coverage of which Der Derian speaks, history was actually marshalled in a much more contradictory field of statements and images that filled the airwaves and ushered audiences back—not just toward nostalgic memories of World War II sacrifice—but also toward the mandates of contemporary consumer culture. On television these "contradictory" statements and images revolved around the paradox of the medium's twin roles as advertiser and public servant.

In the week following 9/11, television's transition back to normal consumer entertainment was enacted largely through recourse to historical pedagogy that ran through a number of television genres, from news to documentaries to daytime talk shows to prime-time drama. The histories evoked were both familiar and familiarizing tales of the "American experience" as newscasters provided a stream of references to classroom histories, including, for example, the history of US immigration, Pearl Harbor, and Vietnam.[16] They mixed these analogies to historical events with allusions to the history of popular culture, recalling scenes from disaster film blockbusters, science fiction movies, and war films and even referencing previous media events, from the assassination of JFK to the death of Princess Diana. Following 24/7 "real time" news strategies that CNN developed in 1991's Gulf War, major news networks provided a host of "infotainment" techniques that have over the past decade become common to war reporting (i.e., fast-paced "MTV" editing, computerized/game-style images, slick graphics, digitized sound effects, banter among "experts," and catchy slogans).[17] On September 12, CNN titled its coverage "The Day After" (which was also the title of the well-known 1980s made-for-TV nuclear disaster movie). NBC sported the slogan "America Strikes Back" based, of course, on the *Star Wars* trilogy. Meanwhile the FBI enlisted the television show *America's Most Wanted* to help in the hunt for terrorists.[18] As we searched for familiar scripts, the difference between real wars and "made-for-TV" wars hardly mattered. History had become, to use Michel de Certeau's formulation, a heterology of science and fiction.[19]

But what did this turn to familiar historical narratives provide? Why the sudden appeal of history? Numerous scholars, from Roland Barthes to Marita Sturken, have analyzed the ways in which history and memory serve to produce narratives of the nation. This work has shown how media (from advertising to film to television to music) play a central role in conjuring up a sense of national belonging and community.[20] Certainly, after 9/11, the media's will to remember was connected to the resuscitation of national culture in a country heretofore divided by culture wars and extreme political partisanship. For the culture industries, however, the turn to history was not only connected to the resuscitation of nationalism; history was also connected to the parallel urge to restore the business routines and marketing practices of contemporary consumer media culture.

At the most basic level, for television executives who were nervous about offending audiences, history was a solution to a programming dilemma. History, after all, occupies that most sought-after realm of "good taste." It is the stuff of PBS, the Discovery Channel, the History Channel—it signifies a "habitus" of educated populations, of "quality" TV, of public service generally. History's "quality" appeal was especially important in the context of numerous critical attacks on television's lack of integrity that ran through industry trade journals and the popular press after 9/11. For example, Louis Chunovic, a reporter for the trade journal *Television Week*, wrote: "In the wake of the terrorist attack on the United States, it's hard to believe Americans once cared who would win *Big Brother* 2 or whether Anne Heche is crazy. And it's hard to believe that as recently as two weeks ago, that's exactly the kind of pabulum, along with the latest celebrity/politician sex/murder/kidnapping scandal, that dominated television news." Chunovic therefore argued,

"We cannot afford to return to the way things were."[21] Ironically, however, the industry's post-9/11 upgrade to quality genres—especially historical documentaries—actually facilitated the return to the way things were. Historical documentaries served a strategic role in the patriotic transition back to "normalcy"—that is, to commercial entertainment and consumer culture.

Let's take, for example, ABC's programming strategy on Saturday, September 15. On that day, ABC became the first major network to return to a semblance of normal televisual flow. Newscaster Peter Jennings presented a children's forum, which was followed by an afternoon lineup of historical documentaries about great moments of the twentieth century. The lineup included episodes on Charles Lindbergh, the Apollo crew and the moon landing, and a documentary on the US press in Hitler's Europe. Interestingly, given the breakdown in surveillance, aviation, and communication technologies that enabled the attacks, all of the chosen histories were about great achievements or great men using great technologies, especially transportation and communications technologies.[22]

Meanwhile, from an economic point or view, these historical documentaries were first and foremost part of the contemporary network business strategy that industry people refer to as "repurposing." The documentaries were reruns repackaged from a previous ABC series narrated by Jennings and now "repurposed" for patriotism. This is not to say that Jennings or anyone else at ABC was intentionally trying to profit from disaster. Certainly, Jennings's forum for children provided a public service. But, as anyone who studies the history of US television knows, the logic of capitalism always means that public service and public relations are flip sides of the same coin. In this case, the public service gesture of running historical documentaries also served to transition audiences from TV news discourse and live reportage back into prerecorded narrative series. Similarly, with an even more bizarre resonance, on the evening of September 15th NBC ran a special news report on *Dateline* followed by a rerun of the made-for-TV movie *Growing Up Brady*.

More generally, history was integral to the transition back to entertainment series programs. On 3 October 2001, NBC's *The West Wing*, one of television's leading quality series, pre-empted its scheduled season premiere to air a quickly drafted episode titled "Isaac and Ishmael." On the one hand, the episode (which teaches audiences about the situation in the Middle East) was clearly an earnest attempt by the cast and Creator/Executive Producer Aaron Sorkin (who wrote the script) to use television as a form of political and historical pedagogy.[23] On the other hand, the episode was also entirely consistent with contemporary business promotional strategies. Like the ABC strategy of repurposing, the NBC network followed the business strategy or "stunting"—or creating a standalone episode that attracts viewers by straying from the series architecture (the live *ER* is a classic example of the technique). In this case, *The West Wing* was in a particularly difficult position—for perhaps more than any other network series, it derives its "quality" appeal from its "timely relevance" and deep, if melodramatic, realism. (The series presents itself as a kind of parallel White House universe that runs simultaneously with everyday goings-on in Washington.)[24]

The credit sequence begins with successive headshots or cast members speaking to the audience in direct address (and in their celebrity personae). Martin Sheen welcomes viewers and announces that this episode is not the previously scheduled season premiere. In a subsequent headshot, another cast member even refers to the episode as "a storytelling aberration," signalling its utter discontinuity from the now routinely serialized/cumulative narrative structure of contemporary prime-time "quality" genres. Meanwhile, other cast members variously thank the New York Fire and Police Departments, while still others direct our attention to a phone number at the bottom of the screen that viewers can call to donate money to disaster relief and victim funds. In this sense, the episode immediately asks audiences to imagine themselves foremost as citizens engaged in an interactive public/media sphere. Nevertheless, this "public service" ethos is embroiled in the televisual logic of publicity. The opening credit sequence ends with cast members promoting the new fall season by telling audiences what kinds of plots to expect on upcoming episodes. The final "teaser" comes from a female cast member, Janel Moloney, who hypes the fall season by promising that her character will have a love interest in future shows.

After this promise of titillating White House sex, the episode transitions back to its public service discourse. Essentially structured as a teach-in, the script follows a group of high school students touring the White House and caught in the west wing after a terrorist bomb threat. Attempting to calm the nerves of the students, various cast members lecture this imaginary high school class about the history of US–Middle East relations. In an early segment, Josh Lyman, a White House "spin doctor," teaches the frightened students about terrorism and Middle East animosity toward the West. After a wide-eyed female student asks, "Why is everyone trying to kill us?" Josh moves to the blackboard, where he begins his history lesson. While he admits that the United States is somewhat to blame (he mentions economic sanctions, occupation of Arab lands, and the US abandonment of Afghanistan), he says all of this at such rapid-fire speed that there is no in-depth consideration of the issues. Instead, the scene derails itself from its "teaching" mission by resorting to the colonialist rhetoric of "curiosities." The scene ends with Josh telling the students of his outrage at the cultural customs of Islamic fundamentalists. The familiar list of horrors—from the fact that women are made to wear a veil to the fact that men can't cheer freely at soccer games—redirects the episode away from ethics toward an ethnocentric celebration of American cultural superiority.[25] Josh concludes by reminding the students that, unlike Islamic fundamentalists, Americans are free to cheer anything they like at football games, and American women can even be astronauts.

In this regard, the episode uses historical pedagogy to solidify American national unity *against* the "enemy" rather than to encourage any real engagement with Islam, the ethics of US international policy, or the consequences of the then-impending US bomb strikes. Moreover, because the episode's teach-in lectures are encompassed within a more overarching melodramatic rescue narrative (the terrorist bomb threat in the White House), all of the lessons the students (and by proxy, the audience) learn are contained within a narrative about US public safety. In other words, according to the logic of this rescue narrative, we learn about the "other" only for instrumental reasons—our own national security.

In all of these ways, *The West Wing* performs some of the fundamental precepts of contemporary Orientalism. As Edward Said argues, in the United States—and in particular after World War II—Orientalism retains the racist histories of othering from the earlier European context but becomes increasingly less philological and more concerned with social-scientific policy and administration that is formulated in federal agencies, think-tanks, and universities that want to "know" and thus police the Middle East. In this configuration, the production of knowledge about the Middle East is aimed at the maintenance of US hegemony and national security, and it winds up producing an image of the Arab as "other"—the antithesis of Western humanity and progress.[26] Indeed, when Josh details the cultural wasteland of Islamic fundamentalism, he enacts one of the central rhetorical principles of Orientalism, for, as Said argues, the "net effect" of contemporary Orientalism is to erase any American awareness of the Arab world's culture and humanity (its poets, its novelists, its means of self-representation), replacing these with a dehumanizing social-scientific index of "attitudes, trends, statistics."[27]

The West Wing's fictional schoolroom performs this kind of social-scientific Orientalism in the name of liberal humanism. And it does so through a pedagogical form of enunciation that places viewers in the position of high school students—and particularly naive ones at that. The program speaks to viewers as if they were children or, at best, the innocent objects of historical events beyond their control. The "why does everyone want to kill us?" mantra espoused by *The West Wing's* fictional students, becomes, to use Lauren Berlant's phrase, a form of "infantile citizenship"[28] that allows adult viewers comfortably to confront the horrors and guilt of war by donning the cloak of childhood innocence (epitomized, of course, by the wide-eyed figure of President Bush himself, who, in his first televised speech to Congress after the attacks, asked, "Why do they hate us?").

In the days following the attacks, the Bush administration spoke often of the eternal and "essential goodness" of the American people, creating a through-line for the American past that flattered a despairing public by making them the moral victims of a pure outside evil.[29] In a similar instance of denial, commentators spoke of "the end of innocence"[30] that the attacks ushered in as if America had been completely without knowledge and guilt before this day.[31] Not surprisingly, in this respect, the histories mobilized by the media after 9/11 were radically selective and simplified versions of the past that produced a kind or moral battlefield for "why we fight." As Justin Lewis shows in his survey of four leading US newspapers, print journalists writing about 9/11 tended to evoke World War II and Nazi Germany while "other histories were, regardless of relevance, distinctly less prominent." Lewis claims that "the more significant absences [were] those histories that signify the West's disregard for democracy and human rights [such as] the U.S. government's support for the Saudi Arabian Theocracy."[32] He argues that the history of World War II and Nazi Germany was mobilized because of its compelling narrative dimensions—especially its good versus evil binary. While this creation of heroes and villains was also a primary aspect of television coverage, it seems likely that many viewers weren't really looking for "objective truth" so much as narrative itself. In the face of shock and uncertainty that seemed to make time stand still, these narratives offered people a sense of historical continuity with a shared, and above all moral, past.[33]

The need to make American audiences feel that they were in the moral position ran through a number of television's "reality" genres. One of the central ways that this moral position was promoted was through the depiction of women victims. According to Jayne Rodgers, journalists tended to frame news stories in "myths of gender," and, she claims, one of the central trajectories of these myths was a reversal of the gendered nature of heroism and victimization. Rodgers points out that even while "male deaths from the attacks outnumbered female deaths by a ratio of three to one," news narratives typically portrayed men as heroes (firemen, policemen, Giuliani) and women as victims (suffering and often pregnant widows). Despite the fact that there were 33 women firefighters and rescue workers on duty on September 11, the media portraits of heroism were mainly of men, which, as Rodgers aptly argues, worked to "restore gender, as well as social and political order."[34]

On television, these myths or gender were often connected to age-old Western fantasies of the East in which "Oriental" men assault (and even rape) Western women and, more symbolically, the West itself. (Cecil B. DeMille's *The Cheat* [1951] or Valentino in *The Sheik* [1921] demonstrate the longevity of this orientalized "rape" fantasy.) In the case of 9/11, the United States took its figural place as innocent victim in stories that interwove myths of gender and the Orient. Both daytime talk shows and nighttime news were filled with melodramatic tales of women's suffering that depicted women as the moral victims of Islamic extremisim. And "women" here meant both the women of Afghanistan and American survivors (the widows) who lost their husbands during the attack. While of course these women are at one level real women who really suffered, on television they were fictionally rendered through melodramatic conventions that tended to elide the complexity of the historical causes of the tragic circumstances the women faced.

For example, in the weeks following the attacks, *Oprah!* ran episodes featuring pregnant survivors who had lost their husbands. These episodes intertwined personal memories (via home videos of the deceased) with therapy sessions featuring the traumatized women. In these episodes, the "talking cure" narrative logic of the talk show format was itself strangely derailed by the magnitude of events; the female guest was so traumatized that she was literally unable to speak. In one episode, for example, a young pregnant woman sits rigidly on stage while popular therapist Dr Phil tells her about the 12 steps of trauma (and Oprah interjects with inspirational wisdom). The episode presents this woman as having lost not only her husband but also her voice and, with that, her ability to narrate her own story. In the process the program implicitly asks viewers to identify with this woman as the moral and innocent victim of *chance*. In other words, any causal agent (or any sense that her suffering is actually the result of complex political histories) is reduced to the "twist of fate" narrative fortunes of the daytime soap.

Writing about the history of American melodramas, Linda Williams demonstrates that this theme of the "suffering" moral victim (particularly women and African Americans) can be traced through cinematic and televisual media representations (including depictions of American historical events). Williams claims that victim characters elicit our identification through sentiment (not only with them but also, allegorically, with historical injustices they face). Following Lauren Berlant and Ann Douglas, she cautions that sentiment and vicarious identification with suffering—in both media texts and politics more generally—are often a stand-in for actual social justice, but, importantly, sentiment is not the same as justice. By offering audiences a structure of feeling (the identification with victims, their revealed goodness, and their pain), melodrama compensates for tragic injustices and human sacrifice. Or, as Williams puts it, "melodramatic climaxes that end in the death of a good person—Uncle Tom, Princess Charlotte, Jack Dawson (in *Titanic*) offer paroxysms of pathos and recognitions of virtue compensating for the loss of life."[35] In political melodramas (like the stories told of 9/11's female victims), pathos can often be an end in itself; the spectator emerges feeling a sense of righteousness even while justice has not been achieved in reality and even while many people feel completely alienated from and overwhelmed by the actual political sphere.

Addressing the public with the same kind of sentimental/compensatory citizenship, President Bush used the image of female suffering in his first televised address before Congress after the attacks. Harking back to Cold War paranoia films like Warner Bros.' *Red Nightmare* (which was made with the Defense Department and showed what a typical American town would look like if it were taken over by "commies"), President Bush painted a picture of the threat that terrorism posed to our freedom. "In Afghanistan," he claimed, "we see Al Qaeda's vision of the world," after which he listed a string of daily oppressions people might be forced to face should Al Qaeda's vision prevail. First on his list was the fact that "women are not allowed to go to school." The rhetorical construction here is important because by suggesting that Al Qaeda had a vision for the world, President Bush asked TV audiences literally to imagine themselves taken over by Al Qaeda and in the women's place—the place of suffering. Having thereby stirred up viewers' moral indignation and pathos, he then went on to justify his own plan for aggression, giving the Taliban a series of ultimatums. Whatever one thinks about Bush's speech, it is clear that the image of suffering female victims was a powerful emotional ploy through which he connected his own war plan to a sense of moral righteousness and virtue (and it is also clear that we had never heard him speak of these women in Afghanistan before that day).

A more complicated example is CNN's airing of the documentary *Beneath the Veil,* which depicts the abuses that women of Afghanistan suffered under the Taliban. Originally made in the spring of 2001 for Britain's Channel 4, *Beneath the Veil* was produced "undercover" by Saira Shah (who grew up in Britain but whose father is from Afghanistan) and with considerable risk to the filmmaker (photography was outlawed by the Taliban, and the fact that Shah is a woman made the whole process doubly dangerous). *Beneath the Veil* outlines not only the Taliban's oppression and cruelty but also the history of global neglect of Afghan women, as well as the need for political action now. Shah is careful to reflect on her own Western assumptions about women, feminism, and Islam, and she shows that it is the Afghan women themselves—a group known as the Revolutionary Association of the Women of Afghanistan (RAWA) —who were the first to fight against the Taliban.

Beneath the Veil opens with footage shot (via hidden cameras) by RAWA. There are images of women huddled in a pickup truck and being brought to a football field turned public execution arena. They are killed for alleged adultery. Interspersed throughout the film are images of and dialogues about the women's oppression, RAWA's own efforts to liberate women, and Shah's documentary witnessing of the events. An accompanying website (still up) provides numerous links to information and zones of action and participation. The program and its website constitute an important political use of electronic media. While there are images of female suffering, the pathos elicited by the pictures is organized around the desire for action (which Williams reminds us can also be part of melodrama) rather than just sentiment as an end in itself.

When *Beneath the Veil* was rerun and repurposed by CNN in the context of the post-9/11 news coverage, however, its politics were significantly altered. In the two months following the attacks, CNN reran *Beneath the Veil* so many times that it became a kind of daily documentary ritual. Although it was certainly important for audiences to learn about this human rights disaster, we should nevertheless wonder why Western eyes were willing to look at this documentary with such fascination after 9/11 (as opposed to, say, on September 10). First, it should be noted that in the wake of 9/11 documentaries of all sorts (but especially ones about terrorism) were, according to *Variety,* a "hot property" in the television industry.[36] Second, whatever the original achievements of the program, in this new context audiences were led to make easy equivocations between the kind of oppression the women of Afghanistan faced and the loss of innocent life on American soil on September 11. In the context of CNN's programming flow, we saw *Beneath the Veil* adjacent to news footage depicting Ground Zero, stories of American victims and heroes, anthrax attacks, public safety warnings, mug shots of the FBI's most-wanted terrorists, and war footage depicting a bizarre mix of bombs and humanitarian aid being dropped on Afghanistan.[37] In this programming context, *Beneath the Veil* could easily be read as a cautionary tale (like *Red Nightmare*) and a justification for the US bombings in Afghanistan. In other words, it might well have conjured up national unity for war as a moral position.

In the midst of the US bombings, Shah produced a follow-up film, *The Unholy War,* which aired on CNN in mid-November 2001. This film documented the lives of women (especially three young Afghan girls) in the midst of the US war against the Taliban. The film showed the destruction caused by bombings, the problems entailed in building a post-Taliban regime, and Shah's own failures in trying to help the three girls (she attempts to get them an education), whose father rejected her humanitarian efforts. *The Unholy War* disrupted the "flow" of CNN's rotation of *Beneath the Veil.* It also punctured President Bush's melodramatic rescue/war narrative and questioned (the usually unquestionable) ideologies of "humanitarianism" that legitimated the US bombings. As Shah said in an interview with *Salon:* "I couldn't believe that we couldn't help them and that money wouldn't solve their problems.... That was a real revelation for me. I rather arrogantly, in a very Western way, assumed that I could solve their problems because I had good will and money. It taught me that their problems are more complex. It also taught me a lot about what's needed in Afghanistan, and how frustrating it is rebuilding a country that's been destroyed to the extent that Afghanistan has."[38]

Event TV and Celebrity Citizenship

While Shah's *Unholy War* suggests that there were indeed counter-histories and anti-war messages to be found on the airwaves and on websites like Salon.com, the news images of unfathomable destruction that aired on 9/11 resulted in industry attempts to match that spectacle with reparative images on a scale as great as the falling towers. In this respect, "event TV" (or television programs designed to take on the status and audience shares of media events) flourished after 9/11, allowing for another staging of national unity after the attacks. These staged events created a "meta-universe" of Hollywood stars enacting the role of patriotic publics.

The first of these events was the celebrity telethon *America: A Tribute to Heroes.* Telecast live from New York, Los Angeles, and London on 21 September 2001, at 9:00 PM, the two-hour program was simulcast on more than 320 national broadcast and cable networks. According to the Nielsen ratings, the telethon garnered a 65 share of US households, making it one of the most-watched programs of the year, behind only the Super Bowl.[39]

America: A Tribute to Heroes featured an overwhelming community of stars recounting the stories of those who died or risked their lives in the struggle. These eulogies were interspersed with musical performances or popular hits from the baby-boom to post-boomer past (the assumed generations of donors). Like all televised funerals, this one deployed television's aesthetics of liveness to stave of the fear of death. In other words, not only the "live" feed but also the sense of unrehearsed spontaneity and intimate revelations gave viewers a way to feel that life goes on in the present. The ritualistic and funereal atmosphere resurrected the recently dead for the living, restoring faith not only in spiritual terms but also in terms of the medium itself (in other words, it was that most "degraded" of media—television—that brought us this powerful sense of healing and community).[40]

While certainly designed to be a global media event, this was a deliberately understated spectacle, achieved through a deliberate display of "star capital" minus the visual glitz and ego. Staged with "zero degree" style (just candles burning on an otherwise unadorned set), the program appealed to a desire to see Hollywood stars, singers, and sports heroes reduced to "real" people, unadorned, unrehearsed (or at least underrehearsed), and literally unnamed and unannounced (there was no variety host presiding over the entertainment, no identification of the stars, and no studio audience). This absence of style signified the authenticity of the staged event, thereby giving stars the authority to speak for the dead. So too, the actual mix of stars (for example, Muhammad Ali, Clint Eastwood, Paul Simon, Julia Roberts, Enrique Iglesias, Bruce Springsteen, Celine Dion, Chris Rock, Sylvester Stallone) combined what might otherwise have been a battle-of-star semiotics (given their often at-odds personas and historical associations) into a compelling and, for many people, moving site of mourning. The program's "interactive" aspect further strengthened the telethon's aura of community, as on-demand celebrity phone operators, from Goldie Hawn to Jack Nicholson, promised to reach out and touch us. In all of these ways, *America: A Tribute to Heroes* is a stunning example of how post-9/11 television has created not a public sphere per se, but rather a self-referential

Hollywood public sphere of celebrities who stand in for real citizens and who somehow make us feel connected to a wider social fabric.

The 53rd Annual Emmy Awards ceremony, which was twice delayed because of the attacks, is another example. Jack Valenti's "show must go on" ethos was everywhere in the publicity leading up to and culminating in this yearly television event. Somehow the industry was convinced that the airing of the Emmys was so important to America that any sign of celebrity resistance to gather (whether for fear of being attacked or for fear of looking crassly self-absorbed) would somehow be tantamount to "letting the terrorists win." As Academy of Television Arts and Sciences Chairman Bryce Zabel told viewers, cancelling the Emmys "would have been an admission of defeat. Like baseball and Broadway, we are an American tradition."[41]

It seems just as probable, however, that the Academy and CBS were also worrying about their own commercial viability in the post-9/11 climate. In other words, cancelling the Emmys would not just be an admission of the defeat of the nation; it would also be an admission that the consumer logics of TV—its annual ceremonies and self-congratulations—had been defeated. In the wake of 9/11, the Emmys came to signify the degree to which the televisual and marketing scene could be revitalized. The broadcast, which took place on November 4 at Los Angeles's Shubert Theatre (almost two months after the originally scheduled broadcast), was carefully orchestrated in this regard. Although there were more "no-shows" than usual, and while the area outside the theatre was reportedly a "surreal" scene of rooftop sharpshooters, the Emmy producers encouraged the stars to perform their roles in the usual fashion. Before the broadcast, Executive Producer Gary Smith coached the stars: "Don't be afraid to be excited.... That's what people are looking for."[42]

The Emmy Awards program was another self-referential celebrity public sphere, this time constructed through appeals to television and Hollywood history. The opening sequence begins with Christian trumpet player/singer Phil Driscoll doing a bluesy rendition of "America the Beautiful" with a backup choir of students from different colleges across the country. The national unity theme is underscored by a large screen display of video images (everything from images of the flag and the Statue of Liberty to historical footage of Charles Lindbergh's lift-off and civil rights protests to landscape images of prairies and cities, all spliced together in a seamless quilt of meaning). This is followed by a female voiceover that announces: "Tonight television speaks to a global audience as we show the world images of an annual celebration. Our presence here tonight does more than honor an industry, it honors those cherished freedoms that set us apart as a nation and a people." After this, the scene cuts to veteran newscaster Walter Cronkite, who appears via satellite from Toronto. Cronkite directly addresses the camera and narrates a history of television's importance to American politics and culture. Evoking the words of the World War II broadcaster Edward R. Murrow, Cronkite says, "Television, the great common denominator, has lifted our common vision as never before, and television also reminds us that entertainment can help us heal."

The Driscoll performance, the video backdrop, the female voiceover, and finally the widely respected Cronkite provide a prelude to what will be the night's apologetic theme: the ritualistic honouring of stars is not narcissistic, commercialized self-indulgence, but instead a public service to America and its image in the world.[43] The opening sequence then transitions to host Ellen DeGeneres, who delivers her monologue as the cameras cut back and forth to a bevy of Hollywood stars seated in the audience. Significantly, among those singled out are stars associated with Hollywood liberalism, including the cast of *The West Wing* and Bill Maher (who had already been in trouble with his sponsors for what they perceived to be unpatriotic comments). In other words, like the telethon, the Emmy ceremony was not simply "right-wing" in its approach to patriotism; it presented well-known Hollywood liberals (including a grand finale by Barbra Streisand and, of course, DeGeneres herself) as part of a national community who leave their identity politics home to join together and defend the larger American cause. Drawing attention to the patriotic mission of this liberal constituency, DeGeneres humorously asks the audience, "What would bug the Taliban more than seeing a gay woman in a suit surrounded by Jews?"

While the opening act establishes television as its own historical reference and television stars as their own public, a sequence near the end of the broadcast is even more blatant in its self-referential memories of Hollywood nationalism and celebrity citizenship. And while the first act uses network-era "hard" newsman Cronkite (who is in Toronto and far removed from the pomp and pageantry), this later segment features the ultimate post-network celebrity journalist, Larry King (who is dressed in a tuxedo and obviously part of the Hollywood community). King introduces a montage of vintage footage portraying Hollywood's efforts in wartime (e.g., the Andrews Sisters; Betty Grable's legs; Bugs Bunny; Bob Hope and the USO; Marilyn Monroe posing for the boys and kissing a wounded GI; Frank Sinatra signing an autograph; Harpo Marx clowning on stage; Bob Hope and a bevy of sexy starlets in Vietnam; Bob Hope, Steve Martin, and Jay Leno in the Gulf interspersed with Vietnam footage of Hope and Phyllis Diller as well as black-and-white images of Nat King Cole and Milton Berle performing for the troops). The rapid, decontextualized series of star fetish icons and the musical accompaniment (from the Andrews Sisters' World War II hit "Boogie Woogie Bugle Boy," to a standard rock riff, to Lee Greenwood singing "I'm Proud to Be an American") establish a "commonsense" and highly sentimental history of Hollywood patriotism (or as Larry King put it while introducing the montage, "Over the years the beat of the music changes, but the heart beneath it never wavers"). This nostalgic display of stars, with its thesis of unchanging Hollywood sentiment, obscures the different historical contexts in which World War II, Korea, Vietnam, and the Gulf War were fought (and obviously also the very different levels of popular support these wars had).

The montage sequence ends with an overhead travelling shot picturing a vast audience of GIs applauding Bob Hope during the Gulf War. The sequence then dissolves back to an overhead travelling shot of the celebrity audience applauding in the Shubert Theatre. This dissolve from the GIs to the Emmy audience—and the fact that the shots are perfectly matched—establishes a visual rhetoric that asks viewers to imagine that soldiers and celebrities are contiguous publics, and perhaps even comparable public servants. Immediately after the dissolve, the show cuts back to Larry King (live) on stage, where he speaks into the camera: "Once again we're in a time when America's armed forces are being sent to defend our freedom, and once again the entertainment industry is giving what it can." The entire segment legitimates future wars through a sentimental journey through Hollywood's wartime past.

The segment is capped off by yet another invocation of Hollywood's self-referential public sphere. Larry King speaks directly into the camera but not, as is usually the case, in order to address the home audience. Instead, he addresses an ailing Bob Hope at home: "We know that Bob Hope is watching at home tonight. And you should know, dear Robert, that we are thinking of you. . . . From all of us here, thanks for the memories." King's direct address to Hope—intercut with stars applauding in the studio audience—creates a completely enclosed universe of citizen celebrities, orchestrating a set of complex relays between popular memories of vintage Hollywood, military history since World War II, and the present-day meanings of nationalism and war. In this televised display of celebrity patriotism, public service and publicity find their ideal meeting ground.

Osama bin Laden Meets the *South Park* Kids

In the introductory pages of his essay "The Uncanny," Sigmund Freud discusses the intellectual uncertainty he faced during World War I when he found it impossible to keep up with the flow of international publications.[44] In the world of electronic "instant" histories, these problems of intellectual uncertainty are compounded in ways that Freud could never have imagined. The "uncanny" seems an especially appropriate trope for the current situation, as nothing seems to be what it was and everything is what it wasn't just minutes before it happened. In this context, the literate pursuit of history writing seems slow to the point of uselessness. This is, of course, compounded by the fact that the publishing industry is painfully behind the speed of both war and electronic media. So rather than partake of either historical "conclusions" or future "predictions," I want to open up some questions about television and nationalism vis-à-vis the changing economics of industrially produced culture.

Given the political divisions that have resurfaced since 2001, it seems likely that the grand narratives of national unity that sprang up after 9/11 were for many people more performative than sincere. In other words, it is likely that many viewers really did know that all the newfound patriotism was really just a public performance staged by cameras. Still, after 9/11 many people found it important to "perform" the role of citizen, which included the performance of belief in national myths of unity. And if you didn't perform this role, then somehow you were a bad American. In this respect, no matter what they thought of the situation, in the wake of 9/11 stars had to perform the role of "love it or leave it" citizen to remain popular (a lesson that Bill Maher learned with a vengeance when his TV show *Politically Incorrect* was cancelled).[45]

But did the performance really work? Just days after the attacks, the limits of performative nationalism were revealed in the televised celebrity telethon *America: A Tribute to Heroes* when, in the final sequence, everyone gathered 'round Willie Nelson to sing "America the Beautiful." Now, this was certainly a bad performance. Most of the celebrities were either too embarrassed to sing, or else they just didn't know the words to this show tune turned national anthem.[46] Some stars were visibly squinting at teleprompters with consternation, hoping to sing a verse. Yet, because the telethon was foremost aimed at baby-boom and post-baby-boom generations, most audiences would have known the popular ballads that were directly aimed at these niche generations. Clearly pop songs like John Lennon's "Imagine" (sung by Neil Young), Bob Marley's "Redemption Song" (sung by Wyclef Jean), or Paul Simon's "Bridge over Troubled Waters" have more historical meaning to these taste publics than any national anthem does.

More generally, I think the post-9/11 performance of nationalism will fail because it really does not fit with the economic and cultural practices of twenty-first-century US media society. The fact that there is no longer a three-network broadcast system means that citizens are not collected as aggregate audiences for national culture. As we all know, what we watch on TV no longer really is what other people watch—unless they happen to be in our demographic taste culture. The post-network system is precisely about fragmentation and narrowcasting. While the new 500-channel cable systems may not provide true diversity in the sense of political or cultural pluralism, the post-network system does assume a culture that is deeply divided by taste, not one that is unified through national narratives.[47] In a multinational consumer culture it becomes difficult for media to do business without addressing the niche politics of style, taste, and especially youth subcultures that have become central to global capitalism. In the end, the new media environment does not lend itself to unifying narratives of patriotism, if only because these older forms of nationalism have nothing to do with the "return to normalcy" and normal levels of consumption. While nationalist popular culture does, of course, exist (and obviously rose in popularity after 9/11), it appears more as another niche market (those people who hang flags on their cars) than as a unifying cultural dominant.[48]

The actual cultural styles in these new narrowcast media markets are increasingly based on irony, parody, skepticism, and "TV-literate" critical reading protocols. For people who grew up watching *The Simpsons'* hilarious parodies of mass culture and national politics; for people who fell asleep to Dave Letterman or Conan O'Brien; and for viewers who regularly watched *Saturday Night Live, In Living Color, The Daily Show,* and *Mad TV's* political/news parodies, a sudden return to blind patriotism (and blind consumerism) is probably not really likely.

In the first week after the September 11 attacks, the cable operators and networks all did cover the same story—and for a moment the nation returned to something very much like the old three-network system.[49] Yet, the case of 9/11 also demonstrates that in the current media landscape it is hard to sustain the fantasy of utopian collectivity that had been so central to previous media events. Comparing media coverage of 9/11 with the coverage of the Kennedy assassination, Fredric Jameson argues that back in 1963 a utopian fantasy of collectivity was in part constructed through news reporters' "clumsiness [and] the technological naiveté in which they sought to rise to the occasion." But, he claims, the media are now so full of orchestrated spectacle and public violence on a daily basis that many people had a hard time seeing media coverage of 9/11 as documents of anything sincere, much less as any kind of intersubjective, utopian communication. As Jameson puts it, despite the many claims that America lost its innocence on 9/11, it was "not America, but rather its media [that had] ... definitively lost its innocence."[50]

Certainly, for industry executives who work in the competitive environment of narrowcasting, sentiments of national belonging and utopian collectivity quickly gave way to the "bottom line." In fact, even in the "good will" climate of September 2001, the industry was still widely aware of the competitive realities of the post-network marketplace. CNN, which then had an exclusive deal with the Al Jazeera network, tried to block other news outlets from broadcasting its satellite transmissions of bin Laden's video address.[51] Even the celebrity telethon was a source of industry dispute. Worried that cable telecasts would undercut audience shares for broadcasters, some network affiliates and network-owned-and-operated stations tried to stop a number of cable channels from simulcasting *America: A Tribute to Heroes.* According to *Variety,* upon hearing of possible cable competition, "some of the vocal managers at the Big Four TV stations ... went bananas and threatened to cancel the telethon and schedule their own local programming."[52] So much for humanitarianism in the post-network age!

Given this competitive media marketplace, it comes as no surprise that industry insiders quickly revised their initial predictions about the fate of American popular culture. By October 4, the front page of the *New York Times* proclaimed, "In Little Time Pop Culture Is Back to Normal," stating that the industry was backtracking on its initial predictions that the events or September 11 would completely change culture. David Kissinger, president of the USA Television Production Group, told the *Times* that the industry's initial reaction to the attacks may have been overstated and that because most industry people were "terror stricken" on September 11, "we shouldn't be held accountable for much of what we said that week."[53]

In fact, within a month, even irony was back in vogue, especially on late-night TV, but increasingly also on entertainment programs. By early November, Comedy Central's *South Park*—a cartoon famous for its irreverence—ran an episode in which the *South Park* kids visit Afghanistan. Once there, Cartman (*South Park's* leading bad boy) meets bin Laden, and the two engage in an extended homage to Warner Bros. cartoons. Bin Laden takes the roles of the wacky Daffy Duck, the dull-headed Elmer Fudd, and even the lovesick Pepe La Pew (he is shown romancing a camel much as Pepe romances a cat that he thinks is a skunk). Meanwhile, Cartman plays the ever-obnoxious Bugs Bunny (like Bugs, he even does a drag performance as a harem girl wooing a lovesick bin Laden, whose eyes, in classic Tex Avery cartoon style, pop out of his head).

Although the episode was the usual "libertarian" hodgepodge of mixed political messages (some seemingly critical or US air strikes, others entirely Orientalist), its blank ironic sensibility did at least provide for some unexpected TV moments. In one scene, when the *South Park* kids meet Afghan children in a war-torn village, American claims of childish innocence (promoted, for example, in *The West Wing's* fictional classroom) are opened up for comic interrogation. Dodging a US bomb attack, the Afghan children tell the *South Park* kids, "Over a third of the world hates America." "But why?" ask the *South Park* kids, "Why does a third of the world hate us?" And the Afghan kids reply, "Because you don't realize that a third of the world hates you." While the episode ends with an over-the-top cartoon killing of bin Laden and an American flag waving to the tune of "America the Beautiful," the program establishes such a high degree of pastiche, blank irony, and recombinant imagery that it would be difficult to say that it encourages any particular "dominant" reading of the war. The laughter seems directed more at semiotic breakdowns, perhaps mimicking the way in which news coverage of the war seems to make people increasingly incapable of knowing what's going on—a point that one of the *South Park* characters underscores at the end of the show, when he says, "I'm confused."

To be sure, programs like *South Park* and the niche cable channels on which they appear might not translate into the old enlightenment dream of "public service" TV with a moral imperative for its national public. Television studies is, of course, riddled with debates over the question of whether these new forms of narrowcasting and multichannel media outlets will destroy what some critics call common culture. In response to the increasing commercialization and fragmentation of European electronic media, scholars like Jostein Gripsrud, Graham Murdock, and James Curran champion European public service broadcast models, and even while they do not advocate a simplistic return to paternalistic models of "cultivation" and taste, they seek a way to reformulate the ideal of an electronic democratic culture.[54] In the United States the situation is somewhat different. The "public interest" policy rhetoric on which the national broadcast system was founded has been woefully underachieved; broadcasters did not engage a democratic culture of diverse interests, but rather for the most part catered to the cultural tastes of their target consumers (which for many years meant white middle-class audiences). Moreover, the networks often interpreted public service requirements within the context of public relations and the strengthening of their own oligopoly power.[55] Meanwhile, the underfunded Public Broadcasting System grew increasingly dependent on corporate funding. And, as Laurie Ouellette argues, by relying on paternalistic notions of "cultivation" and catering to narrowminded taste hierarchies, the network has alienated audiences.[56]

Still I am not saying that the new multichannel and multiplatform system of niche culture is necessarily better. Instead, we need to ask exactly what the new fragmented niche networks, as well as the proliferation of Internet sites, provide. What do the new forms of multinational media outlets offer beyond the proliferation of products and styles? The question is even more complex when we consider the fact that cable and broadcast networks, Internet sites, search engines, television producers/distributors, movie studios, radio stations, newspapers, and publishing companies are increasingly part of global conglomerate media structures (Disney, Rupert Murdock's News Corp., Viacom,

Time Warner, etc.).[57] In the media industries, as in other postindustrial modes of capitalism, there is both fragmentation and centralization at the same time. Any attempt to consider the political effects of the multiplication of channels (and fragmentation of audiences) still has to be considered within the overall patterns of consolidation at the level of ownership.[58]

Perhaps I am a bit overly optimistic but I do want to end by suggesting some alternative possibilities within the highly consolidated, yet also fragmented, global mediasphere. As Daniel Dayan and Elihu Katz argue, although media events may be hegemonically sponsored and often function to restore consensual values, they always also "invite re-examination of the status quo." Following Victor Turner, Dayan and Katz claim that media events put audiences in a "liminal" context, outside the norms of the everyday. Even if media events do not institutionalize new norms, they do "provoke ... mental appraisal of alternative possibilities."[59] In this sense, although I have focused primarily on media myths of reunification and nationalism, it is also true that 9/11 provoked counter-narratives and political dialogues. In particular, 9/11 made people aware of new prospects for communication in a rapidly changing media environment.

Certainly, the Internet allowed for a collective interrogation of mainstream media and discussions among various marginalized groups. According to Bruce A. Williams, while "mainstream media reiterated themes of national unity, the chat rooms allowed different groups of Americans to debate what the impact of the attacks was for them specifically."[60] Internet sites like Salon.com—as well as access to a host of international news outlets—provided alternative views and global discussions. Convergence platforms opened up venues for expression. For example, after 9/11 a chat room hosted by the Black Entertainment Television network included conversations about whether it was possible to reconcile black beliefs about racist police and fire departments with the heroic images of police and firefighters after 9/11. Resistance groups from around the globe used the Internet as a forum for anti-war emails, virtual marches, and group organizing. The Social Science Research Council's website allowed scholars to weigh in on the events at Internet speed. The "low-tech" medium of radio (especially National Public Radio) likewise provided alternative voices.

That said, my point here is not that "new" media or "alternative media" are categorically "better" than TV. Certainly, many Internet sites and talk radio stations were filled with right-wing war fever. As Williams suggests, because the Internet allows for insular conversations, some message boards (such as "Crosstar") discussed ways to draw clear ideological boundaries and to keep "dissident voices" (i.e., liberals) off the board.[61] In this respect, we should not embrace the Internet in some essentialist sense as a pure space of pluralism which is always already more democratic than "old" media. Instead, it seems more accurate to say that the presence of multiple media platforms holds out hopeful possibilities for increased expression, but what this will amount to in terms of democracy and citizenship remains a complex historical question.

In addition to the Internet, the presence of the Al Jazeera news network had a destabilizing effect on the status or information itself. Al Jazeera officials defy the democratic legacy or the "free press" that had been so crucial to US Cold War politics. Whereas the United States used to claim that its so-called free press was a reigning example of "free world" democracy, Al Jazeera now has taken up the same public pose, claiming that it will present all sides of the story from a Middle Eastern vantage point. In their book on Al Jazeera, Mohammed El-Nawawy and Adel Iskandar discuss how the network's post-9/11 coverage—especially its graphic coverage of the US bombings in Afghanistan and the circulation of bin Laden's videotapes—quickly became a public relations crisis for the Bush administration.[62] Troubled by the bad PR, the Bush administration formed a Hollywood summit to discuss the role the industry might play in the war on terrorism. The military also met with Hollywood talent at the University of Southern California's Institute for Creative Technologies, a military/Hollywood alliance that Jonathan Burston aptly terms "militainment."[63] By late November 2001 President Bush had signed an initiative to start the Middle East Radio network (which strives to counterbalance anti-Americanism in the Arab world and is aimed especially at youth audiences).[64] As such federally sponsored efforts suggest, the proliferation of news outlets, entertainment networks, and Internet sites, as well as the mounting synergy between Hollywood and the military, has changed the nature of semiotic warfare, and the United States is certainly keen to play by the new rules of the game.[65]

Back to Normal?

On the one hand, as I have suggested, much of the TV landscape looks like a continuation of the same kinds of programs that aired prior to 9/11, and for this reason it is tempting to say that television's "return to normal" transcended the events of 9/11 and that everything is as it was before. On the other hand, 9/11 haunts US commercial television.[66] The memory of 9/11 now—in 2004—circulates in ways that disrupt the kind of historical narratives and nationalist logic that had been so central to the initial return to the normal TV schedule.

Since 2001 the history and memory of 9/11 have in fact become a national battleground—not only in the notorious fights over Ground Zero's reconstruction but also in the electronic spaces of television. By March of 2002 major networks had begun to feature commemorative documentaries that told the story of 9/11.[67] By March of 2004 President Bush launched a presidential campaign with TV ads that show historical footage of the firefighters, implicitly equating their heroism with his presidency. But whereas nationalist historical pedagogy initially served to solidify consent for the Bush administration, now the history and memory of 9/11 are not so simply marshalled. On 5 March 2004, just one day after the ads began to circulate, CNN interviewed a woman who had lost her husband on 9/11. Unlike the speechless pregnant widows on *Oprah!* back in 2001, this woman had regained her voice and spoke quite articulately of her disgust for the President's use of 9/11 footage for political ends.

In the end, I suspect that the current situation is ripe for new visions of apocalyptic techno-futures, with satellites, guided missiles, surveillance cameras, and communication media of all kinds at the core of an ongoing genre of techno-warfare criticism waged by Jean Baudrillard, Paul Virilio, and many others.[68] But it seems to me that, as forceful and perceptive as this kind of work has been, this is really just the easy way out. Instead of engaging in yet another stream of doom-and-gloom technological disaster criticism, it seems more useful to think about how cultural studies and media studies in particular might hold on to a politics of hope. What I have in mind is in no way the same as utopian claims to transcendence and unity (whether local, national, or global) through new media technologies. Rather, this politics of hope is situated in a confrontation with the actually existing historical divisions around us. This materialist politics of hope should embrace the new global media environment as an opportunity to listen to "the third of the world that hates us" rather than (to use Bush's formulation) clutter the globe with messages about "how good we are." The world has heard enough about America. Time now to tune in elsewhere.

Notes

1. "Disaster Programming," *Variety.com,* 21 September 2001, 1. For more on TV network cancellations of violent movies, see John Dempsey, "Cable Nets Nix Violent Pix in Wake of Tragedy," *Variety.com,* 16 September 2001, 1–2; Joe Flint and John Lippman, "Hollywood Revisits Terrorism-Related Projects," *Wall Street Journal,* 13 September 2001, 82; Joe Flint, "TV Programmers Avoid All Allusions to Attacks," *Wall Street Journal,* 28 September 2001, 136.
2. For speculations on the "end or irony" see Jeff Gordinier, "How We Saw It," *Entertainment Weekly,* 28 September 2001, 12; Peter Bart, "Where's the Snap and Crackle or Pop Culture?" *Variety.com,* 30 September 2001, 1–2. Note, however, that a counter-discourse popped up immediately in venues like the *Onion* and *Salon,* which used irony early on. In an online essay, James Der Derian noted some of the inconsistencies in what he called the "protected zones of language" after 9/11, pointing out, for example, that irony was in some venues under attack: "President Bush was given room to joke in a morale-boosting visit to the CIA, saying he's 'spending a lot of quality time lately' with George Tenet, the director of the CIA." Der Derian also took on *New York Times* reporter Edward Rothstein for taking an "opportunist shot at postmodernists and postcolonialists" by "claiming that their irony and relativism is 'ethnically perverse' and produces 'guilty passivity.'" See Der Derian's "9.11: Before, After, and In Between," Social Science Research Council, After September 11 Archive, SSRC.org, 5 (the original posting date is no longer on the site).
3. Jennifer Netherby, "Renters Flock to Video Stores," *Videobusiness.com,* 21 September 2001, 1–2. *Video On Line* reported that "Wal-mart stores asked the studios for a list of their titles that contain scenes or the World Trade Center, presumably to take some merchandising action on those movies" *(Videobusiness.com/news,* 13 September 2001, 1).
4. "Domain Names Grow after Attacks," *Variety.com,* 25 September 2001, 1.
5. Even while cable outlets are not regulated by the Federal Communications Commission to the extent that the broadcast networks are, they still are widely perceived as "service" industries and protectors of public safety in times of crisis (obviously, this is the platform of cable news outlets like CNN, which dramatically increased its viewership after 9/11).
6. I am borrowing Raymond Williams's phrase "a whole way or life," which he used to define culture. See his *Culture and Society, 1780–1950* (1958; New York: Columbia University Press, 1983), 325.
7. More generally, 9/11 disrupted the familiar/consumer uses of a host of communication technologies, from cell phones to television to satellites to video games, all of which now resonated in an uncanny sense with the militaristic/wartime uses for which their basic technology was developed.
8. Mary Anne Doane, "Information, Crisis, Catastrophe," in *Logics of Television: Essays in Cultural Criticism,* ed. Patricia Mellencamp (Bloomington: Indiana University Press, 1990), 222–39.
9. Venessa O'Connell, "TV Networks Cut $120 Million of Ads in Crisis," *Wall Street Journal,* 19 September 2001.
10. *Variety* reported that "commercial breaks were back across the board Monday [September 17]" (Rick Kissell, "TV Getting Back to Biz and Blurbs," *Variety.com,* September 2001, 1).
11. Jack Valenti, "Hollywood and Our Nation Will Meet the Test," *Variety.com,* 27 September 2001, 1–2.
12. The President said this in a televised address he delivered at Chicago O'Hare Airport with the aim of convincing people to return to plane travel. Note, too, that in subsequent months various advertisers linked their promotional discourses to 9/11 and the idea of patriotic consumption. (For example, ads for United and American Airlines as well as financial corporations did this.)
13. For examples of literature on TV news, 9/11, and Afghanistan, see *Television and New Media* 3 (May 2002); Daya Kishan Thussu and Des Freedman, eds, *War and the Media* (Thousand Oaks, CA: Sage, 2003); Stephen Hess and Marvin Kalb, eds, *The Media and the War on Terrorism* (Washington, DC: Brookings Institute, 2003); Barbie Zelizer and Stuart Allan, eds, *Journalism after September 11* (New York: Routledge, 2002).
14. As other scholars have argued, we should not accept at face value the information/entertainment binary that underpins the ideological logic of mainstream media systems. This binary—and the related binaries of important/trivial, private/public, masculine/feminine, and high/low—not only elide the fact that news is also narrative (and increasingly entertaining) but also fail to acknowledge that entertainment also serves to provide audiences with particular ways of knowing about and seeing the world. See, for example, Richard Dyer, *Only Entertainment* (New York: Routledge, 1992); John Fiske, "Popular News," in *Reading Popular Culture* (Boston: Unwyn and Hymen, 1989); James Freedman, ed., *Reality Squared: Television Discourse on the Real* (New Brunswick, NJ: Rutgers University Press, 2002).
15. Der Derian, "9.11," 2.
16. For an interesting discussion on media references to Pearl Harbor and the rerelease of the film after 9/11, see Cynthia Weber, "The Media, the 'War on Terrorism' and the Circulation of Non-Knowledge," in Thussu and Freedman, eds, *War and the Media,* 190–9.
17. This kind of coverage is, of course, symptomatic of the general rise of "infotainment" in the climate of media conglomeration and a ratings-driven commercial ethos.

For speculation on the social/political effects or the news coverage of the news coverage of 9/11 in terms of "infotainment," see Daya Kishan Thussu, "Live TV and Bloodless Deaths: War, Infotainment, and 24/7 News," in Thussu and Freedman, eds, *War and the Media,* 117–32. There is much additional literature on issues of infotainment. See, for example, Leonard Downie Jr and Robert G. Kaiser, *The News about the News: American Journalism in Peril* (New York: Knopf, 2002); and Pierre Bourdieu, *On Television,* trans. Priscilla Parkhurst Ferguson (New York: New Press, 1998). For analysis of the effect that round-the-clock coverage of "real time" wars has on foreign policy, see Piers Robinson, *The CNN Effect: The Myth of News, Foreign Policy, and Intervention* (New York: Routledge, 2002).

18. Claude Brodesser, "Feds Seek H'wood Help," *Variety.com,* 7 October 2001; Michael Schneider, "Fox Salutes Request by Bush for 'Wanted' Spec," *Variety.com,* 10 October 2001.
19. Michel de Certeau, "History: Science and Fiction," in *Heterologies: Discourse on the Other,* trans. Brian Massumi (Minneapolis: University of Minnesota Press, 1986), 199–221.
20. Roland Barthes, *Mythologies,* trans. A. Lavers (London: Cape, 1972); Marita Sturken, *Tangled Memories: The Vietnam War, the AIDS Epidemic, and the Politics of Remembering* (Berkeley: University of California Press, 1997). For more on the role of memory/nostalgia in film, television, and other popular media, see, for example, the Cahiers du Cinéma interview with Michel Foucault, reprinted in *Edinburgh Magazine* 2 (1977): 19–25; Patrick Bommes and Richard Wright, "Charms of Residence," in *Making Histories: Studies in History Writing and Politics,* ed. Richard Johnson et al. (London: Hutchinson, 1982); George Lipsitz, *Time Passages: Collective Memory and American Popular Culture* (Minneapolis: University of Minnesota Press, 1989); Robert Rosenstone, *Visions of the Past: The Challenge of Film to Our Idea of History* (New York: Belknap Press, 1996); Robert Rosenstone, *Revisioning History: Film and the Construction of a New Past* (Princeton: Princeton University Press, 1994); Marcia Landy, ed., *The Historical Film: History and Memory in the Media* (New Brunswick, NJ: Rutgers University Press, 2000); "Special Debate," *Screen* 42 (Summer 2001): 188–216 (this is a series of short essays on trauma and cinema); David Morley and Kevin Robins, "No Place Like Heimet: Images of Homeland," in *Spaces of Identity: Global Media, Electronic Landscapes, and Cultural Boundaries* (New York: Routledge, 1995), 85–104; Purnima Mankekar, *Screening Culture, Viewing Politics: An Ethnography of Television, Womanhood, and Nation in Postcolonial India* (Durham, NC: Duke University Press, 1999).
21. Louis Chunovic, "Will TV News—or Its Audience—Finally Grow Up?" *Television Week,* 24 September 2001, 15. Note that news executives responded to such criticism. For example, CBS's Mel Karmizan and Fox News Channel's Roger Ailes promised to upgrade news programs and to cover more international issues.
22. So, too, this ABC lineup followed the logic of what Daniel Dayan and Elihu Katz see as integral to media events more generally, namely, a "neo romantic desire for heroic action by great men followed by the spontaneity or mass action" *(Media Events: The Live Broadcasting of History* [Cambridge: Harvard University Press, 1992], 21).
23. Some people have told me that they found it a useful source of "modelling" for their own conversations with their children.
24. Several other series also created special episodes about the attacks or else planted references to 9/11 in preexisting episodes. NBC's *Third Watch* began its season on October 29 with a documentary in which real-life emergency workers recalled their experiences on 9/11. ABC's *N.Y.P.D. Blue* added two scenes acknowledging the attack into its season opener on November 6. As *New York Times* critic Caryn James pointed out, "The creators of 'Third Watch' and 'N.Y.P.D. Blue' have said they felt a responsibility to deal with the events, but the decision was practical, too. Their supposedly realistic characters would have seemed utterly unbelievable if they had ignored such an all-consuming tragedy" ('Dramatic Events that Rewrite the Script," *New York Times,* 29 October 2001, p. E7).
25. Josh lists many of the same Taliban injustices that President Bush listed in his first televised speech to Congress after the attacks.
26. Edward W. Said, *Orientalism* (New York: Vintage Books, 1979), esp. 284–328.
27. Ibid., 291.
28. Lauren Berlant, *The Queen of America Goes to Washington City: Essays on Sex and Citizenship* (Durham, NC: Duke University Press, 1997).
29. As Slavoj Žižek wrote just days after the attacks, this sense of a pure "evil Outside" was the response of a public living in a fake "Matrix"-like existence, a public that had for so long considered itself immune to the suffering endured on a daily basis by other world populations and, in any case, in no way responsible for its own perpetuation of violence around the world. Slavoj Žižek, "Welcome to the Desert of the Real!' posted on Re: Constructions.mit.edu 24 September 2001. The title is taken from a line in the film *The Matrix.* Žižek's short essay was later developed in a book. See his *Welcome to the Desert of the Real* (London: Verso, 2002). Der Derian's "9.11," 4–5, similarly evokes *The Matrix.*
30. Jack Lule, "Myth and Terror on the Editorial Page: The *New York Times* Responds to September 11, 2001," *Journalism and Mass Communication* Quarterly 29, no. 2 (2002): 275–93.
31. Yet, as Marita Sturken argues, this "end of innocence" theme is common to the stories spun around national

disasters (for example, the same language was used after JFK's assassination). See Sturken, *Tangled Memories,* chap. 1.

32. Justin Lewis, "Speaking of Wars ... " *Television and New Media* 3 (May 2002): 170.
33. In this sense, it is interesting to note how television created a *continuous past,* particularly with regard to World War II and Vietnam. In place of the grave generational divides these wars had previously come to signify, television presented unifying narratives that bridged the gap between the self-sacrificing "Greatest Generation" and baby-boomer draft dodgers. This was most vividly displayed when Vietnam POW/Senator John McCain met 1960s youth rebel Stephen Stills on the *Tonight Show,* reconciling their differences.
34. Jayne Rodgers, "Icons and Invisibility: Gender, Myth, and 9/11," in Thussu and Freedman, eds, *War and the Media,* 206, 207.
35. Linda Williams, *Playing the Race Card: Melodramas of Black and White: From Uncle Tom to O.J. Simpson* (Princeton: Princeton University Press, 2001), 24.
36. One month after the attacks, *Variety* reported, "A rash of documentaries—some put together in a hurry—that aim to explain terrorism is a hot property" (Andrea R. Vaucher, "Arab, Terror Docus Heat Up the Market," *Variety.com,* 10 October 2001, 1).
37. US and British air strikes on Afghanistan began on 7 October 2001, and American warplanes attacked the Taliban in the field on 10 October 2001.
38. Saira Shah, cited in Janelle Brown, "Beneath the Veil Redux," *Salon.com,* 16 November 2001, 1–2.
39. Rick Kissell, "Bush Speech, Telethon Both Draw Record Auds," *Variety.com,* 23 September 2001, 1–2.
40. As one of the readers for this article suggested, the telethon's aura of liveness might have also helped to stave off the fear that TV and commercial culture were themselves "dead." To be sure, live "call-in" donations to stars ensured that money was still circulating through the media wires (here, not through the crass commercialism of TV as usual, but through the exchange economies of charity).
41. He said this on the broadcast.
42. Gary Smith, cited in Joseph Adalian, "Show Finally Goes On and TV Biz Takes Heart," *Variety.com,* 4 November 2001, 1.
43. Underscoring the show's global impact, later in the ceremony there is a video montage of leaders from around the globe offering their condolences to the American public.
44. Sigmund Freud, "The Uncanny," in *Studies in Parapsychology* (1919; New York: Collier Books, 1963), 19–60. Freud discusses his lack of bibliographical references vis-à-vis the war in Europe on page 20.
45. When I delivered this paper at a conference at the University of California, Berkeley, Ratiba Hadj-Moussa pointed out that this dynamic of national performance doesn't necessarily suggest that people don't in some way believe in the performance. I want to thank her for this observation. Clearly, through the act of national performance, it is possible to actually to believe in the role you are playing—and even to believe in it more than ever.
46. Note, too, that "America the Beautiful" replaced the actual national anthem after 9/11 because no one seemed to be able to remember the words to the "Star-Spangled Banner."
47. Even news is now a matter of taste and "branded" by networks in ways that appeal to consumer profiles. For example, the news on Fox (especially its markedly conservative talk shows) attracts one of cable TV's most loyal publics, but many on the left mock its pretense of "Fair and Balanced" reporting. Al Franken's best-seller *Lies and the Lying Liars Who Tell Them: A Fair and Balanced Look at the Right* (New York: E.P. Dutton, 2003) and his lawsuit with Fox obviously drew on the more left-associated taste publics that define themselves in distinction—in Bourdieu's sense—not only to Fox News but also to the viewers who (they imagine) watch it. For his discussion of taste as social distinction, see Pierre Bourdieu, *Distinction: A Social Critique of the Judgement of Taste,* trans. Richard Nice (Cambridge: Harvard University Press, 1984).
48. Even before the attacks, patriotic symbols were reemerging as a fashion fad. Corporations such as Tommy Hilfiger, Polo Ralph Lauren, and the Gap Inc.'s Old Navy sported the flag trend, while European haute couture designer Catherine Malandrino unveiled her flag-motif fall collection in the summer of 2001 (which included a skirt that Madonna wore on her concert tour). See Teri Agins, "Flag Fashion's Surging Popularity Fits with Some Fall Collections," *Wall Street Journal,* 19 September 2001, B5. According to Agins, the post-9/11 flag fashions were an extension of this trend, not an invention of it.
49. In 1992 Dayan and Katz speculated on the fate of television, nationalism, and media events in what they saw to be an increasingly multichannel and segmented television system. They argued that while the old three-network or public broadcast systems "will disappear," television's previous functions of "national integration may devolve upon" media events. Their speculation now seems particularly apt. They also predicted that with new technologies and possible erosion of the nation-state, "media events may then create and integrate communities larger than nations." See Dayan and Katz, *Media Events,* 23.
50. Fredric Jameson, "The Dialectics of Disaster," *South Atlantic Quarterly* 101 (Spring 2002): 300.
51. According to *Variety,* news organizations were "furious that CNN wouldn't forego competition" and "rallied against exclusives, saying that they don't serve the

public's interest during a time of national crisis." ABC news spokesperson Jeffrey Schneider disputed any exclusivity deal by arguing fair use. He said, "There was no question in anybody's mind that these images from Al Jazeera were of compelling national interest," and "We felt we had a duty to broadcast them to the American people which far outweighed whatever commercial agenda CNN was attempting to pursue in this time of war." Meanwhile, Walter Isaacson, CEO of CNN News Group, told *Variety* that CNN had a "reciprocal affiliate deal" with Al Jazeera and that "it's Al Jazeera's material and we don't have a right to give it away." Isaacson did admit, however, that "in a time of war, we won't make a big deal about this sort of thing." See Paul Bernstein and Pamela McClintock, "Newsies Fight over Bin Laden Interview," *Variety.com*, 7 October 2001, 1–2.

52. John Dempsey, "Invite to Cablers to Join Telethon Irks Affils," *Variety.com*, 20 September 2001, 1. The underlying reasons for the broadcasters' concern had to do with issues of East Coast–West Coast transmission times. The big four networks—ABC, CBS, NBC, and Fox—aired the telethon at 9 PM eastern time, and because they wanted to make it seem like a simultaneous nationwide event, they also showed it taped via a dual feed at 9 PM on the West Coast. Some single-feed cable networks such as TBS and the National Geographic Channel, however, planned to show the telethon live at 6 PM on the West Coast, and thereby pre-empt the 9 PM taped West Coast network broadcast. Some network affiliates and owned and operated stations were simply unhappy that any cable networks were airing the telethon, even if cablers showed it simultaneously (at 9 PM) with the Big Four.
53. David Kessinger, cited in Rick Lyman with Bill Carter, "In Little Time Pop Culture Is Almost Back to Normal," *New York Times*, 4 October 2001.
54. See, for example, Jostein Gripsrud, ed., *Television and Common Knowledge* (New York: Routledge, 1999), esp. Graham Murdock, "Rights and Representations," 7–17; James Curran, "Mass Media and Democracy Revisited," in *Mass Media and Society*, ed. James Curran and Michael Gurevitch, 2nd edn (London: Arnold, 1996), 81–119.
55. See, for example, Vance Kepley Jr, "The Weaver Years at NBC," *Wide Angle*, (12 April 1990): 46–63, and "From 'Frontal Lobes' to the 'Bob and Bob Show': NBC Management and Programming Strategies, 1949–65," in *Hollywood in the Age of Television*, ed. Tino Balio (Boston: Unwin-Hyman, 1990), 41–62; Lynn Spigel, "The Making of a Television Literate Elite," in *The Television Studies Book*, ed. Christine Geraghty and David Lusted (London: Arnold, 1998), 63–85.
56. Laurie Ouellette, *Viewers Like You? How Public TV Failed the People* (New Brunswick, NJ: Rutgers University Press, 2002).
57. ABC is now owned by Disney (which owns, for example, the Disney theme parks, radio stations, cable networks like ESPN and Lifetime, retail outlets, feature film companies, newspapers, and magazines); the multiple-system operator Comcast has recently bid for the now-struggling Walt Disney Company; CBS is owned by Viacom (which also owns, for example, Paramount Studios as well as cable networks like MTV and Nickelodeon, theme parks, and radio stations); NBC is owned by General Electric (which entered into a joint venture with Microsoft and owns MSNBC); and Fox is owned by Rupert Murdock's News Corp. (which owns, for example, Fox Broadcasting; Fox News Channel; Fox Sports Net; motion picture companies; magazines like *TV Guide*, *Elle*, and *Seventeen*; book publishers; and numerous newspapers and delivers entertainment and information to at least 75 per cent of the globe). Meanwhile, media conglomerate Time Warner owns a large number of cable channels, production companies, home video, magazines, music companies, and book publishers (for example, HBO, Cinemax, TNT, Comedy Central, E! Entertainment, Black Entertainment Television, Time-Life Video, Warner Bros. Television, Book of the Month Club, and its notorious deal with America Online). With telephone and cable operators acquiring and partnering with media corporations and moving into content, the synergy among these sectors, is even more pronounced. These ownership structures make these media organizations more like vertically integrated movie studios of the classical period, as they have controlling stakes in all sectors of their industry—production, distribution, and exhibition—in addition to obvious benefits of owning multiple and related companies that reduce risk and increase opportunities for synergy between different companies in the umbrella corporation. Note, however, that the great instability of the technologies market (including, of course, the fate of AOL and the AOL–Time Warner merger) begs us to ask new questions regarding the future of media conglomeration and convergence.
58. Media conglomerates often say that consolidation of ownership leads to more choice (for example, some media conglomerates claim that consolidation of business holdings allows them to use income from their mainstream media outlets to launch minority channels). A variety of media activists, industry executives, media scholars, and government officials have, however, sharply attacked conglomeration and questioned the degree to which freedom of speech and diversity of representation can exist in a deregulated media system in which just a few major corporations own most of the media sources. See, for example, Patricia Aufderheide, *Communications Policy and the Public Interest: The Telecommunications Act of 1996* (New York: Guilford Press, 1999); Patricia Aufderheide, ed., *Conglomerate and the Media* (New York: New Press, 1997); Robert McChesney, *Corporate Media and the Threat to Democracy* (New York: Seven Stories Press, 1997); Ben H. Bagdikian, *The Media*

Monopoly, 6th edn (Beacon Press, 2000); Dean Alger, *Megamedia: How Giant Corporations Dominate Mass Media, Distort Competition, and Endanger Democracy* (New York: Rowman and Littlefield, 1998).

59. Dayan and Katz, *Media Events*, 20.

60. Bruce A. Williams, "The New Media Environment, Internet Chatrooms, and Public Discourse after 9/11," in Thussu and Freedman, eds, *War and the Media*, 183. It should be noted that the Pew Research Center found that nine out of ten Americans were getting their news primarily from television after the 9/11 attacks. See "Troubled Times for Network Evening News," *Washington Post*, March 10. Citing an ABC News poll, however, Williams claims that "almost half of all Americans now get news over the Internet, and over a third of them increased their reliance on online sources after September 11" ("New Media Environment," 176).

61. Williams, "New Media Environment," 182. Although Williams cites various online attempts to draw ideological boundaries, he doesn't necessary view this as a bad thing. While he admits that some such attempts were disturbing, he also argues that "insular conversations that are not easily accessible to the wider public play a positive role by allowing marginalized groups to clarify their distinct values in opposition to those of the society-at-large within the safety of a sympathetic and homogeneous group" (184). Despite his pointing to the insular nature of the Web and the desire of some groups to draw ideological boundaries, Williams also argues that there was a general air of civility on the Internet (188–9).

62. The administration viewed the presence of Al Jazeera's graphic war footage and bin Laden's videotapes (which were aired around the world) as a grave problem. On 3 October 2001 (a few days before the bombings began), Secretary of State Colin Powell asked the Qatari emir, Sheikh Hamad bin Khalifa, to "tone down" Al Jazeera's inflammatory rhetoric, and the Bush administration specifically requested that the tapes be taken off the network. The International Press Institute sent a letter to Colin Powell, stating that Powell's tactics had "serious consequences for press freedom" (176–7). Al Jazeera journalists defended their coverage of graphic images by stating that they were trying to cover the war objectively, from both sides (Mohammed El-Nawawy and Adel Iskandar, *Al Jazeera: The Story of the Network That Is Rattling Governments and Redefining Modern Journalism*, updated edn [Cambridge, MA: Westview Press, 2002], 176–81). See also El-Nawawy and Iskandar's discussion of Europe's and Al Jazeera's coverage of Afghanistan (ibid., 186–9).

63. Jonathan Burston, "War and the Entertainment Industries: New Research Priorities in an Era of Cyber-Patriotism," in Thussu and Freedman, eds, *War and the Media*, 163–75. For more, see James Der Derian, *Virtuous War: Mapping the Military-Industrial Media Entertainment Network* (Boulder, CO: Westview, 2001). At ICT, technologies such as immersive simulation games are being developed simultaneously for entertainment and military uses.

64. A member of the Bush administration met with Hollywood studio chiefs and network executives in Beverly Hills on October 18 to discuss efforts to "enhance the perception of America around the world." See Peter Bart, "H'wood Enlists in War," *Variety.com*, 17 October 2001, 1–3. A few weeks later, they gathered in what was referred to as a "summit" to discuss more detailed plans for Hollywood's participation in the war effort. See Rick Lyman, "White House Sets Meeting with Film Executives to Discuss War on Terrorism," *Variety.com*, 8 November 2001, 1–3. See also Pamela McClintock, "Nets Rally Stars around Flag," *Variety.com*, December 3, 2001, 1–2.

65. Meanwhile, in a connected fashion, Al Jazeera presence also threatens the hegemony of Western global news sources. Driven by fierce competition for Arab audiences, in January 2002 CNN officially launched its Arabic website, CNNArabic.com. See Noureddine Miladi, "Mapping the Al Jazeera Phenomenon," in Thussu and Freedman, eds, *War and the Media*, 159. Note that CNN launched the website at the same time (January 2002) that Al Jazeera withdrew its exclusivity agreement with CNN because of the dispute over a tape CNN aired without its approval.

66. In a provocative thesis, Bret Maxwell Dawson argues that while TV returned to much of its previous content, television's temporal and narrational forms were "traumatized" by 9/11. He argues that the effects of this trauma can be seen in the way that elements of catastrophe television (e.g., live broadcasts, an aura of authenticity, and an obsession with time) have appeared with increasing popularity in reality TV and programs like Fox's *24*. See his "TV since 9/11" (master's thesis, University of New South Wales, Sydney, Australia, 2003). While I would not posit such deterministic notions of trauma, it does seem useful to think about how 9/11 relates to a particular historical conjuncture in aesthetic ideals of TV realism, and in particular TV's obsession with the reality genre and real time (which, as Dawson admits, began before 9/11).

67. This cycle of memorializing documentaries began with CBS's *9/11* (aired 10 March 2002), which was followed by *Telling Nicholas* (HBO, 12 May 2002), *In Memoriam: New York City, 9.11* (HBO, 26 May 2002), and others. For a seminar I taught at UCLA, Sharon Sharp wrote a very interesting paper "Remembering 9/11: Memory, History, and the American Family," which considers how these documentaries used sentimental images of the family in crisis to tell histories of 9/11.

68. Baudrillard and Virilio both have published monographs on 9/11. See Jean Baudrillard, *The Spirit of Terrorism and Requiem for the Twin Towers*, trans. Chris Turner (London: Verso, 2002); Paul Virilio, *Ground Zero*, trans. Chris Turner (London: Verso. 2002).

Interrogating *24*: Making Sense of US Counter-terrorism in the Global War on Terrorism

Elspeth Van Veeren

Introduction

Celebrated by fans and critics alike, Fox's *24* television series, now filming its eighth season and still averaging over 11 million viewers a week in the United States, has set a new standard for action-drama.[1] Lauded for its innovative split-screen presentation and signature ticking-clock that counts down the seconds remaining in the 24-hour day—time remaining to "save the day"—*24* has nonetheless come under sustained criticism for its depiction of torture and interrogation, most notably by US Army Brigadier General Patrick Finnegan (the Dean of the US Military Academy at West Point), by former US military interrogator Tony Lagourianis, and by Human Rights First, an international human rights organization.[2]

In their defence, *24* producers argue that the fiction of television torture has no influence on reality; that the public can tell the difference between television fantasy and what is acceptable in the "real" world.[3] As a number of scholars increasingly argue, however, popular culture and politics are inseparable.[4] Popular culture (re)inscribes or (re) presents stories about the nature of reality, often (re)telling tales about the rules governing "our" societies and the consequences of transgressing these rules.[5] Like the genre of American "law and order" prime-time television—both fictional and reality television antecedents—from which *24* has evolved, such as *Dragnet* (1967–1970), *Hill Street Blues* (1981–1987), *Miami Vice* (1984–1989), *America's Most Wanted* (1988–present), *Rescue 911* (1989–1996), *Top Cops* (1990–1993), *Law and Order* (1990–present), *NYPD Blue* (1993–2005), and *CSI: Crime Scene Investigation* (2000–present), *24* is saturated with meaning about US society and its response to criminality and violence. However, along with the more traditional police-drama cast of murderers, drug dealers, gangsters, prostitutes, corrupt officials and greedy businessmen (characters who nonetheless remain central to *24* and other recent spy-dramas like *Alias* and *The Agency*), the storylines of *24* focus explicitly on the dangers posed to the US by terrorists. And, just as police dramas in the 1980s and 1990s began to (re)tell the tales of the US "war on drugs," in the process (re)producing the discourse of the Reagan and George H.W. Bush administrations,[6] *24* is fulfilling the same role uncritically with regards to post-9/11 security policies.

As this article will argue, a critical reading of *24* suggests that the series (re)produces key elements of the Bush administration's discourse of the "global war on terrorism" (including the exceptional and pervasive nature of the threat posed by terrorism, and the corresponding need for a militarized and repressive form of counter-terrorism), working with official discourses to constitute a new "reality" of terrorism and counter-terrorism, and therefore facilitating practices such as rendition, detention without charge, and torture. This is accomplished in ways that are no different from the way that popular culture (particularly film and television) and political discourses have traditionally (re)presented crime, conflict and justice. *24* therefore relates more broadly to long-standing US security policy traditions that are a legacy of what Lawrence and Jewett refer to as the American Monomyth, the idea that salvation only comes through extra-legal force.[7]

This in turn relies on a Schmittian understanding of politics: that "authentic" politics is a fatal confrontation between friend and enemy, and is consequently beyond legal regulation.[8] Though the packaging of *24* may be new and exciting, the underlying message remains the same—that America is open, innocent, and law-abiding, but that extralegal force is needed to maintain these qualities when confronted by an existential threat.[9] In the process of transmitting this message, *24* therefore renders commonsensical the construction of the US global war on terrorism and the way that it is waged, helping to offer an explanation as to how the norm prohibiting controversial practices has shifted.[10] In other words, whether intended or not, *24*, like other popular cultural products, cannot be politically neutral but plays an important role in (re)producing political meaning.[11] In order to make this case, what follows is a discussion in three acts (in keeping with the style of *24*), first, of the ways in which the threat from terrorism is represented as exceptional and pervasive in both *24* and the discourse of the global war on terrorism; second, of how the only logical response is constructed as a particular form of militarized and repressive counter-terrorism policy; and finally of how this narrative occludes the rule of law and the role of a legal system as part of countering this new form of terrorism, overall maintaining the construction of America as innocent and law-abiding.

Popular Culture, World Politics, and Counter-terrorism

There is a growing body of literature that explores the linkages between popular culture and world politics, arguing that popular culture, whilst reflecting politics, also plays an important role in producing and popularizing it.[12] As Jutta Weldes explains, popular culture does so by providing "a background of meanings that helps constitute public images of world politics ... [It] helps to construct the reality of world politics for elites and the public alike," thereby helping to produce consent for certain policies and actions.[13] While Weldes' discussion centres on foreign policy, the interconnection equally applies to security policy. What is argued here is that consent and the production of meaning around security is due in large part to intertextuality, a network of textual relations relating to, in this case, counter-terrorism.[14] Any text, whether a presidential address or a film, "is necessarily read in relationship to others [so that ...] a range of textual knowledges is brought to bear upon it."[15] When experiencing a text, these intertextual knowledges—what Fiske refers to as a culture's "image-bank"—"'pre-orient' readers and allow them to make meanings"; to read and therefore respond to texts in certain ways rather than others.[16] The repetitive use of elements from the "image-bank" thereby generates a "common symbolic environment that cultivates the most widely shared conceptions of reality."[17]

More specifically, this interconnection can occur in at least three ways: through an established and longstanding relationship between text producers; through explicit references from one set of texts to another; and thirdly, through the common narratives or tropes that are central to the constitution of meaning in the texts.[18] Through these various levels of intertextuality, the interrelated representations produced by these texts interact to constitute a frame of meaning which, if repeated often enough, can come to be identified as "common sense."[19] By both (re)constituting and drawing on the same (re)presentations of "reality," the intertextuality of popular culture and world politics helps to make the world intelligible. Popular culture therefore can be explored "for insights into the character and functioning of world politics" as it is relevant for insight into what becomes "common sense."[20]

In particular, the mixing of "fictional" and "reality" texts on television can be considered an important and useful example in the production of intertextual meaning.[21] For example, while "drama" and "reality television" may be considered distinct genres, Judith Grant argues they work together to constitute a common (mis)understanding of crime and justice in the US.[22] The recent emergence of "the CSI effect" is one example of this interdependence, whereby prosecutors and police officers have reported an increased tendency among jurors and victims of crime to expect courts and police to work in accordance with the television show.[23] The fiction/reality boundary is therefore important for it is misleading: "fictional" shows draw on elements of "reality" (realities), rearranging them so that their plausibility is accepted to a greater or lesser degree, while "reality" shows are themselves fictional; firstly, as their mediation through a televisual format means that they are edited such that a narrative is imposed by the producers.[24] Secondly, as many have argued before, reality is itself always already socially constructed ("there is nothing outside the (con)text"); however "real" television shows—or counter-terrorism policies, for that matter—purport to be, they remain mediated and therefore fictional.[25] Accepting a fiction/reality binary among texts as unproblematic therefore allows "reality" to continue as the privileged signifier, making it harder to challenge those who claim special access to this "reality" and ignoring the meaning we derive from other sources of information. In other words, conceptualizing fiction and reality as texts which we treat as part of the same "pick-and-mix" (or "image bank") for our constitution of meaning in the world may be more useful for our own understanding of how common sense is produced. Therefore, to explore the way in which meaning and particular conceptions of security emerge, I turn first to a closer examination of the points of intersection between popular culture and conceptions of security "fiction" and "reality," particularly with reference to terrorism and counter-terrorism discourses.

To begin with, as explicitly security-related text producers, the interconnectedness of the US film industry, the Pentagon, security services, and the White House has been described as particularly deep-rooted.[26] This has been especially documented with regards to the connections between the military and producers of popular culture to the extent that, as James Der Derian argues, a military-industrial-media-entertainment network (MIME-NET) has been constituted: a feedback loop that "merges the production, representation and execution of war" such that the distinction between military and civilian, state and public, real and simulation, original and new, produced and reproduced becomes too hard to make.[27] This is accomplished not only through a longstanding relationship when it comes to recruiting and the provision of military resources for filming, but also through the sharing of key ideas regarding the importance of national security strategy.[28] This connection is not limited to the military but extends to the security services more broadly, particularly the CIA, FBI and more recently, the Department of Homeland Security. Overall, this has led to the emergence of "national security cinema," a genre most frequently reproduced in the US and characterized by the rescue of the nation from threat through the actions of a heroic military or security service.[29] As Valantin claims, the "originality of American national security cinema resides in its creation of a highly dramatic portrayal of the life of defence and security institutions, even the most secret of them."[30]

On one level, this interconnectedness is fostered as film and television producers work directly with security services on certain projects: *I Led Three Lives* (1953–1956), *The Man from UNCLE* (1964–1968), and *The FBI* (1965–1974) were produced with the support and endorsement of J. Edgar Hoover, the head of the FBI.[31] More recently, *Alias* star Jennifer Garner, who played an undercover CIA operative, was invited by the "real" CIA to make a recruitment video for the agency as "the character Jennifer Garner plays embodies the integrity, patriotism and intelligence the CIA looks for in its officers."[32] Meanwhile, Fox

Broadcasting Corporation and the producer Brian Grazer from *24*, signed a deal with the "real" FBI to revive the television drama *The FBI*, as the agency was looking for a "primetime vehicle to reflect its new realities."[33] The influence of Hollywood and its ability to shape popular understandings of security is also recognized in the White House. On 11 November 2001 President George W. Bush's political advisor Karl Rove travelled to Hollywood to meet with Jack Valenti, head of the Motion Picture Association of America and the most powerful lobbyist in Hollywood, as well as with several prominent television and film executives to appeal for films and television with "[c]oncrete information, told with honesty and specificity and integrity, [as] important to the ultimate success in [Afghanistan]."[34] According to Jack Valenti, "This was about contributing Hollywood's creative imagination and their persuasion skills to help in this war effort."[35]

However, even without the deliberate and cultivated connections between policy elites and popular culture producers, security-themed films are commonplace with frequent and explicit "intertextual moments" occurring between official and Hollywood texts. Instances of American officials referencing popular culture are well-known: the "Star Wars" missile program after the film of the same name, the naming of the first NASA shuttle the *Enterprise* after *Star Trek*, or Hillary Clinton's presidential campaign advertisement based on the popular finale to *The Sopranos* television show.[36] Discussed with less frequency, however, are the myriad ways in which popular culture draws on official texts. Films frequently refer to "real" agencies and hire consultants to advise on policies or procedures. For example, Chase Brandon, the CIA's representative in Hollywood, acts as an advisor for *24* scripts.[37] The frequency with which popular cultural texts draw on "reality" to *suggest* plausibility is an interesting part of the (re)production of discourses of security and one that is underappreciated.[38]

Specifically, with regards to (re)presentations of terrorism and counter-terrorism, though present in other media such as literary fiction, video games, and comic books, (re)presentations in film have proved particularly popular. Terrorism and counter-terrorism (re)presentations in particular have "become a vital source of narratives, fantasies, and myths that contribute so much to highly entertaining cinema, with its international intrigue, exotic settings, graphic violence, and the putative conflict between good and evil."[39] The "violent high-tech spectacle" that is popular cultural (re)presentations of terrorism (and therefore of corresponding counter-terrorism strategies) can be found in dozens of films produced over the years from James Bond films of the 1960s; to the films of the 1980s and 1990s such as *Delta Force* (1986), the *Die Hard* series, *Speed* (1994), *True Lies* (1994), *Executive Decision* (1996), and *The Siege* (1998), most of which are produced by Hollywood and many of which are dominated by encounters with Arab/Muslim militants. This has continued into the present, albeit arguably with a narrative more critical of counter-terrorism, with films such as *The Sum of All Fears* (2002), *Collateral Damage* (2002), *Munich* (2005), *United 93* (2006), and *The Kingdom* (2007).[40]

Terrorism and counter-terrorism themes are not, however, limited to the big screen but are increasingly (re)presented on television as well. Agents from the CIA, FBI, or military Special Forces also battle terrorists on the small screen on shows such as *MacGyver* (1985–1992), *La Femme Nikita* (1997–2001), *Alias* (2001–2006), and *The Unit* (2006–present).[41] As Boggs and Pollard suggest, "[s]cenes of terrorist and counter-terrorist activity have a … cinematic appeal" which are increasingly finding their way onto television so that viewers can tune in weekly (or more often) to see the inner workings of the security services.[42] With their big-screen equivalents, these representations therefore also become common reference points for understanding terrorism. Overall, the "spectacle" of terrorism has become so familiar that events like the destruction of the World Trade Towers in 2001, however shocking, seemed to many like something out of a movie.[43]

In addition, beyond engaging in intertextual referencing, popular culture and official discourses share common narratives and tropes—structural homologies—that help to generate meaning and an understanding of what constitutes security.[44] While Cold War narratives dominated cinematic as well as political discourses throughout the 1960s, and the "war on drugs" dominated the 1980s, the "war on terror" and international terrorism has come to dominate conceptions of security as reflected in both cinematic and political discourses. Broadly speaking, these themes, as explained by Boggs and Pollard, include "patriotism, the cult of guns and violence, glorification of technology, the hyper-masculine hero, [and] obsession with 'alien' threats."[45] Secondly, these narratives also work so that security services such as the CIA and the FBI are rehabilitated and sanitized, while their very role in producing the insecurity and instability is elided.[46] Therefore, as will be argued here, when it comes to the global war on terrorism, the dominant narratives (re)produced by the Bush administration and within *24* are similarly productive and work together to normalize the existence of a terrorist threat that is constructed as exceptional and ubiquitous, legitimizing certain counter-terrorist strategies that are militarized and repressive, where heroes do "whatever it takes." Just as police dramas "present fables about crime and law" within society and thereby shape our understanding of crime and law as Grant suggests, spy dramas such as *24* present a rationale for a particular conception of security and counter-terrorism policies.

Overall, the intertextuality that occurs between official discourses and popular culture means that, with regards to terrorism, it is impossible to distinguish between fiction and reality; for each point of interconnection, the divide that is most often accepted as existing between reality and fiction is bridged and blurred. When actors imitate spies who are themselves inspired by actors playing fictional spies, or when writers create agencies based on actual agencies, which are in turn modelled by policy-makers on the agencies in fiction, the "commingling of illusion and reality calls both into question."[47] Therefore, once intertextual moments occur that draw on "fact" and "fiction"—as opposed to drawing exclusively from one or the other (if this is ever possible)—a hyper-reality emerges where the blurring that occurs between fact and fiction results in the *recombinant* appearing natural.[48] With regards to counter-terrorism and *24*, the hyper-real emerges when the fusion of little realities of counter-terrorism forms a "fiction" of counter-terrorism in *24*. This in turn interacts with the "reality" of the global war on terrorism as articulated by the Bush administration resulting in an intertext which in turn influences and alters the "reality" of counter-terrorism (most notably the use of torture). In short, "fiction" and "reality" are mutually constitutive, where the "real" influences the "fiction," and the "fiction" influences the "real" working iteratively to produce new meanings.

The result of these interconnections—the intertexts—is the production of a hyper-reality of counter-terrorism in the global war on terrorism, which works to normalize current practices and render them more plausible and commonsensical. If left unchallenged, these meanings therefore become hegemonic and articulations of an alternate approach (as occurred immediately following 9/11) become "unsayable."[49] Therefore, problematizing the distinction between fact and fiction through an analysis of these intertextual moments of *24* and the global war on terrorism discourse becomes more important for understanding terrorism, counter-terrorism, security policy and, more broadly, world politics. A growing body of literature is exploring these links, particularly the interconnections between *24* and torture.[50] What this paper suggests is that *24* is illustrative of a broader argument about the production of meaning within politics; that meaning can be produced through the emergence of intertextual knowledges which often blur, while at the same time taking refuge in, the fact/fiction divide. To explore the production of this common sense of counter-terrorism, the articulations within both *24* and the global war on terrorism will be discussed in terms of their production of exceptional threats and a new form of militarized response, turning first, however, to a discussion of the popularity of *24*.

24: The Clock Is Ticking

As a television show, *24* is successful. Fusing the three popular televisual genres already discussed—law and order, reality television, and Hollywood blockbuster—*24* fits easily within the genre of national security cinema, appealing to a large American audience and exceeding 11 million viewers a week in the US for six of its seven seasons. The show itself depicts, in "real-time,"[51] the efforts of Jack Bauer (Kiefer Sutherland) and the Los Angeles–based Counter-Terrorism Unit (CTU) to stop terrorist threats from being realized on American soil. In particular, its novel techniques such as split-screens and ticking clock, make *24* particularly compelling viewing. However, in addition to its distinct style and format, its producers have also invested heavily in its "realism" by consulting experts in terrorism and counter-terrorism when writing their scripts to increase their believability. As writer Michael Loceff explains:

> We . . . have an investment in plausibility. We've hired writers who have done heavy research in espionage and anti-terrorism and worked with the government. And we've met with consultants from the intelligence community and other parts of the government, just to help stir up ideas and help us come up with something that seems compelling.[52]

Moreover, its timing, airing for the first time shortly after 11 September 2001, also means that *24* exists in a "post 9/11 world." Though the script and the first episodes of Season 1 had been written by the time 11 September 2001 took place, Joel Surnow, the series creator and producer, explains that "the inspiration for seasons two, three, four and five is 9/11."[53]

Based on this success, *24* has run for seven seasons and has been renewed for an additional eighth. There is also the promise of a forthcoming movie, as well as the publication of numerous spin-off books, and board and video games.[54] The show has also won critical acclaim, having been awarded 17 Emmys (including the 2006 Emmy for Outstanding Drama Series) and two Golden Globes (the 2002 Golden Globe for Best Television Series (Drama) and the 2002 Golden Globe for Best Performance by an Actor in a Television Series (Drama) for Kiefer Sutherland).[55] Based on the popularity and influence of *24* and the character Jack Bauer, Kiefer Sutherland has also recorded at least four public service advertisements on US television including (rather ironically for some) advertisements to promote gun safety, to discourage discrimination against Muslim Americans, and to encourage climate-change awareness. *24* has even inspired university courses: Georgetown University Law School Professor, Walter Sharp (who is also associate deputy general counsel for the US Department of Defense), was offering "The Law of '24,'" a course providing "a detailed understanding of a very wide range of US domestic and international legal issues . . . in the context of the utilitarian and sometimes desperate responses to terrorism raised by the plot of *24*.'[56]

Individual viewers are also invested in the series, as evidenced by the number of internet fan websites and listservs devoted to the show, not to mention the distinct ring-tone which fans have downloaded to their personal phones. As one viewer describes:

> From the outset, I was hooked . . . In just a couple months, I had watched all 72 episodes that had previously aired and were available . . . I wondered how Jack would have handled real life situations I learned about on the news or whether discussions of

> national security in the real world pertained to the information gathering techniques utilized on *24*. I often wondered if the strategies worked in *24*, would they also work in the real world? Would they be of necessity? [sic][57]

In other words, *24* is popular; at the level of the public, Americans "care about it, talk about it, and write about it."[58] Its success as a television show is undeniable.

24's reach extends to elites as well—Karl Rove, Deputy Chief of Staff to President Bush, hosted producers of the show at the White House where they also dined with Tony Snow (then White House Press Secretary) and Lynne Cheney.[59] The Heritage Foundation and Rush Limbaugh (the prominent conservative radio talk-show host with 20 million listeners) have also hosted *24*-themed events attended, among others, by Supreme Court Justice Clarence Thomas and Homeland Security Secretary Michael Chertoff; Chertoff himself has corresponded directly with producer Howard Gordon.[60]

In addition to these interconnections, elites have produced explicit intertextual moments: John Yoo, former Justice Department lawyer and author of the Bush administration's "torture memo," used examples from *24* as justification for torture in his book *War by Other Means*; Supreme Court Justice Antonin Scalia suggested that no court in the US would convict Jack Bauer for torturing; Rush Limbaugh described *24* as "pro-America"; even staunch torture-opponent, Senator and Presidential Candidate McCain described himself as "a Jack Bauer kind of guy"; while Army West Point graduates have been reported to believe *24* is how counter-terrorism works.[61] Along with members of the public, elites have therefore also been successfully *interpellated* or "hailed" into subject positions sympathetic with Jack Bauer and which often equate American patriotism with *24* and therefore with a particular narrative of terrorism and counter-terrorism. Viewers find themselves asking, "what would Jack Bauer do?"

Therefore, as these interconnections suggest, whether at the level of the general public or elite policy-makers, the distinction between reality and fiction starts to break down when it comes to developing an understanding of terrorism and counter-terrorism as (re)presented within *24*. However, to understand more fully the production of "common sense" in the "war on terror," it is worth examining more closely the manner in which *24* (re) produces key narratives of the global war on terrorism discourse and the way in which this (re)inscribes beliefs surrounding identities. The themes that are essential to *24* must be explored in order to understand the mutually constitutive nature of these discourses, beginning with the representation of terrorism as an exceptional, ubiquitous, and immediate threat to Americans.

"We're Dealing with Extraordinary Circumstances Here!" The Exceptional Threat of Terrorism

In the world of *24*, Los Angeles is a very, very dangerous place to live. It is a world filled with nasty but familiar threats targeting US citizens: car bombs, chemical attacks, hostage takings, presidential assassination attempts, nuclear explosions, train bombings, and radiological attacks, all the result of terrorism and all on a scale that has never been seen before. In Season 4 alone (4), Bauer and the Counter-Terrorism Unit (CTU) must foil plots masterminded by "Turkish" terrorists and rescue the secretary of defense from public execution, stop a stolen fighter from flying into Air Force One, stop hijacked nuclear reactors from exploding across the country, and stop a nuclear missile from being fired into Los Angeles.[62] And, though these scenarios seem familiar—mostly through popular cultural (re)presentations in police or spy dramas in film or television of the past 40 years—within the series they are constantly articulated as new and exceptional, as well as ubiquitous, immediate, and foreign. This works alongside public discourses to construct the risks posed by terrorism in a way that renders it more "real" and "commonsensical."[63]

As *24* viewers, characters often tell us that these threats spell potential death for "hundreds of thousands of Americans," are "bigger than anyone could have imagined" or "the worst attack in the history of our country." This is because, more often than not, the threats involve "weapons of mass destruction" (WMDs), biological, chemical, radiological, and nuclear weapons that we are told have the capacity to kill thousands, if not millions. This apocalyptic narrative follows a tradition in US popular culture of playing to nuclear anxieties.[64] For example, within the first half of Season 2, which aired 2002–2003, Jack Bauer and CTU work to find a nuclear bomb that Islamic terrorists are planning to detonate in Los Angeles, a scenario easily pulled from the pages of the National Commission on Terrorist Attacks Upon the United States (9/11 Commission) Report.[65] The threat of this super-terrorism in *24* was simultaneously articulated by US officials such as Secretary of State Colin Powell, Secretary of Defense Donald Rumsfeld, and Deputy Secretary of Defense Paul Wolfowitz. Vice-President Richard Cheney in 2003 stated that:

> the next time terrorists strike, they may well be armed with more than just plane tickets and box cutters. The next time they might direct chemical agents or diseases at our population, or attempt to detonate a nuclear weapon in one of our cities ... no rational person can doubt that terrorists would use such weapons of mass murder the moment they are able to do so ... [W]e are dealing with terrorists ... who are willing to sacrifice their own lives in order to kill millions of others.[66]

Meanwhile, as episodes of *24* aired and its fictional officials discussed raising the national threat level, the "real" national threat level stood at Code Orange (the second highest alert level) for an unspecified threat. Similarly, Colin Powell appeared before the UN Security Council in the lead up to the Iraq War just as debates over the manipulation of intelligence were simultaneously aired on *24*.[67] In other words, these "real" and "fictional" moments, based as they are on "plausible scenarios," served to remind Americans that the United States was "really" in danger.[68] These fictional and "real" (re) presentations of catastrophic threat work together through their intertextuality to render the threat recognizable and therefore understandable.

Secondly, the threat from terrorism is presented as ubiquitous—suburban shopping malls are as likely to be targeted by WMDs as Air Force One. Over the first six seasons of *24*, terrorists release a deadly virus in a populated hotel (3); release nerve gas in a shopping mall (3); attempt to explode nuclear reactors near suburban populations (5); explode "suitcase nukes" killing thousands (6), engage in hostage takings in an airport (5); capture, torture or kill individuals who are out camping (4), at work (4,5), driving down the "freeway" (4), or investigating a noise outside their house (4). Individuals can also become victims by being unwittingly related, involved, living next door to, or married to, a terrorist (1,4), or by being a corrupt official (5) or even a corrupt agent (1,4,5). In the world of *24*, targets can be anyone and anywhere: "violent death is possible any time, at any place, from any quarter. Ordinary people are vulnerable as they ride buses, go to work in high-rise buildings, or simply walk along crowded streets."[69]

In the same way, following the September 11, 2001 attacks, President Bush declared that "today's terrorists can strike at any place, at any time, and with virtually any weapon"[70] and the Department of Homeland Security oversaw the identification of over 80,000 sites within the US as likely terrorist targets, including a miniature golf business.[71] The suggestion, like in *24*, is that "we" are all at risk anywhere, including in our homes: terrorism seeks to disrupt "our way of life," to transform a peaceful and innocent society into a fearful one through indiscriminate killing.[72] In this sense, "*24* communicates to its viewers the very sense that American politicians and particularly the Bush administration, have been insisting upon repeatedly since 9/12: '9/11 changed everything,'" providing the space for the raft of new measures implemented in the name of national security.[73] Both *24* and the discourse of the global war on terrorism therefore also work to constitute the threat as new and unprecedented, and therefore requiring a new response.[74]

The history of the United States, however, is replete with identifications of existential threat and "exceptional" events threatening all of "America": the American Civil War, Pearl Harbor and the declaration of unlimited emergency in 1941, the Great Depression, the Cold War and now latterly terrorism and "WMDs."[75] This construction of exceptional threats, as Giorgio Agamben argues, is "a voluntary creation of a permanent state of emergency" that since World War II "has become one of the essential practices of contemporary states," such that the distinction between war and peace is no longer possible.[76] The ubiquity of the threat, along with its exceptional nature, means that, show after show, "*24* offers viewers the exception incessantly" so that "the exception has become the norm."[77] The events of *24*, like the global war on terrorism discourse, are therefore paradoxically represented as both constant and exceptional.

Thirdly, the threat from terrorism is articulated as immediate. Throughout every moment of the series there are ticking clocks, both the overlaying one omnipresent throughout the series with its signature sound-effect, and those embedded within the story itself—either as a part of the surroundings or through the constant reminders from characters—counting down the minutes left until the execution, until the reactors explode, or until the missile hits LA. The ticking clocks, the very premise for the series—and therefore based on a common (mis)understanding of the "reality" of counter-terrorism—provide *24* with one of its most distinctive features, cleverly imbuing the series with its sense of urgency and suspense.[78] The "ticking-time bomb" scenarios of each season render the extraordinary measures of *24* "commonsensical" and "real." For example, from the start of Season 2, the initial scenes feature a source confessing under torture to the existence of a nuclear bomb set to explode in Los Angeles that day—evidence, we are told, that is "highly credible."[79] The initial shots prepare the viewer for an imminent, and catastrophic threat, removing any uncertainty that may lead the viewer to question, first, the method of obtaining the information, and, secondly, the information itself. In the same way, the Bush administration uses the ticking time bomb scenario to caution US citizens that they are in imminent danger from terrorism:

> Thousands of dangerous killers, schooled in the methods of murder, often supported by outlaw regimes, are now spread throughout the world like ticking time bombs, set to go off without warning... tens of thousands of trained terrorists are still at large ... A terrorist underworld ... operates in remote jungles and deserts, and hides in the centers of large cities ... time is not on our side.[80]

It is not enough for the threats to be all around; they must be pressing and immediate, so that the action taken seems urgent and persuasive. This construction of terrorism, more importantly, leaves little discursive space for reflection or critique within the series or the "war on terror." The "ticking time bomb" scenario engenders a sense of immediacy, intensity, and urgency about the threat, limiting the possibility of challenging the claim that a threat exists.

Furthermore, terrorism is constructed through the representation of the terrorists themselves. Within *24*, as with the wider discourse of the global war on terrorism, terrorists are most often constructed as ruthless, devious, resourceful, cunning, dangerous, and evil.[81] They do not hesitate to kill randomly (1–6), they torture (2, 4, 6), and have violent families lives (4), characteristics which are highlighted, even exploited, by CTU. Moreover, their willingness to engage in super-terrorism involving WMDs means that terrorists cease being "normal biopolitical bodies" that can be deterred by conventional means, becoming instead an exceptional threat.[82] Indeed, the construction of terrorists within *24* as willing to engage in extremes of violence make them ideal characters to embody Carl Schmitt's conception of the Partisan—the "real" or "absolute" enemy who is willing to go to all lengths to defend their interests and therefore requires a response in kind. As terrorists, "they show no qualms about the 'real possibility of killing'" and cannot be "opposed by legal, moral or economic devices."[83]

Moreover, terrorists generally originate "over there": Serbian (1), Saudi (2), Turkish (4), Russian (5), and Lebanese (6) terrorists all provide the main threat for a significant portion of each season. This reliance on foreign or "alien" terrorists, as they are commonly referred to in the global war on terrorism discourse, as opposed to "home-grown" ones, is common within "national security cinema." In particular, since the 1980s, Middle Eastern terrorists have served as a main terrorist threat, a powerful construction due to its interplay with existing cultural stereotypes of Arabs.[84] This is wholly consistent with the American tradition of representing threat as originating outside and on an apocalyptic scale, whether in popular culture, or political rhetoric.[85] This construction of terrorists as "outside" therefore also facilitates the understanding of terrorists as "real enemies" in the Schmittian sense as their presence outside means that they are existentially distinct from "us" and "our friends." In other words, the distinction between friend and enemy is clearer and more understandable when it is tied to geography and space. *24* capitalizes on this positioning and on these stereotypes, especially through careful casting, lighting, and musical themes. For example, constructions associated with the character Habib Marwan (played by Arnold Vosloo) who leads the terrorist cell in Season 4 or with Abu Fayed (played by Adoni Maropis) in Season 6—make it impossible to view terrorism as anything other than fanatical. As Marwan or Adoni move through the scenes, they are accompanied by discordant "exotic" sounding music (often in counterpoint to Bauer's heroic theme), with their faces often in shadows, they threaten, torture, and kill civilians and co-conspirators alike without emotion, and, in both cases, flee through the sewers to evade capture.[86]

The general impression of terrorists, therefore, is that they are willing to commit random violent acts that target "civilians" as well as political leaders without restraint. Grievances with US policies and actions that might motivate them are alluded to, but never explored. Therefore, in the same manner that police dramas often set up criminals as "ideological straw men" who represent "agreed upon criminal types,"[87] *24* relies on these terrorists to embody the terrorist threat. The repetition of these images, and their consistencies with the image of the terrorist presented in the discourse of Bush administration officials reinforces the image of the terrorist, making it easier to see racial profiling as common sense, for example.

Overall, *24* is very successful at telling a story about terrorism, of representing the threat of terrorism to the US as exceptional, ubiquitous, and immediate, as well as foreign. Though terrorism as a threat is not new to national security cinema, *24* is successful in (re)producing the elements familiar from the Bush administration's discourse of the war on terrorism. This interplay between the "reality" of terrorism and its simulation/fiction helps to render the threat more commonsensical, and therefore legitimizes a particular form of counter-terrorism—leading to what some have come to refer to as "torture porn."[88]

"We Don't Have Time for Your Rule Book!": Fighting the "New War" through Counter-terrorism

On 1 May 2003, the US Terrorist Threat Integration Centre (TTIC) was created, bringing together 16 agencies involved in counter-terrorism operations as "the nerve centre of the US-led global war on terror."[89] Eight months later, in December 2004, the TTIC became the National Counterterrorism Centre (NCTC), authorized under the Intelligence Reform and Terrorism Prevention Act. The new facilities, located in a non-descript Washington suburb were developed with the help of Hollywood "imagineers" and include large plasma screens which "rise up like something out of a James Bond film."[90]

While the NCTC does not feature explicitly in *24* by name, counter-terrorism operations are carried out by the Counter Terrorism Unit (CTU), which is described as an elite branch of the CIA with local divisions situated in major American cities, including a Los Angeles unit in which the action of *24* is based. And, when images of the new NCTC were released to the public, bloggers commented on how closely the centre resembled the set of CTU Los Angeles in *24*.[91] The willingness of, or even the necessity for, individuals to draw these parallels to communicate is a testament to the longstanding relationship between Hollywood and the security services, which has resulted in the generation of a common "image bank" from which meaning and understanding about security is derived. Just as terrorism has been articulated as an exceptional threat within *24*—working with existing official discourses to tell us what terrorism looks like—counter-terrorism has also been constructed through both "fiction" and "reality." These work together to render counter-terrorism practices commonsensical, specifically the reliance on a particular "war-fighting" model of counter-terrorism, that is not only militarized, but is based on a "new war" model which embraces extralegal force (including extraordinary rendition, indefinite detention without charge, and torture), the use of "exceptional measures" ("going rogue"), and the need for heroic sacrifice in the name of safeguarding "our way of life," freedom, and the homeland. Both the "common sense" of "going rogue" and heroic sacrifice as it relates to the "new wars" will be discussed, but first, I turn to the way in which *24* and the global war on terrorism discourse construct a particular form of militarized counter-terrorism that relies on the maximal use of force.

"The Last Line of Defence"

Through the world of *24* and the discourse of the global war on terrorism, the threat of terrorism is constructed as new, exceptional, ubiquitous, immediate, and foreign. This construction is then articulated to a particular form of counter-terrorism that, firstly, involves the maximum use of force. Force is required to overcome an enemy that, as constructed, cannot be contained or restrained any other way. Most often, this requirement for overwhelming force for counter-terrorism means that high-tech weaponry and military tactics are required, even up to, and including involving, the military directly.[92] As Crelinstein argues, a militarization of counter-terrorism occurs in response to this construction, particularly when the threat is constructed as a war, as was the case with the "war on drugs."[93] Consequently a military model of counter-terrorism is increasingly common and found in many Western European, North American, and Israeli security services and police forces; where, to respond to the needs of these "wars," maximal, as opposed to minimal, use of force is seen as necessary and most effectively delivered with a war-model of counter-terrorism. This means that excessive use of force becomes more likely.

> Excessive use of force has been the primary problem within the war model of counter-terrorism, particularly in the case of political killings whereby a suspect is shot rather than arrested, as in cases of alleged shoot-to-kill policies. This often arises when

> elite commandos, who may be either police personnel with special training or military personnel, are used to capture suspected terrorists.[94]

24 captures the elements of this model nicely, but more importantly, renders it "commonsensical." Towards the start of each season we are offered a view of CTU Los Angeles in operation. Its highly skilled, hard-working professionals monitor suspicious activity, prepared to respond. However, as soon as "action" is required, the real heroes—the field agents and tactical units (with the support of analysts)—are ready to respond with force to eliminate the exceptional threat "in the nick of time" and as "the last line of defense" (3). CTU, with its hierarchies, military-grade communications, command and control systems as well as weaponry and tactics are articulated as de facto military organizations which have the capability—indeed the responsibility—to use maximum force to "save the day."[95] This often results in what could be described as summary executions. By the end of each season, Jack Bauer alone has killed 10 (1), 30 (2), 14 (3), 45 (4), 38 (5), 49 (6), and 25 (7) "terrorists" in a 24-hour period.[96] In many cases this includes the summary execution of the terrorist leaders (1, 3, 4, 5, 6, 7), though drivers and security details are equally dispensable. As this occurs we are told that this is the only option and brought about by the terrorists themselves. The first lesson of counter-terrorism is therefore that force is often the only way of eliminating the threat, meaning that it is a militarized war-model of counter-terrorism that prevails, involving the excess use of force and culminating in a pattern of summary executions.

As a consequence, in *24*, but (re)produced in the global war on terrorism narrative, and therefore consistent with the construction of the threat not only as a war but a "new war," traditional police methods developed for crime (often represented by the LAPD or the FBI) are articulated as insufficient (even ineffective or corrupt) to meet security needs.[97] The criminal justice model which relies on police, courts, and corrections for detection, apprehension, detention, prosecution and/or rehabilitation of accused persons to address conflict and in theory includes operating within the law, using minimal force, careful surveillance, and detailed investigation proves to be too burdensome, even an obstacle to security.[98] "New wars" are constructed both within *24* and the global war on terrorism as beyond the capability and capacity of existing systems, including police, but also legal.[99] Through this emphasis on "new war," one "reality" of counter-terrorism—its detailed research, lengthy surveillance operations, "people debating in a conference room and filling out forms in triplicate"[100]—is overlooked by producers of *24* who have been captivated by the image of a glamorous and adrenaline-fuelled work, focusing on the "pursue" element rather than the "prevent," further perpetuating the myth and (re)producing a new "reality."

"Whatever It Takes"

Secondly, while exceptional measures seem to justify the use of maximum force as part of a militarized approach to counter-terrorism, "going rogue" is presented as the only option when confronted with an exceptional threat and therefore an essential element of the strategy for effectively protecting Americans. As Vice-President Cheney explained in 2001:

> we also have to work sort of the dark side, if you will. We're going to spend time in the shadows in the intelligence world. A lot of what needs to be done here will have to be done quietly, without any discussions, using sources and methods that are available to our intelligence agencies if we're going to be successful. That's the world these folks operate in. And so it's going to be vital for us to use any means at our disposal, basically, to achieve our objective . . . It is a mean, nasty, dangerous, dirty business out there, and we have to operate in that arena. I'm convinced we can do it.[101]

As part of constructing a narrative that relies on the ticking-time bomb scenario and an exceptional threat, agents such as Bauer are presented as having no option but to act, and act such that they step outside the boundaries established either by law—whether by disobeying direct orders or by breaking the law. In this world where there is no time for discussion or debate, only action, Bauer *has no choice* but to constantly shift from operating within the law to operating beyond it. As Bauer explains, "We don't have a choice. We're out of time here" (4.24). As time presses ever onwards and there are no other leads, "going rogue" to get the job done makes sense. We are told there is never any other choice when legal or authoritative obstructions are in the way: whether a suspect with connections is kidnapped from the sanctuary of an embassy (4) or medical assistance is denied (4); whether legal authorities are superseded, disregarded or even incapacitated (1, 2, 3, 4, 5); or whether a court injunction (4) or a presidential immunity deal (5) to stop an interrogation ignored. With regards to the war on terrorism, there is "no choice": as President Bush claimed, "win we must—we have no choice."[102]

More importantly, Bauer's "going rogue," and stepping outside the boundaries of the law is never punished. He may be pursued by the authorities, only to be reinstated as an agent shortly after, when he is again needed. Through Bauer, Schmitt's vision of politics is therefore enacted. In response to the exceptional threat that "real enemies" such as terrorists pose, "we" are required to do "whatever it takes":

> At CTU, exceptional actions not only become regularised, but also are continually made to appear legitimate: the agents pursue leads that *routinely turn out to be true.* And the agents always appear to be working for the good of the country, to stop an indisputably imminent threat.[103]

Other agents within CTU are also continually stepping outside boundaries "to get the job done": holding secret conferences, accessing data from other agencies illegally or countermanding orders from higher ups, all of which are constructed as the logical thing to do to save the day. Even Presidents Palmer (2, 3) and Logan (4, 5), and Vice-President Daniels (6) in *24* are continuously stepping outside accepted parameters for governance, rarely consulting with executive members, Congress, or legal experts in their decision-making; incarcerating journalists (2), even conspiring with terrorists (5), as there is said to be no choice when confronted with terrorism.

These actions outside the legal and established framework of counter-terrorism as constructed within the world of *24*—never a rare occurrence—mirror the justifications provided by the Bush administration in the global war on terrorism. They are what Judith Butler would describe as actions by "petty sovereigns" where unaccountable and decentralized decision-making becomes the acceptable norm as long as it is carried out by the "right people."[104] Together, through their intertextuality, *24* and the global war on terrorism constitute therefore this hyper-real world where counter-terrorism is equated with this type of decision-making. To avoid "the dynamic of perpetual competition and perpetual discussion,"[105] decision-making when the stakes are high must be made in a "fundamentally *norm*-less realm ... in which the executive possesses full discretionary authority" and attempts to tame such conflicts by juridical means are destined to fail.[106] Laws, democracy, transparency, and accountability are constraints in the fight against terrorism when security becomes dissociated and privileged.

In particular, when decision-making is limited under the pressure of a ticking clock, time limits increase the acceptability of the use of violence, especially extralegal violence—euphemistically referred to by Cheney as "working the dark side," "in the shadows," and a "dirty business" or in *24* as "getting your hands dirty"(2.1).[107] This includes the use of torture to extract information from suspected terrorists or their affiliates, which of all the elements of *24* or the global war on terrorism discourse has attracted the most attention.[108] *24* in particular is renowned for its frequent and graphic torture sequences.[109] Torture is a key component of the show, despite the claim to the contrary by producer Loceff who suggests that they often hold back,[110] to the extent that fans specifically expect it and monitor it, particularly through the website *Jack Bauer Torture Report*.[111]

These tortures are often carried out by Bauer, though not always, and all are justified within the narrative and through careful filming and editing by the ticking clock. Credible evidence that a suspect has knowledge of or is affiliated with terrorism is not needed as there is never any doubt that the heroes are torturing, if not always the right person, for the right reason. If an innocent is tortured, they are ultimately either revealed as complicit with the terrorists, or forgive the torturers (4.11, 6.14).

In other words, when laws become an obstacle to security in the war on terrorism, as they do in *24*, a "trade off" between civil liberties and security becomes necessary. The world of successful counter-terrorism requires these sacrifices in order to respond to the new and fast-paced requirements which are too much for "ordinary" police methods. In the Schmittian sense, exceptional threats require exceptional actions. This argument is not only made in *24*, but has also been used to justify interrogation techniques used at Joint Task Force Guantánamo and Abu Ghraib prison by General Miller, the American US Army major general tasked with overseeing detention in Guantánamo in 2003 and later Abu Ghraib. Importantly, these policies have then been perceived as acceptable by a significant proportion of the general public, Congressional elite, and by military personnel.[112] As Scheuerman points out, this "eerily corroborates Schmitt's expectation that the dynamism of modern warfare potentially clashes with any attempt to develop a firm legal framework for the rules of war."[113] Whether in *24* or the global war on terrorism, the "common sense" has become that torture is justified because the clock is ticking; executive discretion or authoritarian decision-making is necessary as legal means are not adequate to address the threat.

Within *24*, however, actions that could be interpreted as morally questionable are always constructed as outside legal boundaries, as "going rogue." This camouflages the reality that the White House and the Pentagon routinely make decisions that involve "permissible" violence—whether it is NSA authorization to listen to domestic phone conversations without a warrant, the use of torture (or "harsh interrogation techniques") as sanctioned by the Bush administration in contravention of international laws, indefinite detention without charge (Guantánamo Bay, Bagram's Pul-i-Charki), or extraordinary renditions—as these are exceptional times and these actions save American lives.[114] The Bush administration has therefore created new legislation and interpreted existing laws in new ways in order to increase the appearance of these acts as acceptable and as a logical and necessary response to the challenges of the "new war." In this respect, the need for CTU agents in *24* to "go rogue" is farcical, as the authority has been constituted through the extension of executive power by the Bush administration and the production of a new common sense of counter-terrorism. Maintaining this construction of "going rogue" within 24, however, preserves the illusion that the US is an innocent and morally upstanding entity.[115]

"Jack's Country Needs Him. Dead": Heroic Sacrifice and Counter-terrorism

Thirdly, the capacity to step outside these boundaries is an essential part of the representation of the hero. Heroes, according to counter-terrorist discourse, are the only characters capable of making this "sacrifice" and therefore deserve our respect and admiration: we must be "inspired by the heroic sacrifices of our fire-fighters, rescue and law enforcement personnel, military service members, and other citizens" (Bush, 4 September 2002).Within *24*, as Audrey Raimes, the show's moral compass in Seasons 4 and 5, expresses: "thank god there are people like you [Jack Bauer] who can deal with that world" (4.24). As heroes, they are the lone authority figure who are able to make difficult decisions, use force, and sacrifice themselves in a selfless manner for a "higher purpose." Individuals who do not abide by that strict code—for example, seeking compensation for being tortured without grounds (4.13)—are expelled or given an opportunity to later redeem themselves by, for example, completing a suicide mission to stop the terrorists (2.1, 3.19).

Heroes, however, are also however positioned apart as a group and cannot be "held back" by laws or "morality" (similar to the way that cowboys were constructed in the American "western" genre).[116] Ordinary members of the community who do abide by the rules and defer to authority to provide security are not capable of heroic action. Like the scared villagers of westerns, members of the community in *24* are never brave or resourceful enough to rescue themselves and must be provided with guns and encouragement in order to fight back (4.13); led to safety and rescued (4.17); or are helpless victims without any agency, too afraid of "the terrorists" to act (4, 5). When individuals do become heroes, it is most often because they "get their hands dirty" and carry out actions that involve sacrificing their own morals and/or welfare. This willingness to "go rogue" and sacrifice themselves sets the heroes of CTU—despite their simultaneous construction as "everyman"—apart from the ordinary members of the community. Their presence as a "super-empowered" individual operating without boundaries is, as Lawrence and Jewett argue, part of the superhero myth unique to America, whereby heroes endowed with the powers to save ordinary citizens are themselves incapable of abiding by the laws of citizenship, maintaining political relationships or responding to the preferences of the majority.[117] Heroes are therefore represented as lonely and singular souls (a very masculine representation), who are able to make these difficult and self-less sacrifices needed to rescue the impotent and terrorized community. For these reasons, fans of *24* buy "Bauer Power" T-shirts and suggest that they are "a Jack Bauer kind of guy." They accept these heroes as representative of the way the world should be, what values they should have, what actions to take, as well as what attitudes bring success, and therefore look to them for inspiration.[118]

Finally, this construction of the hero is therefore also connected to the rehabilitation of security agencies themselves. As Valantin argues, national security cinema has a key role to play in "rehabilitating" agencies like the CIA, eliding the role these agencies have in constituting the threat in the first place.[119] It is in part through what is not shown in this discourse, that security agencies maintain their heroic standing.

Overall, one of the central messages of the discourse of the global war on terrorism and *24* is that a security environment involving exceptional threat demands new security measures, a militarized war-model approach to counter-terrorism that includes new ways of operating that may have previously been considered unacceptable; in an anarchic world, laws and rules interfere with the safety and security of America and exceptional situations require exceptional measures. Television shows such as *24* help to rationalize these extraordinary actions, including torture, as necessary to preserve US national security. The intertextuality at work allows the superheroic myth to be (re) produced not only in popular culture, but also in the global war on terrorism and US security policy, allowing *24* to resonate with viewers as its selfless hero, operating in an anarchic system permeated with new threats, fights terrorism using force without limits and always "saves the day."

Conclusion

This reading of *24* suggests that intricate links do exist between popular culture and world politics, in this case between the discourse of the global war on terrorism and the popular representation of counter-terrorism as depicted in the show—from its (re)presentations of threat to the actions that are required in order to stop terrorism. The intense "liveness" or real-time character of the show which enhances the drama and suspense, making it a critical and popular success, also helps to sustain the illusion that what is presented are the "facts" of counter-terrorism, especially the usefulness of torture as an information-gathering tool.[120] More importantly, the discourse of *24* and official discourses working together have constituted an intertext which overall helps to produce common understandings of security. In other words, *24* and the war on terrorism discourses, by drawing on the same set of factual/fictional tropes, help to constitute a new "common sense" of counter-terrorism.

While we can enjoy these shows and similar ones like *La Femme Nikita*, *Alias*, or *The Unit*, as viewers we must ask ourselves why these shows are so popular and inquire as to how they might influence our perceptions and understandings of security and world politics. Popular television shows and "national security cinema" that depict intelligence operations "in bright and unmottled hues"[121] can have a profound influence on our understanding of counter-terrorism in the same way that popular culture has "profoundly influenced popular understandings of the Vietnam war," for example.[122] And, as much as government rhetoric or news media, these popular television shows are vehicles for communicating and (re)presenting fundamental ideas about how the world works, re-inscribing key myths surrounding security and world politics and therefore must be interrogated.

Notes

1. Daniel Chamberlain and Scott Rudin, "*24* and Twenty-first Century Quality Television," in S. Peacock (ed.), *Reading* 24: *TV Against the Clock* (New York: I.B. Tauris, 2007), pp. 13–24; Associated Press, "List of Top 20 Shows in Prime-time Nielsen Ratings," *Salon.com*, 24 February 2009, available online at: <http://www.salon.com> (accessed 1 March 2009).
2. Jane Mayer, "Whatever It Takes: The Politics of the Man Behind '24,'" *The New Yorker*, 19 February 2007; Martin Miller, "'24' Gets a Lesson in Torture from the Experts," *Los Angeles Times*, 13 February 2007; David Bauder, "TV Torture Influencing Real Life," *Washington Post*, 11 February 2007, available online at: <http://www.washingtonpost.com (accessed 15 February 2007); Human Rights First, "Primetime Torture," (no date), available online at: <http://www.humanrightsfirst.org/us_law/etn/primetime/index.asp> (accessed 14 July 2009).
3. Mayer, op. cit.
4. See for example, Jutta Weldes, "High Politics and Low Data: Globalization Discourses and Popular Culture," in Dvora Yanow & Peregrine Schwartz-Shea (eds), *Interpretation and Method: Empirical Research Methods and the Interpretive Turn* (Armonk, NY: M.E. Sharpe, 2006), pp. 176–86.
5. Like Weldes, I use the term "popular culture" in lieu of "mass culture" which more accurately reflects the relationship between those that produce the type of cultural artifact which *24* represents and those that consume it. Jutta Weldes (ed.), *To Seek Out New Worlds: Exploring Links between Science Fiction and World Politics* (Basingstoke: Palgrave Macmillan, 2003); Jutta Weldes, "Going Cultural: Star Trek, State Action, and Popular Culture," *Millennium – Journal of International Studies* 28:1 (1999), pp. 117–34.
6. Judith Grant, "Prime Time Crime: Television Portrayals of Law Enforcement," *Journal of American Culture* 15:1 (1992), pp. 57–68.
7. John Shelton Lawrence and Robert Jewett, *The Myth of the American Superhero* (Cambridge: Wm B. Eerdmans Publishing, 2004).
8. William E. Scheuerman, "Carl Schmitt and the Road to Abu Ghraib," *Constellations* 13:1 (2006), p. 116.
9. Due to length constraints, several other important constructions and themes at work in *24* are not discussed here, such as the gendered and racial constructions of the terrorists, as well as the troubled relationship with technology in the series.
10. Ryder McKeown, "Norm Regress: US Revisionism and the Slow Death of the Torture Norm," *International Relations* 23:5 (2009), pp. 5–25.
11. Elspeth S. Van Veeren, "The 'Cultural Turn' in International Relations: Making Sense Of World Politics," *e-International Relations*, 10 May 2009, available online at <http://www.e-ir.info/?p=1244> (accessed 11 May 2009).
12. Carl Boggs, "Pearl Harbor: How Film Conquers History," *New Political Science* 28:4 (2006), pp. 451–66; Carl Boggs and Tom Pollard, "Hollywood and the Spectacle of Terrorism," *New Political Science* 28:3 (2006), pp. 335–51; Carl Boggs and Tom Pollard, "The Imperial Warrior in Hollywood: Rambo and Beyond," *New Political Science* 30:4 (2008), pp. 565–78; Andrew Davison, "The 'Soft' Power of Hollywood Militainment: The Case of The West Wing's Attack on Antalya, Turkey," *New Political Science*

28:4 (2006) pp. 467–87; Francois Debrix, *Tabloid Terror: War, Culture and Geopolitics* (London: Routledge, 2007); James Der Derian, "War as Game," *The Brown Journal of World Affairs* 10:1 (2003), pp. 37–48; Lene Hansen, *Security as Practice: Discourse Analysis and the Bosnian War* (London: Routledge, 2006); Gerard Huiskamp, "*Minority Report* on the Bush Doctrine," *New Political Science* 26: 3 (2004), pp. 389–415; Debbie Lisle and Andrew Pepper, "The New Face of Global Hollywood: *Black Hawk Down* and the Politics of Meta-Sovereignty," *Cultural Politics: An International Journal* 1:2 (2005), pp. 165–92; Simon Philpott and David Mutimer, "Inscribing the American Body Politic: Martin Sheen and Two American Decades," *Geopolitics* 10:2 (2005), pp. 335–55; Christina Rowley, "*Firefly/Serenity:* Gendered Space and Gendered Bodies," *British Journal of Politics and International Relations* 9:2 (2007), pp. 318–25; Michael J. Shapiro, *Cinematic Geopolitics* (London: Routledge, 2008); Cynthia Weber, "Flying Planes Can Be Dangerous," *Millennium – Journal of International Studies* 31:1 (2002), pp. 129–47; Cynthia Weber, "Popular Visual Language as Global Communication: The Remediation of United Airlines Flight 93," *Review of International Studies* 34:S1 (2008), pp. 137–53; Weldes, "Going Cultural," op. cit.; Weldes, *To Seek Out New Worlds,* op. cit.; Jutta Weldes, "Globalisation Is Science Fiction," *Millennium – Journal of International Studies* 30:3 (2001), pp. 647–67.

13. Weldes, *To Seek Out New Worlds,* op. cit., p. 7.
14. Graham Allen, *Intertextuality* (London: Routledge, 2000), p. 1.
15. John Fiske, *Television Culture* (London: Routledge, 1987), p. 108.
16. Weldes, "Globalisation Is Science Fiction," op. cit., p. 649.
17. George Gerber, Michael Morgan & Nancy Signorielli, "Living with Television: The Dynamics of the Cultivation Process," in Jennings Bryant and Dolf Zilmann (eds), *Perspectives on Media Effects* (Hillsdale, NJ: Lawrence Erlbaum Associates Inc., 1986), p. 18.
18. Weldes, "Globalisation Is Science Fiction," op. cit.
19. In the Gramscian sense. For an introduction to Gramsci and "common sense," see Mark Rupert, "Antonio Gramsci" in Jenny Edkins and Nick Vaughan-Williams (eds), *Critical Theorists and International Relations* (London: Routledge, 2009), p. 183.
20. Weldes, *To Seek Out New Worlds,* op. cit., p. 7.
21. The complex interplay between fiction and reality has been recognized on some levels since the 1774 publication of Goethe's Werther was linked to an increase in suicides across Europe. The effect of popular culture on reality has subsequently been referred to as "the Werther Effect." Lawrence and Jewett, *The Myth of the American Superhero,* op. cit., p. 9.
22. Grant, op. cit.
23. Andrew P. Thomas, "The CSI Effect: Fact or Fiction," *Yale Law Journal Pocket Part* 115:70 (2006), pp. 70–2, available online at: <http://yalelawjournal.org/2006/02/thomas.html> (accessed 15 March 2008); Jeffrey Toobin, "The CSI Effect: The Truth about Forensic Science," *The New Yorker,* 7 May 2007. I am grateful to David Mutimer for this point.
24. Grant, op. cit.
25. Jacques Derrida, *On Grammatology,* trans. Gayatri Chakravorti Spivak, (Baltimore, MD: John Hopkins University Press, 1974), p. 158.
26. James Der Derian, "Virtuous War/Virtual Theory," *International Affairs* 76:4 (2000), p. 787; Jean-Michel Valantin, *Hollywood, the Pentagon and Washington: The Movies and National Security from World War II to the Present* (London: Anthem Press, 2005), p. ix.
27. Der Derian, op. cit., p. 787.
28. Valantin, op. cit., p. xii.
29. Moreover, whether depicting international conflicts, internal security, or policing issues, national security cinema (like the American western and its reliance on the idea of American Manifest Destiny) (re)produces what Lawrence and Jewett describe as the "American Monomyth," the recurrent narrative in American popular culture that superheroic redemptive violence is essential for US survival. Lawrence and Jewett, *The Myth of the American Superhero,* op. cit.
30. Valentin, *op. cit.,* p. 110.
31. Martin Miller, "'24' Gets a Lesson in Torture from the Experts,' *Los Angeles Times,* 13 February 2007.
32. Christian W. Erickson, "Counter-Terror Culture: Ambiguity, Subversion, or Legitimization?" *Security Dialogue* 38:2 (2007), p. 208; Central Intelligence Agency, "New Recruitment Video on the Central Intelligence Agency Careers Web Site Features Jennifer Garner," *Press Release,* 8 March 2007, available online at: <http://www.cia.gov> (accessed 3 March 2009).
33. Nellie Andreeva, "FBI, Fox on the Case with Drama Series," *Reuters,* 8 August 2007, available online at: <http://www.reuters.com> (accessed 22 November 2007).
34. Doug Saunders, "Hollywood, DC," *The Globe and Mail,* 17 November 2001, available online at: <http://www.theglobeandmail.com> (accessed 20 April 2007).
35. Ibid.
36. Both Sopranos-themed clips are available on *YouTube,* see <http://www.youtube.com/watch?v=9BEPcJlz2wE> and <http://www.youtube.com/watch?v=rnT7nYbCSvM> (accessed 10 May 2009).
37. Mayer, op. cit.
38. For a critique of Hollywood's lack of "reality" with regards to the CIA see Nicholas Dujmovic, "Hollywood, Don't You Go Disrepectin' My Culture: *The Good Shepherd* Versus Real CIA History," *Intelligence and National Security* 23:1 (2008), pp. 25–41.
39. Boggs and Pollard, op. cit., p. 335.
40. For an excellent exploration of the interconnections between Hollywood "fiction" and popular understandings of the terrorist attack on flight United 93 on

11 September see Weber, "Popular Visual Language as Global Communication," op. cit.

41. Other genres other than those explicitly identified as "spy dramas" have also recently explored the theme of terrorism such as science fiction (*Battlestar Galactica*, 2005–present, and *Lost*, 2005–present). A more closely related television genre, that of vigilante police dramas and private investigators (PIs)—especially popular in the 1980s—could also be included, where heroes (usually men) or teams of heroes act on their own initiative to solve and prevent crimes. This includes *Magnum PI* (1980–1988) and *The A-Team* (1983–1987).
42. Boggs and Pollard, op. cit., p. 335.
43. Valantin, op. cit., p. 90. For a discussion of the power of the "spectacle" of the collapse of the World Trade Center towers, see also Jean Baudrillard, *The Spirit of Terrorism*, trans. Chris Turner (London: Verso, 2003), pp. 28–9.
44. Weldes, "Globalisation Is Science Fiction," op. cit., p. 650.
45. Boggs and Pollard, op. cit., p. 347.
46. Valantin, op. cit.
47. Grant, op. cit., p. 62.
48. Jean Baudrillard, *Simulacra and Simulation*, trans. Sheila Glaser (Ann Arbour: University of Michigan Press, 1994). A more obvious and frequently cited popular cultural example of hyper-reality and Baudrillard is that found in the film *The Matrix* (1999). Within the film, the Matrix is a fictional world created by machines to enslave humans. Based on a reality of life before "the machines," the fictional world of the Matrix not only camouflages what life is "really" like for those "plugged in" but can also in turn lead to changes in reality and how it is constituted. W. Irwin, *The Matrix and Philosophy: Welcome to the Desert of the Real* (Chicago: Open Court, 2002).
49. Ernest Laclau & Chantal Mouffe, *Hegemony and Socialist Strategy: Towards a Radical Democratic Politics* (London: Verso, 1985).
50. Christian W. Erickson, "Thematics of Counterterrorism: Comparing 24 and MI-5/Spooks," *Critical Studies on Terrorism* 1:3 (2008), pp. 343–58; Joseph J. Foy, *Homer Simpson Goes to Washington: American Politics through Popular Culture* (Kentucky: The University Press of Kentucky, 2008); Sam Kamin, "How the War on Terror May Affect Domestic Interrogations: The 24 Effect," *Chapman Law Review* 10:3 (2007), pp. 1–17; Richard Miniter, *Jack Bauer for President: Terrorism and Politics in "24"* (Dallas: Ben Bella, 2008); Peacock, op. cit.; Jennifer Hart Weed, Richard Davis, and Ronald Weed, *24 and Philosophy: The World According to Jack* (Malden: Wiley Blackwell, 2008); Slavoj Zizek, "Jack Bauer and the Ethics of Urgency," *In These Times*, 27 January 2006, available online at: <http://www.inthesetimes.com> (accessed 3 March 2009).
51. This device, to have all the action occur in one day, is far from new, but is a return to the classical tradition of the unities as defined by Aristotle in *Poetics* (V): "for Tragedy endeavours, as far as possible, to confine itself to a single revolution of the sun, or but slightly to exceed this limit." Aristotle suggested that respecting the unities (action, place, and time) increases the intensity of the audience's experience. Aristotle, *Poetics*, ed. and trans. Malcolm Heath (London: Penguin Classics, 1996).
52. J. Surowiecki, "The Worst Day Ever: A 24Writer Talks about Torture, Terrorism, and Fudging 'Real Time,'" *Slate*, 17 January 2006, available online at <http://www.slate.com/id/2134395> (accessed 23 November 2007).
53. Cited in Tara DiLullo, 24: *The Official Companion Season 1 and 2* (London: Titan Books, 2006); Suroweiki, "The Worst Day Ever," op. cit.
54. "Fox Orders More '24': Emmy Winner Extended through '08–'09 Season," *Variety*, 15 May 2007, available online at: <http://www.variety.com> (accessed 16 May 2007).
55. Academy of Television Arts and Sciences, "Awards," (no date), available online at: <http://www.emmys.org/awards> (accessed 3 March 2009); Hollywood Foreign Press Association, "Golden Globe Awards," (no date), available online at <http://www.goldenglobes.org/goldenglobeawards> (accessed 3 March 2009).
56. Walter Sharpe, "The Law of '24,'" *Georgetown University Law Courses*, updated 20 November 2008, available online at <http://www.law.georgetown.edu/curriculum> (accessed 3 March 2009).
57. Stephen Keane, "America Exceptionalism in Television Spy Dramas: Mainstreaming America with 'I Spy,' 'Sleeper Cell,' and '24'?" *Aladin Research Commons* (2007), available online at: <http://aladinrc.wrlc.org/handle/1961/4115> (accessed 5 December 2007), pp. 1–2.
58. Weldes, "Going Cultural," op. cit., p. 133.
59. Peter Carlson, "Jack Bauer of '24,' The Interrogator's Marquee de Sade?" *Washington Post*, 20 February 2007.
60. Heritage Foundation, "Public Image of U.S. Terrorism Policy," *C-SPAN Video Library*, available online at: <http://www.cspanarchives.org/library/index.php?main_page=product_video_info&products_id=193133-1> (accessed 10 May 2009).
61. When interviewed on the HBO show "Real Time with Bill Maher," economist Stephen Moore, referred to the Military Commissions Act as "Jack-Bauer justice," suggesting that "He should run the CIA ... I love this guy. I wish it were real life ... This guy knows how to interrogate guys." Michael Brendan Dougherty, "What Would Jack Bauer Do? Fox's hit Drama Normalizes Torture, Magnifies Terror, and Leaves Conservatives Asking Why George W. Bush Can't Be More Like 24's Hero," *The American Conservative*, 12 March 2007, available online at: <http://www.amconmag.com/article/2007/mar/12/00008> (accessed 16 April 2009); Troy Patterson, "Senator, We're Ready for Your Cameo: What Was John McCain Doing on 24?" *Slate*, 7 February 2006; Colin Freeze, "What Would Jack Bauer Do?" *The Globe and Mail*, 16 June 2007; Mayer, op. cit.; James Poneiwozik, "The Evolution of Jack Bauer," *Time*, 14 January 2007;

Saunders, op. cit., John Yoo, *War by Other Means: An Insider's Account of the War on Terror* (New York: Atlantic Monthly Press, 2006).

62. For clarity, I use the media studies tradition of referencing episodes by indicating the season (for example, 4 for Season 4, 5 for Season 5) followed by the specific episode (4.5 for episode 5 in Season 4). Within the world of *24,* seasons are referred to by "Day," for example, Season 1 is Day 1, Season 2 is Day 2 and so on.
63. On the use the term articulate see Jutta Weldes, *Constructing the National Interest: The United States and the Cuban Missile Crisis* (Minneapolis, MN: University of Minnesota Press, 1999), p. 98.
64. Popular cultural (re)presentations of threat in the US tradition often feature an existential threat to a community. It has been suggested that this is a legacy of Protestant millennialism: the belief that the founding of the US represented the establishment of a "city on the hill," in preparation for the new millennium and the apocalypse: "*24* and the Nuclear Narrative," in Peacock, op. cit., pp. 85–96. Lawrence and Jewett, op. cit. Daniel Herbert, "Days and Hours of the Apocalypse: 24 and the Nuclear Narrative," in Peacock, op. cit., pp. 85–96.
65. National Commission on Terrorist Attacks Upon the United States, *9/11 Commission Report* (2004), available online at: <http://govinfo.library.unt.edu/911/report/index.htm> (accessed 5 March 2009).
66. Richard Cheney, "Vice President Cheney Salutes Troops," *The White House*, 9 April 2003, available online at: <http://www.whitehouse.gov/news/releases/2003/04/20030409-4.html> (accessed 5 December 2007).
67. Erickson, "Counter-terror Culture," op. cit., p. 208.
68. Matt Feeney, "Torture Chamber: Fox's 24 Terrifies Viewers into Believing its Bizarre and Convoluted Plot Twists," *Slate*, 6 January 2004, available online at: <http://www.slate.com/id/2093269> (accessed 21 November 2007).
69. Boggs and Pollard, op. cit., p. 344.
70. George W. Bush, *Securing the Homeland, Strengthening the Nation*, Presidential Report (Washington, DC: US Government Printing Office, 2002).
71. Mueller, John, *Overblown: How Politicians and the Terrorism Industry Inflate National Security Treats, and Why We Believe Them* (New York: Free Press, 2006), p. 1.
72. Richard Jackson, *Writing the War on Terrorism* (Manchester: Manchester University Press).
73. Anne Caldwell and Samuel A. Chambers, "24 after 9/11: The American State of Exception," in Peacock, op cit., p. 97.
74. William E., Scheuerman, "Torture and the New Paradigm of Warfare," *Constellations* 15:4 (2008), pp. 561–75. See also, Patricia L. Dunmire, "'9/11 Changed Everything': An Intertextual Analysis of the Bush Doctrine," *Discourse & Society* 20:2 (2009), pp. 195–222.
75. Caldwell and Chambers, op. cit., p. 100. As Scheuerman points out, possibly the first president to declare the need to rid the world of terrorists was Theodore Roosevelt, not Reagan or Bush. Scheuerman, op. cit., "Torture and the New Paradigm of Warfare," p. 564.
76. Giorgio Agamben, *State of Exception*, trans. Kevin Attell (Chicago: Chicago University Press, 2005), p. 2.
77. Caldwell and Chambers, op. cit., p. 99.
78. Suroweicki, op. cit.
79. This scene is set in South Korea rather than the US with the impression given that the torturers are themselves South Korean, though the torture is observed by US government agents (2.1). At the time that this episode was aired little was made of this allusion to the extraordinary rendition program.
80. George Bush, "State of the Union," The White House, 29 January 2002, available online at: <http://www.whitehouse.gov> (accessed 20 April 2007).
81. Jackson, op. cit.
82. Matthew Hannah, "Torture and the Ticking Bomb: The War on Terrorism as a Geographical Imagination of Power/Knowledge," *Annals of the Association of American Geographers* 96:3 (2006), p. 629.
83. Scheuerman, "Carl Schmitt and the Road to Abu Ghraib," op. cit., p. 109.
84. Jack G. Shaheen, "Reel Bad Arabs: How Hollywood Vilifies a People," *The Annals of the American Academy of Political and Social Science* 588:1 (2003), pp. 171–93.
85. Lawrence and Jewett, op. cit.
86. This characterization of terrorists is in contrast to other possibly more "self-consciously critical" films about the US and its relation to terrorism, such as *Syriana* (2005), which sets out to suggest reasons why individuals might engage in such acts without resorting to racist clichés or "othering" practices needed to constitute the state. I am indebted to an anonymous reviewer for this point.
87. Grant, op. cit., p. 59.
88. Surowiecki, op. cit. Though the use of "torture porn" as a label is more of a metaphor than a claim that *24* belongs to the sub-genre of horror film. See Dean Lockwood, "All Stripped Down: The Spectacle of 'Torture Porn,'" *Popular Communication* 7:1 (2009), pp. 40–8 for an exploration of "torture porn" as an allegory of "becoming."
89. Frank Gardner, "The US Counter-terror Nerve Centre," *BBC News Online*, 5 December 2006, available online at: <http://news.bbc.co.uk/1/hi/world/americas/6210090.stm> (accessed 28 November 2007); National Counterterrorism Center, "About the National Counterterrorism Center," 5 August 2007, available online at: <http://www.nctc.gov/about_us/about_nctc.html> (accessed 28 November 2007).
90. Gardner, op. cit.
91. DiLullo, op. cit.
92. The use of the military for counter-terrorism is especially interesting in light of the Posse Comitatus (1878) and Insurrection Acts (1807), which historically have limited the authority of the federal government to use US military

forces for carrying out law enforcement activities on US soil. For the first six seasons of *24*, these acts were in place though that did not prevent the "fictional" world from using the military. However, since 2006, these acts are among those that have been altered in the wake of 9/11. The US president is now authorized to use the military for law enforcement in the event of a "major public emergency."

93. Ronald D. Crelinsten, "The Discourse and Practice of Counter-Terrorism in Liberal Democracies," *Australian Journal of Politics and History* 44:1 (1998), pp. 389–413.
94. Ibid., p. 399.
95. In an interesting case of the interconnection between Hollywood and the Pentagon, where fiction meets reality, real-life marine units and helicopters were loaned to the production for the purposes of "taking down the terrorists" (4.6). When one of the soldiers who participated in the filming was later killed in Iraq, *24* paid tribute to his heroism following the show. "'24' Pays Tribute to Fallen Marine," *Chicago Tribune*, 8 January 2005, available online at: <http://www.chicagotribune.com> (accessed 2 May 2007).
96. For a detailed count of how many "kills" Bauer has carried out in each episode, down to what weapon the character used, see the blog maintained by Wesley Vandlandshoot, "Jack Bauer—Kill Count" (no date), available online at: <http://www.bauercount.com> (accessed 30 November 2007).
97. For the distinction between war and "new war" and its implications, I am indebted to an anonymous reviewer.
98. Thomas Bernard and Robin Shepard Engel, "Conceptualizing Criminal Justice Theory," *Justice Quarterly* 18:1 (2001), pp. 1–30; Crelinstein, op. cit. This model itself is not unproblematic as ongoing problems in the American criminal justice system attest to. See Mark Neocleous, *The Fabrication of Social Order: A Critical Theory of Police Power* (London: Pluto Press, 2004).
99. Scheuerman, "Torture and the New Paradigm of Warfare," op. cit., p. 562.
100. Mike Baker, 14-year CIA veteran, as cited in Erickson, "Counter-terrorCulture," op. cit., p. 201; Vice Admiral Scott Redd, Head of the National Counter Terrorism Centre, as cited in Gardner, op. cit.
101. Interview with Vice President Dick Cheney, NBC *Meet the Press* television broadcast (16 September 2001), transcript available from *The Washington Post* available online at: <http://www.washingtonpost.com/wp-srv/nation/attacked/transcripts/cheney091601.Html> (accessed 14 July 2009).
102. As cited in Jackson, op. cit., p. 139.
103. Caldwell and Chambers, op. cit., p. 104, emphasis added.
104. Judith Butler, *Precarious Life: The Powers of Mourning and Violence* (London: Verso, 2004).
105. Carl Schmitt, *The Concept of the Political*, trans. George Schwab (Chicago: University of Chicago Press, 1998), p. 72.
106. Scheuerman, "Carl Schmitt and the Road to Abu Ghraib," op. cit., p. 118.
107. These metaphors are themselves interesting, with their references to light/dark, good/evil, and clean/dirty associations, and are common in the GWOT discourse generally, working together (along with creating other intertextual moments with texts such as *Star Wars* and "the dark side") to render the argument commonsensical.
108. *24* is not the only show to depict torture as necessary. As Human Rights First reports, primetime depictions of torture have increased from 55 (1995–2000) to 679 (2001–2005), and appear in counter-terrorism shows such as *Alias* (2001), in police dramas such as *CSI Miami* (2002), or science fiction such as *Heroes* (2006) where "good guys" torture, see Human Rights First, "Primetime torture," op. cit.
109. For a discussion of torture in 24, see Douglas L. Howard, "'You're Going to Tell Me Everything You Know': Torture and Morality in Fox's *24*" in Peacock, op. cit., pp. 133–48.
110. Surowiecki, op. cit.
111. Available online at: <http://www.jackbauertorturereport.com>.
112. McKeown, op. cit., p. 18; Scheuerman, "Torture and the New Paradigm of Warfare," op. cit., p. 561.
113. Scheuerman, "Carl Schmitt and the Road to Abu Ghraib," *op. cit.*, p. 121.
114. Barbara Olshansky, *Democracy Detained: Secret Unconstitutional Practices in the U.S. War on Terror* (New York: Seven Stories Press, 2007); Philippe Sands, *Torture Team: Uncovering War Crimes in the Land of the Free* (London: Allen Lane, 2008); Philippe Sands, "Torture Is Illegal—And It Never Works: Jack Bauer and 24 Were Hugely Popular with Interrogators at Guantánamo. Let's Hope the New Series Is More Realistic," *Guardian*, 24 November 2008, section "Comment Is Free," available online at: <http://www.guardian.co.uk> (accessed 2 March 2009).
115. Philpott and Mutimer, op. cit., p. 341.
116. Will Wright, *Sixguns and Society: A Structural Study of the Western* (Berkeley: University of California Press, 1977).
117. Lawrence and Jewett, op. cit., p. 46.
118. Will Wright, *The Wild West: The Mythical Cowboy and Social Theory* (London: Sage Publications, 2001), p. 2.
119. Valantin, op. cit., p. 110.
120. Peacock, op. cit.; Human Rights First, "Torture on TV Rising and Copied in the Field," *Primetime TV Torture Project*, available online at: <http://www.humanrightsfirst.org/us_law/etn/primetime> (accessed 16 May 2007).
121. Saunders, op. cit.
122. Philpott and Mutimer, op. cit., p. 337.

"Get the Puck Outta Here!"[1]: Media Transnationalism and Canadian Identity

Daniel S. Mason

Increasingly, transnational corporations have relied on sport as a vehicle to implement their strategic initiatives; this is a small part of the process of globalization (Denning, 2001; Guillen, 2001; Hedetoft, 1999; Miller, Lawrence, McKay & Rowe, 2001; Robins, 1997; Sassen, 2000). Jackson and Andrews (1999) recognized that "contemporary discussions about globalization are concerned with the basis and consequences of postindustrial capitalism, economic flows, new media technologies, and the influence of largely, but not exclusively, American popular culture on contemporary social life throughout the world" (p. 31). In some instances, a consequence of globalizing processes can be the reassertion of local/national cultures, where "'difference' and 'diversity' have become important labels contributing to the economic and cultural wealth of nation-states" (Preston & Kerr, 2001, p. 125). As explained by De Cillia, Reisigl, and Wodak (1999), a typical response to globalization at the local level is the rediscovery and revitalization of a sense of community and heritage. In many cases, this rediscovery or rearticulation plays out through the discourse of the news media; in other words, the reassertion, or sense of crisis, that emerges as a response to the initiatives of transnational corporations takes place in and through the arbiters of public discourse: the popular, commercial media. Thus, although most nation-states are composed of a diverse group of citizens, "they are convinced that they belong to a unique national community—not least because they read to a large degree the same newspapers, [and] watch widely the same television programs" (p. 154). Therefore, it becomes critical to investigate the means through which discourses of crisis at local levels are manifested and how citizens and the media react to the influences of globalization, which can provide an opportunity to draw together and even (re)create conceptions of unity.

The manner through which local communities react to global pressures varies; Hedetoft (1999) suggested that manifestations of nationalism "oscillate" between scapegoating and reforging identities. In other words,

> the globalization of *culture* (whether American or not) in this threat scenario is invested with a normatively negative sign value; it comes to *stand for* and *represent* the transnational imperatives that in turn are interpreted as eroding the nation-state and its identity. (p. 79)

Although the utility of the term *Americanization* can be contested, Canadians tend to be wary of the influences of American media products and couch these concerns in terms of cultural dependency and a loss of local identity (Jackson, 1994, 2001). This occurs in countries other than Canada, where similar reactionary stances have been made to foreign (and more specifically, American) investments and commodities (Jackson & Andrews, 1999) as a part of a reaction to global processes.

As this article will show, changing technologies instituted by transnational corporations can alter, and/or conflict with, traditional representations of a given sport in a society and the manner through which individuals identify with a sport and their sense of identity. Specifically, discrete incidents can emerge as symbolic of other underlying issues related to the establishment and maintenance of local and national identities. One example of this phenomenon was the reaction in Canada to the advent of the FoxTrax puck, which was introduced during the 1996 National Hockey League (NHL) All-Star Game held in Boston, Massachusetts, as a means of making hockey more viewer friendly for those unfamiliar with the sport. Criticism of the innovation reflected concerns over the utility of a new technological innovation but, more important, represented concerns over the marginalization of Canadian identity. This article reviews the advent of the puck and the reaction it engendered in newspaper coverage in both Canada and the United States, along with sources available on the Internet. In particular, it is hoped that reaction to the FoxTrax puck will provide an example of the contestation of global-local relations in a sporting context. This article begins with a brief overview of the development of hockey in Canada and factors contributing to the "crisis of identity" that faced many Canadians as the FoxTrax puck was introduced (Jackson, 1994). Recent changes to the business of professional hockey are then discussed, followed by an examination of the growing influence of transnational media corporations, such as News Corporation. An overview of the development and implementation of the FoxTrax puck is then provided, followed by a discussion of reaction to the puck in the context of Canada's crisis of identity.

Hockey, Canadian Culture, and the NHL

As noted by Jackson (2001), "Sport has long played a major role in the social construction of national identity in Canada" (p. 171). Since its emergence in major urban centres in eastern Canada toward the end of the nineteenth century, hockey has been described as an integral part of the collective Canadian identity (Kidd, 1996; Kidd & Macfarlane, 1972). Similarly, MacNeill (1996) identified that "over the past century ice hockey has served as a crucial symbol within Canada's struggle to achieve international recognition and in its efforts to create a unifying sense of identity within the country" (p. 103). Hockey has been examined by observers who have attempted to define and explain the Canadian experience (Gruneau & Whitson, 1993) or determine the manner through which hockey has been presented as a defining national cultural practice. In particular, the media has followed and televised events associated with the sport by contextualizing hockey within a broader Canadian social context, while at the same time, the media has been instrumental in creating the experience itself (MacNeill, 1996). In doing so, hockey has been associated with a romanticized vision of national identity (Nauright & White, 1996), a practice found in other sports in other regions throughout the world (Maguire, Poulton & Possamai, 1999). Perhaps the defining moment for the sport as a mechanism for defining Canadian identity occurred in 1972 with the "Summit Series" between Canada and the Soviet Union. As explained by Earle (1995), "For once, disparate notions of class, ethnicity and gender were welded into a rare Canadian moment" (p. 108). Although this comment likely oversimplifies the complex web of relations comprising the Canadian experience, it certainly reflected the sentiment of many social commentators and sports journalists.

However, hockey's evolution into a component of Canadian identity has occurred within a context of the dominating economic and cultural presence of the United States. As a result, how Canadians define themselves is often in terms of how they differ from their American counterparts. In turn, hockey has become a means of defining and distinguishing one's "Canadianness," particularly in the face of American dominance in many sporting pursuits. Thus, anything that appears to infringe on the sport and, in particular, Canadians' conceptions of ownership is highly contested. This contestation is not new; Canadian concerns over the Americanization of hockey have existed since the turn of the century, when Canadian hockey players first left Canada to play professionally in the United States (Mason, 1998; Mason & Schrodt, 1996). Similarly, when Hamilton, Ontario's NHL team, disbanded and reformed in New York for the 1925–1926 NHL season, concerns were expressed that control over the sport was slipping into American hands (Good, 1926). In addition, the trade of Wayne Gretzky from the Edmonton Oilers to the Los Angeles Kings in 1988 was considered a major incident in Canada and received extensive media coverage. As explained by Jackson (1994), "The American media contributed to the discourse of crisis. They did so by perpetuating the myth of the centrality of ice hockey in Canada and by reproducing a discourse that focused on Canada's supposed inferiority complex" (p. 439).

Jackson (1994) described the conditions surrounding the trade as a "crisis of identity" in the Canadian context, linking ice hockey to Canadian identity and placing it within a context of fears of Americanization. Jackson's discussion of Gretzky occurred within a framework of other issues of national importance during the late 1980s, including discussions of the implications of the North American Free Trade Agreement and the manner through which this issue became a focal point in Canada's 1988 federal election. In this situation, Jackson argued that the Gretzky trade was positioned within a broader discourse of concerns surrounding the impact of American interests on Canadian identity and related the circumstances surrounding the trade in terms of its importance in perpetuating/reinforcing Canada's alleged crisis of identity.

In the years following the Gretzky trade, through the early 1990s, several other events occurred that affected the hockey world specifically, that likely only added to this discourse of crisis. One concern for Canadians was the influx of European and other foreign-born players who were playing in a league once composed almost entirely of Canadian-born and -trained players. In 1967, 97 per cent of NHL players were Canadian born (Weiler, 1992); however, this number had decreased to less than 63 per cent by the 1996–1997 season, as more European and American players filled out NHL rosters ("Opening Night," 1996, p. 10). Thus, a sport that had long been the domain of Canadians at the elite level had become a global sport, as the flow of skilled athletes from foreign countries continued. In this manner, the migration of hockey players became another example of the diaspora that remains a hallmark of a broader globalizing process (Sinclair & Cunningham, 2000) and led to concerns regarding Canada's position as a producer of elite-level hockey talent.

In addition to the increasing numbers of foreign-born athletes, concerns were also raised regarding the apparent migration of top players (of Canadian descent or not) from Canadian teams, who opted to play for US-based teams. This provided additional ammunition for critics wary of the economic influence of the United States and another example of the drain of talented and skilled Canadians to US climes. The causes attributed to this were underfinanced Canadian team owners and the reluctance of players to play in Canadian cities with a weaker currency and higher tax rates than found in the United States. The cloudy financial future of several Canadian-based teams, specifically those in Quebec City and Winnipeg, had also led to discussions of franchise sales and relocations to new US markets.

Canadian concerns were exacerbated as the NHL named its first ever commissioner in 1993 and a popular manufacturer of hockey skates and equipment was sold to US interests the following year. Gary Bettman, an American attorney who had worked with the National Basketball Association (NBA), was named commissioner of the NHL and centralized league operations in New York, where Montreal had previously been a centre of league affairs. Shortly afterward, Canstar, Canada's largest and most well-known hockey equipment manufacturer, was bought out by US-based footwear and apparel giant Nike. Such actions, if occurring separately, might not have raised much opposition in Canada; however, in concert with the other events described earlier, they helped contribute to Canada's crisis of identity. Given that hockey was considered by many Canadians to be an integral component of Canadian identity (Earle, 1995; Gruneau & Whitson, 1993; Kidd & Macfarlane, 1972) and the reactionary stance associated with local identities to global processes (Hedetoft, 1999; Hogan, 1999), the FoxTrax puck seemed poised to become a symbolic artifact for discussions of Americanization emerging from Canada's ongoing crisis of identity during the mid-1990s. Thus, reaction to the FoxTrax puck provided a new opportunity for Canadians to find some consensus regarding their perceived "Canadianness": They could all agree to dislike the FoxTrax puck. As will be discussed below, this reaction was also a result of concerns regarding changes to the business operations of the league, which seemed to move the NHL even further away from its Canadian origins.

As the mid-1990s approached, the business of professional hockey continued to expand and change. Until 1967, when the league expanded from 6 to 12 teams, the NHL was considered by many outside Canada to be a small, regional, professional sports league, a view reinforced by the NHL's new commissioner as he assumed his new position in 1993 (Gerlin, 1993). The league has since expanded to 30 franchises, 24 of which are in the United States. In doing so, the NHL has certainly broadened its market beyond what could be considered regional status. In addition to expansion, two Canadian franchises have relocated to US cities. In doing so, a league that as recently as 1991 was composed of one-third Canadian franchises is now one-fifth Canadian.

As Bettman took over leadership of the NHL, an initial mandate of NHL owners was to expand the television presence of the sport in the US. Television has become an increasingly larger source of revenue for professional sports leagues, although the NHL has traditionally derived a much greater percentage (approximately 60 per cent) of its revenues from live attendance when compared to basketball, football, and baseball. In contrast, hockey has had a strong television presence in Canada since the 1950s through its affiliation with the Canadian Broadcasting Corporation (CBC) and its signature program, *Hockey Night in Canada*. According to Earle (1995), "Hockey and television still seem inseparably linked in the [Canadian] popular imagination" (p. 107).

As previously stated, in the United States, despite the increasing revenues generated from media sources in the global sporting community, the sport of hockey did not enjoy the same relationships (and revenues) from television as other North American sports. In fact, up until 1995, the NHL had gone approximately 20 years without a US network television contract. One reason attributed to this lack of interest was that because most NHL teams were located in the northeastern United States, networks would shy away from televising a product that might only have regional interest. For this reason, one of Bettman's first goals when he was hired as the NHL's first commissioner in 1993 was to expand the NHL's presence in the United States, which included expansion into Sunbelt cities without established hockey traditions, such as Miami and Anaheim. As explained by Bettman, "The broader our footprint, the more desirable we become as a network product" (Gerlin, 1993, p. B1).

Thus, one of Bettman's first steps in the process of broadening interest in the NHL product was to negotiate a 5-year, $155 million contract with Fox television, starting with the 1994–1995 season. Although featuring a much smaller number of established viewers than other leagues, the NHL was a desirable commodity to networks due to its potential audience demographics. According to NHL sources, 38 per cent of hockey fans fell into the much-desired age 18-to-34 male demographic; by comparison, the NFL boasted only 32 per cent and basketball only 24 per cent in this group (Goldman, 1994). Thus, using hockey, networks could target specific sponsors trying to reach an increasingly fragmented population of television viewers. These figures were leveraged by Bettman, whose league was coming off an exciting conclusion to its 1994 playoffs, where the New York Rangers won their first Stanley Cup (league) championship since 1940. With a new network contract in hand, the NHL seemed poised to enter a new era of prosperity (Swift, 1994) but was held back by a labour dispute in the fall of 1994 that resulted in a lockout and a shortened 1994–1995 season. As noted by Frank Vuono, president of Integrated Sports International, "This was the first year they [the NHL] were going to move up there with the heavyweights [the other three major professional sports leagues], and they didn't show up for the big fight" (Helyar, 1995, p. B1). Thus, the NHL was at a critical juncture as it entered the 1994–1995 season.

Media and the New Business of Professional Sport

The "heavyweight" professional sports leagues noted above had obtained their status, in part, as a result of strong ties with network television stations in the United States. Increasingly, media companies had begun to become more actively involved in leagues' operations by purchasing interests in teams and showcasing games on their respective stations. In addition, transnational media corporations, through their television networks, were beginning to use sport as a means to penetrate new markets as a part of their global initiatives, a highly debated topic within discussions of the globalizing process (Silk & Andrews, 2001; Tracy, 1999). As television has used sports as a programming option, other business interests have also become involved in sports, viewing professional sport as being part of a greater entertainment industry (Euchner, 1993), and media corporations such as Time Warner and News Corporation have sought to produce products for global audiences (Robins, 1997). To exploit this opportunity in sport, corporations traditionally affiliated with media and entertainment have become more active in owning/operating professional sports franchises. For example, one commentator noted that one of the NHL's newest franchises, the Atlanta Thrashers (owned by Turner Broadcasting), "will be as much a part of Time Warner and Turner Broadcasting as they are a part of the NHL" (Bernstein, 1998, p. 8). Another method has been to use sports programming as a means to enter new markets worldwide. According to Robins (1997),

> Driven now by the logic of profit and competition, the overriding objective of the new media corporations is to get their product to the largest number of consumers. There is, then, an expansionist tendency at work, pushing all the time towards the construction of enlarged media spaces and markets. The imperative is to break down the old boundaries and frontiers of national communities, which now present themselves as arbitrary and irrational obstacles to this reorganization of business strategies. (p. 33)

An obvious potential casualty of such initiatives would be sports with rich heritages and strong existing ties to local communities. Thus, it would seem critical for transnational corporations to be highly aware of the circumstances in which new market opportunities are pursued; otherwise, these same corporations would risk the backlash associated with the response of local identity. For this reason, Silk and Andrews (2001) noted that transnational corporations must negotiate "within the language of the local." With this in mind, penetrating new markets must be done with a keen awareness of the traditions and symbolic meanings of the sports that provide the programming content for these transnational media corporations.

Perhaps, the best example of an individual who has used sport to infiltrate new markets is News

Corporation's Rupert Murdoch. In his own words, Murdoch has told his stockholders that he intended to use sports as a "battering ram and lead offering in all our pay-television offerings" (DeMarco, 1998, p. D01). Fox television, which Murdoch established in 1986, has aggressively purchased regional sports networks in the United States as part of its News Corporation's cable television market strategy. Murdoch has also sought to buy outright or partial ownership of professional sports teams, including a thwarted effort to buy the Manchester United football club. In Los Angeles, this strategy was evidenced by Fox's purchase of the Los Angeles Dodgers baseball team and failed attempts to purchase parts of the NHL's Los Angeles Kings and the NBA's Los Angeles Lakers. According to Neil Begley, senior media analyst for Moody's (a financial data provider), this is a result of Fox's efforts to lock up broadcasting rights to regional sports teams in cities where Fox owns cable networks (Mullen, 1998). In the US network television arena, Fox used sports programming to position itself as the fourth major US television network after obtaining the rights to televise National Football League games in the mid-1990s. Thus, despite losses of more than $100 million on $395 million spent each year on that contract (Martzke, 1997), Fox executives viewed their foray into sport as a wise investment. Certainly, there is likely no better example than Murdoch and his News Corporation of how sport is used by transnational corporations to penetrate new markets and reach new consumers.

Murdoch's business practices have not been without criticism; according to one observer, "As Murdoch has built up his media empire, he has not focused on content to the same extent as others operating in the global media market" ("The Rights Stuff," 1995, p. 10). As a result, criticism has been levelled at Murdoch for presenting arguably "low-brow" programming such as "Married With Children" (Andrews, 2001). Murdoch's ambivalence toward programming content and its target audience can be extended to sport as well. For example, in Australia, a battle between Murdoch and media rival Kerry Packer led to a battle over control of elite-level professional rugby leagues. A war between Murdoch's Super League and Packer's Australian Rugby League resulted in a financial stand-off, where the two leagues eventually agreed to merge. Results of this merger were fan disinterest and confusion over player and team movements; many league clubs eventually folded or merged with others (Brace, 2000). For this, Murdoch was accused of "precipitating the ruin of a national institution and a community resource" (Andrews, 2001, p. 145). Thus, evidence of Murdoch's apparent lack of concern for the long-term interests of local sporting communities does not just appear in Canada with the sport of hockey.

As Murdoch's Fox and the NHL's new leadership commenced their partnership for the 1994–1995 season, both were aware that the NHL needed enhanced exposure to restore any ill will created by the work stoppage of 1994 and to draw a larger (and therefore more lucrative) fan base. The league, with its coveted audience demographic and untapped US network broadcast potential, provided an ideal venue for the transnational News Corporation to expand its global network of media interests. According to Whitson (1998), such practices characterized the new business of professional team sport:

> The most important developments in the sports business, however, follow from the rapid employment of pay-TV technologies (i.e., cable and satellite services) and from the technological and corporate developments that point towards tighter vertical integration in the communication and "infotainment" industries. (p. 67)

Although not familiar with broadcasting professional hockey, Fox likely felt confident that it could connect with hockey's audience demographic in the same way it had done with professional football and other sports. Fox had already experimented with various technological innovations with its coverage of NFL football. One such innovation was the introduction of the Fox box, a small information box that was superimposed on the television screen throughout the duration of a game that gave information such as the current score and time of play. This advancement, although seemingly inconsequential, was in direct contrast to other network executives who feared that such a display would encourage viewers to change channels more frequently (as they could gain an instant update of the game score) (Phipers, 1996). Similarly, Fox entertained various ideas that network executives (and the NHL) hoped would grow the game. For its inaugural season, Fox introduced animated robots to accentuate its graphics; the robots would perform a number of functions after a team scored a goal. In addition, Fox also began developing a new innovation to be introduced during the 1996 NHL All-Star Game, the FoxTrax glow puck, which would dramatically affect its telecasts of hockey games. As such, this study will now focus on the creation and implementation of the FoxTrax puck and the reaction to the innovation as reported in the media.[2]

New Technologies—The FoxTrax Glow Puck

It is important to note that the manner through which television programming is developed, produced, and disseminated is critical in creating the audience experience. Thus, although providing a televised version of a sporting event, television production mediates the event itself in substantive ways (Gruneau, 1989). As explained by Silk (1999),

> It is important then to determine narrative constructions, target markets, and the preferred interpretations of events by networks as they attempt to recreate *meanings* for fragmented markets (p. 115).

Similarly,

> the political, cultural, and economic logic behind these representations, are crucial to our understanding of local/global processes and the possible impact of narrative construction on national cultures (p. 122).

In producing programming, the sports telecast must try to blend features, effects, and other techniques to create an entertaining narrative (one that results from the telecast, separate from the sporting event itself), while at the same time trying not to stray too far from providing an accurate representation of the sporting event itself (Gruneau, 1989). For this reason, the manner in which telecasts reproduce sporting events for viewing audiences is critical.

In hockey, a notion of a "legitimate" way of producing televised programming had slowly evolved from coverage of NHL games in Canada (MacNeill, 1996). In an interview related to Olympic hockey coverage, CBC *Hockey Night in Canada* producer John Shannon intimated that producers cover games largely in the same way, with regard to the use of camera angles and the types of activities occurring during play that were given more exposure (MacNeill, 1996). In contrast, Fox executives professed new ideas of how to go about televising hockey games. According to Sandy Grossman, Fox's lead hockey director, "CBC does a very solid job, but I've just got a different attitude toward the way hockey should be covered. It's not right or wrong, it's what you want to see" (Sandomir, 1998, p. C8). Fitting in with Fox and the NHL's new directive to attract a wider audience, an initial concern of Fox was how to present games in a way that would appeal to inexperienced viewers. Perhaps, the most common reason given for low television ratings for professional hockey games in the United States was the size of the puck (Belsie, 1996; O'Hara, 1996). It was thought that the small size of the puck, combined with the fast and dynamic flow of the game, made it difficult for novice viewers to follow the play and, therefore, grow to appreciate the sport. To combat this problem, David Hill, president of Fox Sports, reportedly approached computer engineers with the following question: "It's difficult to follow the puck on TV. Can you make me an illuminated puck?" (Maney, 1996, p. 1A).

Hockey had earlier experienced a similar attempt to make the game more viewer friendly. A few years prior, a "fire puck" had been used during a Minnesota North Stars practice, video of which was shown during National Broadcasting Company's telecast of the 1993 NHL All-Star Game. The puck featured a computer chip that allowed the puck to glow red when shown on TV (Hackel, 1996b). To develop its own version, Fox contacted ETAK, a company known for making electronic roadmaps used in luxury cars made by General Motors and Mercedes-Benz (Belsie, 1996). The FoxTrax puck was a hollowed-out regulation NHL game puck that was implanted with 20 infrared transmitters (12 on the perimeter of the puck, 4 on top, and 4 on the bottom) that would emit a pulse 30 times per second. Twenty pulse detectors were situated throughout the arena, which would receive the pulses and then determine the puck's location on the ice (http://www.nextstep.com/stepback/cycle10/126/superpuck.html). The data from the receptors could then be used to project a halo or circle, which could be changed in size and colour, that was superimposed over the televised image of the puck on the ice. Thus, the puck could be seen better on television, as it could be shown much larger in size. In addition, the data received by the detectors could be used to determine the speed at which the puck was travelling, and a coloured streak could be created that showed the trajectory of the puck as it moved along the ice surface. The technology also enabled sound accompaniment for the new device (Craig, 1996a).

As Fox developed the puck concept, several questions arose regarding how the innovation would affect established hockey fans, who it could be assumed had no problems following the path of the puck on the ice (Lapointe, 1996a) and were used to the style of telecast that had been accepted as the legitimate way to broadcast games. According to Jerry Gepner, former senior vice president of Fox Sports, "Each sport has its own traditions, lore and legends, the fabric of its soul. Any enhancement must be mindful of these traditions and work to weave itself into the sport itself" (Gepner, 1998, p. 2). Similarly, Rick Cavallaro (1997) of Fox's parent News Corporation reported that

> of course, Fox knew that changing the game in any way might offend long-time hockey fans. We gave a lot of thought to developing an effect that would let would-be fans follow the game without driving away those already watching. (p. 2)

Other industry executives also discussed the issue. Joe Cohen, a former Los Angeles Kings governor who had joined the Madison Square Garden network, reported that the FoxTrax puck "has enough promise to warrant further experimentation. The dilemma you face is alienating your traditional patrons, but the benefits here outweigh that" (Hackel, 1996a, p. 10).

As the project continued and the technology appeared feasible, many involved anticipated the impact that the puck would have on the sport. Ed Goren, executive producer at Fox, proclaimed that "we plan to make FoxTrax become such a normal thing in hockey telecasts that when you see a game without it, you feel something is lacking" (Baker, 1996b, p. 011). Others were cautious, but optimistic, about the puck's potential. Hill stated that "we think it's pretty impressive. We like it but this is brand new technology. If it works on Saturday [at the 1996 All-Star Game] it's a demonstration. If it doesn't, it's an experiment" (Hooper, 1996, p. 2C). Plans were made to have pucks that left the ice surface and entered the seating area of the arena (pucks normally kept by fans as souvenirs) returned so that "autopsies" could be performed on them by Fox technicians (Langton, 1996).

After considerable investment, estimated at $3 million, the FoxTrax puck was to make its debut at the 1996 NHL All-Star Game held in January in Boston. Fox also planned to introduce a "helmet cam," to be worn by one of the goaltenders playing in the game (Baker, 1996a). However, unlike the helmet cam and other innovations, the FoxTrax puck would considerably affect the way in which the game was viewed. When televised, the puck featured a large blue halo, and any time the puck was passed or shot at a speed of more than 70 miles per hour, a red "comet trail" appeared behind the puck. A box also appeared at the bottom of the screen, which displayed the speed the puck had travelled.

A trial run for the puck was organized in Boston in the days leading up to the All-Star Game. Boston Bruins General Manager Harry Sinden attended the demonstration and lauded Fox's efforts. Sinden also acknowledged that he expected some negative reaction to the puck by some Canadian fans (Dryden, 1996). However, FoxTrax received an unexpected endorsement from John Shannon, executive producer of *Hockey Night in Canada*. Shannon reported that he gave the FoxTrax puck "a seven out of ten. . . . I think there are some elements that are distracting. But once the long-term technology is perfected, we may all want to be a part of it" (Longley, 1996b, p. 91). Perhaps, more important for Fox and the NHL, the interest generated by the innovation leading up to the All-Star Game had been a public relations coup. According to one journalist, the FoxTrax puck "was a success even before the opening face-off. In the days before the game, even competing network aired stories about it on their newscasts" (Lapointe, 1996b, p. C8). *Hockey Night in Canada*'s Shannon agreed, noting that "Fox bought at least $3 million worth of publicity with their $3 million investment. I've never been interviewed so many times about something that was not on one of my telecasts" (Hackel, 1996a, p. 10). Major US newspapers featured the puck and its technological aspects (MacKinnon, 1996b), and the Discovery Channel later did a feature on the FoxTrax project (MacGregor, 1997). Following its appearance at the All-Star Game, the puck appeared on American Broadcasting Company's (ABC) *World News Tonight*, and comedian/talk-show host David Letterman later parodied the puck with "DaveTrax" on his late-night television show (Hackel, 1996a). Following its premier, NHL Commissioner Bettman proclaimed that "when FoxTrax is on all cameras and when it becomes a regular part of hockey, we will understand how significant this development is" (Caesar, 1996, p. 8D). However, Bettman may not have foreseen that the FoxTrax puck would become "one of the more controversial features in sports television" (Phipers, 1996, p. D08) and a symbol of Canada's crisis of identity.

"Fox Is Too Glitzy. Just Leave Our Perfect Game Alone." (Respondent to Hockey News "Puck Poll")

Fox's telecast of the 1996 NHL All-Star Game held in Boston received a rating of 4.1, making it the highest rated NHL game in the United States since the sixth and deciding game of the 1980 Stanley Cup Finals between the New York Islanders and Philadelphia Flyers (O'Hara, 1996).[3] Fox reported that the game's rating represented a 64 per cent increase over the previous NHL All-Star Game (held in 1994), which had posted a 2.5 rating. The NHL released a statement reporting that a Neilsen survey of 77 people found that NHL fans liked the FoxTrax puck by a seven to one margin (Hackel, 1996a). Fox's Lou Dermilio announced that a telephone poll among TV critics throughout the United States indicated close to a 90 per cent approval rating for the puck (Craig, 1996b). In Canada, there was some evidence to suggest that Fox was successful in its ability to lure a new audience to the sport. For example, a ratings comparison of Fox and CBC, which both carried the All-Star Game in the metropolitan Toronto area, showed that although CBC enjoyed a 10.6 rating over Fox's 6.1 overall, Fox had higher ratings than its Canada-based rival in the 25-to-54-year-old women category (5.3 to 4.7) and with children aged 12 to 17 (7.6 to 7.4). Given the NHL's male-skewed demographic, it appeared that Fox had reached some of the audience it had targeted with its innovation. After the debut of the FoxTrax puck, Gepner, Fox vice president of field operations and engineering, spoke on behalf of the network, testifying that "we were extremely pleased" (McKee, 1996, p. 5C).

However, it was not long before negative reactions to the puck began to emerge. The *Ottawa Citizen* organized a telephone poll to elicit public response to FoxTrax; 234 of 293 callers strongly disliked the puck (Bray, 1996). Similarly, the *Detroit News* created an online survey, where 78 per cent of 2,600 respondents did not favour the continued use of the puck. ESPN's SportsZone conducted an Internet poll, where 67 per cent of the more than 10,000 respondents shared their displeasure with the innovation (Kent, 1996). *The Hockey News* also developed a reader's poll, where 90 per cent of the 1,813 respondents voiced disapproval of Fox's puck ("No! No! No!" 1996, p. 9). News coverage of the All-Star Game at a local Boston drinking establishment reported that fans disliked FoxTrax virtually unanimously (Lessels, 1996). Thus, it appeared that existing hockey fans, regardless of national origins, did not approve of the new puck. In response to this backlash, several enterprising individuals went to the effort to create anti-FoxTrax websites, where criticisms were shared along with relevant newspaper articles criticizing the FoxTrax project. Within a year, one site had already obtained 4,000 Internet "signatures" for an anti-FoxTrax petition (Sandomir, 1997).

It was also not long before criticism from other industry stakeholders emerged. Former *Hockey Night in Canada* producer Ralph Mellanby reportedly disliked FoxTrax because it drew one's eyes away from the play and made viewers focus solely on the trajectory of the puck itself (MacKinnon, 1996b), an opinion also held by *USA Today*'s Michael Hiestand (Hiestand, 1996). The size of the puck on the screen was also said to diminish one's appreciation of the art of stickhandling the puck (Craig, 1996a). Television hockey analyst and former NHL goaltender John Davidson was later quoted as not being a fan of FoxTrax (Slusser, 1997), and players also began complaining that the puck did not feel the same as regulation NHL pucks (Strachan, 1997). Meanwhile, Tom McClocklin, producer/director of St. Louis Blues telecasts on KPLR and Prime Sports cable network, reported that "I don't like it and haven't talked to anyone else who did. The only advantage I can see is for bar people, sitting a long way away from the television" (Caesar, 1996, p. 8D). Detroit Red Wings captain Steve Yzerman stated that "I really don't care for it, if we're resorting to things like [FoxTrax] to sell the game. I don't think we need gimmicks" (O'Hara, 1996).

Similarly, editorials and letters to various newspapers throughout North America began to feature reports of angry hockey fans describing the puck as "the worst thing to happen to hockey in its entire existence" ("Letter to the Sports Editor," 1996, p. D03). *The Hockey News* printed a number of comments from its poll, with an underlying theme that Fox was not recognizing the rich heritage that hockey had developed ("No! No! No!" 1996, p. 9). Thus, although there was some evidence to suggest that Fox had reached its intended audience (young and inexperienced viewers), FoxTrax "reinforce[d] the complaints of critics who said the network did not intend to cover hockey Saturday night so much as to introduce a new video game" (Craig, 1996a, p. 51).

This discourse was articulated and supported by journalists in both Canada and the United States. One described the use of the FoxTrax puck as a "desecration of a great sport" (Verdi, 1996, p. D10), and the *Boston Globe*'s Dan Shaugnessy said FoxTrax "looked alarmingly like the blue dot (that blocked out) the accuser in the William Kennedy Smith trial" (Hanley, 1996, p. 18). Many journalists ridiculed Fox's efforts (Longley, 1996a), describing the puck as "distracting" (Caesar, 1996, p. 8D) or "that foolish glow thing" (Saunders, 1996, p. 2C). Some tried to make light of Fox and the FoxTrax puck by creating top-10 lists of Fox innovations, including putting a red streak on the Zamboni or creating "cup cam" (Kravitz, 1996) or describing

FoxTrax as "a runaway cockroach in an evening gown" (Chad, 1996, p. C03). Another felt that Fox needed to get rid of its approach to televising NHL games to save itself from further embarrassment (Warmington, 1996). A prevailing view in Canada was that many fans tuned into Fox's inaugural All-Star telecast out of curiosity but then quickly switched channels to watch coverage on Canada's indigenous network, the CBC. Montreal-based journalist Mario Brisebois reported that his children asked to watch CBC's coverage after viewing only a few minutes of Fox coverage. Similarly, Archie McDonald of the *Vancouver Sun* claimed "that noise that occurred across the land 10 minutes into the game was the sound of thousands of sets simultaneously being switched from Fox to CBC" ("FoxTrax Experiment," 1996, p. C3). By all accounts, the debut of FoxTrax was a test run for Fox and the NHL; there were many technological glitches that needed to be fixed. However, one oversight directly led to specific criticism of the puck. According to New Corporation's Cavallaro (1997), the puck was originally designed to be exactly like a regulation NHL puck: "This included the puck's size, weight, balance, rebound and coefficient of friction. What we did not realize initially is that pucks are stored on ice for several hours before being put into play" (p. 8). Because the transmitters inside the FoxTrax pucks could not be cooled, pucks were put into play unfrozen, which changed the manner in which the vulcanized rubber puck rebounded and slid along the ice. This led to player complaints of the puck bouncing too much or not having the right feel. Such an oversight only fuelled critics' claims that Fox executives did not understand the sport of hockey. This and other criticisms of the puck led Bettman to later backtrack and report that the puck remained "in terms of presentation, a work in progress. . . . We hope it will become a work of art that, down the road, will go beyond the Fox broadcasts" ("Commissioner Says," 1996, D4).

The bulk of criticism toward FoxTrax came from established fans of ice hockey, whether they were those who attended games, wrote about hockey, or were involved in the industry in other capacities. Both Fox and the NHL had anticipated this reaction. As mentioned above, it was hoped that established fans would realize that the FoxTrax puck and other innovative efforts were done to expand the fan base of professional hockey by making it easier for novice viewers to understand the nuances of the sport. The response of Fox and the NHL as criticism grew reflected this decision. For example, when told of *The Hockey News* reader poll, Vince Wladika, Fox vice-president of media relations, replied,

> Those are the people we don't need to attract. Those are the same people who, while they're your core audience, they've been the same core audience forever. . . . And unless you build upon it, hockey is going to stay at the same level it is. (Brender, 1996, p. 8)

However, in an effort to attract a new audience, many felt that Fox had gone too far in changing the way the games were televised. One reporter noted that "Fox deserves praise for being innovative with its approach to covering sports. But this time, it has crossed the line" (Longley, 1996d, p. 61). One year later, the same journalist had become much more concerned: "Fox TV already has shown it doesn't give a puck about what hockey diehards think about its coverage—and the network has no plans to start caring now" (Longley, 1997a, p. 11). This comment was likely in response to several remarks made by Fox's Hill regarding future changes to the game of hockey to increase its appeal, one of which was to change the format of games from three 20-minute periods to four quarters (Quindt, 1996a). A puck that was viewed differently when televised was one consideration; suggesting more drastic changes to the sport was another. A perceived lack of knowledge of hockey on the part of Fox executives also led to criticism:

> There is a lack of respect that Fox affords athletes and you could see it again in the broadcast Saturday [at the 1996 All-Star Game]. Hockey can be a violent game

> and it can be a skilled one. Fox treats violence, skill, athleticism and the game's other qualities the same. It trivializes them all. ("Fox's Vapor-Trail," 1996)

Soon journalists began lobbying against Fox and its coverage of NHL games. As Fox and the NHL moved toward the end of their contract, one even went so far as to suggest a boycott: "Don't watch Fox. That may have to be your motto for the next month-and- a-half or so if you want any chance of killing the way the network often televises the NHL" (Caesar, 1998, p. 2D).

"If Those Damn Yankees Can't Watch a Damn Hockey Game without Having an Electric Puck, Well, They Shouldn't Watch It at all." (Telephone Complaint to the Edmonton Journal)

Although response to FoxTrax was equally disapproving by established hockey fans throughout North America, the way in which criticism was articulated was vastly different in Canada as opposed to the United States. The discourse that emerged in Canadian newspapers surrounding the FoxTrax puck placed the innovation within a context of the importance of hockey in Canada, and this was being linked to criticism of the puck, Fox, and the NHL. Specifically, reaction to the puck in Canadian newspapers seemed to emphasize the importance of the sport to the country's identity and the outrage that people had at Fox's arrogance in implementing the new device at the expense of experienced (Canadian) viewers. In Canada, anti-FoxTrax sentiment was rooted in a discourse of ownership and interference and underlying fears of Americanization as perpetuated in newspaper coverage of the FoxTrax puck and as part of Canada's ongoing crisis of identity, where Fox's hockey coverage was yet another example of the economic and cultural influence of the United States. This follows Hedetoft (1999), who described "an increasing reflexive awareness of, and 'strategic' attitude toward, national identity as well as other personal identity structures as resources ... under circumstances dictated by major upheavals in the national and international order" (p. 76). Thus, the reflexive reaction to the FoxTrax puck can be seen as part of a broader Canadian concern over US influences.

At the same time, US-based journalists perpetuated this undercurrent of crisis, which Jackson (1994) had recognized earlier in his examination of Gretzky's trade, as journalists in both countries began to question why Fox was able to make changes that other leagues would surely not allow to occur. That golf balls or baseballs in flight were also difficult for novice viewers to follow, yet were not subject to technological innovation, was brought to light (Baker, 1996c). For this reason, disapproving fans began attributing the autonomy of Fox to make technological innovations to hockey to three factors: (a) Fox's lack of concern/knowledge about hockey's traditions, (b) the leadership of the NHL erroneously allowing outsiders (Fox) to tamper with a great sport, and (c) America's cultural and economic influence on Canada allowing innovations such as FoxTrax to be introduced. Thus, although US-based hockey fans reacted similarly to the efficacy of FoxTrax as a technological innovation, Canadian fans attributed the process to a different phenomenon, which is understood within the context of the globalizing process and Canada's broader discourse of identity.

The NHL had long been considered the weakest of the "Big Four" professional sports leagues in the United States, in terms of both interest and revenues. Thus, in the minds of many FoxTrax detractors in the United States, Fox was able to introduce the new technology because like many others, Fox did not respect hockey in the same manner as other sports. In contrast, Canadian reaction suggests the reassertion of local identities (attempts to reaffirm hockey as an integral part of Canadian identity) in response to the process of globalization (the transnational News Corporation moving into the North American market). Thus,

Canadian reaction manifested itself within a discourse of anti-American sentiment. In the years preceding the arrival of FoxTrax, the concerns described above led to suspicion of ownership or entitlement to the sport beginning to emerge. Calgary Flames radio play-by-play announcer Peter Maher articulated the feelings of many Canadian fans when he said, "People believe they're trying to take away the game from us. There's a real feeling they're trying to Americanize the game" (Helyar, 1994, p. A1). When the FoxTrax puck was introduced, Fox became the equivalent of *they*: The network was simply ruining Canadians' sport (Baker, 1996b; MacKinnon, 1996b).

In this manner, criticism in Canada targeted American viewers in general, rather than novice viewers (who comprised Fox's intended audience). For example, Jim Bray summarized responses to the phone poll conducted by the *Ottawa Citizen* by stating that "Americans who can't follow the puck on their televisions don't get sympathy here. Ottawa-area readers suggest they get glasses, contact lenses, or larger television sets" ("FoxTrax Experiment," 1996, p. C3). Similarly, another Canadian journalist opined, "What has Fox done? Brought high-tech kiddie graphics and a ridiculous glowing puck, and pandered to the parts of the American audience that don't know a hip check from a hippo" (Longley, 1997a, p. 11). Thus, while US critics made comments such as "if your eyesight is sharp enough to tell a colorized black-and-white episode of "Gilligan's Island" from one filmed in living color, surely you can follow a hockey puck on a 27-inch Magnavox" (Quindt, 1996b, p. D2), Canadian journalists announced that "Fox television may just as well have desecrated our flag" (Bray, 1996, p. B1). Similarly, another Canadian journalist decried, "No one, the NHL and Fox included, expected Canadians to buy into the silliness of an expensive high-tech hockey puck" ("They Said It," 1996, p. C1).

The various actions by Fox, such as not considering that hockey pucks are frozen prior to the start of games, were caught up in a much larger discourse in Canada, where many felt a sense of ownership/entitlement with hockey, as "Fox doesn't know hockey" became "Americans don't know Canada." Reaction to FoxTrax revealed underlying concerns Canadian fans (or arguably Canadians in general) had in regard to US influences, which were recognized by both Canadian and US hockey reporters. Seen in this light, concerns about the Americanization of hockey and interpretations of the FoxTrax project were rooted in the traditional relationship between Canada and the United States. As explained by Farrell (1984),

> Virtually all relevant polls and surveys have shown that Canadians are much better informed about the United States than are Americans about Canada. . . . It is nevertheless important that Canadians are sometimes unhappy when they find that most Americans know so little about their country. (p. 5)

Therefore, if, as described above, established Canadian hockey fans saw hockey as uniquely Canadian and proprietary, then it would only follow that suggestions or implementations made by those outside of their group would be viewed with suspicion. Thus, Fox and the NHL's efforts were not seen as "building the game" but rather as "tampering" and reflected the "(re)assertion of cultural differences and distinction in the face of globalizing tendencies" (Robins, 1997, p. 33). In the case of FoxTrax, the reassertion by Canadian fans represented their concerns over having their own sport manipulated, and their response was to compare their situation to that of Americans. For example, one caller to an *Ottawa Citizen* FoxTrax poll stated that "I find it surprising Americans would be so quick to change someone else's pastime when they won't even assist their own [baseball]" (Bray, 1996, p. B1).

In this manner, a simple technological innovation became a lightning rod for issues surrounding the greater relationship that exists between the two countries and the (re)articulation of local identity in the face of globalizing processes. This also explains why established Canadian fans and journalists alike united in their virtually unanimous disapproval of Fox and its American target audience. Doug Ferguson, a founder of one of the anti-FoxTrax websites, recognized that the puck was a symbol of the Americanization of hockey (Sandomir, 1997). In reacting to FoxTrax and its implementation, Canadians seemed to have little trouble expressing their anti-American sentiment. Even American hockey reporters noticed the disdain and scrutiny that Canadian journalists placed on their US counterparts. One US-based journalist complained that "it does become a bit tiresome and even vexing when my Canadian colleagues come to town looking for every little innocent misstep that proves US ignorance on the sport of hockey" (Kravitz, 1997, online).

As criticism of Fox in Canada increasingly continued to take on more anti-American sentiment, other aspects of their telecasts began to be scrutinized, as Canadian critics seemed to be looking for any possible opportunity to deride Fox. For example, during the 1997 All-Star Game, one journalist ridiculed Fox's coverage: "The start of the telecast was a mess with hosts James Brown [an American] and [Canadian-born] Dave Maloney talking over the Canadian anthem and the network almost missed the opening faceoff" (Longley, 1997b, p. 62). Reaction even reached the point of pettiness; the same journalist complained that the onscreen scoreboard ("Foxbox") was bigger and gaudier for hockey than that which Fox used for its (American) football telecasts (Longley, 1997b).

In this manner, what had started for Fox television as a technological innovation designed to make televised ice hockey games easier to follow for novice viewers had now become a means for Canadian fans to articulate their concerns over the state of the sport and to rearticulate hockey as a part of Canadian identity. The manner through which these people reacted also reflected underlying concerns of the fear of Americanization that had manifested under conditions Jackson (1994) described as a "crisis of Canadian identity," which saw resistance to the economic and cultural influences of America. Although the reaction in Canada was unique, it was indicative of the reassertion of local identities that occurs elsewhere in the face of the influence of the globalizing process. For example in England, Maguire et al. (1999) described how newspaper coverage of international sports events revealed

> deep-seated British/English concerns regarding national decline and European integration. This resulted in the dominant discursive themes being nostalgia and ethnic assertiveness/defensiveness (p. 451).

"I Think [the FoxTrax Puck] Is the Most Ridiculous Thing I've Ever Seen. Only Americans Could Think of That." (Telephone Complaint to the Edmonton Journal)

Experienced hockey fans everywhere did not appear to like the innovation; however, Canadians articulated their displeasure within a context of a crisis of identity. In other words, response to the puck was bound up in a larger discourse of crisis related to the cultural and economic influences of the United States. In doing so, Fox, part of a global media company, became equated with Americanization. Fox television, as a subsidiary of Murdoch's News Corporation, was really an example of a transnational corporation trying to use sports programming as a means to increase its media empire, rather than a distinctly American threat. Although Murdoch is now an American citizen, he is from Australia, and despite originating from that country, News Corporation has been described as the "first truly global media business" ("The Rights Stuff," 1995, p. 10). The person who came up with the FoxTrax concept, Hill, is also Australian, yet cries of the "Australianization" of ice hockey were notably absent in this context. With this in mind, reaction to FoxTrax seemed to easily slip into anti-American sentiment and, as the numerous examples provided here suggest, provided what Hedetoft (1999) described as a "scapegoat" for concerned citizens in Canada.

The seemingly nonchalant manner through which Fox approached its innovation and broad casting also fed into this discourse of crisis; possible feelings of inferiority and concerns over Fox's lack of knowledge of the sport may have been reinforced when Fox's Hill responded to Canadian criticism of FoxTrax on Canada's *The Sports Network* (a Canadian cable sports channel) by saying, "If some folks can't see through the glitz for the substance of what we are doing, then that's their problem, not ours" (Longley, 1996c, p. 52). The message here was that Fox did not seem to care what Canadians felt about its technological contribution to the sport.

This lack of concern for Canada's hockey heritage resulted in additional targets for enraged fans. As anti-FoxTrax sentiment increased, another target of criticism emerged. In 1998, Molson breweries created a television commercial that ridiculed the FoxTrax experiment, the alleged foreign cronies who created it, and the hockey executives that endorsed it (Hackel, 1998). The commercial featured an executive proposing a ridiculous idea to overseers of the sport, then being forcibly thrown out of the office, leaving a dramatic red comet trail behind him. Thus, another target of animosity had been revealed, the NHL, in particular its commissioner, Bettman, an American who became NHL commissioner with a strong background in professional sports league operations but with a self-professed lack of knowledge of the intricacies of the sport of hockey. During the final playoff season of the Winnipeg Jets, who were to relocate to Phoenix for the 1996–1997 season, fans booed the "Star Spangled Banner" and displayed protest signs against Bettman with the message "You can take our team but you can't touch our spirit" (Helyar, 1996, p. B10). To many, Bettman and NHL executives had "sold out" to Fox; they had agreed to allow any change to be made to bring back network television coverage, and eventually the revenues associated with it, to the NHL. One commentator noted that

> it's easy to imagine [Fox head] Rupert Murdoch's web trying to coax officials to put a chip inside a golf ball or baseball—to make them glow on-screen and drive up ratings among the young, but can you imagine the PGA saying yes? I can't. (Baker, 1996c, p. 064)

Lending credence to the "selling out" viewpoint was Fox's Hill himself. When asked if he would try to make drastic changes to other sports, such as baseball, as had been done in hockey, Hill replied, "No, don't think so" (Raissman, 1996, p. 94).

According to another report, Fox was interested in adapting the FoxTrax system to baseball; however, Fox insiders privately revealed that they knew that there was no way that baseball owners would allow such a change to their sport (MacKinnon, 1996a). That Hill would not even consider changes in baseball, which had been made in hockey, provided ammunition for Canadian hockey fans who saw Hill, Fox, and NHL executives as having no concern for the traditions of the NHL and its Canadian heritage. In other words, although some sports such as baseball remained untampered, Murdoch was not above changing sport to improve the status of his business interests, where he deemed it possible to achieve. As mentioned earlier, the sport of rugby in Australia was significantly affected by Murdoch's power struggle over control of the sport; thus, that this could be done in some contexts (as opposed to others) would likely exacerbate the fears and insecurities occurring in affected communities. In many respects, for transnational corporations such as News Corporation, any effects on the NHL and fans of hockey were simply an unfortunate consequence of their strategic operations.

Thus, although Fox and the FoxTrax puck continued to be vilified by the newsprint media and editorials in print and on the Internet throughout North America, NHL leaders increasingly came under scrutiny, as they were the ones who allowed Fox to change the sport. Blame then transferred from the puck and Fox, who some critics did not begrudge efforts that Fox saw as being improvements to their televised product, to those in the NHL who gave them the control to do so. One journalist noted that "if only we could blame the network for a well-intended gimmick concocted to nourish its bottom-line ratings. On the contrary, fault lies with the NHL for allowing its product to be demeaned" (Verdi, 1996, p. D10). Commissioner Bettman, in particular, became a focal point of criticism. Bettman, an understudy of the NBA's David Stern, had been hired to replicate the success the NBA had enjoyed during the late 1980s and early 1990s. However, not everyone felt that the success of the NHL should be considered in terms of mimicking the NBA. One vitriolic US-based commentator lambasted Bettman for his efforts: "Nevertheless, there is Bettman, trying to build the bridge of relevance, trying to be Stern, trying to force-feed the Americanization of hockey" (Bickley, 1998, p. W5).

According to Whitson (1998), America is usually blamed for changes to local sports. "Yet, what they are really objecting to is the commodification and marketing that are building renewed (and new) audiences for these games, nationally and globally" (p. 71). In the case of FoxTrax, fans were responding to News Corporation's efforts to build new audiences in North America and the corporation's lack of concern over the relationship between a sport and local identity; the reaction of hockey fans was to stop watching games on Fox. In Canada, this meant watching hockey coverage on other networks such as the CBC. In the United States, it was to watch less hockey altogether. Canadian networks were aware of reaction to Fox and the NHL and sought to distance themselves from the FoxTrax puck. After being awarded NHL telecast rights, Canada's CTV Sportsnet, despite being partially owned by Fox, made sure that viewers knew of their intentions to avoid FoxTrax or any other similar telecasting technique. According to senior vice president of CTV Sportsnet Suzanne Steeves, "To the chagrin of Canadian purists, Fox uses a glowing blue puck to help US viewers follow the game. Sportsnet won't employ any cheap gimmicks like that" (Waal, 1998, p. 47). Obviously, Steeves used the term *cheap* to connote Fox's presentation, given the FoxTrax project's $3 million price tag.

The Audience Speaks

Although Canadians switched to other hockey coverage in Canada, US viewers had fewer options and watched less hockey. Television ratings would suggest that this was the case. Following its initial ratings surge at the NHL All-Star Game in 1996, overall NHL ratings on Fox tumbled from 1.9 in 1997 to 1.4 in 1998 (Caesar, 1998). The FoxTrax puck underwent some significant refinements, as the halo was reduced in size and changed from an obtrusive blue hue to white. The red vapour trail was also reduced in size (Baker, 1996b), and the stability of the image on television was improved (Finder, 1997).

In 1998, both network and cable television contracts for the NHL came up for renewal/negotiation. ESPN had held the previous rights to cable television and were concluding a 7-year, $100 million contract. Fox was heading into the final year of a 5-year, $155 million agreement. When negotiations began for the 1999–2000 season with Fox and ABC-ESPN approached, many felt that the NHL would be hard-pressed to get a similar contract. One observer noted that "it looks doubtful the league will get more money from either network. That is, if the networks agree to another contract at all" (Dater, 1998, p. C01). In 1998, regular season ratings on ESPN had dropped 17 per cent from the previous year, and the coveted age 18-to-34 male demographic saw a 40 per cent decline during the length of Fox's contract (Cauley & Fatsis, 1998). ESPN's ratings for the 1998 playoffs were even more woeful, down 29 per cent (from 1.7 to 1.2) (Manly, 1998b). Fox had lost more than $10 million each year for its $31 million annual contract, yet the ABC portion of the new contract was thought to be in the neighbourhood of $50 million annually ("Disney's ABC," 1998). Surprisingly, when ABC-ESPN first made their offer, Fox still debated whether to match the offer, despite that a reported 95 per cent of Fox's affiliate stations voted not to have hockey return (Manly, 1998a). One Fox executive recounted the dilemma faced by the network: "Some guys say we can't go without it, and others say it's ridiculous to pay that kind of money for a sport that's not doing anything in the ratings" (Schlosser, 1998, p. 16). When Fox chose not to renew, questions were raised regarding honouring the final year of its contract. To one journalist, this was welcome news: "We say the quicker FoxTrax goes off the air, the better" (Felger, 1998, p. B06).

Despite a contract already negotiated between the NHL and ABC-ESPN for the following year, Fox still had one year left on its contract for the 1998–1999 season. NHL officials, responding to alleged (and perhaps warranted) apathy by Fox in its coverage and in an effort to distance itself in anticipation of a new network, complained frequently about Fox's telecasts. Bettman, when asked about coverage, stated, "It's a lame-duck year and I view us in a holding pattern" (Baker, 1999a, p. B05). Boston Bruins owner Jeremy Jacobs reported that "the [NHL] product could've been better presented" (Baker, 1999a, p. B05). FoxTrax was discontinued for the regular season following the 1998 All-Star Game and was not employed at all for Fox's final season of coverage in 1999. In light of the findings of this article, this was not viewed as detrimental to coverage by many. Baker (1999b) explained that "we could all be grateful that Fox, on a last-season economy kick, put away its FoxTrax toy" (p. 106).

Commissioner Bettman, perhaps realizing that FoxTrax had not achieved the prominence he and Fox had hoped, distanced himself from the project. In an interview in 1998, Bettman, who once had high hopes for FoxTrax, commented that "I don't need it, it doesn't bother me. I don't like the blue dot—but if it makes it easier for [television] fans, that's fine" ("Bettman Lukewarm," 1998, p. 3). With this statement and Fox's decision to discontinue using FoxTrax in 1998, the project seemed to have reached an end.

Conclusions

On the surface, FoxTrax would appear simply to be an example of a failed technological innovation implemented by a television network trying to increase the breadth of viewership for a specific sport. However, the underlying issues that emerge from this study are the degree to which large transnational corporations such as News Corporation have affected local identities, the manner through which local communities seek to reassert their own sense of community, and how symbolic objects are revealed as vehicles to articulate broader discourses of crisis. In other situations, reactions have been different, such as the British government's efforts to block Murdoch's purchase of Manchester United, but still reflect the resistance of local communities to the effects of globalization. The response by established fans, particularly those in Canada, attached a significance to the FoxTrax puck that extended beyond its original purpose. As this article has shown, reaction reflected a growing suspicion held toward the NHL and its leaders and, for fans in Canada, a concern over the loss of what was articulated to be "Canada's game." Hockey fans in both Canada and the United States were not sad to see the demise of the FoxTrax puck: The negative response to the puck had been overwhelming.

Both Fox and the NHL did not seem to consider FoxTrax beyond what it was developed for, a device to facilitate the viewing of NHL games on television for potential fans. However, the resistance of hockey fans in Canada suggests that when understood within the context of globalization and the articulation of local identity, technologies such as the FoxTrax puck can become significant symbols of contestation within negotiations of the global and the local. In this instance, the discourse in popular media coverage in Canada framed the issue as part of the Americanization of Canada. However, Americanization tends to be viewed as a one-way process where American cultural forms, products, and meaning are imposed on others (Donnelly,

1996). As this article has shown, the reaction of Canadian fans to the FoxTrax innovation reflects a much more complex phenomenon that fits into discussions of global-local relations. In the current climate of professional team sport, similar changes are sure to be implemented by transnational corporations who see sport as simply one more tool to strengthen their entertainment empires. As Jhally (1989) has suggested, "The search now [for global media corporations] is for new mass audiences for advertisers, rather than the appeal to the 'cultivated' minority who really understand what sports are about" (p. 81). As this example has shown, the expansion of global media interests is sometimes done without due consideration for the cultural significance of specific sports in local communities and with an underestimation of the degree to which resistance will occur.

Notes

1. *Get the Puck Outta Here!* is the name of a website created and maintained by Joe Giammalvo in May of 1997, where concerned fans could "unite in our hatred for the FoxTrax puck" by becoming a member and commenting in an online forum.
2. Data were obtained from major North American newspapers and the Internet. Newspaper articles from throughout North America were sought using the electronic databases ABI/Inform (ProQuest Direct), EBSCO-host, and Lexis-Nexis Academic Universe. Issues of *The Hockey News* were searched between 1996 and 1998 for articles featuring Fox and FoxTrax, along with any editorial correspondence published in the newspapers' letters sections. Using these resources, approximately 600 articles were obtained for analysis.
3. A rating point represents 1 per cent of television households in the United States, or 945,000 homes.

References

Andrews, D.L. (2001). Sport. In R. Maxwell (Ed.), *Culture works: The political economy of culture* (pp. 131–62). Minneapolis: University of Minnesota Press.

Baker, J. (1996a, January 21). Fox dot delivers in all-star fashion. *Boston Herald*, p. B05.

———. (1996b, April 21). Play by play: A dinner view of Fox's laser-lit puck. *Boston Herald*, p. 011.

———. (1996c, January 23). Viewers on the fast trax. *Boston Herald*, p. 064.

———. (1999a, April 4). No goodbye hugs for Fox, NHL. *Boston Herald*, p. B05.

———. (1999b, January 25). There's no defending NHL event. *Boston Herald*, p. 106.

Belsie, L. (1996, April 16). Electronics put a new spin on "inside sports". *Christian Science Monitor*, p. 15.

Bernstein, A. (1998). Thrashers aren't typical expansion team. *Sports Business Journal*, *1*(2), 8.

Bettman lukewarm on FoxTrax. (1998, June 11). *Tampa Tribune*, Sports p. 3.

Bickley, D. (1998, February 1). Bettman's folly bad for hockey. *Arizona Republic*, p.W5.

Brace, M. (2000, November 5). Rugby League World Cup: Last cry of the Rabbitohs. *The Observer*, p. 12.

Bray, J. (1996, January 22).Touchline survey: Chuck that puck! *Ottawa Citizen*, p. B1.

Brender, M. (1996). FoxTrax loses 10-1. *The Hockey News*, *49*(25), 8.

Caesar, D. (1996, January 26). Blue hue did little for fans watching All-Star Game. *St. Louis Post-Dispatch*, p. 8D.

———. (1998, April 24). To derail FoxTrax, fans might have to boycott. *St. Louis Post-Dispatch*, p. 2D.

Cauley, L., & Fatsis, S. (1998, August 5). Disney aims a $400 million body check at News Corp. in seeking NHL rights. *Wall Street Journal*, p. B2.

Cavallaro, R. (1997). The FoxTrax hockey puck tracking system. *IEEE Computer Graphics and Applications*, *17*(2). Retrieved from http://www.computer.muni.cz/pubs/cg&a/1997/g2006.htm

Chad, N. (1996, January 24). Fox's glowing puck: Turn out the lights . . . *Washington Post*, p. C03.

Commissioner says NHL's future is cool. (1996, March 17). *Pittsburgh Post-Gazette*, p. D4.

Craig, J. (1996a, January 23). Fox may have more tricks up its sleeve. *Boston Globe*, p. 51.

———. (1996b, January 21). FoxTrax has them smiling after debut. *Boston Globe*, p. 54.

Dater, A. (1998, June 8). On thin ice: Low television ratings could jeopardize the NHL's network contracts and cause ticket prices to go up even higher. *Denver Post*, p. C01.

De Cillia, R., Reisigl, M., & Wodak, R. (1999). The discursive construction of national identities. *Discourse & Society, 10*, 149–73.

DeMarco, T. (1998, June 15). Too big for baseball? With billionaire Rupert Murdoch in charge, the Dodgers will never be the same. Thanks to his control of the sport's television empire, neither will baseball. *Denver Post*, p. D01.

Denning, M. (2001). Globalization in cultural studies: Process and epoch. *European Journal of Cultural Studies, 4*, 351–64.

Disney's ABC, ESPN get 5-year contract to broadcast NHL. (1998, August 5). *Wall Street Journal*, p. B7.

Donnelly, P. (1996). The local and the global: Globalization in the sociology of sport. *Journal of Sport and Social Issues, 20*, 239–57.

Dryden, S. (1996). NHL, Fox excited about glow puck. *The Hockey News, 49*(20), 5.

Earle, N. (1995). Hockey as Canadian popular culture: Team Canada 1972, television and the Canadian identity. *Journal of Canadian Studies, 30*(2), 107–23.

Euchner, C.C. (1993). *Playing the field: Why sports teams move and cities fight to keep them.* Baltimore: Johns Hopkins University Press.

Farrell, R.B. (1984). *Canada in transition.* Chicago: Chicago Council on Foreign Relations.

Felger, M. (1998, August 23). Stingy Bruins due to deal. *Boston Herald*, p. B06.

Finder, C. (1997, January 16). Hold on! Here come the gizmos. *Pittsburgh Post-Gazette*, p. E6.

Fox's vapor-trail puck drives viewers to distraction. (1996, January 23). *Toronto Globe and Mail.* Retrieved 14 December 1998 from www4.nando.net/newsroom/sports/hkn/1996/nhl/nhl/feat/archive/012396/nhl19874.html. Also available at http://archive.sportserver.com/newsroom/sports/hkn/1996/nhl/nhl/feat/archive/012396/nhl19874.html/index.html

FoxTrax experiment has hockey writers wanting to put the thing on ice. (1996, January 23). *Ottawa Citizen*, p. C3.

Gepner, J. (1998).Too tech or not too tech: New technologies for sports coverage need to bring value to broadcast. *Television Broadcast Online Weekly-stories-98/27.* Retrieved 9 April 1999 from www.tvbroadcast.com/nab/stories-98/27.htm

Gerlin, A. (1993, October 4). Sports: An icy sport heads south to make (it hopes) its fortune. *Wall Street Journal*, p. B1.

Goldman, K. (1994, September 26). Hockey heats up as networks, sponsors seek to fill baseball void. *Wall Street Journal*, p. B10.

Good, C. (1926). Will US cash cripple our hockey? *Maclean's*, pp. 13, 55–56.

Gruneau, R. (1989). Making spectacle: A case study in television sports production. In L.A. Wenner (Ed.), *Media, sports, & society* (pp. 134–54). London: Sage.

Gruneau, R., & Whitson, D. (1993). *Hockey Night in Canada: Sport, identities and cultural politics.* Toronto: Garamond.

Guillen, M.F. (2001). Is globalization civilizing, destructive or feeble? A critique of five key debates in the social science literature. *Annual Reviews in Sociology, 27*, 235–60.

Hackel, S. (1996a). FoxTrax attraction: TV industry applauds puck experiment, but established fans weigh against it. *The Hockey News, 49*(21), 10.

———. (1996b).Will Fox trot out its glowing puck for viewers? *The Hockey News, 49*(18), S-10.

———. (1998, June 14). Backtalk: Cool fads causing meltdown in NHL. *New York Times*, p. 8-11.

Hanley, B. (1996, January 21). NHL's high-tech puck leaves this impression: Dot's all, folks. *Chicago Sun-Times*, p. 18.

Hedetoft, U. (1999). The nation-state meets the world: National identities in the context of transnationality and cultural globalization. *European Journal of Social Theory, 2*, 71–94.

Helyar, J. (1994, November 15). Empty nets: Canadian clubs appear to skate on thin ice amid hockey lockout—Calgary, small-market teams get slammed as pay rises and Sunbelt lures stars—The silence of the fans. *Wall Street Journal*, p. A1.

———. (1995, January 12). Sports: Hockey lives, but how many fans still care? *Wall Street Journal*, p. B1.

———. (1996, April 26). Canada's NHL Jets leave fans in the cold. *Wall Street Journal*, p. B10.

Hiestand, M. (1996, January 22). Fox's new puck generates talk. *USA Today*, p. 2C.

Hogan, J. (1999). The construction of gendered national identities in the television advertisements of Japan and Australia. *Media, Culture & Society, 21*, 743–58.

Hooper, E. (1996, January 19). Fox isn't yet glowing about its puck tracker. *St. Petersburg Times*, p. 2C.

Jackson, S.J. (1994). Gretzky, crisis, and Canadian identity in 1988: Rearticulating the Americanization of culture debate. *Sociology of Sport Journal, 11*, 428–46.

———. (2001). Gretzky nation: Canada, crisis and Americanization. In D.L. Andrews & S.J. Jackson (Eds), *Sport stars: The cultural politics of sporting celebrity* (pp. 164–86). London: Routledge.

Jackson, S.J., & Andrews, D.L. (1999). Between and beyond the global and the local. *International Review for the Sociology of Sport 34*, 31–42.

Jhally, S. (1989). Cultural studies and the media/sport complex. In L.A. Wenner (Ed.),

Media, sports & society (pp. 70–93). London: Sage.

Kent, M. (1996, January 25). Give Fox credit for blazing trail with flashy puck. *Baltimore Sun*, p. 2D.

Kidd, B. (1996). *The struggle for Canadian sport.* Toronto, Canada: University of Toronto Press.

Kidd, B., & Macfarlane, J. (1972). *The death of hockey.* Toronto, Canada: New Press.

Kravitz, B. (1996, June 5). Ten new Fox TV hockey innovations we'd like to see. *Denver Rocky Mountain News*, p. 9N.

———. (1997, May 7). Oh, Canada, we're so sorry—for everything. *ESPN SportsZone*. Retrieved from http://www.rpi.edu/~soucep/canadahockey.html

Langton, J. (1996, February 4). Million-dollar puck is easier on the eye: Infra-red wizardry helps TV capture the dazzling speed of ice hockey. *Sunday Telegraph*, p.19.

Lapointe, J. (1996a, January 21). From Howe to hacker: Hockey finally crosses the high-tech blue line. *New York Times*, p. 8-8.

———. (1996b, September 16). Maple Leaf wilts under Stars and Stripes. *New York Times*, p. C8.

Lessels, A. (1996, January 21). Some fans feeling blue over red streak. *Boston Globe*, p. 54.

Letter to the sports editor. (1996, January 28). *Washington Post*, p. D03.

Longley, R. (1996a, January 26). Fox drops puck—For now. *Toronto Sun*, p. 95.

———. (1996b, January 19). NHL set to enter cyber age. *Toronto Sun*, p. 91.

———. (1996c, January 20). Oh say, can't they see? *Toronto Sun*, p. 52.

———. (1996d, January 22). This time, Fox has gone too far. *Toronto Sun*, p. 61.

———. (1997a, January 17). Fox does what it wants. *Toronto Sun*, p. 11.

———. (1997b, January 20). Reviews of revamped FoxTrax hardly glowing.

Toronto Sun, p. 62.

MacGregor, R. (1997, January 19). Electric Kool-Aid expansion fever. *Montreal Gazette*, p. B3.

MacKinnon, J. (1996a, February 4). CBC sports coverage put under the spotlight. *Ottawa Citizen*, p. B3.

———. (1996b, January 21). Hey, it's hockey, not follow-the-puck. *Ottawa Citizen*, p. B1.

MacNeill, M. (1996). Networks: Producing Olympic ice hockey for a national television audience. *Sociology of Sport Journal*, *13*, 103–24.

Maguire, J., Poulton, E.,& Possamai, C. (1999). Weltkrieg III? Media coverage of England versus Germany in Euro 96. *Journal of Sport and Social Issues*, *23*(4), 439–54.

Maney, K. (1996, January 19). Puck gets high-tech profile. *USA Today*, p. 1A.

Manly, H. (1998a, August 23). Dollars make no sense: Ratings don't justify $600 million for NHL. *Boston Globe*, p. D3.

———. (1998b, June 19). Ice cold ratings. *Boston Globe*, p. E13.

Martzke, R. (1997, January 17). NBC, Fox retool inventions. *USA Today*, p. 2C.

Mason, D.S. (1998). The International Hockey League and the professionalization of ice hockey, 1904–1907. *Journal of Sport History*, *25*(1), 1–17.

Mason, D., & Schrodt, B. (1996). Hockey's first professional team: The Portage Lakes Hockey Club of Houghton, Michigan. *Sport History Review*, *27*(1), 49–71.

McKee, S. (1996, January 22). High-tech puck, hometown hero dot game as one to remember: Fox brass, Bruins' Bourque both excited by outcome. *Baltimore Sun*, p. 5C.

Miller, T., Lawrence, G., McKay, J., & Rowe, D. (2001). *Globalization and sport*. London: Sage.

Mullen, L. (1998). Has the Fox trapped the mouse in LA? *Sport Business Journal*, *1*(1), 7.

Nauright, J., & White, P. (1996). Nostalgia, community, and nation: Professional hockey and football in Canada. *Avante*, *2*(3), 24–41.

No! No! No! Here's what you have to say about FoxTrax: *THN* poll. (1996). *The Hockey News*, *49*(25), 9.

O'Hara, M. (1996, March 28). Fox puck to show up at Wings game. *Detroit News*.

Opening night: 1996–97 NHL season (1996). *The Hockey News*, *50*(9), 10.

Phipers, T. (1996, May 27). Fox tries to revive game with a youthful approach. *Denver Post*, p. D08.

Preston, P., & Kerr, A. (2001). Digital media, nation-states and local cultures: The case of multimedia "content" production. *Media, Culture & Society*, *23*, 109–31.

Quindt, F. (1996a, January 19). Can't keep your eye on the puck? Fox has made it easier to follow. *San Diego Union-Tribune*, p. D2.

———. (1996b, January 22). Fox's puck hockey-impaired. *San Diego Union-Tribune*, p. D2.

Raissman, B. (1996, January 19). Fox scores with high-tech puck. *New York Daily News*, p. 94.

The rights stuff, News Corp's global challenge. (1995). *Managing Intellectual Property*, *53*, 10.

Robins, K. (1997). What in the world's going on? In P. du Gay (Ed.), *Production of culture/Cultures of production* (pp. 12–47). London: Sage.

Sandomir, R. (1997, December 2). Sports column: An Olympic treat awaits for insomniacs. *New York Times*, p. B10.

———. (1998, June 12). Hockey shots being taken from different approaches. *New York Times*, p. C8.

Sassen, S. (2000). Territory and territoriality in the global economy. *International Sociology*, *15*, 372–93.

Saunders, D. (1996, June 3). Puck may not have TV glow. *Denver Rocky Mountain News*, p. 2C.

Schlosser, J. (1998). Fox divided over chasing puck. *Broadcasting & Cable*, *128*(33), 16.

Silk, M. (1999). Local/global flows and altered production practices: Narrative constructions at the 1995 Canada Cup of Soccer. *International Review for the Sociology of Sport*, *34*, 113–23.

Silk, M., & Andrews, D.L. (2001). Beyond a boundary? Sport, transnational advertising, and the reimagining of national culture. *Journal of Sport and Social Issues*, *25*, 180–201.

Sinclair, J., & Cunningham, S. (2000).Go with the flow: Diasporas and the media. *Television & New Media*, *1*, 11–31.

Slusser, S. (1997, January 18). Fox hopes to track puck better: Smoother moves by glowing blue dot. *San Francisco Chronicle.*

Strachan, A. (1997, June 2). Players griping about Fox puck. *Toronto Sun.* Retrieved 14 December 1998 from www.dougf.com/glowpuck/nytimes.htm

Swift, E.M. (1994). While the NBA's image has cooled, the NHL has ignited surprising new interest in hockey. *Sports Illustrated, 80*(24), 30–40.

They said it. (1996, January 23). *Montreal Gazette*, p. C1.

Tracy, J.F. (1999). Whistle while you work: The Disney company and the global division of labor. *Journal of Communication Inquiry, 23*, 374–89.

Verdi, B. (1996, February 11). NHL doesn't need computerized gimmicks to sell hockey. *Pittsburgh Post-Gazette*, p. D10.

Waal, P. (1998). The puck never stops. *Canadian Business, 71*(4), 47–48.

Warmington, J. (1996, January 21). Get the puck outta here. *Toronto Sun*, p. 7.

Weiler, J. M. (1992). Legal analysis of the NHL players' contract. *Marquette Sports Law Journal, 3*, 59–83.

Whitson, D. (1998). Circuits of promotion: Media, marketing and the globalization of sport. In L.A. Wenner (Ed.), *Mediasport* (pp. 57–72). London: Routledge.

Some Notes on Televised Team Sports in North America*

Joseph Kispal-Kovacs

Capitalism, Mass Media, and Commercial Team Sports in the United States and Canada: A Brief History

Throughout the late nineteenth and early twentieth centuries, American city-centres rapidly industrialized. The capitalist factory system expanded, producing more and more commodities for sale on the market. Millions of people moved to urbanizing cities, selling their labour for a wage. Factory work was routinized, dehumanizing, and alienating. The growth of leisure-time consumerism, however, offered workers pleasures and gratifications not available in the sphere of production. The entrepreneurs of a growing culture and mass-media industry produced and sold experiences, information, and entertainment to the working class as leisure commodities. New forms of commodified, spectator-based entertainment emerged in the late nineteenth century to mobilize the working class as a new consuming class. Next to prize fighting and horse racing, spectator sports including baseball and football were among the earliest and most profitable products of this new entertainment "industry" that captured the attention of large sections of US society (McChesney 2008: 219). Late nineteenth-century college football games, for example, were attended by audiences of as many as 30,000 to 40,000 spectators, who were each charged an admission fee for the privilege of watching (Smith 2001: 11).

The commercialization and professionalization of sports as a consumable leisure activity for paying spectators has long served the economic goals of the American colleges. According to Ronald A. Smith (2001), the process whereby US colleges turned sporting games into mass leisure events for consumption began in the 1850s. At that time, competitive rowing was the most popular college sport event and attracted huge spectator audiences: "When a newly built railroad sponsored the first Harvard–Yale crew meet in 1852, giving athletes from the two premier institutions in America an eight-day paid holiday in the vacation lands of New Hampshire, and when, fourteen years, later, Yale hired a professional coach and achieved its first win over Harvard's crew, it was clear that a commercial and professional spirit had invaded college sport"(5). From this point forward, US college sports were divorced from the educational mission for which they were founded and primarily used as a source of additional revenue and public promotion. For more than 150 years, college sports have been one of the most popular forms of entertainment in the United States and a significant source of revenue for universities in the form of tickets sales, merchandising income, and later lucrative radio and television contracts.

Team sports also played an important role in developing and instilling in players and audiences alike the appropriate cultural values necessary to work in an industrial capitalist society. College athletes were also almost exclusively the children of the wealthiest people in US society during this period. At graduation they were expected to assume their place as leaders in the system. The sport values of hard work, repetitive practice, and teamwork, and the division of labour and a clear hierarchy of roles in sports all mirrored the reality of factory and other forms of industrial work. So in a sense, the commercialization of collegiate sports in the United States and later in Canada not only was shaped by the imperatives of capitalism, but was also integral to instilling capitalist values in the players and the audiences that watched them. As in England, the requirements of US and Canadian capitalism required a new way of regulating the populations' play and work (including new forms of discipline):

> The history of the emergence of sport is in the first instance a history of the regulation of popular leisure by the British aristocracy and bourgeoisie. As the first industrial and capitalist power, Britain confronted the unprecedented task of controlling a new urban proletariat which had inherited the kind of time-work discipline associated with the agricultural diurnal rhythms of peasant life. (Rowe 1996: 567)

Throughout the twentieth century, capitalist and technological developments in the mass media regularly turned team sports—baseball, hockey, football, and basketball—into profitable forms of media spectacle. In the early twentieth century, newspapers became a big business. Reduction in newsprint cost and faster printing presses lowered the cost of newspapers. The news became an industry and commodity. The owners of news corporations profited by selling advertising space to industrial corporations. They also profited by selling information about the world to a literate urban population. The mass popularity of professional baseball and college football was initially built up by the newspaper industry. Sports pages became a regular feature in this period, in which inexpensive papers dominated the media landscape (McChesney 2008: 214–19). Eventually this supporting role was taken up by the fledgling new electronic medium: radio.

The radio broadcasting of team sports in the United States began on 5 August 1921, when Pittsburgh commercial radio station KDKA started covering the games of the Pittsburgh Pirates. Other commercial broadcasters in towns where there were Major League Baseball teams quickly followed suit (Catsis 1996: 2–3). The broadcasting of college football games began in 1922 (3). Initially, radio coverage of sporting events was carried out by reporters who phoned in the play-by-play action to their employers from the stands. In some other cases, the telegraph was used to transmit information about games that were taking place far away (3–9).

In Canada, it was ice hockey that became the most popular spectator sport in the late nineteenth century. Advocates of amateur hockey were typically wealthy Canadians who were attracted to the appeal of the tradition of British aristocratic amateurism. Workers, on the other hand, embraced the idea of watching highly skilled professionals engage in a high level of play (Grunneau and Whitson 1993: 65). After this long class-based struggle between supporters of amateur hockey and the advocates of commercialized, professional hockey, a truce was declared with the two forms able to continue to develop side by side (Grunneau and Whitson 1993; Wong 2005). The rising popularity of professional hockey among working class spectators and businessmen team owners led to the eventual creation of the NHL in 1917.

Until the rise of radio broadcasting, professional hockey in North America developed in an uneven way. Most of the teams were located in eastern Canada and the northeast United States. Radio broadcasting of hockey games began in Toronto in 1933 when three local stations began broadcasting Leafs games under the sponsorship of General Motors (Cole 2003: 6). In late 1936, the CBC was founded as the first national broadcasting network in Canada. In 1937, the CBC became the national carrier of the program *Hockey Night in Canada (HNIC)* (6).

The first sports television broadcast in North America was on NBC's experimental station in New York City on 17 May 1939. It was of a college baseball game between Princeton and Columbia (Catsis 1996: 27). However, this was just an early baby step. Limitations imposed by technology prevented full-field coverage of team sporting events. As a result, television broadcasts of team sports were slow to become common and popular (29–30). Later, the use of multiple cameras, the invention of videotape, and the development of satellite transmission greatly improved the arsenal that broadcasters had available to them (32–36).

College basketball and professional basketball were latecomers to this intersection of commerce and media. Basketball was the last of the major team sports to be developed. It was only invented in 1891 and took time to become popular. College basketball began around the turn of the century but was insignificant compared to football as a spectator sport. The first professional league was started in 1937, and the current National Basketball Association (NBA) was established in 1946 when the Basketball Association of America (BAA) was formed. It was renamed the NBA in 1949 (Markovits and Rensmann 2010: 86).

The NBA first appeared on television in 1953 on the now defunct DuMont network. The league was paid $39,000 for the airing of 13 games. Over the years, the NBA television contract with various networks grew slowly but steadily until the late 1980s and early 1990s, when the popularity of the game surged, as did the value of the contracts (Inside Hoops).

Professional football in the United States was effectively created by television. Prior to 1960, pro football was a much less popular sport than either professional baseball or college football. A succession of television contracts between the two football leagues, the NFL and the AFL, greatly increased the revenue stream for team owners; it also increased exposure to the game across the country, especially in places that did not have their own team. The AFL, founded in 1960, had a television contract in place before the first game was played. Later, when the two leagues completed a merger in 1970, the stage had been set for a very lucrative relationship between the new NFL and various TV networks (McChesney 2008: 226–8). The other sports followed suit in the last few decades.

Major League Baseball (MLB) has never been able to achieve the success that the NFL has had on television. Despite the fact that it was the most popular professional sport in the United States for much of the twentieth century (certainly until the 1960s), the league was never very comfortable with TV. Team owners were often worried that people would not show up to games if they could watch them at home. This is particularly a concern for baseball, which has the longest season of any of the major sports (approximately 10 times as many games as football). Nevertheless, baseball has been on television from the very beginning of TV, and although the typical game does not attract the audience numbers of the NFL or NBA, the playoffs and World Series usually generate respectable ratings.

The CBC and its French counterpart, Société Radio-Canada (RDS), began television broadcasting in 1952. For televising of hockey games, a three-camera setup gave television viewers the "best seat in the house" (Cole 2003: 31). *HNIC* quickly became the most-watched television show in Canada and would remain so for many years to come. In the first two decades of television in Canada, Saturday night hockey games were, by far, the most-watched Canadian-made television programs (Rutherford 1990: 228). *HNIC* continues to remain on the CBC and will until at least 2014. Other NHL games are shown on TSN, RSN, and the French-language RDS.

However, the NHL remains the weakest of the big four team sport leagues in the United States. While still extremely popular in Canada, the game is hardly watched south of the border. In the early twenty-first century, the major television networks, broadcast and cable, declined to renew their contracts with the NHL, and the league was subsequently relegated to the Outdoor Life Network (OLN) with a reduced number of games aired nationally (Bellamy and Shultz 2006: 164). OLN has subsequently been renamed Versus.

In addition to TV changing the economics of the team sports industries in significant ways, it has also changed the ways in which the games themselves are played. Television timeouts have changed the flow of games for football, hockey, and basketball. A two-minute warning at the end of each half was introduced in the NFL to allow more commercials to be aired. Television timeouts have slowed the pace of hockey and basketball games, especially at the end of games in which the score is close. All of this has also changed the ways that these games are coached (Klatell and Marcus 41). A pro hockey game that is not televised is quite different: the game's faster pace and flow present a remarkable contrast to the sometimes plodding televised version.

In the twenty-first century, televised sporting events are a multi-billion-dollar industry that attracts significant numbers of viewers and accounts for a large part of the TV schedule, even in the post-network, multichannel era. Television contracts are so large now that many teams rely on these fees to help maintain their operations. All the four major professional team sports have contracts to have their games carried on various broadcast and cable networks. College football and college basketball also have significant television contracts, which provide a significant source of revenue for many colleges and universities.

The most lucrative television contract in the United States is for the National Football League and is worth a total of $20.4 billion over the period between 2006 and 2013. It is divided up between a number of networks: NBC, ABC, Fox, ESPN, and the league's own NFL Network (Wikipedia 2011). The money the NFL receives is divided up among the teams and constitutes a significant portion of their incomes (Battista 2006). In the first year of the new television contract, the NFL had total revenues of $6.4 billion, of which $3.75 billion came from the various television contracts (Vecsey 2006). In Canada, the contract to carry NFL games is currently divided up among a number of networks: CTV, Citytv, TSN, RDS, and Rogers Sportsnet. In addition to NFL games, TSN and RDS carry all the games of the Canadian Football League (CFL).

The biggest American football game of the year takes place in early February. The *Super Bowl* was seen by approximately 106.5 million people in the United States on the CBS television network in February 2010. This made it the most-watched show in the modern era. The Fox network, which aired the next one on February 2011, anticipated a similar success. It had already sold (five months before the actual broadcast) 90 per cent of all the 30-second ad spots for between $2.8 and $3 million each. Advertisers seem to love this show because it is usually watched live and not recorded. For this reason, viewers are less likely to fast-forward through them than they would for other types of programming that they record (Steinberg 2010).

North American television contracts for the other leagues are slightly less: the annual cost of the NBA television contract in 2002 was $660 million; the annual contract for MLB in 2006 was $570 million; and the NHL contract in 2005 was $120 million (Gratton and Solberg 2007: 3). College football is in the same ballpark. It was recently reported, for example, that the ACC (Atlantic Coast Conference) signed a deal with ESPN for $1.86 billion over 12 years (Associated Press 2010).

The CBS television network signed a complicated deal with the National College Athletics Association (NCAA; the body that regulates intercollegiate sports in the United States), which indicates a possible model for the further development of the relationship between corporate media and sports teams in the twenty-first century. It is a $6 billion deal involving "broadcast rights, cable outlet rights, satellite partnerships, digital television and home video rights, plus Internet, electronic commerce rights, marketing, sponsorship, licensing and merchandising rights" (Johnson 2009: 128). As we see, the mid-nineteenth-century capitalist logics that turned college sports into commercial entertainment for a mass audience continue to shape the essence of college sporting events today.

Televised Sports as a Popular Genre and Ideological Form

Televised Sports as Genre—The Case of Football

Televised sport is a hybrid genre combining numerous elements. It blends "news and public service programming with spectacle and epic drama" (Johnson 2009: 125). It is a form of real-time entertainment, generally watched live, although enhanced by technologies that enable the replaying of important moments or referee errors (video review is a regular feature in some sports like football and hockey).

Margaret Morse, in her pioneering study of the generic qualities of televised sport (1983), provides a useful summary of its characteristics as applied to football on TV. The game is shown in "real time," the broadcast lasting as long as the game itself. At times, that broadcast may flow over the scheduled time assigned to the game. As such, it occupies a privileged place in the "flow" of television. Other programs must be delayed until the game is over. Attempts at cutting away have produced enormous outrage on the part of viewers and broadcasters have learned from these painful mistakes (Morse 1983: 60).

The narrative conventions of football on TV are also interesting. On and around the field, dozens of cameras pick up various aspects of the action. A team of editors, in the broadcast centre, allow the story to be told by cutting back and forth between the various television cameras. To help the television audience understand the rather disorienting movement between numerous perspectives, an audio commentary is provided by the "play-by-play announcer" and by the "colour commentator":

> The play-by-play commentator is essentially in charge of game-time, anchoring the narrative of the game by calling out the proairetic code of football. His job implies that the visual movements on screen are not sufficient to name each play but must be supplemented verbally. The color-man is in charge of the "dead-time" when the clock is stopped or players are taking position, time now employed in instant replay analysis, ads or pre-game interviews, etc. Note that the visuals he comments on are neither narrative nor live. The color-man does, however, possess a hermeneutic function in using instant replay to judge individual performance, evaluating it as well as setting it in statistical and biographical perspective. But, as the name implies, the color-man is also responsible for the spectacle aspect of the game, for conveying the enthusiasms of the crowd vocally, inviting discharge. (Morse 1983: 52)

In addition to providing the "choral" commentary on this mythic performance, the colour commentator uses a vast knowledge of statistical matters related to the individuals and their predecessors who are engaged in this contest and those that happened in the past. The vocal commentary is also supplanted by a vast array of superimposed text, which appears on the screen regularly to buttress this expertise. So in this sense the televised sporting event is made up of numerous texts: the visual story told by the cameras, the audio commentators' narrative, and the imbedded text that places this story into a whole tradition and history of similar stories. An additional set of narratives are also imbedded into this pageant: the ads. Televised sports have developed an almost seamless ability to move between the game and the stories told in the ads (Morse 1983: 60). The flow appears to be even less disruptive than the ads that punctuate the narratives found in other television genres. After the game is over, televised sporting events are then rebroadcast in edited form on the nightly news broadcasts that follow and on the sports news programs that are a regular staple on all of the cable sports networks.

The Popularity of Sports Television

All of this contributes to the popularity of televised sports. The endless array of statistical data that sports broadcasts provide gives the audience a feeling of also being a part of the conversation. They can become experts in the arcane world of sports statisticians. The audience is invited to debate the significance of each play and of each game outcome. All the major networks that televise sporting events supplement their programming with an extensive Internet presence, which fans can call upon to acquire additional statistical information. They can supplement the colour commentary of the broadcast by joining a blog, which offers further commentary on the event.

Televised sport is also likely popular among audiences because it entails elements of myth and ritual. According to Michael Real, in his analysis of a typical Super Bowl broadcast, it conforms to the patterns of traditional mythic ritual activities: "The symbolic forms of myth provide personal identification, heroic archetypes, communal focus, spatial and temporal frames of reference, and ecologically regulatory mechanisms" (Real 1982: 215).

Former pro-football player and now sports sociologist Michael Oriard offers another reason for football's popularity. Football provides a forum for fair play that is often unavailable in the conflicts of real life. When a team scores or when they are unable to advance, they must turn the ball over to the other team who then tries to move the ball forward (Oriard 1981: 35). In basketball and baseball, similar forms of reciprocity apply.

Finally, televised sports are popular because the outcome of the game is always uncertain. Bookies may provide a statistical probability on the outcome of the game but there are always "upsets"—any team can win sometimes even if they are the recognized "underdog." This provides a level of narrative pleasure and anticipation that the other more rigidly conventional forms of narrative genres do not possess. We don't always know how the story is going to end; that is part of the appeal.

Sports and Ideology

Taken as a whole, these programs attract large local and often national audiences. They also produce diverse and sometimes contradictory responses from their audiences, varying from local parochialism to feelings of national solidarity. They can stimulate feelings of pride in one's local community as well as hostility to other communities. They are viewed at home or in communally shared spaces such as bars. As spectacle, they can also invoke feelings of admiration in the activities and lives of the performers:

> Today, sports are a major part of the consumer society whereby individuals learn the values and behavior of a competitive and success-driven society. Sports heroes are among the best paid and wealthiest denizens of the consumer society and thus serve as embodiments of fantasy aspirations to the good life. (Kellner 2003: 65)

Television sports in this way partake in the culture of celebrity that all the other entertainment media trade in. The phenomenon of stardom is a complex one and has been theorized by numerous cultural critics, most notably Richard Dyer (1979). Stardom in sports, like its counterpart in other media, serves as a form of product differentiation for the team owners. It also serves as collection of role models for the eager fan. Numerous sports sociologists have commented on the ways in which these programs offer a certain model of masculinity that is presented as desirable.

Ideologically, the sports star most notably embodies the dominant values of the society: patriarchy, profit, and empire (Jhally 1989). Occasionally, dissident voices are allowed tenure—basketball players such as Steve Nash denouncing the ongoing war in Iraq; many basketball and baseball stars voicing their disapproval of anti-immigrant legislation in the state of Arizona; and more recently, the Super Bowl–winning Green Bay Packer players expressing their solidarity with public sector workers in Wisconsin (Zirin 2008; 2011)—but these remain marginal.

Sports celebrities are also the embodiment of the consumer society that we live in. The fabulous wealth that some of them have achieved is partly a product of the transformation of the sports star into a shill for various consumer products: beginning with athletic clothing and shoes and moving on to automobiles and beverages. Some of the biggest sports stars make more money in product endorsements than they draw in salary.

Summary

Television has had a huge impact on the development of team sports in North America over the last 60 years. Initially a small part of the television schedule, televised sport has greatly increased its share of the programming among the different types of TV shows available. It is a multi-billion-dollar boon to the professional leagues in North America and to college football and basketball in the United States. It provides an ideal platform for the celebration of the consumer society and the sales effort required by modern corporate capitalism. The presence of television has also changed the games themselves, which have had to adapt themselves to the interruptions that advertising on television requires. A truly symbiotic relationship has developed between commercial and corporate television broadcasting on the one hand and a number of spectator-based professional team sports in North America on the other.

Note

* Readers who are interested in reading ongoing commentary from a progressive point of view about many of the issues raised in this essay are directed to Dave Zirin's "Edge of Sports" weekly sports column at www.edgeofsports.com.

Works Cited

Associated Press. (2010). "ACC, ESPN Reach 12 Year Deal." http://sports.espn.go.com/ncaa/news/story?id=5363743. 8 July 2010. Accessed 28 February 2011.

Battista, Judy (2006). "Deal Helps Free Agents and Top Draft Picks." *The New York Times,* 10 March 2006.

Bellamy, R., and Shultz, K. (2006). "Hockey Night in the United States? The NHL, Major League Sports, and the Evolving Television/Media Marketplace." In D. Whitson and R. Grunneau (eds), *Artificial Ice: Hockey, Culture, and Commerce.* (pp. 163–80). Peterborough, ON: Broadview Press.

Catsis, J.R. (1996). *Sports Broadcasting.* Chicago: Nelson-Hall Publishers.

Cole, S. (2003). *The Best of Hockey Night in Canada.* Toronto: McArthur & Company.

Dyer, R. (1979). *Stars.* London: British Film Institute.

Gratton, C., and Solberg, H.A. (2007). *The Economics of Sports Broadcasting.* London: Routledge.

Grunneau, R., and Whitson, D. (1993). *Hockey Night in Canada: Sports, Identities, and Cultural Politics.* Toronto: Garamond Press.

Inside Hoops. (n.d.). "NBA TV Contracts." www.insidehoops.com/nba-tv-contracts.shtml. Accessed 4 March 2011.

Jhally, S. (1989). "Cultural Studies and the Sports/ Media Complex." In L.A. Wenner (ed.), *Media, Sports, & Society* (pp. 70–93). London: Sage Publications.

Johnson, V.E. (2009). "Everything Old Is New Again: Sport Television, Innovation, and Tradition for a Multi-Platform Era." In A.D. Lotz (ed.), *Beyond Prime Time: Television Programming in the Post-network Era* (pp. 114–37). New York: Routledge.

Kellner, D. (2003). *Media Spectacle.* London: Routledge.

Klatell, D.A., and Marcus, N. (1988). *Sports for Sale: Television, Money, and the Fans.* Oxford: Oxford University Press.

McChesney, R.W. (2008). "Media Made Sport: A History of Sports Coverage in the United States." In *The Political Economy of Media: Enduring Issues, Emerging Dilemmas* (pp. 213–32). New York: Monthly Review Press.

Markovits, A.S., and Rensmann, L. (2010). *Gaming the World: How Sports Are Reshaping Global Politics and Culture.* Princeton, NJ: Princeton University Press.

Morse, M. (1983). "Sport on Television: Replay and Display." In E.A. Kaplan (ed.), *Regarding Television: Critical Approaches—An Anthology* (pp. 44–66). Frederick, MD: University Publications of America.

Oriard, M. (1981). "Professional Football as Cultural Myth." *Journal of American Culture*, Vol. 4(3): 27–41.

Real, M. (1982). "The Super Bowl: Mythic Spectacle." In H. Newcomb (ed.), *Television: The Critical View*, 3rd edn (pp. 206–39). Oxford: Oxford University Press.

Rowe, D. (1996). "The Global Love-Match: Sport and Television." *Media, Culture & Society*, Vol. 18(4): 565–82.

Rutherford, P. (1990). *When Television Was Young: Primetime Canada 1952–1967*. Toronto: University of Toronto Press.

Smith, R.A. (2001). *Play-by-Play: Radio, Television, and Big-Time College Sport*. Baltimore: John Hopkins University Press.

Steinberg, B. (2010). "Big Marketers to Super Bowl: We Can't Quit You." *Advertising Age*, Vol. 88(33): 6.

Vecsey, G. (2006). "Bridging the Old NFL with the New." *The New York Times*, 10 August 2006.

Wikipedia. (2011). "NFL on Television." http://en.wikipedia.org/wiki/NFL_on_television. Accessed 25 February 2011.

Wong, J.C.-K. (2005). *Lords of the Rinks: The Emergence of the National Hockey League, 1875–1936*. Toronto: University of Toronto Press.

Zirin, D. (2008). *A People's History of Sport in the United Sates: 250 Years of Politics, Protest, People, and Play*. New York: The New Press.

———. (2011). "Wisconsin: Packers Back the Protesters." *The New Yorker*, 28 February 2011. www.newyorker.com/online/blogs/sportingscene/2011/02/packers-wisconsin-unions.html. Accessed 9 March 2011.

Part III | Discussion Questions

Introduction: | Television Genre and Textual Analysis

1. What is a TV genre? Compare and contrast two TV shows that ostensibly belong to different genre categories. Identify commonalities and differences between TV genres (in terms of subject matter, narrative structure, characterization, setting, aesthetics, and so on).
2. Examine how your favourite TV show is "socially constructed" as a distinctive TV genre. What statements and claims do people—creators, industries, advertisers, critics, audiences—make about the TV show? How do they give it meaning as a distinct genre?
3. Select a particular TV show for study. What are the TV show's predominant genre characteristics? What are the major uses of this TV genre by TV networks and TV viewers?
4. How is genre an "industrial" category or "program form"? Discuss the industrial uses of genre by TV production companies, TV networks, advertisers, and viewers with reference to a specific TV show.
5. What is "genre hybridity"? Examine genre hybridity in a particular TV show. Is the TV show a hybrid of pre-existing genres? Which ones? Are there any "intertextual" elements in the TV show?

6 | From Trailer Trash to *Trailer Park Boys*

1. What is a "mockumentary"? What are the main features of a mockumentary? Provide an example.
2. What narrative conventions does the mockumentary use that are not typically found in the traditional sitcom?
3. How does *Trailer Park Boys* represent poverty, crime, and drugs and also law and order?
4. How is *Trailer Park Boys* a "cultural forum" for addressing social class and community issues in Canada?
5. What is "realism"? Is *Trailer Park Boys* a "realist" show?

7 | The *Little Mosque on the Prairie:* Examining (Multi) Cultural Spaces of Nation and Religion

1. What is "orientalism"? Examine orientalist representations in a contemporary TV show.
2. What are some of the ways that *Little Mosque on the Prairie* confronts "Islamaphobia"?
3. How is the debate between modernity and tradition represented in *Little Mosque on the Prairie*?
4. How does *Little Mosque on the Prairie* represent gendered and sexual identities?
5. How is "multiculturalism" represented by *Little Mosque on the Prairie* and other TV shows?

8 | Downloading Dopplegängers: New Media Anxieties and Transnational Ironies in *Battlestar Galactica*

1. How do popular TV shows represent "national security"?
2. What is "allegory"? How does *Battlestar Galactica* allegorize the events and aftermath of 9/11?

3. What does *Battlestar Galactica* suggest about the political relationship between the United States and Canada?
4. What are some of the recent debates about "copyright" and "intellectual property" in Canada and the United States?
5. Select a particular science fiction TV show for study. How does the TV show represent science and technology? Does it represent a dystopian or utopian future? What might this imagined future say about present-day social hopes and fears about technology?

9 | *CSI* and Moral Authority: The Police and Science

1. Does *CSI* legitimize forensic investigation? How?
2. Explain Geertz's definition of culture.
3. In terms of its genre features and thematic elements, how does *CSI* differ from previous police shows?
4. What is the "*CSI* effect"? Do TV shows inform or misinform viewers about the use of science and technology by police as a tool to effectively solve crime? Can science and technology deter or solve crime? Or might crime have deeper social roots?
5. How are gender and sexual relations between characters represented by *CSI*?

10 | Re-Wiring Baltimore: The Emotive Power of Systemics, Seriality, and the City

1. What is "intertextual allusion"? Identify and discuss an example of intertextual allusion in a TV show.
2. What is "seriality"? Select a contemporary TV show and discuss its seriality.
3. How are the civic leaders of Baltimore represented in *The Wire*? Select a Canadian TV show and describe how it represents civic leaders.
4. In what ways is *The Wire* a "cultural forum" for addressing social tensions between public authorities (the police, the schooling system, and municipal government) and economically underprivileged and socially marginalized citizens?
5. How does *The Wire* represent the role and function of commercial media, particularly newspapers?

11 | Making the Most of 15 Minutes: Reality TV's Dispensable Celebrity

1. Do reality TV shows undermine the craft unions that have long been part of the TV industry's creative personnel? How specifically? Are reality TV shows bad for unions?
2. What older TV genres are combined in the reality show genre?
3. What does the term "celebrity as commodity" mean? Provide an example of a contemporary reality TV show that trades on the celebrity as a commodity.
4. Do you think reality TV shows devalue the concepts of celebrity and stardom?
5. How are reality TV shows a form of "unscripted reality," at once "real" and "unreal"?

12 | Reality TV Formats: The Case of *Canadian Idol*

1. What is a TV format? Describe a contemporary TV format. Why did TV networks license it? Why do you think viewers watch the formatted TV show? Does the TV format represent the economic imperatives of TV networks and the tastes and preferences of viewers?

2. Why do TV networks acquire franchised TV formats?
3. How do Canadian reality TV shows promote the cult of celebrity?
4. What elements of the UK and US versions of *Idol* are utilized in the Canadian version?
5. What is "glocalization"? Provide an example of a global TV format that is glocalized for a national audience. What changed and what stayed the same when the TV format was glocalized?

13 | Laughing at Authority or Authorized Laughter?: Canadian News Parodies

1. Does Canadian TV news programming contribute to nationalism in Canada? Are there any examples of American TV news programming contributing to nationalism in the United States? What is similar? What is different?
2. Define and discuss "genre hybridization" with reference to a contemporary TV show.
3. Why do you think news parody TV programs are so popular in Canada, especially among younger TV viewers? Do you feel that news parody TV shows help or harm democracy? Do they encourage or discourage young people to participate in politics?
4. What is the difference between parody and satire?
5. According to Druick, what is the role and purpose of satire on Canadian TV today?

14 | *The Daily Show*: Discursive Integration and Reinvention of Political Journalism

1. What is the "crisis" in broadcast journalism? What are the main causes of the "crisis"?
2. Why do many young people trust Jon Stewart more than actual TV news journalists and anchors?
3. How does the *The Daily Show* engage with political issues? Why might *The Daily Show* be a more popular source of political information for young people than traditional TV news?
4. Why do politicians go on TV programs like *The Daily Show*? Are there any recent examples of politicians appearing on TV shows outside of the traditional TV news frame?
5. What is "fake" news?

15 | Entertainment Wars: Television Culture after 9/11

1. What was the US television industry's immediate reaction to the events of 9/11?
2. In what ways were events in American history marshalled by TV networks to frame what happened on 9/11? How did TV networks try to construct an image of "lost innocence" after 9/11?
3. How and why were critics of US foreign policy silenced after 9/11 by TV networks?
4. How were nationalism and consumerism marshalled as a response to the terrorist attacks of 9/11?
5. How do contemporary TV shows represent national security and terrorism as a threat to it?

16 | Interrogating *24*: Making Sense of US Counter-terrorism in the Global War on Terrorism

1. How does *24* legitimize unlawful detention and torture? Are there any other TV shows that represent unlawful acts by the state that are undertaken on behalf of "national security"? Might these kinds of TV shows function as a kind of propaganda? How?

2. How does *24* depict corruption in the leading institutions of government, business, and the military? Do any other TV shows represent corruption in this way? Why do you think TV shows increasingly represent conspiracy and corruption as a fact of life?
3. What was Hollywood's response to the US government's request that it help out with the "war on terror"?
4. Is *24* a racist TV show? Does it perpetuate stereotypes and popularize hate in society?
5. What is the "ticking clock scenario" on *24*? How is this fictional scenario employed by actual politicians and policy-makers to justify acts of state intervention?

17 | "Get the Puck Outta Here!": Media Transnationalism and Canadian Identity

1. The "FoxTrax" puck was a promotional gimmick, used by Fox network to attract viewers to broadcasts of hockey games. What are some of the current promotional techniques employed by TV networks to attract viewers to televised sporting events?
2. What is the general business relationship between TV networks and sports leagues in Canada and the United States? Why are TV contracts important to sports leagues? Examine the specific business relationship between a TV network and a particular sports league.
3. Discuss the main characteristics of "transnational media." Can you think of some current examples of transnational media? How is transnational media distinct from national media?
4. Why has hockey been such an important component of Canadian national identity? In the twenty-first century, do TV networks continue to associate hockey with Canada? Does hockey continue to be an important part of Canadian national identity? Why or why not?
5. What was the response of Canadian hockey fans to the "FoxTrax" puck? What are some of the current ways that sports TV programming encourages and capitalizes on fandom?

18 | Some Notes on Televised Team Sports in North America

1. What is the "society of the spectacle"? How do TV sporting events participate in the society of the spectacle? Watch a televised sporting event. How many ads for goods and services are represented within the event and between it in TV advertisements? How is the TV sporting event used to communicate commercial values?
2. Why were professional sports popular among working-class spectators in the late nineteenth and early twentieth centuries? Do you think that TV sports are popular primarily among working-class viewers? Why?
3. What is the difference between "commercialization" and "professionalization"? In twenty-first-century sports, is there a tension between commercialization and professionalization?
4. What cultural values do team sports teach? How do televised sporting events communicate the meaning of "sports" to society? How is the "game" represented? What does the game mean? What values and meanings unrelated to the sport are attached to it on TV?
5. Why are televised team sporting events so popular in the twenty-first century of post-network TV?

Suggestions for Further Reading

Television Genre Studies

Allen, R. (1985). *Speaking of Soap Operas*. Chapel Hill: University of North Carolina Press.

Andrejevic, M. (2003). *Reality TV: The Work of Being Watched*. New York: Rowman & Littlefield.

Attallah, P. (2010). "Television Discourse and Situation Comedy." *Canadian Review of American Studies*, Vol. 40(1): 1–24.

Banet-Weiser, S., Cynthia, C., and Freitas, A. (Eds). (2007). *Cable Visions: Television Beyond Broadcasting*. New York: New York University Press.

Boyle, R., and Haynes, R. (2009). *Power Play: Sport, Media and Popular Culture*. Edinburgh: Edinburgh University Press.

Bredin, M., Henderson, S., and Matheson, S.A. (Eds). (2011). *Canadian Television: Text and Context*. Waterloo: Wilfred Laurier University Press.

Brundsdon, C. (2003). "Lifestyling Britain: The 8–9 slot on British Television." *International Journal of Cultural Studies*, Vol. 6(1): 5–23.

Carpignano, P., Anderson, R., Aronowitz, S., and Difazio, W. (1990). "Chatter in the Age of Electronic Reproduction: Talk Television and the 'Public Mind.'" *Social Text*, Vol. 25/26: 33–55.

Creeber, G. (2008). *The Television Genre Book*. London: British Film Institute.

Cushon, S., and Lewis, J. (Eds). (2010). *The Rise of 24-Hour News Television: Global Perspectives*. New York: Peter Lang Publishing, Inc.

Dalton, M.M., and Linder, L.R. (Eds). (2005). *The Sitcom Reader: America Viewed and Skewed*. New York: State University of New York Press.

Davis, G., and Dickinson, K. (Eds). (2008). *Teen TV: Genre, Consumption and Identity*. London: British Film Institute.

Dixon, W.W. (Ed.). (2004). *Film and Television after 9/11*. Carbondale: Southern Illinois University Press.

Dovey, J. (2000). *Freakshow: First Person Media and Factual Television*. London: Pluto Press.

Downing, J. (2007). "Terrorism, Torture and Television: *24* in its Context." *Democratic Communique*, Vol. 21(2): 62–82.

Druick, Z., and Kotsopoulos, A. (Eds) (2008). *Programming Reality: Perspectives on English-Canadian Television*. Waterloo: Wilfred Laurier Press.

Fishman, M., and Cavender, G. (1998). *Entertaining Crime: Television Reality Programs*. New York: Walter De Gruyter, Inc.

Gray, J. (2008). *Television Entertainment*. New York: Routledge.

Gray, J., Jones, J.P., and Thompson, E. (2009). *Satire TV: Politics and Comedy in the Post-network Era*. New York: New York University Press.

Grindstaff, L. (2002). *The Money Shot: Trash, Class, and the Making of TV Talk Shows*. Chicago: University of Chicago Press.

Gruneau, R., and Whitson, D. (1993). *Hockey Night in Canada: Sport, Identities and Cultural Politics*. Toronto: Garmond Press.

Hallin, D. (1989). *The "Uncensored War": The Media and Vietnam*. Berkley, CA: University of California Press.

Heller, D. (2007). *Makeover Television: Realities Remodeled*. London: I.B. Taurus.

Henderson, L. (2007). *Social Issues in Television Fiction*. Edinburgh: Edinburgh University Press.

Hill, A. (2005). *Reality TV: Factual Entertainment and Television Audiences*. New York: Routledge.

Holmes, S., and Jermyn, D. (Eds). (2004). *Understanding Reality Television*. New York: Routledge.

Hogarth, D. (2004). *Documentary Television in Canada: From National Public Service to Global Marketplace*. Montreal: McGill-Queen's University Press.

Hudson, P.J. (2006). "Hockey Night in Canada." *Transition*, Vol. 13(2): 68–85.

Johnson, V.E. (2008). *Heartland TV: Prime Time Television and the Struggle for U.S. Identity*. New York: New York University Press.

Johnson-Smith, J. (2005). *American Science Fiction TV: Star Trek, Stargate, and Beyond*. Middletown, CT: Weslyan.

Jones, G. (2005). *Entertaining Politics: New Political Television and Civic Culture*. Lanham, MD: Rowman & Littlefield.

Jordan, C. (2007). "Who Shot J.R.'s Ratings? The Rise and Fall of the 1980s Prime-Time Soap Opera." *Television & New Media*, Vol. 8(1): 68–87.

Karnick, K.B. (1988). "NBC and the Innovation of Television News." *Journalism History*, Vol. 15(1): 26–34.

Kellner, D. (1992). *The Persian Gulf TV War*. Boulder, CO: Westview Press.

Kompare, D. (2005). *Rerun Nation: How Repeats Invented American Television*. New York: Routledge.

Lewis, T. (2007). "He Needs to Face His Fears with These Five Queers! *Queer Eye for the Straight Guy*, Makeover TV, and the Lifestyle Expert." *Television & New Media*, Vol. 8(4): 285–311.

Lury, K. (2005). *Interpreting Television*. London: Hodder Arnold.

McMurria, J. (2008). "Desperate Citizens and Good Samaritans: Neoliberalism and Makeover Reality TV." *Television & New Media*, Vol. 9(1): 305–32.

Mills, B. (2009). *The Sitcom*. Edinburgh: Edinburgh Press.

Moore, B. (2006). *Prime-time Television: A Concise History*. Westerport, CT: Praeger Publishers.

Munson, W. (1983). *All Talk: The Talkshow in Media Culture*. Philadelphia, PA: Temple University Press.

Murray, S., and Oullette, L. (Eds). (2008). *Reality TV: Remaking Television Culture*. New York: New York University Press.

Neale, S. (1980). *Genre.* London: British Film Institute.

Newcomb, H. (2007). "'This Is Not Al Dente': *The Sopranos* and the New Meaning of Television." In H. Newcombe (Ed.), *Television: The Critical View* (pp. 561–78). Oxford: Oxford University Press.

Nochimson, M.P. (2003). "Whaddaya Lookin' At? Re-reading the Gangster Genre through *The Sopranos.*" *Film Quarterly,* Vol. 56(2): 2–13.

Pach, C.J. Jr. (1994). "And That's the Way It Was: The Vietnam War on the Network Nightly News." In D.R. Farber (Ed.), *The Sixties: From Memory to History* (pp. 90–118). Chapel Hill: University of North Carolina Press.

Philips, D. (2005). "Transformation Scenes: The Television Interior Makeover." *International Journal of Cultural Studies,* Vol. 8(2): 213–29.

Riegert, K. (Ed.). (2007). *Politicotainment: Television's Take on the Real.* New York: Peter Lang.

Rosenberg, H., and Feldman, C.S. (2008). *No Time to Think: The Menace of Media Speed and the 24-hour News Cycle.* New York: Continuum International Publishing Group, Inc.

Selznick, B. (2009). "Branding the Future: Syfy in the Post-network Era." *Science Fiction Film and Television,* Vol 2(2): 177–204.

Snauffer, D. (2006). *Crime Television.* Westport, CT: Praeger Publishers.

Stahl, R. (2010). *Militainment, Inc.* New York: Routledge.

Taylor, P.M. (1997). *Global Communications, International Affairs, and the Media Since 1945.* London and New York: Routledge.

Telotte, J., and Duchovnay, G. (Eds). (2011). *Science Fiction Film and Television: Adaptation across the Screens.* New York: Routledge.

Telotte, J.P. (Ed.). (2008). *The Essential Science Fiction Television Reader.* Lexington: The University of Kentucky Press.

Thompson, K. (2003). *Storytelling in Film and Television.* Cambridge: Harvard University Press.

Timberg, B.M., Erler, R.J., and Newcomb, H. (2002). *Television Talk: A History of the Talk Show.* Austin: University of Texas Press.

van Zoonen, L. (2005). *Entertaining the Citizen: When Politics and Popular Culture Converge.* Lanham, MD: Rowman and Littlefield.

Vest, J.P. (2011). *The Wire, Deadwood, Homicide, and NYPD Blue: Violence Is Power.* Santa Barbara, CA: ABC-CLIO.

Weber, B. R. (2009). *Makeover TV: Selfhood, Citizenship, and Celebrity.* Durham, NC: Duke University Press.

West, P. (2008). "Abject Jurisdictions: *CSI: Miami,* Globalization and the Body Politic." *Critical Studies in Television,* Vol. 3(1): 60–75.

PART IV

Emerging Trends in TV Studies: Interactive Audiences, Advertising, Globalization, and Post-network TV

Introduction: Emerging Trends in TV Studies: Interactive Audiences, Advertising, Globalization, and Post-network TV

In the twenty-first century, the meaning of TV and its audience are changing. The articles included in this section of *The Television Reader* examine interactive audiences, advertising, TV globalization, and post-network TV.

Television's Interactive Audience

The first article in this section, by Eileen Meehan (2007), updates critical political-economy research on the **audience commodity**. Television networks, advertisers, and ratings firms continue to trade commodity audiences. But Meehan argues that there are many varieties of viewer experience: "[W]e approach television as users, drop-in viewers, channel surfers, multiple screeners, casual viewers, focused viewers, engaged viewers, members of interpretive communities, fan consumers, and self-programmers"(165). Meehan's discussion of these novel TV viewer experiences contrasts with the old notion that TV viewers are "passive." Since The channels of mass TV broadcasting only allowed TV shows to flow in one direction, from a dominant sender (TV network) to a passive receiver (TV viewer). The audience was constructed as a mass of passive receivers of TV shows. Though one-way transmission is still a component of contemporary TV, many TV scholars are now less interested in making arguments about what TV networks are ostensibly doing to the audience (whether that be brainwashing them or engineering their pleasure) and more interested in exploring what people are actively doing, saying, and expressing in relation to their favourite TV shows. Using Web 2.0 technology and social networking platforms (Facebook, MySpace, Twitter), millions of TV lovers ritualistically and collaboratively talk about TV shows, create fan websites full of fan fiction, blog about characters, spoil revelations of reality TV shows, and vote for their favourite "idol." Television's mass audience of the network TV era is quickly morphing into groupings of very interactive TV show users.

As the TV set and the computer converge, the relationship between TV and Google-owned **YouTube** has become an important site of inquiry (Strangelove 2010). In 2010, 14.6 billion YouTube videos were streamed per month and the typical YouTube user watched approximately 100 videos per month. YouTube is a new medium for making "public" people's most private lives; it is also a digital cultural forum in which amateur creators of media content vie for public attention. Against predictions that YouTube's user-generated content will displace the mainstream fare offered by established broadcast network, cable, and satellite TV services, Lucas Hilderbrand (2007) argues that YouTube's popularity relies at least in part upon recirculated TV clips, old and new. YouTube is the largest and most popular web-based depot of popular TV clips. Youtube contributes to a "culture of the clip" that allows viewers to search and see particular moments from TV shows. Its clip-based cultural memory tunnel, however, is viewed by the media corporations that own such TV clips as a copyright violation. They regularly order YouTube to remove them. Hilderbrand (2007), sympathetic to millions of YouTube users, challenges the proprietary claims of media corporations: "YouTube does not promote willy-nilly piracy but rather enables access to culturally significant texts that would otherwise be elusive and the ability to repurpose videos in the creation of new derivative works"(56). Should media corporations control (i.e., limit) the use of TV shows they own or should fans creatively mine copyrighted TV shows as raw material to make new expressions?

Throughout the 1990s, there was a legal standoff between corporate-employed copyright lawyers and TV fans. Since the turn of the millennium, media corporations have devised ways of managing, harnessing, and channelling the creative impulses and energies of TV fans toward profitable ends. The relationship between media corporations and new media fandoms are more symbiotic than they are antagonistic: "The culture industry not only produces popular cultural texts but also constitutes their fan cultures, and it does so in order that it may profit from them by selling them its television series, its films and its merchandise"(Gwenllian-Jones 2003: 171). Fans are not "cultural dopes" or "resistant consumers" but the twenty-first-century TV industry's elite tastemakers and unwaged creative workers. Media corporations authorize, observe, and attempt to exploit the interactive practices of fans. While participatory fandom is sometimes optimistically viewed as heralding the democratization of the relationship between the TV industry and TV audiences, Mark Andrejevic (2008) brilliantly argues that it heralds a new stage in the commodification of the audience's labour. Television companies view participatory fandom as a form of "brand loyalty" (a viewer's intense emotional commitment to a TV show). They use brand-loyal fans as a source of unpaid promotion. The online chatter of elite fans influences people to watch the TV show. Fans even function as an unpaid source of demographic market research. Television companies design, monitor, and observe fan websites, mining them for information about audience tastes and preferences. Rather than pay people to say whether they like or dislike a TV show, media firms review fan comment boards. Andrejevic's (2008) critical analysis in "Watching Television without Pity" shows how the previously distinct spheres of TV production and TV consumption are converging. Through their interactive web posts, TV fans become unwaged co-producers of TV shows.

Television Advertising

While viewers work as informal TV show promoters, the formal advertising industry continues to grow. In 2010, globalizing media corporations spent more than $450 billion on advertising; US companies spent roughly $64 billion; and Canadian firms spent more than $8 billion. Advertising, the second thematic focus of this section, is a central feature of the capitalist system in general and the TV system in particular. If goods are not sold, companies cannot make profit and reinvest it in more capital. By cultivating demand for goods, ads—placed on billboards, in magazines, before and during films, and in and around TV shows—help firms avoid an over-accumulation crisis (Jhally 2000). For some critics, advertising is "the most powerful and sustained system of propaganda in human history"(Jhally 2000: 27). Advertising participates in and promotes an environmentally calamitous and emotionally turbulent consumerist culture in which we are told, time and time again, to assess our status and the very meaning of our lives through commodities.

Commercial TV primarily exists to serve the interests of advertising corporations. Raymond Williams (1974) described a typical day seated in front of a TV set, watching traditional network television, as a "planned flow": "the defining characteristic of broadcasting, simultaneously as a technology and as a cultural form"(86). Television shows and ads seamlessly blend or flow together before viewers' eyes. Advertising corporations use TV to reach millions of people with flowing commercial messages that attract and construct the viewers as consumers for specific commodities. Television ads offer them the hope of a commodity-induced lifestyle transformation, which frequently disappoints. The 24-pack of Molson Canadian beer does not lead young men to a wooded Muskoka cabin overflowing with plaid-shirted supermodels, but to a morning hangover. Yet consumers may be aware of TV advertising's magic tricks and false appeals. Following World War II, Max Horkheimer and Theodor Adorno (1972) claimed: "The triumph of advertising in the culture industry is that consumers feel compelled to buy and use products even though they can see through them"(167). Advertising firms are finding it increasingly difficult to manipulative viewers using traditional modes of selling, so they have integrated a postmodern attitude of ironic self-reflexivity ("we know you know we are trying to manipulate you") into their ad campaigns. Viewers, however, may not be susceptible to even the most cleverly designed postmodern ads. Coupled with the migration of viewers to the web and an economic downturn that depressed ad revenue, the skeptical viewer supposedly precipitated a "crisis" in network TV.

Between 2000 and 2010, print media lost advertising dollars to websites, but network broadcast and cable TV remained favoured sellers of time and space to advertising firms. A "tidal wave of commercialism" is represented by twenty-first-century TV and its logic of selling consumer dreams and goods (McChensey 2004). Matthew McAllister and Matt Giglio (2005) examine product placement in TV shows. They argue that this practice blurs the distinction between fictional TV content and other promotional forms. McAllister and Giglio's empirically grounded study of three varieties of "commodity flow" (intra-channel, inter-channel, and synergistic) updates and extends Williams' classic concept of "**flow**" to highlight the intrusion of hyper-commercial advertising priorities and effects into the most benign-seeming of TV forms: children's programming.

Global TV

Television's "globalization" is the third topic explored in this section. Arjun Appadurai (1997) describes globalization as the transborder "flow" of scapes of people (migrants, tourists, workers, businesspeople, missionaries), capital (finance, commodities, industrial corporations), ideas (systems of belief and ideologies: religious, political, commercial), technology (knowledge and innovations), and media (TV shows and films) across national borders, at greater speeds than in the past, resulting in cultural interaction and interdependence. Transnational networks of information and communication technologies (ICTs) enable the movement of cross-border flows of televisual images which render distant places and peoples perceptible to local viewers. According to Williams (1974), TV facilitates "mobile privatization": viewers imaginatively travel the world from within totally privatized settings. Transnational TV broadcasts give audiences a sense of being able to visually access, in real time, what's happening in the world beyond their households. Viewers gain much of their (mis) understanding—about other places and people—through TV images. At the same time, TV reinforces a local viewer's attachment to a national "home" (Morley 2000).

Despite the diffusion of the Internet—in 2010 only 28.7 per cent of the world population was online—TV remains the most transnational of all media, with billions of people watching it every day. More than three billion people worldwide watch more than four hours of TV per day. More than 32 million people watched the opening of the 2008 Winter Olympics in Vancouver. The 2010 World Cup final was the most-watched soccer game in history, with 24 million viewers. More than 41 million people watched the 2010 Academy Awards on TV. Even more watched the 2011 fall of Egypt's dictator, Hosni Mubarak. Satellites orbit the earth in outer space, beaming TV images into privately owned dishes. As Daya Thussu (2007) notes, "Since visual images tend to cross linguistic and national boundaries relatively easily, television carries much more influence than other media, especially in developing countries, where millions cannot read"(1).

Global TV scholarship has long vacillated between the claims of two rival paradigms in international communication studies: media imperialism and media globalization. Early studies of TV's globalization focused primarily on the political economy and cultural consequences of American TV. The US-centrism of early global TV studies was largely due to the fact that US media corporations and the US state were the central proponents of commercial TV's globalization. Since the 1950s, the United States has been the primary base for the transnational expansion of the commercial TV broadcasting model, profit-seeking TV corporations, and TV shows. The US emerged from World War II as an unrivalled postcolonial media empire. Unlike previous territorial empires, it struggled to make the world safe for capitalism by establishing and supporting a system of interdependent liberal democratic (and sometimes authoritarian) market states, connected by technology and media flows. In the context of a Cold War rivalry with the Soviet Union, US corporate and state elite "imagined" the globalization of commercial TV as a support system for US corporate and geopolitical hegemony (Curtin 1997; Schiller 2000). For them, TV shows would efficiently cultivate demand for US exports and sell the "American Way of Life."

Throughout the second half of the twentieth century, the United States became recognized as the world's paramount media imperialist. Oliver Boyd-Barrett (1977) defines "media imperialism" as a "process whereby the ownership, structure, distribution or content of the media in any one country are singly or together subject to substantial pressure from the media interests of any other country or countries without proportionate reciprocation of influence by the country so affected"(117). Cultural imperialism scholars construed US-based yet globalizing media corporations as vehicles for internationally transmitting American capitalist and consumerist ideology (Schiller 1976). Some Latin American scholars feared that the televisual export of American ideology would dominate and destroy local cultures and result in a condition of global cultural homogeneity (Beltran 1978).

To go global, US media corporations set up foreign TV distribution offices, invested in foreign TV network infrastructures, participated in TV co-productions with foreign TV companies, arranged "**block-booking**" deals with foreign TV networks, and licensed discounted TV shows (Segrave 1998). The US state promoted "the free flow of information" doctrine to other countries, championing the movement of media corporations and commercial TV shows between and across the borders of sovereign nation-states as a way to create an interdependent world. Throughout the 1980s and 1990s, the free flow of information was made tantamount to free trade in media products (Comor 1997). By the turn of the twenty-first century, the United States had not only universalized the free flow of information doctrine, but also, generalized neoliberal policies that call for the deregulation, liberalization, and privatization of national TV broadcasters (McChesney 2002).

Between 2001 and 2008, the US media industry achieved record global growth. In 2008, the export of US films and TV shows around the world earned the US culture industry $13.6 billion (MPAA 2009). American TV shows are almost everywhere. In 2010, NBC-Universal licensed the hit show *House* to 250 territories worldwide. In France, *House* averaged 9.3 million viewers per episode; in Italy, 4.7 million; in Germany, 4.2 million; in Poland, 3.3 million; and in the Netherlands, 793,000 viewers. Other popular American TV shows such as CBS's *CSI: Las Vegas* and *CSI: Miami* attracted more than 50 million viewers each (Adler 2010). Do a comparative analysis of the balance of audiovisual trade between the United States and any other country, and you will likely discover that the US has a trade surplus while the other country has a deficit. Canada's audiovisual trade deficit with the US in 2006, for example, was $1.2 billion. Canadian audiences watch a lot of American TV; US viewers don't watch much Canadian TV. There is no reciprocation of economic or cultural influence between the US and Canada. Canada's private TV broadcasters spent a record $775.2 million in 2007–2008 on foreign programming, principally on US TV drama, and only $88.3 million on the production of Canadian TV. From a political-economy point of view, the US is a media imperialist.

However, in the same period that US media corporations accumulated record profits, cultural anti-Americanism boiled over border after border due to the unilateral and militaristic foreign policy of the US state. American TV shows did not "Americanize" the world or cultivate goodwill toward the United States. While the concept of media imperialism helps us examine how US corporate and state actors struggle to control the transnational political economy of global TV, it has many conceptual and methodological problems that scholars have explored in great detail elsewhere (Fejes 1981; Morely 2005; Tomlinson 1991). Media globalization research moves beyond (or at least complicates) the media imperialism hypothesis. Global TV is no longer solely dominated by the US. The United States continues to be a powerful media centre for the production, marketing, and distribution of TV shows, but there is more going on in the global media system than US media imperialism. Joseph Straubhaar's (1991) concept of "asymmetrical interdependence" helps us think outside the box of the media imperialism paradigm by drawing our attention to "a variety of possible relationships in which countries find themselves unequal but possessing variable degrees of power and initiative in politics, economics, and culture"(39). John Sinclair, Elizabeth Jacka, and Stuart Cunningham's (1996) "peripheral vision thesis" highlights the emergence of many regional media centres or what Michael Curtin (2003: 205) aptly describes as "media capitals": regionally based city-centres of media finance, production, and distribution (Hong Kong, Cairo, Bombay, and Toronto, for example). Television is forged in the nexus of transnational, national, and regional economies, polities, and cultures. There is not a universalizing global TV system; the production, distribution, and consumption of TV is unevenly developed and geographically and politically contingent. In globalization scholarship, the notion of TV entails industries, political regimes, technological systems, sets of practices, texts, and audiences that are always rooted in specific times and places. Against generalizing theories of global TV, Lisa Parks and Shanta Kumar (2003) contend TV requires "close examination of the television industries, programs, technologies, and audiences in specific cultural contexts"(6).

Many TV firms are owned by transnational media corporations (media conglomerates that have business operations in two or more countries). They orient their programming to US and transnational viewer sensibilities, customizing their TV shows to appeal to both the local and the global. CNN International and BBC World broadcast a range of TV shows that are tailored to national and transnational media audiences. Rupert Murdoch's News Corporation uses its Fox Broadcasting Company to enrage conservative US citizens and its Satellite Television Asia Region (STAR-TV) to target middle-class audiences in Hong Kong, India, Taiwan, and Singapore. Qatar-based TV network and channel Al Jazeera recently established a 24-hour English-language news TV service to broadcast in the United States, Canada, and European countries. Viacom-owned MTV International mixes its global brand of youth-oriented, commercial, and music video TV with local cultural flare.

Post-Fordist TV media production logics including **glocalization** (customizing products to appeal to local cultural sensibilities) and globalization (manufacturing products that are universally appealing across cultures) are resulting in post-national, hybridized, and cosmopolitan media flows. Television formats represent the most globally popular (and profitable) of all transnationally flowing TV forms. They are global TV show concepts that can be adapted and re-packaged to suit local industry and culturally proximate audience tastes. The *Idol* format, for example, has been locally adapted by TV networks in more than 100 countries, from Canada to the United States, to the cultural zone of East Africa. Why are TV formats so popular? Why do so many national TV networks buy and re-package formats? Silvio Waisbord (2004) presents thoughtful answers to these questions in a seminal critical study of TV formats. For Waisbord, TV formats are cheap to produce, easy to assemble, and flexible. Television networks locally customize foreign-owned TV formats to meet national content quotas and convince audiences that they are watching home-grown TV. Paul Attallah (2009) notes: "[T]he global *Idol* phenomenon tells us not that American culture is homogenizing us but that in a world of increasing competition and fragmented audiences everybody is looking for program formats that are cheap to produce and wildly popular. The truth [. . .] is not that American reality TV dominates us, but that American TV generally now finds itself in the same situation as smaller television markets around the world"(164).

Television is also transnational in terms of its production. It is increasingly manufactured in many countries by many cultural workers as result of what Toby Miller et al. (2004) call the "new international division of cultural labour" (NICL). Television commodities are assembled transnationally within multiple local, regional, and national production zones, whose minor media firms service global Hollywood's major studios. Many TV shows once shot in Los Angeles, California, "runaway" to Canadian cities including Toronto, Vancouver, and Montreal, where cultural labour costs are low and state subsidies are high. Do global Hollywood's runaway productions help or hinder Canada's economic and cultural development goals? What are the benefits and the drawbacks of Canada's attempt to co-produce US TV? Greg Elmer (2002) presents a thoughtful intervention into the runaway production debate. He uses the concept of the "body double" to explore how American TV production companies turn Canadian cities into a "faceless, underpaid, 'stand-in' actor for American landscapes"(431).

American-based media corporations export TV shows (many shot in Canada) to numerous TV markets (as canned programming). There is little to no trade reciprocity between the United States and the many countries to which it exports TV shows. Nevertheless, TV shows do not only flow in one way, from the dominant US media centre to weaker peripheries, spreading a homogeneous global culture based on American nationalist ideology. Globalization entails multidirectional TV flows as well. Canadian TV stations (CBC, CTV, Global, and TVO) are carried by a number of US cable TV providers. Canadian TV shows have been broadcast in the United States too. *Flashpoint, Rookie Blue, Corner Gas, Degrassi: The Next Generation, Little Mosque on The Prairie, Trailer Park Boys, PSI-Factor, Relic Hunter,* and *Stargate SGI* are examples of Canadian TV shows that US viewers watch. And *Slings and Arrows*, "an adult-oriented dramatic series that was resolutely, undeniably about Canada" was exported to the US and global media markets (Beatty and Sullivan 2010).

Next to the United States, Canada is one of the most powerful exporters of TV shows in the world. Like the US, Canada spreads its TV shows worldwide. *Corner Gas*—the most popular Canadian comedy TV show in Canadian history—not only aired in the United States but was also broadcast in 26 more countries. *Rookie Blue* was broadcast by ABC. But NBC-Universal purchased this TV show's broadcasting rights to all international TV markets (excluding Canada, France, Germany, and the US). Does this represent Canadian media imperialism, media globalization, or the inadequacy of both paradigms? How do Canadian and Amercian TV shows enter and become popular in national and transnational markets? Elana Levine's (2009) careful study of the international production history of *Degrassi: The Next Generation* (*DTNG*) examines how and why this Canadian-produced TV show about Canadian youth became successful in Canada, the US, and many other countries. Levine shows how *DTNG* effectively balanced between the particular and the universal in its cultural representation, making it a successful domestic product and global export. *DTNG* was "a critical and commercial success on national and international fronts"(516) that resonated with the sensibilities of Canadian and transnational youth cultures.

What is the local effect of globalizing TV shows? Television scholars have long debated whether or not the globalization of US commercial TV was a force of cultural homogenization or cultural diversification. Canadian cultural nationalists often view the US–Canadian media relationship in terms of a strong imperialist power dominating a weaker periphery's culture. The argument assumes a lot: that pure, unified, and essentially different "American" and "Canadian" cultures exist; that American TV shows are transmission belts for an essentially American culture; that Canadian TV networks are really interested in protecting and promoting Canadian culture (instead of making as much ad money as possible by re-transmitting American TV shows); that Canadian viewers have a shared or collective interest in a system of state subsidizes and protections for capitalist TV networks that ironically fail to "defend" Canada from American imperialist TV.

Ethnographers present a more complex picture of the nexus of global TV and local viewers, in Canada and elsewhere. The movement of American TV shows between nation-state borders almost always involves local interpretation, translation, and adaptation by viewers, who bring their own cultural resources and day-to-day concerns to bear upon the texts of TV shows. While sensitive to the ongoing power of American TNMCs over global TV flows, Jonathan Gray (2007) combines textual analysis with audience ethnography to examine *The Simpsons*' satirical representation of American culture and the transnational audience responses to this globally popular TV show. For Gray, "American television gives us competing images of America and we must study more of them if we are to understand how the world engages in imagining America"(146). Likewise, Canadian TV shows give us competing images of Canada. More critical studies of these national images, with attention to their political economy, textual specificity, and reception contexts, are needed.

Yet, there may still be good reason to maintain a Canadian cultural nationalist policy toolbox. In the era of media globalization, the production and distribution of Canadian TV shows will most likely rely on the maintenance of Canada's cultural policy toolbox. Serra Tinic's (2010) important essay explores a tension within the Canadian TV industry "wherein longstanding goals of nation building compete with economic contingencies in a transnational media environment"(96). Tinic presents a useful synoptic overview of the twenty-first-century Canadian TV industry within the context of global markets, neo-liberal policies, and increasing commercialization. The Canadian TV industry locally reproduces "global generic" TV formats and, through international joint ventures, co-produces TV shows that try to represent the local cultural specificity of Canada. As Canadian and American TV industries continue to undergo deep integration and the commercial logics of advertising-dominated TV limit creativity, state support for public broadcasting (CBC) may successfully enable the production of "diverse" TV shows (distinct from "pluralist" commercial TV shows) "that address controversial issues in all their complexity (and in recognizable Canadian contexts)"(106). Tinic contends that the Canadian state's cultural policy toolbox has been successful at keeping cultural products off the free-trade block in international relations and has enabled the Canadian TV industry to grow and globally compete "without necessarily sacrificing a sense of place or socio-cultural specificity"(111).

The final essay by Tanner Mirrlees presents a political-economy analysis of change and continuity in twenty-first-century American and Canadian TV. Mirrlees presents a systematic overview of the differences between network TV and post-network TV, and engages with current scholarly debates about TV's future. Mirrlees examines the interplay between "what's new," "what's old," and "what's going on now" in twenty-first-century North American TV in the era of corporate and technological convergence. The essay complicates claims about network TV's "death," notions that network TV is undergoing a fundamental "revolution," and assertions that network TV (and society itself) is "irreversibly" or "inevitably" moving toward a scarcely recognizable post-network TV future. Though the network TV landscape is changing, post-network novelties do not signal a radical break with the dominant capitalist logics and political processes of the past. In a period of economic, technological, and cultural change, media conglomerates and the nation-state continue to govern TV.

Works Cited

Adler, T. (2010). "'House' Set To Be Most Popular U.S. TV Export to Europe for 2nd Year." www.deadline.com/2010/01/house-set-to-be-most-popular-u-s-TV-export-to-europe-for-2nd-year-running/

Andrejevic, M. (2008). "Watching Television without Pity: The Productivity of Online Fans." *Television & New Media*, Vol. 9(1): 24–46.

Appadurai, A. (1997). *Modernity at Large*. Minneapolis: University of Minnesota Press.

Armstrong, D. (2006, 4 December). "Peterson Having a 'Gas' Playing Oscar." http://jam.canoe.ca/Television/TV_Shows/C/Corner_Gas/2006/12/04/2621356.html

Attalah, P. (2009). "Review Essay: Reading Television." *Canadian Journal of Communication*, Vol. 34: 163–170.

Beaty, B., and Sullivan, R. (2010). "Surviving the Slings and Arrows of Canadian Television: A Case Study of Success." In L. Shade (Ed.), *Canadian Mediascapes* (pp. 121–34). Toronto: Nelson.

Beltran, L.R. (1978). "Communication and Cultural Domination: USA-Latin American Case." *Media Asia*, Vol. 5(1): 183–92.

Boyd-Barrett, O. (1977). "Media Imperialism: Towards an International Framework for the Analysis of Media Systems." In J. Curran, M. Gurevitch, and J. Woollacott (Eds), *Mass Communication and Society* (pp. 116–35). London: Arnold.

Comor, E. (1997). "The Re-Tooling of American Hegemony: U.S. Foreign Communication Policy from Free Flow to Free Trade." In A. Sreberny-Mohammadi, D. Winseck, J. McKenna, and O. Boyd-Barrett (Eds), *Media in a Global Context: A Reader* (pp. 194–206). New York: Arnold.

Curtin, M. (1997). "Dynasty in Drag: Imagining Global TV." In L. Spigel and M. Curtin (Eds), *The Revolution Wasn't Televised* (pp. 244–62). New York: Routledge.

Curtin, M. (2003). "Media Capitals: Towards the Study of Spatial Flows." *International Journal of Cultural Studies*, Vol. 6 (2): 202–28.

Elmer, G. (2002). "The Trouble with the Canadian 'Body Double' Runaway Productions and Foreign Location Shooting." *Screen*, Vol. 43(4): 423–31.

Fejes, F. (1981). "Media Imperialism: An Assessment." *Media, Culture and Society*, Vol. 3(1): 281–9.

Gray, J. (2007). "Imagining America: *The Simpsons* Go Global." *Popular Communication*, Vol. 5(2): 129–48.

Gwenllian-Jones, S. (2003). "Web Wars: Resistance, Online Fandom, and Studio Censorship." In M. Jancovich and J. Lyons (Eds), *Quality Popular Television: Cult TV, the Industry and Fans* (pp. 163–77). London: British Film Institute.

Hilderbrand, L. (2007). "YouTube: Where Cultural Memory and Copyright Converge." *Film Quarterly*, Vol. 61(1): 48–57.

Horkheimer, M., and Adorno, T.W. (1972). "The Culture Industry: Enlightenment as Mass Deception." In *Dialectic of Enlightenment* (pp. 120–67). New York: Herder and Herder.

Jhally, S. (2000). "Advertising at the Edge of the Apocalypse." In R. Anderson and L. Strate (Eds), *Critical Studies in Media Commercialism* (pp. 27–39). Oxford: Oxford University Press.

Levine, E. (2009). "National Television, Global Market: Canada's *Degrassi: The Next Generation*." *Media, Culture & Society*, Vol. 31(4): 515–31.

McAllister, M.P., and Giglio, J.M. (2005). "The Commodity Flow of U.S. Children's Television." *Critical Studies in Media Communication*, Vol. 22(1): 26–44.

McChesney, R.W. (2002). "The Global Restructuring of Media Ownership." In M. Raboy (Ed.), *Global Media Policy in the New Millennium* (pp. 149–62). Luton: University of Luton Press.

———. (2004). *The Problem with the U.S. Media: Communication Politics in the 21st Century*. London: Monthly Review Press.

Meehan, E.R. (2007). "Understanding How the Popular Becomes Popular: The Role of Political Economy in the Study of Popular Communication." *Popular Communication*, Vol. 5(3): 161–70.

Miller, T., Govil, N., Maxwell, R., and McMurria, J. (2004). *Global Hollywood 2*. London: British Film Institute.

Morley, D. (2000). *Home Territories: Media, Mobility, and Identity*. New York: Routledge.

———. (2005). "Globalization and Cultural Imperialism Reconsidered: Old Questions in New Guises." In J. Curran and D. Morley (Eds), *Media and Cultural Theory* (pp. 31–43). New York: Routledge.

Parks, L., and Kumar, S. (Eds). (2003). *Planet TV: A Global Television Reader*. New York: New York University Press.

Schiller, H. (1976). *Communication and Cultural Domination*. Armonk, NY: M.E. Sharpe.

———. (2000). *Living in the Number One Country: Reflections of a Critic of American Empire*. New York: Seven Stories Press.

Segrave, K. (1998). *American Television Abroad: Hollywood's Attempt to Dominate World Television*. Jefferson: McFarland & Company.

Sinclair, J., Jacka, E., and Cunningham, S. (1996). *New Patterns in Global Television: Peripheral Vision*. Oxford: Oxford University Press.

Strangelove, M. (2010). *Watching YouTube: Extraordinary Videos by Ordinary People*. Toronto: University of Toronto Press.

Straubhaar, J.D. (1991). "Beyond Media Imperialism: Asymmetrical Interdependence and Cultural Proximity." *Critical Studies in Mass Communication*, Vol. 8(1): 39–59.

Thussu, D.K. (2007). *News as Entertainment: The Rise of Global Infotainment*. Los Angeles: Sage.

Tinic, S. (2010). "Walking a Tightrope: The Global Cultural Economy of Canadian Television." In N. Beaty, D. Briton, G. Filax, and R. Sullivan (Eds), *How Canadians Communicate III: Contexts of Canadian Popular Culture* (pp. 95–115). Edmonton, AB: Athabasca University Press.

Tomlinson, J. (1991) *Cultural Imperialism*. Baltimore: The Johns Hopkins University Press.

Waisbord, S. (2004). "McTV: Understanding the Global Popularity of Television Formats." *Television & New Media*, Vol. 5(4): 359–83.

Williams, R. (1974). *Television: Technology and Cultural Form*. London: Fontana.

i. | Commercialism: Audience Commodities, Interactive Audiences, and Advertising

Understanding How the Popular Becomes Popular: The Role of Political Economy in the Study of Popular Communication

Eileen R. Meehan

Political economy is but one of the fields from which scholars of popular communication draw knowledge, methods, and theories. For researchers focusing on commercial artifacts such as television programs (Deery, 2004; Durham, 2003; Weiss, 2005) or on strategic communication such as advertising (Andersen, 1995; McAllister, 1996), political economy contextualizes the objects and practices under study within the larger industrial systems that originate them. That allows scholars to trace market and corporate structures as well as relevant legal and regulatory strictures that set the parameters for expression (Kunz, 2006; Meehan, 2006; Streeter, 1996; Wittebols, 2004). With an understanding of the rules and relationships governing cultural manufacture, we are better positioned to appreciate how the popular becomes popular.

Political economy, then, helps us understand how media conglomerates, media companies, and media-buying corporations work, how they produce the menu of media artifacts, and how we get what we get from the media (Wasko, 2003). This gives us the context from which media commodities originate. For televisual texts, this prepares us to trace the audience's varied negotiations of these texts to understand them as "sites through which meaning about everyday life is shaped, contested, challenged, and reinstated" (Zelizer, 2000). However, the term "audience" takes on different meanings in different contexts.

To illustrate this, I begin by reviewing the debate among political economists over the audience and the commodity audience, and briefly summarize my research on how that commodity audience is defined. I then quickly reference a subsequent debate over theorizing the audience and sketch 10 ordinary approaches that people take to television. I end with a reflection on television as a mundane and hence powerful part of lived experience.

From Audience to Commodity Audience

Thirty years ago, Dallas Smythe published a highly argumentative essay, charging that "Western Marxist analyses have neglected the economic and political significance of mass communication systems" (Smythe, 1977). By this, Smythe meant that most critical media research addressed only the culture side of cultural industries. Within that tradition, scholars deconstructed television programs, films, news articles, and so on, to uncover the ideologies lying below the artifact's surface. For these scholars, media industries produced messages that bore meanings, which generally reinforced the dominant ideology but had potential to be read outside the dominant ideology. In this indirect way, Smythe took on the textual scholarship associated with the Centre for Contemporary Cultural Studies since its founding in Birmingham, England, in 1964.

Noting that advertiser support was the dominant source of revenues for media corporations, Smythe identified the main commodity manufactured by media as the commodity audience. Smythe's analysis took common knowledge about media and put that knowledge into a new context. The television networks' truism that they sold eyeballs to advertisers was more than a clever slogan: Television networks used programming to attract viewers in order to sell them to advertisers that ran their commercials during the programs. Television shows, then, were the "free lunch" that assembled people for sale to advertisers. When Smythe's argument was taken to its logical conclusion, research on the actual content of the programming and what people did with it were irrelevant to television's *raison d'etre*: delivering a commodity audience that was comprised by all viewers.

Smythe went on to argue that watching television indoctrinated viewers, teaching them what to want and what brands to buy. Smythe argued that viewing was a form of work because viewers produced revenues for the watched network and, after viewers purchased advertised goods, for the advertiser. This made viewing economically productive and thus a form of labour. The existence of this working, commodity audience was documented by private companies like the A.C. Nielsen Company.

While insightful and original, Smythe's argument was overdrawn when he applied it to audience-supported media. He was too hasty in positing that firms manufacturing ratings and other measures of the commodity audience exercised no agency. While laying out the abstract relations in the general market for audiences, Smythe ignored the fact that most audiences have neither experience nor analyses of such a market. For television networks, programs may simply be vehicles for commercials and a means to earning high ratings. But for viewers, programs can perform many functions ranging from providing background noise to integrating a person into an interpretive community. Smythe laid bare the root economic relationship in advertiser-supported media as part of the culture industries, but his take on the cultural side was limited by his focus on commercial indoctrination.

Smythe's invitation to debate was taken up by political economists Graham Murdock (1978), Bill Livant (1979, 1982), and Smythe (1978) as well as Sut Jhally (1982). Murdock's response was the most significant, trimming back Smythe's claims to cover only advertiser-supported media and arguing for research that would illuminate both the media's political economy and people's lived experience of media artifacts (Murdock, 1978).

Throughout these exchanges, our colleagues assumed that everybody was part of the commodity audience and that companies measuring the commodity audience were bound by social science and market discipline to produce the most accurate numbers possible. If those assumptions were true for national television ratings, then the programs with the highest Nielsen ratings would be America's most popular programs. With millions of viewers every week, those TV shows should be able to tell us something about the American people and their culture. If so, then commercial television's hits ought to be truly popular and reflect their viewers' culture—just as many idealist cultural scholars had argued (Berger, 1976; Newcomb, 1974).

Commodity Audience and Commodity Ratings

Were those assumptions reasonable? To test them, I undertook research on the political economy of ratings (Meehan, 1986a, 1986b, 1990, 1993, 2006). Here, I will briefly summarize my main findings, starting with a bare-bones account of the television industry.

The television industry comprises multiple markets for equipment, programming, audiences, stations, cable channels, and so on. For our discussion, the relevant markets are focused on national ratings, national audiences, and nationally distributed programming. National ratings describe the commodity audience and guide networks' and cable channels' decisions about the prices that they charge. Ratings also guide advertisers' decisions regarding the purchase of audiences for exposure to commercials. Networks and cable channels use ratings to select programs for cancellation and to commission new programs. Creative personnel, either on contract or employed by networks, cable, and independent production companies, model new programs on current hits. The connection between the market for audiences and the market for programs is the ratings.

If we are all in the commodity audience, then the industrial definition of that audience should be universal and, by extension, everybody should be equally valuable. Neither claim has been historically true. From the beginning, the focus has been on bona fide consumers. For example, when RCA and CBS introduced innovations for television, advertisers were reluctant to abandon network radio given its successful track record in delivering consumers as measured by A.C. Nielsen's metered ratings. RCA, CBS, and their advertisers agreed to continue using ratings derived from Nielsen's radio homes as the standards by which television deals would be made. This ensured the smooth transition from radio to television, defined television as radio with pictures, and significantly limited the impact of television's early adopters on television programming. However, the arrangement ensured that the commodity audience would remain stable.

Times have changed but ratings are still commodities and the market for ratings is still characterized by continuities in demand for measurements of consumers and discontinuities in demand over the price that advertisers should pay networks to get those consumers. But the values attached to types of consumers have changed. In the 1950s and 1960s, advertisers attached most value to the overall numbers of viewers reported by Nielsen, which left CBS consistently ahead of RCA's NBC. In the 1960s, RCA launched a campaign to persuade advertisers that viewers, especially males, between 18–34 years old were the most valuable, noting that NBC excelled in attracting such members of the Nielsen sample. When that sample was turned over between 1963 and 1970 to emphasize younger, more urban viewers, advertisers and all three networks targeted 18–34 viewers in earnest. Since the 1970s, with more middle-class women in the workforce, advertisers have expressed interest in upscale women 18–34.

In the 1980s, Nielsen expanded its metered sample to include cable channels, thus depressing networks' ratings. By the 1990s, white males 18–34 in upscale households subscribing to cable emerged as the subgroup most prized by advertisers. Currently, Nielsen Media Research is responding to demands from advertisers and owners of networks and cable channels to expand the number of viewers aged 18–24 in the People Meter sample by measuring college students living in dormitories, fraternities, sororities, and off-campus housing.

Even this short sketch of the political economy of ratings indicates that all television viewers are not in television's commodity audience and that some parts of the commodity audience are more valuable than others. This implies that networks as well as cable channels will cancel programs that do a poor job of attracting the most valuable subgroups in the commodity audience regardless of a program's overall popularity with the commodity audience. Given that new programs usually recombine elements of programs considered ratings hits (Gitlin, 1983), we can expect that new series will be designed principally for those most valuable subgroups.

By definition, then, the commodity audience is different from the audience, and programs that are popular with its most valuable parts may not be popular with the corresponding portion of television's viewership. Historically and currently, the ratings monopolists' willingness to measure whomever is demanded means that ratings are governed by the market, not by social science. While an unreliable indicator of popular tastes, commodity ratings are a reasonable measure of commercial tastes—of the genres, narrative forms, character types, and iconic elements that advertisers and program providers identify as viable environments for advertisements and as reliable bait for the most valuable subgroups in the commodity audience.

Varieties of Televisual Experience

With the commodity audience debate mostly settled by 1982, questions regarding different conceptualizations of the audience continued to engage scholars. In 1988, Martin Allor critiqued administrative, political economic, post-structuralist, feminist, culturalist, and postmodernist notions of the audience. His purpose was to propose an epistemological framework that would "deconstruct the 'audience's' unity into constituent and constituting moments" in order to reconstruct the concept of the audience as "the unity of the diverse" (Allor, 1988a). The lively debate that ensued was highly theoretical (Fiske, 1988; Hartley, 1988; Lull, 1988; and Newman, 1988) as was Allor's response (Allor, 1988b). Nearly 20 years later, popular communication research on people's relationships with and viewing of television continue to draw from these traditions. The work suggests a variety of experiences with television and hence of ways that we can be audiences (Acosta-Alzuru, 2003; Bird, 2003; Bury, 2003; Hagen and Wasko, 2000; Mayer, 2003; Seiter, 2000; Wasko, 2001). Below I sketch 10 ways in which we approach television as users, drop-in viewers, channel surfers, multiple screeners, casual viewers, focused viewers, engaged viewers, members of interpretive communities, fan-consumers, and self-programmers.

While terms like audience, viewership, active audience, and interpretive community are common, they suggest a person or group of people who are paying attention to what is presented on the screen. Yet, individuals may do other things with television, a fact that mightily worries raters and advertisers. Sometimes we turn on our sets and leave the room, using television to provide background noise. Other times, we use television as a secondary or tertiary activity. While preparing dinner, conversing, doing the crossword puzzle, cleaning up, grading papers, and so on, we turn on a nearby television and ignore it. These sorts of uses fall short of the attention implied by terms like television watcher, viewer, or audience. In such cases, I suggest that we call ourselves television users because we are using television in ways that require no attention and no engagement.

Occasionally when pursuing other activities and apparently ignoring television, we pay some attention to the soundtrack, which uses conventional cues to indicate when something interesting is going to happen. Then we watch the interesting bit, returning to our other activities when it is over. This suggests a minimal level of attention as well as sufficient mastery of television conventions to both recognize when the program is worth watching and to make some sense out of the snippet to which we actually pay attention. That in turn indicates sufficient competence in decoding television texts and familiarity with American commercial culture that we can drop-in and drop-out at will. In this circumstance, I suggest we call ourselves drop-in viewers.

Technological change has provided us with two other ways to watch television: channel surfing and multiple screen viewing. By using a remote control, viewers can "surf" during commercials or whenever searching for something to watch. While some surfers eventually settle on a channel, one can imagine others surfing and resurfing the entire array. In another technological shift, sets have been engineered to show views from multiple channels while still displaying a large image from a single channel allowing us to see (but not hear) different programs simultaneously. Perhaps the best known multi-screeners are sports fans.

When we watch television casually, we pay enough attention to make sense of the program, identify with its characters, and enjoy it. This sort of viewing allows one to admire the product placements, costumes, set decoration, props, or incidental music and perhaps decide to purchase these available goods or licensed merchandise via the show's website, the owning corporation's retail site, or another retailer.

Casual viewing means that we are not so engaged with the characters and narrative that we resent the commercial interruptions. Indeed, our enjoyment of the program may put us in a receptive frame of mind when the commercials appear. The casual enjoyment of a program is a form of reading with the grain: the episode provides its familiar surprises without us having to work very hard. We have sufficient mastery of television's codes and conventions to "get" the show as a piece of entertainment. Perhaps it's very good entertainment but, in the larger scheme of life, it's just entertainment. Again, this level of engagement demonstrates competence with the codes and conventions of American commercial culture. When we view casually, we acquire enough familiarity to chat informally about an episode at work, with friends and family, or in passing conversations with relative strangers. Casual viewing may well be the preferred modus operandi by advertisers, owners of networks and channels, and Nielsen Media Research.

When viewers like a program but dislike a particular character or story, we may selectively ignore what we don't like and attend to those characters or segments that we do like. Viewers who adopt this strategy essentially rework a program to better suit themselves. I call this focused viewing. Program producers use ensemble casts and multiple story arcs to try to manage focused viewers within the commodity audience.

Engaged viewing is a different matter. The engaged viewer is absorbed with a television series. Consistently watching and rewatching episodes, the engaged viewer develops considerable expertise in the series' texts and intertexts, and may seek further information regarding the series' creator, actors, and creative personnel. Through these activities, the engaged viewer becomes an interpreter of the series, generating close readings of episodes. Commercials truly become interruptions and may cause resentment.

When an engaged viewer connects with similarly committed viewers, they may build an interpretive community. Members of an interpretive community organize part of their social life around the symbolic universe envisioned in the program. They extend that universe through personal interactions, group meetings, conventions, and media artifacts ranging from newsletters to semi-professional videos. Most interpretive communities focus on explication, elaboration, and enactment of the symbolic universe and members accrue social status for their expertise.

Such activities are expensive, a fact that has attracted companies intent on substituting fan consumerism for individual and communal production. Television's Big Five—Disney (ABC), General Electric (NBC), National Amusements (CBS and co-owner CW), News Corporation (Fox and My Network), and Time Warner (co-owner CW)—routinely promote programs on their websites via chat rooms, scheduled access to creative personnel, games, contests, clips, episodes for download, and licensed merchandise offers. Networks have fostered engaged viewing through programs with convoluted plots like ABC's *Lost* and *Desperate Housewives* (both 2004–present). The commercialization of engaged viewing and engaged viewers has led Nielsen Media Research to design a way to test if engaged viewing increases viewers' recall of commercials. When firms target engaged viewers as fan-consumers, the companies are mainly focused on shaping how these people spend their disposable income, not how they interpret episodes.

Finally, with VCRs and DVDs, we can watch television without watching what's currently scheduled. As self-programmers, we can view homemade or home-duplicated materials, time-shift television programs, and use prerecorded materials to create our own schedules. Besides the menu of Hollywood movies and old TV shows available for purchase or rental is an array of television and film productions from sources that are international, independent, subcultural, alternative, or oppositional. Having put our selection on the screen, however, we must then decide how to use or watch it.

Television as Ordinary

Of the 10 roles sketched above, only the engaged viewer and the interpretive community seems poised to closely read the televisual text, nevermind contesting or challenging its preferred meanings. The rest of these roles seem profoundly mundane and open to us whenever we wish to assume them. Little work is required to select a program, change channels, drop-in for a few moments, decide to purchase licensed merchandise, or leave the room. The mundane is also targeted by the ratings system: a person's set tuning and viewing status is measured; casual enjoyment and focused engagement are irrelevant.

That this ordinariness undergirds much of our relationship to television may well be the key to television as an agent of socialization and enculturation. Television's position as mundane makes it largely unthreatening, requiring little mindfulness from its users and viewers. As "mere entertainment" that can be easily ignored and still understood, television provides an excellent environment for incidental learning. The symbolic cohesion necessary for each program to be a vehicle for advertising sets up a world view that celebrates commercialism, consumerism, and ultimately contemporary capitalism. When we use or view television as unsuspicious watchers, we expose ourselves to this worldview, which influences us from infancy to senescence.

But, as popular communication research demonstrates, influence is not the same as control. Engaged viewers can regard television with a critical consciousness that does contest, challenge, and struggle with its visions. Cultivating such a consciousness is not part of television's industrial agenda as our analyses of commodity ratings, the commodity audience, and commodity programming make clear. Nor is critical consciousness inherent in our 10 ways to approach television in everyday life: close readers are not necessarily oppositional readers. Our ability to achieve critical consciousness remains rooted in the intersection between the political economy in which we live, the collectivities with whom we live, the sense that we make of lived contradictions, and the agency that we exercise together. In other words, critical consciousness is rooted in both the abstract relationships and lived experiences that constitute our mundane world. This makes dialogue between scholars of popular communication and political economy crucial.

References

Acosta-Alzuru, C. (2003). Tackling the issues: Meaning making in a telenovela. *Popular Communication, 1*(4), 193–215.

Allor, M. (1988a). Relocating the site of the audience. *Critical Studies in Mass Communication, 5*(3), 217–33.

———. (1988b). Theoretical engagements. *Critical Studies in Mass Communication, 5*(3), 251–4.

Andersen, R. (1995). *Consumer culture and TV programming.* Boulder, CO: Westview Press.

Berger, A.A. (1976). *The TV guided American.* New York: Walker & Company.

Bird, S.E. (2003). *The audience in everyday life: Living in a media world.* New York: Routledge.

Bury, R. (2003). Stories for boys girls: female fans read *The X-Files. Popular Communication, 1*(4), 217–42.

Deery, J. (2004). Reality TV as advertainment. *Popular Communication, 2*(1), 1–20.

Durham, M. G. (2003). The girling of America: Critical reflections on gender and popular communication. *Popular Communication, 1*(1), 23–31.

Fiske, J. (1988). Meaningful moments. *Critical Studies in Mass Communication, 5*(3), 217–33.

Gitlin, T. (1983). *Inside prime time.* New York: Pantheon.

Hagen, I., & Wasko, J. (2000). *Consuming audiences? Production and reception in media research.* Cresskill, NJ: Hampton Press.

Hartley, J. (1988). The real world of audiences. *Critical Studies in Mass Communication, 5*(3), 217–33.

Jhally, S. (1982). Probing the blindspot: The audience commodity. *Canadian Journal of Political and Social Theory, 6*(1–2), 204–10.

Kunz, W.M. (2006). *Culture conglomerates: Consolidation in the motion picture and television industries.* Lanham, MD: Rowman and Littlefield.

Livant, B. (1979). The audience commodity. *Canadian Journal of Political and Social Theory, 3*(1), 91–106.

———. (1982). Working at watching: A reply to Sut Jhally. *Canadian Journal of Political and Social Theory, 6*(1–2), 211–15.

Lull, J. (1988). The audience as nuisance. *Critical Studies in Mass Communication, 5*(3), 217–33.

Mayer, V. (2003). Living telenovelas/telenovelizing life: Mexican-American girls' identities and transnational telenovelas. *Journal of Communication, 53*(3), 479–95.

McAllister, M.P. (1996). *The commercialization of American culture: New advertising, control, and democracy.* Thousand Oaks, CA: Sage Publications.

Meehan, E.R. (1986a). Conceptualizing culture as commodity. *Critical Studies in Mass Communication*, *3*(4), 448–57.

———. (1986b). Critical theorizing on broadcast history. *Journal of Broadcasting and Electronic Media*, *30*(4), 393–411.

———. (1990). Why we don't count: The commodity audience. In P. Mellencamp (Ed.), *Logics of television: Essays in cultural criticism* (pp. 117–37). London: BFI Press.

———. (1993). Heads of households and ladies of the house: The political economy of gender, genre, and ratings, 1929–1990. In W. Solomon and R. McChesney (Eds), *Ruthless criticism: New perspectives in U.S. communication history* (pp. 204–21). Minneapolis: University of Minnesota Press.

———. (2006). *Why TV is not our fault: Television programming, viewers, and who's really in control.* Lanham, MD: Rowman and Littlefield.

Murdock, G. (1978). Blindspots about western Marxism: A reply to Dallas Smythe, *Canadian Journal of Political and Social Theory*, *2*(2), 109–19.

Newcomb, H. (1974). *TV: The most popular art.* Garden City, NY: Anchor Press.

Newman, K. (1988). On openings and closings. *Critical Studies in Mass Communication*, *5*(3), 217–33.

Seiter, E. (2000). Making distinctions in television audience research: Case study of a troubling interview. In H. Newcomb (Ed.) *Television: The critical view* (pp. 495–518), 6th edn. New York: Oxford University Press.

Smythe, D. (1977). Communications: Blindspot of western Marxism. *Canadian Journal of Political and Social Theory*, *1*(3), 1–27.

———. (1978). Rejoinder to Graham Murdock, *Canadian Journal of Political and Social Theory*, *2*(2), 120–9.

Streeter, T. (1996). *Selling the air: A critique of the policy of commercial broadcasting in the United States.* Chicago, IL: University of Chicago Press.

Wasko, J. (2001). *Understanding Disney: The manufacture of fantasy.* London: Polity Press/Blackwell Publishers.

———. (2003). *How Hollywood works.* Thousand Oaks, CA: Sage.

Weiss, D. (2005). Constructing the queer "I": Performativity, citationality, and desire in *Queer Eye for the Straight Guy. Popular Communication*, *3*(2), 73–95.

Wittebols, J. (2004). *The soap opera paradigm: Television programming and corporate priorities.* Lanham, MD: Rowman and Littlefield.

Zelizer, B. (2000). Popular communication in the contemporary age. In W. Gundykunst (Ed.). *Communication yearbook 24* (pp. 297–316). Thousand Oaks, CA: Sage.

YouTube: Where Cultural Memory and Copyright Converge

Lucas Hilderbrand

Let's begin with a clip: William Shatner's infamous 1986 appearance on *Saturday Night Live* when he told a convention of Trekkies to "get a life" during a sketch. This scene signalled a defining moment in media reflexivity and public awareness of fan cultures, as well as inspired the opening of Henry Jenkins's 1992 book *Textual Poachers*. The first time I presented some of the material that follows, I used a clip of this sketch as an illustration of content uploaded to YouTube that reflects and replays pop-cultural memory. But by the time I reworked my presentation for a conference about a month later, the clip had disappeared. Perhaps something like this has happened to you, too.

YouTube has become the go-to website for finding topical and obscure streaming video clips, but everyday experiences also indicate how fleeting such access can be. Viewers and academics have quickly come to treat the site as an informal archive of television texts. Yet, as I argue in this article, even though YouTube and sites like it have expanded access to a rich spectrum of such material and suggested the potential for democratization of media memories and flows, they also introduce new ways to regulate and deny access to content under the guise of enforcing copyright protection.

Web Video

At the forefront of web video, YouTube has been called "viral," "revolutionary," and a "phenomenon." Within a few short months of the streaming video website's public launch in December 2005, tens of millions of visitors daily used the site to access television clips online and, in many cases, to post some of their own. Further marking YouTube the medium of its moment, *Time* magazine named "You" (referencing YouTube) the Person of the Year for 2006.[1] Rather than being promoted by multimillion-dollar branding campaigns by major networks or tech firms, YouTube became popular by word of mouth—which in the Internet era means forwarded email links, blogs, and MySpace profiles. (Or, for those older than the "Me Media" generation, articles in the *New York Times* or elsewhere.) The videos available on YouTube include home videos and remixes, up-to-the-minute television excerpts, music videos, trailers, commercials, and highlights from television history posted by users—and increasingly by producers and the networks themselves. (For commentary on the site's content, see the box "The Clip Canon.")

Despite all the hype surrounding the speed of YouTube's popularity, television–computer convergence has been a long-expected prospect. In the mid-1990s, tech companies, networks, and Internet service providers were already speculating about their future merger and the resulting potential for exact target marketing.[2] Microsoft purchased WebTV in 1996 but failed to capture a media monopoly to complement its software empire. In the intervening decade, digital developments such as DVDs, DVRs (Digital Video Recorders, such as TiVo), video-on-demand services, peer-to-peer (p2p) file-sharing networks, and iPods have contributed to the changes in how viewers receive and watch television. The swiftness with which the stakes surrounding YouTube have changed in its first year and a half demonstrate just how difficult it is to rigorously assess cultural and technological developments in their present moment. For instance, an otherwise insightful book about "the transition from network to networked TV" published as recently as 2006 completely missed the YouTube phenomenon.[3] With the expansion of high-speed connections and growing computer memory capacities, Internet video distribution—from BitTorrent downloading to shortform streaming—has at long last become viable on a massive scale. Yet, when the promise of television online finally became palpable, it was not in the way corporations and the digirati had predicted in the 1990s. Indeed, if the histories of communications technologies have taught us anything, audiences rarely adopt and use media in the ways they were originally envisioned. YouTube, like popular p2ps before it, was developed by a couple of young guys who wrote the basic programming code and millions of home viewers who developed its uses.[4]

YouTube and similar sites offer new and remediating relationships to texts that indicate changes and acceleration of spectatorial consumption. YouTube's success has been attributed in large part to its user-friendliness. Users do not need to log-in in order to view clips, and videos start streaming as soon as the webpage loads, so there is no need to worry about software compatibility, downloading files, or even clicking the "play" button. On the interface, videos appear with a scrollable sidebar of other videos that search results have concluded are of related interest, so users can click through from one clip to another without doing multiple searches. This mode of hyperlinking effectively replicates channel-surfing and introduces non-narrative seriality to the viewing experience. Frequently, as well, searches for an iconic or controversial moment of television will yield multiple clips of the same content, with minor variations in image quality, running time, titling, keywords, or spellings. Deciding which clip among the batch to view may depend upon clues such as the thumbnail image or running time (to get the most complete or, contrarily, the most efficient clip) or simply the rules of peer-review popularity (users give clips star ratings, and the number of times each clip has been viewed is also tracked for users' ready reference). Beyond its ease of use, however, its vast collection seems to be the primary draw.

YouTube has contributed to a culture of the clip. The specific moments a viewer wants to see can now be searched and accessed without the hassles of watching live broadcasts, making recordings, or waiting through exposition and commercial breaks. In the process, it fosters a new temporality of immediate gratification for audiences. As soon as the red bar across the bottom of the playback frame indicates how much of the streaming video is ready to view, users can actually drag the cursor to scan ahead to arrive at the moment they seek even quicker. Suddenly, three minutes can seem like a life-sucking eternity, and I, for one, am prone to skipping ahead or moving on before a clip finishes if it is the least bit tedious.

Although I am making a claim for the site's centrality in accessing historical clips, instantaneity is one of its primary virtues. Users post television clips almost as soon as they have been broadcast, which allows viewers who missed a politician's faux pas or bits of incisive satire to see the relevant material in time to participate in water-cooler conversations. Of course, rights owners can and do insist that such popular clips be taken down almost as quickly. It has become fairly common for blog readers to click through an embedded clip from the previous night's television broadcast, only to find that the footage has been taken offline in the few hours that elapsed between the post and the reader's attempted playback. This has become so common that bloggers even signal the likelihood of this outcome, by suggesting readers click through while they can. Even newsworthy public events are not immune. Perhaps the most publicized and outrageous single take-down to date came when public affairs network C-SPAN ordered the removal of Stephen Colbert's tongue-in-cheek speech at the White House Correspondents' Dinner in May 2006, which had been watched 2.7 million times within 48 hours on YouTube and which clearly satirized the state of political journalism.[5] This viewership statistic suggests that more viewers saw the speech on YouTube than during its original transmission, and that, as outrageous as it seems, even official governmental events can be subject to restrictive copyright claims. On the flip side, the site has also been used as a vehicle for grassroots alternative media to expose political gaffes, corporate exploitation, police violence, or the realities of the battlefront in Iraq. Once publicized on YouTube, these events and issues at times get taken up in the mainstream press. In many cases, this feeds the greater good, though at other times a few seconds of video can cause such a scandal that they may ruin a campaign or damage an entire political career. And, rather than diversifying what audiences see, topical viral videos (viral in the sense of epidemic) reinforce the cultural dominance of specific media clips.

The high viewership of short-lived clips—such as those mentioned in blogs or even reported in the traditional press—reintroduce the dialectic of ubiquity and ephemerality that has, historically, been the model of much of popular culture, especially broadcasting. The intervention of home video recording opened up the possibility for home audiences to catch up on live broadcasts that they may have missed or of vintage moments they wish to re-experience. Videotape induced audience expectations for access—whether for home video releases of theatrical feature films approximately six months after their debuts or for film classics, video art, or television shows that someone, somewhere must have recorded. The Internet, Google, and YouTube have accelerated and exaggerated these expectations for availability. But YouTube reminds audiences that such content, once in their grasp, can still be temporary. The initial novelty and glee at finding an unexpected clip soon gives way to frustration and disbelief when searches for something else come up matchless—or, increasingly, when a desired clip has been de-activated for copyright violation. Perhaps more than at any time before, audiences and users seem to reject the content industry's proprietary claims, complaining when a video goes offline or even reposting new versions of formerly disabled clips. Expectations for access have developed into a sense of access entitlement.

Despite many unrealized promises for digital media in the past decade or so, a surprising number of digital technology advocates and scholars remain celebratory in their rhetoric that technology has profoundly changed our culture, and continue to claim that in the near future all content will be digital, interactive, and shared. As a reporter for *Wired* magazine asserted, "Without being overly simplistic or melodramatic, the state of the Old Commercial Broadcasting Model can be summarized like this: a spiraling vortex of ruin."[6] I am far more skeptical. For mass audiences, broadcast, cable, and satellite television still dominate (not least because of class issues such as the digital divide—that is, uneven access to technology—or even the bourgeois pleasures of narrative structures and slick production values), and network content will continue to feed these streams. And I suspect that for many audiences, network content—new or old—still drives users to YouTube, and amateur content is discovered along the way, through the suggested links, alternate search results, or forwarded emails.

Although some cultural critics have predicted that YouTube will displace the established corporate media, YouTube's popularity relies at least in part upon recirculated selections of mainstream media.[7] As has been historically apparent with entertainment technologies, initial novelty often gives way to familiar content. Convergence usually means content redundancy across platforms, and YouTube perhaps relies more on mainstream media for source material than it threatens to displace it.[8] Given this situation, the conflict becomes not only about what media audiences watch, but who can control and profit from it.

Cultural Memory

YouTube has given renewed public lives to thousands or even millions of now-"classic" moments from television, and offers access to a rich spectrum of important footage of history-shaping events and of otherwise unavailable or obscure nuggets of popular culture. Available clips range from CNN coverage of the *Challenger* space shuttle explosion (1986) to footage of Los Angeles police beating Rodney King (1991), from the Disney-animated *The Story of Menstruation* (1946) to Crispin Glover playing up his eccentricities on *Late Night with David Letterman* (1987). In cases such as commercials and talk-show highlights, significant but small-scale ephemera has historically been the hardest content for fans or even historians to track down and re-experience. This Internet library has fed scholarly as well as nostalgic uses.

Culled from users' personal collections of recordings and productions, the site's videos and its search engine offer some evidence of what from television's past now constitutes our cultural memory—a concept that suggests the idiosyncratic ways that personal experience, popular culture, and historical narratives intersect. So much of our personal and social memories are comprised of televised news coverage, commercials, or scenes in bad sit-coms. YouTube allows users to seek out the media texts that have shaped them and that would otherwise be forgotten in "objective" histories. Like memory (cultural or personal), YouTube is dynamic. It is an ever-changing clutter of stuff from the user's past, some of which disappears and some of which remains overlooked, while new material is constantly being accrued and new associations or (literally, hypertext) links are being made. The images are often hazy but may suffice to induce recall or to fill in where we could only previously imagine how things were from written or word-of-mouth accounts. One of the dangers of seeing once-formative content on YouTube is being underwhelmed in the present; such disillusioning effects are probably only enhanced by the low resolution of the video stream. But these disappointments of history alternate with delightful discoveries.

YouTube introduces a new model of media access and amateur historiography that, while the images are imperfect and the links are impermanent, nonetheless realizes much of the Internet's potential to circulate rare, ephemeral, and elusive texts. As documents, the low-resolution postings to YouTube fall far short of archival preservation, and excerpting changes the flow and format of broad/cable-cast content. Archivists and librarians have criticized the site not only for circulating low-resolution copies of unauthorized content but also for skewing general perceptions that sites such as YouTube may render traditional archives irrelevant and introduce unrealistic demands for access.

YouTube functions both as a portal of cultural memory and as a concept, but it does not operate as an archive in the proper sense of the word. Perceptions of its popularity have had a snowball effect on YouTube's prevalence for both uploads and streaming, thus making it the de facto repository for video clips—at least until they are deactivated. YouTube is only the most famous of a proliferation of web video sites, but as the best-known, it has become a centralized repository and probably the first place users search for content. It has not only become the default site, but it is also becoming the generic term for conversational references to web video clips and sharing—much the way Barbie, Xerox, Kleenex, or Coke can be used to describe a type of product beyond a specific brand name.

Memory media are mediated—and look it, as old video clips seem to exhibit a surface haze of worn old video. Streaming clips on YouTube reflect the aesthetics of access; reduced resolution becomes a trade-off for quick and easy use—an issue that has recurred across various technologies, from photocopies to VHS tapes to MP3s. In a word, YouTube clips look and sound terrible. Off-air recordings get compressed, and source webcams and cameraphone images look blocky and jerky from the moment of creation; delays in streaming exacerbate the effects of both. Videos that may look acceptable in miniature reveal low resolution if blown up to full-screen. And digitization of analog source recordings take colour saturation down a few notches while introducing pixelation. The YouTube recordings further remediate content and inscribe its sources onto the recordings. The homemade status of many television clips is marked by station identification logos in the corner of the frame and, in the cases of older recordings, VHS artifacts such as rainbows of discoloration and signal drop-out. Such artifacts and alterations indexically signal the videos' sources and demonstrate bootleg aesthetics.[9] Clips that circulate beyond YouTube, as embedded videos on other websites, feature branded YouTube watermarks. The identities of uploaders and comment posters are also inscribed on the interface, so that there is some record of where the footage came from and where it has gone.

If YouTube can be said to facilitate communication, it is in ways that emphasize video over epistolary exchange. Friends, family, and co-workers can easily email hotlinks for already-posted videos of cute critters or comical blasts from the past to each other, and typically do so with minimal if any written explanations; forwarding YouTube videos can sustain email contact between people with pre-established relationships without the effort of writing personal narratives. In terms of forging new connections, two prevalent types of user-generated posts have emerged: first, talking-head webcam videos of users spouting off extemporaneous rants in response to the clips they watch and, second, more elaborate parodies of popular videos. Despite designated spaces on the YouTube interface for descriptions about videos and for feedback from viewers, the potential for written communication via the site seems to be mostly unrealized. Browsing the posted user comments reveals a lot of plugs for posters' own clips, spam, chain letters, and racist or homophobic flames (insults). When users do make comments, they are typically brief and not terribly enlightening, along the lines of "lol. very funny!!!!!!" Written dialogue remains the domain of blogs and chat rooms.

As a forum for self-syndication and post-broadcast networking, YouTube has elicited considerable discourses of "community" and "sharing." Co-founder Chad Hurley has commented, "People like to share experiences . . . We started it with the idea of solving a problem—how to share video online with your friends."[10] A market analyst was quoted in the *New York Times* as saying, "'YouTube figured out what Google and Yahoo and Microsoft and all the others in the marketplace didn't,' she said. 'It's not about the video. It's about creating a community around the video.'"[11] As its slogan "Broadcast Yourself" suggests, YouTube fosters exhibitionistic and narcissistic amateur video streams; it is tempting to suggest that user-generated content on YouTube is more about promoting oneself than about exchanging ideas with others. Clips that excerpt or rework texts from TV's past, in contrast, indicate a desire to reclaim a shared cultural memory. And, of course, these are the clips most at risk of being taken offline by their rights owners.

Copyright

Copyright has been at the centre of public attention to YouTube, and it sets the terms on which much of personal (and scholarly) access to media texts will be available. It is also the major question that has overshadowed YouTube's success. How long will YouTube survive in an age of aggressive anti-piracy campaigns and lawsuits—content industry movements that have largely been supported by Congress and the courts? Google purchased YouTube for $1.6 billion in October 2006, making it *worth* suing.[12] Videos may easily be found through keyword searches on the site or simply through a general web search on Google. In this sense, its design as a search engine matched Google's business model and allowed for integration with Google's own fledgling video databases when the company acquired YouTube.

With all the attention YouTube has received as the central portal of web video clips, it had seemed inevitable that some media conglomerate or other would sue YouTube for copyright infringement. If anything, it actually took longer than one might have expected. In March 2007, Viacom sued YouTube and Google for $1 billion.[13] The lawsuit followed Viacom's failed attempts to negotiate a co-operative deal (negotiations reportedly continue concurrent with litigation) and hundreds of thousands of requests for YouTube to disable clips of Viacom properties *The Daily Show*, *The Colbert Report*, and *South Park*. Advocates of digital content sharing and remixing have pointed out the irony that Stephen Colbert repeatedly referenced and encouraged YouTube clips and remixes on his show. Whether or not Viacom sees some financial reward for its litigation, this is the type of case that seems bound for the Supreme Court, to follow in the wake of its major precedents: *Sony v. Universal* (1984, known colloquially as "the Betamax case") and *MGM v. Grokster* (2005, which shut down Kazaa-like p2p network Grokster for enabling unauthorized music sharing).

Copyright law was developed to stimulate publication of new works for the edification of culture. At base, copyright allows rights owners the right of publication and, in exchange for offering cultural works for public consumption, of profiting from such publication. This form of legal regulation was intended to foster a vibrant and continuing stream of new cultural works, though legislation and court rulings have increasingly favoured rights owners over their audiences of late. Numerous copyright scholars have suggested that such shifts have betrayed the law's original purpose. For analog media, content owners not only financially benefit from publication, but they also have considerable control in deciding how content will enter the marketplace.

The same basic issues are at stake, if complicated, in the era of digital networks when peer-sharing and video streaming are more or less indistinguishable from publication. In many cases, rights owners request to have streaming YouTube videos disabled not necessarily because they are competing with owners' own residual marketing but because they want to maintain some kind of control over what is publicly accessible and how it is distributed. Digital technologies and policies have facilitated rapid and more drastic methods of disabling the documents that feed cultural memories and enable scholarship. Hardware is now regularly engineered to prevent copying and to disable unauthorized uses, and the 1998 Digital Millennium Copyright Act (DMCA) forbids hacking encryption technologies and allows for offended parties to demand that online content be taken offline without due process to prove infringement. As Lawrence Lessig has suggested, in such situations the layers of "code"—the hardware, the software, and the content—are typically all owned or controlled by corporations with vested interests in regulating them.[14]

Although it should perhaps go without saying, copyright should concern anyone interested in film and media because it has long been the primary legal means of regulating access to texts. When access is restricted or forbidden, not only do viewers lose out, but textual scholars can be severely inhibited as well when key texts simply are not available to be studied or taught. I would go so far as to suggest that YouTube has had a major impact on how television history can be taught by opening up access to a wealth of clips that professors may have longed for but been unable to locate; the site is in credibly useful for reference, just as the Internet Movie Database and Wikipedia—despite (overblown) criticisms of their accuracy—conveniently fill in such information as credits, dates, and historical events. Furthermore, students can make curriculum peer-produced by forwarding relevant links to their instructors and classmates.

To be clear, I am suggesting that YouTube does not promote willy-nilly piracy but rather enables access to culturally significant texts that would otherwise be elusive and the ability to repurpose videos in the creation of new derivative works. In other words, the site and its users (and I) advocate for what copyright is supposed to do. Furthermore, litigation—whether based upon a legitimate legal claim or merely a scare tactic and form of economic intimidation—can have inhibiting effects far more sweeping than the specific rule of law. Copyright matters, and YouTube has become one of the most prominent and popular sites where what's actually legal law is being contested and potentially curtailed.

In terms of copyright, the user-uploaded content streamed via YouTube falls into roughly three categories: copied, appropriative, and original. The copied texts derive primarily from users' television recordings, clipped into bite-sized portions without intended alteration of the source material other than excerpting. This is perhaps the most sought-after category, especially for catching up with topical TV moments or nostalgic clips. Appropriated clips often include copyrighted music or footage used in the service of new derivative works; such uses range from amateur music videos as users dance and lip-synch to popular songs in their bedrooms, to complex fan, slash, or culture-jamming re-edits of footage. Original content would mean any video footage that does not incorporate previously copyrighted works, such as home movies, video diaries, and small-scale productions. There are also innumerable versions, imitations, and parodies of both corporate and amateur content. All three categories are prevalent, including original content, which helps bolster the claim that the site can and is used for substantial non-infringing uses. In many cases, what appears to be the same clip has been uploaded by different users, thus blurring distinctions between authorship, ownership, and distribution rights.

In the wake of court rulings against the p2ps Napster and Grokster, the copyright crisis has haunted otherwise celebratory predictions of the website. In the Betamax case, which legalized home recording with VCRs, the Supreme Court came to three significant conclusions: first, that home video recorders must be allowed because of their potential for non-infringing uses; second, that the dominant uses of the machines were for time-shifting (recording television programs off air for belated viewing), which the Supreme Court considered fair use; and third, that Sony could not be held liable for its customers' misuses of the machines. The court saw fit to expand the definition of fair use—reproduction of copyrighted content for educational uses—to include personal consumptive uses as a way to broaden the potential audiences for television programming and serve a broader public interest. This ruling expanded the domain of fair use beyond orthodox interpretations, thus setting a curious but progressive precedent. The judges were clearly aware that some home tapers did, in fact, elide or fast-forward through commercials when time-shifting, and that some video collectors built home libraries of tapes. But for the court, the legitimate and potentially beneficial uses of the technology outweighed such violations.

Although YouTube may superficially resemble the peer-to-peer networks as a means of unauthorized content redistribution, I suggest that all of the judicial reasons that ultimately protected VCRs can and should reasonably apply to YouTube. YouTube cannot be completely shut down due to the indisputable volume of material that in no way infringes copyright and that can be argued to reflect the experiences and ideas of a generation and possibly even a whole cultural moment. The content industry's interests in the site may suffice to maintain its architecture—and, by extension, to sustain a space for amateur and bootleg media flows. Even if YouTube itself implodes, the technology for video sharing remains available, and viewer desire seems sufficient to drive video sharing to alternative venues.

The failure of the Betamax precedent to save the p2ps should not be seen to limit its viability for YouTube. Judicial perceptions that Napster and Grokster did not have significant non-infringing uses and that the network managers could have intervened to disable infringing content were central to their undoing. Distinguishing YouTube from these peer-to-peer networks, users do not download the video files to their own computers but instead watch them as streaming Flash files and only redistribute them as emailed or embedded links. When the copyright question arises, YouTube representatives have cited the DMCA's safe harbor provision for Internet service providers, which shields companies that provide technical infrastructure from liability for users' infringements.

Further distinguishing YouTube from these peer-to-peer networks, YouTube regulates uses of the site. At the time of the Google purchase, YouTube was portrayed as a "good corporate citizen," one that may actually serve the content industry's interests.[15] YouTube has demonstrated such self-regulations as disabling clips that have been the subject of take-down requests from copyright owners in compliance with the DMCA or that have been deemed obscene by users. The site's inability—or refusal, depending on one's point of view—to stringently and pre-emptively monitor copyright content has led to criticism that it willingly hosts infringing content to boost its bottom line. Meanwhile, YouTube's relatively stringent policies have spawned a proliferation of knock-off sites that use similar technologies and interfaces to provide access to such illicit content. This trend reflects a pre-existing pattern: the rise of alternative peer-to-peer services when popular ones face legal trouble. In fact, killing off YouTube may do more damage to the content industry than good, if doing so eliminates the industry-friendly site.

In contrast to Viacom, some record labels, studios, and networks use YouTube as a promotional platform by uploading previews and pilots through branded "channels" or through paid placement on the website's front page.[16] A handful, including Viacom-owned CBS, have even struck licensing or small-stake ownership agreements with the site. For a time, it seemed that industry licensing agreements and the Google purchase might have signalled a decisive shift in the content industry's war against so-called "piracy" and ensured the site's survival. YouTube has popularized online video viewing generally and very likely driven traffic to other sites, including the networks' own. Such mainstreaming of consumption patterns and collaboration with the entertainment industry invariably entails some compromises, but YouTube might have been part of achieving an access equilibrium—and maybe it still will be. Maybe the site has introduced a new paradigm for online digital video sharing that builds upon the Betamax decision's protections in a way that can be reconciled with the DMCA, but to negotiate these seemingly opposed policies, it must do so in ways as complex, even imaginative, as both the Betamax landmark decision and the digital copyright laws. If YouTube and online video streaming continue to be embraced by the industry, a court ruling may find a way within copyright to ensure the site's survival as a way to protect commerce—just as it did for VCRs.

In a technological, legal, and business sphere that has so far undone most utopian predictions about new media, my initial optimism about YouTube has given way to ambivalence. The site may not be a perfect or perpetual way to preserve content, but it has incredibly expanded access to media content. Ultimately a commercial endeavour, the site is not—and probably never has been—inherently utopian or radical. Whatever YouTube's future, its meteoric rise to popularity and its role at the centre of speculation about the near future of video technology make it historically significant. It should also alert media scholars and audiences to the ways that copyright can regulate video access and, by extension, erase media memory.

THE CLIP CANON

In the main article, I have focused on old content that has become newly accessible through YouTube and on the intellectual property issues that video posting and sharing raise. With millions of different clips posted to the site, it would be impossible to offer a comprehensive analysis of its content. Yet, among all the amateur music videos, fan tributes, talking heads, pet vids, laughing babies, stunts, and TV shows, a minority of clips have been seen and shared millions of times. In the culture of the clip, spectacles, stunts, cuteness, pop culture references, and exhibitionism all trump narrative. Here, then, is a capsule survey of some of the most viewed and most talked-about clips from YouTube's first couple of years—12 candidates for the YouTube canon.

"Evolution of Dance"

http://www.youtube.com/watch?v=dMH0bHeiRNg
Category: most viewed
Copyright status: appropriative (clearing music rights would be both logistically challenging and costly)

With the most viewed clip in YouTube history, "Inspirational Comedian" Judson Laipply performs iconic dance moves to a frenetic megamix of 30 songs in 6 minutes. This clip would seem an unlikely hit: the amateurish footage presents a long take of a balding white guy performing in a glaring spotlight with the acoustics of home video shot in an auditorium. Yet, Laipply cleverly and nimbly switches between dance styles. Most of the songs are instantly recognizable, and the crowd cheers every transition as he moves from Elvis's knee flares to disco, head-banging, the chicken dance, and the Macarena. My personal favourite: the MC Hammer-style sideways shuffle.

lonelygirl15

http://www.youtube.com/profi le?user=lonelygirl15
Category: most notorious
Copyright status: original

One of the most popular video bloggers and arguably the first YouTube star was lonelygirl15, a teenager named Bree. In her postings, she talked about her ambiguously romantic relationship with her best friend, cryptically referenced her religion, attempted to "prove science wrong," and responded to viewer comments. The short episodes began in mid-June 2006. In September lonelygirl15 was exposed as a fictional "soap opera" created by three aspiring screenwriters and an actress. The hoax called into question the authenticity of video blogs generally.

OK Go, "Here I Go Again"

http://www.youtube.com/watch?v=pv5zWaTEVkI
Category: music video
Copyright status: original (posted by record label)

This hipster pop group has staked its fame on ironic synchronized dance routines in videos that have gone viral. In "Here I Go Again," the four band members glide, hop, and turn in sync on a treacherous course of treadmills. The band members perform the number as if it were an elaborate joke—which, of course, it would be if the scene wasn't so well choreographed and rehearsed.

"Dick in a Box"

http://www.youtube.com/watch?v=1dmVU08zVpA
Category: network content
Copyright status: original (posted by network)

The *Saturday Night Live* digital short "Lazy Sunday" became one of the most popular early postings on YouTube—and was the first high-profile clip to be removed at the request of its rights owner. A year later, this *SNL* short became another YouTube favourite, but this time NBC posted the clip—in its un-bleeped, non-broadcast version. In the music video parody sketch "Dick," Andy Samberg and host Justin Timberlake, dressed and sounding like white boy throwbacks to early-1990s sexed-up R&B ballads, sing about giving their girlfriends "something real" for Christmas.

Two Chinese boys

http://www.youtube.com/watch?v=x1LZVmn3p3o
Category: lip-synch
Copyright status: appropriative

Lip-synch videos, featuring teenagers giving exaggerated performances to their webcams, rank among the most pervasive genres on YouTube. To be frank, the appeal of these karaoke videos is pretty much lost on me, but their sheer prevalence and apparent popularity make them one of the central genres of the forum. Cross-cultural interpretations, such as these two Chinese students mugging to the Backstreet Boys' "I Want It That Way" are especially popular. See also the "Numa Numa" post and its copycats.

Nora, the piano-playing cat

http://www.youtube.com/watch?v=TZ860P4iTaM
Category: cute animals
Copyright status: original (possible underlying rights for music played in background)

Home videos of pets rank among the most popular amateur videos on YouTube, especially clips of cats leaping, screeching, or falling down. But probably the most famous single cat is Nora, a feline that purportedly plays piano. Nora sits at the bench and paws one note at a time with apparent concentration, but don't expect any actual melodic progressions. Nora's celebrity was so newsworthy that a sequel clip premiered on CNN.

"Brokeback to the Future"

http://www.youtube.com/watch?v=8uwuLxrv8jY
Category: fan video/trailer slash
Copyright status: appropriative

Trailer re-mixes have become one of the most popular forms of fan subversion in the age of digital video. Amidst the hype surrounding *Brokeback Mountain*'s release, a flood of clips reworked homosocial male buddy films to expose their homoerotic subtexts. Faithfully mimicking the structure of the official *Brokeback* trailer and using its signature score, the best of these slash clips revisits the *Back to the Future* trilogy. Also check out the seminal parody reinvention of Stanley Kubrick's *The Shining* as a light-hearted family comedy.

Hillary Clinton/"1984" parody

http://www.youtube.com/watch?v=6h3G-lMZxjo
Category: political campaign/culture-jamming
Copyright status: appropriative

The first controversial attack ad of the 2008 US presidential election was an instant culture-jamming classic. The creator reworked Apple's famous Ridley Scott-directed "1984" advertisement announcing the Macintosh with video clips of candidate Hillary Rodham Clinton as Big Brother. Clever and technically sophisticated, this unauthorized spot plugged Barack Obama, who in turn refused to condemn it. The original Mac ad can also easily be found on YouTube for comparison—or for a quick tutorial in advertising and computer history.

Mentos and Diet Coke experiments

http://www.youtube.com/watch?v=AkkOUPYNs7I
http://www.youtube.com/watch?v=hKoB0MHVBvM
Category: stunts
Copyright status: original (though trademark owners Diet Coke and Mentos may not be happy)

Mix half-chewed Mentos candies with a large bottle of Diet Coke, and the reaction produces a foamy eruption. YouTube hosts numerous variations on this chemistry experiment–turned-stunt. These are my two favourites. In the first, a guy throws a Diet Coke bottle rocket down against the pavement, and it ricochets clear past the roof of a two-story house. The second, more elaborate clip features two men in lab coats and goggles who unleash 101 bottles in sequence to create a fizzy fountain that unfolds in geyser-tastic spectacle.

Parkour

http://www.youtube.com/watch?v=uUksaD-JJgI
Category: sports/stunts
Copyright status: original (may have underlying music rights to clear)

The numerous videos about Parkour, a French sport of high-speed, daredevil urban acrobatics, suggest that YouTube can introduce audiences to previously obscure athletic forms. Parkour was the *raison d'être* for the hit French flick *District B-13* and made a cameo in *Casino Royale*. But video clips such as this British one take the action back to the streets, with stunning and often dangerous stunts that mix gymnastics, breakdancing, and martial arts, as young men run, jump, and flip. Also on the sports beat, for instant (or incessant) replays, check out Zinedine Zidane's controversial head-butt during the 2006 World Cup.

"Noah takes a photo of himself every day for 6 years"

http://www.youtube.com/watch?v=6B26asyGKDo

Category: self-documentation

Copyright status: original

Blogs, MySpace, cameraphones, and other digital technologies have introduced proliferating modes of autobiography. 2356 days in the making, Noah Kalina shot self-portraits daily between 2000 and 2006, then put them together as an animated slide show. The framing and facial expressions remain remarkably consistent throughout, and the Philip Glass–esque piano score (credited as original music by Carly Comando) accentuate the repetition of the video's structure and its melancholy mood. Unlike many self-indulgent clips that reflect an exacerbated culture of narcissism, this is an arresting and almost moving study of maturing.

Saddam Hussein execution

http://www.youtube.com/watch?v=6tVG5_F5Ado

Category: snuff/current events

Copyright status: unclear

YouTube isn't all crazy cats and teenage goofs. It also appeals to morbid and prurient interest, as the popularity of copies of a cameraphone recording of Hussein's hanging demonstrate.

Notes

1. *Time*, 25 December 2006.
2. See Ellen Seiter, "Television and the Internet," in *Television and New Media Audiences* (New York: Oxford University Press, 1999), 115–30, and Lisa Parks, "Flexible Microcasting: Gender, Generation, and Television-Internet Convergence," in *Television after TV*, eds Lynn Spigel and Jan Olsson (Durham, NC: Duke University Press, 2004), 133–56.
3. Shelly Palmer, *Television Disrupted: The Transition from Network to Networked TV* (Burlington, MA: Focal Press, 2006).
4. YouTube was created by three PayPal alumni, still in their twenties: Steve Chen, Chad Hurley, and Jawed Karim, who left the company to attend grad school before it hit big.
5. C-SPAN later requested the take-down of a clip from Speaker of the House Nancy Pelosi's blog nine months later. See Noam Cohen, "Which Videos Are Protected? Lawmakers Get a Lesson," *New York Times*, 26 February 2006 (accessed online).
6. Bob Garfield, "YouTube vs Boob Tube," *Wired*, December 2006 (http://www.wired.com/wired/archive/14.12/youtube.html, accessed 29 April 2007).
7. See Sonja Baumer, "YouTube vs. Main Stream Media: Kissing Cousins or Feuding Siblings?" *Flow* 5, no. 9 (March 2007). The conventional wisdom that infringing clips are the most popular has been challenged by tracking service Vidmeter, which found that clips subject to take-down requests made up less than 10 per cent of content and only slightly more than 5 per cent of the page views. Dan Mitchell, "YouTube's Favorite Clips," *New York Times*, 7 April 2007 (accessed online).
8. See Henry Jenkins, *Convergence Culture: When Old and New Media Collide* (New York: New York University Press, 2006), 13–16.
9. I previously developed the idea of "bootleg aesthetics," in "Grainy Days and Mondays: *Superstar* and Bootleg Aesthetics," *Camera Obscura* 57 (2004), 57–91.
10. Quoted in Sam McManis, "It's You. It's YouTube," *Sacramento Bee*, 14 March 2006, n.p.
11. Charlene Li, quoted in Andrew Ross Sorkin and Peter Edmonston, "Google Is Said to Set Sights on YouTube," *New York Times*, 7 October 2006. As John McMurria has observed, the "community" rhetoric was rampant and open to dispute following the sale of YouTube to Google. See John McMurria, "The YouTube Community," *Flow* 5, no. 2 (2006), (http://jot.communication.utexas.edu/flow/?jot=view&id=1995).
12. This price reflects market deflation compared to the $5.7 billion Yahoo paid for the short-lived broadcast.com, even during the economic resurgence of the so-called Web 2.0. This figure for broadcast.com appears in John Cloud, "The YouTube Gurus," *Time*, 25 December 2006, 69.
13. See Michael Learmonth, "Viacom Sues YouTube, Google," *Variety*, 13 March 2007, and Jeremy W. Peters, "Viacom Sues Google over YouTube Video Clips," *New York Times*, 14 March 2007 (both accessed online).
14. Lawrence Lessig, *The Future of Ideas: The Fate of the Commons in a Connected World* (New York: Vintage, 2002), 23–5. On "code," see also Lessig, *Code: Version 2.0* (New York: Basic Books, 2006).
15. The description in quotation marks appears in a statement by a representative of the Motion Picture Association of America in Andrew Wallenstein, "Catch YouTube If You Can," *Hollywood Reporter*, 21 March 2006, n.p.
16. Heather Green, "Waiting for the Payoff; The Video-sharing Web site Is a Runaway Success—Everywhere but on the Bottom Line," *Business Week*, 18 September 2006, 56.

Watching Television without Pity: The Productivity of Online Fans

Mark Andrejevic

Mediated interactivity, we are told by its promoters, is a way of recapturing a lost, more participatory past by moving ahead into an era in which viewers can talk back to the TV—and actually be heard. As training wheels for the coming era of interactivity, many television shows have created official websites, and some incorporate the comments of online fans who are encouraged to email comments and requests while they watch. Similarly, reality game shows invite viewers to vote for their favourite contestants via text messaging and offer online contests to build viewer loyalty between shows. Such developments deploy the umbrella promise of interactivity: that new media will challenge the passive forms of media consumption associated with mass society. Consider, for example, the description by J.J. Abrams—creator of the cult spy show *Alias*—of an online fan site as an "integral part" of the production process: "If the Internet is your audience, TV is quite like a play.... Movies are a done deal—there's no give and take—but in a play, you listen to the applause, the missing laughs, the boos. It's the same with the Internet. If you ignore that sort of response, you probably shouldn't be working in TV right now" (Sella 2002, 62). In an era in which the mass audience is becoming increasingly visible thanks to a variety of increasingly sophisticated monitoring technologies, viewers are increasingly encouraged to climb out of the couch to embrace a more "active" approach to their viewing experience. Fan culture is at long last being deliberately and openly embraced by producers thanks in part to the ability of the Internet not just to unite far-flung viewers but to make the fruits of their labour readily accessible to the mainstream—and to producers themselves.

The digital embrace of viewer activity requires a rethinking of any approach to media audiences that seeks to orient itself through recourse to the opposition between passive and active viewership, where the former is associated with the straw man figure of the manipulated dupe and the latter with the subversive textual poacher (Jenkins 1992; Fiske 1987). Although Jenkins (1992, 287) once noted that fandom proves "not all audiences are passive," the advent of interactive media highlights what has been true all along: that *all* audiences are active, although perhaps not in the progressive sense the term has come to imply. What is perhaps distinctive about the advent of interactive media is the development of strategies for promoting, harnessing, and exploiting the productivity of this activity. To observe that such strategies are doubtless facilitated by celebratory portrayal of the creative, subversive potential of an active audience (as an antidote to the implied passivity of the mass audience) is not to discount or dismiss this potential. Rather, it is to attempt to understand and elucidate the ways in which creative activity and exploitation co-exist and interpenetrate one another within the context of the emerging online economy. This article draws on a case study of the Television Without Pity (TWoP) website to explore the role of mediated interactivity in facilitating what Terranova (2000, 45) has described as the "simultaneity of labor as something which is voluntarily given and exploited."

The Productivity of TWoP: An Overview

For producers, fan sites such as TWoP can serve as an impromptu focus group, providing instant feedback to plot twists and the introduction of new characters even as they help to imbue the show with the kind of "stickiness" coveted in the online world by creating a virtual community as an added component of the show. As a *New York Times* article about online fan sites put it, "It is now standard Hollywood practice for executive producers (known in trade argot as 'show runners') to scurry into Web groups moments after an episode is shown on the East Coast. Sure, a good review in the print media is important, but the boards, by definition, are populated by a program's core audience—many thousands of viewers who care deeply about what direction their show takes" (Sella 2002, 62).

As in the case of other forms of consumption, viewer feedback promises to become increasingly integrated into the production process in a cybernetic cycle that offers to reduce uncertainty and, at least according to the marketing industry, increase customer satisfaction (Pine 1993). Indeed, many of those who visit TWoP, which includes forums devoted to some three dozen shows, are convinced that their feedback has had some sort of impact on writers or producers. As one respondent to my online survey of TWoP participants put it, "The decision makers can come and see what specifically the audience liked and disliked about the way they handled various things, and why... which, if they choose to pay attention, can help them to improve their work." Although the site, as its name suggests, encourages critical, "snarkastic" commentary, many of those who post do so in the spirit described by the respondent, adopting the viewpoint of assistants who can help producers and writers do their job better by providing detailed commentary not just on plot development but also on technical aspects of the show, including continuity, wardrobe, and make-up. The "recappers"—hired by TWoP to craft lengthy, detailed, and humorous summaries of the shows—often focus on production details including lighting and editing, thereby helping direct the attention to the formal aspects of the shows they describe.

The result is the merging of two forms of audience participation: the effort viewers put into making the show interesting to themselves and the effort they devote to taking on the role of production assistants and attempting to provide feedback to writers and producers. Part of the entertainment value of a site such as TWoP is the implicit promise to erode the boundaries between the sites of ostensibly passive consumption and those of the sequestered power of media producers—what Couldry (2000) has called the "place of media power." If interactive technologies help dedifferentiate sites of consumption and production according to this account, they also pose a challenge to the boundaries that reinforce the concentration of control in the hands of the few. In keeping with the celebratory predictions of those who champion the democratizing potential of new media (Gilder 1994; Kelly 1996), respondents to an online survey I posted to TWoP overwhelmingly agreed with the assertion that online fan sites will make TV producers more accountable to viewers. As one respondent put it, "I think producers/writers etc. would be well served to see what their 'constituents' want. TV should be more viewer driven and I think TWoP is a foundation for a movement toward that."

Interestingly, the promise of accountability seems to cut both ways: if TWoP provides producers with direct and immediate access to the viewpoints of the audience, it also fosters identification on the part of audiences with the viewpoint of producers. Market and production imperatives such as show promotion, mass audience appeal, and technical details are taken up in depth by TWoP posters, who, in elaborate postings directed to producers, suggest ways to more effectively tailor a particular show to its viewers. The promise of virtual participation in the production process, in short, invites viewers to adopt the standpoint of producers, and thereby facilitates the conversion of viewer feedback into potentially productive marketing and demographic information.

TWoP posters, who pride themselves on their savvy, can be quite cynical about the prospect of shared control and the willingness of producers to pay attention to fan feedback. Several respondents suggested that producers view Internet fans as mildly obsessed cranks representing the geek fringe of a show's audience. This perception was highlighted by an infamous incident in TWoP lore: the fallout from a visit to the forums by Aaron Sorkin, creator of the popular show *The West Wing.* After a heated exchange with critical fans, Sorkin scripted an episode that, according to a *New York Times* account, portrayed "hard-core Internet users as obese shut-ins who lounge around in muumuus and chain-smoke Parliaments" (Sella 2002, 66). Still, the incident was taken as a sign that the producers were, at the very least, paying attention, and TWoPpers are perpetually on the lookout for other "shout-outs" that directly or indirectly refer to the site and to their activities. The recapper for a show on the WB network called *Popular* noted, for example, that in a backhanded gesture of recognition for his praise of the show, the writers named a character after him: a junkie who was killed in a car accident. He also received email from cast members who reportedly told him that the show's executive producer, in an effort to find something positive written about the show, printed out his recaps and distributed them to the cast and crew. As he put it, "That was weird because all of a sudden we weren't students sitting around snarking on shows anymore. We were a focus group whose comments were heard by the executive brass" (personal correspondence). Other shout-outs included the use of the recapper's name by the writers for NBC's *Ed* and the appearance of the TWoP logo on a bag in an episode of *Once and Again.* A TWoP recapper who goes by the online moniker "Shack," and who repeatedly criticized the producers of *American Idol* for the misleading way in which they reported the number of audience votes (equating the number of votes cast with the number of voters), said that he heard from someone at Fox that they changed their reporting format in part because of his criticism (personal correspondence). However, the line between real and perceived impact is not always clear. Fans and recappers have a tendency to interpret changes in the show that seem to be direct responses to online criticism as having been prompted, at least in part, by their comments.

The embrace of new media, interactive sites, and online communities by marketers does not go unacknowledged by posters, some of whom expressed concern that fan sites might be reduced to one more marketing strategy. As one poster put it, "The majority of producers/execs either fear the Internet community or feel that if they try hard enough, they can manipulate it right back." However, direct manipulation by producers is not necessary to make even a critical site like TWoP an effective form of promotion. Almost one-third of the 1,800 respondents to my online survey indicated that they felt they watched more television because of TWoP, and a large majority said that the site made television more entertaining to watch. Indeed, it is the collective effort of viewers to enlist the Internet to enhance the entertainment value of their televisions that emerges as a recurring theme in the remarks of respondents. Interactivity, in short, allows the viewers to take on the work of finding ways to make a show more interesting.

The following section considers the productive character of viewer participation as a form of audience labour to suggest the role played by the promise of interactivity as an incitation to participate in the work of being watched. Subsequent sections explore the importance to posters of having a public forum for their comments, a forum in which their savvy responses can be seen and registered by the TWoP community. If, for fans, the promise of online forums is to have their voice heard within the confines of the sequestered site of production, the promise to producers is the ability to monitor viewers. The responses referred to throughout the following argument are drawn from two online surveys posted to the TWoP website for one week in May 2003. The first survey, which was largely quantitative, received more than 1,800 responses; the second, composed of open-ended questions, received more than 500 responses. Statistics in the remainder of this article come from the first survey, quotes from the second. About 87 per cent of the responses to the first survey were from women, a fact that will be discussed in the following section. Seventy per cent of the respondents indicated they were in the 18 to 34 age range, which represents the demographic group most prized by advertisers and marketers. The respondents, of course, were self-selected—they represented visitors to the website who clicked on a link to the survey—but the large number of responses provided a rich set of observations, and several clear trends, discussed below, that demonstrate the ways in which viewer participation, while providing perceived benefits to viewers, doubled as what I will characterize as a form of free labour for producers.

Talking Back to the TV

If, as Antonio Gramsci (1971, 286) suggested, the implementation of a new economic regime requires the elaboration of "a new type of man suited to the new type of work and productive process," the same might be said of the emerging interactive economy, and even for the advent of interactive television: it requires the creation of new, more active—or "interactive"—types of viewer and consumer. The evolution of the television remote control is suggestive of the type of transformations underway: early remotes that facilitated the growing passivity of the couch potato stressed simplicity and ease—the goal was to reduce the amount of effort, such as it was, associated with the viewing experience. Over time, the drive has been toward an increasing range of functions and the convergence of devices, including remote controls for video recorders, sound systems, and cable boxes. Now, mastering a remote control device can require a fair amount of time and effort pouring over lengthy instruction manuals, and some of the more advanced devices come equipped with their own screens: the TV screen has split into one to be watched and one to be interacted with. Remote control has transformed itself from a passive activity to a hyperactive one. Consequently, one of the central problems facing the promoters of interactive television is how to reconfigure the viewer's relationship to the screen along the lines of the computer user who both watches and interacts.

A site such as TWoP provides a neat transition to this era of interactive viewing. Many of my respondents told me that even if they were not online while watching TV, they often took notes as they watched, writing down choice morsels of dialogue and observations to help them prepare for their posts. The TWoP forums, in short, provide a pool of research expertise available not just to fellow fans but also to producers. The result is both a ready resource for fans and, at times, a resource for writers and producers who learn from attentive viewers that an upcoming script includes a continuity flaw or plot inconsistency.

TWoP contributors collectively put a significant amount of time and energy into the creation of a detailed and productive online resource. One-fourth of the survey respondents indicated that they spent between five and ten hours a week in the TWoP forums, and 13 per cent said they spent more than 10 hours a week on the site (much of which, according to several of the comments in the qualitative portion of the survey, takes place at work). In addition, many TWoPpers devoted time not just to watching (and sometimes taking notes on) particular shows but to gathering information about them from other sources. This is precisely the type of effort that Terranova (2000, 33) has described as the "free labour" characteristic of the relationship between the online economy and what, following the Italian autonomists, she terms "the social factory." She invokes this term to describe the process "whereby 'work processes have shifted from the factory to society, thereby setting in motion a truly complex machine.'"

The notion of the social factory coincides with the creation of an interactive consumer–viewer, one prepared to devote time and energy to developing the skills necessary to participate in an increasingly interactive media economy. The list of such skills is becoming increasingly long and includes the ability not only to operate a computer and surf the Internet but also to master an array of devices including

VCR programmers, cell phones, palm pilots, video games, and so on. To the extent that such effort generates useful demographic feedback to producers (as in the case or interactive devices that record, save, and aggregate viewer preferences), it is productive not just in the sense that it facilitates the consumption of an increasingly technologically sophisticated array of media products and services but also insofar as it allows producers to, as one business futurist put it, "save costs by off-loading some of the duties of consumer interactions onto consumers themselves" (Mougayar 1998, 174). Work that used to be the province of producers is being redefined as that of the active consumer, who is increasingly becoming responsible for developing a unique demographic profile and relaying the information it contains to producers.

It is perhaps not insignificant that the work off-loaded onto the consumer is referred to by marketers as a "duty" of interaction. The notion that consumers are increasingly required to take on a broad array of interactive responsibilities neatly ties in with the forms of "governing at a distance" elaborated by the Foucault-inspired literature on governmentality. The interactive consumer is the market analogue of the "active" citizen interpellated by the proponents of the neo-liberal post-welfare state. As Rose (2001, 164) puts it, the model of the active citizen is that of the "entrepreneur of him- or herself" who "was to conduct his or her life, and that of his or her family, as a kind of enterprise, seeking to enhance and capitalize on existence itself through calculated acts and investments." It does not seem farfetched to extend this analysis into the realm of consumption, where the consumer is increasingly encouraged to make the investment of time and energy it takes to be an interactive consumer responsible for his or her own viewing and consumption practices and experiences.

Similarly, many TWoPpers suggest that the effort that they put into the shows they watch increases their own viewing pleasure. As one fan put it in a column about her passion for collecting behind-the-scenes and advance information about her favourite show, "At the most basic level, being plugged-in means becoming invested in the creation of the show, rather than simply a passive recipient" (Nussbaum 2002, 1). To the extent that such sites, even those that are ostensibly critical, promote this sense of investment, they consolidate a multiplatform involvement with the show, the type that producers covet in an era of multitasking and channel surfing. As one respondent put it, "TWoP has definitely made me pay closer attention to the shows I watch (i.e., script, direction, set decoration, etc.). While at times I can be more critical of a show, for example more aware of continuity errors and obvious audience manipulation, it also makes me more appreciative of the work that goes into creating a show, and insanely, more loyal to a show." This post and several similar ones suggested that the more the boundary between the "offstage" site of production and that of consumption is eroded, the greater the sense of participation-based loyalty.

Although TWoPpers pride themselves on belonging to a knowing and critical subset of viewers, many nonetheless find themselves captivated by those moments when producers, actors, or writers participate in the forums or agree to be interviewed online for the site. One respondent described the experience of hearing from those involved in a favourite show as "unbelievably weird and simultaneously wonderful. Their feedback and insights made my love for the show grow exponentially! If actors and other persons affiliated with shows regularly showed up, I might end up watching much more TV, simply because of the stronger connection I would feel." TV shows attempt to capitalize on such loyalty by creating official websites, the savviest of which provide interactive interviews and the kind of behind-the-scenes information that gives fans the sense of at least partial entry into an inner circle of producers and writers.

Official sites, however, do not have the luxury of deliberately fostering the critical, sarcastic repartee that has become the staple of TWoP, which provides visitors with not just tightly monitored and witty forums but also lengthy, often sarcastic and savagely funny recaps of selected shows. The combination of enthusiasm and criticism that infuses the site is in part a function of the fact that there are two, not entirely distinct, types of forums: those populated by serious fans who admire the show and those devoted to viewers who love to mock the show being discussed. The former "fan"-oriented forums tend to coalesce around dramatic shows that have included the likes of *24*, *Buffy the Vampire Slayer*, *Dawson's Creek*, and *Alias*, whereas shows such as *Joe Millionaire* and *The Bachelor* serve as the brunt of the more "snarkastic" forums. The boundary between the two types of forum is far from clear: fans of shows such as *Dawson's Creek* enjoy criticizing it, and snarky viewers become invested in the show that they follow online. In both cases, the goal is not uncritical fannishness but rather for viewers to use the site as a springboard for entertaining one another. The show itself can in some cases become merely a precursor to the real entertainment, which takes the form of its online comeuppance: the gleeful dissection that takes place after it airs.

I first noticed this phenomenon when I was spending a fair amount of time in the official chat rooms for the first US version of the *Big Brother* reality game show. Despite much hype, the show was often mind-numbingly boring, as were the round-the-clock live Internet video feeds. The chat rooms became, for at least some viewers, one way to make the show interesting and entertaining. While watching the contestants attempt to entertain themselves in a drab, media-free ranch house on a lot in Studio City, online viewers similarly took on themselves the task of amusing themselves by speculating on plot twists that might make the show more interesting, by sharing information about the various contestants, and by starting online debates. Viewers created their own web pages devoted to the show, including the popular BigBrotherBlows.com. There was, in short, more to host Julie Chen's closing observation to fans that "your participation made this a truly interactive show" than she might have realized. Faced with a show that was routinely dull and contrived, online viewers did the creative work of making the show entertaining to themselves, often by coming up with innovative ways to poke fun at it.

Similarly, TWoP fans focus their attention on the lengthy recaps written by paid freelancers and on the ongoing discussions of fellow fans and critics in the forums. Within this context, the show is no longer the final product but rather the raw material to which value is added by the labour—some paid, some free—of recappers and forum contributors. Not only did roughly one-third of the respondents indicate that they watched more TV because of TWoP, but a similar number noted that there were shows that they would not have watched without the TWoP recaps. The most frequently mentioned of these shows were the reality shows *Joe Millionaire*, *Married By America*, *Are You Hot*, and *The Bachelor*. Respondents said that, taken on their own, such shows were too contrived and poorly produced to merit watching but that they provided wonderful raw material for the TWoP recaps and forums. As one respondent put it, "I watched parts of *Married by America* simply because Miss Alli [one of the favourite recappers] was recapping it and I wanted to see what she was so hysterically mocking. This week, during *For Love or Money*, I had to visit the site because I knew that people would be hilariously mocking the 'robot' bachelor and I was not disappointed. So, yes, TWoP can get me to watch bad TV, at least for a short period." Another viewer expressed similar enthusiasm for Miss Alli's sardonic prose: "I absolutely *will* watch a show just to be able to keep up—*The Amazing Race*! Miss Alli's recaps were just so damn SMART, I had to know what she was skewering." Others said that they tuned into a show after reading a particularly amusing recap and continued to watch to enjoy future recaps. Interestingly, a few respondents said they followed some shows entirely online because the recaps were entertaining and thorough enough to stand on their own. Although not the norm, these "viewers" had found a way to consume TV-based entertainment without having to watch, not least because the musings of other viewers may well be more creative and interesting than the story lines produced by the culture industry. As Baym (2000, 216) observed in her study of soap opera fans, "The Internet gives fans a platform on which to perform for one another, and their informal performances might please fans more than the official ones do." Perhaps out of a desire to encourage the kind of participation that fosters loyalty to a show—even if it is a program that viewers love to hate—producers have publicly said that they find websites to be useful sources of feedback. The executive producer of *ER*, one of TWoP's staple shows, said, "I don't overreact to the boards, but I pay real attention to messages that are thoughtful. If you ignore your customer, you do so at your peril" (Bradberry 2003, 11).

As in the case of other forms of interactive commerce, the information provided by viewers does not just add value to the product; it doubles as audience research. Fan communities have been around for a long time, but the growth of online bulletin boards received a boost with the reality TV boom, perhaps in part because of the way in which such shows foster a sense of participation by proxy (Gardyn 2001). Indeed, several formats incorporate fan participation online or by cell phone to exploit the promise of an ersatz democratization, a promise that is often repeated in the media coverage. As a research article in *American Demographics* explains, "The popularity of this format with youth also has a lot to do with their growing up in a democratized society, where the Internet, webcams, and other technologies give the average Joe the ability to personalize his entertainment" (Gardyn 2001, 38).

The ready equation of commodity customization with democratization echoes the marketing rhetoric of the interactive revolution. If the implicit message of reality TV is one of increasingly shared control, it is not surprising that CBS spokesman Chris Ender said the power of the web-based fan groups first caught his attention during the airing of the smash hit reality series *Survivor*: "In the first season there was a groundswell of attention in there.... We started monitoring the message boards to actually help guide us in what would resonate in our marketing. It's just the best market research you can get" (Sella 2002, 68). TWoPpers may be working for free, but that does not mean they are not producing value. The work they do—the work of making their preferences transparent, of allowing themselves to be watched as they do their watching—is an increasingly important component of the emerging interactive economy.

One of the ancillary effects of the promise of shared control mobilized by producers who publicize the impact that their online fans have on a show is that of an implicit bridging of the production–consumption divide. If viewers are, to some limited extent, allowed to participate in the production process, then the notion that a new set of duties has devolved on them becomes much more palatable. Furthermore, the promise of shared control, the invitation to participate in the production process, doubles as an invitation to internalize the imperatives of producers. There are entire threads on TWoP devoted, for example, to the marketing of a favoured show. Posters frequently bemoan the ineffectiveness of promotional ads for the shows they follow and offer suggestions as to which characters and images ought to be included to increase audience appeal and viewership. Even in the face of a still relatively nonresponsive industry, the formal introduction of an interactive element helps foster a sense of identification with producers. While there are instances in which the feedback seems to have had an impact, for the most part the impact from the boards is limited and indirect. The fun comes not so much from watching the implementation of viewer suggestions—since very few of these have any directly discernable impact—as from embracing the modicum of interactivity that makes it possible to identify with the position of the producer.

The work that viewers do for producers emerges as a necessary corollary to their entrepreneurial activity: the work that they do for and on themselves. If, in other words, the advent of advanced neoliberalism is associated with the constellation of practices that promote the "responsibilization" of the citizen, a similar logic emerges in the realm of consumption, wherein viewers are invited to take on some of the "duties" associated with their media consumption. If reality TV provides a representative version of this process by allowing selected members of the audience to stand in for the viewer, websites such as TWoP broaden the potential scope of participation via interactivity. Viewed within this context, the recurring refrain that TWoP promotes critical and intelligent viewing on the part of its participants appears as a form of self-optimization. If, as Rose (2001, 164) suggests, the emergent society of control operates on the assumption that "one is always in continuous training, lifelong learning, perpetual assessment, continual incitement to buy [and] to improve oneself," the imperative for consumers is to become not only more efficient but also more informed and even more critical viewers. To borrow some loaded terms from the political sphere, if the passive viewer is associated with the welfare "culture of dependency," the active viewer is associated with the post-welfare culture of individual responsibility and self-activation. If TV is low quality, unentertaining, or unintelligent, the viewer can take on the duty of making it more interesting, entertaining, and intelligent. As one respondent put it, "I would like my TV to be smarter, better written, more intellectually stimulating, and more emotionally engaging. With TWoP, at least my watching of TV can be those things."

In contrast to the image of television as a mind-numbing addiction that promotes a culture of passivity, that of TWoP-enhanced TV is one of active participation, self-improvement, and actualization, even creativity, the benefits of which, it might be added, redound on the producers by increasing the value of TV content without in any way realigning the relations of production. As the deployment of the promise of interaction suggests, shared production does not necessarily entail shared control. Respondents repeatedly reiterated their assertion that TWoP allowed them to develop and hone their critical skills, the very skills that were ostensibly threatened and eroded by the "plug-in drug." One respondent summed up this recurring refrain as follows: "My inner critic was always apparent, now it is a better, more intelligent form." Or, as another respondent put it, TWoP has "certainly made me more snarky/critical of television. However, it's also made me more critical of my own writing in that it's highlighted some clichés and contrivances that we systematically use without thinking about them. All in all it's made me more creative."

The portrayal of interactivity as a means for revitalizing a self-actualizing form of participation parallels the marketing of the digital economy as one that counters the stultification and homogenization of mass society. Indeed, one of the recurring marketing strategies of the new economy is the suggestion that with the addition of the interactivity prefix—the telltale lower case *i*—forms of media that were once passive and mind numbing are transformed into means of creative self-expression and empowerment. Thus, as one survey respondent put it, a site such as TWoP "changes TV from a brain-dead pastime to an art and a science." Or, similarly, "bad TV becomes good TV when combined with TWoP." The element of reflexivity, combined with a "snarkastic" savvy, inoculates the viewer against the ostensible depredations of passivity.

The intriguing result is that, thanks to the inclusion of the formal element of interactivity, the character of a particular show changes from that of a mass-produced product of the culture industry into a tool to hone and develop one's critical thinking and viewing skills. As one response put it, "Being able to see through the stereotypes and clichés bad shows propagate is a useful skill, much like being able to deconstruct and analyze advertising. At least if you are able to hone your critical thinking skill during a tasteless show, it's not a total waste." Another TWoPper invoked the terms of the famous indictment of the mass media for fostering a form of "narcotizing dysfunction" (Lazarsfeld and Merton 1948), suggesting that the ostensibly stultifying effects of the mass media can be overcome by reflexive, critical humour: "Applying such a smart, dark sense of humor to the thing that pervades our lives takes away some of its hypnotic power. When you look at it critically it is something you are experiencing and participating in, rather than something that is narcotizing you." Several respondents suggested that the development of critical viewing skills, combined with the feedback supplied by increasingly sophisticated viewers, might result in improved programming. However, even if such a result is not forthcoming, savvy reflexivity serves as a kind of coping mechanism, a strategy for salvaging the very same advertisements and programming that, viewed uncritically or nonreflexively, are relegated to the category of the shallow manipulations of the culture industry. In other words, it is not the content itself but the attitude taken by the viewers, the way in which they watch—or, more precisely, the way in which they are *seen* to watch (or see themselves watching)—that makes the difference. TWoPpers esteem savvy, critical posts highly, and those who are active contributors to the site say that while they like the idea that producers may be paying attention, they post mainly for the benefit of fellow posters and the moderator. The goal is not so much to influence the group of producers and production assistants referred to in posts as TPTB (the powers that be) as it is to entertain and impress the TWoP community with wit, insight, and, above all, "snark."

"Thanks for Listening (Or Not)!"

Despite the stories of shout-outs and other examples of the impact of the online community on producers and writers, the savvy attitude of TWoPpers includes a marked skepticism toward the notion that they might actually be making a difference. As one poster put it, "The producers are such prostitutes to advertisers and whatever other show may be popular that giving advice would be pointless. It is all about the Benjamins." Indeed, most of the respondents took pains to suggest that they did not have any illusions about transforming or improving the culture industry. The recurring theme in the responses was that contributors post primarily for one another and that if producers feel like paying attention, so much the better. Some respondents cautioned against the dangers of TWoPpers believing the intermittent media hype about the influence of the boards: "Although the artistic personnel of some shows probably read TWoP, I think the posters on the forums think they have more influence than they probably do. If they write posts for the series creators, they are deluded as to their influence." The more cynical posters note that there is a certain amount of public relations value to be gained from suggesting that online fans influence the production process: it helps foster the multiplatform (Internet plus TV) marketing of the show and thus build loyalty.

For those who claim to have few illusions about the impact they're having on the industry, the appeal of online critique is not just its entertainment value but also the recognition that they receive online. Respondents repeatedly emphasized the satisfaction they received from having their posts noticed and responded to in the online forums. A typical example was the observation by one regular poster that "when posting, my main goal is to make the other posters laugh, to be witty. If I get a 'word' out of the deal, my day's pretty much made." Another respondent, highlighting the work done by viewers in making the viewing experience more entertaining, wrote, "My 'job' on TWoP is the class clown—almost all of my posts are humorous in nature and I love it when posters respond to them in their posts. I guess I enjoy the validation that I can indeed be funny." A premium was placed on the ability to get some kind of shout-out, not from the producers or writers but from fellow viewers: "The pleasure kicks in when I've helped to expand someone's knowledge or worldview and when I'm quoted or declared funny. (I like making other people laugh.)" The high expectations that posters have for the level of wit, sarcasm, and snark in some of the forums apparently has the unintended result of keeping some readers from posting, in part because they are worried their own posts will not live up to the standard set by the regulars. As one avid TWoP fan put it in a parenthetical aside to an effusive description of the quality of the discussion on the boards, "I should note that I'm a lurker—too afraid to post!"

But for those who do post, the goal is not just to be heard—but to be seen in a particular way: as savvy viewers who are not taken in by the transparent forms of manipulation practised by producers. The ability of the viewers to make themselves seen is perhaps the characteristic attribute of the impending era of interactivity, and its implications are worth exploring in a bit more detail. The celebratory promise of the interactive era is that transparency will result in greater democratization, in both the political and the economic spheres (although the latter is often conflated with the former). This promise is underwritten by the unexamined equation of participation with shared control: that any medium that promotes interaction is politically progressive and empowering.

However, the exploitation of participation as a form of audience labour—and even as a source of demographic information that can be appropriated and commodified—suggests that this equation needs to be approached with a bit more caution. Jodi Dean (2002, 173) argues that the interactivity fostered by new media promotes a form of publicity without publics: a drive to advertise one's own opinion that falls short of the political commitments of the public sphere. For her, the characteristic mode of subjectivity associated with new media is that of universalized celebrity: "The subject is driven to make itself visible over and over again. It has to understand itself as a celebrity precisely because the excesses of cyberia make it uncertain as to its place in the symbolic order." Dean is here following Zizek's (1999) diagnosis of the pathologies associated with the ostensible decline of the symbolic order ("Big Other") in postmodernity, understood as an era in which the grand narratives that underwrote and guaranteed a shared sense of meaning and values have been debunked, or, perhaps more precisely, an era in which such narratives have debunked themselves. The result is a generalized skepticism, a universal savvy that places a premium on irony, detached cynicism, sarcasm, and, of course, snark.

Furthermore, as Dean (2002) suggests, this skepticism translates into the self-contradictory (and self-stimulating) logic of the attempt to make some kind of impression on a symbolic register whose very existence is in doubt. The savvy subject, wary of metanarratives, repeatedly attempts to assert this wariness as a sign that he or she is no dupe. The paradox lies in the attempt to register the fact of one's own non-duped status—a process that, of course, implicitly smuggles back in the efficacy of the symbolic register. The impasse of the desire to be seen as savvy results in the properly perverse logic of celebrity described by Dean, one in which the subject gets off on the very failure of the attempt to make an impression on a debunked symbolic order. Savvy contemporary subjects know better than to imagine that interactivity would actually allow them to make an impression on TPTB of the entertainment industry, one whose claims to represent the demands of consumers is little more than a ruse of the marketing process. As one respondent put it, "TV producers are kind of like politicians, I think, in that no matter what they do some people will complain, so they just do what they want and/or follow the advertising dollars." Or, as another post put it, "Producers of TV (and here I include the entire range from network execs through creators, writers, actors down to the grips) firmly and completely believe that they are the Gods who know 'how to tell the story' and that we the viewers are the idiots watching the shadows on the cave wall."

In the face of this uncanny autonomy—uncanny because of the persistence of the functioning of the market and political system in the wake of the debunking of their ostensibly foundational ideologies—it is perhaps not quite enough to observe, with Dean (2002), that viewers are compelled to continually attempt to publicize themselves because they are unsure of whether their presence has been registered. Rather, the failure of these attempts has become, in some sense, the goal in itself. Translated into the terms of TWoP, the savvy, snarkastic response is not incidental to the prevailing skeptical attitude toward the promise that the boards will democratize the viewing process. Rather, one of the apparent goals of posters is to be seen by others as not being duped, to make it clear to one another that they have not been caught up in the illusory, breathless promise of a kind of immaculate revolution, painlessly effected by technological developments.

Surely, there are those on TWoP who imagine a world in which producers will pay more attention to viewers and in which viewers may play an active and creative role in producing the culture they then turn around and consume. However, the characteristic attitude encouraged by the site and its posters is much more skeptical. Even if feedback is taken into account, would this not just be one more form of market rationalization, the use of "just-in-time" focus groups to fine tune a show or the exploitation of online communities as a form of viral marketing, a way to spread buzz by word of mouth rather than solely relying on advertising promotions?

In a world in which the half-life of the cooptation of ostensibly subversive cultural forms seems to have shrunk almost to zero, in which revolution itself has become a marketing slogan, the savvy subject looks askance at the promise of power sharing. Rather than buying into the promise that interactive technology will fundamentally alter the power relations between consumer and producer, the interactive viewer enlists the proffered technologies to, if nothing else, let others know that he or she has not been taken in by the ruse. The minimalist, defensive pleasure that remains for the savvy subject is, at the very least, that of ensuring he or she is seen to not be a dupe. This might be described, in the Lacanian terms enlisted by Dean, as a strategy for "getting off" on the very failure of the promise of power sharing.

The consequence is a sense of political inertness—only the dupes imagine that things could be otherwise; the non-duped may well crave social change, but they are not so naïve as to be fooled by their desire into believing that it is actually possible. Rather, they are invited to perform (and exhibit) their own voyeurism as a form of participation. The promise of interactive television is to take this equation literally; in the digital future, watching will really be a form of participation precisely because we will be able to "talk back" to the tube. The savvy subject will be realized in the form of the active viewer. If the viewers cannot be insiders, at least they can make it clear that they are not being fooled by the insiders, and this is the closest that the interactive technologies can bring them to the inner sanctum.

As Gitlin (1990) notes, savvy encourages viewers to identify with insiders by defining the issues as they define them, which is an apt description of much of what goes on in the production-oriented strands of the TWoP boards. Posters who identify problems in continuity, in plot and character development, in make-up and lighting, and even in publicity and promotional material are using the interactive forum as one in which to imagine themselves in the position of the producer so as to understand the imperatives that shape the programming they consume. In this respect, they adopt a standard critical procedure, an attempt to demystify and explain the behind-the-scenes functioning of the media. And it is in this very dynamic that a consideration of the TWoP website reflects back on the process of criticism itself. The danger, in a savvy era, is that the goal of self-reflexive knowledge is not so much to reshape the media—to imagine how things might be done differently—as it is to take pleasure in identifying with the insiders. The next best thing to having power, on this account, is identifying with those who do rather than naïvely imagining that power can (or should) be redistributed or realigned. In this respect, the snarkiest and most critical of the fan sites runs the danger of partaking in what Gitlin describes as "the postmodern fascination with surfaces and the machinery that cranks them out, a fascination indistinguishable from surrender—as if once we understand that all images are concocted we are enlightened" (21).

The stance of the savvy viewer is twofold: an insider's skepticism toward the notion that real insiders are paying any attention to the boards combined with a sense that understanding the insider's perspective sets the savvy viewer apart from the rest of the viewing audience. Thus, one respondent described the pleasure of TWoP as follows: "It is hard to explain, but I feel like an 'insider' when I read TWoP. Like we are a community of those in the know, not a bunch of clueless losers." Another poster observed that "reading and participating in the forums makes me feel that all hope for humanity is not lost. If there are so many people watching reality TV, at least not all of us are taking it seriously. At least the folks at TWoP are looking at it mostly as a theater of the absurd. TWoP makes it easier for us to convince ourselves that we are smart, while watching DUMB television."

Such is the fate of the savvy viewer: to search for the redeeming value of the media not in the content—over which their newly enhanced, interactive participation has little influence—but in understanding why their participation *must be* ineffective, in their insider knowledge of how the system works. Within this context, the lure of interactivity loses some of its lustre. Rather than a progressive challenge to a nonparticipatory medium, it offers to divert the threat of activism into the productive activity of marketing and market research. Interactivity turns out to be rather more passive than advertised. The drive of savvy viewers to make themselves seen (as non-dupes) overlaps with the invitation proffered by interactive media: for audiences to reveal themselves in increasing detail to producers. The logic of a savvy site such as TWoP, which allows viewers to take pleasure in critiquing the programming within which they are immersed, seems to stage Zizek's (1999, 284) formulation of the drive as the ability to derive "libidinal satisfaction from actively sustaining the scene of one's own passive submission." This Lacanian formula applies to the savvy stance in general—and perhaps more generally to the version of interactivity being prepared for the viewing public by the promoters of the digital economy.

Conclusion: Refeudalization and the Publicity Sphere

If, as Habermas (1991) has argued, the political public sphere can trace its origins to the literary public sphere, perhaps we can discern its definitive decline in the form of participation modelled by the interactive, televisual publicity sphere anticipated by sites such as TWoP. Such sites exhibit many of the attributes of the public sphere: open admission, discussion of topics of communal interest, and, at least on TWoP, a relatively scrupulous adherence to norms of noncoercive speech. TWoP moderators, for example, ban anyone who directly insults another poster and generally ban offensive, sexist, and other forms of inflammatory or insulting commentary. Many posters described the site as a variant of public sphere that allowed them to intelligently discuss topics with strangers and thereby to develop their own critical and analytical skills and to learn from one another. Moreover, the Internet is, at least in some respects, more open than the literary societies and secret societies described by Habermas. One poster suggested that it remains more open than other venues of social interaction "in which men still tend to dominate conversations, meetings, and classrooms, and women's opinions are often ignored or marginalized, even if they have something valuable to contribute. Online forums give us the chance to be heard, and the reader can choose to ignore it or pay attention—but the point is, WE GET THE CHANCE TO BE HEARD. It isn't any wonder that the majority of posters in most chatrooms are female?" Such sentiments may help explain the high number of female respondents to the survey even as they echo cyberfeminist Sadie Plant's (1997, 144) suggestion that the medium lends itself to a dismantling of gendered power relations in part because of the decentralized forms of communication it facilitates: "The roundabout, circuitous connections with which women have always been associated and the informal networking at which they have excelled now become protocols for everyone."

Removed from traditionally male-dominated public spaces and accessible not just from home but from the privacy of one's workspace, bulletin boards such as TWoP make it hard to differentiate posters based on gender. Perhaps not insignificantly, the form of unpaid labour that goes into a site such as TWoP bears a certain similarity to the unpaid labour of the homemaker. The ability of the new media to dedifferentiate sites of production, domesticity, and leisure has been portrayed by the promoters of the new economy as a form of liberation from spatial constraints: the telecommuter will be able to live wherever he or she wants, skip the traffic, and work from home (or the beach, corner coffee shop, or any other "wired" location). At the same time, as Darin Barney (2000, 147) points out, dedifferentiation makes it possible for employers to off-load the costs of the workplace onto workers and encourages the transformation of the home into a workplace in which domestic labour and paid labour simultaneously take place: "When performed at the same site where cooking, cleaning, and diaper-changing waits to be done, network-mediated telework enables women to exceed even Aristotle's designation of their utility: they can be, simultaneously, unpaid domestic managers as well as poorly paid... wage slaves." The flip side of the fact that online discussion forums facilitate the forms of audience activity that Bacon-Smith (1992) describes as fostering "a women's art/communication system" is that it simultaneously makes possible the exploitation of forms of dedifferentiated and networked labour that have historically characterized the sites of women's work.

The forms of interactivity enabled by networked media also allow formerly nonproductive activities to generate valuable information commodities to the extent that they take place within the monitoring capacity of an interactive digital enclosure. The work of being watched doubles as yet another form of unpaid labour. In this respect, it is tempting to read Plant's (1997) techno-utopianism in the opposite direction: if the traditional gender hierarchy is challenged online, the result is not necessarily an emancipatory privileging of decentralized networking but the universalization of forms of exploitation associated with unpaid labour. As Witheford (2004, 14) suggests, the invisibility of free labour in the "social factory"—the fact that an increasing variety of activities double as value-generating labour thanks to the information-gathering capacity of interactive media—echoes the invisibility of forms of "female domestic drudgery" that are functional to capital "which profited by avoiding the full costs of recreating the successive generations of the labor force."

Viewed in this light, the exploitation of free labour represents the obverse of fan participation as the potentially subversive form of textual "poaching" described by Jenkins (1988, 1992). Jenkins's (1988, 86) formulation relies on and compounds a potentially misleading appropriation of a production-oriented metaphor suggested by de Certeau: "Readers are travelers; they move across lands belonging to someone else, like nomads poaching their way across fields they did not write, despoiling the wealth of Egypt to enjoy it themselves." The metaphor breaks down in the transition from fields to texts: the consumption of crops is exclusive (or, as economists, put it, "rival"), the productive consumption of texts is not. Far from "despoiling" the television texts through their practices, TWoPpers enrich them, not just for themselves but for those who economically benefit from the "added value" produced by the labour of viewers. This is one of the defining characteristics of the contemporary deployment of interactivity: the ability to enfold forms of effort and creativity previously relegated to relatively unproductive (economically speaking) realms within the digital embrace of the social factory.

This is not to dismiss the claims that fan or viewer groups may be engaged in creative activity, nor is it to write off the notion that such groups serve as "communities of practice" (Baym 2000) or sources of enjoyment, culture building, and relationship building (Bacon-Smith 1992; Jenkins 1992). Nevertheless, the point of exploring the ways in which the interactivity of viewers *doubles* as a form of labour is to point out that, in the interactive era, the binary opposition between complicit passivity and subversive participation needs to be revisited and revised. It is one thing to note that viewers derive pleasure and fulfillment from their online activities and quite another to suggest that pleasure is necessarily either empowering for viewers or destabilizing for entrenched forms of corporate control over popular culture. If, as Jenkins (1992, 278) observes, "fandom constitutes the base for consumer activism," it would be misguided to regard all viewer participation as activist. Activity and interactivity need to be clearly distinguished from activism. This becomes a particularly important distinction in an era when the simple equation of participation with empowerment serves to reinforce the marketing strategies of corporate culture. It is precisely the creative character of viewer activity that makes it more valuable to producers: the better the contributions to TWoP, the more likely viewers are to continue to tune in to a particular show; the more work viewers put into researching a program, the more likely they are to form an affective attachment to it. Thus, to note with Baym (2000, 16), following Radway, noting that audience practices have the "potential" for empowerment is not to valorize audience practice "as is." Rather, Radway (1986, 116), in reflecting on her own work on women's romance novels, makes a clear distinction between the potential invoked by the contradictions in audience response and what would count as progressive action: not just transformations in romance narratives themselves but transformation of "real social and material relations as well as the way they are conceived within symbolic forms." By the same logic, fan activity that—even in the form of a communal activity with all of its attendant benefits—ends up reinforcing social and material relations might be considered a form of active participation in the constitution of those relations rather than a challenge to them. The workplace can be a site of community and personal satisfaction and one of economic exploitation. Thinking of these characteristics together is crucial to any critical approach to the current deployment of the promise of interactivity. The Internet helping to promote the formation of communities of practice around TV shows in the era of relationship marketing community is, as Fernback (2002, 11) notes, an increasingly valuable marketing apparatus. The advantage to marketers of online communities is that they help build allegiance to particular products, serving as forums for practices of self-disclosure that generate detailed information about consumers. As one company quoted by Fernback puts it, the systematic development of product-related sites represents "a trend toward the transformation of ad hoc e-communities into established forums that drive product innovation and contribute to profits."

TWoP, which remained an independent site for several years, was purchased by Bravo (whose parent company is NBC-Universal) in early 2007, but its posters continue to make the most of its largely critical approach to the TV shows it recaps. The site may have the potential to serve as an instant focus group, as one respondent put it, but perhaps even more importantly, it helps draw viewers to particular shows and allows them to build up social and information capital that increases their commitment to viewing. Several posters noted that they continued to watch shows that they once enjoyed but no longer really liked because they wanted to participate in the ongoing online dissection of the program, its characters, and its writers. As a public sphere, the site also retains certain pathologies of online community, including the passion for a friction-free form of community, what Kevin Robins (1999, 166) has described as "the desire to be free from the challenge of difference and otherness" and a "a culture of retreat from the world." As one respondent put it, echoing Robins, "The site... provides a sense of community, without the tangles of actually knowing the people."

TWoP also provides a form of publicity without—as Dean (2002) suggests—a public, or, put in slightly different terms, a public that has dispersed its activity into a savvy but domesticated interactivity. Publicity as a counter-hegemonic principle enacts not the drive toward self-exposure associated with the celebrity subject of cyberia but the exposure of the secret of power. The challenge was not directed toward those private secrets associated with the personal lives of public figures but toward the principle of secrecy governing public affairs. The contemporary Habermasian diagnosis of refeudalization suggests a return to the principle of the secrecy of power accompanied by the pomp of public display. What the diagnosis of refeudalization misses—and what is highlighted by the form of savvy critique associated with sites such as TWoP—is the way in which the emerging (interactive) constellation of voyeurism and self-disclosure facilitates identification with the "insiders" on the part of outsiders. One of the aspects of the reverse form of the scopic drive—the exhibitionistic obverse of voyeurism in an increasingly voyeuristic culture—is the impulse to show what one knows. A savvy identification with producers and insiders facilitated by interactive media fosters an acceptance of the rules of the game. In an era of interactive reflexivity, the media turn back on themselves: new media mock the old while tellingly failing to deliver on the promised transformative shift in power relations. It is perhaps possible to discern in the criticism of the commercial mass media a certain resentment over a failed promise, that information would double as a form of power sharing, that once the secret of power were exposed it would be shared. The perceived dissolution of the democratic promise of publicity, in an era in which information is increasingly available and in which power and wealth (and the media) are simultaneously becoming increasingly concentrated in the hands of the few, feeds a savvy attitude toward the media itself. The critical impetus shifts away from political leaders—witness a Pew poll that indicated almost half of the population felt the media were becoming too critical (Pew Research Center for the People and the Press 2003)—and toward the media themselves. The result, however, is not a transformed media but participatory submission. As in the online world of TWoP, spectators take their pleasure in knowing—with the insiders—just why things are as bad as they are and why they could not be any different.

References

Bacon-Smith, Camille. 1992. *Enterprising women*. Philadelphia: University of Pennsylvania Press.

Barney, Darin. 2000. *Prometheus wired: The hope for democracy in the age of network technology*. Chicago: University of Chicago Press.

Baym, Nancy. 2000. *Tune in log on: Soaps, fandom, and online community*. London: Sage.

Bradberry, Grace. 2003. Review: Get a shave, Carter: Forget TV criticism. *The Observer*, January 5.

Couldry, Nick. 2000. *The place of media power: Pilgrims and witnesses of the media age*. London: Routledge.

Dean, Jodi. 2002. *Publicity's secret: How technoculture capitalizes on democracy*. Ithaca, NY: Cornell University Press.

Fernback, Jan. 2002. Using community to sell: The commodification of community in retail web sites. Paper presented at the annual conference of the Association of Internet Researchers, Maastricht, the Netherlands, October.

Fiske, John. 1987. *Television culture: Popular pleasures and politics*. London: Methuen.

Gardyn, Rebecca. 2001. The tribe has spoken. *American Demographics*, 34–40, September.

Gilder, George. 1994. *Life after television: The coming transformation of media and American life*. New York: Norton.

Gitlin, Todd. 1990. Blips, bites and savvy talk: Television's impact on American politics. *Dissent*, 18–26.

Gramsci, Antonio. 1971. Americanism and Fordism. In *Selections from the prison notebooks of Antonio Gramsci*, ed. and trans. Quintin Hoare and Geoffrey Nowell Smith, 279–318. London: Lawrence and Wishart.

Habermas, Jurgen. 1991. *The structural transformation of the public sphere: An inquiry into a category of bourgeois society*. Cambridge, MA: MIT Press.

Jenkins, Henry. 1988. Star Trek rerun, reread, rewritten: Fan writing as textual poaching. *Critical Studies in Mass Communication* 5: 85–107.

———. 1992. *Textual poachers: Television fans & participatory culture*. New York: Routledge, Chapman and Hall.

Kelly, Kevin. 1996. What would McLuhan say? *Wired*, 4.10. http://www.wired.com (accessed 5 April 2005).

Lazarsfeld, Paul F., and Robert K. Merton. 1948. Mass communication, popular taste, and organized social action. In *The communication of ideas*, ed. Lyman Bryson, 95–118. New York: Harper and Row.

Mougayar, Walid. 1998. *Opening digital markets: Battle plans and business strategies for internet commerce*. New York: McGraw-Hill.

Nussbaum, Emily. 2002. Confessions of a spoiler whore: The pleasures of participatory TV. *Slate*, April 4. http://slate.msn.com/id/2063235/ (accessed 2 October 2003).

Pew Research Center For the People and the Press. 2003. *Strong opposition to media cross-ownership emerges: Public wants neutrality* and *pro-American point of view*. http://people-press.org/reports/display.php3?ReportID=188 (accessed 4 October 2003).

Pine, Joseph. 1993. *Mass customization: The new frontier in business competition*. Cambridge, MA: Harvard University Press.

Plant, Sadie. 1997. *Zeros + ones: Digital women and the new technoculture*. London: 4th Estate.

Radway, Janice. 1986. Identifying ideological seams: Mass culture, analytical method, and political practice. *Communication* 6: 93–123.

Robins, Kevin. 1999. Against virtual community: For a politics of distance. *Angelaki* 4(2): 163–70.

Rose, Nikolas. 2001. *Powers of freedom: Reframing political thought*. Cambridge, UK: Cambridge University Press.

Sella, Marshall. 2002. The remote controllers. *New York Times Magazine*, 20 October.

Terranova, Tiziana. 2000. Free labor: Producing culture for the digital economy. *Social Text* 63(18): 33–57.

Witheford, Nick. 2004. Autonomist Marxism and the information society. *Endpage*. http://www.endpage.com (accessed 20 April 2005).

Zizek, Slavoj. 1999. *The ticklish subject*. London: Verso.

The Commodity Flow of US Children's Television

Matthew P. McAllister and J. Matt Giglio

Viewers watching the 8:30 AM telecast of *Rocket Power*, a program on the children's cable network Nickelodeon on Saturday, 26 January 2002, may have noticed at its conclusion (at 8:55 AM) a common technique called "living end credits." Also called "squeezed credits," these occur when the closing credits are reduced to a small portion of the television screen while the bulk of the screen is used to promote an upcoming program. In this case, however, the promotional space is not used to tout a future Nick show, but features a music video by heartthrob singer Aaron Carter. The song is part of the soundtrack for the film *Jimmy Neutron, Boy Genius*, at that time still in theatrical release. The Nick logo and the web address nick.com also appear on the bottom of the screen. Four minutes later, at 9:00, a government-mandated "program separator" (or "bumper") signals that a commercial break is about to start or end. In this case, the program separator airing before *Rugrats* features the character of Jimmy Neutron controlling an orange robotic monster with a Nickelodeon logo on its head.

At 9:10 AM a video "bug" appears for several seconds during the *Rugrats* program. A bug is a small video icon in the screen's bottom corner; often this identifies the network being watched. In this case, the bug is quite elaborate. Appearing on the screen are the words, "Grab a pencil and paper. Nickelodeon Milk Mustache. Coming up." True to its word, at 9:12 a minute-long spot promotes a contest co-sponsored by Nickelodeon and the dairy industry. The spot states that the winner, along with a Nickelodeon character, will be featured in a "Got Milk?" advertisement in *Nickelodeon* magazine. When a copy of the magazine is displayed on screen, Jimmy Neutron is pictured on the cover.

Fifteen minutes later (9:27 AM), a traditional spot commercial for the *Jimmy Neutron* movie airs. A promotion for a Jimmy Neutron computer game available at nick.com airs at 9:44. At 9:56 and 10:26, different versions of the commercial and squeezed credits for *Jimmy Neutron* air. At 10:58, a milk mustache commercial featuring the video-game character Mario completes the commercial circuit: the ad portrays live-action children interacting with a licensed property, just as promised to potential winners of the Nickelodeon contest.

The Jimmy Neutron example from Nickelodeon, although particularly licensing-oriented (Pecora, 2004), is not uncharacteristic of the often-seamless movement of product images and corporate branding that is increasingly a defining element of US children's television. It thus illustrates "commodity flow," a concept that highlights the embeddedness of promotional and commercial techniques throughout television generally but especially in children's television. To explore how the phenomenon applies to commercial programming aimed at children, we first discuss commodity flow as a construct, including its establishment in the work of Raymond Williams (1975). The concept is valuable for deconstructing children's television, given the genre's long-established roots in commercial culture and more current role in media corporate synergy. The existence of different manifestations of commodity flow—including intra-channel, inter-channel, and synergistic flow—will then be demonstrated by an analysis of specific commodity flow patterns in several hours of children's programming. The analysis shows how the flow of commodities on children's television often blurs the distinction between content and promotional forms, dramatically illustrating the intense level of commercialism targeted at this audience.

From Television Flow to Commodity Flow

Television executives have probably understood the idea of flow, especially as manifested in audience viewing patterns and programming strategies, since the beginnings of commercial broadcasting. Raymond Williams is largely credited with introducing the scholarly concept of television flow, now one of the most commonly used concepts in television studies (Corner, 1999). Williams argued that television is a technological and cultural experience that brings together discrete phenomena (events that occur outside of the medium in different locales and contexts) by framing them in a continuous stream of images and sound channelled through television. Specific techniques such as television program promotions, cliffhangers in programs timed before a commercial break, and strategic program scheduling combine with television's characteristics as a medium to decrease the incongruence between images on the screen and enhance their ability to flow into one other. Content categories such as different program genres and product commercials therefore are enacted not as fragmented and isolated forms but more as the experience of "watching TV." The ease of channel switching (even in the pre-remote control 1970s, when Williams developed the concept), the similarity of program structure, and uniform scheduling on nearly all stations and networks render flow an inter-channel experience, "perhaps the defining characteristic of broadcasting" (Williams, 1975, p. 86).

The idea of television flow has been critiqued and transformed. Modleski (1983), for example, argues that flow does not adequately explain all television genres and "dayparts" (an industry term for sections of the broadcasting day), especially daytime television, which she contends is characterized by repetition and interruptability, to match the reception context of stay-at-home wives and mothers. Similarly, Corner (1999) regards Williams' concept as undertheorized and often misapplied. He concludes that over-zealous use of flow essentializes the medium and masks fundamental differences in its programming forms.

Revisionists also contend that Williams attributed too much agency to the technology of television in his explanation of flow, therefore downplaying the influence of economic factors (Corner, 1999). The "product" of commercial television is, after all, the audience, which the television industry sells to advertisers (an idea first attributed to Smythe, 1977). Viewers who switch channels or turn the television off can no longer be sold to advertisers. It is in the best economic interests of television, then, to reduce the disjointed nature of the transition between "switchable" moments, such as when a program breaks to a series of commercials, and thus keep viewers in their television place.

Budd, Craig, and Steinman (1999) point out another increasingly important way that advertisers influence television flow. They argue that the "flow of commodities," characterized by the similarity of specific elements in product commercials, promotional spots, and programs, is intended not just to keep an audience in front of the television, but also uses all possible televisual forms to sell, including but not limited to the traditional 30-second spot commercial. Their analysis of one night's broadcast of CBS, for instance, identifies such commodity-flow characteristics as the presence of one actor both as a character in a program and as a narrator for a commercial that airs during the program, and product placements.

Budd et al.'s (1999) emphasis on the pervasiveness of commodity flow is well aligned with other critiques of the increased level of commercialism in broadcasting (Andersen, 1995; Jacobson & Mazur, 1995; McAllister, 1996). These scholars argue that, beginning in the mid-1980s, television advertising was plunged into crisis as several developments unfolded. These included: (1) dissemination of technologies like the remote control and personal recording devices that facilitate viewers' avoidance of discrete commercial spot advertisements; (2) increased competition for viewers from cable, video games, and other sources that eroded traditional television network viewership; and (3) the large number of television commercials/promotions ("clutter") that may undermine the effectiveness of any single television spot ad. The result was an increased aggressiveness on the part of advertisers. In this context, television's commodity flow is cultivated when advertisers try to prevent viewer zapping, enhance the promotional power of ad campaigns with the help of increasingly accommodating television networks, and create connections between ads and beloved programs to help campaigns stand out from the clutter. Resulting examples of commodity flow on prime-time television include college football bowl sponsorships, "long-form" advertisements like infomercials, and aggressive product placement in such genres as reality-based programs.

Adding to the increased influence of commercial product flow on television are the synergistic strategies of many key corporations involved with the television industry. The increased emphasis on media promotion is one side-effect of the growth of large media entertainment conglomerates (see, for example, Bagdikian, 2004; McChesney, 1999). Corporations owning different media outlets often exploit promotional and licensing linkages between the properties to create corporate efficiencies. Television holdings, then, may be used to promote (and be promoted by) music, book, film, and other media subsidiaries. As manifested by such synergistically driven companies as Time Warner, Disney, Viacom, and News Corp., the temptation to create a "promotional flow" among different programming and commercial elements may be as great as—and complementary to—commodity flow driven by advertisers (McAllister, 2000).

A more salient example of this phenomenon is found in children's television, an especially commercialized genre of television, both historically and in the current hyper-promotional environment. The next section briefly discusses traditional connections between advertising and children's programming, as well as recent trends in synergistic ownership of children's media.

Children's Commercial Television in Historical and Corporate Contexts

Early children's programming was in many ways more crassly (if less strategically) influenced by advertising's influence than later versions. Advertisers began aggressively using the medium to sell directly to kids at least by the mid-1950s with the success of the Mickey Mouse Club to promote Disney and other brands (Kline, 1993).

Many early TV ads targeted at children in retrospect were highly "flow oriented." Sponsorship of programs by one dominant advertiser was common. In the late 1950s, for example, Kellogg Company owned the syndicated *Huckleberry Hound* (Mittell, 2003). Over 60 per cent of children's programs sampled from the 1950s contained sales pitches by the program's host for sponsored products. These programs routinely used "integral ads" (seamless commercial messages in the program featuring established program characters) and "segue ads" (touting of products by program actors, but often in a neutral setting and conducted between program segments or before a more circumscribed commercial break) (Alexander, Benjamin, Hoerrner & Roe, 1998).

Legislation eventually banned practices such as explicit host-selling. Nonetheless, other commercial and promotional techniques encouraged commodity flow. Fast-food restaurants, breakfast cereals, and other products are sold on children's television, but it is perhaps the toy industry that is the most integrated in the programming mix. Describing the relationship as symbiotic, Pecora (1998) says the "programs offer the toy industry advertisements for characters, and the toys present the entertainment industry with readily identifiable characters" (p. 40). Creating toys that feature licensed characters—characters that appear in a variety of program and commodity forms—allows advertisers to grab the child viewers' attention and break out of commercial clutter (Seiter, 1993). In 1997, approximately half of all toys were based on licences from television or movies (Kapur, 1999). This also works in the other direction: beginning in the 1980s programming based upon toy and game characters became common (Pecora, 1998). Significant money is at stake. In 2000–2001, advertising on children's network television earned $700–750 million a year for the cable and broadcast networks (Larson, 2001). This figure actually underestimates the value of children's television programming, given the promotional benefits this provides its corporate owners. As a market, children in the 4–12 age group directly control as much as $29 billion a year, and influence family purchases in the $290 billion range (McDonald & Lavelle, 2001), including media products such as DVDs.

Four corporate giants have been especially involved in producing and distributing children's television to tap the advertising and media-product purchasing potential of this market. Typically owning both a broadcast and cable outlet for their programming, these corporations use a synergistic philosophy to build multimedia brand identity. These four are briefly profiled below.

- News Corp, via its FoxKids Network programming block, was a dominant player in the 1990s, triggered by its embrace of the Power Rangers franchise earlier that decade (Kinder, 1999; Pecora, 1998). Fox's audience share dwindled in the early 2000s and the network's sale of the Fox Family Channel to Disney in 2001 left it without the potential for all-important cable/broadcast "cross-platform promotions" (quoted in Bernstein, 2001, p. 30).
- Viacom, through its Nickelodeon cable network and franchise, was the ratings leader after the Fox drop-off, and is one of the top-rated US cable networks of any type (Sandler, 2004). Nickelodeon often uses its corporate siblings such as Paramount to carry and promote licensing. CBS, also owned by Viacom, typically programs an abbreviated block of children's shows on Saturday morning, most of it heavily influenced by the Nickelodeon brand.
- Disney is, of course, a visible force in children's television, using ABC to reach younger child viewers early in its schedule, and its cable networks The Disney Channel and ABC Family (bought from Fox) to attract the slightly older "tween" market (Dempsey, 2001a). Although the Disney Channel is "commercial-free," it is hardly promotion-free: It generates revenue from cable licence fees, licensing/merchandising activity, and sponsorship deals (Schmuckler, 2002).
- Time Warner uses both its cable-based Cartoon Network and its broadcasting subsidiary Kids WB to compete for the market. Each of these TW outlets is a separate entity with its own organizational culture, but the goal is to develop synergistic projects and approach advertisers as a combined unit (Bernstein, 2001; Schmuckler, 2002). In fact, the two networks frequently share or "repurpose" each other's programs (Sandler, 2003, p. 102).

Commodity flow in children's television is not wholly without constraints. Applying to both broadcast and cable (Kunkel & McIlrath, 2003), the Children's Television Act of 1990 established restrictions on the amount of "commercial time" during children's television (10.5 minutes per hour on weekends; 12 minutes per hour on weekdays) and broad requirements for the airing of children's educational programming. Host-selling and program-length commercials are prohibited; bumpers between programs and commercials are required. However, several loopholes in this Act, as well as recent media developments, leave much room for the cultivation of commodity flow, as will be illustrated. For example, the ambiguities embedded in the definitions of both commercial time and educational programming problematize the effectiveness of such measures (Kinder, 1999; Kunkel, 2001). Public service announcements (PSAs) and program promotions—

both of which can incorporate commodity imagery—are not considered advertising by the Act (Kunkel & McIlrath, 2003). In addition, the definition of program-length commercial used by the Act, a result of policy compromise, essentially restates the definition of host-selling: "a program associated with a product in which commercials for that product are aired" (quoted in Kunkel, 2001). Programs based upon toys and media licences, then, are perfectly legal, as long as ads for those same products do not air during the program on that same channel. *On that same channel*, it will be argued, becomes a significant factor in the modern multichannel environment. Although their existence is mandated, bumpers can become tools for, rather than against, "connected selling" in a medium dominated by corporate branding.

Method

To capture the possibilities for commodity flow in children's television, several hours of programming from five different networks were taped and analyzed on two separate dates. Three continuous hours of programming (from 8 AM to 11 AM, EST) were collected on Saturday, 29 July 2000, and Saturday, 26 January 2002, for a total of 30 hours. Two different time periods were chosen to prevent analyzing an atypical historical moment, such as the highly commodified Pokémon craze in the late 1990s. In addition, two seasons, summer (from 2000) and winter (2002), were selected to avoid a sample skewed by calendar-based promotions or contests. The five networks (three cable and two broadcast) videotaped were ABC, Cartoon Network, Fox, Nickelodeon, and the WB. These five networks were chosen for study, given their uninterrupted three-hour block of children's programming (unlike NBC or CBS), their stable nature (unlike the troubled Family Channel, see Dempsey, 2001b), and their acceptance of product advertising (unlike PBS or The Disney Channel).

Tapings were coordinated so that analysis began at exactly 8 AM, to enable cross-channel comparisons of images and content types. The authors took detailed notes about iconography, sounds, language, and other textual characteristics. They also noted the beginning and ending time of the discrete units of content types found on children's television: program credits, program segment beginning and endings, program separators, product commercials, promotional spots for programs, network and station IDs, and PSAs. The resulting 131 pages of single-spaced notes were then extensively re-read and compared to uncover points of convergence and emerging themes and groupings. Moreover, video tape segments were often viewed again to expand the analysis.[1]

Guiding the analysis of the programming and the subsequent notes was the idea of commodity flow, the main "sensitized concept" of the study. Sensitized concepts are "taxonomical systems that discover an integrating scheme within the data themselves" and facilitate analytical focus in qualitative research (Christians & Carey, 1989, p. 370). Using commodity flow as a significant sensitized concept enabled a focus on connections between content categories, especially when these connections involved commercial and promotional forms. These connections were then used to generate styles and categories of commodity flow. Various forms in the enhanced commercial and synergistically promotional environment of children's television often blur the distinctions among traditional content types, different networks, and even different media. The remainder of this article analyzes three kinds of commodity flow emerging from the programming: intra-channel commodity flow, inter-channel commodity flow, and synergistic commodity flow.

Intra-channel Commodity Flow

Among the most common of the commodity flow categories found during the telecasts was intra-channel commodity flow, where commodity images are interwoven throughout the lineup of one network. The researchers found several subcategories of intra-channel commodity flow.

Shared Textual Elements between Programs and Commercials

Seiter (1993) notes that children's television commercials are "rapidly paced, musical, and filled with special effects and animation. Children behave raucously, outsmarting adults and escaping the dull restrictions of home and school" (p. 3). This, of course, also describes much of the children's programming that airs between the commercials. The visual styles and sounds of commercials and children's programs are strikingly similar.

Animation, obviously, is a common modality found throughout children's television. Often, the specific style of the animation of commercials matches that of other content types such as programs, program promos, and program separators. For example, in the 2002 ABC sample, similar visual styles mark the 8:00 AM cartoon program *Mary Kate and Ashley in Action!* This program features the animated adventures of the Olsen twin sisters as secret agents, but the beginning and end of the program are live-action segments featuring the actors Mary Kate and Ashley Olsen. This mix of live action and animation continue in a program separator at 8:27:35, which presents a live-action small girl (about the same age as Mary Kate and Ashley) dancing with an animated "1" (as in "Disney's 1 Saturday Morning," the network's branding slogan at the time). Immediately following, at 8:27:41, a commercial for Honeycombs cereal airs, with a plot involving a live-action snowboarder morphing into the animated Honeycomb "Craver." This is followed at 8:28:11 by a Three Musketeers candy bar ad, where the animated Musketeers accept a "Chocolately Award" at a live-action ceremony. Following this is a 15-second promotion for *Disney's Teacher's Pet* (all animated), back to the girl-dancing program separator, and then finally the life-action epilogue with Mary Kate and Ashley. Similar matching of styles continues throughout Saturday morning.

Sounds between commercials and other program types also match. In prime-time television, the sound difference between programs and commercials is often significant. Adult television programs tend to be fairly sedate in terms of music and sound effects; the ads feature such elements more prominently. However, jarring sound effects and loud rock or hip-hop music are much more common in children's programming, matching the surrounding commercials. Sounds of conflict and strident music may be found in action-adventure cartoons and commercials for toys, such as a sequence on Fox 2002 that featured violent conflict and action music in a *Power Rangers Time Force* episode (8:31), a Lego commercial featuring Star Wars characters (8:34), and a promo for the spin-off *Power Rangers Wild Force* (8:35).

Similarly, the role of laughter varies more widely in prime-time content forms than in children's television. Most prime-time situation comedies feature a laugh track or live audience reactions, an audio characteristic missing in most commercials. Alternatively, laugh tracks from real or virtual audiences are absent from children's programming, matching their absence in the ads. Tellingly, though, children's laughter itself (emanating from characters) is found in nearly all content forms, including programs and ads, depending upon the target demographic. One such example was a two-minute stretch on ABC 2002 that featured similar sounds of children laughing/playing on the opening credits of the *Recess* program, and the subsequent ABC program separator and Kool-Aid commercial.

Programming Featuring Licensed Characters

Virtually all Saturday morning programming involves licensing to some degree. Even a commercially sedate program like *Doug* (aired in 2000 on ABC at 8:30 and 9:00 AM) has been available in video games (for Game Boy), theatrical film (with the franchise hopeful title *Doug's 1st Movie*), video tapes, and books (well over 20 different titles).

Much Saturday morning programming is more definitively embedded in ancillary licensing. Many of these programs have their roots in video games, toys, or other merchandise. The WB and Fox in particular aired programming spun off from licensed commodities (see Tables 22.1 and 22.2). Nearly 80 per cent of programs aired or promoted during the period sampled were based upon characters with strong ties to other media or commodities, including comic books (*Batman/Superman Adventures, Static Shock, X-Men*), movies (*The Mummy, Alienators: Evolution Continues, Jackie Chan Adventures*), book series (*R.L. Stine's The Nightmare Room*), and toys (*Transformers, Action Man, Dinozaurs*).

Strikingly commodified are *Pokémon* and variations of this model, such as *Digimon, Monster Rancher, Medabot, Cubix, Mon Colle Knights, Yu-Gi-Oh!*, and *Card Captors. Pokémon*, a dominating brand in the child market from 1996 to 2001 (Tobin, 2004), represents the genre; plots ask characters to collect items such as cards or small creatures (Pokémon is an abbreviation of "Pocket Monster"), with the outcome of a key competition or even the fate of the world often hanging in the balance. In the programs these items are magical; in real life they are for sale. Specific plot points often emphasized the importance of amassing large collections (*à la* the *Pokémon* brand slogan "Gotta Catch 'Em All"). In a *Pokémon* episode on the WB 2000, one character states explicitly, "The more Pokémon you have, the better position you are in to win battles." Given the emphasis on collecting implied in nearly all of the above listed cartoons, the programs function as virtual commercials for the licensed collectables featured in the cartoons and related subsidiary properties.

One commodity flow element driving this point home was the use of multiple content

Table 22.1 | List of Children's Morning Programs Shown or Promoted on FOX during the Time Sampled (in order of first appearance)

July 29, 2000	January 26, 2002
Power Rangers LightSpeed Rescue[a]	Transformers: Robots in Disguise[a]
Action Man[a] (based upon a Hasbro property[c])	Digimon[ab]
Beast Machine[a]	Power Rangers Wild Force[a]
Digimon[ab]	Galidora (a "Lego-collaboration action show"[d])
Angela Anacond[a]	Medabots[a]
NASCAR Racers[a]	Power Rangers Time Force[a]
Cybersix	Ripping Friends
X-Men[ab]	Mon Colle Knights[a] (stands for "Monster Collector Knights")
Dinozaurs[a] (based on action figures created by Bondai[c])	Alienators: Evolution Continues[a] (based on the movie Evolution)
Flint the Time Detective	
Escaflowne	
Pokémon[ab] (syndicated version: local promo)	
Histeria!	
Monster Rancher[a]	

[a] A program that is heavily commodity-oriented through licensing activities in the U.S.
[b] A program with specific characters also used in commercials or other forms to promote product licensing during telecast.
[c] From Hall (2000).
[d] From Finnigan (2002).

Table 22.2 | List of Saturday Morning Programs Shown or Promoted on the WB during the Time Sampled (in order of first appearance)

July 29, 2000	January 26, 2002
Batman/Superman Adventures[a]	Cubix[a]
Poke'mon[ab]	Jackie Chan Adventures[a]
Men in Black[a]	Pokémon[a]
Cardcaptors[a]	Static Shock[a]
Batman Beyonda[a]	Scooby-Doo[a]
Detention	Magic Schoolbus (local promo for a program on a competitor station)
	The Mummy[a]
	X-Men: Evolution[a]
	R.L. Stine's The Nightmare Room[a]
	Yu-Gi-Oh! a

[a] A program that is heavily commodity-oriented through licensing activities in the U.S.
[b] A program with specific characters also used in commercials or other forms to promote product licensing during telecast.

forms to create a flow of licensed programming icons on a given network. As promoted programs *and* advertised products *and* cross-promoted/cross-mediated characters, images from licensed properties are sprinkled throughout the lineup. An example of this is seen in Table 22.3, which lists the promotional and commercial moments aired between 8:13 and 10:58 AM for *Digimon*, which in July 2000 was Fox's highest rated children's program (Hall, 2000). The promotions and product commercials create a steady flow of licensed images that connect the *Digimon* program with the Digimon website, the then-upcoming *Digimon the Movie*, Digimon video games, the brand identity of FoxKids, its website, and the various programs that Digimon promotions are connected to through "bug" symbols. Although only promotions for the *Digimon* television program aired during the *Digimon* program (i.e., no product commercials, thus fulfilling the letter of the Children's Television Act of 1990), the multi-licensed commodity orientation of the Digimon brand makes such distinctions irrelevant. Indeed, some forms, such as a "promotion" for the FoxKids *Digimon the Movie* tie-in contest, are difficult to classify. It could be legitimately labelled both a promotion for *Digimon* on FoxKids and an advertisement for the *Digimon* movie.

Programming Icons in Commercials

While the above practice integrates the commercial function into programs, another strategy creates "camouflaged ads" (McAllister, 1996) by making product commercials look like programs. A primary mechanism for this is integrating television program characters into these product commercials.

For example, an ad for "The New Rugrats Edition Gateway Astro PC" (at 10:43:29) that aired on Nickelodeon during a 2000 installment of *Spongebob Squarepants*—and one that is part of a larger cross-promotional campaign between network and advertiser (Sandler, 2004)—uses clips and sounds from *Rugrats*. Although the commercial itself combines animation and live action, it begins with animation directly lifted from a *Rugrats* episode;

Table 22.3 | Flow of *Digimon* Images, FOX, July 29, 2000

Time	Image
8:13:02	Promotion for *Digimon* summer reruns, framed with FOXKids logo (:20 seconds)
8:23:58	Promotion for *Digimon* summer reruns
8:34:36	Product commercial for Digimon website, which shows Digimon-licensed merchandise available in eight different product categories (:25 seconds)
8:41:51	Promotion for *Digimon* summer reruns
8:49:20	Promotion for FOXKids *Digimon* The Movie tie-in contest (:40 seconds); winners receive "Digimon Game Guide"
8:50:20	Promotion for *Digimon* summer reruns
8:57:27	Promotion in bug: Digimon character appears in bottom corner during the program *NASCAR Racer* (:10 seconds)
9:00:01	Program: Digimon first episode begins (:30 minutes)
9:14:37	Promotion for *Digimon* upcoming season (:20 seconds)
9:17:34	Promotion: Digimon character appears in promo for FOXkids.com website
9:28:27	Promotion during credits, for *Digimon* summer reruns
9:43:17	Promotion for *Digimon* summer reruns
9:43:37	Promotion: Digimon character appears in promo for FOXkids.com website
9:51:16	Promotion of FOXKids *Digimon The Movie* tie-in contest
10:10:05	Promotion for *Digimon* summer reruns
10:20:50	Promotion of FOXKids *Digimon The Movie* tie-in contest
10:27:10	Promotion in Bug: Digimon character appears in bottom corner during the program *Monster Rancher* (:10 seconds)
10:30:39	Program: *Digimon* second episode begins (:30 minutes)
10:43:30	Promotion for *Digimon* upcoming season
10:57:57	Promotion: narrator promotes *Digimon* upcoming season during closing credits

the first sounds heard are the title music that also begins the program. The ad uses seven different clips from *Rugrats*, all intercut between live-action clips of a little girl laughingly using her *Rugrats*-branded personal computer. An episode of *Rugrats* had concluded on the network just 43 minutes earlier. Similarly, in 2000 a cross-promotional ad for Pokémon toys at Burger King featuring Pokémon animation aired on the WB in 2000—also carrying *Pokémon* the network program—and on the local Fox affiliate that also carried *Pokémon* the syndicated program. At 9:12 AM in 2000, the Cartoon Network characters Cow and Chicken appear in a Got Milk ad on that network.

Kunkel & McIlrath (2003) argue that some product advertising may mask selling intentions by resembling the more benign public service announcement (PSA). PSAs likewise can be integrated into the larger licensed promotional flow of children's television. Resembling both the Fox cartoon *NASCAR Racer* and promotions for the program, a "wear your seatbelt" PSA aired on Fox 2000 (10:33AM, 90 minutes after the program ended) integrates icons, footage, music, and sounds of the cartoon with a message from real-life NASCAR racer Jeff Gordon and stock footage of a NASCAR race. Gordon is visually framed by a FoxKids graphic and wears his racing outfit, which prominently displays sponsor logos such as Pepsi and GMAC. The PSA—essentially a promotion for the cartoon, NASCAR, and its merchandise and sponsors—ends with the same group voice from the cartoon's opening credits that shouts "NASCAR!" As a PSA, it is not counted toward the commercial limits imposed by the Children's Television Act of 1990.

Inter-channel Commodity Flow

Although a significant part of television scheduling and advertising placement is still premised on the idea of the "lazy viewer," the remote control and channel surfing that results has nevertheless affected much programming placement strategy (Bellamy & Walker, 1996). Channel surfing by potentially short-attention-span child viewers is assumed to occur especially frequently. The same commercial is sometimes placed on different channels at the same time to try to "roadblock" those trying to escape ads via the remote control (McAllister, 1996).

With children's television, it is unclear how much inter-channel placement results from strategy, and how much is a matter of sheer redundancy. Many advertising and merchandising campaigns purchase multiple placements on the networks, so that even active channel surfers cannot avoid these ads. One common advertisement found during the 2002 sample, for instance, was for *MVP2: Most Vertical Primate*, a direct-to-DVD movie about a skateboarding chimpanzee (and sequel to *Most Valuable Primate*, about a hockey-playing chimpanzee). This advertisement aired 21 times during the three-hour sample across the five networks: ABC (six times), Cartoon (two), Fox (six), Nickelodeon (two), and WB (five). Inevitably, then, a roadblock, whether intentional or not, occurred on four of the six networks during one four-minute stretch: This ad appeared at 8:47:16 on WB; 8:50:09 on ABC; 8:51:07 on Fox; and 8:51:10 on the Cartoon Network.

This inter-channel commodity flow across networks was also true not just for one ad placed many times, but also for licences that appear in many promotional forms. In 2002, 15 minutes before a promotion for *The Flintstones* program on the Cartoon Network, its sibling the WB aired a Fruity Pebbles cereal ad featuring Fred and Barney in a commercial mock-up of another program, *Survivor*. More extensive was Pokémon, still a hot property during the 2000 sample. Commercials for Pokémon products and for cross-promotional activities with fast-food restaurants as well as promotions for movies and TV were ubiquitous on the five-channel schedule of the sample. Table 22.4 focuses on 12 minutes when an active channel surfer could view promotional iconography of Pokémon on all five cable networks. Forms include ads for Pokémon products (a trading

Table 22.4 | *Pokémon* Iconography "Roadblock" on Five Networks, July 29, 2000

8:21:42, ABC	Commercial with cross-promotion (Burger King ad with a *Pokémon the Movie* tie-in)
8:27:40, WB	Program promotion (*Pokémon* mentioned as part of summer line-up)
8:28:15, NICK	Commercial for licensed product (Pokémon Trading Card League)
8:28:52, CN	Commercial for licensed product (Pokémon Trading Card League)
8:29:10, WB	Commercial for cross-promotion and licensed product (Pokémon video game shown in a Fruit-by-the-Foot tie-in with Nintendo)
8:33:36, FOX	Commercial with cross-promotion (Burger King ad with a *Pokémon the Movie tie*-in)

card league) and media extensions (the movie version), a promotional spot for the program, and tie-ins in advertisements for Burger King and the snack food Fruit by the Foot. Perhaps exploiting the potential for these multichannel lead-in promotions, *Pokémon* the program begins a half-hour later on the WB.

Synergistic Commodity Flow

Besides the encroachment of product advertisements on other content categories in children's television, another influence on commodity flow is the corporate interests of the network's conglomerate owner. As noted earlier, all five networks studied are owned by entertainment media corporations. These corporations advocate promotional synergies, whereby any given property is used to promote other properties or an overarching corporate brand. Such activity adds a layer of media product promotion upon the traditional toy, cereal, and snack food product commodity flow in children's television. This strategy was especially evident for the corporations with significant multimedia branding targeted at children: Disney, Viacom, and Time Warner.

Disney has been especially aggressive in using its broadcasting and cable outlets to create a corporate brand. Many critics accuse Disney of appropriating culturally rich stories through corporate ownership and then transforming these texts into ideological visions of life that connect to the interests of corporate capitalism and patriarchy (see, for example, Giroux, 2001). Often the specific texts that Disney is accused of appropriating are classic fairy tales, such as Snow White and Cinderella. However, Disney stamps its identity on more recent cultural materials as well. As Table 22.5 shows, most of the ABC programs shown during the sample have a possessive modifier in their title: "Disney's—." This title characteristic explicitly signals Disney's ownership and connects the brand identity of the corporation with the specific program. This is true even for a program like *Doug*, which originally aired on Nickelodeon in 1991. Disney's name in the altered official title of the program, the result of a production company purchase in 1996, may be legally correct. However, the title *Disney's Doug* symbolically overwhelms the important role and original authorship of the program's creator, Jim Jinkins.

Even the other non-"Disney's" programs on ABC's Saturday morning schedule ultimately have their own synergistic purpose. *Sabrina, the Animated Series* (the title of which connotes "spin-off") in 2000 helped to plug the prime-time *Sabrina, the Teenage Witch*, at that time still airing on ABC. In 2002, *Mary Kate and Ashley in Action!* helped create an inter-channel flow, as other Olsen programs like Two of a Kind and *So Little Time* were shown on the ABC Family Channel. *Two of a Kind* on ABC Family aired at 7:30 AM, immediately before its cartoon

Table 22.5 | ABC's Program Line-Up, 8–11 am, July 29, 2000 and January 26, 2002

2000[a]	2002
Disney's Recess	Mary Kate and Ashley in Action!
Disney's Doug	Disney's Teacher's Pet
Disney's Recess	Disney's Recess
Disney's The Weekenders	Disney's Recess
Sabrina, The Animated Series	Lizzie McGuire
NASCAR Racers[a]	Even Stevens

[a] Interstitial programming ("One Saturday Morning") filled the remainder half-hour.

equivalent on ABC, creating a quasi-inter-channel lead-in. *Lizzie McGuire* and *Even Stevens* are "Powered by Zoog," as ABC program separators and other promotions informed viewers. "Zoog" was a "tween-targeted" programming brand strongly tied with The Disney's Channel's lineup. Both *Lizzie* and *Stevens* were shown on ABC and The Disney Channel during this time. One ABC promotional spot (10:54) tells viewers that *Lizzie McGuire* may also be found on The Disney Channel: this promotion aired about a half-hour after the ABC version of the program ended. Thus, a paradox in the new synergistic media environment is the promotion of a cable network by a broadcast network owned by the same corporate owner, essentially urging viewers to switch channels.

Other content forms besides the programs tout the Disney brand on ABC Saturday mornings. In 2000, the interstitial programming "Disney's One Saturday Morning" promoted Disney and featured Disney characters like Timon and Pumbaa from *The Lion King* in short skits. In a very similar manner, the shorter program separators (with a narrator saying "Disney's One Saturday Morning will be right back" and the word Disney prominently displayed) do not separate Disney content from the Disney ads and Disney promotions at all. Instead, they become modern versions of "segue ads" from the 1950s, playing up the Disney brand and connecting programs to more conventional forms of commercial culture. ABC telecasts commercials for Disney products (*Atlantis* on DVD, 2002, for example) and promotions for Disney programs (*Disney's Mickey Mouse Works* on ABC, which aired after 11 AM that day and therefore not part of the sample) to fill any potential void in the flow of Disney branding. As Table 22.6 illustrates, in the 2002 broadcast nearly all content types (with the exception of the few PSAs) mentioned or showed Disney, often quite extensively. This, then, creates a promotional flow whereby Disney's name is displayed or uttered 178 times during the three-hour span, nearly once a minute in ads, promotions, and programs. ABC essentially becomes, at least on Saturday mornings, a Disney branding channel.

Other networks also use their children's daypart to promote synergistic holdings. The Nickelodeon/Jimmy Neutron example cited earlier highlights the influence of synergy in that venue. For Time Warner holdings, an ad for *Pokémon the Movie 2000* airs on the Cartoon Network 2000 (9:26) at the same time that the *Pokémon* program is shown on the WB. This strategy subverts restrictions against program-length commercials and host-selling by using two different channels to link product (the movie) to the program. In addition, synergy was at the heart of the Pokémon property for Time Warner,

Table 22.6 | Instances of Visual Appearance and Vocal Mentions of "Disney" on ABC, 8–11 am, January 26, 2002

Content type	Visual Appearance	Vocal Mention
Program title/opening credits	9	0
Program ending credits	16	6
Program seperators	43	43
Product advertisements	8	4
Program promotions	32	11
Network/station ID	6	0
Public service announcements	0	0
Totals	114	64

creating an added incentive. Warner Brothers Pictures and Nintendo were involved with the production/distribution of *Pokémon the Movie 2000.* Meanwhile, Atlantic Records, a subsidiary of Time Warner, produced the soundtrack, which is also touted on the commercial for the movie.

The Internet is a large part of the synergistic strategy, encouraging an "inter-media" commodity flow, or an "overflow" (Brooker, 2001). The major children's programming players all have websites aimed at children (disney.com, foxkids.com, kidswb.com, cartoonnetwork.com, nick.com), and sometimes more than one; toonami.com, a Time Warner website hyped by both WB and Cartoon Network, for example, is devoted to action cartoons and anime. These sites are promoted through bugs (that often transform from the corporate name to the website address), squeezed credits, and their own promotional spots.

Such sites help to extend the brand, create sites to sell merchandise, and further encourage the flow of audiences through corporate programming. In a promotional spot for both *The Mummy* and kidswb.com that was shown on WB 2002, a contest is touted called "Ask Imhotep." The spot is shown at 9:52, during *The Mummy*, and repeated at 10:17. The narrator says, "Kids WB is giving you a chance to ask Imhotep [the Mummy's name] anything you want to know . . . . Go to kidswb.com and ask your question. And then watch Kids WB on Saturday, February 9th, and Imhotep might read your question on TV." This spot, then, directs audiences from the TV to the Internet (where online shopping opportunities exist) and back to the TV. A similar tactic is used by the Cartoon Network in its 2002 Batman/Superman voting competition where viewers can "go to toonami.com, choose your favorite [character], and play them in a new online game . . . The winner is announced at 5 [on Cartoon Network]." One difference, as the narrator in a later version of the spot informs us, is that this network/Internet promotion is also a type of product ad, because it is "Brought to you by Gatorade . . . Is it in You?" In fact, the narrator for this promotion, although of course uncredited, sounds very much like Kevin Conroy, the actor who is the voice for Batman and has narrated earlier, stand-alone Gatorade commercials. This promotional spot pulls extra duty, plugging with the same images and sounds: (1) Cartoon Network; (2) Batman licences; (3) Superman licences; (4) DC Comics (owned by Time Warner); (5) the toonami brand and website; and (6) Gatorade.

Conclusion

This analysis of commodity flow on children's television shows the intrusion of selling and branding strategies across many content forms, and the erosion of distinctions between these forms that this intrusion fosters. The heavy commercialism found throughout the history of US children's television notwithstanding, the increasingly strategic nature of commodity flow and the promotional synergy of entertainment corporations add levels of integration. Specific forms of flow subvert policy restrictions designed to decrease commercialism. Program separators and PSAs, for instance, become part of the branding mix rather than barriers to commercial blurring.

Both samples showed strong indicators of flow. However, even in the modest time that elapsed between 2000 and 2002, increases in promotional flows may be seen. Although the 2000 sample featured the visibility of collector programs like Pokémon and Digimon that were nearing the end of their reign, the 2002 sample offered more systematic integration of cross-promotion between corporate holdings, such as the multi-licensed promotion of Jimmy Neutron and the repurposing (Sandler, 2003, 2004) of programs like *Lizzie McGuire* from the Disney Channel to ABC, promoting and branding the former while decreasing production costs for the latter. Web addresses and promotions of websites were frequent in 2000, but the strategic movement of children to commercially friendly sites—such as the Mummy and Superman/Batman "contests" mentioned above—indicates that new techniques are evolving to fully integrate the Internet.

As noted earlier, some critics of the concept of television flow claim that it essentializes television and masks key distinctions among content categories found on television (discussed in Corner, 1999). In fact, there were moments of *dis*junction in the sample. Many PSAs were more sedate, shorter, and less sales-oriented than many of the forms around them, such as a 10-second PSA for the music-oriented website playmusic.org (ABC, 2002, 9:51, repeated at 10:31). Especially on the cable networks, an occasional "old school" commercial featured a traditional authoritarian male narrator discussing an educational product targeted more to parents than children, such as a two-minute long Zoobooks commercial on the Cartoon Network, at 8:41 AM in 2002. But these differences were rare in the larger promotional environment, which featured other forms that were more synergistically and stylistically a part of the flow.

Another criticism of flow research is that it is typically "source-biased," and does not take into account the variability in reception contexts and interpretative frameworks that audiences bring to bear (see Budd et al., 1999). In particular, Seiter (1993) argues that children are perhaps more sophisticated television viewers than many researchers assume. It is true that this study did not analyze audience reception of flow, and no doubt children vary in how they view the images targeted to them.

Yet implied by this analysis is a concern about differences in social power between sources and audiences in children's television. Through collective ownership, media corporations are increasingly joined; audience members are isolated from each other. Corporations have collected much proprietary research about audience behaviour, research that they are not compelled to make public. Children collectively have significant purchasing influence, but little political influence. Perhaps more significantly, children's self-concept is still being formed, while advertising and media brands have been solidly formed through a torrent of marketing research and branding messages. Children face waves of images of themselves and things they love that are increasingly connected together by a dominant message: "You should buy/watch this as part of being a kid." What, then, does this power difference between sources and audiences lead to? Although more research is needed, evidence exists that children's advertising may cultivate materialistic values among young viewers (Smith & Atkin, 2003). As media synergy and branding have come to dominate children's television as much if not more than more traditional toy and cereal advertising, the message of "you are what you watch" may contribute to the historically commodified ethos of product advertising by encouraging the purchasing and consuming of media products that connect so many different content forms.

More precise and assertive policy may help considerably. So may the viewing context. Parents as mediators—watching television with their children, for example—can blunt the cultivation of material values with children's television viewing (Smith & Atkin, 2003). But constantly evolving forms of promotion challenge the effectiveness of slow-moving policy development and the role of adult mediators. Much of the research about the effects of children's television examines the extent to which children can distinguish between commercials, which primarily have a selling function, and programs, which primarily have entertainment or educational function (Smith & Atkin, 2003). How do parents respond when there is little distinction? What happens when devices that were mandated to circumscribe the selling function (like program separators and PSAs discussed earlier) actually enhance it through their integration with branding strategies? How may regulation deal with new, more subtle forms of selling and promotion that are difficult to separate from other television forms, and that seem designed to undermine existing policy? Children may be at risk of growing up in a world with fewer "ad-free" cultural zones, zones that can serve as important high ground above commodity tidal waves.

Note

1. One author analyzed all of the programming from the 2000 tapes, and the 2002 programming was divided up for analysis by the two authors (with one author taking ABC, Cartoon Network, and the WB; and the other taking Fox and Nickelodeon). Although the primary method is not a quantitative content analysis per se, training and double checks were conducted to increase the validity of the analysis. The researchers discussed their notes and analysis of textual characteristics. In addition, one stretch of programming was viewed by both researchers to check for similarities in uncovering textual nuances and similarities. Finally, the separate notes of the two researchers were compared for agreement when the same commercial or other program type was analyzed by both researchers, a common occurrence given the repetition found in children's television.

References

Alexander, A., Benjamin, L.M., Hoerrner, K., & Roe, D. (1998). "We'll be back in a moment": A content analysis of advertisements in children's television in the 1950s. *Journal of Advertising*, 27, 3, 1–9.

Andersen, R. (1995). *Consumer culture and TV programming.* Boulder, CO: Westview Press.

Bagdikian, B. (2004). *The new media monopoly* (7th edn). Boston: Beacon.

Bellamy, R.V., & Walker, J.R. (1996). *Television and the remote control: Grazing on a vast wasteland.* New York: Guilford.

Bernstein, P. (2001, 17 December). Ayem kid biz losing fizz. *Variety*, 30–1.

Brooker, W. (2001). Living on Dawson's Creek: Teen viewers, cultural convergence, and Television overflow. *International Journal of Cultural Studies*, 4, 456–72.

Budd, M., Craig, S., & Steinman, C. (1999). *Consuming environments: Television and Commercial culture.* New Brunswick, NJ: Rutgers University Press.

Christians, C.G., & Carey, J.W. (1989). The logic and aims of qualitative research. In G.H. Stempel III, & B.H. Westley (Eds), *Research methods in mass communication* (2nd edn, pp. 354–74). Englewood Cliffs, NJ: Prentice-Hall.

Corner, J. (1999). *Critical ideas in television studies.* Oxford: Clarendon.

Dempsey, J. (2001a, 3 September). Disney Channel primo with tweens. *Variety*, p. 24.

———. (2001b, 28 May–3 June). Fox Family put up for adoption. *Variety*, 13–14.

Finnigan, D. (2002, 17 June). When it comes to pitching properties almost everything old is new again. *Brandweek*, pp. 10–11.

Giroux, H.A. (2001). *The mouse that roared: Disney and the end of innocence.* New York: Rowman and Littlefield.

Hall, W.J. (2000, 10 April). The toys are back in town. *Variety*, p. 55.

Jacobson, N.F., & Mazur, L.A. (1995). *Marketing madness: A survival guide for a consumer society.* Boulder, CO: Westview.

Kapur, J. (1999). Out of control: Television and the transformation of childhood in late capitalism. In M. Kinder (Ed.), *Kids' media culture* (pp. 122–8). Raleigh, NC: Duke University Press.

Kinder, M. (1999). Ranging with power on the Fox Kids Network: Or, where on earth is children's educational television? In M. Kinder (Ed.), *Kids' media culture* (pp. 177–203). Raleigh, NC: Duke University Press.

Kline, S. (1993). *Out of the garden: Toys and children's culture in the age of TV marketing.* London: Verso.

Kunkel, D. (2001). Children and television advertising. In D.G. Singer & J.L. Singer (Eds), *Handbook of children and the media* (pp. 375–93). Thousand Oaks, CA: Sage.

Kunkel, D., & McIlrath, M. (2003). Message content in advertising to children. In E.L. Palmer & B.M. Young (Eds), *The faces of televisual media: Teaching, violence, selling to children* (2nd edn, pp. 287–300). Mahwah, NJ: Erlbaum.

Larson, M. (2001, 13 August). Kids anticlimax: Upfront is a dud. *Mediaweek*, p. 4.

McAllister, M.P. (1996). *The commercialization of American culture: New advertising, control and democracy.* Thousand Oaks, CA: Sage.

———. (2000). From flick to flack: The increased emphasis on marketing by media entertainment corporations. In R. Andersen & L.A. Strate (Eds), *Critical studies in media commercialism* (pp. 101–22). New York: Oxford University Press.

McChesney, R.W. (1999). *Rich media, poor democracy: Communication politics in dubious times.* Urbana, IL: University of Illinois Press.

McDonald, M., & Lavelle, M. (2001, 30 July). Call it "kidfluence." *U.S. News and World Report*, p. 32.

Mittell, J. (2003). The great Saturday morning exile: Scheduling cartoons on television's periphery in the 1960s. In C.A. Stabile & M. Harrison (Eds), *Prime time animation: Television animation and American culture* (pp. 33–54). New York: Routledge.

Modleski, T. (1983). The rhythms of reception: Daytime television and women's work. In E.A. Kaplan (Ed.), *Regarding television: Critical approaches—an anthology* (pp. 67–75). Los Angeles: The American Film Institute.

Pecora, N. (1998). *The business of children's entertainment.* New York: Guilford.

———. (2004). Nickelodeon grows up: The economic evolution of a network. In H. Hendershot (Ed.), *Nickelodeon nation: The history, politics, and economics of America's only TV channel for kids* (pp. 15–44). New York: New York University Press.

Sandler, K.S. (2003). Synergy nirvana: Brand equity, television animation, and Cartoon Network. In C.A. Stabile & M. Harrison (Eds), *Prime time animation: Television animation and American culture* (pp. 89–109). New York: Routledge.

———. (2004). "A kid's gotta do what a kid's gotta do": Branding the Nickelodeon experience. In H. Hendershot (Ed.), *Nickelodeon nation: The history, politics, and economics of America's only TV channel for kids* (pp. 45–68). New York: New York University Press.

Schmuckler, E. (2002, 1 April). Looking for a fight. *Mediaweek*, pp. 23–26.

Seiter, E. (1993). *Sold separately: Children and parents in consumer culture.* New Brunswick, NJ: Rutgers University Press.

Smith, S.L., & Atkin, C. (2003). Television advertising and children: Examining the intended and unintended effects. In E.L. Palmer & B.M. Young (Eds), *The faces of televisual media: Teaching, violence, selling to children* (2nd edn, pp. 301–25). Mahwah, NJ: Erlbaum.

Smythe, D. (1977). Communications: Blindspot of western Marxism. *Canadian Journal of Political and Social Theory*, 1, 3, 1–27.

Tobin, J. (2004). Introduction. In J. Tobin (Ed.), *Pikachu's global adventure: The rise and fall of Pokémon* (pp. 3–11). Durham, NC: Duke University Press.

Williams, R. (1975). *Television: Technology and cultural form.* New York: Schocken.

McTV: Understanding the Global Popularity of Television Formats

Silvio Waisbord

Back in the 1980s, global television seemed headed toward becoming a "wall-to-wall Dallas," as Hollywood's domination of television screens was dubbed in Europe. In the context of profound changes in the structure of European television, such a prospect raised concerns about the future of national television and cultural imperialism amid the onslaught of US media. Lately, it seems that global television is likely poised to be a "wall-to-wall format." Around the world, television is filled with national variations of programs designed by companies from numerous countries. Formats are programming ideas that are adapted and produced domestically. The commerce of formats is not new. For decades, formats of "reality" and "fiction" programming have been produced and sold in international markets (Moran 1998). But, as the trade press has recently described it, "format television" has taken the industry by storm. In recent trade fairs, studio executives have pontificated about the virtues of formats and industry panellists have discussed the differences between formats of "reality" and "scripted" programs.

The popularity of formats is more than just another trend in an industry perennially hungry for hit shows and eager to follow them. It reveals two developments in contemporary television: the globalization of the business model of television and the efforts of international and domestic companies to deal with the resilience of national cultures. The analysis of these developments allows us to re-examine how economics and culture are related in the process of media globalization. In the first section of this article, I argue that when understood as a set of media policies and technological developments, globalization has intensified interconnectivity among television industries worldwide. Interconnectivity happens through structural and institutional linkages among television systems and industries worldwide. The result is the emergence of an increasingly integrated business governed by similar practices and goals. In the second section, I delve into what the popularity of television formats reflects about national cultures in a globalized world. On the surface, the global dissemination of formats may suggest not only the global integration of the economy of the industry but also the standardization of content. What better evidence of cultural homogenization than format television? A dozen media companies are able to do business worldwide by selling the same idea, and audiences seem to be watching national variations of the same show. At a deeper level, however, formats attest to the fact that television still remains tied to local and national cultures. Bringing up examples of Latin American cases, I argue that television is simultaneously both global and national, shaped by the globalization of media economics and the pull of local and national cultures.

Privatization and Demand for Format Programming

The massive changes in the structure of television systems in the 1980s and 1990s have connected television systems that, until then, functioned in relative isolation. When television was conceived as a national, protected industry, the global trade of programming ran into regulatory stonewalls. In the past decades, privatization, liberalization, and deregulation of the airwaves removed such limitations and opened television systems to flows of capital and programming. The result has been the increasing homogenization of systems on the principles of private ownership and profit goals.

Together with structural changes, technological developments increased the demand for programming. Before the last wave of globalization, most television industries had a limited number of hours that they needed to fill. The emergence of a multichannel, liberalized environment raised the possibility that large producers would benefit from increased demand generated by the explosion in the number of television hours. With extensive libraries, well-established distribution networks, and an unparalleled marketing machine, Hollywood companies were poised to profit enormously from those changes. The globalization of television industries seemed unequivocally designed to benefit Hollywood. The fact that most systems shifted toward an "American" model of television gave a substantial advantage to the industry that had invented it.

However, as the principles of commercial television became standardized and industries matured, other domestic industries could also produce and export programming, particularly if they catered to audience niches. What was good for Hollywood could, under the appropriate conditions, also be good for other production companies based in other countries as long as they could master the game of commercial television. Consequently, dozens of television companies based in Western Europe, Australia, and New Zealand gained more than a foothold in the global television market. This is put in evidence by the trade of program formats. Many Western European companies are the copyright holders of recent hit formats. The trade press has dubbed Europe "the leader of reality programming" (Fry 2000). The success of Britain's Celador and Pearson, Holland's Endemol, or Sweden's Strix television is evidence that the pool of producers is no longer limited to traditional Hollywood companies. Pearson Television boasts to be "Britain's only truly global television producer, with over 160 programs currently in production in almost 35 countries around the world." Its hit *Who Wants to Be a Millionaire* has been sold to 79 countries (Schneider 2000). The BBC has sold *The Weakest Link* to 38 countries. Telefónica-owned Endemol has blanketed the world with *Big Brother* and other reality programming. Strix created the widely popular *Expedition: Robinson* (known as *Survivor* around the world) and *The Bar*. Moreover, the success of these companies has been mentioned lately as evidence of important changes in the European media and tougher competition for Hollywood (Andrews 2000; Carter 2000). They have accomplished what seemed reserved only to a handful of British productions until not so long ago—that is, to sell formats in the almost impenetrable US television market (see O'Regan 2000). These developments have led some observers to talk of a "two-way transatlantic" flow (Guider 2000), while others, stretching the point, conclude that "U.S. influence is slipping" (Jensen 2000) and that "TV imperialism goes into reverse" (Moyes 2000).

Although it is true that some European production companies are able to capitalize on the changes that globalization promoted in the last decades, such statement rush to conclusion, failing to recognize the enormous inequalities that still exist in the global trade of audiovisual products. To speak of Hollywood's influence as "slipping" or facing "competition" based on the strength of a handful of non-US companies is absurd considering that Hollywood has expanded its worldwide presence through the promotion of globalization policies. No question, in addition to European firms, a number of non-Western companies also became important producers and exporters of television programming. The number of booths at international trade fairs, such as National Association of Television Program Executives (NATPE) and Marche International des Films et des Programmes pour la TV, la Video le Cable et les Satellites (MIPCOM), grew steadily, featuring new sellers of diverse television programs. Japanese firms, whose traditional exports consisted mainly of cartoons and documentaries, now sell dramas and game-show formats. Hong Kong, Egyptian, and Indian producers consolidated their presence in their respective linguistic regions as well as in diasporic markets (Sinclair, Jacka, and Cunningham 1996). Mexican and Brazilian media powerhouses found new opportunities in global television, mostly through the sale of telenovelas (Sinclair 1999; Straubhaar 1991). In recent years, some Latin American producers have also exported formats to the United States and many European countries.

However, the rise and consolidation of television exports from several regions can hardly be considered evidence that Hollywood's dominant position in global television is challenged or, more generally, that inequality in the flows of television and information has been eliminated (Biltereyst and Meers 2000; Golding 1998). Notwithstanding the success of some third world producers, Western domination of the global television market remains undisputed in terms of program sales (and, more broadly, the structure of the industry). Although the pool of global exporters has expanded beyond traditional Hollywood studios as industries matured, companies based in big and wealthy countries have better chances to become global exporters. The largest ten exhibitors at recent MIPCOM meetings were companies based in the United States, Western Europe, or Japan. In the late 1980s, the "US accounted for 71 per cent of the total world traffic in television material." As television industries matured and domestic programming topped ratings, it was estimated that the percentage of US shows dropped to 60 per cent in 1995 (Segrave 1998). Local preference for domestic or regional shows does not necessarily mean that Hollywood's fortunes have decreased. Recent calculations are that the six major Hollywood studios raked in $4.5 billion to $5 billion in 2001, more than the rest of the world combined (Pursell 2001). Although it has become more diversified in terms of the number of producers and more complex in terms of patterns of programming flows, the field of television exports hardly seems levelled.

Explaining the Popularity of Television Formats

The popularity of formats has been the result of many developments. First, it has been the unintended by-product of the existence of protectionist laws in some television systems. In some countries, such as Indonesia, the use of subtitles is banned, and programs are broadcast in English or local languages. Such protectionist restrictions prompted broadcasters to purchase foreign scripts (instead of canned shows) and produce them domestically without subtitles. Also, quota policies favour formats over canned shows. Informed by concerns about national culture and the promotion of "national" television, many European countries, for example, have quotas that primarily aim to curb the import of Hollywood programs (Grantham 2000; Tunstall and Machin 1999). Programming quotas have loopholes that allow foreign ideas (rather than foreign shows) to enter as long as they are produced domestically. Format programming, then, is part of business strategies to bypass local programming quotas. If stations broadcast domestic versions of foreign shows, those versions help to satisfy quota requirements; if they buy canned foreign shows, they do not. So peddling formats allows Hollywood studios and Latin American producers, for example, to enter protected markets in Europe by selling scripts, packaged formats, or partnering with domestic companies in coproduction arrangements.

Besides protectionist laws, television formats have recently caught on like wildfire partially because of the huge success of "reality shows" such as *Survivor* and *Big Brother*, particularly in the United States. Like other cultural industries, the television industry is ruled by the "nobody knows" principle

(Craves 2000; Gitlin 1983), with constant ebbs and flows in programming trends. Because there is no certainty about the prospects of specific programs and genres, hit shows inevitably engender trends that are followed until exhaustion. Coping, imitation, and jumping on the bandwagon of whatever seems to work at the moment have been typical in the television industry since its origins and, arguably, have become even more common lately as conglomerization has increased pressures for higher profits in shorter periods of time.

Before the latest phase of globalization, trends tended to be limited to national boundaries. Back in the days when television systems were organized around different principles, station executives could not easily adopt successful trends from US or European commercial television. What worked in private television could not necessarily be applied in public broadcasting systems or in government-controlled television and vice versa. Structural regulations and institutional expectations limited programming choices. For programming trends to become truly globalized, television systems needed to be patterned along the same principles. Once such limitations were eliminated and commercial principles became dominant, then, what works in one television system could be adopted elsewhere. In standardizing the structure of television, globalization encouraged the tendency toward imitation and reluctance to promote innovation that underlies commercial broadcasting.

Globalization also accelerated the integration of television systems through business and professional networks. The global presence of media corporations has laid the ground for standardization of television output. International corporate networks are conduits for information about what works and what doesn't. Corporate executives may not be completely familiar with programming trends and audience preferences in every country, but they carry around the world their own experiences that in most cases have been nurtured in television industries in the West and are likely to be updated about current trends in the United States. Although they may be sensitive to local tastes and may give autonomy to domestic personnel familiar with local audiences, their commercial and aesthetic judgments are likely to be informed by trends and production values that are common in the West. Such experiences inform decisions to green-light programming ideas. So domestic programming chiefs are more likely to get approval if they acquire a format that is known to their bosses in Miami, London, or Los Angeles or if they pick a show with aesthetic and production values that are familiar to corporate executives. The growing homogenization of the professional sensibilities among television executives worldwide, embedded in Hollywood's worldview, is an important aspect of "the new international division of cultural labor" (Miller et al. 2001) that needs to be studied. Globalization has nurtured the formation of a cosmopolitan class of industry professionals who, from New York to New Delhi, increasingly share similar concepts and attitudes about "what works" and "what doesn't" in commercial television. Moreover, the globalization of the television business has introduced and improved the formation of informal networks for the dissemination of information about the industry. Television executives are more likely to be familiar with programming hits and duds, trends and preferences, particularly in the United States. Hollywood, arguably, may not be the undisputed seller of television programming worldwide as it was in the early decades of television. US television, however, remains the fishbowl of the global television industry. Executives from around the world immediately take note of whatever seems to work (or fail) in US television.

Attendance at annual trade meetings, exposure to the same trade publications, and regular electronic communications have helped maintain frequent interpersonal contacts that facilitate familiarity with global trends. The number of participants in trade fairs and conferences substantially grew in the last decade. These meetings are places for cultivating a similar business mindset among industry executives. MIPCOM's motto frankly states it: "MIPCOM speaks the unifying dialogue of the industry: Business." Also, the number of trade publications with international distribution and readership grew. Some weeklies and monthlies regularly feature special sections devoted to international television and to the state of the industry in regions and countries from around the world. Finally, the availability of communication technologies such as cable, satellite, and the Internet provide easy access to a wealth of information about programs worldwide. With these interpersonal and technological networks in place, it has become easier, and also professionally imperative, for television executives to know about global trends.

In this sense, the popularity of television formats reflects the globalization of television trends; the adoption of programming that circumstantially offers some predictability in terms of its potential commercial success. In times when such dynamics are almost universal, then, formats satisfy the double demand of finding low-cost programming with a track record. Private television, no matter where it is situated, constantly demands new and cheap programming that can deliver audiences to be sold to advertisers. Buying formats, then, is a cost-saving strategy that eliminates some of the highest fixed costs that fiction programming demands. Some of the most popular formats such as game shows and "reality" shows usually require smaller investments than fiction as they don't need to hire actors and well-known writers. The average cost of ABC's *Who Wants to Be a Millionaire* is \$750,000 compared to \$1.2 million for ABC's *The Practice*; NBC's *Twenty-one* costs not more than \$700,000 versus \$1.4 million for an episode of *Law and Order*; and an installment of *Survivor* costs \$200,000, three times less than \$600,000 for each episode of *King of Queens* (Weinraub 2000). In Britain, it was estimated that an hour of a high-rating quiz show costs £200,000 compared to £1 million for a drama (Hughes 2001). Not surprisingly, then, from Argentina to the United States, labour unions representing actors, writers, and technical staff have resisted the rush to format television on the grounds that it threatens their jobs.

Besides lower costs, imported formats offer some measure of predictability based on their past performances in numerous countries. The constant and increasing pressures for turning profits means that there is little, if any, time for innovating or trying new ideas. All incentives are to reach out for proven ideas that can help diminish uncertainty. Formats, then, are the ultimate risk-minimizing programming strategy. Format owners provide extensive experience that includes the record of shows in different countries, what worked and what didn't, and details on national variations. Game-show producers, for example, bring a plethora of statistics about the records of different games and detailed information about production that draws from hundreds of hours of programming in several continents.

Some format shows (particularly "reality" shows) are also attractive to television companies because they give the opportunity to draw large audiences to their websites that feature interactive games, polls, and details about the contestants. Format copyright owners have been pitching their wares worldwide, stressing that their productions are able to integrate television and the Internet, thereby increasing revenues and much-needed net traffic. Also, companies can make additional revenues through the publishing of fanzines and magazines about the shows and newfound celebrities.

Formats and the Globalization of Intellectual Property Rights

Whereas successful programs and trends, especially in the United States and a few other Western countries, used to be blatantly imitated, the illegal copying of programs has become problematic. Using someone else's ideas in the production of television shows is certainly not new. Since the beginning of the industry, television executives have freely appropriated program ideas without acknowledging their origin or paying royalties. In an industry that has long been characterized by sameness and repetition, borrowing ideas across geographical borders has been common. This practice has not disappeared. Producers continue to find inspiration in other shows. More interconnectivity among television industries and easy access to what is playing around the world means that executives have better and faster information about an expanding pool of potential ideas. Moreover, controversies over the legal rights of program ideas and shows continue. Because intellectual property laws across countries do not grant similar rights, television companies have intensified lobbying efforts to pass legislation that protects their programs. Although violations are more closely monitored than in the past, companies have battled in each other in court over "original" authorship of highly profitable program formats. In the past years, there have been various copyright lawsuits and accusations. UK-based companies Planet 24 and Castaway Television Productions have unsuccessfully sued Endemol for "theft of format," arguing that the latter's *Big Brother* resembled *Survivor*. CBS initiated legal actions against Fox claiming that *Boot Camp* stole ideas from *Survivor*. Celador sued Denmark Radio for copyright infringement of *Who Wants to Be a Millionaire*.

These legal battles illustrate the rising importance of intellectual property issues in the agenda of global cultural producers and Western governments. The reasons for why these debates have become prominent recently are many (e.g., the coming of digital technologies, the separation of form and content) and are common to all cultural industries. Issues specific to the television industry need to be mentioned, however. Globalization has facilitated the "stealing" of programs by fostering increasing interconnection among industries. The expansion of cable and satellite signals and the gradual articulation of integrated global business networks provide a constant source of programming ideas that can be appropriated. Simultaneously, globalization has improved the chances for companies to monitor and litigate copyright violations. Like large content producers in other industries, television companies have become increasingly interested in detecting and persecuting violators. Having extensive operations in the most important television markets, large producers have better chances to find transgressors. As a result of these concerns, format producers gathered at the 2000 Cannes Marche International des Programmes de Television (MIPTV) launched the Format Recognition and Protection Association (FRAPA). Members of the Monaco-based organization include major television companies interested in investigating and preventing piracy. FRAPA created an International Television Paper Format Registry.

In terms of intellectual property rights, the effects of globalization on television companies have been similar to the ones on the "copyright industries" at large. For all content producers, globalization has posed a challenge—namely, how to harmonize copyright laws and improve enforcement at a global level, particularly in markets where piracy is rampant and governments are "unco-operative" in meeting corporate objectives.

In summary, the popularity of formats is largely the result of fundamental institutional changes in the global television industry—namely, the domination of the private model of television, the standardization of commercial practices, and rising concerns about copyright infringements.

Television Formats and National Cultures

It would be limiting to try to understand the popularity of formats by only addressing changes in the structure of television systems. It also reflects where economics and culture meet in global markets. International flows of standardized, delocalized formats prove that audiences cling to local and national consciousness. This may seem ironic only if we assume that globalization inevitably eliminates cultural diversity and breeds homogenization. The dichotomy between globalization as the agent of cookie-cutter commercial cultures or the force for cultural hybridity and resistance is false, however. Global media and the national are not antithetical but, actually, are integrated in complex ways.

The popularity of television formats is at the crossroads of global and local dynamics of the cultural economy of television. Contemporary television is a Janus-faced industry that in the name of profitability needs to commodify real and imagined nations while being open to global flows of ideas and money. The global circulation of formats responds to programming strategies to bridge transnational economic interests and national sentiments of belonging. Such strategies neither follow patriotic concerns nor suggest that television dutifully respects the diversity of national cultures. Rather, they result from the intention to maximize profits while "the national" continues to articulate cultural identities. In turn, television programming recreates and perpetuates national sentiments. Formats reflect the globalization of the economics of the television industry and the persistence of national cultures in a networked world. They make it possible to adapt successful programs to national cultures. In comparison to canned shows, they provide television executives with a reliable and malleable solution to produce potential hit shows. Most foreign shows often run into cultural barriers and, thus, are less likely to become ratings boosters. They can be cheaper than domestic productions and a low-cost strategy to fill more television hours, but they are unlikely audience magnets.

Compared to canned programming, the question of culture is thematized differently in formats. Formats carry meanings that are not necessarily attached to national cultures. Formats are culturally specific but nationally neutral. The DNA of formats is rooted in cultural values that transcend the national. Textual readings of popular formats such as game shows suggest that they champion the culture of consumption (Fiske 1990; Otnes 1996). "Reality shows" like *Survivor* can be read as the global projection of capitalism, naked individualism, and competition. However, format shows are less prone to have specific references to the local and national, precisely because they are designed to "travel well" across national boundaries. Formats purposefully eviscerate the national. Could we say that *Survivor/Expedition: Robinson* is unequivocally a Dutch show? What makes *The Bar* Swedish and *Taxi Orange* Austrian? How does *Waku Waku* represent Japanese national identity? What is British about *Who Wants to Be a Millionaire*? Because formats explicitly empty out signs of the national, they can become nationalized—that is, customized to domestic cultures. For commercial television, this is the advantage of television formats over ready-made shows. Because formats are conceived as flexible formula, traces of national belonging are downplayed and even eradicated. The result is a pasteurized, transnational product detached from national cultures. Formats, then, reveal the dynamics of "glocalization" (Robertson 1992) in the pursuit of profit: the adaptation of programming formula to the tastes of domestic audiences.

Hollywood-filled television schedules around the world might suggest that domestic audiences prefer US programs or that the latter enjoy the "competitive advantage of narrative transparency" (Olson 1999). Neither audience preference nor the presumed textual universality of programs account for the wide presence of Hollywood fare, however. Such arguments downplay or simply ignore the structure of the global cultural economy and the institutional workings of the television industry that make certain choices available. Audiences' choices follow industrial dynamics and decisions. To suggest that schedules accurately reflect audience tastes falls into "consumer sovereignty" arguments that ignore the variety of forces and decisions that shape programming schedules. When television is organized on the basis of commercial principles, explanations for why schedules feature foreign or national programming depend on profit calculations and the business savvy of producers in selling their wares in different markets.

More than audience tastes, trade practices and costs better explain the content of schedules. Programming decisions are often contingent on whether owners believe that substantial investments are required to turn a profit. Those calculations depend on the fact that not all television industries offer similar conditions for national production. When the economic conditions are propitious (e.g., substantial economy of scale, advertising investments, sizable domestic market), companies are more likely to produce programming even though the costs are higher than buying foreign shows. Even under these conditions, television companies might opt to produce cheap (talk shows, news, variety shows, game shows) over expensive genres (fiction, documentaries), particularly in countries with small economies of scale and infant television industries. However, even when domestic conditions could allow some production, filling schedules with foreign canned programming is preferred because it's significantly cheaper.

In the last decade, ratings have confirmed that when given a choice, audiences prefer domestic and regional content to foreign programs (Hoskins, McFayden, and Finn 1997; Langdale 1997; Waisbord 2000a; Waterman and Rogers 1994). This is hardly an indication of the levelling of opportunities for television industries to produce content that, at least in principle, reflects better local realities. Audiences might prefer local content, but domestic industries might not produce it. Only under specific economic and industrial circumstances is local programming able to knock Hollywood shows off prime-time schedules, and Hollywood productions are used as fillers in off-peak hours when audiences and advertising revenues are smaller. Not all television industries have the capacity to produce a significant number of hours to satisfy demand, however.

Against the backdrop of different possibilities for domestic production, audiences' localism is an important factor, particularly when markets are sizable and wealthy. This is the reason why many cable and satellite networks decided to split their signals along cultural lines by offering regional services. MTV, ESPN, and other cable networks have realized that programming in local languages that taps into local talent and preferences is more profitable than monolingual, "American"-only broadcasts (Hils 1998; Koranteng 1999). These services increasingly feature a higher percentage of locally and regionally produced content. It is not easy to pin down exactly what it is that audiences prefer about domestic content. The industry comes up with mostly ad hoc, post facto explanations about why certain programs were hits. Explanations do not necessarily guarantee that programs with similar characteristics would perform similarly. It is generally believed that audiences choose programming that resonates with their own cultures. To examine this issue, I analyze the relation among formats, narratives, and language by looking at the experience of Latin American television.

Formats and Narratives

The conventional wisdom in the industry seems to be that audiences like to recognize familiar themes, places, and characters on television. Humour and drama are favourites because they are commonly rooted in local and national cultures. Likewise, the appeal of news and mediated sports lies in the fact that they continue to cultivate linkages to the local and the national. Newscasts anchor a sense of community by relaying information about current events. Televised sports provide opportunities for representing and re-enacting local and national sentiments. It continues to operate as an arena in which national identities retain important commercial and ideological functions (Whannel 1993).

Although universal stories and foreign places may be appealing, television audiences consistently prefer narratives that incorporate familiar elements. This is why audiences prefer productions coming from countries that share "cultural proximity" (Straubhaar 1991). However, audiences may find remote even co-productions among companies based in countries that share cultural elements such as language. A case in point is the commercial failure of Latin American telenovelas that featured multinational casts and stories that evolved in many countries in the region. According to television executives

I interviewed, these programs flopped because they were a hodgepodge, a "Latino-pudding" that unsuccessfully tried to articulate a common regional identity. The result was that they featured a collection of scattered references to national cultures that ultimately lacked cultural specificity. Even the presence of popular, national stars did not help to deliver bigger ratings in their own countries.

Audience preferences for domestic content presents television executives with a dilemma: content that is strongly embedded in local and national cultures has a better chance to be successful domestically, but it is less likely to find interested buyers and enthusiastic audiences abroad. Because foreign sales are, for most Latin American companies, secondary business strategies, the success of telenovelas hinges mainly on the domestic market. Moreover, because metropolitan markets capture the lion's share of audience ratings and advertising revenues, it is not unusual that telenovelas unmistakably reflect the local culture of big cities (where production companies usually are based). In Argentina, for example, the greater Buenos Aires area has 78 per cent of media advertising and 60 per cent of television homes. No wonder, then, that audiences in the interior find that most productions are too "*porteñas*" (as Buenos Aires culture/people are called).

Because domestic and, particularly, metropolitan markets continue to be central to television economics, producers are inclined to incorporate local stories, humour, and characters in their programs, even though it potentially deters marketability abroad. This is why productions that in the industry lingo are "too local," such as "period" telenovelas or those heavily immersed in local politics, have a harder time finding international markets than programs that are detached from the local. In Latin America, there is a long tradition of telenovelas that place classic love stories and family conflicts amid historical and political struggles. It has been argued that many have been profitable domestically precisely because they offer audiences opportunities to recognize themselves as members of a cultural community (Allen 1995; Martin-Barbero 1993). Their exportability is limited, however. If they are sold, it is usually because of their low costs. The relative higher costs of Hollywood productions in small and impoverished television markets in Eastern Europe and Asia benefited Latin American productions in the 1980s and 1990s.

In contrast to "national" productions, telenovelas that tell universal love stories (e.g., rags-to-riches, Cinderella-themed plots), without specific local references and featuring known stars have fewer problems in crossing cultural boundaries. The best example has been Mexico's Televisa-produced telenovelas. Their remarkable success in countries as diverse as Russia and the Philippines has been explained by the fact that besides the charisma of lead stars, national references are almost absent from the stories. Particularly compared with Brazilian "period" and contemporary telenovelas (Trinta 1998) or TV Azteca's telenovelas that address political "headlines" issues, Televisa's productions typically feature universal stories.

Unlike canned shows that are steeped in specific national cultures, formats are open texts that can be adapted. Within the constraints dictated by their owners, domestic productions can fit local narratives, histories, humour, events, and characters into the basic formulas that they purchase. Because formats are essentially open, they cannot be seen simply as transmission belts for Western values. In his thoughtful study of formats, Albert Moran (1998) argues that formats are places for negotiation between domestic and foreign cultures rather than Trojan horses of Western culture. Formats neither crystallize a static notion of national culture nor are pure impositions of external values. They are texts in which different understandings of national identity are projected and redefined against the backdrop of imported formulas. To conclude that national cultures are the casualties of television formats, Moran suggests, is to ignore the flexibility of formats and the active role of audiences in consuming television (also see Skovmand 1992).

Format television shows, then, organize experiences of the national. Even "reality" shows, which unlike "period" or "contemporary" fiction are not ostensibly designed to articulate national narratives, provide spaces for the representation of national cultures. Particularly in times when private television has little incentives to produce fiction and prefers to churn out low-cost shows, one should not ignore the fact that game shows, variety shows, or "reality" shows also offer opportunities for audiences to recognize themselves as members of national communities. The question of how the national is expressed and recreated in those genres, however, has not received sufficient attention. Studies have generally prioritized the textual analysis of "highbrow" programs (dramas, documentaries) that purposefully delineate cultural boundaries through historical narratives and appealing to collective memories. Aside from the textual characteristics of specific genres, television is intertwined with the national in multifaceted ways. More than in specific moments when programming appeals to nationalistic discourses, television has the power of naturalizing cultural connections in everyday viewing.

Language and Formats of Television Fiction

One way in which television turns "the national" into a pre-given, constitutive reality is through broadcast languages. Arguments about globalization qua cultural homogenization pay inadequate attention to the fact that language remains a pillar of cultural distinctiveness and national identities in a globalized world. Notwithstanding the consolidation of English as the world's lingua franca, the linkages between language and nation are still important and, in some cases, fundamental to an understanding of processes of cultural unification and difference. The formation of national identities continues to be inseparable from language (De Swaan 1991; Edwards 1985). Language is the basis for the politics of inclusion and exclusion that are at the centre of processes of identity formation (Anderson 1983; Hall and du Gay 1996).

From this perspective, it is important to consider the relation between media and language. Languages delineate cultural boundaries that articulate flows of television programming. This is the main finding of the argument that global patterns of television flows are articulated around "geo-linguistic markets" (Sinclair, Jacka, and Cunningham 1996). So, even at a time when global television audiences arguably seem to be watching the same or similar shows, television programs in vernacular languages continue to anchor a sense of cultural belonging and function as a privileged site for the reproduction of nations. In a world saturated by Hollywood content, mediated vernaculars are both cultural binders and reminders of belonging to distinctive cultural communities.

The force of broadcast language (or mediated language, in general) lies in its invisibility, on the fact that we rarely notice it. Language constitutes an example of "banal nationalism" (Billig 1995). Billig (1995) argues that the ideological habits that enable nations to be reproduced "are not removed from everyday life. . . . Daily, the nation is indicated, or 'flagged,' in the lives of its citizenry" (p. 6). For him, the image of "the flag hanging unnoticed on the public building" (p. 8) is one of the best illustrations of banal nationalism. Language can be understood along similar lines. The common belief that languages and nations are "naturally" inseparable hides, for Billig, the artificiality of such relation (also see Anderson 1983).

Following Billig's argument, we can understand broadcast language as a way in which nations are daily reproduced. Television normalizes the ties between language and nations. The force of televised language lies in its ordinariness, in continuously weaving a seamless linkage between nation and language. Television "flags" nationhood often through regular programming in specific languages. This is different from "media events" (Dayan and Katz 1992) that purposefully appeal to the nation through communal media experiences. "Media events" such as official funerals, the signing of international treaties, or global sports are moments of collective mobilization in the name of the nation; television is put in the service of nationalism as a political movement. Every day, however, television perpetuates national bonds in the mould of "banal nationalism." It is the active reminder more than the active mobilizer of national consciousness. While the broadcast of momentous occasions that congregate extraordinarily large audiences is sporadic, television regularly keeps nationhood alive by "flagging" spoken languages and drawing and sustaining linguistic boundaries such as "diasporic" media that maintain national identities through perpetuating linguistic bonds among immigrant communities (Sinclair and Cunningham 2000).

Perhaps because of the invisibility of broadcast language, this point has not been sufficiently emphasized. Whereas literary studies have focused on how media narratives and storytelling articulate nations, historical-sociological studies have addressed the role of public broadcasting and media industries in "imagining" nations (Scannell and Cardiff 1991; van der Bulck 2001). It is also necessary to consider that the media propagates and reinforces national sentiments through perpetuating linguistic bonds. Contemporary television, like newspapers in the nineteenth century (Anderson 1983), contributes to the perpetuation of national cultures by spreading a vernacular and reinforcing linguistic bonds among populations. Thus, programs in vernacular languages that are not explicitly interested in articulating national cultures also provide a place for the representation of the national. In legitimizing some and excluding other languages, television allows for the recognition of language-based cultural communities. The need for dubbing and subtitling imported programs and films implicitly acknowledges that any attempt to produce cultural uniformity clashes with the resilience of vernacular languages.

The global popularity of formats attests to the resilience of language as a constitutive element of national identities. Compared with "reality" programs, fiction is more difficult to be formatted and adapted. Scripted programming, including fiction, tends to be more culturally specific and is more expensive to produce. Despite these difficulties, fictional programming has also been formatted for two main reasons: linguistic barriers and the cultural nature of drama and comedy. Even when countries have a similar linguistic and cultural base such as Britain and the United States, original programs are steeped in different webs of meaning that are lost when they cross borders (Miller 2000). Formats, then, offer a way to adapt not only the content but also the language of original productions.

Latin America offers an interesting case to examine this issue because amid the intensification of regional trade of programming in the last decades (Sinclair 1999), the Spanish/Portuguese divide continues to be one of the most visible fault lines in the region's cultural geography. The division is certainly not as pronounced as in Europe, where media projects intended to create a regional culture have run up against linguistic fragmentation and the strength of vernacular languages (Kilborn 1993). Still, the issue of language divisions remains an important one, particularly in relation to regional trade of television. Serialized fiction, namely telenovelas, continues to be the backbone of television programming in Latin America. Although schedules feature a heavy diet of "reality" programming, television executives view telenovelas as the fundamental pillars of daily schedules. Language has been a sticking point in the regional trade of telenovelas. Since the 1970s, many Spanish-dubbed Brazilian telenovelas have been shown in Spanish-speaking Latin America (as well as in Spain), and some continue to be very popular. But as television industries matured and state-owned television stations were privatized (Waisbord 2000b), more Spanish-language productions from different countries became available in the international market. This made programming executives from Spanish-speaking countries less enthusiastic about importing Brazilian telenovelas. Although the latter generally have superior production values, gripping stories, and often feature breathtaking outdoor scenery that is appealing to audiences, they hit a cultural wall. One obstacle is arguably the fact that some of the most popular Brazilian telenovelas are embedded in national histories, politics, and myths that do not resonate with global audiences. Simultaneously, however, these characteristics work in favour of Brazilian productions, branding them as "the exotic other" in international markets. In many Latin American countries, however, the main obstacle has been linguistic. Even the best dubbing cannot make up for the fact that they are not originally spoken in Spanish. This cultural distance has been more acute in countries with substantial domestic production (such as Mexico), where audiences are accustomed to programming in their own language both domestic productions and dubbed Hollywood shows.

Something similar happens on the other side of the linguistic divide. In Brazil, a country that produces a significant amount of programming, only a small amount of foreign programs is aired on terrestrial television. As one of the largest global media corporations and the country's longstanding dominant television company, Globo has produced thousands of hours of programming for decades. Its annual production was estimated at 2,239 hours in 2000 (Fernandez 2001). It produces 80 per cent of its schedule (Cajueiro 2000). Sistema Brasileiro de Televisão (SBT) and Bandeirantes also produce a considerable number of hours, particularly variety and talk shows. Hoping to chip away at Globo's audience share, both networks occasionally decided to import programs from Spanish-speaking countries to keep costs down, particularly when a downturn in the economy slowed down advertising revenues. Because of language differences that Portuguese dubbing cannot completely bridge, they purchased formats of successful telenovelas. SBT has purchased formats of Televisa telenovelas that are produced in Brazil with local actors. Bandeirantes acquired from Argentina's Telefe the hit children-oriented novela *Chiquititas*. Under Telefe's supervision, the Portuguese version with Brazilian actors was filmed in Buenos Aires. Globo, which did not buy programs from Spanish-speaking Latin American countries for decades, bought the script of the Colombian hit "Betty la Fea" for $100,000, a paltry sum considering that the cost of an hour of its lavish telenovelas is several times higher. Whereas Globo justified the purchase by stating that it would produce a version adapted to Brazilian culture and television, observers speculated that Globo's decision was motivated by a different interest—namely, to prevent SBT and Bandeirantes, who traditionally rely on successful telenovelas from Spanish-speaking countries, from acquiring the Brazilian rights of a potential hit.

But linguistic screens are not limited to the presence of different languages; the multiplicity of Spanish accents is another cultural barrier in the trade of television shows in the region. One could argue that accents, not simply Spanish, became visible markers of national identity in Spanish-speaking Latin America. As Nancy Morris (1999, 55) writes, "accent . . . is perhaps one of the strongest ways of establishing a local identity."

The old quip is that Latin America is a region divided by the same language. In a region where the Spanish empire imposed cultural homogeneity through language over a variety of indigenous languages, language did not become the distinctive marker of national identity in the post-independence period, as it did in other postcolonial societies (see Mar-Molinero 2000). Because most states (excluding Brazil and the English-, Dutch-, and French-speaking Caribbean islands) shared the same language, they could not be defined as nations in terms of language. Only in a few countries did indigenous languages (e.g., Guarani in Paraguay) gain official acceptance as part of the national imaginary, but they had limited, if any, presence in the national media. With little sensitivity to linguistic diversity within Latin American nation-states, radio, film, and television have greatly contributed to making specific accents distinctive signifiers of the nation. Not only did they nationalize Spanish, particularly among illiterate populations scattered through vast and hard-to-reach territories, but they also nationalized the accents of the capital cities, where the largest media industries historically have been based (Martin-Barbero 1993).

At the regional level, television was responsible for the expansion of Mexican accents. This was the consequence of two developments. First, for decades, Latin American audiences have watched Hollywood film and television productions dubbed mainly into Mexican-accented Spanish. Second, Televisa has exported telenovelas and children's shows throughout the region, some of which were massively popular, since the early 1970s. The result was that Mexican accents became the lingua franca of Latin American television and are widely believed to be more "neutral" than any other accent. This gave Televisa a huge competitive advantage over television producers from other countries. Televisa's success was based on the fact that audiences were familiar with Mexican accents, a familiarity that its productions reinforced. This advantage was not limited to South America, but it also extended to the United States given Televisa's longstanding presence as the leading program provider in the Spanish-language television market. Besides culture, Televisa certainly enjoyed other economic advantages; it expanded regionally earlier than other television industries and produced a substantial number of television hours.

Because Spanish-speaking audiences are generally used to Mexican accents, productions in any other accents sound "foreign." This fact certainly has not escaped Brazilian producers, who prefer Mexican dubbing of their productions for Latin American distribution. It has also been a main difficulty for other Latin American producers to enter regional markets. Besides business obstacles, they have also faced accents as a cultural wall. For Argentine programs, for example, accents are a major cultural hurdle to export their productions north of Ecuador. The situation is different in the Southern Cone as well as in Bolivia and Peru where audiences are more familiar with Argentine accents, particularly after the satellite signal of Telefe and other Buenos Aires–based regional cable networks started operations in the 1990s. But elsewhere, audiences reject the Argentine accent, particularly in countries where, given the absence of indigenous fiction and the reluctance of media moguls to support production (such as in Central America), audiences have watched Mexican programming for decades.

Having been exposed mostly to national accents, Mexican audiences find other accents foreign. Equipped with an enormous production capacity and vast libraries, Televisa has accustomed domestic audiences to Mexican accents. Its limited foreign programming is overwhelmingly Hollywood productions, particularly films (Sanchez-Ruiz 2000). Aiming to reduce Televisa's audience share, newcomer TV Azteca resorted to in-house and independent productions and, in some opportunities, to regional shows. But recognizing the difficulty of jumping over the accent barrier, it opted to produce versions of popular shows from the region, such as the Argentine hit *Chiquititas*.

Accent barriers are also evident in the trade of programming between Spain and Latin America. Television audiences are not used to each other's accents. Only a small amount of Spanish productions has been aired on Latin American television. Spanish audiences have been accustomed to national accents in both domestic and foreign programming. If interested in shows from across the Atlantic, Spanish networks are more likely to buy the libretto and formats instead of canned shows. In recent years, for example, they bought formats of Argentine programming (variety shows, novelas, game shows, and dramas) and produced domestic versions that incorporated news headlines, local references, and characters.

To Globalize, McDonaldize

The traffic of television formats in Spanish- and Portuguese-speaking countries suggests that formats allow companies to jump over linguistic barriers. This is what Hollywood companies recently learned: because of domestic preference for "national languages" (and national programming), they cannot rely solely on the old practice of dumping programs to conquer international markets. The time when television systems went on a buying binge and loaded up on Hollywood productions to fill increasing demand for terrestrial television has changed, particularly in large and wealthy markets. In a world of linguistic diversity and more developed television industries, Hollywood television studios had to find new and creative ways to do business. Co-producing local-language programs with domestic companies and other forms of partnership illustrate the "think globally, program locally" mantra that currently dominates the global television industry. Format television shows "glocalization" at work—that is, the merits of a business "multicultural" strategy that is "sensitive" to cultural diversity. Such sensitivity is not informed by respect for or interest in preserving "multiculturalism" but rather to maximize opportunities for commercial gain. For global television companies, cultural difference is not an obstacle, but, if incorporated properly, it could be a boon. Programming hybridity makes sense because it makes money. In the international division of cultural labour, domestic companies are more attuned to local sensibilities than global corporations and, consequently, are better at manufacturing programs that incorporate the local and the national. In the traffic of global television brands, the partnership of global and domestic companies aims to address cultural diversity as a component of global markets. Cultural difference is a business matter rather than a political project.

Grappling with the reality of globalized economics and localized cultures, the global television industry has found formats as convenient instruments to leap over cultural boundaries while taking economic advantage of the substantial transformations that domestic television industries experienced in the past decades. Formats are a form of McTelevision. Shorthand for the McDonald's fast-food chain, the prefix *Mc* stands for a business model characterized by efficiency, calculability, predictability, and control that caters products to specific local requirements, usually informed by cultural factors (Ritzer 1998). Applied to the television industry, formats represent the global commercialization of an efficient and predictable program that can be tweaked according to local tastes. McTelevision is the selling of programming ideas with a track record that are sufficiently flexible to accommodate local cultures to maximize profitability. The national origin of the format is less important than its effectiveness. Formats are de-territorialized (see Tomlinson 1999); they have no national home; they represent the disconnection between culture, geography, and social spaces that characterizes globalization. Signs of cultural territories are removed so domestic producers can incorporate local colour and global audiences can paradoxically feel at home when watching them. Locality needs to be evicted so it can be reintroduced as long as it does not alter the basic concept. Although any television company can come up with such formula and market it globally, Hollywood and some European television companies maintain substantial advantage in the selling of formats. The popularity of formats suggests that global television industry is becoming a giant cultural vacuum cleaner that constantly sucks in ideas from around the world and turns them into commodities. In a global world, capital flows encounter fewer obstacles in crossing borders than in the past, but canned programming continues to run into cultural and linguistic barriers. Economic and cultural boundaries do not seem to be eroding similarly.

Where the Global Meets the Local

The evolution of the global television industry has largely shaped arguments about the circulation of television programming. Since the 1960s, analyses have reflected not only political and theoretical debates but also the state of international television flows. Theories of media imperialism and "one-way street" flows expressed the first phase in the 1960s and 1970s, which can be characterized by the domination of Hollywood productions and infant industries worldwide. In the 1980s and 1990s, arguments about multiple flows responded to a new phase that featured the rise and consolidation of new producers and exporters, particularly in the third world. At the cusp of a new century, a new phase seems to be emerging, one characterized by the increasing complexity of flows of capital and programming and novel developments in the economics, production, and export of television.

One of the new developments is the appeal of television formats both for exporters and buyers. The contemporary trade of formats puts in evidence that the globalization of media economics and culture are intertwined but are not identical. Globalization has been responsible for major transformations in the structure of television systems. Privatization and deregulation have opened the doors to cross-border flows of capital and technology. Those changes opened new ways for media business to expand into international markets through output deals, joint ventures, programming sales, and production arrangements. Globalization has unsettled past linkages between state and capital, geography and business, the local and the global. No longer do conflicts neatly fit in the "national versus foreign" mould. Multiple alliances and conflicts have emerged. Governments and domestic companies tried to fend off foreign powerhouses through requirements of national citizenship for media owners and limitations on the percentage of foreign ownership of domestic business (Morris and Waisbord 2001). Such attempts to harness the global traffic of capital are bypassed by international and domestic corporations, who, having realized that they mutually need each other, decide to partner in different ways.

Amid these dynamics, the industry became more integrated as a whole. The structure of television systems became streamlined along the lines of the private model. Business is the name of the game, regardless of where company headquarters are located. As some domestic industries matured, a new slew of producers began peddling programs worldwide. Consequently, flows of capital and television programming are more complex than in the past. The globalization of television economics has not made national cultures irrelevant. Even when screens have been inundated with Hollywood fare, television remains a central place for articulating the national. Media narratives and spoken language continue to organize a sense of cultural belonging.

Formats are not the catalysts for cultural sameness or the loss of cultural diversity; adaptations provide opportunities for reimagining nations in various ways (Moran 1998). Global audiences are watching the same formats, but they engage culturally in ways that are not predetermined. Formats are ultimately contained in local and national meanings. It would be a mistake, however, to celebrate formats as harbingers of cultural diversity. Just because formats are "glocalized," they do not necessarily usher in multiculturalism or stimulate cultural democracy. First, formats are not entirely malleable. Copyright holders ultimately determine what changes can be incorporated; they remain "the author" of the text despite a variety of national adaptations and audiences' interpretations. Second, adaptations run a whole gamut of possibilities, partially related to the fact that some genres (drama) are more open-ended than others (game shows) (Moran 1998). We can't simply assume that because formats are adapted, they express national cultures in similar ways. How is the national expressed in formats? Unlike versions in Northern Europe, the Spanish producers of *Big Brother* decided to include outdoor swimming pools because of better weather. The Russian producers of *Who Wants to Be a Millionaire* eliminated the "ask the audience" lifeline because people intentionally give the wrong answer to contestants. The Argentine edition of *The Price Is Right* had to make room for winners to celebrate effusively with the friendly host and to include more games with low-price prizes (people there prefer more opportunities to win cheaper items than fewer chances to win big-ticket consumer goods). The Brazilian version of a Mexican telenovela brings home settings and references familiar to domestic audiences. These adaptations evoke and materialize different meanings of local/national cultures. Can we say that format adaptations equally reflect national culture or nurture a sense of local/national community? What kind of opportunities do different television genres and format adaptations offer for organizing a sense of cultural belonging?

These questions need to be examined by expanding our thinking about the consequences of globalization in the television industry. The issue of the "effects" of international television flows needs to be asked not only in terms of "effect/audience activity" but also in terms of "missing opportunities" for cultural diversity to be expressed. The contemporary popularity of "reality show" formats as a cheap programming alternative arguably elbows out genres such as drama and comedy that, when compared with "reality" programming and game shows, offer different possibilities for the expression of national experiences. When profit is the bottom line and "reality" formats are available at a fraction of the cost of fictional programming, commercial television does not have to bother to produce fiction, to paraphrase Manuel Alvarado (2000). Format television does not eradicate national cultures, but as a reflection of a global industry solely concerned with quick commercial success and no patience for innovation, it decreases opportunities for diverse and complex representations of "the ties that still bind" (Waisbord 1998) local and national communities.

References

Allen, Robe. 1995. To be continued: Soap operas around the world. London: Routledge.

Alvarado, Manuel. 2000. The "value" of TV drama: Why bother to produce it? *Television & New Media* 1(3): 307–19.

Anderson, Benedict. 1983. *Imagined communities: Reflections on the origins of nationalism.* London: Verso.

Andrews, Edward L. 2000. Europe's "reality" TV: Chains and Big Brother. *The New York Times*, April 11.

Billig, Michael. 1995. *Banal nationalism.* London: Sage.

Biltereyst, Daniel, and Philippe Meers. 2000. The international telenovela debate and the contra-flow argument: A reappraisal. *Media, Culture and Society* 22(4): 393–413.

Cajueiro, Marcelo. 2000. "If it ain't broke," *Variety*, April 3.

Carter, Bill. 2000. At TV Bazaar, US companies look to buy, not just sell. *The New York Times*, October 9.

Craves, Richard. 2000. *Creative industries: Contracts between art and commerce.* Cambridge, MA: Harvard University Press.

Dayan, Daniel, and Elihu Katz. 1992. *Media events: The live broadcasting of history.* Cambridge, MA: Harvard University Press.

De Swaan, Abram. 1991. Notes on the merging global language system: Regional, national, and supranational. *Media, Culture and Society* 13: 309–23.

Edwards, John. 1985. *Language, society and identity.* Oxford: Blackwell.

Fernandez, Angel. 2001. El boom de la telenovela. *El Mundo* (Spain). http://www.elmundo.es/2001/02/22/television/957968.html.

Fiske, John. 1990. Women and quiz shows: Consumerism, patriarchy, and resisting pleasures. In *Television and women's culture: The politics of the popular*, edited by Mary Ellen Brown. London: Sage.

Fry, Andy. 2000. Europe secure as leader of reality programming. *Variety*, September 25, M4–M8.

Gitlin, Todd. 1983. *Inside prime time.* New York: Pantheon.

Golding, Peter. 1998. Global village or cultural pillage? The Unequal inheritance of the communications revolution. In *Capitalism and the information age*, edited by Robert W. McChesney, Ellen Meiksins Wood, and John Bellamy Foster. New York: Monthly Review Press.

Grantham, Bill. 2000. *"Some big bourgeois brothel": Contexts for France's cultural wars with Hollywood.* Bedfordshire, UK: University of Luton Press.

Guider, Elizabeth. 2000. Two-way transatlantic. *Variety*, September 25, M1–M2.

Hall, Stuart, and Paul du Gay. 1996. *Questions of cultural identity.* London: Sage.

Hils, Miriam. 1998. MTV sings in local lingos. *Variety*, August 10, p. 24.

Hoskins, Colin, Stuart McFayden, and Adam Finn. 1997. *Global television and film.* Oxford: Oxford University Press.

Hughes, Janice. 2001. Rewriting the traditional broadcast revenue model. *Financial Times* (London), June 19, p. 2.

Jensen, Elizabeth. 2000. The changing face of international TV. *Los Angeles Times*, October 27, F1.

Kilborn, Richard. 1993. "Speak my language": Current attitudes to television subtitling and dubbing. *Media, Culture and Society* 15: 641–60.

Koranteng, Juliana. 1999. TV goes local: Pan-regional networks launching local channels. *Advertising Age* 70(2): 32–3.

Langdale, John V. 1997. East Asian broadcasting industries: Global, regional, and national perspectives. *Economic Geography* 73: 305–21.

Mar-Molinero, Clare. 2000. *The politics of language in the Spanish-speaking world.* London: Routledge.

Martin-Barbero, Jesus. 1993. *Communication, culture and hegemony: From the media to mediations.* London: Sage.

Miller, Jeffrey S. 2000. *Something completely different: British television and American culture.* Minneapolis: University of Minnesota Press.

Miller, Toby, Nitlin Govil, John McMurria, and Richard Maxwell. 2001. *Global Hollywood.* London: BFI.

Moran, Albert. 1998. *Copycat TV: Globalization, program formats, and cultural identity.* Luton, UK: University of Luton Press.

Morris, Nancy. 1999. US voices in UK radio. *European Journal of Communication* 14(1): 37–59.

Morris, Nancy, and Silvio Waisbord, eds. 2001. *Media and globalization: Why the state matters.* Lanham, MD: Rowan & Littlefield.

Moyes, Jojo. 2000. TV imperialism goes into reverse as British shows invade the US. *The Independent* (London), August 4.

Olson, S.R. 1999. *Hollywood planet.* Mahwah, NJ: LEA.

O'Regan, Tom. 2000. The international circulation of British television. In *British television: A reader,* edited by Edward Buscombe, 303–22. Oxford: Oxford University Press.

Otnes, Cele. 1996. A critique of daytime television game shows and the celebration of merchandise: *The Price Is Right. Journal of American Culture* 19(3): 51.

Pursell, Chris. 2001. To import or to format? That is the question. *Electronic Media,* January 15, 64.

Ritzer, George. 1998. *The McDonaldization thesis: Explorations and extensions.* London: Sage.

Robertson, Roland. 1992. *Globalization: Social theory and global culture.* London: Sage.

Sanchez-Ruiz, Enrique. 2000. Globalization y convergencia: Retos para las industrias culturales Latinoamericanas. Typescript.

Scannell, Paddy, and David Cardiff. 1991. *A social history of British broadcasting: Serving the nation, 1923–1939.* Oxford: Blackwell.

Schneider, Michael. 2000. Whiz quiz hits global jackpot. *Variety,* July 17.

Segrave, Kerry. 1998. *American television abroad: Hollywood's attempt to dominate world television.* Jefferson, NC: McFarland.

Sinclair, John. 1999. *Latin American television: A global view.* Oxford: Oxford University Press.

Sinclair, John, and Stuart Cunningham. 2000. Go with the flow: Diasporas and the media. *Television & New Media* 1(1): 11–31.

Sinclair, John, Elizabeth Jacka, and Stuart Cunningham, eds. 1996. *New patterns in global television: Peripheral visions.* Oxford: Oxford University Press.

Skovmand, Michael. 1992. Barbarous TV international. In *Media cultures: Reappraising transnational media,* edited by Michael Skovmand and Kim Christian Schroeder, 84–103. London: Routledge.

Straubhaar, Joseph. 1991. Beyond media imperialism: Asymmetrical interdependence and cultural proximity. *Critical Studies in Mass Communication* 8: 39–59.

Tomlinson, John. 1999. *Globalization and culture.* Chicago: University of Chicago Press.

Trinta, Aluizio R. 1998. News from home: A study of realism and melodrama in Brazilian *telenovelas.* In *The television studies book,* edited by Christine Gerghty and David Lusted, 275–86. London: Arnold.

Tunstall, Jeremy, and David Machin. 1999. *The Anglo-American media connection.* Oxford: Oxford University Press.

van der Bulck, Hilde. 2001. Public service television and national identity as a project of modernity: The example of Flemish television. *Media, Culture and Society* 23: 53–69.

Waisbord, Silvio. 1998. The ties that still bind: Media and national cultures in Latin America. *Canadian Journal of Communication* 23: 381–411.

———. 2000a. Industria global, cultural y política locales: La internacionalización de la televisión Latinoamericana. *America Latina Hoy* (Salamanca) 20 (August): 77–85.

———. 2000b. Media in Latin America: Between the rock of the state and the hard place of the market. In *De-Westernizing media studies,* edited by James Curran and Myung-Jin Park. London: Routledge.

Waterman, David, and Everett M. Rogers. 1994. The economics of television program production and trade in Far East Asia. *Journal of Communication* 44(3): 89–111.

Weinraub, Bernard. 2000. Sudden explosion of game shows threatens the old TV staples. *The New York Times,* February 9, E1, E3.

Whannel, Gary. 1993. *Fields in vision. Television sport and cultural transformation.* London: Routledge.

National Television, Global Market: Canada's *Degrassi: The Next Generation*

Elana Levine

The tension between heterogeneity and homogeneity, specificity and universality, has become the central problematic of global media culture (Appadurai, 1996: 32). While media scholars have largely discounted claims of total cultural homogenization by examining vibrant local production and reception contexts, the threat of a universal—usually Americanized—cultural colonization continues to operate in tension with those localizing forces. As one of only two nations to share a border with the United States, Canada and its domestic television industry seem particularly vulnerable to the cultural power of their southern neighbour. Thus, as in many countries worldwide, Canadian cultural policy has sought to protect the status of broadcasting as a "public service essential to the maintenance and enhancement of national identity and cultural sovereignty" (Canada Department of Justice, 1991) and scholars have identified "the Canadian media-identity problematic" as being "at the forefront of the major debates concerning the relationship between places, media representations, and community formations in a global cultural economy" (Tinic, 2005: viii). This article examines the production and distribution of the Canadian teen drama, *Degrassi: The Next Generation* (*DTNG*) as a case study of Canada's "media-identity problematic." As a program supported by and successful within its domestic, national market as well as the global TV trade, *DTNG* balances the tension between the specific and the universal so central to global media culture and so heightened in the case of Canada.

Recent discussions of Canada's positioning between the poles of cultural specificity and universality tend to see the global and homogeneous winning out over the local, regional, or national. For example, the Vancouver-based television producers Serra Tinic interviewed repeatedly spoke of a "perceived need to universalize the culturally particular" as a strategy for survival (2005: 110). With a tighter and tighter national broadcasting market, dominated as it is by American imports, for many Canadian producers "there appear few alternatives to diluting domestic content and participating within the global cultural economy instead of the regional or national arena" (2005: 92). Ravindra N. Mohabeer has criticized *DTNG* along similar lines, describing it as "plastic, generic and universal," "a product for and about a generic and glamorized adult-take on a commodified youth culture" as opposed to being "a social forum for and about *Canadian* youth" (2005: 100–1). In this article, however, I argue that what is most significant, and most revealing, about *DTNG* as a product of Canada's contemporary television industry and the "media-identity problematic" it faces is the way in which the program's success is predicated upon its servicing of both national-specific and global-universal ends, its ability to balance the heterogeneous and the homogeneous such that it can stand as a proud symbol of Canadian culture while simultaneously circulating as a desirable international property. The tension and subsequent balance between these poles pervades the program's production and distribution; these sites are the focus of my analysis.

DTNG is part of a 25-year-old Canadian television franchise centring on a fictional group of Toronto teens and produced in Toronto by Epitome Pictures. A half-hour program, *DTNG* combines comedic and dramatic elements to narrate the lives and loves of its ensemble cast. The series, along with its franchise predecessors, has been on the whole well regarded both within and outside Canada for its age-accurate casting and unflinching, open-minded treatment of social issues, from teenage pregnancy to multicultural identities. *DTNG* thus emerged in 2001 with a built-in fan base and automatic audience interest in Canada, but also in the many other countries in which the earlier series, namely *Degrassi Junior High* and *Degrassi High*, had achieved popularity more than 10 years previously. Airing its seventh season in fall 2007, the program is funded not only by its domestic broadcast licence (from the private, commercial network CTV), but also by Canada's public-private production funds and global sales to such channels as The N, an American outlet for MTV Networks' tween/teen viewers, Filles TV in France, MTV's Latin American channel, and Australia's national public broadcaster, ABC. The different iterations of the *Degrassi* franchise have won multiple Gemini Awards (Canada's highest TV industry award), International Emmy Awards and a Teen Choice Award in the US. Scholars of Canadian and youth media have typically praised the series, as seen in the 2005 volume *Growing Up Degrassi: Television, Identity and Youth Cultures* (Byers, 2005) and in favourable mentions in such publication as Beaty and Sullivan's *Canadian Television Today* (2006) and Grant and Wood's *Blockbusters and Trade Wars* (2004). *DTNG* is thus a critical and commercial success on national and international fronts. For an English-language Canadian television industry that struggles to survive in the face of the massive influence of Hollywood, *DTNG* is a somewhat unusual victory for home-grown production.

In what follows, I detail the ways in which this victory is dependent upon the *DTNG* producers' ability to manage the tension between local/national and global forces. How does the program manage to achieve the status of a legitimately Canadian cultural product yet not suffer a "cultural discount" on the global TV market? What production factors enable this dual positioning? And what are the implications of that positioning for the survival of the Canadian television industry and for non-Hollywood television productions more generally? If media culture is increasingly global, and if *DTNG* might serve as a case study for the successful negotiation of the heterogeneous and the homogeneous in that global context, what does this case suggest about the costs and the benefits of producing television programming for the global market in general and the global youth market in particular?

DTNG as Canadian Content

DTNG's well-established position in the Canadian television industry and in Canadian culture more generally suggests that the program has somehow managed to capture a Canadian sensibility or identity. Yet research on the global media industries contends that any product that too fully embraces the local specificity of its point of origin will have little chance of success on the international market; it will suffer a "cultural discount" that will fundamentally devalue it (Havens, 2006: 15–16; Hoskins and Mirus, 1988). I argue that *DTNG*'s "Canadianness"—an inherently ambiguous identity—conversely helps its global marketing, in part because of its very ambiguity. What is this seemingly ambiguous Canadian identity and what part does it play in the production and distribution of *DTNG*?

Serra Tinic (2005: 20) has explained that: "The search for Canadian identity has often been regarded as a defining national characteristic in and of itself." This uncertainty and ambiguity may be largely due to the fact that Canadianness is most often defined in the negative, by what it is not. As Seymour Martin Lipset (1990: 53) writes: "Canadians have tended to define themselves not in terms of their own national history and traditions but by reference to what they are *not*: Americans. Canadians are the world's oldest and most continuing un-Americans." Tinic adds that a perception of marginalization pervades Canada, generated by a sense of subordination not only to the US, but also to "the legacy of Britain's imperial past" or, for many regions of the country, to the national power centres of Toronto and Ottawa (2005: 134).

The Canadian identity of the not-American and the marginalized has been particularly central to the country's television history, and especially to the cultural policy that has shaped it (Beaty and Sullivan, 2006: 18). Canadian broadcasting policy has sought to preserve distinctly Canadian programming as a means of preserving Canadian national identity and protecting it from US dominance, as well as encouraging Canadian economic health. The imperative to protect television's Canadianness filters down into the way Canadian producers conceive of their work. As Tinic found in her interviews with Vancouver-based producers, television creators' choices of what stories to tell and how to tell them are informed by their "Canadian sensibility," an outlook related to their experiences of marginality (to the US) as Canadians and (to central Canada) as British Columbians (2005: 13–14).

Scholarly, industry, and regulatory discourses have all identified DTNG as a distinctly Canadian show. Grant and Wood (2004: 15) cite the program's "uniquely Canadian" take on multicultural identities. Similarly, an industry-sponsored 2007 study heralding the importance of children's and youth programming in Canada named the *Degrassi* franchise as a leader in Canada's effort to expose its youth to "Canadian values," particularly its "commitment to developing a tolerant and just society that is open to all cultures" (Nordicity Group Ltd: 1). And *Degrassi* creator and executive producer Linda Schuyler (2005: 297) has claimed that: "*Degrassi* is unabashedly Canadian. It is liberal, multicultural and proud of its roots in east-end Toronto." While such discourses do not explicitly construct the Canadian as the not-American, their adherence to constructions of Canada as multicultural and tolerant echo the longstanding conception of Canada as a cultural mosaic, with multiple ethnic and cultural groups distinctively and equally celebrated, a metaphor meant to contrast that of America as a cultural melting pot, an amalgamation of groups whose differences disappear as they come together.

Despite these attempts to label *Degrassi* as Canadian, in my conversations with multiple members of the DTNG production staff I found a consistent hesitancy to assert such an identity. Actor and producer Stefan Brogren (personal communication, 2 Aug. 2006), who was also one of the teenage actors on the earlier *Degrassi* series, pointed out that: "nothing on the school [set] hides the fact that it's Canadian ... if they're gonna talk about sports it's usually the Jays or the Raptors." But he also wondered, "What would you actually do to be a Canadian show?" Similarly, director Phil Earnshaw (personal communication, 2 Aug. 2006) told me:

> Well we have Canadian flags, we don't hide them, which is Canadian but ... that's a good question. [Pause] I don't know. I mean it's hard to distinguish on television the difference between American and Canadian in a way because Canadians are so ... [shifts topic].

At first, executive producer and creator Linda Schuyler (personal communication, 2 Aug. 2006) told me, "I don't feel the show is any different than if I would be an American doing it," but she later speculated:

> I suppose the one way being Canadian influences our storytelling [is] that as a country and as a nation we are probably more small and liberal than America ... and there certainly is a lot of liberalism in our storytelling.

Executive producer and head writer James Hurst (personal communication, 3 Aug. 2006) also mentioned the left-leaning tendencies of Canadians as compared to Americans, but denied that they alone could explain the show's Canadianness. He suggested: "I don't think you could do *Degrassi* in America but ... it's not exactly for the obvious reasons; it's very complex." Clearly, the purported national characteristic of uncertainty about Canadian identity and the unifying principle of the Canadian being most often identified as the not-American inform all of these responses.

While it is understandable that those who produce *DTNG* might spend little time conceiving of what makes their series Canadian, occupied as they are with their daily work, it is notable that the Epitome Pictures personnel had such an ambivalent perspective on the matter, particularly when their comments are contrasted with those of the producers Tinic studied. Tinic's interviewees repeatedly referenced the impact of a Canadian sensibility on their work; "they felt their stories could not help but be informed by their experience of place" (2005: 81). The *DTNG* producers had some awareness of this "sensibility" as well, but their comments on the matter were even more vague and ambiguous than were those of Tinic's Vancouver producers. In part, this may be accounted for by the fact that the Toronto-based *DTNG* is positioned much more centrally in the Canadian television industry than are the regionally remote producers Tinic studied. The added marginality of those producers' location may have increased their awareness of regional and national identities. However, the Epitome staff's hedging around the question of their show's Canadianness is also understandable as a function of the program's somewhat unique positioning in the tension between the national and the global, the heterogeneous and the homogeneous.

As I will consider shortly, the international circulation of *DTNG* makes any claims of the show's national specificity a potential detriment to its success in the global TV marketplace, which may in part explain the Epitome personnel's reluctance to declare the series' Canadianness. But the series is equally, if not more fully, indebted to the Canadian television industry and its funding practices as it is to the revenues of global distribution. Thus, while Epitome personnel may have a difficult time describing the program's Canadianness they are also mindful, even proud, of its Canadian roots. Such roots may have an impact on the program's characters, narratives, or themes, but they most certainly have an impact on the program's economic viability. Epitome and *DTNG* are expert in negotiating the complexities of the Canadian television industry and its funding; however, this structure also shapes the production and distribution of the program in ways that help define its identity. The series' reliance on the Canadian system thus determines its "Canadianness" in fundamental ways that may have little to do with any kind of essential national character.

DTNG and many other Canadian television productions are financed by a combination of domestic sources. Not only do they receive a licence fee from their broadcaster, but they can also receive funding through a number of public/private organizations meant to boost the Canadian production sector. That sector needs boosting because Canadian broadcasters and cable/satellite channels can achieve greater profits from purchasing American series than they can from licensing domestically generated content. Because of the large licence fees US producers receive from the networks that carry their shows, they can sell those same programs to foreign markets for less than those foreign broadcasters pay for indigenous content. Thus, while a US drama series might accrue a $1.4 million/hour licence fee from its domestic broadcast network, a Canadian network could purchase the same hour for $50,000 (US). In contrast, a Canadian-produced series might cost that network much more per hour. For example, in 2002–3, Canadian private broadcaster CTV licensed one hour of *DTNG* (two half-hour episodes) for $165,000 (US) (Grant and Wood, 2004: 19). These factors make a production like *DTNG* expensive for Canadian broadcasters (compared to US shows), even as, for the show producers, those "expensive" licence fees are inadequate for the creation of programming with production values anywhere close to those of a US-based series.

DTNG and other Canadian productions thus depend upon financers such as the Canadian Television Fund (CTF). Independent film and television production first became viable in Canada in 1983 with the government's creation of Telefilm Canada as a funding source.[1] In 1996, the Canadian Television Fund (CTF), a private-public partnership supported in part by Telefilm, was created, and it eventually became the central funding venue for Canadian TV. CTF support is dependent upon a given production receiving 10 of a possible 10 points in the Canadian content requirements established by the Canadian Audio-Visual Certification Office. These points are awarded by virtue of the number and kind of Canadian personnel employed on a given production. The CTF also requires that productions be shot and set primarily in Canada, that the producers are Canadian, and that significant portions of the budgets are paid to Canadian individuals and firms. In addition, only certain kinds of programming are funded by the CTF; genres such as sports, news, reality, and talk are not eligible.[2] Instead, CTF support is divided among documentary, drama (fictional programming, either comedic or dramatic, in series or special form), children's/youth, and variety/performing arts categories, and is shared between English-, French-, and Aboriginal-language productions. The CTF declares its mission to be supporting:

> ... the production and broadcast of a specific type of culturally significant television production. These productions speak to Canadians about themselves, their culture, their issues, their concerns and their stories. These productions reflect the lives of Canadians across the country and reveal Canadians and their society to the viewer. (CTF, 2007–08)

The CTF's policies and practices are thus rooted in a rhetoric of Canadian national identity, but, practically speaking, that identity and the funding it allows is predicated more upon a given production's employment of Canadian labour and ability to substitute for the kinds of programming that Canadian broadcasters can buy relatively cheaply from US producers than it is upon any kind of essential national character.

DTNG fits these criteria well and thus has been well supported by the CTF. But the production also has supplemented its CTF backing by taking advantage of domestic funding sources designed to support new media and web-based initiatives, including the Bell Broadcast and New Media Fund, and Telefilm's New Media Fund. This choice of financing not only marked the program as a product of a Canadian system, but also shaped the kind of show *DTNG* would become, one in which viewers are invited to engage with the characters through technological means, initially through an interactive website but in more recent years through mobisodes and other new media content. According to Raja Khanna (2002), president of Snap Media, Epitome's partner in developing the transmedia component of the series, the plan was to make *DTNG*:

> ... reflect the culture of the young people today, a culture that has been revolutionized in terms of the way it communicates ... . So the idea was from the very beginning to produce this property as a cross-platform piece of entertainment ... . This meant doing it on television, on the web, and on wireless devices all at once. Throughout the project there would be no separation.

DTNG was thereby designed from its inception as a multiplatform show that would not only attract young viewers but also would take advantage of the various new media funds available in Canada. The *DTNG* creators had an incentive to produce this kind of transmedia content years before it would become more standard practice in television around the world because of the Canadian funding structure.

Of course, the Canadian system places constraints around *DTNG* as much as it offers opportunities, and these constraints shape the program's Canadianness. These constraints come into play, for example, in the relationship between the show's producers and its domestic distributor, private broadcaster CTV. The prime-time schedules of Canada's private broadcast networks are largely made up of US imports, thus working with the producers of original, scripted drama is not a central part of their programming efforts. In addition, because the private networks' profits are so heavily dependent on ad sales for the US shows they purchase, they do not have a strong financial stake in the small amount of home-grown content they carry. Economically speaking, they license such shows not because they are profitable but because national broadcasting policy mandates it. This results in domestic productions being scheduled during times when they are unlikely to succeed (such as on Saturday evenings opposite hockey broadcasts), as well as generating strained interactions between broadcast executives and Canadian creative personnel. A number of Canadian television writers have criticized the networks, both public and private, for their unwillingness to embrace creative experimentation, to put the time and energy into making a home-grown series into a hit. For example, writer Denis McGrath (2006) argues that the secret to success in the US network television business is the network executive who "speaks up for a project, and really pushes it, believes in it, tends to ride their way to the top." But, he asks:

> Is there anyone at CBC or CTV or Global or other Canadian networks willing to be that person? Or is that even relevant here? . . . before the current shake-up, the people making the calls about what went on the schedule at CBC had been in their jobs for twenty years. People can fail here, and not get fired . . . . Is anyone going to stop being quite so Canadian for a second and do what needs to be done to generate a creative hit and make some money?

McGrath's reference to the network executives' Canadianness is notable for its construction as the not-American, with a supposed disinterest in profit and an apathy about the commercial success of domestic content as the marked opposites of the American TV industry's practices.

Although *DTNG* is a relatively successful Canadian production for CTV, the network's interactions with the show's creators reveal the ambivalence in the private network's attitude toward domestic content. CTV executives seem uncertain about the role a series like *DTNG* is to play in its program lineup. Because the program cannot generate the advertising profits that American imports can, the network seems uninterested in using the show as a money-maker. Thus, CTV (as well as other Canadian networks) typically license just 13 episodes per season of domestic series, while the American programs they purchase often run for 24 episodes per season. *DTNG* has managed to offer between 19 and 22 episodes most of its seasons, but these additional episodes have been funded either through a government mandate that CTV extend the number of episodes per season for some Canadian series, or through the support of *DTNG*'s US distributor, digital cable/satellite channel The N. CTV's reluctance to see the show as a profit generator is also evident in the fact that the network only began to promote *DTNG* with any real presence and to invite its cast members to industry events once the series became a niche hit on the American cable station. Its US popularity additionally has led CTV to charge more for ad time during the *DTNG* broadcasts (Stephanie Cohen, Vice-President, Communications and Marketing, Epitome Pictures, personal communication, 2 Aug. 2006). Investing in the promotion of a domestic series is not a high priority for CTV dollars, although the network can be moved to promotional action when a series garners US approval.

The more typical treatment of home-grown series like *DTNG* by Canadian private network executives is to handle such series as if they are public service programming. The fact that *DTNG* and other domestically produced programs help the network fulfill its mandated responsibility to carry a particular percentage of Canadian content motivates this attitude, although *DTNG*'s subject matter—teens facing myriad social issues and problems—most certainly encourages such a stance, as well. This approach can result in CTV attempting to guide creative decisions toward unspoken ideals of social responsibility. For example, head writer James Hurst (personal communication, 3 Aug. 2006) told me about CTV executives challenging story decisions, such as having a 17-year-old female character "acting dumb" with a choice she makes because, as Hurst claimed the executive put it, "Well, I have a 14-year-old daughter and I don't want to put this out there."[3] In this case, the CTV executive was focused on the potential social impact of the representation, while the *DTNG* creatives were focused on the dramatic resonance and truthfulness of the character's actions.

Television producers and distributors often have competing interests. In the American context, this can result in network executives wanting to temper producers' desires to represent an admirable main character as a feminist or to depict stories of racial inequality, given network anxieties about advertiser and audience approval (D'Acci, 1994; Lotz, 2004). In the Canadian context, executives at a network such as CTV may be most interested in having the Canadian content the network carries offer a "positive" or educational message as a way of affirming the network's support for the proud national identity embedded in the country's broadcasting policy. Meanwhile, program producers and/or writers may be more invested in their creative vision, in telling an involving story with fully realized characters, a goal that does not necessarily intersect with pretensions toward national cultural uplift. Indeed, in the Canadian context, these sorts of tensions can even play out between a given program's producers and its writers, as the executive producers of Canadian series are rarely also their head writers, unlike American prime-time series in which the show runner (who is in charge of all creative and business dimensions of US TV series production) is nearly always a hyphenate writer-producer. The particularities of the relationships between producers, writers, and network executives are elements of *DTNG*'s production context that are specific to Canada and thereby part of its identity as a Canadian show.

DTNG's Canadianness is not an essential trait, embedded in the very stories and characters of the series. Yet aspects of the Canadian location of the program's production and initial distribution do make *DTNG* Canadian. From the perspective of the program's production personnel, the Canadian identity of the series they create is both a matter of significance and pride and a matter of uncertainty and disadvantage. The multiple economic and cultural forces working against the success of home-grown television make *DTNG*'s ongoing existence a clear triumph for Canadian TV, and yet those same constraining forces make understandable the desire of those involved to downplay the production's Canadian roots. In a context in which the very meaning of Canadianness is a matter of ambiguity and debate, in which the trait that most unifies Canadian national identity is its non-Americanness, categorizing any given series as truly Canadian is an inherently frustrated act. This very ambiguity of identity helps make *DTNG* a valuable property in the global TV market, a place where universality and homogeneity—a rejection of geographic or cultural specificity—is a distinct advantage.

DTNG as Global Television

The difficulty inherent in articulating *DTNG*'s essential Canadianness works to the program's advantage on the global TV market, where a lack of local specificity is a plus. As Epitome's director of digital media and merchandising, Chris Jackson, has put it in a promotional push for the series' graphic novel tie-ins:

> It's easy to say that *Degrassi* is uniquely Canadian for we Canadians, because it's been a part of our consciousness for so long, but is it really? When we see and hear how teens around the world (and not just in English-speaking markets, either) react to *DTNG* . . . . the argument could be made that the show totally transcends any nationalistic considerations. (Singh, 2006)

Jackson's market-savvy remarks point out the centrality of a transnational teen identity to *DTNG*'s successful global circulation. In this section, I examine the ways in which the assumed universality of youth helps *DTNG* to sell well internationally, but I also consider two other aspects of *DTNG*'s positioning as universal that operate in tension with its positioning as Canadian. The tension, ultimately kept in balance, between *DTNG* as Canadian and as global demonstrates the costs and the benefits for non-Hollywood productions in a transnational media age.

DTNG's success on the global TV market is indebted, at least in part, to its connections—linguistic, cultural, and economic—to the US, and to the US's positioning as globally desirable. In the global market, the national origins of television programming play an important part in establishing a hierarchy of desirability for those productions. US series are often the most coveted worldwide. Data from 2006 reveal that US sales make up 70 per cent of the total hours sold to foreign broadcasters, while UK sales make up 10 per cent. The distant third place TV exporter is Canada, with 3.7 per cent of the sales market (Nordicity Group Ltd, 2006). Because US television is omnipresent and favoured worldwide, any association with the US benefits a program's fortunes. Thus, the fact that *DTNG* is produced in English and that its actors have accents difficult to differentiate from those of US performers works in its favour. So, too, does the program's generic and narrative similarity to US teen series. Finally, as the number of Hollywood-based productions that shoot in Canada makes clear, a Canadian location—especially an English-language metropolis like Toronto—can stand in for the US on screen, offering yet another advantage to Canadian productions seeking success on the international stage.

All of these factors make Canadian programming sellable within the US as well as around the world. This even further advantages the program purchased in the US, as a US sale makes sales elsewhere in the world all the more likely. As one Canadian entertainment executive has explained: "Around the world, one of the first questions a Canadian selling a product will hear is, 'Who is buying it in the United States?'" (Rice-Barker, 1996). Another Canadian TV distributor adds:

> As much as some countries are anti-American, it really helps them feel comfortable with a series if it's run in America . . . . We can get a great review anywhere in the world—it won't matter as much as a great American review. (Davidson, 2006)

Degrassi's long-time relationship with US broadcasters and audiences has thus been central to its longevity. *Degrassi Junior High* and *Degrassi High* were co-produced with Boston's public television station, WGBH, and ran on PBS stations across the US. *DTNG*'s relationship to its US outlet, digital cable caster The N, is, technically speaking, less closely entwined than was the earlier generation's relationship to WGBH. Yet, *DTNG*'s positioning on The N has been one of the most significant factors in the program's viability. Until the end of 2007, when it became a stand-alone station, The N was the evening programming block of Noggin, a preschool-targeted channel during the day; both ventures are part of Viacom's MTV Networks. The N began as a "tween"-targeted channel, seeking to attract pre-teen viewers, and thus *DTNG*'s cast of characters, in grades 7 and 8 when the series began, was an appealing match. Unlike WGBH, however, The N is not a co-producer of *DTNG*. Instead, the network is one of 70 international licensees (Vlessing, 2007). Still, The N has a much more prominent role in the show's production than does any other international buyer.

Executives from The N preview *DTNG* scripts and offer input to the show's writers and producers, just as do representatives of CTV. The N affects the show's production in multiple ways, some of which place constraints around its storytelling and some of which open up possibilities both narrative and economic. Early in the program's run, executives from The N went so far as to urge *DTNG*'s creators not to shoot certain scripted episodes such as season four's "Secret," which dealt with the phenomenon known as "rainbow parties," where teenage girls perform oral sex on one or several boys (J. Hurst, personal communication, 3 Aug. 2006). The Epitome staff has largely resisted these censorship efforts although, as Linda Schuyler (2006) notes, it is always a challenge "to not let the economic contributors to your show become the dictators of your content." In addition to supporting the production of extra episodes in certain seasons, The N has also initiated and funded the production of *DTNG* webisodes, special behind-the-scenes episodes, and other online content, helping to extend the brand across media (S. Cohen, personal communication, 3 Aug. 2006). The N thus supplies a direct financial benefit to *DTNG*'s production and promotion; this connection to the US helps the producers to generate content that circulates not only within the US, but also in Canada and around the world.

The popularity of the series in the US not only enhances the production's budget and increases its cachet on the global market, it also has a psychological impact on the program's cast and crew that shapes the way they experience their work. The program's success in the US is a point of great pride for the Epitome staff. Studio hallways are papered with photos from the cast's summer 2005 US shopping mall tour, where the thousands of fans screaming with excitement at meeting their idols surprised and somewhat overwhelmed the cast, used to the more decorous responses of Canadian viewers. Many Epitome staffers told me about the remarkable turnout of fans during that mall tour, perhaps because of my status as an American but nonetheless suggesting their sense of pride and accomplishment in the show's transnational appeal. This pride is clearest in Cohen's tale of Epitome's efforts to acquire the surfboard trophy awarded to *DTNG* at the 2005 US Teen Choice Awards, where the show was voted Choice Summer Series. Epitome happily paid to have their own board shipped to Canada, where it is now displayed in Cohen's office, signifying, as Cohen (personal communication, 2 Aug. 2006) laughingly put it: "Oh my God, we're good! They like us!" The emotional component of The N's involvement—and the success with US viewers that involvement has brought—is a significant matter in the culture of the Epitome workplace; in the Canadian context, achieving the admiration of Americans is seen as a victory, even while maintaining one's difference from Americans, one's identity as the "not-American" is equally prized. Thus, *DTNG*'s success in the US offers the production direct economic and psychological benefits. Its popularity south of the border signifies a kind of global acceptance; it secures the series a status of universality that flatters the participants in its production for its ability to overlook—or at least not be deterred by—the program's Canadian roots.

The show's creative workers have a significant investment in their series having a universal appeal. Not only does such a position secure some of the funding so necessary in the Canadian context, but also it enhances the creators' own visions of the work they do. Linda Schuyler has long treated her work on *Degrassi* as an educational mission. As she explained to me: "We are working with a double mandate. We are working to entertain and educate" (personal communication, 2 Aug. 2006). While she emphasized the importance of strong storytelling and entertainment as the series' first priorities, she also reminded me of her personal history as a teacher, a biographical fact often mentioned in media coverage of the series, and one that is clearly meant to imply an educational foundation to her work as a producer. Schuyler's investment in education makes her belief in the show as universally appealing all the more flattering to her efforts, and thus she is eager to assert its broad reach (and thus its lack of Canadian specificity).

Head writer James Hurst also benefits from a conception of the series as universally appealing. Artists' desires to speak to a universal human condition have long been central motivators of creative expression and Hurst's motivations are no different. While he described the ways that personal experiences and contemporary social issues feed into

DTNG's storytelling, he also insisted that attention to any given issue was not the focus of the series, not the purpose or the primary appeal of the *DTNG* narratives. As he explained, the show's writers:

> ... think more in terms of characters and just emotional stuff... they're all love stories, all of them, every single one of these stories is a love story. So the issues frankly are bullshit .... [the issues give] us the excuse to talk about this stuff, whether it's questions about love, questions about revenge, guilt, grief, depression, anxiety. (personal communication, 3 Aug. 2006)

Hurst heralds emotions and themes that may be taken as universal, thereby allowing him to ascribe a kind of humanist breadth to his creative labour that understandably informs his identity as an artist. Thus, whether imagining their work as the educational discussion of contemporary social issues or as the creative expression of fundamental human emotions, the *DTNG* creators have a significant investment in their program's identity as universally resonant.

In addition to an economic dependence on international sales and a creative commitment to universal appeal, *DTNG* is also positioned as a global commodity through its affiliation with youth. As a category of age rather than of a more culturally specific identity, an association with youth easily translates into an association with the global and the universal. Charles Acland (2004: 44–5) notes that debates about the Americanization of global culture have youth culture as their subtext: "This cohort is taken as the embodiment of the potentials of a global village and of the anxieties about the social change implied by international connection in general." This conception of youth as a global identity is a logic regularly articulated by corporations as well as by cultural commentators. As Coca-Cola's Director of Global Marketing has noted: "There is a global teenager. The same kid you see at the Ginza in Tokyo is in Piccadilly Square [sic] in London, in Pushkin Square, at Notre Dame" (quoted in Campbell, 2004: 1). Such thinking also pervades the *DTNG* creators' conceptions of their work and its wide appeal. As Schuyler (personal communication, 2 Aug. 2006) remarked: "the teenage years, there's a huge commonality of experience regardless of what culture you come from." The assumed universality of youthful identity has helped to generate a vibrant market for youth-targeted television around the world; *DTNG*'s articulation to such an identity has thus helped to negate any "discount" resulting from its national origins.

The global market for youth-targeted TV grew strongly in the late 1990s and early 2000s when the "tween" audience, described as ranging anywhere from 8 to 14 years old, became a new target of television programmers worldwide. In certain respects, this was a surprising turn, as animation targeted to younger kids had long been the focus of the youth-oriented international TV trade (understandable given the ease with which animation can be dubbed into different languages and dialects) (Esposito, 2004; Mesbah and Kirchdoerffer, 1998). Animation is still a primary seller in the global children's marketplace, not to mention a primary export of Canadian producers, but the tween market became especially significant in the early 2000s, no doubt because advertisers believed such a market had been theretofore undertapped. Live-action programming, rather than animation, is often preferred for this slightly older market, a fact that boosted *DTNG*'s foreign sales potential when international distributor AAC Kids first offered it to buyers such as The N and France's Filles TV, which went to air in September 2004 as a channel aimed specifically at 11- to 17-year-old girls and for which live-action drama series make up 75 per cent of its schedule (Esposito, 2004).

As much as the assumed universality of youth and the new tween market enabled *DTNG*'s robust sales globally, the series has also had to negotiate the aging of its initial tween target audience since its early 2000s debut. As the 2000s have progressed many of the new tween-oriented outlets have begun to skew a bit older, fashioning themselves as tween/teen stations, or simply as teen-targeted channels. Following the tweens of the early 2000s into their teen years is a worthwhile business practice for such channels because of the impressive numbers of this cohort. These young viewers are the children of the baby boom generation, the upsurge in people born post–Second World War throughout the Western world. The "echo boomers," the progeny of the baby boomers and the primary target of the new tween channels, were born between the late 1970s and the early 1990s. Thus, by the mid-2000s, the youngest of these kids were exiting their tween years, necessitating a gradual upward shift in the target age for those channels trying to reach this large cohort. *DTNG*'s commitment to age-accurate casting—a feature that has helped to earn the program some of its critical plaudits and its educational credibility—has kept the series a sellable commodity over the years, for the cast members have aged alongside the target audience, moving from tweens to teens across the 2000s.

DTNG's success on the global TV market is thus a product of a number of aspects of its production and distribution, from the alignment of the program's young cast, the growth of tween/teen outlets worldwide, and the assumed universality of youth to its secure position in the US and its creators' investment in seeing their work as having resonance across national borders.

In all of these ways, *DTNG* is able to balance its status as a Canadian product with its status as a global one, a factor crucial to the economic survival of Canadian-produced television. Still, however, I argue that *DTNG*'s global vitality is not a result of its ability to deny or reject its Canadian origins; instead, it is the specificity of its Canadian identity, at least as applied to its cultural products, that centrally enables its global reach.

A Global/Canadian Series

Canadian television productions, particularly when they take the form of a series such as *DTNG*, do not succeed internationally simply because of their similarity to Hollywood product. Instead, such series, and *DTNG* in particular, benefit from their slight differences from American programming, from the very elements of Canadianness that are typically constructed as the not-American, as such differences can become the brand identity with which buyers worldwide connect. Andrew Higson identifies this flash of cultural specificity as the "Unique Selling Point" for non-Hollywood products. To Higson, such products can be sold because of "their exoticism, their foreignness—so long as the sense of cultural difference is not too great" (2006: 213). Tinic (2005: 108) has noted the same of European buyers' interest in Canadian-produced programming, in which both a similarity to and a difference from American TV establish that programming's value. This is potentially *DTNG*'s greatest global selling point, as well. As Beaty and Sullivan (2006: 82) contend: "The success of *Degrassi* as a distinctly Canadian show is defined through its ability to emulate American television, but only because it is more edifying, less commercial." Beaty and Sullivan are referring to the series' success in the US, but their claims apply equally to *DTNG*'s global circulation, in which the series benefits from both its similarity to and its difference from Hollywood-produced fare.

Canada's worldwide reputation for exporting well-regarded children's and youth programming (Nordicity Group Ltd, 2007), combined with the Canadian television industry's structural incentive to create "culturally significant" products (CTF, 2007–8) and *DTNG*'s specific mandate to educate as well as entertain help *DTNG* to acquire the air of the more edifying and the less commercial, the air of the not-American. Those factors specific to the context of the series' Canadian production and domestic distribution have been important to its global reach in that they have helped to differentiate *DTNG* from otherwise similar US productions. Such factors also operate within the context of Canadian national identity more generally. However, because Canadian identity is most typically conceived in terms of vagueness or negation, as marginal or as not-American, the very lack of specificity inherent to Canadianness allows the difference and distinctiveness of Canadian fare such as *DTNG* to be taken up and read in any number of ways—as rather like US-produced teen series (as in *DTNG*'s attractive and fashionably dressed cast), or as definitively unlike typical US programs (as in *DTNG*'s willingness to confront core characters with controversial circumstances such as abortion or testicular cancer). The flexibility of *DTNG*'s identity as Canadian—its ability to seem American, or to seem not-American—is thus central to its assumed universality. In the end, *DTNG* depends heavily upon the very Canadian roots it finds it economically necessary to transcend. The vagueness, flexibility, and connection to American fare that assist *DTNG*'s successful circulation in the global TV trade are not only central to the program's status as Canadian, but also are key attributes in the economic sustainability of non-Hollywood products as they work their way through today's transnational media industry.

Notes

1. Additional factors also encouraged independent production in Canada, among them the government's requirement that the CBC acquire programming from outside sources, instead of producing programming solely in-house. Independent film production has had additional means of support since the late 1960s origins of the Canadian Film Development Corporation.
2. This is not to say that such productions have no place on Canadian television. In fact, a 1999 Canadian Radio-television Telecommunications Commission policy made it easier for broadcasters to substitute this cheaper form of programming for drama in their Canadian content requirements.
3. Hurst did not specify what choice the character, Manny Santos, was to make that was so undesirable to the network executives. However, I suspect that it was Manny's one-time use of cocaine when she feels out of place at a dinner party with her boyfriend and his friends in "What's It Feel Like to be a Ghost?" (Part 1, 2 Jan. 2007).

References

Acland, C.R. (2004). "Fresh Contacts: Global Culture and the Concept of Generation," pp. 31–52 in N. Campbell (ed.) *American Youth Cultures*. Edinburgh: Edinburgh University Press.

Appadurai, A. (1996). *Modernity at Large: Cultural Dimensions of Globalization*. Minneapolis, MN: University of Minnesota Press.

Beaty, B., and R. Sullivan (2006). *Canadian Television Today*. Calgary: University of Calgary Press.

Byers, M. (ed.) (2005). *Growing Up Degrassi: Television, Identity and Youth Cultures*. Toronto: Sumach Press.

Campbell, N. (2004). "Introduction: On Youth Cultural Studies," pp. 1–30 in N. Campbell (ed.) *American Youth Cultures*. Edinburgh: Edinburgh University Press.

Canada Department of Justice. (1991). "Broadcasting Act," 1 Feb., URL (consulted April 2007): http://laws.justice.gc.ca/en/showdoc/cs/B-9.01/bo-ga:l_I-gb:s_3//en#anchorbo-ga:l_I-gb:s_3

Canadian Television Fund. (2007–8). "Introduction to the Canadian Television Fund: Spirit and Intent," in *Broadcaster Performance Envelope Guidelines*, URL (consulted April 2007): www.canadiantelevisionfund.ca/producers/bpe/

D'Acci, J. (1994). *Defining Women: Television and the Case of* Cagney & Lacey. Chapel Hill, NC: University of North Carolina Press.

Davidson, S. (2006). "*Da Vinci*'s Leads Cancon Pack in US," *Playback*, 20 March, URL (consulted September 2006): www.playbackmag.com/articles/magazine/20060320/syndie.html?.

Esposito, M. (2004). "Children's Channels—A Niche Too Far?" *C21Media.net* 20 October, URL (consulted September 2006): www.c21media.net/common/print_detail.asp?article=22202

Grant, P.S., and C. Wood (2004). *Blockbusters and Trade Wars: Popular Culture in a Globalized World*. Vancouver: Douglas and McInytre.

Havens, T. (2006). *Global Television Marketplace*. London: British Film Institute.

Higson, A. (2006). "Crossing Over: Exporting Indigenous Heritage to the USA," pp. 203–20 in S. Harvey (ed.) *Trading Culture: Global Traffic and Local Cultures in Film and Television*. Eastleigh, UK: John Libbey Publishing.

Hoskins, C., and R. Mirus. (1988). "Reasons for the US Dominance of the International Trade in Television Programmes," *Media, Culture & Society* 10: 499–515.

Khanna, R. (2002). "Creation," *Canadian Journal of Communication* 27(September), URL (consulted March 2007): www.cjc-online.ca

Lipset, S.M. (1990). *Continental Divide: The Values and Institutions of the United States and Canada*. New York: Routledge.

Lotz, A.D. (2004). "Textual (Im)possibilities in the US Post-network Era: Negotiating Production and Promotion Processes on Lifetime's *Any Day Now*," *Critical Studies in Media Communication* 21(1): 22–43.

McGrath, D. (2006). "Desperate Canadian Networks and the 'Permanent Downturn,'" *Dead Things on Sticks*, 24 May, URL (consulted March 2007): heywriterboy.blogspot.com/2006/05/desperate-canadian-networks-and.html

Mesbah, M., and E. Kirchdoerffer. (1998). "Mipcom Jr. Market Intelligence," *Playback* 21 September, URL (consulted 15 September 2006): www.playbackmag.com/articles/magazine/19980921/23252.html?

Mohabeer, R.N. (2005). "Changing Faces: What Happened When *Degrassi* Switched to CTV," pp. 96–112 in M. Byers (ed.) *Growing Up Degrassi: Television, Identity and Youth Cultures.* Toronto: Sumach Press.

Nordicity Group Ltd. (2006). *Green Paper: The Future of Television in Canada*, 8 June, URL (consulted September 2006): http://www.nordicity.com/reports/The_Future_of_Television_in_Canada.pdf

———. (2007). *The Case for Kids Programming: Children's and Youth Audio-Visual Production in Canada*, February, URL (consulted April 2007): www.act-aet.tv/PDF_aet_act/The_Case_for_Kids_programming.pdf

Rice-Barker, L. (1996). "The Ins and Outs of the International Market," *Playback* 20 May, URL (consulted September 2006): www.playbackmag.com/articles/magazine/19960520/5350.html?

Schuyler, L. (2005). "Afterword," pp. 295–9 in M. Byers (ed.) *Growing Up Degrassi: Television, Identity and Youth Cultures.* Toronto: Sumach Press.

———. (2006). "The Future of Television in Canada," Plenary Panel at the "Two Days of Canada: Television in Canada" conference, November, Brock University, Ontario.

Singh, A. (2006). "School Is in Session and on Television as the *Degrassi* Comic Hits TV," *CBR News: The Comic Wire* 1 November, URL (consulted November 2006): http://www.comicbookresources.com/news/printthis.cgi?id=8780

Tinic, S. (2005). *On Location: Canada's Television Industry in a Global Market.* Toronto: University of Toronto Press.

Vlessing, E. (2007). "Today Canada, Tomorrow the World," *Playback* 16 April, URL (consulted April 2007): www.playbackmag.com/articles/magazine/20070416/mip.html

Imagining America: *The Simpsons* Go Global

Jonathan Gray

Cultural imperialism was supposed to be dead. Defined by Beltran as a "process of social influence by which a nation imposes on other countries its set beliefs, values, knowledge and behavioural norms as well as its overall style of life" (1978, p. 184), cultural imperialism posited a world media and cultural order in which Western and particularly American products were killing other cultures. Championed by academics, artists, and politicians alike, the belief in cultural imperialism flourished in the 1970s and 1980s, becoming, as Sarakakis (2005) argues, one of the few academic theories to have been directly incorporated into the world of international politics, through its corporeal existence in the New World Information and Communication Order (NWICO). Filmmaker Wim Wenders prominently announced that "the Americans have colonized our subconscious" (quoted in Miller, Govil, Maxwell & McMurria, 2001, p. 1); Herbert Schiller (1976) wrote of the threat of American cultural domination of the world via American media (see also Gans, 1985; Herman and McChesney, 1997; Mattelart, 1983); George Ritzer worried that "America will become everyone's 'second culture'" (1998, p. 89), as we all become citizens of a "McDonaldized" planet, and many culture ministers wrote similar fears into their policy documents. However, starting in the 1990s, cultural imperialism came under attack from various angles, and at least in academia, for several years it seemed damaged and discredited by a collection of audience researchers and theorists who balked at its assumptions of cultural weakness, cultural authenticity, and audience passivity.

In recent years, though, a "revived" cultural imperialism (Harindranath, 2003) has returned. Many culture ministers never gave up believing in cultural imperialism, and the academics are once more on-side too. Even in their 1993 promise to go *Beyond cultural imperialism*, many of the contributors to Golding and Harris' collection refused to leave behind notions of gross power imbalance, as the editors themselves noted that "Whatever the form and character of the new international order, it remains deeply and starkly inegalitarian" (p. 7), "itself the transnationalization of a very national voice" (p. 9). In recent years, too, Ramaswami Harindranath (2003) has argued for cultural imperialism's continued existence; and edited collections by Artz and Kamalipor (2003), Hamm and Smandych (2005), and Mosco and Schiller (2001), and Miller, Govil, Maxwell, and McMurria's *Global Hollywood* (2001) provide accounts that either explicitly or implicitly give renewed life to cultural imperialism, albeit in updated forms. Many of these accounts implore us not to suffer from the illusion that global media imperialism and Americanization are either myth or history. However, if cultural imperialism is indeed experiencing a rebirth, particularly given its first incarnation's power in policy debates, it is imperative that we interrogate the precise nature of countervailing global media flows, so that it does not suffer its former fate. Global media and cultural power inequities need to be taken seriously, and thus a continuing risk exists of exaggerated accounts of cultural imperialism that will only hurt the careful analysis of media globalization. In particular, while the first wave of anti-cultural imperialism research adequately pointed out the theory's crude analysis of audiences and reception, and hence while cultural imperialism "revivalists" are now avoiding this Scylla, there remains cultural imperialism's Charybdis of its inadequate analysis of texts and of the encoding of "American" values.

In this article, then, I wish to complicate notions of global cultural flows by discussing the case of *The Simpsons* and its reception by a group of non-American viewers. *The Simpsons* is one of the world's most successful American television exports, broadcasting in 70 countries at its peak (Pinsky, 2001), and even now, in its seventeenth season, expanding into new markets through freshly dubbed versions (El-Rashidi, 2005). If anything, then, it should be regarded as one of the key culprits of Americanization, its animated figures invading households and minds from Brazil to Korea. Yet, as textual analysis will show, *The Simpsons* has turned on its family sitcom brethren, and situates its action within an anti-suburb that is depicted as xenophobic, provincial, and narrow-minded. Parodying the traditional family sitcom neighbourhood, *The Simpsons*' Springfield often satirizes rather than expostulates the American Dream. The show's depiction of America, the American suburb, and American capitalism are a far cry from flagwavingly chauvinistic, as with its individuals, institutions, and mindsets. Moreover, adding weight to what textual analysis suggests, audience research into a specific group of non-Americans who watch the program will show that, to some, *The Simpsons* is read as an at-times incisive criticism of America and the American Dream. Thus, where the Americanization and cultural imperialism thesis at times comes close to positing the existence of a unitary and strictly managed vision of America beaming down from satellites above, this article will suggest that, in fact, there exist numerous competing Americas in the American global media, some of them satirically looking back at and attacking other Americas as presented in the more happy, glowing, and affirmative of American media products. My point will not be to further discredit cultural imperialism, nor to offer foolish apologism, but I will argue that in order to continue down the road of revival, we must first improve our analysis of the cultural content of global exports.

Global/American Cultural Flows

That Americanization is not a monolithic, all-powerful force should be no revelation. Numerous writers have paid attention to how American currents will always need to contend with other flows of identity and meaning (see Appadurai, 1990; Butcher, 2003; Katz & Liebes, 1990; Mankekar, 1999; Sreberny-Mohammadi, 1997; Strelitz, 2003), creating a process whereby no text or meaning can simply enter a country and hypodermically, without problem, inject itself into a populace. In general, drawing on the work of Mikhail Bakhtin (1986), John Fiske (1989) in particular has pointed communication scholars to the realization that popular texts are always "polysemic" and dialogic to one degree or another, not only offering various meanings, but also being read against the grain, "actively" by audiences, as part of the process of textual play and consumption. Hence, examining international flows of meaning specifically, Katz and Liebes' (1990) seminal study of the global reception of *Dallas* showed that while some international viewers found the text's glamour and dazzle highly attractive, others saw in it an allegory for the cultural emptiness that they regarded American capitalism to offer, a finding that is echoed by more recent work by Kraidy (1999) and Strelitz (2003). Certainly, foreign media can be, as Tripathy (2005) notes, carnivalized. Or, writing of the utility of foreign media, Gillespie (1995) charts how the very White (here, Australian) soap *Neighbors* is used in meaningful ways by Punjabi teens growing up in Southall, London to construct their own sense of group and personal identity. Thus, as Garofalo (1993) documents, one of the cultural imperialism thesis' key weaknesses lay in assuming a passive audience, and, in doing so, conflating economic power with cultural effects.

Nevertheless, the complications to the cultural imperialism thesis offered by work such as Katz and Liebes' and Gillespie's are at the level of interesting, or even resistive, localized *decoding*. As is active audience theory more generally, then, this work is open to criticism or the qualification that an audience's ability to "make do" (de Certeau, 1984) with the media on offer is hardly equal to the ability—the *power*—to create and circulate other, better messages. As Sarakakis observes, "the power of free interpretation and recreation—in other words, human agency—can only with difficulty be compared to systemic mechanisms that assure the propagation of capitalism in general and its major agents, the US and the West, in particular" (2005, p. 82).[1] Solely deflecting messages cannot be the basis of a culture's, or an individual's, sense of identity and communal and personal meaning, as adept as that culture or individual may be at textual play. Hence, while the existence of active audiences points to a key blind spot of the cultural imperialism thesis, and somewhat deflates its at-times alarmist rhetoric, such audiences alone are not enough to discount the theory in its entirety.

Another prominent counter-criticism to the cultural imperialism thesis comes from John Tomlinson, who argues that "No one denies that there is a lot of US product around. But if we look closer, it almost always turns out that: (a) it is home-produced programs which top the ratings; and (b) that foreign imports generally operate at a 'cultural discount' in terms of their popularity with audiences" (1997, p. 180). Thus, *Friends*, *24*, and *ER* may have travelled the globe, but we should not assume that their presence in a foreign television set equates to predominance in either qualitative or quantitative terms. As Sreberny-Mohammadi (1997) observes, culture is not created by media alone, and as easy as it may be for media scholars to fall into, we must be careful to avoid the trap that Couldry calls "the myth of the mediated centre" (2003), a myth that sees everything of substance, and all of social reality as processed by and only accessible through the media.

Many American programs will play on global televisions with the indelible stamp of "foreignness," perhaps amusing and profitable, yet not regarded as at the very centre of popular culture. Even when decoded as they were written, then, and hence even if we disregard an active audience altogether, some American programs may carry little cultural impact (just as they might in America itself). Thus, for instance, conducting a cultivation analysis of Greek viewers watching American television programs, Zaharopoulos (2003) found only a small cultivation of a US-influenced view of reality (see also Strelitz, 2003), and saw many other non-media-related variables playing a seemingly more important role in cultivating such values. Indeed, there is often something quite patronizing about imagining foreign viewers and cultures as woefully endangered by American programs; debates about media effects are often debates about others perceived to be lesser-skilled viewers than ourselves, such as children, women, and the working classes, and foreign Others have been added to this list.

Nevertheless, the sheer presence of American television worldwide is still cause for considerable concern. Hollywood's might at forcing foreign nations to abandon or weaken cultural protectionist policies is well-established (see Miller et al., 2001), and the American television industry's near-blanket coverage of the world, whether in globalized or "glocalized" form, is similarly undeniable. Increasingly, turning on television in Sri Lanka or Costa Rica, one is just as likely to find CNN Headline News or NBC sitcoms as in Louisville or Tucson. As Harindranath argues, moreover, this imperialism is insidiously facilitated by "compador" classes of "local" elites (2003, p. 162) complicit with foreign media ownership and control of key cultural mouthpieces. Active audience or "cultural discount" defences, therefore, would appear to be threatened by time, forcing us to ask how long foreign nations and their citizens can hold out when the likes of *CSI*, *Everybody Loves Raymond*, and their many colleagues are at the least a perpetual, and at the worst a growing, presence in global prime time. Meanwhile, as Harindranath argues in his "plea" (2003, p. 155) for the reinstatement of cultural imperialism, the theory's critics have often been too quick to leap from a belief in complete threat to one of no threat, "which belies the fundamental inequality in the flow of the media, the flow of capital, and the international division of labor" (p. 157). I do not here have space enough to detail the many ways in which Hollywood and America still control a great deal of international cultural flows, but said documentation is the basis for a major growth area of media studies (see Artz & Kamalipor, 2003; Hamm and Smandych, 2005; Harindranath, 2003; Miller et al., 2001; Mosco and Schiller, 2001). With even most of the current wave of international audience ethnographers (see, for instance, Juluri, 2003; Kraidy, 1999; Strelitz, 2003) lodging few systemic attacks on a "revived" cultural imperialism thesis, and with American and Hollywood policy and practice producing ever yet more supporting evidence, the cultural imperialism thesis appears once more on the rise, and once more moving to the position of dominant paradigm for the study of international media flows.

This article makes no attempt to disagree with such scholars as Harindranath. However, in reading such contemporary accounts, there is the faint air that we have already dealt with cultural imperialism's weaknesses. I contend, though, that we must first correct the theory's inadequate and oversimplified understanding of textual encoding. For, in the rush to oppose cultural imperialism's assumptions about audiences, to date media studies has failed to challenge cultural imperialism's beliefs in the unitary, essentialized nature of American media cultural products. While Fiske's insistence that audiences resist and actively watch television (1989) has been raised to a position of particular prominence and infamy in media studies, Fiske also observed that popular texts frequently open up cracks in the hegemonic order, inviting audiences in, whether actively *or* passively. As such, to assume that any given American product will be imbued with a flagwaving pro-American message requires a crude and indefensible notion of production. Similarly, though, this assumption would require that the semiotics of "America" had already been universally determined, agreed upon, and recognized as such by all. Particularly in light of the current and divisive "Culture Wars" between culturally conservative America and its progressive opposite, to ascertain exactly *which* America is supposedly being encoded into all American media products would itself be an impossible and problematic task, for the degree to which American media content represents and speaks of and to a single idea of the nation and Americanness is hardly evident. If this is the case within the country's borders, we cannot assume that on an international stage, a single America will rise to the top of every American media product. Rather, we could hypothesize that, on a textual level, a variety of American depictions of America are circling worldwide, some (perhaps even many) deeply chauvinistic and garish (as in films such as *Independence Day* or *Pearl Harbor*), but some nuanced, complex, and even focusing on the country's shortcomings and failings. It is with this in mind that I turn to *The Simpsons.*

The Simpsons on America

The Simpsons began as a series of animated shorts on *The Tracey Ullman Show* in 1987, before becoming its own half-hour sitcom in January 1990 on the then fledgling Fox network. The show quickly shot to popularity, and was soon being exported, both in English and dubbed into a variety of other languages. Seventeen seasons later, it is still popular both in the US and abroad. In England, in particular, a recent bidding war between BBC2 and Channel 4 drove its price per episode up from £100,000 to £700,000; the show regularly places in British ratings; and it is single-handedly responsible for nearly one-fifth of Sky One's viewership (Cassy & Brown, 2003). It has also proven particularly popular in former English settler colonies, including Australia (see Beard, 2004), Canada (see Turner, 2004), and South Africa, is estimated to have reached 60 million viewers worldwide each week at its peak (Chocano, 2001), and recently began broadcasting in Arabic to Middle Eastern nations (El-Rashidi, 2005). The show follows the lives of the Simpson family—father Homer, mother Marge, and children Bart, Lisa, and Maggie—in the fictional small town/suburb of Springfield, USA. However, while many of its traditional American family sitcom predecessors situated themselves in the suburbs so as to sing a love song to small town America, *The Simpsons* is deeply parodic of the sitcom lifestyle and regularly satirizes all manner of American institutions and ideals. A great deal of its satiric-parodic powers derive from its characters so clearly inverting family sitcom norms. Named after the idyllic Springfield of *Father Knows Best*, *The Simpsons*' town is anything but a warm, embryonic, and nostalgic space in which the American Dream can be imagined and mythologized.

At once the fattest town in America ("Sweets and Sour Marge") and the town with the lowest voter turnout ("Two Bad Neighbors"), Springfield is run by a corrupt mayor and an incompetent police chief ... if mob rule does not prevail first. With the exception of poor Lisa Simpson and sometimes her mother, most people in Springfield are stupid; family life—as embodied by the Simpsons—is relatively dysfunctional; and most of the townspeople are under the thumb of local nuclear power plant owner C. Montgomery Burns, a man whose power is such that to console him, his assistant can arrange for the Australian population to join hands and spell his name with candles ("Rosebud"), and yet who pays three dollars a year in tax ("The Joy of Sect"). People lose jobs in Springfield, people fight, and people fail.

At the head of the traditional sitcom family was the noble father, perhaps domestically inept, goofy (Bill Cosby) or rather boring (Ozzie Nelson), and even ineffectual at times, but nearly always warm and approachable, moral, a hard worker, and a model citizen. Compared to this is Homer, an overweight, oafish man who may do the right thing sometimes, but more often by accident. He drinks and eats his family's money away, throttles his son regularly, usually even forgets he has a third child, has an astoundingly low intellect (looking up "photography" in a dictionary, for instance), is not registered to vote, and his greatest dream was to become a "pin monkey" at the local bowling alley. *The Simpsons* takes the sitcom father's talent for conservative inertia (see Grote, 1983; Jones, 1992; Marc, 1989) and ironically attaches it to a human being desperately in need of any form of change. As opposed to the hardworking ethic of sitcom fathers—the ethic that engines the American Dream—Homer's rare words of fatherly advice to his son are that "If something's hard to do, it's not worth doing" ("The Otto Show"). Homer can be a remarkably selfish man, guided less by civic or parental responsibility than by childish amusement and hunger. And unlike his counterpart sitcom dream father, Homer cannot simply laugh or pray all his problems away, resorting more often to anger. Yet he is often revered by the town for these very qualities, and just as the ethos of many suburbs radiated outward from the sitcom father—as, for example, with Andy Griffith and Mayberry—Homer is emblematic of Springfield's ethos.

Springfield's ignorance is regularly satirized in *The Simpsons*. Grote observes that what goes unmentioned amidst most sitcoms' glowing depiction of comfy suburbia is the "intense exclusivity" required to keep this situation, whereby "the people from outside who cause problems are overcome and excluded" (1983, p. 82), creating "a world of Us and Them, and there is room for only so many of Us and no more" (1983, p. 105). Traditionally in family sitcoms, as in fairytales, troubles come from outside the home or immediate community. However, if White Flight to the suburbs and racist exclusivity are the unspoken truths of traditional sitcoms, *The Simpsons* highlights this racism and xenophobia. Here, the episode "Much Apu About Nothing" is illustrative, as the plot sees the town spuriously blame illegal immigrants for higher taxes. What follows is a hilarious yet chilling depiction of suburban provincialism, as the townspeople plaster the streets with Uncle Sam posters demanding

"I Want You OUT!" and get caught up in the push to deport all "foreigners." This action culminates at the port, with Police Chief Wiggum calling out: "Okay, here's the order of deportations. First, we'll be rounding up your tired, then your poor, then your huddled masses yearning to breathe free." As does the entire episode, the ironic recontextualization of the Statue of Liberty's promise criticizes how the very spirit with which America was supposedly founded has been inverted by the intense gate-keeping mentality of many American neighbourhoods.

Throughout other episodes, too, criticisms of the American Dream and suburban provincialism are common. In "The City of New York vs. Homer Simpson," Lisa must lecture Homer on not judging places he has never been to, to which an impervious Bart responds, "Yeah, that's what people do in Russia"; and the school comptroller's rousing speech on the value of courage in "Lisa Gets an 'A'" ends with, "Where I come from—Canada—we reward courage." Similarly, the judge in "Bart the Fink" explains, "this is America. We don't send our celebrities to jail," and when Selma learns the "Beeramid" (a massive, promotional object, created out of beer cans to resemble a pyramid) killed 22 immigrants, she comments, "Big deal. They were only immigrants" ("Selma's Choice"). Meanwhile, Homer is prone to mindless "USA! USA!" chants at random moments of personal victory, numerous townspeople have used "Go Back to Russia!" as a taunt at illogically inopportune moments, and the kids cannot even find Canada on a map, commenting it is "tucked away down there." Even over-zealous pro-American rhetoric is mocked, as in "Bart vs. Thanksgiving," in which a Super Bowl half-time show announcer introduces a band called Hooray For Everything, and their "Salute to the greatest hemisphere on Earth—the Western hemisphere, the dancing-est hemisphere of all!"; or in "New Kids on the Blecch," an episode that lampoons the disturbing link between the American military and popular entertainment by focusing on a boy band backed by the Navy for propaganda purposes. While most sitcoms celebrate America and the average American, *The Simpsons* presents a notably darker view. Granted, the town comes together at other moments, and can show itself capable of great things, for the criticism is by no means scathing, but overall, Springfield is no safe, enlightened zone of happiness, equality, and perpetual tolerance, as its sitcom predecessors purported to be. Indeed, by referencing other countries, *The Simpsons* also goes where few other family sitcoms in history have, by actually drawing connections between its world and the world outside, refusing the generic requirement of the hermetically sealed community (see Grote, 1983; Jones, 1992).

Moreover, the criticism of American culture goes beyond home and suburb to the very nature of consumerist capitalism. Again, the critique is neither all encompassing, nor by any stretch of the imagination stridently Marxist, but *The Simpsons* is well known for its irreverent play with and ridicule of consumer culture. Ads, marketing, and merchandising come under frequent attack, most notably through the figure of Krusty the Clown, an anti-Ronald McDonald children's entertainer; corporate greed and ecologically perilous avarice are personified by Mr. Burns; and Homer is playfully drawn as a drone-like ideal consumer, subject to all fads and advertising plugs. Most episodes, moreover, contain at least one, if not several satiric-parodic attacks on advertisements and their inescapability (see Gray, 2005), so that, for instance, various episodes have seen the church and the school overtaken by corporate interests, the local cigarette company sponsor a children's beauty pageant, and, in a special Hallowe'en segment called "Attack of the 50 Ft. Eyesores," the town's corporate mascots come to life and ransack the town. In recent years, too, *The Simpsons* have occasionally turned their eyes to international inequalities—albeit very briefly—as we have seen inside Krusty's Chinese sweat shop (with "Tomorrow—Mandatory Bring Your Daughter to Work Day" sign outside), and as Burns hires Señor Spielbergo, "Spielberg's non-union Mexican equivalent," to make a movie. Consumerism and capitalism, in short, are hardly given the candy-coated, reverential treatment and adrenalin shot that they receive in much American media fare. Instead, as Homer says to Lisa and the family's Albanian exchange student in "Crepes of Wrath," "Maybe Lisa's right about America being the land of opportunity, and maybe Adile has a point about the machinery of capitalism being oiled with the blood of the workers."

American life and culture are under scrutiny in *The Simpsons*, not always with venom in the bite, but with a bite nonetheless. And aside from the many one-off lines regarding America and American consumerist capitalism, as suggested earlier, much of this scrutiny comes through the relentless depiction of Springfield's inhabitants as variously subjects or objects of the American Dream's failure. To see *The Simpsons* as such is not to read against its grain, and it requires no "active audience" position; rather, it is part of the explicitly stated text. As a parody, though, the force of its depiction of suburbia comes from its negation of depictions offered by countless other traditional family sitcoms. The family sitcom, suburban paradise, and the American Dream have traditionally gone together, in good cliché style, like ball-games and hot dogs. From *Father Knows Best* to *Family Ties*, the Cleavers to the Tanners, many sitcoms and their families have served stalwart duty in illustrating all that is supposedly wonderful and idyllic about nuclear family life in the American suburb. While the genre has moved on somewhat from these days, and as other sitcoms such as *Roseanne* or *South Park* similarly took aim at the white picket fence image of American life, many of the older family sitcoms such as *The Cosby Show*, *Full House*, and *Happy Days* have travelled the globe (see Havens, 2000). Thus, to fully appreciate *The Simpsons*' parodic message, we must regard it intertextually as one that talks back to previous and other contemporary media messages and depictions of America, seeking to *replace* these images with a new, considerably less flattering picture. The show is still predominantly light in tone, and thus the criticism is measured, and its targets limited. Nevertheless, if perpetual happiness, conspicuous consumption, endless wealth, familial bliss, and friendly and open communities frequently formed the sitcom depiction of America from the 1950s to the 1980s (and still today, as reruns), *The Simpsons* contributes to a debunking of that myth, offering an alternate image of the American family, community, and nation. Reception can never be predicted from textual analysis alone, though, and so for this, I turn to my audience research.

Watching *The Simpsons*

From late 2001 to early 2002, I conducted a series of interviews with *Simpsons* viewers in London, England. The interviewees were all between the ages of 22 and 37, with a mean age of 27, and most were international students from Canada, Greece, England, Singapore, South Africa, Denmark, Scotland, and Australia. The purpose of the study was to inquire into *Simpsons* viewers' responses to the show's parody and satire. Thus, unless led by the interviewee, at no point did I bring up issues of America, or of the national tone of the program. Instead, in interview after interview, they gravitated toward such issues and I found them bringing up how much they felt the show portrayed another, less flattering view of Americans. Echoing what both Beard (2004) from an Australian context, and Turner (2004) from a Canadian context have suggested, I saw a clear indication that outside of America's borders, the show is often read as being about America, Americans, and American life. Thus, this section draws from the 30 interviews conducted with non-Americans, in order to offer some preliminary observations on the international decoding of *The Simpsons*' America(s).

Interviewees were largely self-selecting, having either answered a call for interview subjects placed in an overseas student residence, or having been recommended by other participants. They hailed from many disciplinary backgrounds, but were all well-educated and were frequently affluent international students. I make no claim to representativeness of the sample, for this was not a heavily scientific study, nor are its findings "representative," particularly as regards class or educational background. Many came from globally privileged elite groups, so undoubtedly responses from less privileged individuals from developing nations may have offered starkly different data. Furthermore, most spoke English as a first language, or with considerable fluency, and so all watched the program in English, not dubbed. This further limits the scope of these findings, as they cannot fully address concerns of linguistic imperialism, nor do they chart non-elite readings.[2] Nevertheless, despite the lack of any mention of America or even the American sitcom in my questions, their near-uniformity of response on the show's "Americanness" was striking; indeed, I underline that I came to this research topic deductively because of these responses, not inductively because I set out to find them. After first asking questions of how long they had watched and how loyally, I proceeded to ask after favourite characters, episodes, and scenes, why they liked or disliked the show, if they felt it had any specific politics or values, if its humour had any targets, and if they felt the show was merely fun, or if it held any more resonant role. All of the following audience commentary came in response to one of those broad questions.

The show was watched and enjoyed for many reasons, including its visual style, its slapstick, its love of parody, and its intelligence. Most of the viewers were particularly quick, though, to point out the "foreignness" of *The Simpsons*. In discussing George Bush Sr's comments on *The Simpsons* as being opposed to "family values," for instance, Wei[3] struggled with applying the assertion to her native Singapore, explaining:

> the Simpsons are *not* Singapore. Even if Bush commented on the Simpsons, he would have been commenting on American society, and, umm, I don't think Singaporean families identify themselves with *The Simpsons*; they would have watched it and enjoyed it and had a good laugh, but I don't think anyone would have thought "That's my family on TV."

Similarly, South African Judy offered, "I don't think that it has any relationship at all with South African society, to be honest with you. I think it's completely. . . . Like, to me, I can draw no parallels." Later, she expanded upon her comment, saying that "it's very much an American thing. Like, I don't think that Europe ... that it reflects on European society, on African, on Asian, on ... it's very American." Or, as fellow South African Zach iterated, "they model themselves as an all-American family, and you've got Springfield, which is this little suburban ... it's suburbia. And from our point of view, it's America, and it's Americans." Most of the interviewees did not read *The Simpsons* wholly as commentary on the "us" of "everyone," but rather on the "them" of Americans. In his study of South African youths' responses to American media and *Ally McBeal* in particular, Strelitz (2003) found a similar process, whereby the youth were clearly aware of, yet remained critically distant from, *Ally McBeal*'s Americanness and American values. Here, too, my interviewees' shared frame through which they watched the show was as an "American" program with clearly American cultural codes, characters, and settings.

More than just *being* American, though, *The Simpsons* was seen as actively *talking about* America. In asking what if any targets the show's parody and satire had, I regularly received answers highlighting the program's satire of American values and institutions. Thus, for instance, Canadian-English Al said "It does a *great* job of satirizing sort of a so-called middle class or lower-middle class milieu in the United States," while, to be compared with Beard's observation that many Australians feel *The Simpsons* "takes the piss out of [i.e., satirizes] Americans" (2004, p. 276), Australian Leo stated that "it certainly takes the piss out of the American ideal of truth, fairness, and all that way." Likewise, Scottish Ryan declared, "It's a satire on the modern American"; Canadian Sunshine noted, "I like the satire. I love the fact that they make fun of, you know, so much American culture"; and Canadian Katy observed that, "It highlights how abnormal things in the U.S. are. Like Springfield is just an example of the larger context in which it exists."

Discussing the program's interest in suburban provincialism in particular, Greek Thanos laughed before noting:

> I mean, their main target must be the middle-class American family: obviously, the whole show is about that [...] Umm, you see that they never, they never make something extraordinary: they always move in the same town with the same people, and rarely do anything out of the ordinary. So I think this kind of life is targeted by the show.

Canadian Mary, too, was clear in saying she felt the program spoke back directly to the idea of an American Dream of prosperity within the reach of any and all citizens, as she stated, "it is a little bit of a dig, uh, on that [...] whole idea of 'gotta get ahead,' and endless ambition of the American Dream. Homer's very much against that." These responses were not always the first "targets" mentioned by the interviewees, but in all cases they were listed along with others, with little if any delay required to ponder the question. The idea that the show targeted America was clearly a given to most interviewees, so much so that some even apologized for not coming up with "more creative" or "deeper" responses: the targeting of America was regarded as wholly *obvious.*

Moreover, while many of the above quotations address a more generic Americanness, numerous interviewees would list specific aspects of American life under attack. For example, Canadian Joanne felt that "the public education system in the States is a major target, and I think they pull that off quite well [...] I think it's shown that well, and the crumbling with the lack of funding, which the Americans just suffer with." Or, the more frequent target listed was American television, or America as a television culture. "TV news," Al noted, is a target, "especially American TV news I laugh about a *huge* amount, and American so-called documentary shows, like *Hard Copy* and stuff like that, which they have fun satirizing." Or, elaborating on her above-quoted comment on the show's attack on the American Dream, Mary noted that the show parodies the American sitcom, turning it "inside-out," for it "does have a darker message to it. Umm, so yes it is a family sitcom, but it's definitely not as 'everything's all wonderful' as, like, *The Cosby Show,* or like *Full House,* and those horrible ones that used to be on. It's *much* darker, in that everything doesn't turn out." Certainly, I received many answers to my question about the show's targets, and yet frequently these were offered with the important adjective "American" attached.

If interviewees discussed America as a clear target, though, they mentioned this targeting with amazing frequency when asked why they liked *The Simpsons,* or when asked whether they felt the show was "important." While numerous ethnographic studies of active audience readings reveal either the work or the ambivalence involved in reading against a text's grain (see Gillespie, 1995; Katz & Liebes, 1990; Strelitz, 2003), here the viewers expressed significant *pleasure* in being able to read critical commentary of America *with* the grain. After being asked what sort of things he finds funny, for instance, Canadian-Japanese Reid answered, "The put-offs on, like, on Americans." English Whitney stated that he used to watch it because, "the thing I like about it was it pokes fun at hometown, Springfield type of.... Every place in the States has a Springfield [...] It's quite political and ripping the piss [...] out of red-neck America, and hometown USA." Similarly, when I posed Rupert Murdoch's statement that *The Simpsons* is the most important show on television to Danish-Canadian Angie, unfazed she answered "Yeah," and when asked why, she elaborated, "Well, just the statements, again, that it says about American culture and the American lifestyle, and the American politics." Behind some of these comments was a pre-existent and fairly strong construction and dislike of "America" to begin with, and *The Simpsons* occasionally became merely an excuse to discuss America. But this was not always the case. Rather, for instance, Mary was careful to separate America from the American Dream of comfy suburbia, saying she felt the program was powerful and "kind of sits with you," because "it can burst your bubble of, you know, constant progress and everything's gonna get better." Later, she added:

> I think *The Simpsons* is important for the sense that it tries to peel away that sugar coating, and I think it gives everybody a pretty serious dose of reality [...] There *are* a lot of people out there who just have a job, and don't do a very good job, and not everyone's Bill Cosby, and this is a more relevant "sample," or it's a nice counterpoint.

More noticeably than any other respondent, Mary talked of the show precisely as an intertextual attack on American family sitcoms, and it was this that she valued the most about the program.

Admittedly, most of these interviewees are students, and so are perhaps more prone than others to (over)rationalize their consumption patterns. Thus, it might seem prudent to regard their remarks on the importance of, or society's need for, *The Simpsons* somewhat suspiciously. And yet, if this is the script that they hold to, it suggests this is how they rationalize it *to themselves* too, and thus, either way, it becomes an important part of their consumption of, and relationship to, *The Simpsons.* It is worth reflecting upon the huge cultural caché that *The Simpsons* carries amongst not only twenty- and thirty-somethings, but amongst many in academia: it is generally and widely regarded as a media literate, astutely critical text. *The Simpsons* is one of the few mainstream television texts that left-wing academics can talk openly about watching without feeling somewhat ashamed. Consequently, and as these interviews certainly suggest, the text is surrounded by an approving interpretive community, one that recognizes and applauds its critical stance toward American media and consumer culture. Text and audience, in other words, are working together to stand back from and dissect American society.

In contrast, though, two viewers felt it is yet another mindless product of the American media. In soliciting interviewees, I was clear that I welcomed anyone, including non-fans and anti-fans, and it is noteworthy that both of these viewers had watched very little *Simpsons* (coming to the interview with a partner), and thus were making conclusions based on little evidence. This is not to detract from their position or reading. On one level, after all, it raises interesting questions about how the show is marketed worldwide, since these quasi-viewers may simply have been interacting more with *The Simpsons'* commercial intertexts, ads, and merchandise than with the program itself, gleaning what they knew of it from MasterCard and KFC ads, for instance. Certainly, one of the non-watchers adamantly claimed to have disliked the show before ever watching it. Their reading is under-informed, but it is a reading nonetheless, and it should serve as a rejoinder that *The Simpsons* is hardly spreading a gospel of suspicion of pro-American rhetoric to every viewer worldwide, and that if my research was replicated with a different group of viewers from non-English speaking nations or from different socio-economic backgrounds, for instance, the findings may have changed radically. One might read some of the humour in *The Simpsons,* say, as aimed at fictional characters who fail to live up to the ideals that proper Americans are suggested to be succeeding at living up to, but this was not a position adopted by any of my respondents.

At the same time, however, lest this article suggest *The Simpsons* was being read as unrelentingly "anti-American," although some viewers found it commensurate with their own negative feelings toward America, the majority felt the criticism was good-natured, seeing it as necessary and important, but not caustically destructive. To begin with, while viewers such as Judy, Wei, and Zach, quoted earlier, saw few connections with their own country or culture, some viewers reflected on how part of *The Simpsons'* appeal to them lay in the relevancy of some of its criticism and humour to their own environment. Canadian Charlie, for instance, noted that "it stabs at Americans in the nuclear family and blablabla, but it's universal in that a lot of the stuff, you know, it's like what good humor is, where it's like, 'That happened to *me*' kind of thing. 'How did they get a camera inside my house?'" Or, as South African Daphne offered, "they're kind of middle-class America, but they needn't be." In other words, while *The Simpsons* was seen as critical of America and Americans, some viewers saw how this criticism could also apply to them and their own countries.

Beyond just applying *The Simpsons*' criticism to their own situations, though, to some viewers, the show and/or the criticism actually served as a positive sign of America. To Judy, for example, "it makes Americans look buffoonish," but "ultimately they're likeable, the Simpsons." As critical of Americans as many viewers felt the show was, they still saw *The Simpsons* as providing a rather endearing picture of family life, with Ryan glossing that "The average American is pretty dumb, but that's okay, 'cause he loves his family," and with others perplexed at Bush, Sr's attack on its family values, regarding them as entirely laudable. As Ryan's comment suggests, therefore, we should regard *The Simpsons* not as an "anti-American" show, but simply as a show that is uncomfortable towing the line that so many other American family sitcoms, dramas, and movies pull of mythologizing and romanticizing the American Dream into a tenuous existence. Richard closed his interview by noting that "in Australia, the perception is that America, in general, does not have a facility for irony or satire or anything like that, but clearly it's not the case when something like *The Simpsons* is far better than anything else that has been produced." The point is, then, that *The Simpsons* offers an/other view of America, and with it, therefore, another America. This other image and these viewers' response to it may be read by some as evidence of hegemonic incorporation; however, although *The Simpsons* hardly poses a serious structural challenge to America, it does circulate images that question and interrogate some mainstream constructions of the nation. Katz and Liebes' work on *Dallas* (1990), and Strelitz's work on *Ally McBeal* (2003) suggest that active audiencehood can easily equate to outright rejection of and scorn toward America and American values, but perhaps here, the American text's involvement in the act of criticizing America helps produce a more negotiated response in between (crude) rejection and (crude) wholehearted acceptance. Thus, although Matheson (2001) charges *The Simpsons* with nihilism for failing to present a better option, the show takes a small step toward embodying this other option—an America capable of laughing at itself, and willing to realize its shortfalls, a counter-hegemonic America that honestly accepts it is not the pinnacle of all greatness, enlightenment, and progress, and that at many places and times it is failing its people.

Conclusion

To talk of *The Simpsons* as counter to the mainstream, however, is paradoxical. After all, with very few exceptions, media texts do not come more mainstream internationally than *The Simpsons*, and when 70 countries import a program, it is hardly marginal. Rather, *The Simpsons* has received ample marketing and distribution, and is a key prime-time offering in many countries, attracting many millions of viewers weekly worldwide. Moreover, it is not alone in its mix of popularity and alternative presentation of American suburbia, as *Roseanne*, *Married ... With Children*, *King of the Hill*, *Malcolm in the Middle*, *South Park*, *Arrested Development*, and their reruns work in similar ways. Or, weighing in with arguably an even starker picture of strange and dysfunctional America, *The Jerry Springer Show* (or, to a lesser degree, *Judge Judy*) has travelled the globe replacing or supplementing tract housing and happy nuclear families from the picture of American life with the trailer park and multiple layers of infidelity, poverty, anger, and bad personal hygiene. American viewers may well detect the cultural signs in programs such as *The Simpsons*, *King of the Hill*, or *The Jerry Springer Show* that these characters and the lives being toyed with represent small town, "middle America"; but, outside of the nation, such a distinction might be lost on or irrelevant to international viewers without the cultural codes to distinguish between types of Americans, who will look at a cheap joke on *Springer* directed at "redneck trailer trash" as a joke on Americans in general.[4] Thus, as international viewers sail through their channels with their remote controls, it is possible that any American image of America and Americans they might find is mitigated. The American Dream and the idyllic suburban existence must now share the box with satire of America and the anti-suburb. Moreover, television is not alone in the production of contestatory images, as the international success of Michael Moore as both filmmaker and writer bears witness to. Thus, even when American texts experience no "cultural discount" (Tomlinson, 1997), and attract large audiences, not all are selling American fairy tales.

Admittedly, and importantly, to regard contestatory images as equal in number or reach as their chauvinist counterparts would be utterly foolish. Likewise, as the case of *The Simpsons* also illustrates, these texts are often plagued with other problems. As Beard discusses in his analysis of some angry Australian reactions to an episode in which the Simpsons go to Australia, opening the door for countless Australian stereotypes, "the broader symptom of [*The Simpsons*'] critique of American insularity often leads to the relegation of foreign nations to the status of backdrop for major characters to dramatically enact such satirical circumstances" (2004, p. 286). As Beard argues, the program can all too easily slip into a process of Othering, whereby all non-Americans serve, like the faceless Africans on the shores of Conrad's Congo, as props for inner reflection. As important as such reflection may be, then, the strategy may leave little room for international identification, nor does it *correct* the substance of the stereotypes by presenting more accurate and careful depictions. A different version of America may be on offer, but the subject and topic of discussion is still America. Furthermore, just as audience research discovered with one of *The Simpsons*' progenitors, *All in the Family* (Jones, 1992), while some audience members read Homer and his xenophobia as worthy of ridicule, others may find it as endearing as some found Archie Bunker's bigotry, meaning that back in America, the program may be engendering some of the imperial values that other viewers see it as attacking.

Meanwhile, due to economies of scale pricing, Fox is able to flood the world market with the show, and in doing so, self-deprecating humour or not, *The Simpsons* takes space on television channels that might otherwise be occupied by local programs focusing on local issues, culture, and values. Indigenous, and even hybrid, television programming has often shown itself particularly resilient and resourceful in facing the challenge posed by Hollywood's bargain basement prices for programs (see Butcher, 2003; Mankekar, 1999), but the economics of American television's pricing nevertheless remains a challenge for all countries. The show's use of Korean animators to finish up cells also perpetuates the "new international division of cultural labor" (Miller et al., 2001), whereby Americans get to tell stories and non-Americans are often consigned merely to touch them up as below-the-line workers.

Ultimately, then, we must be wary of over-exaggerating *The Simpsons*' power, for it represents no magic tonic. Nevertheless, we must also be wary of underplaying the importance of such widely circulating parodic messages. The case of *The Simpsons* tells us that at least some American programs appear to be engaged in an active debate over the semiotics of Americana, and this debate is being exported. What is more, the texts in which an alternate America is presented serve an intertextual function. As Bakhtin argues (1986), no text operates in a vacuum. Instead, texts talk to each other, and to each other's meanings. *The Simpsons*, therefore, is not just an alternative view of America: it is an alternative view that talks back to and can intertextually attack other, more traditional views/texts, so that our reading and interpretive process of such programs is inf(l)ected by it. *The Simpsons*, and with it other programs, might plague once comfortable and secure discourses, clearing the suburb and American life of some of their over-easy meanings and replacing them with a more critical picture.

This should not be read as a naïvely uncritical celebration of the end of Americanization or the complete reversal of cultural imperialism. After all, if *The Simpsons* serves as a tool for "speaking back" to another, more prevalent image of America, this presupposes the entrenched power, volume, and frequency of delivery of that other image. I doubt my findings here would be replicated with *CSI* or *Friends*. Hence, the findings and arguments of cultural imperialism revivalists still stand, as does the gross disparity in power, ownership, and capital that threatens the global flow of cultural products. Here, *The Simpsons* is complicit, too, for despite its semiotics, as one of the vanguards of Murdoch's News Corporation, bringing the company billions in rental, sales, merchandising, and licensing revenue, as a purely economic product, it is as guilty as are most programs in perpetuating Hollywood's vice grip on international global media flows.

Nevertheless, my research findings complicate the debate. Firstly, the presence of such texts as *The Simpsons* demands that we stop conceiving of the meanings of media flows leaving America and Hollywood as so unitary, standardized, and predictable. To assume that all American texts are saying the same things about America is as ludicrous as to assume that all American people share the same image of the nation. Secondly, and at a broadly methodological level, these findings argue for the necessity of making considerably more use of textual analysis and of qualitative audience research together in examining questions of globalization and cultural imperialism. While culture and meaning cannot simply be read off texts and audience response alone, nor can they be read off ownership and economics alone, as *The Simpsons* proves, for if this were so, *The Simpsons* would be—and would be read as—one of the most pro-American, flag-waving, and pro-capitalist products the world has ever seen. As we talk, therefore, of the American Dream and its export, it is imperative that we twin more traditional approaches with careful textual analysis and qualitative audience research (for the latter, see Clark, 2005; Ginsburg, Abu-Lughod, & Larkin, 2002; Kraidy, 1999; Mankekar, 1999; Murphy & Kraidy, 2003). The point is not at all one of dispelling fears of global media inequalities; rather, it is one of treating the topic with due complexity, and not discounting the relevancy of our findings by making things too simple. American television gives us competing images of America, and we must study more of them if we are to understand how the world engages in imagining America.

Notes

1. Furthermore, Patrick Murphy (2005) sagely observes that much active audience ethnography to date has focused on limited aspects of the full "negotiation" of power and meaning, particularly as regards the researcher's own positioning in the research.
2. However, several issues are imbedded in this point, for first there is no adequate data available to indicate how elite or non-elite the *Simpsons*' international audience in fact is. Second, some readers may see my choice of interviewing elites as an elitist act in itself; yet I believe that elite audiences are no more invincible to cultural effects, and hence no less worthy of examination, particularly when it is these audiences who frequently have greater access and exposure to all manner of foreign texts. Non-elite audiences, of course, must also be studied, and their responses may differ greatly; however, I repeat that this article makes no claim to have found a "representative" audience, nor to offer a complete picture of *The Simpsons*' relationship with international cultural flows.
3. All interviewee names are pseudonyms.
4. Of course, they may instead create other, different divisions, something which further research could examine.

References

Appadurai, A. (1990). Disjuncture and difference in the global cultural economy. *Public Culture, 2*(2), 1–24.

Artz, L., & Kamalipor, Y.R. (Eds). (2003). *The Globalization of Corporate Media Hegemony.* Albany, NY: SUNY Press.

Bakhtin, M.M. (1986). *Speech Genres and Other Late Essays.* (V.W. McGee, Trans.). Austin: University of Texas Press. (Original work published 1978)

Beard, D.S. (2004). Local satire with a global reach: Ethnic stereotyping and cross-cultural Conflicts in *The Simpsons.* In J. Alberti (Ed.), *Leaving Springfield: The Simpsons and the possibility of oppositional culture* (pp. 273–91). Detroit, MI: Wayne State University Press.

Beltran, L.R. (1978). Communication and cultural domination: USA-Latin American case. *Media Asia, 5,* 183–92.

Butcher, M. (2003). *Transnational Television, Cultural Identity and Change: When STAR Came To India.* Thousand Oaks, CA: Sage.

Cassy, J., & Brown, M. (2003, 10 February). Homer is where the heart is. *The Guardian,* Retrieved 17 November 2004, from http://www.media.guardian.co.uk

Chocano, C. (2001). Matt Groening. *Salon,* Retrieved 17 November 2004, from http://www.salon.com/people/bc/2001/01/30/groening/print.html

Clark, L.S. (2005). New directions in popular communication audience studies: Understanding meaning in a transnational, market-oriented, and interdisciplinary context [Special issue]. *Popular Communication, 3*(3).

Couldry, N. (2003). *Media Rituals: A Critical Approach.* New York: Routledge.

de Certeau, M. (1984). *The Practice of Everyday Life.* (S.F. Rendall, Trans.). Berkeley: University of California Press.

El-Rashidi, Y. (2005, 14 October). D'Oh! Arabized Simpsons aren't getting many laughs. *The Wall Street Journal,* p. B1.

Fiske, J. (1989). *Understanding Popular Culture.* New York: Routledge.

Gans, E.L. (1985). *The End of Culture: Toward a Generative Anthropology.* Berkeley: University of California Press.

Garofalo, R. (1993). Whose world, what beat: The transnational music industry, identity, and Cultural imperialism. *World of Music, 35*(2), 16–22.

Gillespie, M. (1995). *Television, Ethnicity and Cultural Change.* New York: Routledge.

Ginsburg, F.D., Abu-Lughod, L., & Larkin, B. (Eds). (2002). *Media Worlds: Anthropology on New Terrain.* Berkeley: University of California Press.

Golding, P. & Harris, P. (Eds). (1993). *Beyond Cultural Imperialism: Globalization, Communication and the New International Order.* Thousand Oaks, CA: Sage.

Gray, J. (2005). Television teaching: Parody, *The Simpsons,* and media literacy education. *Critical Studies in Media Communication, 22*(3), 223–38.

Grote, D. (1983). *The End of Comedy: The Sit-Com and the Comedic Tradition.* Hamden, CT: Archon.

Hamm, B., & Smandych, R. (Eds). (2005). *Cultural Imperialism: Essays on the Political Economy of Cultural Domination.* Peterborough, ON: Broadview.

Harindranath, R. (2003). Reviving "cultural imperialism": International audiences, global capitalism, and the transnational elite. In L. Parks & S. Kumar (Eds), *Planet TV: A global television reader* (pp. 155–68). New York: NYU Press.

Havens, T. (2000). "The biggest show in the world": Race and the global popularity of *The Cosby Show. Media, Culture and Society, 22*(4), 371–91.

Herman, E.S., & McChesney, R. W. (1997). *The Global Media: The New Missionaries of Global Capitalism.* Washington: Cassell.

Jones, G. (1992). *Honey, I'm Home! Sitcoms: Selling the American Dream.* New York: Grove Weidenfeld.

Juluri, V. (2003). *Becoming a Global Audience: Longing and Belonging in Indian Music Television.* New York: Peter Lang.

Katz, E., & Liebes, T. (1990). *The Export of Meaning: Cross-Cultural Readings of Dallas.* New York: Oxford University Press.

Kraidy, M. (1999). The global, the local, and the hybrid: A native ethnography of globalization. *Critical Studies in Media Communication, 16*(4), 456–76.

Mankekar, P. (1999). *Screening Culture, Viewing Politics.* Durham, NC: Duke University Press.

Marc, D. (1989). *Comic Visions: Television Comedy and American Culture.* New York: Unwin Hyman.

Matheson, C. (2001). *The Simpsons,* hyper-irony, and the meaning of life. In W. Irwin, M.T. Conard & A.J. Skoble (Eds), *The Simpsons and philosophy: The d'Oh! of Homer* (pp. 108–25). Chicago: Open Court.

Mattelart, A. (1983). *Transnationals and Third World: The struggle for culture.* South Hadley, MA: Bergin and Garvey.

Miller, T., Govil, N., Maxwell, R., & McMurria, J. (2001). *Global Hollywood.* London: BFI.

Mosco, V., & Schiller, D. (2001). *Continental Order? Integrating North America for Cyberspace.* New York: Rowman & Littlefield.

Murphy, P.D. (2005). Fielding the study of reception: Notes on "negotiation" for global media studies. *Popular Communication, 3*(3), 167–180.

Murphy, P.D., & Kraidy, M.M. (Eds). (2003). *Global Media Studies: Ethnographic Perspectives.* New York: Routledge.

Pinsky, M.I. (2001). *The Gospel According to The Simpsons: The Spiritual Life of the World's Most Animated Family.* Louisville, KY: Westminster John Knox.

Ritzer, G. (1998). *The McDonaldization Thesis: Explorations and Extensions.* Thousand Oaks, CA: Sage.

Sarakakis, K. (2005). Legitimating domination: Notes on the changing faces of cultural imperialism. In B. Hamm & R. Smandych (Eds), *Cultural imperialism: Essays on the political economy of cultural domination* (pp. 80–92). Peterborough, ON: Broadview.

Schiller, H. (1976). *Communication and Cultural Domination.* Armonk, NY: M.E. Sharpe.

Sreberny-Mohammadi, A. (1997). The many faces of imperialism. In P. Golding & P. Harris (Eds), *Beyond cultural imperialism* (pp. 48–68). Thousand Oaks, CA: Sage.

Strelitz, L. (2003). Where the global meets the local: South African youth and their experience of global media. In P. Murphy & M. Kraidy (Eds), *Global media studies: Ethnographic perspectives* (pp. 234–56). New York: Routledge.

Tomlinson, J. (1997). Cultural globalization and cultural imperialism. In A. Mohammadi (Ed.), *International communication and globalization* (pp. 170–90). Thousand Oaks, CA: Sage.

Tripathy, B.K. (2005). Redefining cultural imperialism and the dynamics of culture contacts. In B. Hamm & R. Smandych (Eds), *Cultural imperialism: Essays on the political economy of cultural domination* (pp. 301–16). Peterborough, ON: Broadview.

Turner, C. (2004). *Planet Simpson: How a Cartoon Masterpiece Defined a Generation.* Cambridge, MA: Da Capo.

Zaharopoulos, T. (2003). Perceived foreign influence and television viewing in Greece. In M.G. Elasmar (Ed.), *The impact of international television: A paradigm shift* (pp. 39–56). Mahwah, NJ: Lawrence Erlbaum.

Walking a Tightrope: The Global Cultural Economy of Canadian Television

Serra Tinic

In 2003, Alliance Atlantis Communications Inc. (AAC)—Canada's largest vertically integrated television and film production company—announced that it was moving out of dramatic television series production due to the decreasing profit potential of this programming sector. The exception to the company's long-range strategy would be the number-one-rated *American* franchise series *CSI: Crime Scene Investigation*. At the same time, AAC announced that it would be closing down its recently acquired production company, Salter Street Films. The highly regarded Salter Street had been an important contributor to the Canadian television arena with its incredibly popular sketch comedy *This Hour Has 22 Minutes* and had dispelled the industry notion that Canadians had no interest in homegrown television content. Salter Street entrenched its risk-taking reputation when it produced Michael Moore's Oscar-winning documentary *Bowling for Columbine*, a project that was too controversial for production in the Hollywood system.

The Alliance Atlantis decision is indicative of larger global production strategies wherein economic objectives increasingly take precedence over creative and cultural concerns. As members of a small-market nation, Canadian television producers have come to rely on access to global markets as a means to generate revenue for domestic productions. This has sometimes led to the dilution of cultural specificity due to the perceived need to universalize (often read as "Americanizing") televisual stories for greater international distribution. The presence of the few large companies like Alliance Atlantis had, to some extent, militated against this process by offering alternative avenues of support for television series production that emphasized the local cultural narratives of the national community. Thus, with an eye to shareholders' profit potential, the company dealt a serious blow to the Canadian television production community.

This chapter explores the contemporary landscape of the Canadian television industry wherein longstanding goals of nation-building compete with economic contingencies in a transnational media environment. It examines the tensions between television series based on the model of the "global generic" and those that speak to the cultural specificity of the domestic market. The emphasis here is not on a false dichotomy between global and local cultural forces but rather on the ways in which market considerations infuse and inform cultural decisions in television production. Consequently, the discussion focuses on the emergent global framework of the television industry and illustrates the impacts of strategies such as format purchasing and international co-production agreements on Canadian television. Consideration is also given to the ways that the global restructuring of national broadcasting policies and practices has changed the production and programming strategies of the Canadian Broadcasting Corporation (CBC) and the impact that this has had on the domestic television industry. It should be noted that the emphasis throughout is on the production of Anglo-television drama as this has long been the weak link in English Canadian broadcasting.[1]

Given the parameters of this essay, what follows is neither an in-depth research analysis of current Canadian television programming nor a close reading of policy discourse. Rather it is a broad overview of the potential possibilities and pitfalls facing the

Canadian television industry within the context of global, neo-liberal strategies to subsume political, social, and cultural spheres into economic decision-making models. Consequently, its objective is to sustain debate about the present and future directions of Canadian television in an era of increasing transnational media commercialization. The discussion begins with an overview of the tensions between market and cultural development goals as evidenced in two dominant forms of global drama programming: international format purchases and co-productions. Set within the context of the different structural constraints of public and private broadcasting sectors, this section argues that there is no inevitable outcome in terms of cultural homogeneity or hybridity in these types of programs. The central problematic, rather, is one of diversity of cultural representations as opposed to mere plurality of domestic incarnations of global forms and the importance of different modes of audience address. The second half of the essay brings the issue of global cultural diversity into sharper relief through a consideration of the challenges facing domestic broadcasting policy measures within the framework of multilateral trade agreements and organizations. As many nations, and most notably the United States, seek to define media content as just another commodity form to be "freely" traded across borders, policy-makers must now contend with the fact that cultural decisions are subject to arbitration outside the borders of the nation and within the halls of WTO (World Trade Organization) meeting rooms. As the conclusion indicates, the recent global success of explicitly domestic Canadian television dramas should be seen as a direct result of federal funding and cultural regulations.

Trading in Culture: Global Markets versus Global Publics?

It has been noted that television is a "contradictory industry" in that it is both a site of artistic expression as well as a business concerned with the maximization of markets and profits.[2] The reference here is, of course, to the American model of private broadcasting where creative decision-making is always tempered by considerations of advertiser and shareholder interests. As this commercial model is becoming increasingly prevalent worldwide, countries whose systems had once been predominantly public and national are now experiencing the tensions of a landscape where public and private broadcasting goals compete on an unequal economic terrain. A problem that becomes ever more acute as governments globally retrench from investing in the public sphere in general and the cultural industries in particular. This is not, however, a new dilemma for the Canadian television industry. It is, in fact, the story of the history of Canadian broadcasting. Since the 1960s, the Canadian Broadcasting Corporation (CBC) has been in direct competition with national commercial television networks. Moreover, this dual market/public model is replicated within the structure of the CBC itself, as the national broadcaster is also expected to generate 30 per cent of its revenue from advertising support. The expectation that the CBC produce culturally relevant programming while simultaneously competing for advertisers with private networks, who are able to more cheaply import popular American programs for broadcast, has placed unique structural constraints on cultural production at the national public network. The problem is exacerbated by the small domestic audience "market" for both private and public broadcasters. Consequently, global program sales and production strategies have long been crucial to Canadian television producers—a situation that has marked Canada as a model of the contemporary television industry in a global media arena.

In March 2005, the British Broadcasting Corporation (BBC), arguably one of the strongest national public broadcasters internationally, announced that it would be cutting 4000 jobs in an effort to streamline the institution and reduce overhead costs. The resulting protests and labour strikes eerily echoed similar events during the drastic cutbacks at the CBC throughout the 1980s. The question now facing the BBC is the same one that CBC personnel encountered 25 years ago: how will "content" be developed and produced with fewer workers, less funding, and a new television environment with hundreds of competing channels in need of "product"? Similar to its colonial offspring, the BBC has found the answer in the move to out-of-house production agreements with independent drama production companies.

The CBC's experience with out-of-house production should provide some reassurance to BBC staff who argued that their own: "savage cuts ... will damage programming as well as the organization and will unravel British broadcasting traditions. The BBC is a unifying British institution which acts as the nation's conscience, but these redundancies will damage the UK at its core."[3] Indeed, over the past decade some of the CBC's most lauded (and watched!) programs were developed in partnership with independent producers whose programs ushered in a greater diversity of domestic regional voices to the national public network. The aforementioned Salter Street Films is one of the penultimate examples of these new out-of-house production partnerships. Yet, Salter Street's experience under the ownership of AAC is instructive to the new dilemmas facing national broadcasters, for it is no longer solely the whims of government funding bodies that determine the level of support for public institutions but also the overall financial health of the domestic independent production community that largely affects the future of culturally specific programming. It is here that global diversification strategies, in both private and public television production strategies, have come to shape the Canadian industry.

There is a growing body of literature on the rationales behind, and relative successes of, Canadian international television co-productions measured in both market and cultural terms.[4] Despite this recent interest in the proliferation of international joint ventures, they are not a strikingly new global phenomenon, as their origins can be traced back to the postwar period in which the nations of Europe developed partnerships to rebuild their film and cultural industries during a time of economic devastation.[5] Today, they provide a means for independent producers in small-market nations both to share the high costs of dramatic television production and to access transnational audience markets in territories often circumscribed by national cultural content regulation measures. Having signed official co-production treaties or agreements with 50 nations, Canada has become a world leader in the area of international joint ventures (IJVs). Because of these partnerships, the sheer amount of Canadian television programming increased to the extent that by the early 1990s, Canada was the second-largest exporter of audiovisual products after the United States.[6] The fact that between 2002 and 2008 Canadian producers were involved in 343 new and continuing international television projects underlines the significance of the transnational production sector.[7]

Employing such quantitative output measures as barometers of success could lead us to believe that Canada had overcome the longstanding issue of cultural representation in a domestic television arena long dominated by American programming. However, a closer examination of the *types* of programs often produced through IJVs tells a different story—one that often leans toward the business, rather than the creative side of the contradictory institution of television. IJVs are an integral production strategy for independent Canadian drama producers who have very few domestic television networks at which to pitch their program ideas. For those who seek to develop projects deemed highly culturally specific or "proximate" to Canadian experiences then the CBC is often the only game in town. Although the private television networks, of which only CTV and Global can be seen as *national* in scope, are governed by Canadian content regulations (CanCon), they prefer to satisfy these requirements with less expensive news and sports programs. This programming practice became further entrenched after 1999 when the Canadian

Radio-television and Telecommunications Commission (CRTC) relaxed the rules concerning the specific amount of dramatic television programming required to fulfill CanCon guidelines. Consequently, there are few dramas produced for private television that speak to the specificity of Canadian settings, issues, and social processes. Despite a few recent exceptions—such as CTV's *Corner Gas*—when the commercial broadcast networks do purchase Canadian dramas, they often prefer the globally generic form produced through IJVs with the goal of reaching an international market. These types of international co-productions are marked by their tendency to follow established Hollywood television formulas and set their stories in American cities although they are usually filmed in Vancouver or Toronto. They qualify as Canadian content through the citizenship of the key creative participants in the production agreement. Some examples include *StarHunter 2003* (Canada/UK), *Riverworld* (Canada/UK/New Zealand), *Queen of Swords* (Canada/UK/Spain), *Relic Hunter* (Canada/France/UK), and *Stormworld* (Canada/Australia). The advantages of this type of market-oriented productions are manifold. First, as science fiction/fantasy or action-adventure genres they escape the "cultural discount" that affects dramas too closely tied to the social, political, and linguistic experiences of a particular country.[8] Second, they operate as mimetics of dominant American television narratives that have increasingly become the *lingua franca* of global television markets. Together, these factors enhance the global sales value of these forms of IJVs which, in turn, allows for production cost amortization and a lower selling price. This makes them particularly appealing to private Canadian broadcasters who seek to fulfill CanCon regulations with less expensive "product."

A newer and increasingly popular variant of these globally generic productions is the format program, which is the licensing and sale of a television program that has achieved success in one country. Here, the complete production "recipe" from sets to story organization is packaged and sold to producers in other nations. Examples of these format programs abound in the proliferation of reality TV, game shows, and makeover programs. Consequently, some of the more popular programs on Canadian television screens are *Canadian Idol*, *Canada's Next Top Model*, *So You Think You Can Dance Canada*, and *Project Runway Canada*. Format products hold a special attraction to broadcasters due to the low cost of production and their ability to draw sizeable audience cross sections, thereby attracting greater advertiser interest.

Market-oriented IJVs and format television purchasing fuel the fires of ongoing debates over cultural homogenization in contemporary studies of media globalization. Unlike older charges of cultural imperialism wherein the film and television programs of cultural superpowers, such as the United States, were seen to dominate the media landscape of small-market nations (and Canada is often the most cited example in this regard), these new production arrangements find producers throughout the world contributing to the generation of standardized television genres and narratives. Moran presents a more optimistic perspective of this process in his comparative analysis of national variants of formats ranging from soap operas to game shows. He argues that despite the generic rigidity of licensed formats, these programs are subject to adaptation to local cultural experiences to militate against their "foreignness" and make them more appealing to domestic audiences.[9] His conclusions correspond with Robins' conceptualization of "structures of common difference" whereby audiences across national borders increasingly engage with the same *types* of programs but see localized variation in the treatment of issues and thematics.[10] In many respects, these arguments present a production-side version of the cultural hybridity argument wherein cultural resistance is written into the dominance of genre and format structures. This negation of the influence of format structure over cultural content, however, elides the standardizing impact that often follows market models of cultural production.

A parallel example from the global magazine industry is instructive here. In their study of international versions of *Cosmopolitan* magazine, Machin and Van Leeuwen found that the overall "formula" of the magazine and its emphasis on individually based problem-solution case presentations affected a discursive closure of alternative cultural framings:

> [T]he local becomes an adornment or decoration which is embedded in a basic architecture of the global . . . this kind of globalization is the deliberate strategic embedding of certain local discourses into Western/capitalist models. . . . Global corporate media may tell stories set in different settings and dealing with people that have slightly different values and looks, but the fundamental structural reasons for how they behave, for what they want and how they might attain it will follow the same logic.[11]

Whether or not we agree that local cultures are "deliberately" incorporated into Westernized discourses of global capital, it is evident that the structures of commercial television provide specific constraints as to the types of stories produced and how they will be told. Moving away from reductionist theories of cultural imperialism, Barker argues that television as an institution formed within the context of industrial modernization is also a cultural forum for the generation of narratives supportive of capitalist modernity; and with the transnational encroachment of commercial television, these narratives become the global cultural currency.[12] Herein, homogenization is not about the erasure of cultural differences but, instead, the synchronization of bounded discourses underlining modernity and the merits of capital accumulation, such as rugged individualism, consumption, and the importance of personal success. So, yes, *Canadian Idol* localizes a format by placing Canadians into the pop music game show genre but once there they follow the same steps as British, American, Italian, and all other "idols" to compete their way to the brass ring of a recording contract with a multinational music company.

This is intended neither to cast dispersion on commercialized television programming nor to enter into debates about "quality" television. Rather, it is to highlight the different structural constraints that govern private and public broadcasting. In brief, different organizational and purposive logics result in different types of televisual storytelling. As it is Hollywood that has perfected the market model of television entertainment it can be said that the story of US television is also, largely, the story of the private Canadian broadcasters. It has become a truism that the market model of television treats audiences as consumers, as opposed to the public model's emphasis on audiences as citizens. However, as most contemporary global audiences engage with both types of broadcasting simultaneously, this bifurcation of modes of address becomes significantly more complex. In a mixed media system like Canada's, audiences more closely approximate Miller et al.'s depiction of the hybrid "citsumer," doubly hailed into national cultural belonging as well as popular participation in the global market of consumption.[13] The "consumer" side is invoked in classical economic arguments of supply and demand that assert that specific television programs are produced because audiences desire them. The implication is that the invisible hand of the market will satisfy the diversity of audience demand and thus the consumer is sovereign. However, this is not how commercial television works. The real target audience for private network executives are advertisers and shareholders—viewers are crucial to the extent that they can attract advertisers whose financing will generate profits for shareholders. Profits, in turn, are dependent on minimizing production cost and risk in an uncertain creative environment. This strategy actually militates against diversity in television storytelling as commercial network executives develop defensive strategies to reduce the odds of producing programs that will fail to fulfill the economic logic of the industry. Here we return to the centrality of the "formula" or "format" in private television.

To speak to cultural diversity by providing a range of cultural representations and methods of incorporating them into innovative narrative forms would be an incalculable risk for commercial broadcasters who seek never to divide the potential audiences available to advertisers. The reliance on television formulas becomes a means by which to control the volume of failed programs (read as ratings flops). Following the adage that "nothing succeeds like success," commercial television at times resembles a manufacturing assembly line where all networks schedule virtually identical programs because of high ratings experienced by particular genres or story premises. The 2004–2005 television schedule in the United States exemplified this standardization process and how the system of risk aversion proved to be an imperfect gauge of audience programming tastes. In preparing their schedules for the 2004–2005 season, network executives felt secure in their decisions that franchise television (four *Law and Order* programs and three versions of *CSI* as examples) and a heavy schedule of reality programming would guarantee ratings success. The bonus of low production cost in the genre of reality programming combined with track-record genre programming spoke to the conservative tendencies of the major broadcasters. Consequently, CBS and NBC decided to pass on the character drama that would be the only breakout audience hit of the season, *Desperate Housewives.* ABC found itself the overall winner of the television season due to its decision to air the series—a risk taken because the network trailed CBS and NBC and, thereby, had little to lose in taking a chance on the series. In the end, *Desperate Housewives* showed that the death of drama predicted by the major networks had been greatly exaggerated. Interestingly, it was the perceived lack of profit potential in the sector of original dramatic television that led to the AAC decision mentioned at the outset of the chapter. And, not surprisingly, the success of ABC's new series eventually led to the proliferation of a host of new dramas on the 2005–2006 schedules of all the American networks—many of which interestingly resembled *Desperate Housewives* or ABC's other ratings' winner, *Lost.*[14]

As Richard Williams comments, commercial television is a conservative industry when it comes to taking chances with new or untested ideas and: "the trouble with television ... is that even at the fringes it is staffed by people who think of themselves as radical, yet whose idea of progress is to clone the last thing their peers raved about... . This is perhaps not surprising, in view of television's wholesale capitulation over the past decade to the imperatives of market forces."[15] The particular manifestation of homogeneity, mixed with moments of creativity and innovation, evidenced in American network programming strategies replicates itself at the global level of television production. It is the type of decision-making that sets the foundation for the more generic forms of IJVs that I have outlined. Globally, market-oriented programs produce not "diversity but plurality" wherein there are "more products but they're spin-offs of a limited set of master templates."[16] Nevertheless, success in global terms continues to be measured in economic terms of output and scope of presence in media buying markets, regardless of cultural content. In fact, Marc Doyle emphasized this business logic in his praise for Canada's leading presence in the field of international co-productions.[17] In a study for the (American) National Association of Television Program Executives (NATPE), Doyle invoked the supply and demand argument in his prediction that the proliferation of Canadian IJVs would translate into a substantial increase of domestic programs on Canadian television networks. Unfortunately, 16 years later, Doyle's prediction has yet to be realized. The Canadian private networks have long known that the financial bottom line is better served by purchasing original American programming for prime-time scheduling as opposed to cheap Canadian imitations of these shows. As such, Global and CTV found themselves in a race to have the most shows in the "Top 20" as they went on a buying frenzy of the new American successors to *Desperate Housewives* and *Lost* for their own 2005–2006 season schedules.[18] Meanwhile, there remained a dearth of culturally proximate programming on Canadian network television despite the quantity of Canadian co-productions circulating globally. In fact, there were approximately 16 domestic dramas set explicitly in Canada on the three national English networks that season and nine of those were broadcast on CBC.

Turning to national public broadcasting provides us with another perspective as to how Canada's global presence in television might develop in ways that need not sacrifice issues of cultural specificity while simultaneously providing domestic audiences with stories that dramatize the conditions of their own society. The CBC's mandate to "reflect Canada to Canadians" provides the public broadcaster with a different set of structural constraints from those of its private network counterparts. The expectation that the public broadcaster would be home to culturally proximate programming while, at the same time, generating advertising revenue for part of its production budget has meant that the CBC addresses its audience as the ultimate "citsumers." In an era of government cutbacks and competition with private broadcasters for audiences, the CBC has had to develop new types of programming and production strategies to remain a relevant presence in the Canadian broadcasting and cultural arena. These measures have included developing out-of-house production partnerships, limiting the number of episodes per dramatic series (as well as the numbers of ongoing dramatic series, in general), and more aggressively pursuing international sales of its programming. It is in the area of co-productions and international sales that the CBC experience provides a different vantage point from which to view globalizing processes in television. It shows how, with some measure of government support, the turn to global markets does not necessarily mean that all television production must be homogenized into standardized generic "products." Three examples will be briefly discussed here to illustrate the relevance, indeed importance, of global public broadcasters to the maintenance of alternatives to the global generic versions of dramatic television. The first two are domestic co-productions with independent Canadian production companies: *Da Vinci's Inquest* and *Human Cargo*. The third is *Sex Traffic*, an international co-production with Britain's Channel 4—a television movie that illustrates promising possibilities of work between transnational broadcasters with similar cultural mandates.

As mentioned earlier, the CBC had the dubious advantage of a head start in the government cutbacks that would eventually also affect public broadcasters in other countries. When it was announced that dramatic production would have to move "out-of-house," people began to predict the demise of the nation's public network. However, over the past decade, these domestic co-productions have resulted in some of the most popular Canadian programs in the country's broadcast history as well as provided indications as to how the CBC might begin to resolve some of the tensions between the market and cultural development goals that define its structure. In this regard, the CBC's partnership with the former Salter Street Films generated domestic comedy programming that frequently won audiences away from the private network's broadcasts of American programs; and its much earlier partnership with Sullivan Enterprises resulted in extraordinary international sales of the period drama *Road to Avonlea*. More recently, the CBC's partnership with Barna-Alper Productions and Haddock Entertainment gave the public broadcaster the top-rated Canadian television drama *Da Vinci's Inquest*. *Da Vinci's Inquest* was based loosely on the "real-life" of former Vancouver coroner and current mayor, Larry Campbell. The character of Dominic Da Vinci drew on Campbell's actual crusade for the poor and marginalized living in Vancouver's Downtown Eastside and when the series headed into its eighth season in 2005 it was renamed *Da Vinci's City Hall*, following Campbell's own career trajectory into the mayor's office. At first glance, it would be easy to define *Da Vinci*'s success in generic terms as an urban crime drama—a popular formula with audiences. However, what distinguished the series from its commercial equivalents was the direct referencing of the lived experiences of its location, Vancouver, as a source of storytelling. There was no attempt to erase the cultural markers of its domestic setting and, given the show's premise, it engaged with the issues of crime, poverty, and class struggle within this globalizing metropolis. It was also a relatively expensive production, in Canadian terms, at over $1 million an episode.[19] The production value and genre factored into the show's international success and it was quickly sold to over 25 countries after the first season. *Da Vinci* also exhibits other aspects of domestic cultural production that go against the grain of the American commercial mode of storytelling—notably, the ambiguity of good and evil in central characters and the lack of happy endings that wind up the episode's hour. These subtle cultural differences actually enhance the global sales of Canadian dramas, particularly in European markets where buyers enjoy Hollywood genres with less of an American cultural sensibility.[20]

Government funding for the CBC thus provides a buffer that allows the national public broadcaster to avoid complete capitulation to advertising interests and thereby produce projects that address controversial issues in all their complexity (and in recognizable Canadian contexts). The result is that public broadcasting is able to take greater risks in all aspects of the production process from story selection to narrative development. Two of the CBC's co-produced dramatic mini-series elaborate this point: *Human Cargo* and *Sex Traffic*. Similar to *Da Vinci's Inquest*, these two programs make no attempts to mask their production origins and they have garnered critical acclaim, both domestically and internationally, while simultaneously drawing a sizeable viewership. What is particularly striking about these two mini-series is the fact that while they speak from a specific and recognizable cultural positioning, they both address the human costs of globalizing forces at the intersection of national borders. *Human Cargo*, a CBC partnership with Canadian producers Force Four Entertainment and Howe Sound Films is a stark dramatization of the lives of refugees beginning with the experiences of their persecution in their homelands to the tribulations they endure as they negotiate their way through the labyrinthine mechanisms of the Canadian immigration system. Kate Nelligan, one of the lead actors in the project, described *Human Cargo* as something she had "never seen before"—a mini-series that would "scare most networks with its content." *Sex Traffic*, a CBC co-production with Britain's Channel 4, pursues a similar theme in its dramatization of the plights of East European women sold into the global sex trade in the post-Soviet era. We probably should not be astonished that two productions that explicitly address the darker side of global capital would find little purchase in commercial broadcasting.[21] Indeed, John Yorke, the former Head of Drama at Channel 4 and current Head of Independent Production at the BBC, described *Sex Traffic* as "controversial and provocative ... a big talking thing that rarely gets made these days" and which is the "job as public broadcasters to make."[22] What is most striking about productions like *Human Cargo* and *Sex Traffic* is that they underline that national public broadcasting does not mean a retreat into parochial, isolationist dramas that invent the nation as a bounded cultural terrain that is immune from competing definitions of what it means to be a citizen of that place. Rather, unlike IJVs that seek to exploit market borders by homogenizing cultural narratives into the global generic, these types of projects speak forthrightly to the intersections of global and local processes and emphasize the subnational tensions and fissures that characterize the experiences of people of all nations. While never losing sight of the local, or the "idea" of the national, these types of public broadcasting productions exemplify "diversity" in contrast to the forms of "plurality" generated within commercial television.

Yet, the future of national public broadcasting in Canada and elsewhere remains precarious. As Murdock notes, "we live in a climate of increasing 'marketization' where market measurements of success [are] the yardsticks against which all institutions are judged, including those still formally in the public sector."[23] It, therefore, becomes imperative to keep issues of the exclusionary aspects of market forces at the forefront of public and policy discourse; continually to remind decision makers that publicly funded institutions produce and distribute the cultural "products" that do not appeal to the commercial imperatives of market logic. Rather, they redress "the market's failures."[24]

In the meantime, the story of Canadian public broadcasting remains one of "two steps forward, one step back." There have been promising signs in terms of the rhetoric of ensuring domestic cultural representation in the tightening of guidelines governing the subsidization of Canadian television production. For example, Telefilm Canada, as the primary government granting institution, has recently stipulated stricter rules for accessing the Canadian Television Fund (CTF) that supports domestic production. Herein, the guidelines posted on Telefilm's website (www.telefilm.gc.ca) now insist that productions must meet the "spirit and intent" of Canadian content regulations and, therefore: (1) must "reflect Canadian themes and subject matter"; (2) must achieve 10/10 points on the content regulation scale; (3) "the project may not be based on foreign television productions, foreign format buys, foreign feature films ... or foreign fully developed final-version scripts"; and 4) the project must be "shot and set primarily in Canada." Another positive step forward is the revival of Salter Street Films after its closure by AAC. Now reconstituted as the Halifax Film Company (HFC), this strong contributor to the domestic television scene underscores the importance of independent production companies being committed to diversity in their willingness to produce television and films that may be political and economic anathema to the powers that be both at home and internationally (as was the case with the company's support of the work of Michael Moore). However, Telefilm guidelines and the presence of innovative, risk-taking independent producers are moot points without the concomitant government will, politically and financially, to support both the CBC, as the primary broadcaster of culturally specific programming, and the CTF. This support continues to be lacking in Canadian cultural policy decisions and becomes even more crucial as new transnational trade agreements attempt to reduce culture to the category of a general commodity exempt from protectionist measures. The following section, therefore, provides a very brief glimpse of the challenges facing Canadian cultural policy in an age of cultural and economic globalization.

Cultural Exchange or Trading Away Culture?

McChesney argues that "neoliberalism is a superior term to globalization" in describing the transnational momentum of capital encroachment into all aspects of public life, including corporate domination in the global media sphere.[25] I am not quite prepared to evacuate the term globalization despite my general agreement about the prevalence of neoliberal philosophies governing the decisions of most contemporary Western nations. Globalization also encompasses transnational activism, resistance, and cultural sharing that militate against atrocities that can be committed within the "iron walls" of isolated nation-states and, therefore, I would caution against reducing all conceptualizations of globalization to the conservative forces of neo-liberal economic strategies. I do agree, however, that the discourses of neo-liberalism have been executed in the attempt to place cultural productions under the purview of transnational bodies such as the World Trade Organization (WTO) and, thereby, subject them to unprotected free trade policies.[26] If governments capitulate to the strictures of these organizations, then the sustenance of national public broadcasting institutions and support for non-market-oriented television programming will inevitably be termed economic protectionism and thus open to arbitration under GATT and GATS regulations. Indeed, Canada again provides an important case of foreshadowing here, when the government's attempt to support the domestic magazine industry was deemed an unfair trade practice against the United States under NAFTA. As McDowell (2001) underlines, current efforts to use principles of "cultural exemption" in global trade negotiations have failed to garner the support of countries that seek to exploit the market potential for their own cultural products across national borders. As such, McDowell argues for a new rhetoric in global media trade debates that emphasize the need for "cultural diversity" as a driving principle in WTO negotiations.[27] His statements parallel my preceding analysis of the contradictory forces between market and public structures in the broadcasting industries. The goal here is to convince cultural power brokers, such as the United States, that investments in the public media sector are not intended as trade barriers but, rather, as correctives to market imperfections. Magder's conceptualization of "media and cultural products as public goods" is particularly compelling and provides a framework for effective negotiating at the transnational level. In persuasive terms, he uses the analogy of public parks—a customarily non-negotiable trade sector—to explain the value of national measures to support domestic media forms:

> Public parks are public goods, goods for which one's personal use or benefit does not affect its use or benefit for another person (littering aside). Public goods have another aspect: while the benefit they provide may be significant, generally speaking no single person is able to pay the full costs for their production. This too is an obvious characteristic of many media products and cultural goods, from news to drama and entertainment. The strongest version of this argument begins with the acknowledgment that a robust and diverse sphere of public expression is a fundamental prerequisite for a healthy democratic polity. We don't rely on markets to provide us with an efficient allocation of parks; we shouldn't rely on the market to provide us with a sufficient supply of media or cultural diversity.[28]

The force of Magder's analogy is strengthened in his implication that national subsidization of cultural industries is not intended to bar entry of another nation's cultural products but, instead, is put into place to ensure that alternative modes of cultural expression are allowed to exist and flourish in a globally competitive economic environment. This is especially instructive to the Canadian case as the increased permeability of borders to the flow of media products has been an integral component of the growth of the Canadian television industry, both public and private. Indeed, the ability to maintain a thriving global presence through the generic forms of IJVs has generated significant ancillary benefits to domestic—and more culturally proximate—television production.[29] Canada also holds a stronger bargaining chip than many other countries in that policy emphasis has always focused on domestic content regulations as opposed to import quotas. This is crucial to trade negotiations in that you cannot argue for protecting cultural diversity (as a democratic measure) while denying Canadians the right to engage with media products from all over the world. And there is much to be learned from the cautionary tale of New Zealand, which after trading away cultural subsidization measures under GATS, lost in its attempt to later resurrect national content quotas in broadcasting.[30]

Thus far, Canada, in co-operation with France in particular, has been one of the leading nations to keep culture off the free-trade block in transnational economic negotiations.[31] Through the efforts of ministers of culture and media professionals, a global co-operative—the International Network on Cultural Policy (INCP)—was formed and with the tentative support of UNESCO hoped to set the framework for future rounds of debate on cultural production within the WTO.[32] However, such international efforts are undermined if the Canadian government fails to support existing measures to foster culturally specific programming and institutions on home territory. Without a funding structure to support independent producers who want to challenge market formulas and speak to the cultural experiences (both global and local) of a "small-market" nation, there will be little incentive to produce programs that fulfill the spirit of Telefilm guidelines. As the concluding section indicates, the combination of government regulation and funding, albeit never ideal, has enabled the cultural and industrial growth of a domestic television industry that is now in a position to compete globally without necessarily sacrificing a sense of place or socio-cultural specificity. The question, as always, is whether policy-makers see the benefit of continuing to foster an industry that some producers argue is as important a resource as "water and wheat."[33]

Back to the Future: Opportunity in Uncertain Times

The proliferation of new technologies, distribution channels, and the concomitant fragmentation of audiences has led to an environment of "indeterminacy" in the global television industries. In the transition to the "neo-network era," there is a new momentum to "organize and exploit diverse forms of creativity toward profitable ends."[34] Here we see even American program buyers, working in one of the most closed import markets, competing to purchase programs with an "edge" that allow them to compete against upstart US specialty channels buffered from the more conservative influence of advertising support. Perhaps not surprisingly, many of these programs originate in countries with strong histories of public broadcasting. Canadian producers, due to their cultural proximity to the United States and extensive experience in global production, have benefited greatly from Hollywood's content crises over the past several years. The reliance on reality programming, in the previously mentioned 2004–2005 American network schedule, resulted in a dearth of syndicated scripted programming available to fill the off-prime-time schedule. Consequently, CBS took a calculated risk and purchased *Da Vinci's Inquest* for broadcast in 98 per cent of its market during the 2005 television season. The series was a major ratings success for the network and defied Hollywood's conventional wisdom that American audiences would not watch programs set in other countries and particularly those that did not follow the rigid formula structures of American television genres. CBS renewed *Da Vinci* through the 2007–2008 season and the network's confidence in the series eventually opened the door to other Canadian programs. In fact, when the Writers Guild of America (WGA) went on strike in 2007, the American networks quickly turned to the Canadian television industry in anticipation of a lack of prime-time programming. A bidding war amongst the networks resulted in CTV successfully selling two domestic dramas: *Flashpoint* and *The Listener*, to CBS and NBS. In the end, the networks did not need to rely on these insurance policies. However, CBS decided to air *Flashpoint* as part of its prime-time summer schedule and the series not only won the night but also continued to dominate the ratings throughout its run. *Flashpoint*'s unforeseen success led *MediaWeek*'s Marc Berman to state: "There is every reason to now believe the broadcast networks will rely more on quality Canadian programming in the future."[35]

Hollywood's recognition of "quality Canadian programming" may prove to be a double-edged sword for domestic producers. It inspires a new sense of confidence about the maturation of the industry to the extent that masking cultural references may no longer be required to access the world's largest single-language market. However, it also provides politicians with a rationale to divest themselves further from supporting domestic production and broadcasting. The fact remains that these programs probably would not have been produced if it were not for the combination of government financing, content regulations for private broadcasters, and the maintenance of a national public broadcaster. Moreover, there is no guarantee that American interest in Canadian television will continue; this may be a liminal moment in the restructuring of their broadcasting strategies in an era of "indeterminacy." There remains one insurmountable fact in Canadian television: the potential domestic audience will never be large enough to sustain drama of high production quality. As this chapter has indicated, the globalization of the Canadian television industry is rife with both opportunity and constraint but it is too soon to dismantle the infrastructure that ensures a site of domestic cultural expression in television. It is fitting to conclude here with a statement from Laszlo Barna, one of the executive producers of *Da Vinci's Inquest*:

> Are people entitled to see 100-percent Canadian [content] if it doesn't sell in Yemen? I say absolutely. The day we only make shows that are for export would spell the end to highly personal Canadian storytelling. And that would be a tragedy.[36]

Notes

1. Serra Tinic, *On Location: Canada's Television Industry in a Global Market* (Toronto: University of Toronto Press, 2005).
2. E. Meehan, "Conceptualizing Culture as Commodity: The Problem of Television," in *Television: The Critical View*, ed. H. Newcomb (York: Oxford University Press, 1994): 563–72.
3. www.tv.msn.com/tv/article.aspx?news= 91805.
4. Paul Attallah, "Canadian Television Exports: Into the Mainstream," in *New Patterns in Global Television: Peripheral Vision*, eds J. Sinclair, E. Jacka, and S. Cunningham (New York: Oxford University Press, 1996): 161–91; C. Hoskins and S. McFadyen, "Canadian Participation in Co-Productions and Co-Ventures," *Canadian Journal of Communication* 18 (1993): 219–36; Tinic 2005.
5. P. Taylor, "Co-Productions—Content and Change: International Television in the Americas," *Canadian Journal of Communication* 20 (1995): 15–20.
6. A.B. Albarran and S.M. Chan-Olmsted, *Global Media Economics: Commercialization, Concentration and Integration of World Markets* (Ames, Iowa: Iowa State University Press, 1998).
7. www.telefilm.gc.ca.
8. C. Hoskins, S. McFadyen, and A. Finn, "The Environment in which Cultural Industries Operate and Some Implications," *Canadian Journal of Communication* 19 (1994): 353–75.
9. A. Moran, *Copycat Television: Globalisation, Program Formats and Cultural Identity* (Luton, UK: University of Luton Press, 1998).
10. K. Robins, "What in the World's Going On?" in *Production of Culture/Cultures of Production*, ed. P. Du Gay (London: Sage and the Open University Press, 1997): 11–66.
11. D. Machin and T. Van Leeuwen, "Global Media: Generic Homogeneity and Discursive Diversity," *Continuum: Journal of Media and Cultural Studies* 18:1 (2004): 118–19.
12. Chris Barker, *Global Television* (London: Blackwell Publishers, 1997).
13. T. Miller, N. Govil, J. McMurria, R. Maxwell, *Global Hollywood* (London: BFI Publishing, 2001): 178–81.
14. G. MacDonald, "Smart Dramas Welcomed Back," *Globe and Mail*, 31 May 2005: R1, R3.
15. In D. Berkeley, "Creativity and Economic Transactions in Television Drama Production," in *Cultural Work: Understanding the Cultural Industries*, ed. A. Beck (London: Routledge, 2003): 104.
16. Graham Murdock, "Back to Work: Cultural Labour in Altered Times," in *Cultural Work: Understanding the Cultural Industries*, ed. A. Beck (London: Routledge, 2002): 15–36.
17. M. Doyle, *The Future of Television: A Global Overview of Programming, Advertising, Technology, and Growth* (Lincolnwood, Illinois: NTC Business Books, 1992).
18. MacDonald, "Smart Dramas Welcomed Back"; G. MacDonald, "CTV Now Tops on All Seven Nights: Fecan," *Globe and Mail*, 7 June 2005: R3.
19. G. MacDonald, "Made in Canada, Big in Syria," *Globe and Mail*, 18 December 2001: R1, R7.
20. Tinic 2005.
21. Serra Tinic, "Between the Public and the Private: Television Drama and Global Partnerships in the Neo-Network Era," in *Television Studies after TV: Understanding Television in the Post Broadcast Era*, eds G. Turner and J. Tay (London: Routledge, 2009).
22. www.channel4.com/corporate/4producers/commissioning/documentarytranscript_Drama.pdf.
23. Graham Murdock, "Back to Work: Cultural Labour in Altered Times," in *Cultural Work: Understanding the Cultural Industries*, ed. A. Beck (London: Routledge, 2002): 19.
24. Murdock 2002, 27.
25. R.W. McChesney, "The Global Restructuring of Media Ownership," in *Global Media Policy in the New Millennium*, ed. Marc Raboy (Luton, UK: University of Luton Press, 2005): 149.
26. McChesney 2005, 152–7.
27. S.D. McDowell, "The Unsovereign Century: Canada's Media Industries and Cultural Policies," in *Media and*

Globalization: Why the State Matters, eds N. Morris and S. Waisbord (New York: Rowan and Littlefield Publishers, 2001): 117–32.

28. Ted Magder, "Transnational Media, International Trade and the Idea of Cultural Diversity," *Continuum: Journal of Media and Cultural Studies* 18:3 (2004): 394.
29. Tinic 2005.
30. Magder 2004.
31. B. Goldsmith, J. Thomas, T. O'Regan, and S. Cunningham, "Asserting Cultural and Social Regulatory Principles in Converging Media Systems," in *Global Media Policy in the New Millennium*, ed. Marc Raboy (Luton, UK: University of Luton Press, 2005): 93–109.
32. Magder 2004.
33. C. Haddock, "Lights, Magic and Spider Venom," *Globe and Mail*, 7 April 2003: R1.
34. Michael Curtin, "On Edge: Culture Industries in the Neo-Network Era," in *Making and Selling Culture*, eds R. Ohman, G. Averill, M. Curtin, D. Shumway, and E. Traube (Hanover, NH: Wesleyan University Press, 1996): 181–202.
35. Marc Berman, "Continued Summer Success for CBS' *Flashpoint*," www.mediaweek.com (accessed 1 August 2008).
36. MacDonald 2001.

iii. / *Post-network TV*

The Future of Television: Revolution Paused, Media Conglomeration Continued

Tanner Mirrlees

Since the turn of the millennium, TV business representatives, TV broadcasting policy agencies, TV creators, journalists, and viewers have participated in numerous discussions and debates about TV's "future." Graeme Turner (2001) noted: "at the present conjuncture, we confront more than the usual repertoire of genuine uncertainties about the future of television and about the kinds of interventions that should be made by academics in taking this future seriously"(372–3). In the field of television studies, edited collections by Lynn Spigel and Jan Olsson (2004), Amanda Lotz (2009), Graeme Turner and Jinna Tay (2009), and Michael Kackman et al. (2010) have examined how new corporate strategies (vertical and horizontal integration), technological transformation (the broadbanding of networks, wireless systems, and digitization), new media (computers, the Internet, websites, mobile devices, and video game consoles), and interactive viewers are reshaping TV. As an industry, technological form, viewer experience, and object of scholarly inquiry, TV—broadcast TV specifically—is changing.

What is the future of broadcast TV? Will TV "as we know it" be eclipsed by a "post-broadcast era" (Turner and Tay 2009), "post-network era" (Lotz 2007; 2009), or "convergence culture" (Jenkins 2006)? Many authors project broadcast TV's demise. In "TV Is Dead, Long Live Viral!," Craig Pearce (2010) declares: "[B]roadcast TV as we know it, or more specifically the networks themselves [sic], is dead." Kim Moses, co-producer of CBS's TV show *Ghost Whisperer*, claims: "Traditional TV won't be here in 7 to 10 years. It's changing so fast that I don't know if it's even going to be that long"(cited in Berland 2007). Jason Kirby (2009) notes: "A perfect storm of the recession, new technologies and shifting tastes has threatened the way conventional broadcasters [...] have operated for decades. [...] [This] is the death of TV as we've known it and the future will be scarcely recognizable." Wilson Rothman (2010) declares: "The End of TV (as we know it)." Ian Macdonald (2009) writes: "It's now very clear that conventional over-the-air television as we know it is in irreversible decline." Even Lotz (2007) anticipates a future of TV that is much different from its present configuration: "These changes are so revolutionary that they have initiated a new era of television, the effects of which we are only beginning to detect"(3). She further asserts: "[T]he eventual dominance of post-network conditions does appear to be inevitable"(8).[1]

In post-network discourse, network TV is represented as in irreversible decline (TV is in a "crisis" that will lead to its collapse) or experiencing revolutionary changes (TV is being reconfigured for a fundamentally new future). Though the TV landscape is indisputably changing, there are important continuities with the past that tend to be overlooked in work that writes TV's obituary and speculates about radically different futures. Laura Grindstaff and Joseph Turow (2006) emphasize the importance of change and continuity when studying TV.

They argue that the TV "industry's transformation of television into continually emerging sets of multifaceted digital-interactive technologies challenges researchers to draw enduring perspectives from the older work and assess how they apply to the new media environment"(104). This essay examines the interplay between "what's new," "what's old," and "what's going on now" in twenty-first-century North American TV. By focusing on this interplay, I wish to complicate claims about network TV's "death," notions that TV is undergoing a fundamental "revolution," and assertions that network TV (and society itself) is "irreversibly" or "inevitably" moving toward a "scarcely recognizable" post-network TV future.

Network TV and the commercial functions that sustain it have not been terminated; the political-economic power structure that has historically governed TV has not been overturned; and the future of TV is not inevitable. There are important changes associated with post-network TV, but they do not signal a radical break with the dominant capitalist and political logics of TV's past. To highlight "what's new," the first part of this essay reviews the "emergent" characteristics of post-network TV. To situate the "new" within the "old," the second section of the essay emphasizes the resilience, responsiveness, and re-invention of network TV by media corporations. Post-network TV has not precipitated a "crisis" for broadcast TV, nor has it heralded a "revolution" in media capitalism. Though important economic, technological, and cultural changes are reconfiguring TV, features of the new and the old co-exist and mix in the present moment. This essay, then, illuminates the dialectic of change and continuity in twenty-first-century TV.

Network TV and Post-network TV: What's New?

Post-network TV is often represented as part of a new historical "period." Lotz's (2007) seminal account of post-network TV, for example, cleaves TV history into three distinctive periods: the classical network TV era (the early 1950s to the mid-1980s), the multichannel transition stage (the early 1980s to the mid-2000s), and the "final" post-network era (the mid-2000s to the future). Television history is rendered as a narrative of modern progress entailing forward-moving eras, one following and improving upon the next in a linear sequence. Though Lotz's "periodization" identifies the general characteristics (industrial, technological, and cultural) of specific moments in TV's history, periods are not internally unified. The precise beginning and end of a period are often difficult to find. For Raymond Williams (1977), periodization (and epochal and teleological history-telling itself) is too broad, if not reductive. In every historical moment, there are many pressures and limits shaping the society, all at once. To capture the dynamism of history, Williams says we must examine how every moment entails complex relations among dominant, residual, and emergent forms. Each moment is a contradictory mix of the present, past, and future. This is a methodologically useful way to grasp the interplay between the past, present, and future of TV. Within the present moment, characteristics associated with the classical network era (the residual), the multichannel transition era (the dominant), and the post-network era (the emergent) exist simultaneously. In 2011, a small number of TV viewers relied on rabbit-ear antennas to capture analog TV signals in their living rooms. Suburban teenagers watched their favourite cable TV shows on personal TV sets in their bedrooms. Many college and university students didn't own rabbit ears or subscribe to cable. Instead, they watched YouTube clips of their favourite TV shows on their laptop computers. The point: TV history does not exhibit radical ruptures between distinct periods with internally unified viewing characteristics. Very different experiences of TV exist in the same historical moment.

Lotz (2007) nonetheless uses the term "post-network era" to describe a new period that heralds the demise of "the network era" of TV, "when television meant the networks NBC, CBS, and ABC"(11). Lotz (2007) notes: "Television as we knew it—understood as a mass medium capable of reaching a broad, heterogeneous audience and speaking to the culture as a whole—is no longer the norm in the United States. But changes in what we can do with television, what we expect from it, and how we use it have not been hastening the demise of the medium. Instead, they are revolutionizing it"(2). What are the main features of post-network TV? How are they different from classical network and multichannel TV? I review a number of the "emergent" (though certainly not universally shared) characteristics of post-network TV. My discussion encompasses the following: (1) what we use to watch TV; (2) when we watch TV; (3) where we watch TV; (4) the "audience" watching TV; (5) what kinds of TV shows we watch; (6) the experience of TV; and (7) the way TV stories are told.

What We Use to Watch TV

Network TV and multichannel TV involves people watching TV shows on TV sets. Shows are received through free-to-air broadcast transmission or through cable or satellite subscription. As Lotz (2007) notes, "Not so long ago, television use typically involved walking into a room, turning on the set, and either turning to specific content or channel surfing"(2). The TV set is the "go-to" technology for TV shows. Shows are tied to a specific technological medium and interface. In post-network TV, technological convergence decouples the longstanding one-to-one relationship between the medium and its content, TV sets and TV shows. Henry Jenkins (2006) argues that "a process called the convergence of modes is blurring the lines between media, even between point-to-point communications [...]. A single physical means—be it wires, cables or airwaves—may carry services that in the past were provided in separate ways. Conversely, a service that was provided in the past by any one medium—be it broadcasting, the press or telephony—can now be provided in several different physical ways" (10). Due to convergence, TV shows are "no longer limited to the TV medium"(Brooker 2001: 457). Flow destabilizes the idea of a singular TV text; convergence unseats the notion of TV as a singular object.

Viewers use all kinds of technological devices to watch TV. In addition to using high-definition flat-screen TV sets equipped with set-top boxes like Roku, Apple TV, or TiVo premier, viewers use their personal computers to stream TV shows from websites like MegaVideo, Fast Pass TV, and Side Reel. Downloaders plunder the digital treasure chest of TV episodes from BitTorrent websites like Pirate's Bay, described as "one of the world's largest facilitators of illegal downloading"(Sarno 2007). "Prosumers" produce and consume TV content for YouTube, a massive user-generated archive of TV show clips, fan reels, and mash-ups. Mobile viewers watch TV on mobile devices including iPods, iPhones, and iPad tablets. In sum, post-network TV entails watching TV shows through new-fangled TV sets and many interactive computer-mediated screens.

When We Watch TV

In network TV, people's TV viewing time is determined by TV networks. Network TV rules leisure time and meticulously schedules it on behalf of advertising clients. In post-network TV, new technologies and services enable TV audiences to become self-schedulers and do-it-yourself programmers. DVD or Blu-ray box sets of TV shows allow entire seasons of TV series to be consumed in one or two weeks. On-demand and pay-per-view TV services enable audiences to watch whatever TV shows they want, at whatever time they like. By legally and illegally downloading TV shows, people develop vast libraries stored on their personal computers. Digital video recorder (DVR) technologies enable viewers to miss regularly scheduled TV shows, record them, and watch them at a later time. Lotz's (2007) post-network media viewers are "in control." This signals a "break from a dominant network-era experience in which viewers lacked much control over when and where to view and choose among a limited selection of externally determined linear viewing options—in other words, programs available at a certain time on a certain channel. Such constraints are not part of the post-network television experience in which viewers now increasingly select what, when, and where to view from abundant options"(15).

Where We Watch TV

In network TV, TV shows tend to be watched within the household. Network TV is "family TV"(Spigel 1992). The TV set is a domesticated appliance that is integrated with family leisure space and time. Each home is expected to have at least one TV set, and family members watch TV shows together. In multichannel TV, TV sets continue to be domesticated objects, but start to multiply and take up space in many rooms: one TV for Dad's den, one for Mom's study, and one for the kids' playroom. The living-room-bound family TV audience is dispersed "into the kitchen, into the den, study or computer room, into the home theatre, into the bedroom"(Turner and Tay 2009: 2). While multichannel TV fragments the TV family into individualized consumers of brand-specific TV shows within the place of the home, post-network TV leaves the home. Drinking beer and eating chicken wings at the local pub, fans have their eyes transfixed on big-screen sporting events. Reclining in giant leather chairs at an electronic retail store such as Best Buy, shoppers watch the same blockbuster film simultaneously played on hundreds of price-tagged TV screens. Walking through city squares and shopping malls, pedestrians gaze up at gigantic media towers equipped with massive advertising projection screens. Riding the bus, subway, or airplane, travellers and tourists watch digital TV shows on their netbooks or PSPs. Seated in the backseat of a minivan, children stare at a pre-recorded episode of an animated TV show on the 9-inch dashboard screen. Tuning out of the TV studies class at university, students plug in their earphones and watch the TV image on their laptop computers. In post-network conditions, television "has moved from the domestic sphere and reappeared in all of these other places"(Dowler 2002: 58).

The "Audience" Watching TV

The "audience" of network TV is constructed by TV networks, advertisers, and ratings agencies as a homogenous "mass." Viewers presumably tune into a specific TV show that the TV network schedules at a specific time and watches it (and the ads surrounding it). Ron Becker (2006) notes of network TV: "Reaching as broad an audience as possible was the primary concern for the nation's wealthiest companies, their ad agencies and the mass media companies used to reach customers"(83). In multichannel TV, mass TV and mass marketing give way to niche TV and lifestyle marketing (Turow 1997). "Instead of homogenizing consumers into a uniform mass, target marketers sort them into different demographic groups by age, race, income, gender and location," says Becker (2006). TV shows are "increasingly shaped so as to appeal to the perceived interests of specific consumer niches"(84). In multichannel TV, cable TV networks target specific viewers with particular TV shows that are created to attract and deliver specific audience commodities to tailored ads. Network TV's audience share is reduced as the mass audience is segmented into different narrowcast niches. TV firms court and encourage the fan activities and meaning-making practices of TV viewers.

In post-network TV, TV networks and ad companies reconceptualize viewers as members of brand-loyal TV communities whose identities are forged through a shared emotional investment in copyrighted TV shows (Jenkins 2006: 70). The Internet enables new forms of interactivity and participation, and significantly alters "the way in which TV is created and understood"(Ross 2008: 27). Media corporations are less interested in what TV shows are "impressing" upon viewers and more interested in mapping what people are doing, saying, and "expressing" in relation to TV shows (Jenkins 2006: 63–5). TV viewers are asked to respond to "various kinds of calls to tele-participation—invitations to interact with TV shows beyond the moment of viewing and 'outside' of the TV show itself"(Ross 2009: 4). Opportunities for audience interactivity and self-expression once denied by TV networks are now regularly designed by TV networks. TV fandom is normative. People create websites and write fan fiction. They blog about TV shows and post YouTube mash-ups that combine their favourite TV clips and songs. Post-network conditions entail more participation, but new forms of exploitation as well. More and more work related to TV production, distribution, and marketing is downloaded to interactive consumers who essentially perform tasks once done by paid creative professionals. Post-network TV viewers are invited to collaborate, participate, and share ideas with the TV show's marketers and writers; their creative agency and desire to express are exploited as a source of viral marketing, unpaid demographic research, and content generation (Andrejevic 2007).

What Kinds of TV Shows We Watch

Network TV entails limited TV show choice. There are a few big TV networks (ABC, NBC, CBS; CBC and CTV), a select number of TV stations, and a few TV shows scheduled. Anxieties about dumbing down, massification, and cultural assimilation due to the production and regularized scheduling of "lowest common denominator" TV (TV shows for everybody) abound. Network TV creates mass mega-hit TV series like *The Cosby Show*, which during the mid-1980s delivered as many as 50 million viewers per episode to advertisers (Harris 2008). Multichannel TV diversifies the TV programming selection. Associated with the rise of MTV, CNN, and ESPN in the United States and specialty TV channels in Canada including MuchMusic, TSN, Newsworld, YTV, Vision, Bravo!, Space, and Talk TV, multichannel TV offers several TV networks, cable TV, speciality channels, and TV programs to many different audience niches. Television networks and production companies manufacture heterogeneous TV shows for "lifestyle" groups. G4, for example, targets teenage men who play video games. A Canadian pornography channel called Northern Peaks titillates cultural nationalist porn lovers. Baseball TV pitches itself to baseball fans. Radical Tele grapples with the attention of extreme sports viewers. For Michael Curtin (1999), worries that TV is a force of cultural homogenization and mass unification are out of touch with neo-network capitalist logics which recognize, segment, commodify, and sell a multiplicity of diverse audience niches to advertisers. The postmodern TV market thrives on endless differentiation. Multichannel TV shows with "edge" (risky, untraditional, and culturally diverse content that would not be aired in the network era) are common fare. The "narrowcasting" exception to the uniformity of network TV rules is the new rule.

Post-network TV opens up even more space for diverse and particularized cultural expressions that were hitherto marginalized by network TV. Using multimedia platforms like Facebook, YouTube, MySpace, and Twitter, viewers of prepackaged TV shows become the producers and distributors of personalized media content. The source of entertainment is not only TV networks and multichannel cable firms, but anyone who has access to a computer, camcorder, and Internet connection and who uses these new media technologies to create and share media content. In this self-producing post-network peep culture, "we are all learning to love watching ourselves and our neighbours"(Niedzviecki 2009: 3). Motivated by a desire for community or the digital dream of Justin Bieber, do-it-yourself celebrities, self-broadcasters, and wannabe talk show hosts share and overshare, screening the most banal and intimate facets of their private lives to viewers everywhere. On 1 April 2011, The YouTube homepage displayed a number of mundane and maddening user-generated videos: "Angry Dad finding cat in house"; "my reaction to Russian neo nazi behading video"; "The American Experiment – No Money = No Harmony"; "Canadian conservatives not so conservative"; "The Illuminati and the New World Order"; "baby dancing to Beyonce – baby breakdancing." In post-network conditions, user-generated media content becomes an important source of mass entertainment. The unwaged "prosumers" independently create personalized media content for the networked masses of Web 2.0. Post-network TV overflows with personalized videos made by anyone and for everyone to see.

The Experience of TV

In network TV, the experience of watching TV is described as a "flow." Williams (1974) states that flow is "the defining characteristic of broadcasting, simultaneously as a technology and as a cultural form"(86). Television networks try to hold the audience's attention from the content of the scheduled TV show to the content of featured ads and back to the TV show, hour after hour. Viewers are delivered from TV clip to ad segment in a calculated and controlled fashion. They turn on TV sets, change channels with dials or remote control devices, and watch TV shows; they have a generally passive relationship to the medium. In post-network TV, technological convergence enables viewers to interactively access TV flows through what Daniel Chamberlain (2010) calls "interfaces." Viewers retrieve TV shows by engaging with digital menu screens. TV's new interfaces "require viewers to make choices about how they will negotiate the streams and databases of possible viewing options, calling on viewers to scroll through choices, make selections, respond to prompts, and otherwise engage with the devices that control the delivery of content"(Chamberlain 2010: 86). In post-network TV, the flow does not stay within the time and space constraints of a network schedule, nor is it limited to the apparatus. Television shows "overflow" into the viewer's everyday life and onto multimedia platforms. According to Brooker (2001), post-network TV "structures are there to enable an immersive, participatory engagement with the program that crosses multiple media platforms and invites active contribution; not only from fans, who after all have been engaged in participatory culture around their favoured texts for decades, but also, as part of the regular 'mainstream' viewing experience"(470).

The Way TV Stories Are Told (and Sold)

With the exception of open or closed serial soap operas, most network TV shows are stories with beginnings, middles, and ends. These story narratives are contained by the temporal boundaries of the TV network's scheduled slot. The typical TV show for a 60-minute slot entails about 42 minutes of fictional TV show content and 18 minutes of ads. In post-network TV, "we are seeing the emergence of new story structures, which create complexity by expanding the range of narrative possibility rather than pursuing a single path with a beginning, middle and end"(Jenkins 2006: 120). We are watching synergistic transmedia TV: bits and pieces of TV stories are told and sold to viewers through multiple and interactive media platforms. Unlike traditional storytelling, wherein one story is contained by one media form (e.g., a TV show), transmedia stories are spread across many media forms such as TV shows, films, radio programs, comic books, video games, product tie-ins at fast food chains, and children's toys. Jennifer Gillan (2010) refers to these transmedia synergies as "must-click TV." Indeed, "on-air, online, and on-mobile [TV show] elements are created simultaneously and held together through a combination of trans-media marketing and storytelling. Television studios strive to keep their audiences in constant interaction with elements of the show franchise in between airings not only to boost ratings, but also to move viewers through the different divisions of a media conglomerate"(1). Though standardized network TV storytelling persists, transmedia stories are the new interactive digital commodities of vertically integrated media conglomerates. Barbara Williams, executive vice-president of broadcasting at CanWest Global Communications, says this about transmedia and multiplatform TV: "Cannibalization is the great unknown as we all move our content all over the place"(cited in Krashinsky 2010a).

In sum, the concept of post-network TV represents a number of important changes pertaining to the technological medium used to watch TV, the temporal boundaries of watching TV, the place of watching TV, the conceptualization of the TV audience, the kinds of TV shows produced and distributed, the experience of TV, and the way TV stories are told. Though significant, these changes have not led to a situation in which network TV is in "crisis," which implies a negative or dangerous situation for TV networks and advertisers. Nor do these corporate, technological, and cultural changes represent a "revolution" (a fundamental transformation of the existing political-economic power structure of a society in a short period of time). Network TV has not suffered a crisis; post-network TV has not revolutionized existing social relations. "Reports of TV's death [are] greatly exaggerated," contends Susan Krashinsky (2010b). Vanessa Richmond (2010) says, "TV is not dead." *The Economist* (2010) frames TV as "The Great Survivor." Post-network TV should be viewed as an extension of network TV and the interests of the media conglomerates that control both. All major private TV networks (in Canada and the United States) continue to prosper as central appendages of much larger and vertically and horizontally integrated media conglomerates. Post-network TV is not network TV's antithesis, but a structural adjustment by large media corporations to flexible business models, digital technologies, and viewer practices.

Network TV: Crisis or Reconsolidation?

To reveal how old network models cannibalize new TV possibilities, I assess four problematic claims associated with the "network TV in crisis" hypothesis: (1) TV networks are experiencing an advertising slump due to new media drain, recessionary economics, and audience segmentation; (2) TV networks are losing the confidence of advertisers, and commercialism is being undermined as result of personal video recorders (PVRs); (3) TV viewers have migrated from TV network–scheduled TV shows on TV sets to web TV on computers; and, (4) conventional TV broadcasters are being undermined by cable TV. As we will see, TV networks have adjusted to post-network conditions and expanded existing strategies for commodifying audiences.

Network TV: Still Advertising-rich, Over-the-air and On-the-web

The "network TV in crisis" hypothesis contends that TV networks are suffering a profitability slump because advertising firms have withdrawn their cash from TV networks and opened their wallets to new media and cable. Between 2001 and 2010, print media (including magazines and newspapers) and old media (such as radio) lost ad dollars, which ad firms funnelled into commercial websites. According to the Interactive Advertising Bureau of Canada, online ad revenues for 2009 were $1.82 billion. They reached approximately $2.1 billion in 2010. During the 2008 and 2009 recession, major American and Canadian TV networks reported a decline in ad revenues (James 2009). The online market for advertising is slowly growing (Clifford 2009), but the displacement of network TV ad revenue by websites is minimal. Advertising on social media networks like MySpace and Facebook accounted for less than 1 per cent of worldwide ad spending in 2010 (Powell 2011).

In 2008–2009, recessionary economics did depress TV network ad revenue, but TV broadcasters and cable networks remained the most attractive sellers of ad space and time (Pfanner 2010). By 2010, ad spending was recovering. The four major American TV networks boosted ad revenue: CBS earned $6.48 billion (up 8.2 per cent); Fox, $4.49 billion (up 2.2 per cent); ABC, $5.12 billion (up 1.1 per cent); and NBC, $4.82 billion (up 17.7 per cent) (Szala 2011). In 2011, American TV networks reported further increases in ad revenue ("CBS Shares" 2011). Canadian TV network ad revenue was up in 2010 and 2011 as well (Vlessing 2011). Advertising revenue accumulated through the sale of audience attention to corporations continues to profit TV network shareholders and executives very handsomely. Television, not the Internet, remains corporate capitalism's favourite means of exposing audiences, mass and niche, to imagery for branded goods. "Television is the core of advertisers' spending plans," says Jonathan Barnard, director for publications at ZenithOptimedia. "Even when they're cutting back in other places [such as the web and new media], they are sticking with television"(cited in Pfanner 2010).

Television networks have responded to the migration of viewers from network TV schedules to web TV's spaces of self-scheduling by expanding the presence of network TV shows in the Web 2.0 environment. Networks have recaptured viewer attention using Web 2.0 platforms that enable profitable forms of viewer self-scheduling. All major American and Canadian TV networks stream their own licensed TV episodes from their websites. Paid advertisements are featured before, within, and after streamed TV shows; a variety of different ads are also embedded within the webpage. This model continues to use TV shows as a means of delivering audience attention to ads (though this is not nearly as profitable as over-the-air TV). In 2009, web revenue for TV broadcasters and specialty and pay TV channels was approximately 2.3 per cent of overall ad revenue that year (Krashinsky 2010a). TV network websites are not facing serious competition with social media platforms. Rather, they regularly link to Facebook, Twitter, and MySpace to "share" promotional material that regularly generates attention and channels the eyes of TV viewers to TV shows. The move of TV show consumption from the TV set to computer screen is a move from one kind of viewer commodification to another. Both help TV networks to profit.

The segmentation of the audience has not caused a network TV crisis either. Scheduled mass TV events, not narrowcast cable spots or personalized web viewings, still deliver the largest number of viewers to advertisers. Why? The postmodern market's fragmentation of society and the hyper-individualism of self-scheduling rituals result in nostalgia for a collective TV experience. Mass TV is still a solid societal referent point. Unlike cable narrowcasts and YouTube videos, mass broadcast TV shows still have the "ability to provide a voluntary point of social cohesion, of being-together while being-apart"(Ellis 2000: 176). Advertisers know this. "Many big advertisers remain loyal to television," says Vincent Letan, an industry analyst at Screen Digest. "At the end of the day, it's about audience. Despite all the hype about digital growth, spending goes were the eyeballs are"(cited in Pfanner 2010). People continue to be attracted to mass TV shows and big scheduled TV events. *American Idol* is the most sought after TV show by North American TV advertisers. In 2010, Fox TV network sold about $7.11 million in ad space for every half hour of the *American Idol* broadcast. *Two and a Half Men* was the second largest TV ad revenue generator, bringing in $2.89 million every half hour to its broadcaster (Sergeant 2011). *Super Bowl XLV* was the most commercially successful sporting event of all time, reaching 111 million viewers for three hours. In Canada, 16.6 million people watched the men's gold medal hockey game at the Vancouver 2010 Winter Olympics. This was Canada's largest mass TV broadcast ever ("Oh Canada!!" 2010). Web and cable TV are accumulating ad dollars, but this has not caused a crisis for TV networks. They still profit-maximize by delivering viewers to ads on behalf of the international advertising firms that employ them.

Personal Video Recorders (PVRs): Data Surveillance and Branded Entertainment

A second claim connected to the "network TV in crisis" hypothesis is that personal video recorders (PVRs) have jeopardized network TV's ability to deliver viewers to ads and thwarted commercialism. PVRs—an extension of the video cassette recorder (VCR)—allow viewers to record and replay broadcast TV shows at their convenience and in accordance with their own schedule. With PVRs, they can watch TV programs at a different time than originally scheduled by TV networks. PVR-enabled "time-shifting" of TV shows, in turn, allows viewers to resist exposure to traditionally scheduled 30-second advertisements. When replaying personally recorded TV shows on PVRs, viewers can fast-forward past ads, escaping "commodification." Advertising firms complain that the traditional 30-second TV ad spot is being undermined by PVRs. They are more hesitant to pay top dollars for TV network ad time and space. PVRs (new technology) and time-shifting viewers (the interactive audience) supposedly put the traditional TV broadcasting model in crisis. Advertising firms and their larger industrial sponsors started to demand "accountability" from TV networks and their ratings clients. They wanted guarantees that viewers are watching their ads and the ads were having an impact (Hamp 2008; Jaffee 2005).

This technologically deterministic argument overstates the impact of the PVR on viewer receptivity to TV ads. PVR diffusion has increased over the past five years, especially since PVRs are regularly designed into new cable and direct broadcast satellite (DBS) set boxes. But PVR use is not generalized. In 2010, approximately 20 per cent of Canadian TV households owned a PVR, while in the United States only 38 per cent did (Nielsen 2010). PVR presence in households doesn't determine viewer use either. "Live" television, not playback TV, is still being watched by most (Debusmann 2010). In Canada, almost all weekly TV viewing abides by the real-time schedule. And when people do use PVRs, they do not always skip ads. In the United States, 5 per cent of TV is time-shifted and only 3 per cent of ads are skipped. When viewers do use PVRs to fast-forward through ads, they are still exposed to brand imagery. Advertising firms have modified ads so that they are still visible and still have an impact, even when they are being time-shifted. PVR playback rituals can actually be a more effective means of exposing viewers to ads, especially those ads they might have otherwise skipped by taking a "commercial break" to the washroom. As Duncan Stewart, director of research for technology, media, and telecom at Deloitte Canada, remarks: "If I am skipping the ads, I am holding down the little button. I have to pay attention to the screen so I know when the commercials are over. At some level, you are paying more attention than you might be if you were just walking away during a normal commercial break"(cited in "PVRs Will Not Eliminate TV" 2011).

PVRs do not eliminate TV advertising. On the contrary, they help corporations to more effectively target viewers with customized ads and trade in monetized audience data. TiVo, for example, is a TV data surveillance system that collects and commodifies TV viewer information (Carlson 2006). It tracks every move of its viewers; it monitors how many people watch TV shows, at what times, and whether or not people are watching the ads. TiVo then sells this data to advertisers, providing them "with the most detailed information possible about viewers [...] the ability not just to determine which households are watching what shows, but the minutiae of how they are watching and when, including how often they rewind, fast forward, pause, and so on"(Andrejevic 2007: 11). PVRs monitor TV viewing practices, assemble recorded viewer information into data profiles, assign price tags to these data profiles, and then sell them to marketing firms. Marketing firms, in turn, use data profiles to make inferences about the kinds of commodities viewers may be interested in buying and then place customized ads accordingly. In fact, PVRs place "addressable" ads to viewers. PVRs "store and forward addressable ads in the set-top box, and when a break comes up, the PVR sends an ad [to the viewer] that is more relevant and targeted demographically and geographically," says John Boland, vice-president of advertising systems at US communications technology company Arris ("PVR Survey Says" 2010). While the PVR personalization of the TV schedule purports to increase the power of TV audiences by allowing them greater control over their viewing experience, it actually serves the profit-interests of digital surveillance firms that trade in personalized data commodities.

PVRs have not killed the 30-second ad spot or given TV viewers the power to escape dominant and emergent audience commodification strategies. In fact, the total time TV networks allocate to ads per hour has increased. In the prime-time US slot, ad time is approximately 16 1/2 minutes per hour. The daytime level of advertising is nearly 21 minutes per hour. TV advertisers and TV networks are nevertheless strategizing to ensure that the small portion of PVR users who do not want to be exposed to the 30-second ad during and between TV shows will be exposed to products placed within TV shows. "The beauty of product placement, a.k.a. brand integration," explain business writers Erick Schonfeld and Jeanette Borzo (2006), "is that viewers can't TiVo past it because it's part of the show, and it lives on in any reruns or DVDs." According to Phil Hart, president of Canada's MMI Product Placement Inc., product placement "protects" the interests of advertising firms by pre-empting audiences from "zipping, zapping and muting" ads (cited in Moretti 2010). **Product placement** refers to when branded products and services are placed into the fictional content of TV shows by TV production studios and TV networks on behalf of ad clients. There were more than 200,000 product placements in American TV shows between January and June 2008 (Harris 2009). This practice collapses the boundary between fictional TV content intended to entertain or inform and ad content intended to cultivate desire for branded goods.

A recent extension of product placement in TV is called "branded entertainment"(Donaton 2004). Branded entertainment refers to the process of weaving or integrating a branded commodity or service into the story of a TV show, so as to associate a corporate brand image with a particular TV character or theme. Traditional TV product placement inserts commercial products or brand logos into scenes after a TV script is written. Brands are not meaningfully integrated with the TV show's story, but featured mainly as set-dressing and props. Branded entertainment writes specific products and branded logos into the scripts. Advertising considerations precede script development and shape TV show concepts. Staples (the office supply retailer) worked with NBC producers of *The Office* to integrate the MailMate paper shredder into a 2006 episode (Sassone 2007). In another episode of *The Office*, Dwight quits his job at Dunder-Mifflin and is soon after employed by Staples (Sassone 2007). More examples: a 2003 episode of the ABC series *Alias* featured a car chase in which characters drive the Ford Focus; ABC's *Extreme Makeover: Home Edition* regularly stars household goods, compliments of Sears; Fox's *Bones* and ABC's *Modern Family* entail mini-subplots entirely around Apple's iPad; *American Idol* judges drink Coke from Coke logo cups; and TD Canada Trust appears in CBC hits including *Being Erica*, *Little Mosque on the Prairie*, and *Heartland* (Castillo 2009).

The placement and integration of corporate brands into TV shows represents contemporary media capitalism's struggle to supplant all non-commercial forms of viewer identification—as citizens, members of a social class, or even partisan party hacks—with immersive, affective, and entirely depoliticized subject-positions that belong to managed brand-loyal communities. As Jenkins (2006) notes: "Marketing gurus argue that building a committed 'brand community' may be the surest means of expanding consumer loyalty and that product placement will allow brands to tap some of the affective force of the affiliated entertainment properties"(63). These brand-loyal communities are forged within the nexus of sets, computer and mobile device screens, and branded TV content, which is designed, controlled, and delivered by TV networks. Clearly, the age of the PVR does not signal the diminishing power of ad corporations to hyper-commercialize the TV experience.

Network TV Shows: Every Screen, Anytime

A third claim associated with the "network TV in crisis" hypothesis is that TV networks and domesticated TV sets are being abandoned for web-streamed TV shows and the screens of mobile devices, laptops, and personal computers. The "mass audience" presumed by TV networks to watch TV shows on TV sets is being disaggregated and dispersed into many screens. People are searching for and watching TV shows in a variety of web-based contexts and spaces, using a variety of new post-TV set screens. In February 2009, a reported 21 million Canadians (88 per cent of Internet users in Canada) watched an average of 10 hours of video online. Canadian viewers reportedly watch more hours of videos on average than Internet users in the US, UK, Germany, and France (Chung 2009). While the computer does constitute a new TV space for many viewers, this is certainly not a universal phenomenon, nor has it led to the demise of the TV set.

One reason why TV sets will continue to be the primary tool for watching TV shows is generational. Arguments about post-network TV on the Internet rely on a generalized image of the twenty-first-century "TV audience." Post-network viewers are represented as part of a youthful 18- to 24-year-old demographic ("generation Y"). This group of "early adopters" is supposedly on the move, media savvy, and computer literate. They do not watch TV shows according to a conventional schedule—they are "tethered" to mobile screens and refuse to pay for TV shows. The post-network TV cohort is regularly depicted as empowered agents who are driving and benefiting from technological change. What often is not represented is the fact that post-network youth are part of a disempowered "generation of toiling freelancers and part-timers [...] lucky to get shift work, temp work and piecework [...] the biggest losers in a worldwide casualization of labour"(Breen 2009). The flexible, do-it-yourself ethos and disaggregated leisure-time rituals of post-network TV viewers fit the precarious experience of a brutalizing post-Fordist labour regime. That much-advertised practice of "watching whatever you want, whenever you want" makes sense to this youthful "audience" because they do not work regularized daily 9-to-5 jobs. They do not return from a day's work at 5 PM and start watching TV at 7 PM. They start and stop work throughout all hours of the day and night. They are hired and fired. Service sector employers compel these workers to be transient and networked with technology and information flows at all times. Tasks are assigned and completed from a variety of networked places, public and private. Post-network TV corresponds with this group's way of work (and way of life).

The representation of youth as techno-revolutionaries, pushing the frontiers of technological possibility, is an old marketing trick. This emergent experience of young flex-workers as flex TV watchers, however, does not represent the dominant experience of TV. People born in the 1950s who grew up watching TV shows on TV sets still do so. Their "couch potato" TV leisure rituals have not disappeared because of YouTube. Many young people prefer to watch broadcast TV shows on TV sets as well. Between 1998 and 2007, the number of people in the 18–34 demographic who watched broadcast TV fell only 2.4 per cent. "It's remarkable how stable TV audiences have been," says Nordicity Group representative Peter Lyman (cited in Kirby 2009). Network TV normalized a practice of watching that is habitual for millions of people: sitting down in a couch or chair, turning on a TV set with a remote control in hand, surfing for a TV show, and watching it. The post-network practice of "leaning forward" to type for TV shows on a computer takes much more time and effort than "leaning back" and surfing for pre-scheduled TV shows. The notion that people will opt out of the network TV experience and cancel paid TV subscriptions to engage in the time-intensive process of cobbling together their own schedules every day and night from web-based multimedia platforms removes the lazy leisure from TV time.

Television sets are used to watch TV shows for aesthetic reasons too. Many viewers prefer watching TV shows on TV sets because web TV on small computer screens is often a very low-quality experience: "[V]ideos routinely freeze, stutter, take forever to load or show 'missing plug-in' error messages. We are used to that. We have low expectations on the Web," says David Pogue (2010). To keep TV shows on TV sets, electronics corporations are mass-producing and promoting larger and larger TV sets as "must-have" commodities for high-quality televisual experiences. High-definition flat-screen TVs, energy-saving TVs, digital TVs with built-in download services, 3D TVs: each year, corporations market bigger and better TV sets, fuelling conspicuous consumption. Growth in the "home theatre" market represents the continued centralization of the TV set as the site for watching. Living rooms are regularly transformed into interactive "home theatres" equipped with big-screen TVs; projectors for TV shows, movies, and games; furniture; and ancillary products including sound systems and multimedia storage devices (O'Donnell 2011). The global market for home theatre technologies is estimated to grow from $1.9 billion in 2006 to $2.9 billion in 2013 (O'Donnell 2011). TV sets remain the favoured technological mediums for watching TV shows.

There are socio-economic reasons for the resilience of the TV set (as opposed to the computer) as the site of TV viewing. Post-network "TV on the computer" presumes an ideal-type user that owns a personal computer, can afford an Internet connection, and possesses the computer literacy skills required to be interactive. While TV sets are staple commodities in North America, computers are not. Computer ownership, ISP connections, and computer literacy skills are not provisioned to the population as public goods, but rather reserved for only those that have the ability to pay. Due to social class divisions and the unequal distribution of wealth, knowledge, and power, many people (in the United States, Canada, and worldwide) are excluded from the experience of post-network TV. There is a digital divide within North America (Marlow and McNish 2010). In Canada, a little over 75 per cent of the population has Internet access ("Canada Internet Usage" 2009). Until digital divides are overcome, TV sets will likely remain the go-to technology for TV shows.

Television shows will continue to be watched on TV sets for political reasons as well. The Internet gave TV viewers what paid TV networks didn't: access to an abundance of free-to-view high-quality TV shows. Post-network TV's early adopters learned to watch TV on the Internet because they did not have the means to pay for expensive cable subscriptions (or because they really believed information should be free!). But their pirate practices violated the proprietary interests of many TV studios and networks, which then aggressively lobbied governments to crack down upon illegal BitTorrent and streaming TV sites. In 2010, some of the world's largest TV downloading and streaming sites—Channelsurfing.net, Ninjavideo,

ThePirateCity.org, and PlanetMoviez.com—were shut down by the US state. Some site owners were charged with copyright infringement. In 2011, days before *Super Bowl XLV*, the US state shut down 10 unauthorized sports-streaming websites, including Rojadirecta.org, Channelsurfing.net, and ATDHE.net. Upon arrival to the homepages of these websites, viewers faced a message: Immigration and Customs Enforcement officials seized domain names through warrants obtained by the US Attorney's office for the Southern District of New York (Hsu 2011). As large-scale TV networks use the power of the state to track and eliminate unauthorized TV websites and engineer network-friendly, -owned, and -sponsored websites as alternatives to digital piracy, the ability and inclination of TV viewers to illegally file-share, download, and stream copyrighted TV shows may be significantly diminished.

The movement of viewers from TV sets to computer-based web TV may also be deterred by usage-based billing schemes (Marlow 2011). Usage-based billing allows Internet service providers (ISPs) to impose bandwidth caps (typically between 25 gigabytes and 175 gigabytes) on the amount of data that users can upload and download in a set period of time, usually a month. When users exceed the bandwidth cap, extra fees apply. Watch a lot of TV shows and films streamed by Netflix? Be prepared to pay between 1 and 2 dollars extra per gigabyte. Classified as a "heavy user" by your ISP due to your participation in peer-to-peer networks? Be prepared to pay for your sharing. Usage-based billing, an ISP profit-maximization strategy, takes the "free" out of web TV. It is a powerful deterrent to watching TV on the Internet.

In response to those viewers who refuse to watch TV shows on TV sets, TV networks have started profiting from the distribution of commercialized TV shows through the streaming and video-on-demand websites they own. In 2008, Hulu.com—a US web-based TV service—was promoted as the future of TV on the Internet; it supposedly "liberated" viewers from the tyranny of the TV set and TV network schedules by helping "people find and enjoy the world's premium video content when, where and how they want it"(Stelter 2011b). Major and minor American TV networks—NBC, ABC, Fox, PBS, USA Network, Bravo!, and Syfy—license TV shows to Hulu. Viewers access the Hulu.com website, select the TV show they want to watch (from a limited selection), and then stream it on their computer or mobile device. Hulu generates revenue by exposing viewers to about 2 minutes of ads per each 22-minute TV show. Hulu is not a threat to the dominant TV networks. Hulu is basically owned by them. ABC owns 27 per cent, NBC-Universal owns 27 per cent, and Fox Entertainment owns 27 per cent. Providence Equity Partners and Hulu.com employees own the remaining 19 per cent of Hulu. The TV networks that own Hulu accumulate between 50 and 70 per cent of Hulu's ad revenue. Viewers that wish to escape exposure to ads on Hulu and access a wider selection of premium TV shows must subscribe to Hulu Plus (for 8 dollars a month). Hulu certainly does not diminish the power of TV networks. Without access to a supply of TV shows provided by TV networks and their production companies, Hulu is an "empty jukebox" (Stelter 2011b).

The "empty jukebox" metaphor can be applied to many online and on-demand video-streaming firms that grant viewers access to TV shows and films on a subscriber or pay-per-view basis. Like Hulu Plus, Netflix provides on-demand Internet streaming video in the United States and Canada to its more than 20 million subscribers, who each pay 9 dollars a month to access and stream TV shows and films from its library of licensed content. Netflix sources its digital content from the major TV networks. For $1.99 per download, iTunes grants Apple users temporary viewing rights to specific TV shows. Video game console web stores (on the Xbox 360 and Playstation 3) invite their users to download network

TV shows for a few dollars as well. Bell Canada and Rogers profit on subscriber-only online TV services. Though unpopular with advertisers, YouTube serves network TV too, excerpting, commenting on, and promoting it (Miller 2010: 15). Networks are not suffering a crisis as result of new media distribution and consumption platforms. As *The Economist* (2009) points out: "Far from being cowed by new media, TV is colonizing it."

The colonial metaphor is appropriate. Television networks are carving up and building within the de-territorialized global space of Web 2.0 digitized territorial borders to consolidate nation-state website-viewing parameters. For example, I recently tried to watch a streaming episode of *Grey's Anatomy* from US-based Hulu.com. I went to the site, selected the episode, and clicked "play." The following message appeared: "We're sorry, currently our video library can only be streamed in the United States. For more information on Hulu's international availability, click here. If you're inside the United States and believe you've received this message in error, please click here." Blocked by Hulu.com, I moved on to NBC's website, where I tried to stream *Celebrity Apprentice*. Geo-blocked again: "We're sorry, but the clip you selected isn't available from your location. Please select another clip." I went to CBS. There, I was informed that *The Price Is Right* "is not available for your geographic region." I finally went to the website for CTV, one of Canada's TV networks. There, I streamed *Grey's Anatomy*. I also streamed *The Colbert Report* and then *The Daily Show*, two of my favourite American TV shows.

American and Canadian and TV networks are digitally re-engineering the territorial borders of the Canadian and US state so as to reassert the permanence (as opposed to web-supported permeability) of nationalist boundaries. Television network websites use software to determine the Internet Protocol (IP) address of a visitor's computer (the IP address is numeric code assigned to every computer connected to the Internet). TV network websites use geo-blocking to guarantee that national audience commodities will be produced and delivered to the national ad clients that pay for them. "It costs money to distribute content over the Internet because each stream has an incremental cost to it," says a new media consultant. "It's not like the broadcast world where the signal costs the same whether one person or a million people are tuning in. American advertisers don't want to pay to have Canadians watching"(cited in Kritsonis 2010). Canadian TV networks also rely on US geo-blocking practices to make sure US digital TV streams don't draw presumably Canadian viewers away from the Canadian-focused TV broadcast (or the Canadian TV stream-cast). When viewers go to the CTV.com website in search of a TV show to stream/watch, CTV pinpoints their computer's IP address and geographical location. So long as the IP address and location are in Canada, CTV lets the viewers to stream TV shows. Viewers located in other countries are blocked. Geo-blocking is deployed by TV networks to construct and control a national audience, protect national licensing rights, and fill advertiser orders for a national audience.

The general TV network strategy is to prevent the rise of the Internet as an alternative medium for television (Winseck 2010: 373). Networks are also designing ways of controlling web TV delivery. The practice of watching TV shows on TV sets will co-exist with rather than replace the practice of watching TV shows on computers. "The Internet is our friend, not our enemy," says Leslie Moonves, chief executive of the CBS Corporation. "People want to be attached to each other"(cited in Stelter 2010). As Miller (2010) notes, "even the cybertarians at MySpace and Jupitermedia [...] insist that viewers want TV to remain TV, with a few add-ons—their preference is for watching programs, albeit with some added elements, while flat-screen sets are generally already constructed with connections to computers"(179). While viewers watch their favourite TV shows on TV sets, they simultaneously use computer-screened social networking sites like Facebook, MySpace, and Twitter to chat about the TV shows they are watching. Viewer vision is split between computer screens and TV sets; bodies and fingers are extended through keyboards and TV remote controls; imaginations shift between person-to-person TV talk and TV show fictions. Television networks are facilitating and monitoring this blurring of screens, bodies, and discourse. The emergence of Web TV does not signal the end of network TV shows on TV sets.

Broadcast TV, Cable TV, and Web TV Networks: Same Owners

A fourth tacit claim associated with the "network TV in crisis" hypothesis is that TV networks are being outcompeted by cable TV service providers, which draw more and more viewers each year. American and Canadian cable and satellite TV firms are accumulating super-profits. But while cable TV captures viewers, subscription fees, and ad dollars by creating and scheduling edgy TV shows, TV networks still rule audience share. In 2010, "[T]he smallest of the big four broadcast networks, NBC, still retained more than twice as many viewers as the largest basic cable channel, USA"(Stelter 2011a). Discussions about competitions between broadcast TV and cable TV, however, are misplaced. It is inappropriate to speak of genuine competitive conflict between broadcast TV, cable TV, and web TV, because all of these modes of TV production and distribution are owned by a handful of large media conglomerates that continue to profit-maximize. In the United States and Canada, TV (broadcast networks, the multichannel cable TV universe, satellite TV, and web TV) is owned by a few transnationalizing media conglomerates. Almost everything we watch on TV is owned and controlled by a few large media firms.

In the United States, five vertically and horizontally integrated and globalizing mega-corporations own most of TV.

The **Walt Disney Company** (WDC), perhaps the largest media conglomerate in the world, owns the American Broadcasting Company (ABC). WDC owns cable TV networks including Disney Channel, Disney Junior, Disney XD, ABC Family, SOAPnet, Lifetime, Lifetime Movie Network, Lifetime Real Women, a third of the A&E Network, The History Channel, The Biography Channel, History Channel International, Military History Channel, Crime & Investigation Network, and ESPN (Hearst Corporation owns 20 per cent). It possesses vast TV and film production and syndication capacities as well including ABC Studios, Walt Disney Television Animation, Disney-ABC Domestic Television, Buena Vista Studios, and more.

Time Warner controls the Warner Bros. Television Group (WBTVG) and Warner Bros. Home Entertainment Group, which produce and distribute TV content across many media platforms. WBTVG is responsible for the entire Warner Bros. portfolio of TV businesses including worldwide production, distribution, and broadcasting of more than 40 TV shows, from scripted and unscripted prime-time shows for broadcast and cable networks to first-run syndicated TV programs. Time Warner owns and operates some of the leading cable television networks including HBO, CNN, HLN, TNT, TBS, Cartoon Network, Turner Classic Movies, Adult Swim, and truTV.

News Corporation (owned by Rupert Murdoch) has many TV broadcast, cable, and satellite operations. The FOX Broadcasting Company controls 27 Fox TV stations. News Corporation's Cable Network Programming produces and licenses TV programming for distribution on cable TV systems and direct broadcast satellite platforms in the United States and in Asia. It includes the FOX News Channel and FOX Business Network, FX, STAR, and many other popular pay-per-view TV channels (The Big Ten Network, FOX Business Network, Fox Movie Channel, FOX News Channel, FOX College Sports, FOX

Sports Enterprises, FOX Sports Net, FOX Soccer Channel, Fuel TV, FX, National Geographic Wild, National Geographic Channel, Speed, and STAR).

NBC-Universal (owned by Comcast and General Electric) produces, distributes, and markets TV and film entertainment and news products worldwide. The conglomerate owns and operates NBC Television Network and numerous cable networks (NBC Entertainment, NBC News, NBC Sports & Olympics, Bravo!, Chiller, CNBC, CNBC World, Comcast Sports, E! Entertainment Television, Exercise TV, G4, Golf Channel, MSNBC, mun 2, Sleuth, Style Network, Syfy, Universal HD, USA Network, VERSUS, The Weather Channel, and one-third of A&E). It also owns film and TV show content production capacities including Universal Media Studios, Universal Cable Productions, Universal Pictures, Focus Features, Universal Studios Home Entertainment, and many digital media content production and distribution platforms as well as theme parks.

CBS Corporation (owned by media mogul Sumner Redstone) controls broadcast TV, TV production and distribution, cable TV, and more. CBS Corporation owns CBS TV Network, The CW (50 per cent co-owned by Time Warner) and 28 TV stations. CBS Corporation owns many cable TV networks including the College Sports Network and Showtime Networks (Showtime, N4Q, The Movie Channel, FLIX, CBS College Sports). CBS Corporation's TV content production studio is CBS Entertainment, which develops, acquires, and schedules the entertainment programming on CBS TV network. CBS Television Studios is one of the industry's leading producers of prime-time TV network programming (including the popular *CSI* franchise).

In addition to owning CBS Corporation, Redstone owns **Viacom**, the world's most global cable TV corporation. Viacom's portfolio of media brands designed for specific cultural demographics includes BET Networks ("media and entertainment for African Americans and consumers of Black culture"), MTV Networks (more than 160 music video entertainment channels), Nickelodeon (TV for kids), Spike (a TV brand that "speaks to the bold, adventuresome side of men with action-packed entertainment"), the Country Music Channel (CMT), Comedy Central, and LOGO ("TV for the lesbian, gay, bisexual, and transgender community"). Viacom also owns more than 500 digital and web-based platforms/properties including TheDailyShow.com, RateMyProfessors.com, Movietickets.com, and Neopets.com (a network for virtual pet lovers!). Viacom owns film entertainment studios including Paramount Pictures, Paramount Vintage, MTV Films, Nickelodeon Movies, and Home Entertainment.

Talk of genuine competition among conventional TV networks, cable TV, and web TV obscures the fact that all of these sectors of media capitalism tend to be owned by a few conglomerates. Canada's media market is similarly ruled by a few vertically and horizontally integrated multimedia conglomerates including Bell Canada Enterprises (owner of CTV), Rogers Communication (owner of Citytv), Shaw (owner of Global), and Quebecor (owner of TVA).

Bell Canada Enterprises (BCE) owns CTV (Canada's largest TV broadcaster), 27 TV affiliates, 30 specialty TV channels (including TSN, Discovery Channel, The Comedy Network, and Business News Network), CHUM Radio (including 34 radio stations), 15 per cent of *The Globe and Mail* national newspaper, and several websites including CTV.ca, TSN.ca, RDS.ca, MuchMusic.com, MTV.ca, and TheComedyNetwork.ca. BCE is Canada's most powerful converged media conglomerate. "Today's regulatory and technological environment allows integrated players to leverage content ownership for differentiated offers across all three screens (TV, computer, mobile)," Bell said, boldly announcing its corporate convergence strategy in 2010 (cited in Lam 2010).

Shaw Communications Inc., a telecommunications and cable TV giant owned by the Calgary-based Shaw family, controls the Global TV network (and its 11 stations) and at least 19 specialty TV channels (including TVtropolis, Showcase, HGTV Canada, Food Network Canada, and History Television). In addition to controlling 80 per cent of Corus Entertainment (another giant media firm), and a large intellectual property portfolio of TV shows, Shaw owns telecommunications firms too. "We believe the combination of content with our cable and satellite distribution network, and soon to be wireless service, will position us to be one of the leading entertainment and communications companies in Canada," says Shaw Chief Executive Jim Shaw (cited in Rocha and Jordan 2010). "The number-one driving force for us in this strategic acquisition has been this notion of content," says Shaw's president Peter Bissonnette. "Over the next decade, to be successful as a distributor over many platforms we will require strong content capacity"(cited in Beer 2010).

Rogers Communications, controlled by the Rogers family, owns five Citytv stations, several specialty TV channels (including OMNI, Sportsnet, and The Shopping Channel), 53 radio stations, and more than 55 magazines including *Macleans*, *Chatelaine*, *Canadian Business*, and *Flare*. Rogers Communications also owns the Toronto Blue Jays baseball team.

Quebecor Media, controlled by the Péladeau family, owns Quebec's largest cable TV company, Videotron, and its largest French-language TV network, TVA. Quebecor also owns Sun Media's newspaper chain, 8 dailies, and 200 other newspapers.

In sum, less than 10 mega-corporations own most all conventional TV networks, cable TV networks, specialty TV channels, and major digital entertainment platforms in North America.

Conclusion: Revolution Paused, Media Conglomeration Continued

Between 2000 and 2008, the giant media corporations that control the means of producing and distributing TV restructured and adjusted their operations in order to exploit new digital media opportunities. But the TV industry never faced a crisis: its shareholders, CEOs, and managers profited handsomely. A revolutionary transformation of existing social relations did not occur. The 2008 recession hit the North American automotive industry and other large-scale industrial corporations hard, resulting in a downturn in TV network ad revenue. "Belt-tightening by major industries thus trickled down to advertiser-supported television"(Lotz 2010: 186). Some TV networks worried about their future. And in Canada, CanWest Global Communications collapsed (due to its own mismanagement). But there was never an overall profitability crisis in network TV or any sector controlled by North America's largest media conglomerates. As Winseck (2010) states: "the network media industries—television, cable, satellite distribution, newspapers, Internet access, advertising, radio and magazines—expanded substantially from $21.4 billion to $32 billion between 2000 and 2008"(369). Television will likely strengthen its "super-media status" and "continue to command a growing share of the world's attention and wallets and will retain its leadership among all media in terms of total revenues" including ad sales, subscriptions, and pay-per-view and license fees (Powell 2011).

The recession and changes associated with post-network TV were perhaps "a blessing in disguise for Canada's private broadcasters"(Tinic 2010: 197). Corporate arguments about an irreversible economic downturn and radical technological change drew public attention away from the root causes of network TV's financial difficulties: debt-financed media conglomeration and skyrocketing expenditure on American TV shows. The recession and technological change represented a "perfect 'crisotunity' for the private broadcasters to attain long-sought-after objectives"(Tinic 2010: 194). These included the diminishment of Canadian content quotas, the elimination of advertising time caps, fee-for-carriage policies, and the deepening of neo-liberal media policies of liberalization, deregulation, and privatization. In sum, "[we] are witnessing a transformation of TV, rather than its demise. What started in most countries as a broadcast, national medium, dominated by the state, is being transformed into a cable, satellite, Internet, and international medium, dominated by commerce—but still called television"(Miller 2010, 19).

Economically and politically, the future of North American TV may share similarities with TV's past. Capitalism, conglomeration, and commercialism will likely continue to constrain the emancipatory and democratizing potential of the media, old and new. The problems humanity, the environment, democracy, and the media face are immense. They establish conditions for a revolution that could be televised. But TV will not be revolutionized until the revolution is. Public or private, activist or mainstream, network or post-network, twenty-first-century TV is society's to make.

Note

1. Lotz (2007) recognizes that not everyone has "completed the transition" to the post-network era and says her use of "post" does not mean "the death or complete irrelevance of what we have known as television networks and channels"(254). Nonetheless, Lotz still posits a periodization that represents the completion of the post-network future as inevitable or forthcoming.

Works Cited

Andrejevic, M. (2007). *iSpy: Surveillance and Power in the Interactive Era.* Kansas: University of Press of Kansas.

Becker, R. (2006). *Gay TV and Straight America.* Rutgers University Press.

Beer, J. (2010, 28 September). "Media News." www.marketingmag.ca/news/media-news/according-to-jim-5135

Berland, J. (2007, 6 March). "The TV Is Dead. Long Live TV." www.wired.com/entertainment/hollywood/news/2007/04/tvhistory_0406

Breen, K. (2009, 9 June). "Young and Restless, Gonna Watch on My Terms." www.cbc.ca/news/canada/story/2009/06/08/f-vp-breen.html

Brooker, W. (2001). "Living on Dawson's Creek: Teen Viewers, Cultural Convergence and Television Overflow." *International Journal of Cultural Studies,* Vol. 4(4): 456–72.

"Canada Internet Usage." (2009). www.internetworldstats.com/am/ca.htm

Carlson, M. (2006). "Tapping into TiVo: Digital Video Recorders and the Transition from Schedules to Surveillance in Television." *New Media & Society,* Vol. 8(1): 97–115.

Castillo, D. (2009, 2 October). "TD Canada Trust Product Placement Triggers Debate." http://productplacement.biz/200910021310/news/television/td-canada-trust-product-placement-triggers-debate.html

"CBS Shares, Profit Jump on Fivefold Higher TV Ad Revenue." (2011, 17 February). www.nationalpost.com/todayspaper/shares+profit+jump+fivefold+higher+revenue/4298983/story.html

Chamberlain, D. (2010). "Television Interfaces." *Journal of Popular Film and Television,* Vol. 38(2): 84–8.

Chung, E. (2009, 27 April). "Who Will Cash in on Canada's Love for Online Video?" www.cbc.ca/news/technology/story/2009/04/27/tech-090427-online-video.html

Clifford, S. (2009, 31 March). "Ad Sales Up on Internet, but '08 Pace Was Slower." www.nytimes.com/2009/03/31/business/media/31netads.html?pagewanted=print

Curtin, M. (1999). "Feminine Desire in the Age of Satellite Television." *Journal of Communication,* Vol. 49(2): 55–70.

Debusmann, B. (2010, 21 October). "Most Americans Still Watch TV in Real Time: Poll." www.reuters.com/article/2010/10/21/us-poll-idUSTRE69K56U20101021

Donaton, S. (2004). *Madison & Vine.* New York: McGraw-Hill.

Dowler, K. (2002). "Television and Objecthood: The 'Place' of Television in Television Studies. *TOPIA,* Vol. 8(1): 43–60.

Ellis, J. (2000). *Seeing Things: Television in the Age of Uncertainty.* London: I.B. Tauris Publishers.

Gillan, J. (2010). *Television and New Media: Must-Click TV.* New York: Routledge.

Grindstaff, L., and Turow, J. (2006). "Video Cultures: Television Sociology in the 'New TV' Age." *Annual Review of Sociology,* Vol. 32(1): 103–25.

Hamp, A. (2008, 29 February). "Advertisers Seek TV Ad Effectiveness and Accountability." www.ana.net/content/show/id/464

Harris, M. (2008, 13 August). "Saving TV." www.portfolio.com/culture-lifestyle/culture-inc/arts/2008/08/13/Tracing-the-Decline-of-Network-TV/

Hsu, T. (2011, 3 February). "U.S. Shuts Down 10 Streaming Websites." http://articles.latimes.com/2011/feb/03/business/la-fi-superbowl-stream-shutdown-20110203

Jaffe, J. (2005). *Life after the 30 Second Spot: Energize Your Brand with a Bold Mix of Alternatives to Traditional Advertising.* Hoboken, NJ: John Wiley & Sons, Inc.

James, M. (2009, 4 May). "TV Networks Are Uneasy about Declining Advertising." http://articles.latimes.com/2009/may/04/business/fi-ct-cbs4

Jenkins, H. (2006). *Convergence Culture: Where Old and New Media Collide.* New York: New York University Press.

Kackman, M., Binfield, M., Payne, M. T., Perlman, A., and Sebok, B. (Eds). (2010). *Flow TV: Television in the Age of Media Convergence.* New YorK: Routledge.

Kirby, J. (2009, 19 October). "Is There a Future for Canadian TV?" www2.macleans.ca/2009/10/19/is-there-a-future-for-canadian-tv/

Krashinsky, S. (2010a, 9 March). "Online Challenge: Getting TV Viewers to Pay Up." www.theglobeandmail.com/news/technology/online-challenge-getting-tv-viewers-to-pay-up/article1495477/

———. (2010b, 12 April). "Reports of TV's Death Greatly Exaggerated." www.theglobeandmail.com/report-on-business/reports-of-tvs-death-greatly-exaggerated/article1532303/

Kritsonis, T. (2010, 23 September). "Media-hungry Canadians Seek Access to Geoblocked Hulu." www.theglobeandmail.com/news/technology/media-hungry-canadians-seek-access-to-geoblocked-hulu-spotify/article1322574/

Lam, E. (2010, 13 September). "Bell Communications to Buy Broadcast Giant CTV for $1.3 billion." www.canada.com/business/Bell+Communications+broadcast+giant+billion/3506356/story.html#ixzz1J1qhx4O

Lotz, A. (2007). *The Television Will Be Revolutionized.* New York: New York University Press.

———. (Ed.) (2009). *Beyond Prime Time: Television Programming in the Post-network Era.* New York: Routledge.

———. (2010). "US Television and the Recession: Impetus for Change." *Population Communication*, Vol. 8(3): 186–9.

MacDonald, I. (2009, 7 March). "The Future of Television in Canada." www.friends.ca/news-item/7896

Marlow, I. (2011, 25 January). "Usage-based Internet Ruling Draws Fire." www.theglobeandmail.com/news/technology/tech-news/usage-based-internet-ruling-draws-fire/article1882339/

Marlow, I., and McNish, J. (2010, 2 April). "Canada's Digital Divide." www.theglobeandmail.com/report-on-business/canadas-digital-divide/article1521631/

Miller, T. (2010). *TV Studies: The Basics.* New York: Routledge.

Moretti, S. (2010, 6 April). "TV Takes Product Placement One Step Further than Hollywood." http://money.canoe.ca/money/business/canada/archives/2010/04/20100406-175127.html

Niedzviecki, H. (2009). *The Peep Diaries: How We're Learning to Love Watching Ourselves and Our Neighbors.* San Francisco: City Lights.

Nielsen. (2010, December). "DVR Use in the U.S." http://blog.nielsen.com/nielsenwire/wp-content/uploads/2010/12/DVR-State-of-the-Media-Report.pdf

O'Donnell, J. (2011, 1 April). "Home Theatre Gear Is a Booming Business." www.usatoday.com/tech/products/2011-01-04-home-theater-gear_N.htm#

"Oh Canada!! 16.6 Million Watch Team Canada Ignite a Nation." (2010, 1 March). www.friends.ca/news-item/9260

Pearce, C. (2010, 1 October). "TV Is Dead – Long Live Viral!" http://craigpearce.info/marketing/tv-is-dead-%E2%80%93-long-live-viral/

Pfanner, E. (2010, 13 June). "TV, the 'Old Medium,' Holds Its Own in an Ad Spending Recovery." www.nytimes.com/2010/06/14/business/media/14adspend.html

Pogue, D. (2010, 17 November). "Google TV, Usability Not Included." www.nytimes.com/2010/11/18/technology/personaltech/18pogue.html

Powell, C. (2011, 18 January). "Social Media Ad Revenue Limited, TV to Stay Super Media." www.marketingmag.ca/news/media-news/social-media-ad-revenue-limited-tv-to-stay-%25E2%2580%2598super-media%25E2%2580%2599-deloitte-21395

"PVR Survey Says TV Ads Get Through." (2010, 13 August). www.mediacastermagazine.com/issues/story.aspx?aid=1000381886&ref=rss

"PVRs Will Not Eliminate TV Advertising's 30-Second Spot, Experts Say." (2011, 28 February). www.tvb.ca/pages/pvrs+will+not+eliminate+tv+advertisings+30second+spot,+experts+say_htm

Richmond, V. (2010, 26 January). "TV Is Not Dead: 3 Ways Television Makes the World a Better Place." www.alternet.org/media/145423/tv_is_not_dead%3A_3_ways_television_makes_the_world_a_better_place

Rocha, E., and Jordan, P. (2010, 3 May). "Shaw to Acquire Canwest Cable Channels." http://investdb4.theglobeandmail.com/servlet/ArticleNews/story/ROC/20100503/2010-05-03T162817Z_01_TRE6422E8_RTROPTT_0_CBUSINESS-US-CANWEST

Ross, S.M. (2008). *Beyond the Box: Television and the Internet.* Oxford: Blackwell-Wiley.

Rothman, W. (2010, 8 July). "The End of TV (As We Know It)." http://today.msnbc.msn.com/id/38007802/ns/today-entertainment/#

Sarno, D. (2007, 29 April). "The Internet Sure Loves Its Outlaws." www.latimes.com/technology/la-ca-webscout-29apr29,0,5609754.story

Sassone, B. (2007, 19 January). "*The Office* Takes Product Placement to the Next Level." www.adjab.com/2007/01/19/the-office-takes-product-placement-to-the-next-level/

Schonfeld, E. and Borzo, J. (2006, 2 October). "The Anti-TiVo: Product Placement Beats the 30 Second Spot."

http://money.cnn.com/2006/09/15/technology/disruptors_nextmedium.biz2/index.htm

Sergeant, J. (2011, 17 March 17). "'American Idol' King of TV Advertising Revenue." www.reuters.com/article/2011/03/17/us-moneymakers-idUSTRE72G9FB20110317

Spigel, L. (1992). *Make Room for TV: Television and the Family Ideal in Post-war America*. Chicago: University of Chicago Press.

Spigel, L., and Olsson, J. (2004). *Television after TV: Essays on a Medium in Transition*. Durham: Duke University Press.

Stelter, B. (2010, 23 February). "Internet Can be TV's Friend." www.nytimes.com/2010/02/24/business/media/24cooler.html

———. (2011a, 2 January). "TV Viewing Continues to Edge Up." www.nytimes.com/2011/01/03/business/media/03ratings.html?ref=cabletelevision

———. (2011b, 23 July). "Hulu, Billed as Tomorrow's TV, Looks Boxed In." www.nytimes.com/2011/07/24/business/media/hulu-billed-as-tomorrows-tv-looks-boxed-in-today.html?pagewanted=all

The Economist. (2009). "The Revolution that Wasn't: DVRs Were Supposed to Undermine Television. They Have Done the Opposite." www.economist.com /node/13528310

Tinic, S. (2010). "The Global Economic Meltdown: A Crisotunity for Canada's Private Sector Broadcasters?" *Popular Communication: The International Journal of Media and Culture*, Vol. 8(3): 193–97.

Turner, G. (2001). "Television and Cultural Studies: Unfinished Business." *International Journal of Cultural Studies*, Vol. 4(4): 317–84.

Turner, G., and Tay, J. (2009). *Television Studies after TV: Understanding Television in the Post-broadcast Era*. New York: Routledge.

Turow, J. (1997). *Breaking up America: Advertisers and the New Media World*. Chicago: University of Chicago Press.

Vlessing, E. (2011, 13 January). "Ad Market Recovery Drives Canadian TV Revenue Momentum." www.mediapost.com/publications/?fa=Articles.showArticle&art_aid=129920&nid=115346

Williams, R. (1974). *Television: Technology and Cultural Form*. London: Fontana.

———. (1977). *Marxism and Literature*. London: Oxford University Press.

Winseck, D. (2010). "Financialization and the 'Crisis of the Media': The Rise and Fall of (Some) Media Conglomerates in Canada." *Canadian Journal of Communication*, Vol. 35(3): 365–93.

Part IV | Discussion Questions

Introduction | Emerging Trends in TV Studies: Interactive Audiences, Advertising, Globalization, and Post-network TV

1. What is the interactive audience? Select a specific TV show and examine how its members interact within the Web 2.0 environment. What are viewers interactively doing, saying, and expressing in relation to their favourite TV show using Web 2.0 technology and social networking platforms (Facebook, MySpace, Twitter)?
2. How does a particular TV ad cultivate desire for a particular good or service? How does TV advertising attach cultural meanings to goods or service that are inherently meaningless? What non-utilitarian meanings does a TV ad communicate about a good or service? Do you agree or disagree with Jhally's (2000) argument that TV advertising is a form of corporate propaganda that promotes an environmentally calamitous and emotionally turbulent consumerist culture?
3. What is a "media capital"? Describe how a "media capital" outside of the United States attempts to export TV shows to the US. What kinds of TV shows made by non-US culture industries for export to the US tend to be most popular in the American market? Why?
4. What is a runaway production? Examine a runaway TV production from Los Angeles to a Canadian city. Do runaway TV productions help or hinder Canada's economic and cultural development goals? What were the benefits and the drawbacks? Did a Canadian city become a "body double" (Elmer 2002) for a US city?
5. Do you watch TV shows on TV sets or computer screens? Do you adhere to the schedules of TV networks or do you make up your own TV schedule? In your opinion, what is the future of TV?

19 | Understanding How the Popular Becomes Popular: The Role of Political Economy in the Study of Popular Communication

1. What is the "audience commodity"? Why do TV networks commodify the viewers of specific TV shows? Select a specific TV show and watch the ads scheduled alongside it. What kind of audience demographic does the TV show attempt to attract? What audience members are not targeted by the TV show and ads? Why?
2. What is the "political-economy" approach to TV? How is it different from "textual" and "reception" studies of TV?
3. What is the difference between "distracted" and "engaged" viewership? What kind of viewer are you?
4. What are the different ways in which ratings have been collected? What are some of the new ways that Nielsen is gathering ratings about particular TV shows? Have you or anyone you've ever known been asked to participate in a Nielsen rating study? If not, why might you and your friends "not count" as TV ratings? Do you feel that TV networks attempt to represent your viewing tastes and preferences? Why or why not? Do you "count" as part of the audience for prime-time TV shows?
5. How have recent technological developments transformed the ways that ratings are determined? Do you feel that ratings provide reliable data about contemporary TV viewers?

20 | YouTube: Where Cultural Memory and Copyright Converge

1. What does going "viral" mean? Can you provide an example of a contemporary YouTube video that went "viral"? Why do you think the video went "viral" when it did?
2. Is YouTube a profitable business venture? How does YouTube make money? What is the primary source of YouTube's profit: Ads? User-generated content? Users? All of the above?
3. What are some of the copyright conflicts between YouTube and media corporations?
4. What are the three types of content on YouTube? Describe them, using current examples.
5. Is YouTube changing the way we communicate? How specifically? What is lost and what is gained?

21 | Watching Television without Pity: The Productivity of Online Fans

1. What is "participatory exploitation"? Provide a contemporary example of this practice.
2. What uses do TV networks and marketing firms make of online fan sites for TV shows?
3. Provide an example of a web-based community surrounding a TV show. How are the members of this web-based community different from other types of TV show viewers?
4. How are fan sites like Television Without Pity (TWoP) different from the official websites of TV shows?
5. What is the "public sphere"? Is Internet fandom an indication of the decline of the public sphere?

22 | The Commodity Flow of US Children's Television

1. What did Raymond Williams mean by "flow"? Define "flow" and discuss examples with reference to a prime-time network schedule.
2. What is "commodity flow"? Identify "commodity flow" in a contemporary TV show.
3. What are the different forms of commodity flow? Describe them with reference to current examples.
4. Discuss the importance of licensing and branding in children's TV shows. Provide an example of a contemporary children's TV show that is utilized by advertisers to promote brands.
5. How do TV shows target and attempt to turn children into brand-loyal consumers? Give some examples.

23 | McTV: Understanding the Global Popularity of Television Formats

1. Examine the acquisition of a American TV show by a Canadian TV network. What kind of distribution deal occurred? How did the American TV distributor export the TV show to Canada?
2. Select a recent TV format. How is it global? How is it local?
3. Is the global dominance of TV formats evidence of Hollywood's domination of transnational media markets?
4. What is the difference between national and global culture? Are globalizing TV formats evidence of the emergence of a "global culture"? Why or why not?
5. How are global formats "localized" by national TV networks and for national viewers?

24 | National Television, Global Market: Canada's *Degrassi: The Next Generation*

1. How did the producers of *Degrassi: The Next Generation (DTNG)* try to make this show accessible to foreign audiences?
2. What makes *Degrassi: The Next Generation (DTNG)* "Canadian" and "universal" at the same time?
3. What is a "multiplatform" show and how is it different from TV shows that were produced in the network era? Provide a current example of a "multiplatform" TV show.
4. Does *Degrassi: The Next Generation (DTNG)* fit into the tradition of "public service" programming? Why or why not?
5. Select a contemporary Canadian TV show. How does this TV show represent Canadian national identity?

25 | Imagining America: *The Simpsons* Go Global

1. What is "cultural imperialism"? What are some of the weaknesses of the cultural imperialism thesis?
2. To what extent does *The Simpsons* show celebrate and/or criticize American society?
3. Select an American TV show. How is America "imagined" by the TV show? Does the TV show's representation of America affirm or contest dominant values in US society?
4. How might a Canadian or American TV show be locally interpreted by non-Canadian and non-American TV viewers? Do a reception study of how a North American TV show is locally interpreted, received, or adapted by an audience within another country.
5. What is a "polysemic" text? Give some examples from *The Simpsons*.

26 | Walking a Tightrope: The Global Cultural Economy of Canadian Television

1. What is the main "tension" between the economic and cultural goals of Canadian TV production in the twenty-first century?
2. What is the difference between a "global generic" TV series and a TV series that speaks to the cultural specificity of a domestic market? Compare and contrast a Canadian TV series based on the "global generic" model and one that speaks to Canadian cultural specificity.
3. What is an international joint venture (IJV)? Select a Canadian TV series that is the outcome of an IJV. Does the type of TV series produced through the IJV lean toward the business, rather than the creative side of the contradictory institution of television?
4. What are some of the main economic and political challenges faced by the Canadian Broadcasting Corporation (CBC) in the twenty-first century? Why, according to Tinic, is the CBC still relevant?
5. What is the difference between "pluralist" and "diverse" representations of Canada? Select a Canadian TV series produced by the CBC and one produced by a private Canadian TV network. Does the CBC's Canadian TV show entail a more "diverse" representation of Canada than the one produced by Canada's private TV network?

27 | The Future of Television: Revolution Paused, Media Conglomeration Continued

1. What are the main differences between network TV, multichannel TV, and post-network TV?
2. Do personal video recorders (PVRs) compromise the commercial functions of TV networks?

3. What is the difference between product placement and branded entertainment? Provide an example of product placement and branded entertainment in a contemporary TV show.
4. Describe "geo-blocking." Why are Canadian viewers blocked from watching TV shows on Hulu.com?
5. Will Internet TV on computer screens replace the experience of watching TV shows on TV screens?

Suggestions for Further Reading

Interactive Audiences and TV Fandoms

Costello, V., and Moore, B. (2007). "Cultural Outlaws: An Examination of Audience Activity and Online Television Fandom." *Television & New Media*, Vol. 8(2): 124–43.

Cover, R. (2006). "Audience Inter/active." *New Media & Society*, Vol. 8(1): 139–58.

Gray, J. (2005). "Antifandom and the Moral Text." *American Behavioural Scientist*, Vol. 48(7): 840–58.

Gray, J., Sandvoss, C., and Harrington, C.L. (2007). *Fandom: Identities and Communities in a Mediated World.* New York: New York University Press.

Gwenllian-Jones, S., and Pearson, R.E. (2004). *Cult Television*. Minneapolis: University of Minnesota Press.

Hills, M. (2002). *Fan Cultures*. New York: Routledge.

Harrington, C. Lee, and Denise D. Bielby.(1995). *Soap Fans: Pursuing Pleasure and Making Meaning in Everyday Life.* Philadelphia: Temple University Press.

Holmes, S. (2004). "'But This Time You Choose!' Approaching the 'Interactive' Audience in Reality TV." *International Journal of Cultural studies*, Vol. 7(2): 213–31.

Jancovich, M., and Lyons, J. (Eds). (2008). *Quality Popular Television: Cult TV, the Industry and Fans.* London: British Film Institute.

Jenkins, H. (1988). "Star Trek Rerun, Reread, Rewritten: Fan Writing as Textual Poaching." *Critical Studies in Mass Communication*, Vol. 5(2): 85–107.

———. (1992). *Textual Poachers: Television Fans & Participatory Culture*. New York: Routledge.

———. (2006). *Fans, Bloggers and Gamers: Media Consumers in a Digital Age.* New York: New York University Press.

Jenson, J. (1992). "Fandom as Pathology." In L.A. Lewis (Ed.), *The Adoring Audience: Fan Culture and Popular Media* (pp. 9–29). London: Routledge.

Lewis, L. (Ed.). (1992). *The Adoring Audience: Fan Culture and Popular Media*. London: Routledge.

Livingstone, S. (2004). "The Challenge of Changing Audiences: Or, What Is the Audience Researcher to Do in the Age of the Internet?" *European Journal of Communication*, Vol. 19(1): 75–86.

Russo, J.L. (2009). "User-Penetrated Content: Fan Video in the Age of Convergence." *Cinema Journal*, Vol. 48(4): 125–30.

Television Advertising and Commercialism

Anderson, R. (1995). *Consumer Culture & TV Programming.* Boulder: Westview Press.

Cross, G. (2000). *An All-consuming Century: Why Commercialism Won in Modern America.* New York: Columbia University Press.

Debord, G. (1983). *Society of the Spectacle.* Detroit: Black and Red Press.

Ewen, S. (1976). *Captains of Consciousness: Advertising and the Social Roots of Consumer Culture.* New York: McGraw-Hill.

Goldman, R., and Papson, S. (1994). "Advertising in the Age of Hypersignification." *Theory, Culture & Society,* Vol. 11: 23–53.

Gunster, S. (1007). "'On the Road to Nowhere': Utopian Themes in Contemporary Auto Advertising." *Review of Education, Pedagogy, and Cultural Studies,* Vol. 29(2): 211–38.

Haug, W.F. (1986). *Critique of Commodity Aesthetics: Appearance, Sexuality, and Advertising in Capitalist Society.* Cambridge: Polity Press.

Jhally, S. (1987). *The Codes of Advertising: Fetishism and the Political Economy of Meaning in the Consumer Society.* New York: Routledge.

Leiss, W., Kline, S., and Jhally, S. (1990). *Social Communication in Advertising.* New York: Methuen.

McAllister, M.P. (2010). "But Wait, There's More!: Advertising, the Recession, and the Future of Commercial Culture." *Popular Communication,* Vol. 8(3): 189–93.

Meehan, E. (2005). *Why TV Is Not Our Fault: TV Programming Viewers and Who's Really in Control.* Lanham, MD: Rowman & Littlefield.

Morris, M. (2005). "Interpretability and Social Power, or, Why Postmodern Advertising Works." *Media, Culture & Society,* Vol. 27(5): 697–718.

O'Guinn, T.C., & Shrum, L.J. (1997). "The Role of Television in the Construction of Consumer Reality." *The Journal of Consumer Research,* Vol. 23(4): 278–94.

Spurgeon, C. (2008). *Advertising and New Media.* London: Routledge.

Turow, J. (2005). "Audience Construction and Culture Production: Marketing Surveillance in the Digital Age." *Annals of the American Academy of Political and Social Science,* Vol. 597(1): 103–21.

Watts, E.K., and Orbe, M.P. (2002). "The Spectacular Consumption of 'True' African American Culture: 'Whassup' with the Budweiser Guys?" *Critical Studies in Media Communication*, Vol. 19(1):1–20.

Wernick, A. (1991). *Promotional Culture: Advertising, Ideology and Symbolic Expression*. New York: Sage Publications.

Williams, R. (1980). "Advertising: the Magic System." In R. Williams (Ed.), *Problems of Materialism and Culture* (pp. 170–95). London: New Left Books.

Television and Globalization

Allen, R.C. (Ed.). (1995). *To Be Continued ... Soap Operas around the World*. New York: Routledge.

Ang, I. (1994). "In the Realm of Uncertainty: The Global Village and Capitalist Postmodernity." In D. Crowley and D. Mitchell (Eds), *Communication Theory Today* (pp. 193–213). Cambridge: Polity.

———. (2003). "Culture and Communication: Toward and Ethnographic Critique of Media Consumption in the Transnational Media System." In L. Parks and S. Kumar (Eds), *Planet TV: A Global Television Reader* (pp. 363–76). New York: New York University Press.

Bagdikian, B. (2004). *The New Media Monopoly*. Boston, MA: Beacon Press.

Barker, C. (1997). *Global Television: An Introduction*. Oxford: Blackwell.

Bielby, D.B., and Harrington, C.L. (2008). *Global TV*. New York: New York University Press.

Bicket, D. (2005). "Reconsidering Geocultural Counterflow: Intercultural Information Flows through Trends in Global Audiovisual Trade." *Global Media Journal*, Vol. 4(6): n.p.

Boyd-Barrett, O. (1998). "Media Imperialism Reformulated." In D.K. Thussu (Ed.), *Electronic Empires: Global Media and Local Resistance* (pp. 156–76). New York: Arnold.

Chalaby, J.K. (2005). *Transnational Television Worldwide: Towards a New Media Order*. London: IB Taurus.

———. (2006). "American Cultural Primacy in a New Media Order: A European Perspective." *The International Communication Gazette*, Vol. 68(1): 33–51.

Coutas, P. (2006). "Fame, Fortune, Fantasi: Indonesian Idol and the New Celebrity." *Asian Journal of Communication*, Vol. 16(4): 371–92.

Curtin, M. (1999). "Feminine Desire in the Age of Satellite Television." *Journal of Communication*, Vol. 49(2): 55–60.

———. (2007). *Playing to the World's Biggest Audience: The Globalization of Chinese Film and TV*. Berkley and Los Angeles, CA: University of California Press.

Davis, C., and Kay, J. (2009). "'Runaway' Film and Television Production in Canada; The Good, Bad and Ugly of Foreign Location Production." Paper presented at the 12th Uddevalla Symposium: the Geography of Innovation and Entrepreneurship, Bari, Italy, 11–13 June 2009.

———. (2010). "International Production Outsourcing and the Development of Indigenous Film and Television Capabilities: The Case of Canada." In G. Elmer, C. Davis, J. McCullough, and J. Marchessault (Eds), *Locating Migrating Media* (pp. 57–78). New York: Rowman & Littlefield.

Dorfman, A., and Mattelart, A. (1975). *How to Read Donald Duck: Imperialist Ideology in the Disney Comic*. New York: International General Editions.

Elmer, G., and Gasher, M. (2005). *Contracting out Hollywood: Runaway Production and Foreign Location Shooting*. Latham, MD: Rowman & Littlefield.

Freedman, D. (2003). "Who Wants to Be a Millionaire? The Politics of Television Exports." *Information, Communication & Society*, Vol. 6(1): 24–41.

Gordon, N.S.A. (2009). "Globalization and Cultural Imperialism in Jamaica." *International Journal of Communication*, Vol. 3(1): 307–31.

Havens, T. (2001). "Subtitling Rap: Appropriating The Fresh Prince of Bel-Air For Youthful Identity Formation in Kuwait." *Gazette: The International Journal for Communication Studies*, Vol. 63(1): 57–72.

Herman, E., and McChesney, R. (1997). *The Global Media: The New Missionaries of Corporate Capitalism*. London: Continuum.

Johnson-Yale, C. (2008). "So-Called Runaway Film Production: Countering Hollywood's Outsourcing Narrative in the Canadian Press." *Critical Studies in Media Communication*, Vol. 25(2): 113–34.

Keane, M., and Moran, A. (2008). "Television's New Engines." *Television & New Media*, Vol. 9(2): 155–69.

McChesney, R., and Schiller. D. (2003). "The Political Economy of International Communications: Foundations for the Emerging Global Debate about Media Ownership and Regulation." United Nations Research Institute for Social Development (Technology, Business and Society Programme Paper Number 11).

Miller, J.L. (2010). "Ugly Betty Goes Global: Global Networks of Localized Content in the Telenovela Industry." *Global Media and Communication*, Vol. 6(2): 198–217.

Miller, T., Govil, N., McMurria, J. Maxwell, R., and Wang, T. (2005). *Global Hollywood 2*. London: British Film Institute.

Moran, A. (2009). "Global Franchising, Local Customizing: The Cultural Economy of TV Program Formats." *Continuum: Journal of Media & Cultural Studies*, Vol. 23(2): 115–25.

Morley, D., and Robins, K. (1995). *Spaces of Identity: Global Media, Electronic Landscapes and Cultural Boundaries*. New York: Routledge.

Morris, N. (2002). "The Myth of Unadulterated Culture Meets the Threat of Imported Media." *Media, Culture & Society*, Vol. 24: 278–89.

Raboy, M. (2007). "Global Media Policy – Defining the Field." *Global Media and Communication*, Vol. 3(3): 343–61.

Schiller, H. (1976) *Communication and Cultural Domination*. Armonk, NY: M.E. Sharpe.

Selznick. B.J. (2008). *Global Television: Co-producing Culture*. Philadelphia: Temple University Press.

Sinclair, J. (2003). "The Hollywood of Latin America: Miami as a Regional Center in Television Trade." *Television & New Media*, Vol. 4(3), 211–29.

Sinclair, J., Jacka, E., and Cunningham, S. (1996). *New Patterns in Global Television: Peripheral Vision*. Oxford: Oxford University Press.

Sparks, C. (2007). *Globalization, Development and the Mass Media*. Los Angeles: Sage Publications.

Steger, M.B. (2009). *Globalization: A Very Short Introduction* (paperback, 2nd edn). New York: Oxford University Press.

Thussu, D.K. (2000). *International Communication: Continuity and Change*. London: Arnold Press.

Tinic, S. (2004). "Global Vistas and Local Identities: Negotiating Place and Identity in Vancouver Television." *Television and New Media*, Vol. 7(2): 154–83.

———. (2005). *On Location: Canada's Television Industry in a Global Market*. Toronto: University of Toronto Press.

———. (2008). "Mediated Spaces: Cultural Geography and the Globalization of Production." *Velvet Light Trap*, Vol. 62(1): 74–5.

Tomlinson, J. (1991). *Cultural Imperialism*. Baltimore: The Johns Hopkins University Press.

———. (1999). *Globalization and Culture*. Chicago: Chicago University Press.

Straubhaar, J. (1997). "Distinguishing the Global, Regional and National Levels of World Television." In A. Sreberry-Mohammadi, D. Winseck, J. McKenna and O. Body-Barret (Eds), *Media in a Global Context: A Reader* (pp. 284–98). London: Edward Arnold.

Strelitz, L. (2004). "Against Cultural Essentialism: Media Reception among South African Youth." *Media, Culture & Society*, Vol. 26(5): 625–41.

Ward, S., and O'Regan, T. (2007). "Servicing 'the Other Hollywood': The Vicissitudes of an International Television Production Location." *International Journal of Cultural Studies*, Vol. 10(2): 167–85.

Wasko, J., and Erikson, M. (Eds). (2009). *Cross Border Cultural Production: Economy Runaway or Globalization?* New York: Cambria Press.

Weeks, E. (2010). "Where Is There? The Canadianization of the American Media Landscape." *International Journal of Canadian Studies*, Vol. 39–40(1): 83–107.

Post-network TV

Andrejevic, M. (2007). *iSpy: Surveillance and Power in the Interactive Era*. Kansas: University of Press of Kansas.

Bolter, J.D., and Grusin, R. (2000). *Remediation: Understanding New Media*. Cambridge, MA: MIT Press.

Brooker, W. (2001). "Living on Dawson's Creek: Teen Viewers, Cultural Convergence and Television Overflow." *International Journal of Cultural Studies*, Vol. 4(4): 456–72.

Burgess, J., Green, J., Jenkins, H., and Hartley, J. (2009). *YouTube: Online Video and Participatory Culture*. Cambridge: Polity Press.

Carlson, M. (2006). "Tapping into TiVo: Digital Video Recorders and the Transition from Schedules to Surveillance in Television." *New Media & Society*, Vol. 8(1): 97–115.

Gillan, J. (2010). *Television and New Media: Must-Click* TV. New York: Routledge.

Grindstaff, L., and Turow, J.(2006). "Video Cultures: Television Sociology in the 'New TV' Age." *Annual Review of Sociology*, Vol. 32(1): 103–25.

Jenkins, H. (2004). "The Cultural Logic of Media Convergence." *International Journal of Cultural Studies*, Vol. 7(1): 33–43.

———. (2008). *Convergence Culture*. New York: New York University Press.

Kackman, M., and Binfield, M. (2010). *Flow* TV: *Television in the Age of Convergence*. New York: Routledge.

Lotz, A. (2007). *The Television Will Be Revolutionized*. New York: New York University Press.

———. (Ed.) (2009). *Beyond Prime Time: Television Programming in the Post-network Era*. New York: Routledge.

Manovich, L. (2002). *The Language of New Media*. Cambridge: MIT Press.

Niedzviecki, H. (2009). *The Peep Diaries: How We're Learning to Love Watching Ourselves and Our Neighbours*. San Francisco: City Lights.

Ross, S.M. (2009). *Beyond the Box: Television and the Internet*. Oxford: Blackwell-Wiley.

Spigel, L., and Olsson, J. (2004). *Television after* TV*: Essays on a Medium in Transition*. Durham: Duke University Press.

Strangelove, M. (2010). *Watching YouTube: Extraordinary Videos by Ordinary People*. Toronto: University of Toronto Press.

Vonderau, P., Snickars, P., and Burgess, J. (Eds). (2009). *The YouTube Reader*. Stockholm: National Library of Sweden.

Glossary

Advanced Television Systems Committee (ATSC): A set of technical standards for the digital transmission of television signals. It replaces the older **NTSC** standard in North America.

Advertising buys or media buys: When a company buys a spot in the commercial media to promote their product or service. Examples include print ads in newspapers or magazines or 30-second commercials on television.

Aspect ratio: Ratio indicating the width of the TV screen to its height. Older TVs in North America had a 4:3 (1.33:1) aspect ratio. Newer (HD) TVs have a wider 16:9 (1.78:1) aspect ratio. This is sometimes referred to as "widescreen".

Audience commodity: This term describes the way in which TV networks bundle audiences and sell them to advertisers for commercial gain. Networks treat the viewers who watch particular programs as a product to be exchanged with TV advertisers for cash. Canadian communications scholar Dallas Smythe coined the term "audience commodity."

Block-booking: The practice of forcing television networks to buy a bundle of shows from a TV producer rather than buying series individually. The business practice is commonly used by American TV producers to sell their shows in foreign markets.

Broadcasting: The wireless distribution of audio and video content from one point to another; when television networks transmit signals to the widest audience possible. It is the opposite of **narrowcasting**.

Broadcasting distribution undertakings (BDU): Fee-for-carriage regulations in Canada, which require cable and satellite operators to pay funds to over-the-air (OTA) broadcast networks for carrying their signals.

Canada New Media Fund (CNMF): A state institution that funds the development of video games, podcasts, and streaming video for social media platforms and mobile devices. Name changed to Canadian Media Fund (CMF) in 2010.

Canadian Broadcast Standards Council (CBSC): A non-governmental organization set up by Canadian Broadcasting Association (CBA) to administer standards established by its members. The CBSC encourages TV broadcasters to self-regulate and self-censor TV content.

Canadian Media Fund (CMF). A state-subsidizing institution that on 1 April 2010 was the result of the combination of the Canada New Media Fund (CNMF) and the Canadian Television Fund (CTF). The CMF supports the development of TV shows, video games, podcasts, and streaming video for social media platforms and mobile devices.

Canadian Radio-television and Telecommunications Commission (CRTC): Institution of the Canadian federal government that regulates all radio and television broadcasting and telecommunications technologies, such as telephone and the Internet.

Canadian Television Fund (CTF): A state institution that provides funding to Canadian television producers to produce "Canadian" programming. Name changed to the Canadian Media Fund (CMF) in 2010.

Commercialization: A term used in sports to indicate the practice of using amateur athletics to raise money for various institutions such as universities and colleges. An example would be charging admission to see college football games in the United States.

Community Antenna Television (CATV): The original name for cable TV. Cable television started as a means of distributing TV signals to remote rural communities that could not receive the signals from broadcasters located in large cities. These communities used a very high antenna tower to receive signals from afar. They then distributed the signals to local television viewers by way of coaxial cable, for which these viewers paid a subscription fee.

Consumerism: An ideology rooted in the development of the modern advertising industry. This ideology promotes the idea that human happiness can be found in buying of products and services.

Copyright: Copyright is a set of state-granted exclusive rights to private authors that regulates the public use of a particular expression. It is "the right to copy" an original creative expression, such as a TV show. Media corporations (private "authors") are holding companies for a diverse range of developed or acquired copyrighted creative expressions (TV shows, films, books, etc.). Copyright gives corporations control over the use and reproduction of creative expressions in society.

Critical theory: A branch of Marxist theory that examines the relationship between culture and society. Its most prominent representatives are those individuals who were associated with the Frankfurt Institute of Social Research or the "Frankfurt School."

Cultural determinism: The idea that cultural factors are the most important component in the development of a social order including its social, political, and economic institutions.

Cultural nationalism: A form of nationalism, which privileges the role of culture in the manufacture of national identity. Usually a defensive posture, such as when Canadian "cultural nationalists" bemoan the negative impact of American media on their "culture."

Cultural studies: An approach to the study of culture, economics, and politics established by Richard Hoggart, Raymond Williams, Edward Thompson, and Stuart Hall at the Centre for Contemporary Cultural Studies (CCCS) at the University of Birmingham, England. The CCCS studied subcultures, popular culture, and how race, class, and gender identities were being transformed by economic, political, and technological changes.

Digital Millennium Copyright Act (DMCA): An American copyright law enacted in 1998 that was designed to try to stop the copying of digital media texts such as music files, television shows, and movies.

Federal Communications Commission (FCC): A US government body that regulates the broadcast and telecommunications industry. Historically, it has tended to support the interests of private media and communications corporations.

Financial Interest and Syndication Rules (Fin-Syn Rules): A set of rules adopted by the FCC in 1970 to curtail the power of the Big Three television networks. It was an anti-trust initiative designed to open up competition in the market for the production of television shows. It was repealed in 1993 as part of the neo-liberal political culture, which favoured abandoning the regulation of markets.

Flow: A term used by Raymond Williams to describe how TV viewers experience a continuous process where TV shows and commercials flow seamlessly from one to the other.

Glocalization: A Japanese business term that emphasizes how the globalization of a product is more likely to succeed when the product is adapted specifically to each locality or culture in which it is distributed. The term combines the concept of globalization with the word *local*. In media studies, the term is commonly used to describe how Transnational Media Corporations (TNMCs) adapt their products to suit local tastes. MTV India, MTV China, and MTV Latin America are examples of "glocalization."

Hegemony: A term used by Italian Marxist theorist Antonio Gramsci to describe the way a small elite can rule over a society by getting the majority of citizens to go along with (or "consent" to) its rule. Subsequent media scholars have suggested that the corporate media plays a vital role in the process of organizing the consent of the many to the rule of the few. Hegemony is the opposite of coercion since it involves ideological mechanisms of control as opposed to physical force or threat to keep people compliant.

Ideology: A dominant system of ideas that represent the point of view of a dominant class; a false system of ideas that mystify or mask the real power relations in society or actual state of affairs; a set of views that people hold to make sense of the world.

Infomercial: A 20-minute long advertisement placed in an official TV network timeslot. The whole program is a commercial for a product (for example, a new household appliance). Sometimes an infomercial is disguised as a documentary. Television producers and advertisers are now blurring full-length infomercials into full-length TV shows. For example, General Motors (GM) financed a 30-minute infomercial called *Monster Garage* in 2003.

Local Programming Improvement Fund (LPIF): A state fund financed by 1 per cent of the annual gross revenue of Canadian cable TV and satellite TV firms; it is a state subsidy that supports the production of diverse local programming (news and entertainment) for local markets.

Mass media: A term to describe all mass-produced and mass-distributed forms of mechanical and electronic communication. Mass media includes newspapers, magazines, radio, television, and the Internet.

Mediated interactivity: Communication and interaction between people that is mediated by some form of communications technology. Online gaming is an example.

MIME-NET (military-industrial-media-entertainment network): A term used to describe the ways in which the military works with media firms to make media products (TV shows, films, and video games) that valorize war, militarism, and imperialism.

Mockumentary: A recent word for "mock documentary," it is a fictional work that uses the techniques and forms of documentary. An example is the Canadian TV show *Trailer Park Boys*.

Multiculturalism: A political ideology that celebrates, encourages, recognizes, and promotes diversity among peoples. In Canada, it is a policy used to encourage mass immigration from the rest of the globe and to help newcomers adjust to Canadian society.

Narrowcasting: When a TV network customizes and schedules TV shows for a very particular audience niche (defined by tastes and preferences or demographic characteristics). For example, the American cable TV channel Nick Jr. (owned by MTV Networks) is aimed at 2- to 6-year-old viewers; it schedules TV shows that reflect this niche's presumed tastes and preferences.

National Television Systems Committee (NTSC): A set of technical standards developed for analog television systems in North America, parts of South America, and parts of East Asia. Originally adopted in 1941, it has been phased out in the United States recently and will soon be gone in Canada as well with the adoption of digital television (see **ATSC**) as the sole form of television transmission in North America.

Neo-liberalism: A dominant political ideology over the past three decades; it argues that markets should regulate all facets of human life (opposed to government regulation). Neo-liberal media policy calls for the liberalization of media markets (audiovisual free trade), deregulation (abolishment of public interest regulation and re-regulation on behalf of powerful business interests), and privatization (commercialization of publicly owned telecommunication and broadcasting systems and content).

Online community: A community comprised of people who ritualistically interact and communicate with each other using the Internet. Players of massive multiplayer online role-playing games (MMORPGs) such as *World of Warcraft* (*WOW*) and TV fans participate in online communities.

Orientalism: A term coined by Edward Said to describe the ways in which western scholars and media represent eastern (particularly middle eastern) cultures in negative ways in order to define and distinguish the positive qualities of the West. Orientalism supports, informs, and sustains negative stereotypes about Muslim and Arab peoples.

Police procedural: A film and television genre that looks at the activities and lives of various police forces and their employees. Examples include the *CSI* franchise and *NYPD Blue*.

Political economy: The study of economic matters that takes into consideration the ways in which they are shaped by governmental laws, regulations, and political power.

Post-Fordism: A term used to describe the more flexible forms of industrial production that have come to replace the older assembly-line-based mass production techniques developed in the early twentieth century. It is also used to describe the decline of jobs in the industrial sector in North America and its replacement with jobs in the service and information sectors.

Post-network era: A term to describe the recent period in which the traditional broadcast networks have significantly diminished in power and audience share while television transmission systems have seen the rise of hundreds of other TV stations and networks instead.

Product placement: The practice of putting "brand" products into TV shows to increase the amount of commercial impressions viewers are exposed to in each hour of programming they watch.

Progressivism: A late-nineteenth- and early-twentieth-century political ideology in the United States that held that the state should play a large role in controlling the behaviour of individuals and corporations. Examples of progressivist legislation include the Sherman Anti-Trust Act (1890), The Volstead Act or prohibition, (1919–1933) and the Radio Act of 1927.

Public sphere: The space in society between the private sphere (individuals and family) and the state where citizens and communities freely discuss and debate significant political matters in their society. The outcome of public deliberation is public opinion, which is ideally recognized by government and translated into public policy. The public sphere can be a physical space like the central square in Cairo where the recent Egyptian revolution took place. It can also be a virtual space like online communities in social media platforms, where virtual citizens discuss and debate politics.

Rating: A measurement category uses by TV ratings corporations such as Nielsen and BBM Canada to represent the number of households that watch a particular TV network, TV channel, or TV show for a particular length of time. Nielsen has had a near monopoly on gathering and selling rating information to TV networks and TV advertisers for the last 60 years in North America. Ratings help TV networks determine the cost of ad time/space and give advertisers confidence that their ads will reach an audience.

Reality TV: A TV show genre that features non-professional actors (often ordinary people) improvising within loosely scripted dramatic situations for the purposes of entertainment.

Reception studies: A branch of cultural studies that focuses on the ways in which readers and viewers interpret and respond to media texts within particular social contexts.

Share: The percentage of television viewing households watching a particular program among those who have their TV sets turned on. This number is always higher than the show's **rating**.

Simulacra: This term once referred to a "false copy of something." Postmodern TV theorists such as Jean Baudrillard describe "simulacra" as a copy of something without an original. Television simulates reality. Since TV images of reality stand in for and become reality to many people, it is no longer possible to distinguish between a true and false copy of reality.

Situation comedy or sitcom: A radio and television comedic genre that focuses on the trials and tribulations of a small group, often a family or the employees of a workplace.

Society of the spectacle: A term used by French philosopher Guy Debord to describe the late capitalist media system's transformation of authentic and face-to-face social relations between people into artificial and distanced relations between images. In the society of the spectacle, image is everything. All social relationships are mediated by images, which degrade human perception, knowledge, and critical-thinking skills.

Spot: A short period of time in a network TV schedule that is used for broadcasting 30-second advertisements; also, a TV advertisement that is broadcast by a TV network.

Syndication: The selling of the airing rights of a show to multiple television stations and/or networks. This is usually done after the initial broadcasting of a program on a particular network. For example, new episodes of *The Simpsons* air on the Fox network, but older episodes can be found on many different stations. The exception to this is first-run syndication, where a TV show's producer allows numerous networks to show a new program at the same time. Some of the later *Star Trek* series where broadcast in this way.

Technological determinism: The belief that technological development is the single most important factor underlying social, political, cultural, and economic change or transformation.

Technological instrumentalism: The belief that technology is a tool that rational human actors determine, develop, and actively use for a variety of purposes upon which they decide.

Transnational media corporations (TNMCs): Very large vertically and horizontally integrated media corporations that dominate the media landscape of many countries. Examples include The Disney Company, Time Warner, and News Corporation.

UHF (ultra high frequency): A range of television broadcast frequencies that was developed after **VHF**. They corresponded to channels 14 to 83.

VHF (very high frequency): A range of television broadcast frequencies that were originally used in the first television sets. They corresponded to channels 2 through 13.

YouTube: An Internet video-sharing website that enables people to upload, share, and view videos (that they and others have created). YouTube is owned by Google Corporation and is intensely policed by **TNMCs** that are looking for copyright violations.

Credits

Andrejevic, Mark. (2008). "Watching Television without Pity: The Productivity of Online Fans." *Television & New Media*, 9(1): 24–46.

Attalah, Paul (2007) "A Usable History for the Study of Television." *Canadian Review of American Studies*, 30(3): 325–45. Reprinted with permission from University of Toronto Press Incorporated (www.utpjournals.com).

Baltruschat, Doris. (2009). "Reality TV Formats: The Case of *Canadian Idol*." *Canadian Journal of Communication*, 34(2): 41–59.

Baym, Geoffrey. (2005). "*The Daily Show*: Discursive Integration and Reinvention of Political Journalism." *Political Communication*, 22(2): 259–76.

Cañas, Sandra. (2008). "*Little Mosque on the Prairie*: Examining Multicultural Spaces of Nation and Religion." *Cultural Dynamics*, 20(3): 195–211.

Cavender, Gray and Deutsch, Sarah. (2007). "*CSI* and Moral Authority: The Police and Science." *Crime, Media, Culture: An International Journal*, 3(1): 67–81.

Collins, Sue. (2008). "Making the Most of 15 minutes: Reality TV's Dispensable Celebrity." *Television & New Media*, 9(2): 87–110.

Defino, Dean. (2009). "From Trailer Trash to *Trailer Park Boys*." *Post Script*, 28(3): 47–57.

Druick, Zoë. (2008). "Laughing at Authority or Authorizing Laughter?" *Programming Reality: Perspectives on English-Canadian Television*, edited by Zoë Druick and Aspa Kotsopoulos. Waterloo: Wilfred Laurier University Press, pp. 107–128.

Goodman, Mark and Gring, Mark. (2000). "The Radio Act of 1927: Progressive Ideology, Epistemology and Praxis." This work originally appeared in *Rhetoric and Public Affairs*, Vol. 3, No. 3, 2000, published by Michigan State University Press.

Gray, Jonathan. (2007). "Imagining America: *The Simpsons* Go Global." *Popular Communication*, 5(2): 129–48.

Hilderbrand, Lucas. (2007). "YouTube: Where Cultural Memory and Copyright Converge." *Film Quarterly*, Fall, 61(1): 48–57.

Kinder, Marsha. (2009). "Re-Wiring Baltimore: The Emotive Power of Systemics, Seriality, and the City." *Film Quarterly*, 62(2): 50–7.

Levine, Elana. (2009). "National Television, Global Market: Canada's *Degrassi: The Next Generation*." *Media, Culture & Society*, 31(4): 515–31.

Mason, Daniel. (2002). "'Get the Puck Outta Here!': Media Transnationalism and Canadian Identity." *Journal of Sport & Social Issues*, 26 (20): 140–67.

McAllister, Matthew P. and Giglio, J. Matt. (2005). "The Commodity Flow of US Children's Television." *Critical Studies in Media Communication*, 22(1): 26–44.

McCutcheon, Mark. (2009). "Downloading Doppelgängers: New Media Anxieties and Transnational Ironies in *Battlestar Galactica*." *Science Fiction Film and Television*, 2(1): 1–24.

Meehan, Eileen, R. (2007). "Understanding How the Popular Becomes Popular: The Role of Political Economy in the Study of Popular Communication." *Popular Communication*, 5(3): 161–70.

Raboy, Mark. (1998). "Canada." In Anthony Smith (ed.) *Television: An International History*. Oxford: Oxford University Press, 161–8.

Spigel, Lynn (1992). "Women's Work." *Make Room for TV: Television and the Family Ideal in Postwar America*. Chicago: Chicago University Press, pp. 73–8, 206–11.

Spigel, Lynn. (2004). "Entertainment Wars: Television Culture after 9/11." *American Quarterly*, 56(2): 235–70.

Tinic, Serra. (2010). Excerpt from "Walking a Tightrope: The Global Cultural Economy of Canadian Television." In Bart Beaty, Derek Briton, Gloria Filax, and Rebecca Sullivan (eds) *How Canadians Communicate III: Contexts of Canadian Popular Culture*. Edmonton: Athabasca University Press, 95–115.

Van Veeren, Elspeth. (2009). "Interrogating *24*: Making Sense of US Counter-terrorism in the Global War on Terrorism." *New Political Science*, 3(3): 361–84.

Waisbord, Silvio. (2004). "McTV: Understanding the Global Popularity of Television Formats." *Television & New Media*, 5(4): 359–83.